2

The History of
SCOTTISH LITERATURE

Volume 3

THE HISTORY OF SCOTTISH LITERATURE
general editor Cairns Craig

Volume 1   Medieval and Renaissance *editor R D S Jack*
Volume 2   1660 to 1800 *editor Andrew Hook*
Volume 3   Nineteenth Century *editor Douglas Gifford*
Volume 4   Twentieth Century *editor Cairns Craig*

DICTIONARIES from AUP

THE SCOTTISH NATIONAL DICTIONARY
(18th century to the present day)
in ten volumes

THE COMPACT SCOTTISH NATIONAL DICTIONARY
in two volumes

A DICTIONARY OF THE OLDER SCOTTISH TONGUE
From the twelfth century to the end of the seventeenth
Volumes 1 to 6 (and continuing)

THE CONCISE SCOTS DICTIONARY
editor-in-chief Mairi Robinson

GAELIC DICTIONARY
Malcolm MacLennan

The History of
Scottish Literature

Volume 3

Nineteenth Century

edited by Douglas Gifford

general editor Cairns Craig

ABERDEEN UNIVERSITY PRESS

820 .9 941
14 13

First published 1988
Aberdeen University Press
A member of the Pergamon Group

© The Contributors 1988

The publisher acknowledges subsidy from the Scottish Arts Council towards the publication of this volume.

British Library Cataloguing in Publication Data

The History of Scottish literature.
　Vol. 3: The nineteenth century
　1. English literature ——— Scottish authors
　——— History and criticism 2. Scottish
　literature ——— History and criticism
　I. Gifford, Douglas, *1940–*
　820.9′9411

　ISBN 0-08-035056-9

Printed in Great Britain
The University Press
Aberdeen

Contents

List of Contributors   vii

Introduction *Douglas Gifford*   1

1   'The Last Purely Scotch Age' *Paul Scott*   13

2   Industry, Religion and the State of Scotland
    Christopher Harvie   23

3   'A Ferment of Change': Aspirations, Ideas and
    Ideals in Nineteenth-Century Scotland *Donald
    J Withrington*   43

4   Walter Scott *David Hewitt*   65

5   James Hogg: The Play of Region and Nation
    Thomas Crawford   89

6   The Scottish Fiction of John Galt *Keith Costain*   107

7   John Wilson (Christopher North) and the Tory
    Hegemony *Andrew Noble*   125

8   Carlyle: The World as Text and the Text as Voice
    Roderick Watson   153

9   Nineteenth-Century Non-Fictional Prose   *Ian
    Campbell*   169

10 Reviews and Magazines: Criticism and Polemic
    Joan Milne and Willie Smith   189

11 Popular Literature: The Press, the People, and the
    Vernacular Revival *William Donaldson*   203

12 Myth, Parody and Dissociation: Scottish Fiction
    1814–1914 *Douglas Gifford*   217

13 Heroes and Hero-makers: Women in Nineteenth-
    Century Scottish Fiction *Jenni Calder*   261

14 Realism and Fantasy in the Fiction of George Mac-
    Donald *David S Robb*   275

15 Robert Louis Stevenson in Prose *Francis R Hart*   291

16 The Kailyard *Gillian Shepherd*   309

17 Language and Nineteenth-Century Scottish Fiction
    Emma Letley   321

18 Scottish Poetry in the Nineteenth Century *Edwin
    Morgan*   337

19 Reclaiming Local Literature: William Thom and
    Janet Hamilton *William Findlay*   353

20 Gaelic Poetry in the Nineteenth Century *John
    MacInnes*   377

21 The Study of Folk Tradition *Mary Ellen Brown*   397

22 Exile and Empire *Alan MacGillivray*   411

23 Scottish Drama in the Nineteenth Century *Alas-
    dair Cameron*   429

General Bibliography   443

Index   447

List of Contributors

MARY ELLEN BROWN was educated at Mary Baldwin College and the University of Pennsylvania. She is Professor of Folklore and Women's Studies at Indiana University, and currently Director of the Women's Studies Program. Her research and teaching interests have always centred on the inter-relationships of oral and written literature, on cultural traditions (especially balladry and folksong)—with attachments to eighteenth and nineteenth century Scotland. *Burns and Tradition* represents one attempt to deal with these interests. She has published widely in the leading Scottish literary and folklore journals.

JENNI CALDER is Publications Officer of the National Museums of Scotland. This involves planning and editing Museum publications. Her own publications include *Women and Marriage in Victorian Fiction* (1976), *The Victorian Home* (1977) and *RLS: A Life Study* (1980). She is currently working on a book on Margaret Oliphant.

ALASDAIR CAMERON is a lecturer in Theatre Studies in the University of Glasgow. He is assistant editor of the Journal, *Theatre Research International* and is a member of the Board of Tay Theatre Company. He is at present at work on a history of the theatre in Scotland, planned in conjunction with the Scottish Theatre Archive for which he has academic responsibility.

IAN CAMPBELL, Reader in English Literature at the University of Edinburgh, is a specialist in Victorian and modern literature of England and Scotland. He is Associate Editor of the *Duke-Edinburgh Edition of the Carlyle Letters*, and author of editions and critical studies of Carlyle, Grassic Gibbon, the Kailyard, Stevenson. He is at work on an extended history of nineteenth and twentieth century writing in Scotland.

KEITH COSTAIN studied at Keele and Nottingham, going on to a PhD at Washington University, Missouri, where he began lecturing. He is presently Professor of English at the University of Regina in Canada. He has been President of the Western Canada Victorian Studies Association; and is working towards a study of the English *Bildungsroman*. He has published on Ramsay, Fergusson, and (extensively) Galt.

THOMAS CRAWFORD was until his recent retirement a Reader in English at the University of Aberdeen. His best-known books are *Burns: a study of the poems and songs* and *Society and the Lyric*, and he is joint editor of *Longer Scottish Poems Volume Two 1650–1830*. A founder member of the Association for Scottish Literary Studies, he was for several years its President, and continues active within it.

WILLIAM DONALDSON has written widely on Scottish Literature and history and is a collector and composer of Scottish traditional music. He co-edited *Grampian Hairst: an anthology of North-East Prose*; edited *David Rorie: Poems and Prose*, and William Alexander's previously unattributed novel *The Laird of Drammochdyle*. He is author of two recent major studies, *Popular Literature in Victorian Scotland* and *The Jacobite Song*. He has been a Leverhulme Fellow in the University of Aberdeen, where he was made an honorary fellow.

WILLIAM FINDLAY pursues the modern calling of househusband and writes for *Scotland on Sunday*. He is a founder editor of *Cencrastus* magazine. His translation into Scots of Michel Tremblay's *Les Belles-Soeurs* is to be staged in 1989.

DOUGLAS GIFFORD is Senior Lecturer in the department of Scottish Literature at Glasgow University. He has published widely in the field of Scottish literature, especially on Hogg, Stevenson, Gunn and Gibbon and modern Scottish fiction.

FRANCIS RUSSELL HART teaches English at the University of Massachusetts at Boston. His several books and articles have focused on Scottish fiction and biography, on theory of biography and autobiography, and on English fiction and social history of the nineteenth century. His fifth book, *Teachers, Learners, and Literature*, will appear in 1989, the year of his retirement. He and his wife Lorena are now beginning a book-project in local history.

CHRISTOPHER HARVIE is Professor of British Studies at the University of Tubingen in West Germany. Born in Motherwell and educated at the High School and University of Edinburgh, he was formerly Senior Lecturer in History at the Open University and is the author of *Scotland and Nationalism* (1977) and *No Gods and Precious Few Heroes, Scotland since 1914* (1981) and several articles on Scots history, literature and politics.

DAVID HEWITT is Senior Lecturer in English in the University of Aberdeen. He has been Treasurer of the Association for Scottish Literary Studies since 1973, and is Editor-in-Chief of the Edinburgh Edition of the Waverley Novels, which will appear during the nineties. He is author of many articles on Scottish literature and his books and editions include *Scott on Himself*, a selection of Scott's autobiographical writings.

EMMA LETLEY graduated in English Language and Literature at Oxford. She is currently Lecturer at Roehampton Institute in London. Her previous publications include editions for Oxford University Press of some of Robert Louis Stevenson's novels and, more recently, a major study of nineteenth century fiction and its use of Scots language, *From Galt to Douglas Brown*.

ALAN MACGILLIVRAY has been a teacher in secondary schools and Senior Lecturer in English at Jordanhill College of Education. Over many years he has worked extensively on the teaching of Scottish literature in schools. Currently he is teaching English as a foreign language at Glasgow University, is a visiting lecturer at Strathclyde University, and edits the Scotnotes Study Guide series for the Association for Scottish Literary Studies.

JOHN MACINNES is a native Gaelic speaker. He first specialised in English language, Germanic philology, and philosophy, subsequently turning to Celtic studies. He is Senior Lecturer in the School of Scottish Studies at Edinburgh University, and is responsible for research in Oral poetry. He is presently engaged on the study of Ossianic and other heroic Gaelic ballad texts. He has published widely in the field of Gaelic tradition and is well-known as a broadcaster.

JOAN MILNE studied at Hamilton College and Strathclyde University, doing postgraduate work in Scottish literature, and helping develop the university's 'outreach' scheme. She currently teaches at Earnock High School, Hamilton.

EDWIN MORGAN was Titular Professor of English at the University of Glasgow until 1980, and is now Visiting Professor at the University of Strathclyde. His books include *Essays* (1974), *Hugh MacDiarmid* (1976), and *Poems of Thirty Years* (1982). He edited an anthology of *Scottish Satirical Verse* (1980), and is co-editor of *New Writing Scotland.*

ANDREW NOBLE is a graduate of Aberdeen and Sussex Universities and is presently Senior Lecturer in the Department of English Studies, Strathclyde University. His most recent publications include an edition of critical essays on Stevenson, and *From The Clyde to California* a critical edition of Stevenson's emigrant journey.

DAVID S ROBB is a lecturer in English at the University of Dundee. He is the author of a book and of several articles on George MacDonald and has published essays on various aspects of twentieth-century Scottish literature. He is General Editor of the Scottish Classics series and joint Series Editor of the Scottish Writers series. He is Secretary of the Association for Scottish Literary Studies.

PAUL H SCOTT was born and educated in Edinburgh. He spent many years abroad as a diplomat, returning to Edinburgh in 1980. Since then he has been active in Scottish causes and has written extensively on historical, literary and political subjects. Publications include: *1707: The Union of Scotland and England, Walter Scott and Scotland, John Galt, In Bed with an Elephant.*

GILLIAN SHEPHERD graduated in English in 1970 from Strathclyde University where she studied Scottish literature. Her undergraduate thesis was on George Douglas Brown and the reaction to the Kailyard School; and the Kailyard has continued to exercise a morbid fascination on her ever since. Other special interests in Scottish literature include the women novelists as well as Neil Gunn. She has worked in publishing and in public relations and is now a management consultant in Glasgow.

WILLIE SMITH studied at Glasgow University and Jordanhill College. He lectures extensively for the Association for Scottish Literary Studies, the Scottish Language Society, and the extra-mural departments of Strathclyde and Glasgow universities. He is currently principal teacher of English at Lornhill Academy in Alloa.

RODERICK WATSON lectures at the University of Stirling. He graduated from Aberdeen University and taught for a year at the University of Victoria in British Columbia. The Lucy Fellowship took him to Cambridge and a PhD on the poetry of Hugh MacDiarmid. Publications include numerous critical articles and essays as well as *True History on the Walls* (poetry), *The Penguin Book of the Bicycle* (with Martin Gray), *MacDiarmid* (Open University Study Guides, 1985), and *The Literature of Scotland* (a literary history).

DONALD J WITHRINGTON is a graduate of Edinburgh University and taught there before moving to Aberdeen in 1964. Since 1969 he has been Senior Lecturer in Scottish History at the University of Aberdeen, where he was the first Director of the Centre for Scottish Studies (1970–80) and in that period edited *Northern Scotland*, the journal for the Centre. From 1972 until 1981 he was joint editor, with Professor Gordon Donaldson and G W S Barrow, of *The Scottish Historical Review*; he was also general editor (1973–82) of the 20-volume reprint of Sir John Sinclair's *Statistical Account of Scotland, 1791–99*. He has been Schools Liaison Officer for Aberdeen University since 1976. His main research interests are in Scottish ecclesiastical and educational history since the Reformation.

Introduction

DOUGLAS GIFFORD

The student of nineteenth-century Scottish literature is faced with a bewildering variety of critical perspectives and questions which at times lead to doubt as to the validity of thinking that there is a cultural tradition which can be called 'Scottish literature', or whether writers like Scott, Carlyle, Stevenson and John Davidson should be read along a different cultural axis of English literary tradition, with due recognition of eccentric Scottish preoccupations of theme, style, and language. No brief introduction can substantiate the claim that there remains in this and other periods a separate Scottish tradition. Instead, I prefer to indicate to the intending student of the literature of the century produced by Scots and about Scotland, who seeks a historical and cultural context, some of the varieties of perspective among which the student's judgements have to be made, to suggest a positive revaluation of the literary achievement of the period, and to explain the not immediately obvious *rationale* of the volume's arrangement.

The orientation of this volume (and the *History* generally) is one in which works of literature are seen as products of their time and background. But what background? Failure to contextualise writers like Scott, Hogg and MacDonald within their immediate Lowland Scottish ideological territory denies them their most intense and universal readings. To see Scott's earlier fiction as essentially Lowland Scottish is to recognise *Waverley*, *Old Mortality* and *The Heart of Midlothian* as operating within cultural and ideological limits different from those of Austen, Thackeray, and Dickens. Scott's symbolism and patterning in these earlier novels attempt to create a myth of Scottish national regeneration, and his richness of metaphor and irony cannot be fully understood without placing this work within the context of novelists like Hogg, Galt, and Stevenson, and non-fiction writers like Cockburn and Miller. On the other hand, Scott and many of the major writers crossed over the cultural border to locate themselves within a wider audience and market; their work must then equally be 'placed' in this wider context. The paradoxes which dominate Scottish literature demand that the student allows a kind of critical ambivalence to operate in his mind in his revaluation of the century's achievement, permitting a sense of alternative traditions to co-exist. Most of the essays here work within this dual perspective.

That said, the main object of this volume is to allow the reader to see much more clearly how the Scottish writer grows from native roots and out of a Scottish ideological context. But what are the roots, and what is the appropriate native context? The student reading behind the literature in modern social and cultural commentary, turning to the work of the *doyen* of the social historians, T C Smout and *A Century of the Scottish People: 1830–1950* (1986) (his continuation of *A History of the Scottish People: 1560–1830*) might well conclude that, while the first volume honoured Burns, Scott and Hogg in terms of the Scottish Enlightenment and native cultural traditions, after 1830 Scottish cultural history (let alone literature) merited no serious consideration at all. Smout traces the life-history of a Scottish Everyman, from a background somewhere between peasant and semi-skilled worker, living more often than not in conditions of degradation, with a compassion which regards the inheritance of *Literati* and Enlightenment as irrelevant. William Alexander's *Johnny Gibb* is mentioned, as 'the best of the Kailyard tradition'; Hugh Miller represents the tension between scientific rationalism and theology; Carlyle's effect on earlier Scottish working class leaders is emphasised as a continuation of Scots religion and metaphysics. And that is virtually all. The implication that Scottish literature had nothing significant to say with regard to the actuality of change and its attendant social horror is clear. And wider cultural issues, such the validity of school and university education, or attempts by prominent figures like John Stuart Blackie and Patrick Geddes to achieve Scottish national revival in politics and culture, are marginalised. Scottish experience is reduced to that of the bulk of ordinary people living through profound social change, from Scotland as rural to Scotland industrial.

To turn to George Davie's *The Democratic Intellect* (1961), the pioneering and profound study of Scottish educational and cultural values from the Enlightenment's pride in Scottish general metaphysical enquiry to the 1889 'Anglicising' introduction of specialist university study, is to discover a radically different perspective; virtually a diametric opposite, but in its own terms equally justifiable. Davie's central defence of the indigenous Scottish philosophical tradition of 'commonsense', running from Francis Hutcheson down through Smith, Brown and Stewart to William Hamilton in the eighteen-forties, argues that the Scots lost an authentic, fundamental (if pessimistic) analysis of the nature of man which was the centre-piece of mature Scottish education and culture. Elsewhere Davie continued his argument (specifically against Smout's view that Scottish philosophy, inhibited by Calvinist pessimism, lacked the vision to see that industrial change would transform the restricted Scottish polity) to suggest that Scottish philosophical 'pessimism' actually foresaw the fruits of English radical specialisation— 'the dangerous consequences of an intellectual atomisation of society—the dreaded alienation'.[1] At the core of Davie's argument is the notion of a continuity of older native humanist culture, surviving in the Scots-classical orientation of Ruddiman and Fergusson in the eighteenth century, through to a nineteenth century 'commonsense' native adaptation, which, despite its later disengagement from Scots language, is defensive about Scottish ideals and cultural integrity. From the philosophers of the Enlightenment through the period of Scott, Cockburn and Francis Jeffrey in the first quarter of the nineteenth century, to Sir William Hamilton and James Frederick Ferrier, outstanding representatives of the commonsense tradition in the eighteen-forties and -fifties, Davie sees an underlying core (despite superficial and notorious disagreements) of belief in indigenous Scottish values.

His argument suggests that for the century 1750–1850 a kind of compact between church and university allowed moderatism in religion to agree loosely with commonsense in overall cultural and educational ideology. It must be understood that inherent in the idea of 'commonsense' was a kind of secularised admission of faith—since central to the Smith-Hamilton line of thought was the idea that a kind of instinctive, holistic awareness was common to all humanity, an awareness of how to 'place' moral actions in an ethical context which lay beyond mere theories of association. This secular 'conscience', set in an unknowable metaphysical background, accorded sufficiently with moderate religious opinion, so that as long as moderatism controlled the Scottish kirk, the 'compact' endured, all the more socially effective because Westminster government took little to do with internal Scottish affairs, leaving them to the Dundas family to negotiate with Scottish church, legal and educational leaders. For Davie, the rise to power of the evangelical movement in the church in the 'ten years' war' before the Disruption of 1843 is the real ominous sign of the break-up of Scotland's precarious and astonishingly fruitful balance of religious and secular interests. This division and disintegration within Scottish church and society resulted in evangelical interference in culturally critical Scottish appointments, and in the weakening of unified resistance to 'Anglicising' tendencies in education and cultural values. Thus Scotland lost the vigour of its Humanist and Enlightenment inspired culture; the integrity of rational *and* moral ideological background to Scott and his contemporaries disappeared.

Within the extremes of the Davie-Smout interpretations of the time lie a host of theories identifying different reasons for the decline of Scottish cultural achievement after the Enlightenment. Probably the most forceful contemporary account came from the leading cultural historian of his time in Britain, Henry Buckle. In *On Scotland and the Scotch Intellect* (1861) he argued powerfully that nineteenth-century narrowness of outlook and achievement arose from the philosophy of common sense itself, since its deductive and *a priori* methodology led to widespread and negative Scottish authoritarianism; 'In no other Protestant nation, and indeed, in no Catholic nation except Spain, will a man who is known to hold unorthodox opinions, find his life equally uncomfortable . . . a whisper will quickly circulate that such a one is to be avoided, for he is a free-thinker . . . in no civilised country is toleration so little understood . . . in none is the spirit of bigotry or of persecution so extensively diffused.'[2] Other and later perspectives merely shift the emphasis on religious bigotry to a sort of superficial 'holier-than-thou' vying for greater outward shows of respectability and kirk worthiness, like Willa Muir in *Mrs. Grundy in Scotland* (1936); while David Daiches sees 'gentility', born with New Town Edinburgh, as a creeping blight on older, more robust expression,[3] Andrew Noble develops this argument in this volume, identifying John Wilson ('Christopher North'), a powerful Edinburgh establishment figure as editor of *Blackwood's* and Professor of Moral Philosophy after 1820, as the baneful influence on Scottish literature after Scott, with his rulings that certain subjects were 'improper' for poetry. Noble's perspective also identifies another rapidly developing and strident Scottish attitude as seen in its infancy with Wilson and *Blackwood's*; that identification with England and Empire, which Wilson saw as 'established under divine Providence in these islands . . . as the mainstay of England, as the bulwarks of the Protestant faith', so that 'kingly government, checked and balanced by a proud aristocracy, and a due mixture of a popular representation' will fight off Whig, Jacobin, Radical, Deist, Demagogue. A rhetoric begins here which will be found in Norman Macleod, Ian Maclaren, Robertson Nicoll and John Buchan, which sees in Scotland the sense of a British and God-ordained imperial mission, managing to combine with an anachronistic parochialism, in a way which many of the essays in this volume find significant and paradoxical.

Other perspectives on the period identify further sources of cultural dis-integration. In *Scott and Scotland* (1936) Edwin Muir argued that the linguistic schizophrenia of Scotland since the Reformation had destroyed wholeness of critical and creative thought, so that by Scott's time no healthy critical awareness existed in Scotland; consequently Muir simply 'wrote off' Scott as impressive failure and the rest of the century as blighted spiritual wasteland— failing to see (as I argue in my essay on the fiction) that a far deeper 'dissociation of Scottish sensibility' was frequently and successfully expressed by Scott and his followers—a sense of Scotland divided between its past and present, between perceptions of nationality swayed in opposite directions by nostalgic emotion and materialistic reason, successfully expressing what even Smout was to recognise as 'duality of consciousness' representing 'a real emotional tension, a contradiction within the citizen that is never resolved'.[4] David Craig argued that emigration of talent from Carlyle on 'created gaps in the imaginative records of the country and tempts our writers into indulgence of their weaker sides'—and, elsewhere, that a 'hypertrophication' of moral sensibility in Scotland developed (here approaching Buckle and Willa Muir), an exacerbation of conscience detached from specific belief in predestination or the truth of the Bible, so that 'keeping up appearances' became the obsession of a materialist and 'polite' Scottish society.[5] And the student of the century is further bewildered when, in addition to such arguments involving the religious heritage, the linguistic predicament, and plain snobbery, Tom Nairn's powerful analysis of *The Break-up of Britain* (1977) suggests that the real paradox of nineteenth-century Scotland lay in its separation of its sense of historical identity from its practical involvement with England, thus developing a 'quasi-national inheritance'. Nairn argues that Scotland's singular arrangement of Union with England prohibited its participation in nineteenth century European movements of liberal nationalism, separating 'new popular-national consciousness from action', or, as he summarises, a separation of Scotland's heart from its head. In an earlier article, Nicholas Phillipson anticipated Nairn's attitude towards Scott by concluding that the 'patriot' Scott of *The Letters of Malachi Malagrowther*, who, 'for one wild moment . . . is about to raise the spectre of revolt', characteristically climbed down, bathetically suggesting that the English attempt to foist their banking system on Scotland, although unwanted, was 'kind and friendly'. 'By validating the making of a fuss about nothing, Scott gave to middle-class Scotsmen and to Scottish nationalism an ideology—an ideology of noisy inaction', argued Phillipson.[6] But Paul Scott, here and in his edition of *Malachi Malagrowther* (1981) profoundly disagrees, arguing that Scott's defence of Scotland's national character as well as its economy and banking system is the true beginning of modern nationalism.

What is the student to make of such a variety of perspectives? Despite the apparent diversity, certain major issues do emerge as seen in similar and agreed ways. The social 'compact' underlying the Enlightenment was threatened as resentment over patronage developed evangelical strength in the church. Phobia concerning the effects of French revolution in Scotland increased Whig-Tory polarisation, so that increasingly religious and political pressures disrupted what remained of the cultural-religious compact. While the 1832 Reform Act revealed that the Whigs in Scotland were not in fact as far from their Tory opponents as polemic of the time might have suggested, much more serious social unrest emerged from 1832 onwards, as the massive population shifts from country to industrial town began. Nevertheless, Scottish radicalism was muted, compared to English chartist violence; a traditional religious moderation limited Scottish violence to the 1820 'Weaver's rebellion' or the land agitation in the Highlands in the 1880s. The spectre of revolution so feared by Wilson and Chalmers, by landed interest and church, was never, with hindsight, a serious possibility. Much of the literature shared this neurotic fear of radicalism and revolution from Scott, Galt, Wilson and Cockburn to Miller, Carlyle and Stevenson, and to this extent it is true that what has hitherto been considered as the 'canon' of the creative literature failed to respond imaginatively to society's changes, and failed to interpret and empathise with the mass of ordinary people whose plight Smout so movingly records. Instead, anachronistic, sentimental and patronisingly distorted representations in fiction, poetry and essay are too frequently given, especially by Wilson and his descendants. Here, perhaps, an analogy can be drawn with Thomas Chalmers and the predicament of the church in 1843. Chalmers's desire to combat industrialisation and the alienation of the individual in the new city with ideals of traditional rural parochialism was probably altruistic; but it led to failure to understand both the nature and extent of the new urban and political problems and the people who sought radical action to solve them. Like the 'kailyard' writers of poetry, fiction and essay, Chalmers simply could not accept what Donald Withrington aptly describes as 'a ferment of change'. And, like so many of the writers, Chalmers preferred 'equality of souls without disturbing equality of ranks'; thus Scottish presbyterianism's democratic tradition was fatally flawed as an ideology suited to rapid social change. Recent studies have emphasised the failure of the church to grapple with the crying problems of the century.

And the centrality of the church's position (and thus the centrality of its failure) is a point which the student should understand from the beginning. The schizophrenic Act of Union in 1707 contained the seeds of Scotland's nineteenth-century crises of identity, though it took till 1843 for them to ripen fully. The church had maintained a sense of separate Scottish identity. As Christopher Harvie puts it, 'the annual General Assembly looked more like a parliament than many of the provincial assemblies of continental Europe'. George Davie asked the question why this autonomous, self-respecting and identity-carrying Scottish body avoided all thought of directly and collectively challenging Westminster's authority on patronage matters in Scotland, instead of self-destructing; the failure of Scotland's main representational body to assert its constitutional rights must indicate a loss of Scottish confidence, identity and will, rather than being seen as Cockburn saw it, as the last *heroic* act of the old Scotland. With the Disruption went the church's place as secular organiser of poor relief and education; not immediately, but inevitably, as infighting between the established and free church led to disintegration of services and duplication of effort. Such rivalry for the moral high ground, together with the need for alternative channels of social protest, created the new evangelicism's next wave of success, as it moved from its earlier hold in fishing village and manufacturing town throughout society, till Buckle in 1861 deplored its zealous ubiquity and intolerance. As Davie records, the last efflorescence of traditional Scottish humanism and the commonsense philosophy under William Hamilton and Frederick Ferrier in the 1840s was to be doused by evangelical intrusion of less-than-liberal appointments in university and education. Instead of the old 'compact' of church and intellectual culture which had underpinned the Enlightenment, the second half of the century saw the energies of the broken church dissipated in internal quarrels, in neurotic suspicion of deviation from orthodoxy (culminating in the expulsion from his free church Professorship of the brilliant Robertson Smith of Aberdeen for heresy in 1881) and increasing unease concerning advances in scientific rationalism. It may be too glib to assume that Hugh Miller's suicide in 1856 was symbolic of the tensions and inconsistencies arising from such pressures, but there is no doubt that Miller's writing captures the essence of the century's unsureness of how to cope with scientific materialism and its unsureness of procedure in remedying social injustice or reconciling progress with tradition. Miller's place at the centre of religious debate, periodical culture and geological enquiry adds a poignancy and archetypal quality to his predicament.

   Scott, Harvie and Withrington examine the main issues of the century in this volume, so here I merely suggest further contexts for the literature. As the reader seeks to 'frame' the essays in this volume, the following considerations will reinforce an awareness that there is a pervasive dualism of national attitudes running down the century. How else can one reconcile on one hand the 'commonsense' and 'democratic intellect's' emphasis on *a priori* and deductive science, logic, ethics and metaphysics (and the popular evangelicism which succeeded it) with the *a posteriori* and inductive emphasis of Thomas Reid and 'the School of Scottish Realism' and the advances in practical science, in medicine and engineering in the work of figures like Charles Tennant, Joseph Lister, Clark Maxwell and Lord Kelvin? Davie records how Kelvin recommended that the young Scottish scientist should go to England to find proper instruction—so where, if not in formal courses of education at university, did the outstanding European expertise of ventures like Tennant's Glasgow chemical works originate? How indeed do we account for the basic split in nineteenth century Scotland between the materialism of science and the idealism of evangelicism? Beyond this, how do we reconcile the apparent simultaneous identification with Empire, British and English military and social aspirations (even, as MacInnes shows here, in the Gaidhealtachd, torn apart by Clearance, land reform and evangelicism) with parochial and sentimental yearning for a lost or imagined community simplicity summed up in Alexander Smith's ideal and timeless community in *Dreamthorp* (1863)? And, as Emma Letley shows, the century echoed this dualism in complex and paradoxical attitudes towards Scots and English language choices and strategies. It won't do simply to assume that Scots steadily withered as English became the socially acceptable norm. William Donaldson shows clearly that popular usage of Scots burgeoned in the second half of the century in popular presses, deploying the vernacular in new, outward-looking, urban-and-industry conscious varieties of genres. And perhaps linked to this are the equivocal attitudes of the century towards traditional folk culture. Mary Ellen Brown helps focus for us the tension between the increasing interest of collectors like Motherwell, Campbell, Child and Greig in authentic and orally transmitted folk material, and the new Scottish anthropological interest in folk ritual and belief of scholars like Robertson Smith, Clouston and Frazer, which was less interested in aesthetic value or cultural authenticity than—particularly in the case of Frazer—exploiting the world-wide congruences of pagan irrationalism as evidence of man's abiding need to invent dark gods, and thence attacking all varieties of Western religion. The student of the century's evolving ideologies should not forget in this respect Walter Scott's earlier and significant redefinition of cultural attitudes towards folklore and literature's exploitation of its resources, like the rich supernatural background so colourfully deployed by Burns and Hogg. Scott relegated such traditional *diablerie*, with its brownies and wraiths, wizards and kelpies, to 'the cottage and the nursery', thus declaring such a strong and organic part of Scottish cultural heritage off limits to 'sophisticated' writers and society at large.

And Scott's influence in this respect relates to a literary and aesthetic question which increasingly engages modern critics. How far must the student of Scott, Hogg, Galt and later writers of the century read them with reference to the dominating ideas and modalities of Romanticism? Andrew Hook closed volume 2 of this History by acknowledging Scott's movement of Scotland 'squarely to the centre of the romantic map of Europe', completing Europe's sense of Scotland as Ossianic landscape of noble savages. Are we therefore to identify in Scott and his contemporaries the intrinsic values and statements of Romanticism? Several of the essays here engage with this question; while others suggest that the student must not only identify versions of 'romanticism', but look at these writers from a counter-perspective which suggests that at the heart of Scottish fiction of the period—and later, in Alexander, Oliphant and Stevenson—there lies a debt to the 'Scottish Realism' of Thomas Reid as well as profound anti-romance and a reductivism more deeply rooted in Scottish cultural attitudes from Dunbar, Henryson and the Ballads to Ramsay, Fergusson and Burns, than the eighteenth century Scottish romantic expressions which Scott apparently took to triumphant fruition. 'The reductive idiom' has long been identified, if somewhat vaguely, in Scottish literature by critics like Spiers and Craig; arguably Scott, Hogg, Galt and Stevenson employ varieties of it as a kind of ironic juxtapositioning with high-flown assertions of romantic idealism, in a kind of self-mockery or parody within the fiction's *apparent* romanticism, in novels like *Waverley*, *The Brownie of Bodsbeck*, *The Entail*, and *The Master of Ballantrae*. The fiction is well represented in the essays here; the student must decide which claim, romantic or realist, carries most weight.

In all this a sense of recurrent pattern will, I think, strike the reader. There is something of a Jekyll-and-Hyde dualism manifesting itself through these cultural ambivalences, in that the sophisticated, the genteel, the bourgeois and respectable, and perhaps the Anglicised voice of Victorian Scotland is constantly undercut by an older, rougher, and often vernacular assertion that the professed new and improved identity is not the real essence of the country. In the Highlands, for example, the Ossianic-Scott-Victorian line of representation which did so much for Scotland's tourist industry developed into the Balmorality and Celtic Twilight of William Black, James Grant and 'Fiona McLeod'; into a representation divorced from the actuality of despoliation of the Highlands through militarisation, clearance, famine and religious bigotry. Two voices speak of the Gaidhealtach; the stronger and socially acceptable 'improves' it beyond all recognition; while, as John MacInnes shows us, the traditional and authentic voice of John Smith, Mary MacPherson and William Livingstone, is neglected, although persistent. History repeats itself; where 'Ossian' drowned out Duncan Ban MacIntyre and Rob Donn in the previous century, the new, romanticised, and marketable versions of Gaeldom drown the native poets in the nineteenth. The Lowland and Anglicised version of the Highlands wins, reminding yet again of the difficulty of arguing for a 'true' Scottish identity at all in the century in which identities were being constantly broken down and reformed in the ferment of change. Davie has shown how complex for Victorian leaders of church and education was the problem of national identity, showing the chameleon changes of Scottish-English identification in figures like Ferrier, Caird and Forbes, as they swithered between native and English models of educational value. W E Aytoun's activity at the heart of cultural education in Edinburgh at mid-century onwards clearly shows a split set of cultural identifications, with the older traditions of Scottish poetry set against the English tradition, each with a separate claim on the orientation of his teaching. As the century wears on, the major writers like Oliphant, Stevenson, Smith and Buchan develop an ability to turn with remarkable celerity from assertion of Scottish identity to casual reference to their position as 'English'. By 1895, Oliphant's *A Child's History of Scotland* gives a mere seven pages of over two hundred to post-1707. A sense of national identity may be gained from the past, she suggests, but 'prosperity and peace brought common sense and cool judgement along with the realisation that the independence of a separate kingdom had become a thing impossible . . . even now a hot-headed Scot may dream foolish dreams, or a thick-headed Englishman repeat the old insults; but I think the one is as harmless as the other'. Once again it is impossible to avoid the notion of a Scottish psychological syndrome in which a basic separation of emotional indulgence in the mythology of the past somehow co-exists with the calculating assessment of opportunity in the present and future. Every major cultural figure of the century betrays this dualism of values, from Scott and Wilson to Chalmers and Cockburn; from Carlyle and Miller to Oliphant, Stevenson, Davidson and Buchan. Individual criticism of these figures has continually pointed to Scott's divided allegiances or Cockburn's separation of private self from public *persona*, Carlyle's and Chalmers's engagement with contemporary problems set against their dream of a simpler communal past, or Miller's inability to reconcile what his radical and evangelical heart wants him to believe with the evidence of scientific rationalism. By the end of the century the recurrent Scottish authorial crisis of identity created a rash of 'aliases'; William Sharp/Fiona McLeod, Neil Munro/Hugh Foulis, and the later examples of Grieve/MacDiarmid and Mitchell/Gibbon, all exhibiting tension between opposing selves and subject-matters.

A final and crucial question remains. Is the student to accept that Scottish literature, tormented by these ambivalences of identity and purpose, lost its way and dropped its standards drastically after the death of Scott, failing to engage with the changes in Highlands and Lowlands, country and city? Before attempting a direct answer, it is worth stressing an outstanding aspect of Victorian Scotland on which all social and cultural critics agree. It was 'an exceptionally male-dominated society', says Smout. Harvie points to Trollope's Robert Kennedy, the Scottish magnate of *Phineas Finn*, as the archetype seen beyond Scotland as uniquely authoritarian and materialistic. Drummond and Bulloch, in their *The Church in Victorian Scotland* (1975) saw Scotland's achievements in the century as industrial and technological; 'leadership in this new Scotland belonged to men who had made money and meant to make more'. Culture and nationality were unimportant to such, especially after the Disruption. The Checklands put it vividly:

> The magnates of the Scottish basic industries at the end of the century may perhaps be taken as a distillation of the Victorian ethic. It centred upon the dominant male of middle age or over, brooking no interference, speaking only with his equals in so far as there was any conferring at all, keeping under authority not only his labour force but also his wives and daughters. Even his sons could be kept under tutelage until old age or death broke his grip. Perhaps some of these magnates saw themselves as living legends, naming their forges *Vulcan, Atlas,* or *Phoenix . . .*[7]

Such energies would hardly sympathise with the survival of folk culture, or the Scottish vernacular. Their social and religious attitudes encouraged respectability, often combining with evangelicism to add a secular disapproval to any attempts of drama, poetry, or fiction genuinely to engage with the condition of women, sexuality, radical social problems, disruptive Scottish nationalism. Cockburn laments the passing of the earthy, vigorous women of smeddum, women like Galt's Leddy Grippy or Ferrier's Violet McShake. He is noting not merely the sinking status of women, and it is significant that Scottish literature recovers in the period of the 'Scottish renaissance' of the nineteen-twenties and -thirties when sexual balance is once again acknowledged as essential to full creativity, as well as the need of the arts to engage with the reality and fullness of human problems and change.

Poetry in our period is too often derivative, parochial, and escapist. In their essays, Morgan, Findlay and MacInnes accept the verdict of Victorian decline—although Morgan's and Findlay's qualifications should be taken together with Donaldson's suggestion that further research into popular literature should be undertaken. Once again, the underlying Scottish voice beneath that of the establishment, the voice of the 'autodidacts', the self-taught, humble poets who speak directly and are not afraid to experiment with form in an age chronically limited in experimental confidence, emerges as the voice worth revaluing, in the work of William Thom, Janet Hamilton, and, outstandingly, James Young Geddes, whose astonishing satire on the archetype of the Scottish magnate in 'Glendale and Co.' has all the innovatory boldness of Whitman. Prose is more striking, from Scott and Lockhart to Carlyle, Cockburn and Miller; Roderick Watson makes an impressive case for Carlyle's anticipation of modernism and semiotics, and Ian Campbell describes a rich variety. But one can't help feeling that even with the best of the resident Scots a stolid conservatism eventually damps down the originality and passion of writers like Lockhart and Cockburn, in *Peter's Letters to His Kinsfolk* or *Memorials of His Time*. Even with the frankest, most passionate and radical voice of the century, Hugh Miller's, there is a sense of wasted potential. His anger which argued against the debasement of the bothy system, or against social injustice like that of the virtual slavery of Niddry coalminers in 1824, or the Duke of Atholl's closing of public roads, was to dissipate itself in issues which seem sadly irrelevant now. And drama, for all Alasdair Cameron points to a flourishing theatre-going, went from bad (in its early elevation of *Rob Roy* to the crown of Scottish theatre) to worse, in Alfred Wareing's 1911 attempt to inaugurate a Scottish National Theatre with an adaptation of J J Bell's best-selling urban rival to *Peter Pan*, *Wee MacGreegor*. That said, Cameron, like so many of our essayists, warns us to look beyond 'library shelves' to rediscover a now-forgotten, but in its time, lively popular culture.

Only the fiction can, however, argue against the assertion that literature collapsed after Scott. Arguably, Scott begins a tradition or school of Scottish fiction which does engage with the central issues of the day in work like that of Hogg, Galt, MacDonald, Oliphant, Alexander, Stevenson, Brown and MacDougall Hay. The period 1814 to 1914 sees these novelists using recurrent narrative structures, protagonists, symbolism and comment. In this fiction the essential dualism of perspective of the century in Scotland is exploited in conscious artistry which often deploys a kind of creative ambivalence to sum up the tensions of the age between rationalism and supernaturalism, values of the heritage of the past and the new values of the developing future, and Scotland's chronic uncertainty as to final choice of identity not so much in terms of political choices between Anglicised and materially advantageous membership of Empire, or Scottish nationalism, as an awareness of historical complexity and a consequent tendency to morbidity, infantilism and disintegration of sense of identity in nineteenth century Scottish personality. The essays on specific novelists and groups of novelists all illustrate this, to greater or lesser degrees; and I make no apology for trying to indicate the major characteristics of the Scottish novel in the period 1814–1914 in what is the lengthiest of the essays here. Scotland's major genre in a neglected period deserves extensive if (as I am all too aware) subjective and exploratory investigation.

This volume gives an overall impression of great range and energy (if not consistent quality) in the literature of the period, but with a sense that, apart from the fiction, Scottish literature had lost its sense of identity and direction by the end of the century. Awareness of a 'Scottish Renaissance' in the nineteen-twenties tends to heighten the student's sense of previous decline and stagnation—witness T F Henderson's influential and negative description of a darkening land at the close of his *Scottish Vernacular Literature* (1898). I close this introduction with the suggestion that Wittig's idea of Scottish Literature's 'heaving again' with the work of Stevenson and others is a fair perspective; that, although the 'Celtic revival' of the eighteen-nineties was bound to fail, unlinked as it was to any strong lowland Scottish traditions, or social realities (let alone any real Gaelic traditions!) it showed a resurgence of Scottish aspirations to native expression which gathered with increasing strength, in the work of painters like 'the Glasgow Boys' and the Scottish colourists, architects like Rennie Mackintosh, and novelists from those discussed here to, outstandingly, Willa Muir and Catherine Carswell, whose *Open the Door!* of 1920, with its awareness of European fiction and its feminist sympathy, its Lawrentian exploration of new sexual, psychological and social issues, and its modern symbolism and methodology, should have been recognised by MacDiarmid as part of a profound stirring in Scottish literature prior to his magnificent contribution. The Great Exhibition of 1911 in Kelvingrove was directed towards the founding of a chair of Scottish History and Literature at Glasgow University, and towards reasserting a sense of Scottish identity and an awareness of its indigenous culture. Looking beyond Victorian and Edwardian Scottish culture, and beyond the Great War, to the Carswells, MacDiarmid, the Muirs, Gunn, Soutar, Bridie, Linklater and Mitchison, we realise that they were all rooted in Victorian Scotland, and were all in their different ways drawing both nourishment from and developing antipathy towards aspects of their home background. As we come to appreciate the complexity of nineteenth century Scottish culture more fully, I believe that we shall, by revaluing neglected authors and re-reading those accepted, begin to see much more significant literary achievement before the 'Scottish renaissance', and much more continuity from Scott to the present, than we have considered to be the case.

The rationale of the volume is an attempt to combine a chronology of development and change down through the period together with a rough grouping of types and genres. To this end the three first essays approach the period in terms of social, political and cultural background history, so that the student has some idea of the major issues of the century, from the

Disruption to issues of home rule under Gladstone, from the Highland Clearances to land reform in the 'eighties. The major figures in the time of Scott follow thereon, while the essays from Watson's on Carlyle, to Milne and Smith on 'Reviews and Magazines' take us into mid-century and Scottish Victorian love of polemic and weighty debate. At the centre, fittingly, lies William Donaldson's challenging discussion of popular literature in the second half of the century; his emphasis on the need to reconsider our previous generalisations about the range, subject-matter and aesthetic achievement of the literature of Scotland in the period has rightly provoked more of the contributors here to debate or argument than any other critic. Thereafter till Letley's study of Scots and English in Scottish fiction the essays continue consideration of the developing fiction; while Morgan, Findlay and McInnes look specifically at the achievement and problematics of poetry in English, Scots and Gaelic. The last three essays consider other aspects of nineteenth century literature; folk tradition, the writing of Scottish exiles, emigrants, and, energetic in activity if not outstanding in quality, Scottish Drama. The volume does not pretend to do more than open up further debate. The period lacks primary socio-cultural investigations. Major study of this kind, to take up from works like those of Craig and Smout which ended at 1830, is urgently needed, as a basis for more authoritative and definitive description and analysis of the literature of the century.

NOTES

1   George Davie, 'The Social Significance of the Scottish Philosophy of Common Sense' (The Dow Lecture, University of Dundee, 1972).
2   Henry Thomas Buckle, *On Scotland and the Scotch Intellect*, ed. H J Hanham (Chicago and London, 1970), pp. 393–394. This emphasis on the deductive bias of the Scottish mind must be tempered with an awareness of an opposing tendency in Scottish philosophy. The inductive character of the school of Scottish Realism of Thomas Reid profoundly affected the 'theoretical histories' of John Galt. Keith Costain demonstrates this in his essay here and opens up a fascinating new line of enquiry.
3   David Daiches, *Literature and Gentility in Scotland* (Edinburgh, 1982).
4   T C Smout, *A Century of the Scottish People 1830–1950* (London, 1986), p. 238. Smout sees nationalism 'in happy times' as a 'lesser consciousness', only asserting itself as 'sentimental expression of regional loyalties. In less happy times, when an empire falls or an economy receives a jolt . . . the lesser consciousness may grow obsessionally powerful . . .' (p. 239).
5   David Craig, *Scottish Literature and the Scottish People 1680–1830* (London, 1961), p. 293; and in his introduction to J G Lockhart's *Adam Blair* (Edinburgh, 1963), pp. xxi–xxiii.
6   Tom Nairn, *The Break-up of Britain* (expanded ed., London, 1981), p. 150; N T Phillipson, 'National and Idealism' in *Government and Nationalism in Scotland*, ed. J N Wolfe (Edinburgh, 1969), pp. 183–186.
7   Sidney and Olive Checkland, *Industry and Ethos: Scotland 1832–1914* (London, 1984), pp. 178–179.

Chapter 1

'The Last Purely Scotch Age'

PAUL H SCOTT

The late 1830s mark one of the most obvious and drastic turning points in the literary history of Scotland. Before lay a long period of high achievement: Ramsay, Fergusson and Burns, the Gaelic poets of the eighteenth century, the philosophers and historians of the Enlightenment, Scott, Galt and Hogg. Afterwards there was a loss of cohesion and self-confidence, a decline which lasted about 50 years. In George Davie's famous and precise phrase, it was a time of 'failure of intellectual nerve'.[1] Historians of Scottish literature all take a similar view of the period. Kurt Wittig, for instance: 'The less said about the two generations after Scott the better. . . . The tradition seemed really to have come to an end, and not with a bang, but a whimper.'[2] In Roderick Watson's recent history there is a chronological table of important publications. It is conspicuously thin from 1830 to 1880.[3] William Power says of the 1830s that 'Scots literature fell at once from a national to a provincial level'.[4] David Craig makes fun of this suggestion that the change was abrupt ('overnight?'), but himself gives an even more final significance to the year 1830 in which he ends the period of this *Scottish Literature and the Scottish People; 1680–1830*. With a sublime indifference to what was going on around him as he wrote, he says that his period 'includes the last flowering of the vernacular poetry and the rise and hey-day of the native novel'. He takes an even more terminal view of what happened to Scotland as a whole at that time, 'the point at which Scotland was all but emptied of native talents during the early Industrial Revolution and the increase of emigration'.[5]

William Power had good reason for using language which implied that the change was sudden and abrupt. The great figures of the previous age all died within a few years of one another, Scott in 1832, Hogg in 1835 and Galt in 1839. Of the writers who survived them, many left Scotland. Lockhart emigrated to London to edit the *Quarterly* in 1825 and Carlyle also finally moved there in 1834. Nor were they by any means alone in yielding to the pull of what Lockhart called the 'immense magnet' of 'triumphant and eclipsing England',[6] or more specifically London. Walter Scott remarked in his *Journal* on 24 March 1829: 'Thus London licks the butter off our bread, by opening a better market for ambition. Were it not for the difference of the religion and laws, poor Scotland could hardly keep a man that is worth having.' The most accomplished and prolific novelist between Galt and Stevenson, Margaret Oliphant, became in J H Miller's words, 'thoroughly acclimatised in

England'.[7] James Thomson of *The City of Dreadful Night*, the most interesting poet of the same period, also lived in, and wrote of, London, even if he was not so happily acclimatised. By death or emigration, therefore, Scotland was emptied of major writers in the ten years or so before the Disruption of 1843, which was itself a turning point with far-reaching consequences.

Scotland's loss was England's gain as John Gross recognised in his book, *The Rise and Fall of the Man of Letters*:

> It would be hard to exaggerate the part played by Scotsmen in the development of the English periodical press. They helped to create not only the great quarterlies and monthlies, as is well known, but the weeklies as well; the first editors of the *Spectator*, the *Economist* and the *Saturday Review*, for example, were all Scotsmen. And right through the nineteenth century critics and essayists made their way south across the border. Lockhart, Masson, Andrew Lang, William Archer are a few random instances. The list could easily be extended—and it would become positively daunting if one were allowed to include the second generation of the diaspora: men like Ruskin, who still spoke with traces of a Scots accent, or Macaulay, whose features in repose struck Carlyle as those of 'an honest good sort of fellow, made out of oatmeal'.[8]

Recently, William Donaldson has challenged the 'prevailing view' that 'the nineteenth century after the death of Scott was a period of decline and failure'. He does this by examining articles, stories and novels published in the Scottish newspapers. His conclusion is that the later nineteenth century so far from being a period of failure of writing, especially in Scots, was one of 'resurgence, renewal and growth almost without precedent'.[9] This is an exciting theory which may make us all change many of our old ideas and assumptions, although we can only test it when more of the texts become generally available. But even if Donaldson is right, I do not think that his discoveries fundamentally challenge the view that there was a marked change for the worse in the literary climate in the late 1830s. In the first place, Donaldson tells us that the newspapers got into their stride only with the repeal of the Stamp Act in 1855. Much of the writing that he discusses appeared towards the end of the century when there were many other signs of the recovery of self-confidence. Also, if the best writing in Scotland was driven out of the 'London-dominated booktrade'[10] and forced to take refuge in the newspapers, that in itself would be a very telling sign of a loss of status and self-assurance.

In his *Life of Sir Walter Scott*, John Buchan described the Edinburgh in which Scott lived as 'a true capital, a clearing-house for the world's culture and a jealous repository of Scottish tradition.'[11] David Craig would argue that already Scott and his contemporaries were 'deeply conditioned by provincialism'.[12] But if provincialism threatened before the 1830s, it became infinitely more destructive afterwards when the drift to the south became a flood. As the symbolic date for the change, we might take 1834 when Carlyle decided that Scotland could not hold him. A generation earlier he would have found sufficient challenge, stimulation and opportunity in Edinburgh. Why did he opt for London in 1834? What had gone wrong?

The classic and contemporary statement of the problem is in Henry Cockburn's *Life of Lord [Francis] Jeffrey*, published in 1852. Towards the beginning of the book he describes Edinburgh as it was in the early years of the nineteenth century, shortly after Jeffrey, Scott and Cockburn himself had all passed through the High School and university there. The whole passage is well worth reading in full, but the following are the key sentences:

> The society of Edinburgh was not that of a provincial town, and cannot be judged of by any such standard. It was metropolitan. . . . It was the seat of a university famous throughout the world, of the supreme courts of justice, of the government offices, and of the annual convocation of the church, formerly no small matter. . . .
>
> Many of the curious characters and habits of the receding age, *the last purely Scotch age that Scotland was destined to see*, [my italics] still lingered among us. . . . Almost the whole official state, as settled at the union, survived; . . . unconscious of the economical scythe which has since mowed it down.
>
> Over all this there was diffused the influence of a greater number of persons attached to literature and science, some as their calling, and some for pleasure, than could be found, in proportion to the population, in any other city in the empire. . . . Philosophy had become indigenous in the place, and all classes, even in their gayest hours, were proud of the presence of its cultivators. Thus learning was improved by society, and society by learning. . . .
>
> And all this was still a Scotch scene. The whole country had not begun to be absorbed in the ocean of London. . . . The operation of the commercial principle which tempts all superiority to try its fortune in the greatest accessible market, is perhaps irresistible; but anything is surely to be lamented which annihilates local intellect, and degrades the provincial spheres which intellect and its consequences can alone adorn. According to the modern rate of travelling, the capitals of Scotland and of England were then about 2,400 miles asunder. Edinburgh was still more distant in its style and habits. It had then its own independent taste, and ideas, and pursuits. . . . This city has advantages, including its being the capital of Scotland, its old reputation, and its external beauties, which have enabled it, in a certain degree, to resist the centralising tendency, and have hitherto always supplied it with a succession of eminent men. But, now that London is at our door, how precarious is our hold of them, and how many have we lost![13]

No doubt, Cockburn's account of the Edinburgh of his youth is coloured by nostalgia. He was born in 1779 and wrote the *Life of Jeffrey* when he was in his seventies. He was looking back at the great days of his youth 'when there were giants in the land',[14] as Scott said of the time of the Scottish Enlightenment. Perhaps Cockburn romanticises the past a little, but he is evidently convinced that during his own life-time Edinburgh and Scotland had lost much of their 'independent taste and ideas' and their own 'style and habits' because of increasing centralisation from London. He implies that very little independence in these things remained by the time he was writing, that there was increasing pressure from centralisation and that Edinburgh had indeed become provincial.

When Cockburn spoke of the 'modern rate of travelling', he meant, of course, the railway and the steamboat. He recorded a similar thought in his *Journal* on 11 August 1844; 'Railways and steamers, carrying the southern into every recess, will leave no asylum for our native classical tongue.' Here he is thinking of the Scots language (although the same point might be made even more strongly of Gaelic). 'Scotch has ceased to be the vernacular language of the upper classes, and this change will go on increasing with the increasing intercourse which rolls the language of the greater (in the sense of more numerous) people over our surface.'[15] The erosion of a language is bad enough, but Cockburn was also afraid of an even more fundamental loss, of all independence in taste, ideas, style and habits. If that happened, Scotland would become no more than a geographical expression and there could be no question of a Scottish literature. This erosion has not continued at anything like the exterminating pace which Cockburn feared. Both languages have retreated but they have survived, and confidence in a distinctive national character has recovered. Were there special circumstances which made Cockburn so pessimistic in the 1850s, so soon after a long period of achievement?

The invention of the steam engine, which he mentions, can hardly be the whole story. Certainly, it made a radical difference. Edinburgh and London suddenly became readily accessible to one another for the first time. We have had many drastic revolutions in communications since then, and they have made English voices and English ideas audible in every house in Scotland. Perhaps the first abrupt jump, from the horse to the railway engine, was a greater shock because people were not yet accustomed to rapid technological change. Even so, the languages, literature and culture of Scotland would have been frail plants indeed if the steam engine alone was a threat to their survival.

In fact, the steam engine, and with it the Industrial Revolution, was only one of a number of powerful changes which struck Scotland at about the same time. For one thing, the government in London had started to intervene actively in Scottish affairs. This was quite new. The previous practice of London governments since the Union of 1707 had been to ignore Scotland as completely as possible, except for the suppression of the Jacobite risings and the subsequent destruction of Highland society. In 1761, for example, when James Stuart Mackenzie became the minister responsible for Scottish affairs, he was surprised to find no papers in his office and no sign that any business was being carried on.[16] In any case, the roles of governments anywhere at that time were very limited. In Scotland, education and such social services as existed were the concern of the Kirk and the burghs. The Union had left intact the Scottish legal system, the Kirk and the burghs, removing only the Parliament which could have given cohesion and expression to the society as a whole. The consequence was that Scotland had been left 'under the guardianship of her own institutions, to win her silent way to national wealth and consequence'.[17]

This last phrase comes from Walter Scott's *The Letters of Malachi Malagrowther* of 1826. These three famous letters to the *Edinburgh Weekly Journal*, which were immediately re-issued as a pamphlet, ostensibly dealt with a proposal for the abolition of the Scottish bank-notes. In fact, as is very clear from Scott's *Journal* and from his letters, he seized the chance to raise the whole question of the treatment of Scotland by England. It had been troubling him for years. 'I will sleep quieter in my grave', he wrote to James Ballantyne, 'for having so fair an opportunity of speaking my mind.'[18] England, he argued, had been content to leave Scotland alone as long as she was poor. Now that Scotland by her own efforts had increased in prosperity by a ratio five times greater than England, the government had begun to intervene with a vengeance. Scotland had become 'a sort of experimental farm'.[19] 'A spirit of proselytism has of late shown itself in England for extending the benefits of their system, in all its strength and weakness, to a country, which has been hitherto flourishing and contented under its own.'[20] He goes on to write what amounts to the first manifesto of modern Scottish nationalism, a plea for diversity and for Scotland to be free to handle her own affairs in her own way without external interference. 'For God's sake, sir, let us remain as Nature made us, Englishmen, Irishmen, and Scotchmen, with something like the impress of our several countries upon each!'[21]

Scott argues that much of the interference in Scottish affairs was contrary to the safeguards in the Treaty of Union and was imposed just for the sake of uniformity in spite of the differences in conditions and attitudes between the two countries. The legal system and the universities were both affected. Lockhart records an episode in 1806 when Scott was deeply disturbed by an attempt to change the procedure in the courts closer to the English model: 'Little by little, whatever your wishes may be, you will destroy and undermine, until nothing of what makes Scotland Scotland shall remain.'[22] In spite of the outstanding reputation of the Scottish universities, there was pressure on them to conform to English models. The first move in this campaign was in 1826, the year in which Scott wrote *Malachi*.[23]

Writing in 1826, Scott said that this interference, treating Scotland with 'absolute contempt' had begun in 'the last fifteen or twenty years and more especially in the last ten'.[24] In other words, it began at about the same time as the Napoleonic Wars and increased after Waterloo. It therefore coincided with the period when London became the capital of the richest, most successful and powerful of the World Powers, which it continued to be for about a hundred years. England was then in a mood of assertive self-confidence, the 'Falkland spirit' writ large and on a much larger scale. It was a mood which had little patience with the divergent ideas and aspirations of a smaller neighbour.

The Napoleonic Wars had other effects within Scotland itself. Even before the war started, the threat of revolutionary ideas from France reduced the establishment to paranoia and panic. Only a few people, like Muir of Huntershill, were actually condemned for sedition; but it was a time when you had to watch what you said. Both Cockburn and Scott, for instance, record that the worthy Dr Adam of the High School of Edinburgh was 'watched and traduced for several years' because 'a Latin and Greek schoolmaster naturally speaks about such things as liberty, and the people, and the expulsion of the Tarquins, and republics.'[25] Such an atmosphere was obviously destructive of the spirit of free enquiry which had made the Scottish Enlightenment. This is perhaps the main reason why Scottish thought became less innovative and wide-ranging about the end of the eighteenth century.

The Napoleonic Wars also introduced another element into Scottish life,

British patriotism. They were the first wars of the modern kind, wide in scale and involving a self-conscious sense of nationhood among the participants. In Scotland this took an additional turn. The Scots Greys may have charged at Waterloo with a cry of 'Scotland for ever', but for the first time Scots also began to share patriotic feelings in common with their neighbours and old enemies across the Tweed. It was expressed by Scott, as in the Introduction to Canto First of *Marmion*. Even Burns, in some moods or under some pressures at least, was capable of expressing it. You find it, for instance, in the song with the significant first line, 'Does haughty Gaul invasion threat?':

> 'Be Britain still to Britain true,
> Amang ourselves united!
> For never but by British hands
> Maun British wrangs be righted!'

There is plenty of evidence, of course, that Burns and Scott continued to feel passionately Scottish at the same time.[26] Ever since, most of their compatriots have continued to feel this dual allegiance, at least from time to time and in certain circumstances. This new British consciousness did not destroy the Scottish identity, but it inevitably tended to weaken and confuse it. Probably this was especially true in the early nineteenth century when Britishness was a fresh idea and one associated with the triumph of Waterloo.

The confusion was compounded by the disproportionate part which the Scots played in the British Army and in the development of the British Empire. This was a consequence of the vacuum inside Scotland itself without control over her own affairs and therefore unable to provide or stimulate outlets for talent and energy at home. For generations, Scots who were denied opportunities in Scotland turned to the Empire instead. 'India', Scott wrote in a letter in 1821, 'is the Corn Chest for Scotland where we poor gentry must send our younger sons as we send our black cattle to the south.'[27] It is impossible to calculate the effect on Scotland of this haemorrhage over the years of millions of intelligent and enterprising people. As long as the Empire lasted, it accustomed the Scots to think of themselves as partners in a joint British endeavour.

At the same time, Scotland was being radically transformed by the Clearances in the Highlands, which destroyed a whole way of life, and by the Industrial Revolution in the Lowlands. Workers for the new industries were sucked away from the countryside to congregate in urban slums. The parish system of the Kirk had served the rural communities, but it could not cope with the scale and intensity of the new social problems in the towns. As these new stresses developed, the Kirk was preoccupied with its own internal controversies. They came to a head in the 'Ten Years Conflict' which began in 1833, but they had their origin in an Act of the British Parliament of 1712. The Patronage Act, passed in that year in violation of the Union settlement, gave rights to the heritors (or landowners) in the appointment of ministers. This had become increasingly intolerable to the Evangelicals who gained control of the General Assembly in 1834. They passed the Veto Act in the Assembly to give an absolute right to the congregations to refuse a minister presented by the heritors. When the Court of Session and the House of Lords upheld the authority of State against the Church, the Evangelicals saw no alternative to withdrawal from the established Church. In the Disruption of 1843, 470 of the 1,200 Church of Scotland ministers abandoned their manses and their salaries and walked out of the General Assembly to form the Free Church.

This wholesale sacrifice of status, home and income for the sake of principle was, in the words of Cockburn, 'one of the rarest occurrences in moral history. I know no parallel to it. . . . It is the most honourable fact for Scotland that its whole history supplies.'[28] It was magnificent, but it was also disastrous. The Kirk had been 'the great unifying institution of the Scottish nation'[29] and a bulwark of the national identity. Since 1707 the General Assembly of the Church had been a substitute for a Parliament, where representatives of the whole people could meet and discuss great national issues. The parish organisation embraced the whole country and most of the population. The Kirk embodied, fortified and expressed many of the strengths, as well as the weaknesses, of the distinctive Scottish attitude to life. When the English divine and wit, and one of the founders of the *Edinburgh Review*, Sydney Smith, arrived in Edinburgh in 1798, he remarked on the influence of the Clergy:

> In England I maintain that (except amongst Ladies in the middle class of life) there is no religion at all. The Clergy of England have no more influence over the people at large than the Cheesemongers of England have. In Scotland the Clergy are extreemly active in the discharge of their functions, and are from the hold they have on the minds of the people a very important body of men. The common people are extreemly conversant with the Scriptures, are really not so much pupils, as formidable critics to their preachers; many of them are well read in controversial divinity. They are perhaps in some points of view the most remarkable nation in the world, and no country can afford an example of so much order, morality, oeconomy, and knowledge amongst the lower classes of Society. Every nation has its peculiarities, the very improved state of the common people appears to me at present to be the phoenomenon of this country.[30]

Smith was right to speak of the ministers and the national character together like this because the two were inextricably intermingled.

With the Disruption, this great force for the cohesion of Scottish society was shattered in two. In every parish in the country there were now two congregations and soon two church buildings. The new building was financed by the contributions of the people and few of the supporters of the Free Church were wealthy. It was yet another sacrifice for the sake of principle, but a distraction from the other work of the Church, including education. Eventually, the Church gradually overcame its divisions and by 1929 it was re-united, apart from a small minority. By then, conditions had radically changed. Life in general had become more secular and the Government had assumed responsibility for education and social welfare. 'Religion was no longer the very pith and core of Scottish life.'[31] The Chuch of Scotland never regained its importance as the central institution in Scottish life which it lost in 1843. It was particularly incapacitated as a custodian of the Scottish identity in the period from the beginning of the conflict in 1833 until the schism began to heal towards the end of the century.

Remarkably enough, this decline in the influence of the Kirk coincides precisely with the period of literary decline. There is, of course, no simple, direct relationship of cause and effect between the two, but the decline of the Kirk affected all aspects of Scottish life. It meant that Scotland was deprived of an important line of defence and force of cohesion at a time when strong pressures were tending in any case to undermine national identity and self-confidence and reduce the country to a provincial backwater. The other two great institutions left intact when political independence was lost in 1707, the law and the universities, were simultaneously under pressure. If the Kirk had not been distracted, the General Assembly might have provided a focus for resistance. As it was, there was no natural centre to hold things together. Under the force of all the circumstances, it is hardly surprising that there was a loss of collective nerve and a weakening of the will for national survival. Perhaps without such nerve and such a will there can be no distinctive literature. Perhaps the best that a writer can do in such a case is, like Carlyle, to seek elsewhere the tradition, the community and the atmosphere which has disappeared at home.

If there is substance in these propositions, one would expect a literary revival only with a recovery of national self-confidence and a general assertion of identity. This is, in fact, what happened. Literary, political and institutional developments all reappeared at the same time. In the 1880s the Scottish Home Rule Association was formed and the Scottish Liberal Party adopted a policy of Home Rule for Scotland. The Government revived the office of Secretary of State for Scotland in response to Scottish pressure. The Scottish National Portrait Gallery, the Scottish History Society and the Scottish Text Society were established. Stevenson wrote *Kidnapped* and *The Master of Ballantrae*. By 1895 Patrick Geddes in his periodical, *The Evergreen*, was speaking about a Scottish Renaissance, long before the term was associated with Hugh MacDiarmid. In spite of the gloom of the mid nineteenth century, the Scottish tradition had not after all ended with a whimper. It still had a long struggle ahead, but that is the theme of Volume 4 of this history.

NOTES

1. George Elder Davie, *The Democratic Intellect: Scotland and her Universities in the Nineteenth Century* (Edinburgh, 1961), p 337.
2. Kurt Wittig, *The Scottish Tradition in Literature* (Edinburgh & London, 1958), pp 253, 254.
3. Roderick Watson, *The Literature of Scotland* (London, 1984), pp 467, 468.
4. William Power, *Literature and Oatmeal: What Literature has Meant to Scotland* (London, 1935), p 117.

5 David Craig, *Scottish Literature and the Scottish People, 1680–1830* (London, 1961), pp 12, 13.
6 John Gibson Lockhart, *Peter's Letters to his Kinsfolk*, 3 vols (Edinburgh, 1819), II, p 356. (Letter LV). In selection edited by William Ruddick (Edinburgh, 1977) p 145.
7 J H Millar, *A Literary History of Scotland* (London, 1903), p 615.
8 John Gross, *The Rise and Fall of the Man of Letters; English Literary Life since 1800* (Harmondsworth, 1973), pp 19–20.
9 William Donaldson, *Popular Literature in Victorian Scotland* (Aberdeen, 1986), pp. xii, 71.
10 Ibid, p. xii.
11 John Buchan, *Sir Walter Scott* (London, 1932) 1961 edn, p 210.
12 Cf. Craig, p 13.
13 Henry Cockburn, *Life of Francis Jeffrey* (Edinburgh, 1852) 1872 edn, pp 150–4.
14 Sir Walter Scott, *The Lives of the Novelists* (London, 1928), pp 294–5.
15 Henry Cockburn, *Journal*, 2 vols (Edinburgh, 1874), II, p 89.
16 Alexander Murdoch, *The People Above: Politics and Administration in Mid-Eighteenth Century Scotland* (Edinburgh, 1980), p 106.
17 Sir Walter Scott, *The Letters of Malachi Malagrowther* (1st published Edinburgh, 1826), Paul H Scott (ed) (Edinburgh, 1981), p 10.
18 *The Letters of Sir Walter Scott*, H J C Grierson (ed) 12 vols (London, 1932–37), Vol IX, p 437
19 Cf. *Malachi Malagrowther*, p 10
20 Ibid., p 9
21 Ibid., p 143
22 John Gibson Lockhart, *Life of Sir Walter Scott* (1837–8), 1900 edn (London) 5 vols, I, p 460, Chapter XV.
23 George Elder Davie, *The Democratic Intellect: Scotland and her Universities in the Nineteenth Century* (Edinburgh, 1961), Chapter 2.
24 Cf. *Malachi Malagrowther*, p 4.
25 Henry Cockburn, *Memorials of his Time*, 1872 edn (Edinburgh) p 5
26 On Walter Scott's attitude, *see* Paul H Scott, *Walter Scott and Scotland* (Edinburgh, 1981), especially Chapter 7.
27 Cf. *Letters of Scott* Vol VI (1934) p 489.
28 Cf. Cockburn's *Journal*, Vol II pp 30, 32.
29 Sydney and Olive Checkland, *Industry and Ethos, Scotland 1832–1914* (Vol 7 of *The New History of Scotland*) (London, 1984), p 122.
30 *The Letters of Sydney Smith*, Nowell C Smith (ed), 2 vols (Oxford, 1953), I, pp 21–2.
31 William Ferguson, *Scotland 1689 to the Present* (Vol IV of *The Edinburgh History of Scotland*) (Edinburgh & London 1968), p 339.

FURTHER READING

Although all the standard histories of Scottish Literature necessarily record the decline between the 1830s and the 1880s, there has been no sustained attempt to consider the factors which may have contributed to it. For literature there is no equivalent book to George Elder Davie's classic work on the universities, *The Democratic Intellect* (Edinburgh, 1961 and reprinted as a paperback in 1982). There are valuable comments on the general problem of cultural pressure in Michael Hechter's *Internal Colonialism; The Celtic Fringe in British National Development, 1536–1966* (London, 1975). My own Saltire Pamphlet, *In Bed with an Elephant* (Edinburgh, 1985) is a brief account of the Scottish experience.

The main primary text is Sir Walter Scott's *The Letters of Malachi Malagrowther* (Edinburgh, 1826). It is included in the various collections of Scott's miscellaneous prose and there is a recent reprint which is mentioned in the Notes. The works of Cockburn and Lockhart, also mentioned in the Notes, throw light on the literary climate at the beginning of the period of decline. See also works identified in the Notes.

Chapter 2

Industry, Religion and the State of Scotland

CHRISTOPHER HARVIE

'No century in modern Scottish history has been subject to so little close scrutiny as the nineteenth' was the comment of one researcher in the 1960s.[1] This is certainly not the case today, after several substantial investigations of the economic and social transformation of the country from its predominantly agrarian existence in 1801. In that year 46 per cent of Scots still lived in the North, and 42.5 per cent in the Central counties; by 1871 the latter accounted for 61 per cent and two-thirds of the total population lived in towns.[2] The work of Christopher Smout, Iain Hutchison, Stuart Jay Brown and Robert Anderson—among many others—has meant that, although *lacunae* remain, we now know a great deal about how this happened. Our problem now is to try to synthesise accounts which demonstrate that a remarkable plurality of experiences were contained within this transition, and were only imperfectly assimilated into the cultural expressions of those who had undergone them.

In 1935, for example, Edwin Muir wrote in *Scottish Journey* that

> from another point of view one may say that it [Glasgow and its industrial hinterland] is not Scotland at all, or not Scotland in particular, since it is merely one of the expressions of Industrialism. . . . Glasgow is consequently far more like Manchester than like Edinburgh.[3]

Muir's statement manages to be both true and misleading. Glasgow was of course dependent on technological change, and this marked life in it off from life in the administrative capital. Yet ships-and-engineering-based Glasgow was as different from textile-and-engineering Manchester as both were from jute-jam-and-journalism Dundee. Muir's own fall from edenic Orkney to purgatorial Glasgow was only one biography among millions, but his itinerary contributed to his critical stance. Others with different biographies (one thinks of John Wheatley, for example, shifting from rural poverty in Ireland to success in Glasgow business and politics) responded in more optimistic ways, recapturing community and fellowship where Muir found only alienation and death.

This is emblematic of a more general confusion, with explicitly literary elements embedded in it. The onset of turbulent industrial change in Scotland was accompanied by a failure to integrate the experience of it into an explanation, and thus into a social doctrine, which would be politically or intellectually convincing. The period between 1831 and 1881, when the population of Glasgow rose 153 per cent, the economic structure shifted from agriculture and textiles to coal, iron and engineering, and (uniquely in Europe) economic growth coincided with large-scale emigration, is also that of the great 'black hole' in Scottish creative literature and social thought. Not only do Scott and Galt fall silent, but the massive social documentation associated with Sir John Sinclair's *Statistical Accounts* ends in the 1830s. Just at the point where they could have proved most useful in attempting to cope with the assault of industrialisation, competence and confidence deserted the Scots elite. In 1843, confronted with widespread distress and the creation of a Royal Commission to enquire into poverty in Scotland, Henry Cockburn wrote in his *Journal* in tones of near-panic:

> During all this period, extending from 1785 to 1825, it was our monopoly of the steam engine that made us. There were then probably more of these wealth producers in Glasgow than in all the continent of Europe. That monopoly is now gone forever. A richer world may make us a richer people, but still we must feel its vicissitudes, which, if it be a world whose wealth depends mainly on manufactures, must be as periodical as our own. . . I see no ground for expecting . . . that we can ever be uncursed by these heartrending visitations—visitations which are bad enough as productive of misery, but far worse when viewed as instruments of political danger.[4]

The 1842–43 depression moved the young Manchester-German Friedrich Engels to a more optimistic revolutionary diagnosis—in part by drawing on the dramatic rhetoric of one powerful and unmistakably Scots literary figure, Thomas Carlyle—but the conflagration Engels predicted, and Cockburn feared, did not come about.[5] What did happen in Scotland in 1843, however, had serious and lasting consequences for Scotland's political role in Britain. The Church, when united, had controlled education and poor relief in the Scottish parishes, and its influence penetrated deep into the Scottish 'clerisy' of lawyers, academics, journalists and politicians. The split within it on 18 May 1843, when over a third of the clergy left to form the Free Church, effectively ended the form of semi-autonomous government which had been the single most significant element in Scottish civil society.

The apparent evaporation of the 'great' literature of the Scots bourgeoisie coincides with this loss of direction. Are the two linked? Or has the literary collapse been exaggerated, perhaps through the application of standards derived from an English 'great tradition' which are inappropriate for Scotland? In the 1960s the prosecution case, out of Marx by Leavis, was set out at some length by David Craig in *Scottish Literature and the Scottish People* (1961). After the flowering of a rare demotic voice in Burns, Craig saw the debasing of standards, both through Anglicisation and through the creation, by a widespread but unimaginative educational system, of a large and undemanding Scottish literary public. The elite had settled for assimilation; no other group was capable of providing that crucial artefact of 'print capitalism', the 'novel of ideas'; so the novel of ideas hung fire at least until the beginning of the twentieth century. And probably beyond. As far as Craig was concerned, the flawed achievement of Sir Walter Scott was a terminus. All that followed was the eccentric, isolated contribution of Hugh Mac-Diarmid. In this Craig echoed earlier Scoto-Oxbridge scholars like George Gordon, President of Magdalen and a member of the influential 1921 Newbolt Committee on English in the Schools, whose dismissal of Scottish literature after Scott was even more sweeping:

> The Scottish Muse has many things to her credit in the century and more since Burns died, but singly they are slight and innovate little about the past . . . Scotland . . . continues to produce its occasional writer of genius, its Stevenson and the rest, but not one has kept his roots there and stayed where he was planted . . . it leaves Scotland bare and the old altars smokeless.[6]

Even if a nationalist position were adopted, which did not accept this national eclipse as inevitable, the failure of Scottish literature to evolve any equivalent to Fontane or Flaubert, Manzoni, Perez Galdos, Ibsen or Turgenev, seemed an integral part of the weakness which characterised what ought to have been the country's liberal-nationalist phase. When the keynotes for a national resistance were needed, the national *litterateurs* were not there to sound them. Scott, a nationalist but also an ultra-conservative, knew what he was about when he settled for innocuous antiquarianism. According to Edwin Muir, his writing

> skims over every aspect of experience that could be obnoxious to the most tender or prudish feelings and in fact renounces both freedom and responsibility. Scott, it seems to me, was largely instrumental in bringing the novel to that point; with his enormous prestige he helped to establish the mediocre and the trivial.[7]

This has been countered by two theses of which the earlier was the more fundamental. Writing, in the same year as Craig, the Edinburgh logician George Davie argued (in *The Democratic Intellect*) that attempts after the 1820s to anglicise higher education stimulated a steady resistance from philosophic defenders of the 'democratic intellect'. They were worn down by persistent attacks but never totally surrendered. The principle of Davie's position was that the Scottish *Weltanschauung*, derived from the 'common sense' school of the eighteenth century, with its enthronement of reason and personal judgement, still conformed to an essentially republican rationalism. This found fiction inherently misleading, a position broadly held by radical movements in Britain until the 1830s,[8] by Carlyle, who had little time for the 'long ear of the novel', and by Carlyle's disciple Walt Whitman in his prescription of an epical, philosophic poetry—'bold, modern and all-surrounding and kosmical'—as the keystone of a democratic American culture.[9] Not only was Whitman a major influence on Scottish working-class culture, but this programme bears a considerable resemblance to that of Hugh Mac-Diarmid, another sceptic about the worth of fiction, and Davie's mentor.[10]

More recently the Aberdeen economic historian William Donaldson, in his ground-breaking *Popular Literature in Victorian Scotland: Language, Fiction and the Press* (1986) has applied John Sutherland's analysis of the literary production process to the conditions which appertained in industrialising Scotland around the mid-nineteenth century, with remarkable results, arguing that

> ... Scottish culture was (and is) a popular culture, and that its major vehicle during the period was not the London-dominated booktrade, but the Scottish newspaper press, owned, written and circulating within the country ... in the Scottish context fiction published in the press was more significant than fiction published in book form as well as being infinitely greater in extent ... use of the Scots language was much more extensive and important than might otherwise be concluded ... and that during this period newspapers provided the environment for a vernacular prose revival of unprecedented proportions.[11]

The Scottish novel not only has life, but has it (perhaps) in over-abundance, Donaldson having hinted at the existence of upwards of 5,000 novels buried in the back-files of provincial weeklies.[12]

But is a mute inglorious Dickens likely to lurk in the files of the *Kelso Chronicle*? And even if he does, can a genius who remained obscure outwith his locality be granted cultural significance? Certainly, even if we can't unearth a Thackeray, a George Eliot or a Trollope, an equivalent to a Wilkie Collins or a Mark Rutherford would be an interesting find. But figures like Scott and Burns had been—and still were in Victorian times—unavoidable in national life. They had no successors. Stevenson and Barrie were cult figures of a sort, but of *British* cults, and no amount of reappraisal of the likes of George MacDonald, Mrs Oliphant, and Alexander Smith is going to change this. Donaldson may have a strong case to press on behalf of William Alexander, but the fact that—apart from *Johnny Gibb of Gushetneuk* (1871)—Alexander's *oeuvre* has taken over a century to penetrate beyond the North-East reflects the absence of that apparatus of public political criticism, the erection of a national *canon*, which characterised national movements in Europe and indeed profoundly affected Scotland once MacDiarmid got into his stride in the mid 1920s.

Donaldson's study in fact ends on a note of decline, with the commercialisation of the weekly press, and the sensationalism of the 'new journalism' evicting realism as well as radical liberalism.[13] Matters became worse between the wars with the local amalgamations which produced Conservative monoliths like the D C Thomson group, attaining its apogee in the founding of the *Sunday Post* (1931) just as the national critic MacDiarmid reached the height of his powers. The old Tories at Blackwoods and London publishers, notably T S Eliot, were to do more for the Scottish renaissance than the Scottish popular press.

Elsewhere, I have raised a more tentative thesis that a national literature of some sophistication emerged in the nineteenth century which was neither 'reasonable' nor demotic but a more conservative recovery of folklore and tradition akin to that pioneered by the brothers Grimm and Karl von Savigny in Prussia, which had its culmination in the Scots contribution to the rise of social anthropology in the persons of Robertson Smith, Andrew Lang, W A Clouston, J F MacLennan and J G Frazer.[14] This drew heavily on the ethnic variety of Scottish society, and on the survival of a pre-literary culture along-side industrial communities, but the point of literary production occurred for the most part furth of Scotland, and hence could not restore a Scottish cultural centre.

The existence of four competitive theses suggests that the main problem in creating such a centre may have been that individuals and social groups faced choices diffused among a range of moderately-powered cultural options. The argument of this essay is that these choices were, moreover, presented at a critical juncture to a political structure too pluralistic to concentrate its efforts on the most effective mechanisms of cultural dissemination.

The situation which resulted is by now familiar: a 'high' intelligentsia which ran—rather than drifted—south in the decades after the Enlightenment, to occupy university chairs, parliamentary seats, and editorial offices, and what R G Collingwood would term the con-creation—by this group, the 'red' Scots and its parochial native brethren the 'black' Scots—of a nostalgic, ruralist fetish to stand guard over the but-an'-bens remaining: the Kailyard, Balmorality, Tom Nairn's 'great Tartan monster'.[15]

This was what happened. How it happened is another matter. Nairn followed Nicholas Phillipson in seeing assimilation as a necessary consequence of the Enlightenment, that premature anticipation of the modernisation ethic of mid-nineteenth-century liberal-nationalism.[16] Improvement generated intellectual and political ambitions which could no longer be realised in the context of a nation of two millions: the move to the larger arena of Britain and the Empire was inevitable and profitable. David Craig and, following him, Andrew Noble, posited darker motives: a loss of nerve by an elite confronted by the new and terrifying challenge of industry, urbanisation and economic fluctuations, which both in its literature and in its politics, fled from civic reponsibility to rural sentimentalism—'a wholly artificial and politically corrupt treatment of town versus country'[17]—and an acquiescence in English administration.

It is, however, a mistake to grant a calculated quality to political processes which were usually more hit-or-miss affairs. This is a major problem with socio-cultural critiques which tend to assume a straightforward relationship between ideology and action. Robert Anderson, for example, has shown that class interests and institutional and local loyalties did much, in the course of nineteenth century eductional policy-making, to rearrange the participants whom George Davie classifies as 'Anglicisers' and 'Scots'.[18] Later on, when Tartanry attained its fullest extent in the shrewd marketing of the Kailyard authors in the 1890s, a counter-current was already setting towards Labour representation, social reform, native MPs and realist literature. It bore substantial fruit in a nationalist revival in the 1900s which could have attained its political goal of home rule but for the outbreak of war in 1914.[19] The Scotland of Ian MacLaren was also the Scotland of J M Robertson, Cunninghame Graham, and George Douglas Brown.

The fact that the debate about Scotland's unquestionable cultural 'inferiorism' in the nineteenth century has been conducted to a great extent by philosophers has given it a pronounced Weberian tang: nationalism and religious change are seen as tending to proceed from ideas to political action. Yet political interactions can exert at least as powerful an influence on cultural ethos as *vice versa*. To link these to a social context is not to succumb to crude Marxian reductionism: early nineteenth-century Scotland presented a society politically and economically so deeply-faulted that it was virtually impossible that any national intellectual consensus would emerge.

In literary terms the Scottish failure to emulate the English 'great tradition', is distinctive enough to appear autonomous. It took five main forms. Literacy and authorship appear to have remained much more widespread than in England. Subjected to a rough and ready sample, John W Cousin's *Everyman Biographical Dictionary of English Literature* (1910) showed around 15 per cent of its nineteenth-century entries as drawn from Scotland, a disproportionately high number (although one perhaps attributable to a Scottish editor!). Something like 20 per cent emigrated to England, the rest remained in the north. The overall impression they give is of a timebound respectability; essayists who would never bear reprinting; theologians, hymn-writers, editors, scientific popularisers. In many ways it is the literary cast-list of an average European nation; but the national history, which 'fixed' the significance of similar men, whose statues grace squares in provincial towns in Finland or Portugal, is simply not present.

The problem of these 'average men' was not just that they coincided with the literary capitalism of the world's most powerful nation working next door and at full throttle, but that they had so little impact in their own country. Industrial growth was accompanied by problems of poverty and sanitation, drunkenness and disorder, to which the traditional institutions of a literate country brought little relief. The government commissioner who wrote of New Monkland in 1842

> a population has been growing up immersed more deeply than any I have met with in the most disgusting habits of debauchery.[20]

reflected the breakdown of civil society under such stresses. No less palpable was the fact that nearby Airdrie's library owned only 500 books, to serve over 12,000 people, in 1856.[21]

Industrialisation ought, as Edwin Muir assumed, to have been a homogenising factor, yet the structures of Scottish middle-class society, of church politics, education and the universities, remained sufficiently remote from those of England to deny them any British representative quality. Scotland could not provide a Barchester or a Coketown. Scots society could occasionally be attractive to the literary market, but consistent success required skilful tactics. An anecdotal, mildly nationalistic, ecumenical sort of literature came into vogue in the 1850s—Dean Ramsay did well with *Reminiscences of Scottish Life and Character* (1855) and Dr John Brown with *Rab and His Friends* (1859)—but no Scots writer commanded the literary market in the style of Dickens or George Eliot. This was partly due to the politics of copyright. There was little sense in addressing the potentially huge exile market, only to be ripped off by American pirate publishers. Significantly, the conquests of the Kailyard followed hard on the heels of the Anglo-American Copyright Treaty (1891).

Scotland also lacked the Darwinian seed-bed of literary bohemia on which the publishing machine fed.[22] For all the Scots dominance of London publishing, journalism and circulating libraries, Scotland itself was a country of pin-money *litterateurs*, otherwise secure in the professions, and constrained by their intense internal politics and *amour-propre*. The serious Victorian novel, the result of close collaboration between author and publisher, was often launched as carefully as a railway company, or was even the work of 'in-house' authors,[23] while the Scottish social novel had plainly lost vogue after Galt and Scott had overstocked the market. It did not recover until the end of the century, despite the opening-up of the country by rail and steamer for middle-class tourism—or perhaps because of it.

The new Scotland thus projected was emphatically not an urban, industrial country but Walter Scott's sanitised version of the clan system, offered to tourists in the aftermath of Queen Victoria's discovery of the Scottish Highlands in 1842 and her settlement at Balmoral in 1848. The decade which witnessed the breakdown of Scottish semi-autonomy, and the evictions which completed the rationalisation of the Highland economy, ended with Prince Albert 'composing' the Highlands as the first British Heritage Trail. As his biographer, Theodore Martin (a Tory of the Aytoun-Wilson breed) wrote, 'He loved the people, he admired their character, and he respected their prejudices as the antique vestiges of other days'.[24] For most of the century Scotland presented a beguiling mixture of the demotic and the picturesque. Just as Arthur Hugh Clough's Chartist undergraduate hero (in the *Bothie of Tober-na-Vuolich* (1848)) fell for the simplicities of Highland life while on an Oxford reading-party, and carried the crofter's daughter off to New Zealand, Queen Victoria, in her forays *incognito* through the Highlands, cast back to the legendary 'Gaberlunzie kings' of the middle ages. Until the 1870s, and at a time when republican ideas might have been expected to be popular, royal prestige was probably higher than that of most parliamentarians and, because of religious divisions, higher than that of church leaders. When it started to recede, after the mid 1870s, it was replaced by a veneration of 'sympathetic' figures from the metropolitan elite, in particular Gladstone and Rosebery, reading-party veterans who received a truly remarkable degree of native indulgence.[25]

For most of the period 1843–1914, Scottish politico-cultural life was, therefore, marked by the 'long swings' of 'tendencies' rather than the more febrile relationships of 'transactional' politics.[26] The latter could have given a much more elaborated range of flashpoints, but essentially it was eliminated after the 'resolution' of the 'Ten Years' Conflict' in 1843, and not restored—except momentarily—until during World War I, and more lastingly in the period after 1945.

The key to Scottish culture-politics in the nineteenth century, therefore, lies in the crisis of the 1830s and 1840s, and it is significant that one of the most important twentieth-century Scots novelists, Robin Jenkins, has been driven to consider this *Zeitbruch* in *The Awakening of George Darroch* (1985): significant, too, that he finds it deeply unsatisfactory as a climacteric; less a matter of burning conviction than of obscure issues of ecclesiastical politics which are all but impossible to comprehend from the secularised standpoint of the late twentieth century.[27]

Jenkins echoes the emphatic rejection of the cosmology of Victorian Scotland in J M Robertson's *The Perversion of Scotland* (1886), which contributed considerably to the socialist and secularist movement of the turn of the century. Yet, with recent experience of how technological and political modernisation can be coupled with 'reactionary' and simplistic religious beliefs—in the Islamic world, in the USA and, painfully close to home, in Ulster—we can perhaps better appreciate the political power of evangelical protestantism in an early nineteenth century Britain undergoing unprecedented transition, than could an earlier, more optimistic, generation.

Evangelicalism was, at one level, a Britain-constructing, Anglophone ideology. *The Pilgrim's Progress*, the great bequest to demotic belief of the Civil War period (which saw the most drastic centralisation ever of British government) became a fixture in practically every working-class household in the eighteenth century; Wesley took care to include the peripheries of Britain in his preaching tours, which were at least of indirect importance in 'naturalising' his brand of vital religion.[28] Even in Wales, where Methodism broke up the Established Church, and largely used the Welsh language as its means of communication, its social goals were integrationist. On top of all this, the wars with France after 1793 meant that government placed considerable stress on broadcasting an uncomplicated faith which would promote cross-class solidarity and, at a time of rapid industrial growth, quarantine dangerous, democratic ideas. Victor Kiernan has noted that evangelicalism had

> the great merit, in the face of egalitarian ideas, of throwing into relief the equality of souls without disturbing the inequality of ranks. All men were not equally good, as Rousseau had made people think, but they were all equally bad.[29]

The problem was that evangelicalism's postulates were themselves paradoxical, and became grotesquely so once conservative political pressure was
removed. The notion of the equality of souls may have been employed against
democracy—this was particularly true of Scotland in the age of Dundas and
Braxfield—but it was a challenge to ideas of church authority which were
derived from social hierarchy. The 'enthusiastic' urban middle classes, with
their church extension and mission enterprises, assaulted the careful balances
of the old rural order; even their 'Britishness' menaced the privilege of the
Scots political elite.[30] Finally, the causes evangelicalism furthered, like abol-
ishing slavery and, later, fighting the drink trade, extended a sort of 'arm's
length' political participation to groups—the lower middle classes, artisans,
women—who had not hitherto experienced such involvement.

Scots evangelicalism was far from revolutionary radicalism and the dissenting tradition of 'Commonwealth man', yet it had contacts with the more
fastidious liberalism which was incubated by the *Edinburgh Review* and waxed
in the aftermath of the Napoleonic wars, while its capacity to massage social
tensions concurred with the desire of Scottish civil society, the legal profession in particular, to 'incorporate' industrial workers through equitable treatment.[31] In Scotland both had a political structure to operate on which was
ostensibly favourable. The Kirk could indeed claim jurisdiction over what
Henry Cockburn, a fairly representative figure in both groups, called 'the
whole Christian and civic economy' of Scotland.[32] Its annual General
Assembly looked more like a parliament than many of the provincial assemblies of continental Europe, and acted as the *locus* of a type of transactional
politics. As Ian Clark has written:

> It has often been remarked that, lacking a parliament of her own, Scotland has
> found in the General Assembly a forum for national debate and self-expression
> far more resonant than one might expect of a Church Court. The Moderates
> welcomed and encouraged this, and towards the end of the century actually
> deplored the fact, that the Assembly was being deserted by the judges, statesmen
> and nobility who had, a little earlier, adorned it as elders.[33]

The problem was that the Evangelical ideal of the Godly Commonwealth
was contested both by the political elite and by most radicals. The landed
classes still regarded church matters as an extension of the authority they
exercised by appointing to livings under the Patronage Act of 1712. The
church was subordinate to the Court of Session in Edinburgh and ultimately
to Parliament in London, in both of which the landed interest was supreme.
To radicals the Church had, by its acquiescence in patronage, forfeited its
claims to autonomy, and many had left for dissenting groups, some claiming
to be the 'true' Kirk, and willing to accept establishment on their own terms,
others rejecting the principle completely. English politicians tended to mistake
the 'Voluntaries' for a Scottish version of English dissent. But in many ways
they were further from the Non-Intrusionists (the Evangelicals who wanted
to make the presentation of ministers subject to a parochial veto) than

they were from the Moderates, the traditionally dominant group among the ministers.

Yet because Scottish evangelicalism was a broad social movement, not a purely political response, prominent laymen could exercise patronage on its behalf, while 'enlightenment' within the universities actually increased the power of 'vital religion', by showing up the increasingly time-serving ethos of the *fin-de-siecle* Moderates.[34] The 'popular' or 'wild' party was favoured by the Crown in over a third of preferments to its own livings (particularly dense in the Highlands and in new urban areas) and many private patrons concurred, with the result that Robert Dundas, nephew of the Scotch manager, Viscount Melville, could write in 1808:

> The Popular Party in the Church, like the Opposition in the State, are infinitely more assiduous in their Measures . . . and by applying through every possible Channel they have in the case of every Vacancy of a Church in Scotland, succeeded as often in putting in Clergy of their way of Thinking, that many Presbyteries . . . are now gradually converted into Wild Presbyteries, and uniformly send to the Assembly members of that description.[35]

As the Moderates retreated from their 'national' ideal of a Kirk 'treating with government in equal terms',[36] their opponents, the 'popular party' came to resemble an embryonic national liberal movement of the sort currently emerging in Europe.

It was into this inchoate situation that a particularly talented Scots generation inserted itself, chief among whom was Thomas Chalmers (1780–1847). Only eight years younger than Scott, one year younger than Henry Cockburn, and an almost direct contemporary of such religious nationalists as the Irishman Daniel O'Connell (1775–1847) and the Danish bishop N F S Grundtvig (1783–1872), Chalmers has been one of those figures treated with idolatry by one generation, and almost totally dismissed by its successors. For the purposes of the Free Church in the nineteenth century his career had to be described in the heroic terms of his son-in-law William Hanna's massive biography (1849–52); others—and the number grew—came to see him as

> an 'evil genius'. . . . whose personal ambition and drive to create an ecclesiastical despotism destroyed the unity of the Church of Scotland, embittered Scottish religious life for nearly a century, and permanently ended the social influence of Christianity in Scotland.[37]

Recent reappraisals by Stewart Brown and A C Cheyne have revealed a fascinating, contradictory figure of much more contemporary interest, as complex and psychiatrist's-couch-worthy as Henry Cockburn himself.[38] What is evident in Chalmers' career is not the rationalist Moderate's conversion to scriptural literalism but the awkward coexistence of both impulses within the intellect of a moody, energetic man, deprived of any stable political or social structure through which these could be resolved. Chalmers' scientific interests show him in the direct Enlightenment line, yet he recoiled both from its social atomism and from its contemptuous rejection of the embattled tradition of seventeenth-century Calvinism. His 'Godly Commonwealth' was less a forerunner of Herbert Spencerian individualism[39] than, in its recreation of the parish as an active, interdependent social unit, a strongly communitarian ideal which restated the 'active' society associated with Adam Ferguson and his *Essay on the History of Civil Society* (1767). Andrew Noble has denounced Chalmers' attempt to resuscitate an essentially rural ideal as absurd,[40] yet, although he used the government's fear of social disorder as a means of getting purchase for his plans, his programme of parochial regeneration was nationalistic rather than reactionary.

Tradition has also insisted on Chalmers' Toryism, yet Stewart Brown has shown how this was the product of manoeuvre rather than conviction or conversion. Chalmers was a Tory of a far different stamp to Sir Walter Scott, whose Moderatism had gone sour by the 1820s. In 1829 he took the liberal, Canningite line in the dispute over Peel's Catholic Relief Bill—although many of his followers wanted a more emphatic expression of Protestantism—and he favoured Reform in 1832. Only the Whigs' continuing hostility to the 'Non-Intrusionist' cause pushed him in 1841 into the Peelite camp—to no good effect.[41]

The events of the 'Ten Years' Conflict' are well enough known. The Evangelicals gained a majority in the General Assembly in 1834, passed the Veto Act and sided with the parishioners of Auchterarder in 1834 and Marnoch in 1837 in rejecting their patrons' nominees. The Court of Session abrogated the Veto Act in 1838; but the Assembly reaffirmed it in the following year, and suspended the Presbytery of Strathbogie, which had upheld the rights of the patrons. In 1841 a 'Claim of Right', signed by the majority of the Scottish clergy, affirmed the autonomy of the Church.[42] It was the rejection of this, in 1842, which prompted the withdrawal of a majority of the Evangelicals from the General Assembly in May 1843 and the founding of the Free Church.

This sequence of religious politics was, however, paralleled by events in the economic and political spheres which substantially determined the ultimate outcome. The 1830s saw a revival in Scottish labour organisation after the repression of 1819–20, with cotton-spinners and coal-miners struggling to maintain their position as a working-class elite against cheap labour—from the Highlands and Ireland—and new technology. This came to a head in 1837, when the Glasgow spinners, fighting the attempt by a combination of employers to reduce wages, were attacked and, as a trade union, effectively destroyed by Archibald Alison, Sheriff of Lanarkshire since 1834. Alison, a highly-ideological Tory of the Blackwood type, repeated the prescription against the miners in 1842. The same year saw the climax of his brother, Professor William Pulteney Alison's, assault on the old Scottish Poor Law, somewhat eased by the depression of 1842, the worst in the century, which forced members of the government to take personal responsibility for relieving the desperate poverty of Paisley, the fourth largest town in Scotland. The pressure of such philanthropic Tories brought about the Royal Commission on the Scottish Poor Law, and the whole notion of Church responsibility in the social domain came under threat.[43]

When the Assembly presented the Claim of Right, the Tories had a new resolution. They had been prepared to make appointments to their own livings in the spirit of the Veto Act, but although leaders like Sir James Graham and the Earl of Aberdeen were sympathetic to the Non-Intrusionists, the Claim, and any attempts at legislation on its basis, failed. As substantial landowners, Graham and Aberdeen were reluctant to deal a blow against their order, while the Whigs remained pro-Voluntarist.[44] Chalmers' statesmanship then broke down. He could not hold the Evangelicals together in their confrontation course with the government, so he led most of them—but a minority of the whole clergy—out.

For many clergy the fateful trip to Edinburgh meant two new encounters: with the railway, opened from Glasgow in the previous year, and with the photographers David Octavius Hill and Robert Adamson, who were preparing for the former's huge (and hideous) painting 'The Signing of the Deeds of Demission'. The Disruption took place at a critical juncture, as—with a labour force cowed and, helpfully, low-paid—the country moved into an age of new technology.[45] With ever-more-powerful engines, Napier's steamers threshed their way down a dredged and tamed Clyde; in five years the railways would offer two routes to the English system. Neither a nationalistic clergy nor a radical labour force could—although Chalmers would claim that all good radicals were Free Churchmen[46]—do much to impose a Scottish element on the results.

Church-building was a sort of material compensation for the fact that the Godly Commonwealth ideal had been destroyed for good. The aim of regulating 'Christian and civic life' was impossible in a divided church and, with the secularisation of the Poor Law in 1844 and the more gradual withdrawal of educational authority, the agenda of the General Assemblies of both churches shrank in a couple of decades to purely religious business.[47] Hill's 'Sun Pictures' are now much more familiar than the grounds for the Disruption and, indeed, than the mass of churches that the Free Church heroically erected throughout the country, until there was scarcely a large village in the land which did not have three solid Gothic-revival barns, half-empty then and garages or warehouses today.

Perhaps the element of disaster can be exaggerated. Scotland lost an Assembly which had, proportionate to the activities of government, as much if not more authority as that proposed in 1978–9, but the united Church had failed to make way against Westminster in 1834–43, and the General Assembly remained a religious forum in a pluralistic and increasingly secular society. It could have developed towards a form of parliament, but—given Irish immigration and the class nature of Scottish society—it could also have become a focus for religious and racial intolerance, which Protestant divisions and the two-party system eventually worked to defuse. Chalmers was personally capable of a far-sighted ecumenicism, but some of his lieutenants, notably James Begg, cooked up a potentially toxic mixture of anti-Catholicism, dogmatic scripturalism, social reform and Scottish nationalism which could in practice have been unpleasantly divisive.[48]

Although the Free Church bridged one enormous gulf in Scottish society— it was the first body to create a common concern on the part of Highlander and Lowlander—the sudden evaporation of the issue of church government after 1843 left a peculiar void at the heart of Scots political identity. The issue had been the focus for a wide range of political concerns, not the least being the confrontation of the territorial aristocracy and the bourgeoisie. Although the Free Church was all too eager to publicise its aristocratic backers, these were few, while Scottish Chartists seem to have been notably religous.[49] How far did the rights of the parishioners become important in radical politics? The young William Latto, editor of the *People's Journal* after 1861, had started off his career in Ceres as a weaver, Free Churchman, and physical force Chartist, and while such a combination would have worried Chalmers, Latto was probably not alone.[50] When Johnny Gibb defied the 'muckle farmers' and helped the Free Kirk in his Aberdeenshire parish he was rebelling against the same hegemony which the thrawn radical John Guthrie would challenge in *Sunset Song*.

Yet the marginal issues which remained contentious after the Disruption— patronage itself was straightforwardly abolished by Disraeli in 1874—meant that the whole process of church creation was pervaded with unreality. As James Kellas, himself a son of the manse, has written:

> ... it brought out the worst in Scottish Presbyterianism—intolerance, arrogance and irrelevance. The more they were alike, the more they hated each other; the more they argued about mundane matters, the more they attributed them to divine intervention; and while industrial Scotland wallowed in the slums of Glasgow and the crofters starved in the highlands, the Scottish middle classes argued about church attendances and the size of members contributions to the church plate . . .[51]

Politically the Disruption led to a Liberal dominance which lasted, with only a short hiatus at the end of the century, right up to World War I. But at a deeper level there seems to have been a revulsion—a 'scunner'—against the business of government, linked to Westminster's myopia on the issues which had brought the Disruption about. Although there was a myth that Scottish members could get what they wanted because they acted as a 'little parliament'[52]—a coherent interest group—this seems to have been a fairly rare occurrence, increasingly contradicted by the religious-based divisions between Liberal Free Churchmen and Voluntaries in a powerful position in the Commons, and Tory supporters of the Establishment, solidly grouped in the Lords. In the absence of a specifically Scottish minister, something bemoaned by the short-lived Scottish Rights movement in the 1850s, such splits caused repeated failure to create an adequate educational settlement.[53] What eventually emerged was a rather slavish copy of Forster's English Act of 1870, more democratic in certain aspects, but controlled from Whitehall by a succession of convinced Balliol unionists.[54] And this was a success compared with the almost total inability of central government to control the course and consequences of the breakneck industrialisation which produced a lop-sided economy and an inequitable society.

Not until the late 1870s, when economic depression and in particular the catastrophic collapse of the City of Glasgow Bank in 1878 coincided with Gladstone's rediscovery of Scotland, did a 'Scottish' politics re-emerge. Even then, it was a tentative affair. Whoever described Ramsay MacDonald (who made his *debut* in the mid 1880s as a Scottish home ruler) as having the vertebrae of a jellyfish made a telling point. The years 1843–78 had removed the spine of the 'Scottish Question'. Putting it back was to prove a long and tedious business, periodically interrupted by the incursions of MacDiarmid's 'wunds wi 'warlds to swing'—Communism, depression, war.

This had profound cultural and literary implications. In England in the 1840s the novel was used to debate issues of social reform—less positively than is usually assumed, but the agenda is there. Between 1865 and 1880, from George Eliot's *Felix Holt* to Trollope's *The Duke's Children*, the novel of political practice and public doctrine was at the centre of English literary consciousness.[55] It was almost totally absent from Scotland: Alexander's *Johnny Gibb*, whose subtitle is *Glimpses of the Parish Politics about AD 1843*, is the exception that proves the rule.

The disjunction, however, goes further. There is a sense that in mid-nineteenth-century Scotland the problem of engaging with contemporary society was so difficult that the flight of talented writers such as William Black, 'Fiona MacLeod' and George MacDonald to the other extreme—fantasy—was facilitated. Scotland was at one level too fractured, composed of too many disparate societies, each possessed of its own dialect and social categories.[56] At another, it was divided vertically into fearsome degrees of privilege and deprivation, numbing for the few from the middle classes who penetrated into them. Trollope essays a portrait of a Scottish plutocrat in Robert Kennedy in *Phineas Finn* (1867) and the result is both realistic and chilling, while it's possible to see in much of Stevenson's work a coded expression of a middle class *grand peur*—of the underprivileged surfacing in violent revolt.[57]

But there does seem to be a way out, or at least of constructing an observation platform over the 'black hole'. Douglas Gifford has suggested that a central element in the Scottish fiction tradition is the 'unreliable narrator',[58] and I would like to extend this concept. In a period which sees civil society in turmoil, the creative writer is unlikely to aim for the ideal-type 'truth' of Scott or Galt, in which fictional examples validate an accepted notion of historical pattern. Instead he will tend to record personal experience, and then trim and adapt it, to produce an artificial equilibrium in an otherwise constantly-changing, baffling society.

One instance is the great exile himself. The Scottish predicament would have come as no surprise to the man who wrote, at Craigenputtock in 1831:

Given a world of knaves, to produce an Honesty from their united action? Were not experiments enough of this kind tried before all Europe, and found wanting, when in that doomsday of France, the infinite gulf of human Passion shivered asunder the thin rinds of Habit, and burst forth all-Devouring, as in seas of Nether Fire? Which cunningly-devised 'constitution', constitutional, republican, democratic, sansculottic, could bind that raging chasm together?[59]

Carlyle had met Chalmers during his Glasgow ministry in 1820, and while he found him personally sympathetic, he was sceptical about his social and religious aims.[60] Carlyle was also to see his talented friend Edward Irving (then Chalmers' assistant) go right over the edge. His own view, perhaps obtained via wary borrowings from Saint-Simonianism, was that in the 'critical' period that European civilisation had entered only 'provisional solutions' were possible. His rhetorical flirtations with Irish and Italian nationalism, and that appreciation of the human consequences of *laissez-faire* which impressed Engels, could be combined with endorsements of individualism which commended themselves to such full-blooded parliamentary opportunists as Disraeli and John Morley.[61] An existential cultivation of strength of character and the work ethic was all that could combat *anomie*.

The rationale behind this—and the link to Scotland—was conveyed by biography; Carlyle on Burns, Carlyle on Scott, Carlyle on Heroes, Carlyle—interminably—on Carlyle. It was not that a British, or imperial, loyalty replaced his Scottishness: the last years of his creative life were devoted to boosting the ego of Britain's emergent European rival, Germany. But the stress placed on character-formation in that sequence of sermons-cum-autobiographies that poured out between 1829 and 1841 could only have a locus in a Scottish experience. Educational possibilities unimaginable in the south for someone of his social class were necessary to create those glittering, allusive texts.

Yet what followed was a leap into a void: although he visited the place regularly, and was always in contact with his family, Carlyle contributed in the last forty years of his life little to Scotland. The contrast with Ibsen, far more of an exile from his native Norway between 1864 and 1891, is salutary. Norwegian politics always provide the frame of his moral dramas. The big questions that face *Peer Gynt* (1867), the riddles of the Boyg and the Button-Moulder, are those that face him on his return to the Gudbrandsdal after his travels, as indeed they faced Ibsen in his last Norwegian years. Carlyle never returned.

If Carlyle's was a sort of psychic suicide, Hugh Miller was psychologically torn and literally destroyed by cultural tensions. Miller's reputation as the polemicist editor of the *Witness* after 1839, in its day a more important paper than the *Scotsman*, seems conservative (or at least Whiggish) in everything but his commitment to the Free Church. As a scientist he was hamstrung by his religious fundamentalism. Yet this greyness is banished by the vitality of his autobiography, *My Schools and Schoolmasters* (1854). This is neither 'reliable' nor sentimental but a remarkably comprehensive survey of the pressure-points of a changing Scotland, viewed by a man vertiginously on the edge of so many divides: on the edge of the highland line, the sea, the oral tradition, the working class, of sanity itself.[62] At the very least *My Schools and Schoolmasters* was a huge reservoir of experience for the likes of Stevenson and Buchan to draw on. But, more importantly, it was that rare thing in Britain—though Carlyle had tried hard to naturalise it—an individualistic *Bildungsroman*. When compared with a contemporary, influential English novel about education, Tom Hughes's *Tom Brown's Schooldays* (1857), the difference between the ascriptive ethos of English class society and the 'open' commitment of Miller to experience and change leap out at us—this despite the fact that Hughes was politically the more radical figure.[63]

Hughes's ideal is the autochthonous English gentleman (the prelude, set in the Vale of the White Horse, is a paean to Anglo-Saxonism) good-hearted, energetic and dim. Miller, on the other hand, conveys the almost sensual quality of knowledge, the excitement of acquiring it, the near-inebriated condition of the adept. Both books recognise the intrinsic value of childhood, but where Hughes foresees a life governed by the rules of team games (parliament itself being an obvious example) Miller's voyage is towards an unknown region, possibly exciting, possibly (as in his own case) disastrous.

Douglas Gifford characterises the themes of the 'serious' nineteenth-century Scottish novel as 'the divided self; the divided family which contains the broken self; the divided nation behind the fragmented family'.[64] This discouraging agenda seems only to offer 'ideal types' of frustration, and is scarcely consonant with the liveliness of the Scottish contribution to education and what Patrick Geddes (a typical magus-figure) called 'civics' in the first half of the twentieth century. Against this constriction of the fictional imagination, the 'autobiography', or the documentary *Bildungsroman*, seems both a way out of the chaos of Victorian Scotland, and a means of dramatising the role of education in the processes of individuation and socialisation. Elements are common between it and the novel, in particular the flawed, severe, ultimately pathetic father-figures, who could stand for the generation which failed so emphatically to create a national identity, while the cultural schizophrenia is embedded in a classic of the genre, John Ruskin's *Praeterita*, published in 1885–89. But if one reads an all but forgotten book, the *Reminiscences* of James Stuart (1913), centred on his Fife boyhood in a family influenced by Godwinianism, one is struck by an energy and openness to experience similar to Miller's, which later went into the creation of the university extension movement. In the same tradition stand the *Memorials* (1907) of Thomas Davidson, founder of the Fabian Society and later of the summer school movement in the United States, and other autobiographical writings by R B Haldane, John Muir's *The Story of my Boyhood and Youth* (1924), Edwin Muir, A S Neill and Jennie Lee, varied in standpoint and literary quality but united in their preoccupation with childhood and education. As with Carlyle, the inadequacies of adult life in a depoliticised Scotland can provoke flight, but Lord Jeffrey's dismissal of the Scots language—'All its pleasures conjure up images of schoolday innocence, and sports, and friendships which have no part in succeeding years'—approvingly echoed by Nicholas Phillipson, cannot be extended to Scots education.[65] It was in the Langholm Library and the Arbuthnott schoolroom that the Scottish renaissance would begin.

NOTES

1   J Williams, 'Edinburgh Politics, 1832–1852'. Unpublished PhD thesis, Edinburgh University 1972, p 377.
2   S G E Lythe and John Butt, *An Economic History of Scotland*, (Glasgow, 1975) p 95.
3   Edwin Muir, *Scottish Journey*, (London, 1935) pp 102–3, quoted in G F A Best, 'The Scottish Victorian City' in *Victorian Studies*, Vol XI, 1967–8, p 330.
4   *The Journal of Henry Cockburn* (Edinburgh, 1874) Vol II, p 5 (entry for 6 February 1843).
5   F Engels, *The Condition of the Working Classes in England* (1845, English trans London 1892, 1969) pp 301–2.
6   G Gordon, 'Scottish Literature' in *The Discipline of Letters*, (Oxford, 1946) p 96.
7   Edwin Muir, quoted in Andrew Noble, 'Urbane Silence: Scottish Writing and the Nineteenth Century City' in George Gordon (ed), *Perspectives of the Scottish City*, Aberdeen, 1985, p 75.
8   See Horst Rössler, *Literatur und Arbeiterbewegung, Studien zur Literaturkritik und Frühen Prosa des Chartismus* (Frankfurt, 1985), p 54.
9   Walt Whitman, *Democratic Vistas*, 1871, Nonesuch 1938, pp 708–9; Whitman took the Scottish ballads—'subtly expressing their past and present, and expressing character'—as a model.
10 See Hugh MacDiarmid, *The Company I've Kept* (London, 1966) pp 19, 237–55.
11 William Donaldson, *Popular Literature in Victorian Scotland* (Aberdeen, 1986) p xii; and see John Sutherland, *Victorian Novelists and Publishers* (Athlone, 1976).
12 Donaldson, op. cit., p 148.
13 Ibid., p 149.
14 *See* Christopher Harvie, 'Legalism, Myth and National Identity in Scotland in the Imperial Epoch' in *Cencrastus*, Summer 1987; and Richard Dorson, *The British Folklorists*, (London, 1968) pp 115ff.
15 *See* Christopher Harvie, *Scotland and Nationalism, 1707–1977* (London, 1977), p 17; and Tom Nairn, *The Break-up of Britain*, (London, 1977) p 168.
16 *See* Nicholas Phillipson, 'Nationalism and Ideology' in J N Wolfe (ed), *Government and Nationalism in Scotland* (Edinburgh, 1969) pp 168–86.
17 Noble, 'Urbane Silence' p 81.
18 Robert Anderson, *Education and Opportunity in Victorian Scotland* (Oxford, 1983) pp 253–94 and 358–61.
19 *See* Ian Hutchison, *A Political History of Scotland, 1832–1922*, (Edinburgh, 1985) pp 232ff.
20 Quoted in Alastair R Thompson, 'The Use of Libraries by the Working Class in Scotland in the Early Nineteenth Century' in *Scottish Historical Review*, vol XLII, 1963, p 27.
21 Ibid.
22 Nigel Cross, *The Common Writer: Life in Nineteenth Century Grub Street* (Cambridge, 1985) p 5.

23   Sutherland, *Victorian Novelists* pp 53–60.
24   Sir Theodore Martin, *Life of HRH the Prince Consort* (London, 1880), Vol 2, p 319.
25   *See* Christopher Harvie, 'Gladstonianism, the Provinces and Popular Politics' in Richard Bellamy (ed), *Victorian Liberalism* (London, 1988).
26   This is discussed at greater length in Harvie, *Scotland and Nationalism*, pp 163–5.
27   Robin Jenkins, 'Speaking as a Scot' in *The Scottish Review*, No 27, August 1982, pp 19–25.
28   Callum G Brown, *The Social History of Religion in Scotland since 1730* (London, 1987), p 52.
28   *See* Ieuan Gwynedd Jones, 'Language and Community in Nineteenth Century Wales', in Dai Smith (ed), *A People and a Proletariat*, (London, 1980) p 59.
29   Victor Kiernan, 'Evangelicalism and the French Revolution' in *Past and Present*, Vol I, 1952, pp 49–50.
30   Linda Colley, 'Whose nation? Class and National Consciousness in Britain, 1750–1830', in *Past and Present*, No. 113, 1984, pp 104ff.
31   W Hamish Fraser, *Conflict and Class, Scottish Workers 1700–1838* (Edinburgh, 1988), pp 3–10.
32   Henry Cockburn, *Journal*, 2 vols (Edinburgh, 1874), II, p 181.
33   Ian D Clark, 'From Protest to Reaction: the Moderate Regime in the Church of Scotland, 1725–1805', in N T Phillipson and R Mitchison (eds), *Scotland in the Age of Improvement* (Edinburgh, 1970), p 203, and see Iain MacIver, 'The Evangelical Party and the Eldership in General Assemblies, 1820–43', in *Records of the Scottish Church History Society*, Vol xx, part 1, 1978, pp 1–13.
34   Ibid., p 222.
35   Ibid., p 219.
36   Ibid., p 204.
37   Stewart Jay Brown, *Thomas Chalmers and the Godly Commonwealth in Scotland* (Oxford, 1982), p xiii.
38   *See* Karl Miller, *Cockburn's Millenium*, (London, 1977).
39   *See* Rosalind Mitchison, 'The Making of the Old Scottish Poor Law', in *Past and Present*, May 1974, and *see* Stewart Brown, *Godly Commonwealth*.
40   Noble, 'Urbane Silence', p 83.
41   Callum Brown repeats the traditional assessment (Brown, *Social History of Religion*, p 40), but see Iain Hutchison, *A Political History of Scotland, 1832–1924* (Edinburgh, 1985), pp 17–19.
42   G I T Machin, 'The Disruption and British Politics', in *Scottish Historical Review*, vol LI, 1972, pp 20–51; and *see* Harold Laski, 'The Political Theory of the Disruption', in *Studies in the Problems of Sovereignty* (Yale, 1917), p 208.
43   T C Smout, *A Century of the Scottish People, 1830–1950*, (Glasgow, 1986), pp 25, 40.
44   *See* J T Ward, *Sir James Graham* (London, 1967), pp 198–202.
45   T C Smout, *A Century of the Scottish People* (Glasgow, 1987), p 112
46   Stewart Brown, *Godly Commonwealth*.
47   Hutchison, *Political History of Scotland*, p 60.
48   For Begg as a nationalist *see* H J Hanham, *Scottish Nationalism* (London, 1968) p 74; as a militant protestant *see* Tom Gallagher, *Glagow, the Uneasy Peace* (Manchester, 1987) p 201.
49   Dorothy Thompson, *The Chartists*, (London, 1984) pp 341–68, records 23 Scottish Chartist Churches in 1839; and *see* Callum Brown, op. cit., p 106.
50   Donaldson, *Popular Literature*, p 28.

51   James Kellas, *Modern Scotland* (London, 1968) p 61.

52   *See* Charles Cowan MP, *Reminiscences*, Privately Printed, 1878, p 263

53   Hanham, op. cit., p 77; and *see* Michael Fry, *Patronage and Principle: a Political History of Modern Scotland* (Aberdeen, 1987) pp 59ff.

54   J D Myers, 'Scottish Nationalism and the Antecedents of the 1872 Education Act', in *Scottish Educational Studies*, Nov 1972, vol IV, No 2, pp 73–92.

55   *See* Sheila M Smith, *The Other Nation: the Poor in English Novels of the 1840s and 1850s*, (Oxford, 1980), and C T Harvie, *The Centre of Things: Political Fiction in Britain from Disraeli to the Present*, forthcoming.

56   *See* Donaldson, *Popular Literature* p 133 for the geographic limitations to Alexander's realism.

57   *See* Christopher Harvie, 'Stevenson's Politics', in Jenni Calder (ed), *Stevenson and Victorian Scotland*, (Edinburgh, 1981), pp 116ff.

58   Douglas Gifford, '*The Master of Ballantrae* and the Tradition of Scottish Fiction', in *Stevenson and Victorian Scotland*, pp 69ff.

59   'Characteristics', in *Edinburgh Review*, 1831, repr in *Scottish and Miscellaneous Studies* (London, n.d.), p 221.

60   Fred Kaplan, *Carlyle* (Cambridge, 1983), p 62.

61   For Disraeli *see* Morris Speare, *The Political Novel* (Oxford, 1924) pp 124ff; for Morley *see* D A Hamer, *John Morley: Victorian Intellectual in Politics* (Oxford, 1968), pp 88–90.

62   For an introduction to Miller see George Rosie, *Hugh Miller: Outrage and Order* (Edinburgh, 1980); and *see* Miller, *First Impressions of England*, (Edinburgh, 1847), pp 16, 46, for his contrast between the Scots and English intellects.

63   Clive Emsley reminds me that, a century after its publication, *Tom Brown's Schooldays* prompted the discovery of the most unreliable of narrators, George MacDonald Fraser's *Flashman*.

64   Gifford, 'Stevenson and Scottish Fiction', p 69.

65   Quoted in Phillipson, *Age of Improvement*, p 178.

FURTHER READING

Anderson, Robert, *Education and Opportunity in Victorian Scotland* (Oxford, 1983).

Brown, Callum, *The Social History of Religion in Scotland since 1730*, (London, 1987).

Brown, Stuart Jay, *Thomas Chalmers and the Godly Commonwealth in Scotland* (Oxford, 1982).

Donaldson, William, *Popular Literature in Victorian Scotland: Language, Fiction and the Press* (Aberdeen, 1986).

Fraser, W Hamish, *Conflict and Class, Scottish Workers 1700–1838*, (Edinburgh, 1988).

Harvie, Christopher, *Scotland and Nationalism, 1707–1977*, (London, 1977).

Hutchison, Ian, *A Political History of Scotland, 1832–1922*, (Edinburgh, 1985).

Smout, T C, *A Century of the Scottish People 1830–1950*, (Glasgow, 1987).

Chapter 3

'A Ferment of Change': Aspirations, Ideas and Ideals in Nineteenth Century Scotland

DONALD J WITHRINGTON

Scotsmen throughout the nineteenth century—at least those who have bequeathed us records of their opinions—sensed vividly that they were living in times of swift, dramatic, often bewildering, and apparently irreversible change. And they were not wrong. In May 1870 Sheriff Barclay of Perth, an elder in the Established Church, echoed many observations made in the thirty years or so before—and exemplified many which would be made in the succeeding thirty:

> No attentive observer of the signs of the times in which we live, and of that mysterious element called the spirit of the age, but must note the restless state of public feeling in every sphere of national life—political, moral, social and, perhaps most prominently, religious. The edict seems to have at length gone forth, Overturn! Overturn! Overturn![1]

Certainly, to take one example, even by 1870 the century had seen a quite extraordinary transformation in the direct political involvement of the people in the government of the country. In 1832 there were only 4,500 voters (in a Scottish population of two millions); in that year this number rose at one stroke to 65,000 and for fifty years and more in Scotland everything 'was saturated in politics'.[2] In 1868, the franchise was extended to include male householders, including substantial numbers of the urban working classes; and in a town like Glasgow the proportion of local votes held by skilled and unskilled manual workers rose from some 35 per cent to over 65 per cent— bringing a huge alteration in the character and political influence of its enfranchised population.[3] Sheriff Barclay's observation came on the heels of that substantial change: yet within another twenty years came an act which would give voting rights to virtually the entire adult male populace, with the vast bulk of the crofters in the Highlands and Islands and the small tenants of the rural Lowlands being enfranchised for the first time.

Even in and after 1868 existing political groupings had experienced terrifying problems in coming to terms, as well as they could, with the greatly enlarged mass of the new voters (and their novel and distinctive demands on 'management' structures). These were as nothing to the impact of 1884, which was to introduce something very novel indeed—the formation of the first effective, popular political party in Britain, the Crofters' Party, set up specifically in order to press for a radical programme of legislative action on behalf of one newly-powerful section of the people. The old mould of British politics was certainly broken. The author of a recent book on the political history of Scotland has claimed, not unfairly, that the mid 1880s constitute 'a turning point in modern Scottish history', a time when Scotland became 'a country with a modern, pluralistic political system of organised group interests' instead of one dominated by a single party; as a result 'the class politics of the future had been germinated in Scotland, even if it took thirty years before class differences were to a significant extent defined and articulated in political terms'.[4]

There was, of course, dramatic reconstruction in the Scottish economy too; yet despite a huge shift into manufacturing in the nineteenth century, it is work recalling that not until the 1870s were a majority of Scots in work to be found in non-agricultural employments. Industrial revolution in the nineteenth century was, in national terms, a slower business than is sometimes imagined. Indeed, even the 'agricultural revolution' had not, as is still often implied, been completed in the previous century—far from it, in fact. In the 1790s, and as late as the 1830s, even neighbouring parishes, sometimes within the estate of the same landowner, had responded very differently to reforming ideas in agriculture; many parishes in both Lowlands and Highlands were slow to alter their time-honoured methods, only gradually responding to the undoubted strength of market forces (e.g. in choice of crops, the rise of dairy-farming and market-gardening) and of the working-out of prevalent economic theories (e.g. clearances in the Highlands). There were still considerable variations, in Highlands and Lowlands alike, in the response which was being made to reforming ideas and practices, in the economy as in so much else.

Let us look more closely at the way in which attitudes could change, quite dramatically, on one issue of continuing concern in our period. The over-population of the Highlands and Islands was the core element in the so-called 'Highland problem' and was to cause constant confusions in, and reconsideration of, landlord policy. In the later eighteenth and early nineteenth centuries, both landlords and governments resisted emigration by the tenantry, especially the more able, the more ambitious and the wealthier 'spirits' who constituted potentially a vital economic resource. But two especially severe periods of dearth and famine in 1837–8 and 1845–6 led, with or without the support of the Highland landlords, to much emptying of the countryside through migration and emigration; and latterly, government itself was persuaded into an extensive policy of subsidising emigrant passages to the colonies. Large-scale emigration had become the accepted, if not the only possible, solution to the increasing destitution of the superfluous population. Yet, if we look forward thirty years or so, there is a startling change, and we find instead much concern—voiced loudly in government circles too—about the impoverishing effects on Scotland of rural depopulation. There were by the 1870s and 1880s new sensitivities about landlord policies in the Highlands and Islands, at a time when there were increasing demands for land-nationalisation (much influenced by the speeches and writings of Henry George) and when attitudes were being much affected also by a new 'rural romanticism'. These shifts in attitude were underlined in the warnings of social moralists, and found additional support among the devotees of the new science of eugenics, who concluded that urbanisation was leading inexorably to the physical as well as to the moral deterioration of the national stock. The only assurance for the future, it was claimed, would be in genetic renewal and that would have to depend on the maintenance of a burgeoning, vibrantly healthy and virtuous rural population. There was also a more general, public awareness of the problem, and of the need to review existing policies, evident in government reports on the future of rural Scotland. As early as 1883, tucked away among their arguments for more sympathetic treatment of Highland crofters and cotters, the Napier Commissioners commented:

> The crofting population of the Highlands and Islands is a nursery of good workers and good citizens for the whole Empire. The stock is exceptionally valuable. It cannot be indifferent to the whole nation to possess within its borders a people, skilful, intelligent and prolific, as an everflowing fountain of prolific life.[5]

Another commission on the Highlands and Islands, the Congested Districts Board, would demand in 1897 that the inhabitants of the Western Isles should be granted more land, better housing and better schooling in order 'to prevent the crofting population from being ill-nourished and in such depressed circumstances that the stock would suffer'.[6] And in 1911 when the security of tenure and the fixing of rents which had been granted to crofters in 1886 was at last extended to Lowland smallholders, these improvements were made (in part at least) to stabilise and then to increase the numbers of rural inhabitants throughout the country:

> Every country should have a strong, vigorous and abundant agrarian population fixed to the soil . . . As long as the urban population increases at the expense of the rural, so long will the position of the nation be unhealthy and insecure. Men and women are the most valuable crop that a nation can cultivate. Small holdings provide admirable conditions for the growing of that crop, for building up a vigorous and healthy population.[7]

But was it just a matter of 'stock', of numbers and of 'rude health'? Was this the only or the most effective way of meeting the social problems of the late nineteenth century, whether in the Highlands and Islands or in Lowland Scotland? In a speech to the United Free Church general assembly in 1900, Lord Provost Chisholm of Glasgow had his own warning to give:

> Society is honeycombed with religious indifference. The race for wealth, the rush for pleasure, the constant cry for increasing sensationalism in one's excitements, all these things have deadened the sense of unseen things, and in too many cases have reduced life to the merest and most sordid struggle . . . In addition to that, I am afraid we must cease to talk about the sins of our great cities, because intemperance and impurity and gambling have seized and taken

hold of our towns and country villages [applause] and these have become great crying national sins. Then there is the poverty of which one does not like to speak, because there is so much poverty . . . But there is poverty worse than that . . . what one might call godless poverty, the poverty that is the fruit of lust, the poverty that is the result of self-indulgence . . . and which is being accompanied with a moral deterioration that is reducing man below the normal level of his kind. And then, in and through and over and above all that, we have persistent intemperance in our midst, that intemperance which, more than anything else, lies at the root of poverty and . . . has become such a power in our midst.[8]

Thus, for him and for the majority of commentators, eugenics alone would not overcome the degeneration of society, especially if the social evils were now infiltrating rural as well as urban communities. The larger questions still remained. There was certainly some evidence that Scotland was generally much more prosperous than half a century earlier; and one particular barometer of economic distress, the rate of emigration, had fallen markedly in the 1890s. Yet poverty was widespread and demoralisation continued. In fact, Provost Chisholm's insistence that the root causes lay in self-indulgence, that the major social ills were essentially self-inflicted, was—as we shall see—already an increasingly outmoded view (at least outside certain groups of conservative evangelicals). The problems which beset society at the close of the century were, generally, those which had shocked and perplexed generation after generation before: it was in the matter of their treatment, in choosing the most hopeful antidote to them, that successive periods reveal their social ideals.

If church-going was an essential requirement for the moralising, and generally for the social good, of Scotland, then had the churches failed the nation? It certainly seemed so to some observers. A Free Church magazine in 1871 concluded sadly that 'thirty-five years ago the state of Glasgow was relatively much the same as it is now' and that the 'indifferent classes destitute of all connection with the Church of God are doubtless the growth of past ages of neglect—the children and the children's children of a past century of ungodliness'.[9] Somewhat earlier, in 1866, a presbyterian seceder, a minister in Haddington, was more specific about his view of the effects of continuing detachment from church influence:

We have had our lot cast in evil times—times of spiritual declension and decay . . . in the market, the warehouse, the office or the shop you can scarcely meet a man on whose integrity, honesty, veracity and fidelity you can with safety depend . . . Luxury, licentiousness, intemperance, profanity, desecration and all manner of vice and prodigality are increasing at a fearful rate . . . and this among people who are almost all baptised Christians.[10]

At the close of the century little seemed to have changed, and the parish minister of Liberton near Edinburgh was sadly reporting in 1897 that even in his well-heeled district 'very many sit loosely to Christian ordinances; very many never go to Church at all (true of the classes as well as the masses);

young men especially are not joining the Church as they used to do; many who have joined have lapsed?'[11] Was religion dying? Was the decline in formal church attachment both a reflection of moral degeneration and also its progenitor? Were matters, in effect, even worse in the 1890s than they had been in the 1830s?

What is clear enough, in fact, is that even in an era in which the institutional influence of the churches may have been distinctly weaker, there was in the last decades of the nineteenth century a still strong commitment to the concept of religious belief as a 'good' (for example, the numbers of and attendance at Sunday Schools increased markedly; even non-Church-going parents wished their children to be exposed to Biblical instruction) and there was also still a widespread acceptance of the distinctive importance to Scotland of its 'Christian values' (however these were defined, as for example in the 1880s in Fabian and Labour ideals in matters of social and political policy). Apart from a few, relatively uninfluential, secularist groups, there was no break during the century in the general acceptance that schools should retain a Christian religious element in their teaching and that the schools had still the prime function of inculcating Christian moral values in the young.

In the earlier decades of the century the 'godly partnership' of Church and school had been perceived as the essential, if not the sole, means of saving a society which was then in deep decline. Thus in January 1820, in the aftermath of a period of strikes and rioting and of intense social distress in Glasgow, Dr Thomas Chalmers wrote from there to William Wilberforce: 'The infidelity of this neighbourhood has been much over-rated. There is a fearful majority of practical ungodliness amongst us, as there is everywhere, and I believe some few hundred, even of the labouring classes, who avow Deism or Atheism; but I think I am quite sure that the irreligion of the Radicals did much at length to neutralise their political influence amongst our people.'[12] For Chalmers the nascent underlying religious feelings of the people only needed to be brought to life again, to ensure the security of the nation. A renewed Church and a re-energised Church life, particularly in the new urbanised areas, was necessary; so too was greater support for the efforts of the 'godly schoolmaster' in urban and also in rural parishes—for the labours of these schoolteachers would be the surest means of converting (into the next generation of faithful attenders) the sons and daughters of those currently lost to church-going.[13] But a strongly religious-backed schooling, under the supervision of the local minister and presbytery of the Established Church, would also offer much wider social benefits. When Chalmers in 1820 opened two new 'parochial' schools in the newly-established industrial parish of St John's, Glasgow, he was at pains to emphasise for his audience the wider social implications of their task:

> Each scholar comes upon the same equal and independent footing. There is nothing to elevate one but his superior scholarship—and this is an elevation which may be attained by the very poorest in attendance . . . The great peculiarity of these schools is that the education is so cheap as that the poor boy may pay. But at the same time it is so good that the rich may receive . . .

It is well to learn there the lesson of respect for our common nature. It is well to have observed there that neither talent nor character are the prerogatives of rank alone. It is well to acquire there such friendships as will be retained in future life . . . It is exceeding well that the prosperous and distinguished citizen should have to recognise on some future day in some obscure artisan the school-fellow of his now fading remembrance, with whom he strove for mastery in the class and perhaps was overcome by him . . . (and thus) would learn to bear a friendly and respectful homage to the class of society to which he belonged; and therefore it is, that so far from wishing the children of the various ranks in the parish not to mingle at these schools, I want them to mix as extensively as they may. A far blander and better state of society will at length come out of such an arrangement. The ties of kindliness will be multiplied between the wealthy and the labouring classes of our city, the wide and melancholy gulf of suspicion will come at length to be filled up by the attentions of a soft and pleasing fellowship . . .[14]

But still more reassurance was needed for Chalmers' mainly middle-class audience, for would not such common schooling—of such quality—begin to weaken their superior position within the existing class structure?

But for what purpose, it may be asked, the above style of education for the labouring classes? Is it to help them in their preferment in life, that from labourers they may be fitted for the business of the higher situations in society? No! Some of course will in the vicissitudes of human history attain such an eminence, and their learning will serve to grace and guide them in the place they have reached. But most assuredly it is not that they may aspire after an elevated condition that I would want them all to be learned . . . Were all to aspire many would be disappointed; for be assured, that to the end of the world the men of opulence will be few and men of industry will compose the multitude. The structure of human society admits of no other arrangement . . . And what then is the object, it may be asked? It is not to turn an operative into a capitalist: it is to turn an ignorant operative into a learned operative, to stamp upon him the worth and respectability of which I contend he is fully susceptible, though he rise not by a single inch above the sphere of life in which he now moves, to transform him into a reflective and accomplished individual—not to hoist, as it were, the great ponderous mass of society into the air where it would have no foundation to support it, but . . . to diffuse through it the light of common and Christian intelligence.

There was, however, also a word or two of some comfort for the lower orders, to reassure them that a good education would in the end improve their lot in life too:

I know that there has been a most severe and overwhelming pressure of late on the labouring classes, and that between sleep to recruit their exhausted nature and labour to subsist, there are many who for months together have not had a single hour of recreation, and that thus the privilege of reading to store their minds either with general or religious information has by circum-stances been witheld from them. But it will not be always so. There will, I prophesy, if the world is to stand, there will be a great amelioration in the life of general humanity. The labouring classes are destined to attain a far more secure place of comfort and independence in the commonwealth than they have yet occupied, and this will come about not as the fruit of any victory gained on the arena of angry and discordant politics, but far more surely as the result of growing virtue and intelligence and worth among the labourers themselves . . .

These views of Thomas Chalmers are of particular importance because they had a wide acceptance. For Scots within the Established Church—and as worried about the drift of the religious into dissenting churches, as they were about the increase in non-church-going—it soon became something of a war-cry that only the state-supported Established Church, in close alliance with a state-supported and much extended school system, would be able to regenerate Scotland. In their view it was the government's undeniable duty to fund both.[15] But Liberal governments in the 1830s virtually refused all such aid to the national church or to the extension of national schooling under the close supervision of the Establishment; they were too dependent on the votes of the Scottish 'voluntaries' and the English dissenters to dare to act against these sectarian interests. More than that, government enquiries in the 1830s into the amount of church accommodation and into the numbers and quality of available schools,[16] followed by the results in 1851 of the first and only census of church attendance,[17] all seemed to confirm that non-church-going could not be blamed on lack of seating and that the apparent increase in illiteracy in Scotland could not be entirely blamed on lack of opportunity for schooling.[18] Worse still in many respects, neither problem appeared by mid-century to have been in the least assuaged by the Disruption; no real advance had been achieved by the 'spiritual release' which the evangelicals believed they had brought to Scotland by the foundation of the Free Church in 1843.

Indeed, the 1840s and 1850s were to attest the very intransigence of those problems which Chalmers and so many others had believed must soon diminish and disappear. In these decades even the most obvious and evident social evils seemed only to increase, for all the money and effort expended on attempts to combat them. The reports of the Prison Board for Scotland, and those of the county police committees up and down the country, distressingly showed ever-larger expenditures on the courts, on prisons and on policing, and yet levels of crime—especially by juveniles—increased; even after the passing of the Poor Law Amendment Act of 1845, the relief of poverty and provision of medical support for the poor called on more and more financial support, and yet pauperism was rife; the state of public health forced governments, local and national, into expensive measures of sanitary reform; and drunkenness and prostitution seemed ever more prevalent. But there are, nonetheless, changes in attitude to be found. Thus, Dr Thomas Guthrie in the 1850s preached and wrote 'against drunkenness' but 'on behalf of drunkards';[19] he and others still railed against pauperism, but they offered more temperate criticism of the supposed fecklessness of the individual poor; there was plenty of bitter comment about the continued rise in criminality, but more sympathetic consideration for the unchurched and unschooled petty thief and for the juvenile delinquent. What is certain, and is different, is that the environmental influences in human behaviour were becoming clearer, and were being effectively highlighted by social reformers such as Guthrie and James Begg, Frederic Hill, Sheriff William Watson and Alexander Thomson of Banchory.[20]

We must, however, be careful not to overstress these changes in attitude: they had their limitations. If the lower orders occupied an unfairly weak position in the battle of life, and while it could be agreed that their depressed state was not necessarily or entirely of their own making, nonetheless it was commonly assumed that the way out of it certainly was: it was the churches' main task 'to stand by and to shout encouragement to them'.[21] That such encouragement was, generally, expected of the Scottish churches and that it was thought that, of all agencies, it would still best come from them is worth remarking; moral and social improvement was still seen as being intrinsically bound up with religion. What was wanted in effect was a moral reformation and that this was the churches' business was generally accepted in mid-century by the vast majority of Scots of all classes, of all political persuasions and, more or less, of all sectarian sensitivities.

In the early and very unsettling days of Chartism, for example, the Scottish supporters of the movement had gone out of their way to placate their middle-class opponents by declaring their loyal attachment to Christianity: 'As the Scottish Chartists are believers in the creed established by the law of Scotland, the term infidelity applied to them is utterly false and unjust'—even if they were in the throes of setting up their own churches, to signify their distaste for the existing sects and their class-ridden organisations.[22] In August 1842, some three years later, an English secularist and Owenite came to Edinburgh to lecture to one of the oldest zetetic or free-thinking societies in Britain and was much shaken by what he found—nothing less, it seemed, than a deeply-held religious conviction which demanded that commitment to liberty of thought should somehow be closely associated with a continued attachment to Christian ideals (but not at all to the existing church structures):

> The members were fond of hearing the nonsense sometimes spoken about 'socialism being genuine, primitive, practical or some other form of Christianity'. A word against religion nearly frightened them out of their seats.[23]

We should not be surprised indeed, half a century later, to find signs of much the same acceptance of the place of religion; perhaps more covert, even unconscious in some, but still there for all that. Keir Hardie, for instance, keenly attacked 'churchianity' and the bourgeois domination of organised religion, but the many Biblical allusions in his speeches reveal clearly enough what might be seen as essential religion in his socialism. We should not, in other words, equate the undoubted fact of increased non-church-going with a turning away from all religious belief and attachment—even in the 1890s when there was certainly a sharpened anxiety among the churches themselves at their apparently growing unpopularity and when there was even a drying-up of good candidates for the ministry in all the major presbyterian sects.[24] In fact secularism drew relatively little of its support from Scotland, through-out the latter half of the nineteenth century; instead, there was an almost voracious public appetite for such writings as Henry Drummond's *Natural Law in the Spiritual World* (1883) and *The Ascent of Man* (1894) which set out to neutralise the anti-religious thrust of the new sciences of geology and evolutionary biology and argued vehemently that both could be accommodated readily within a system of faith that was itself being revised (in the light of the new 'scientific theology' and of new strides in the historical analysis of the Bible and of Biblical times). The Scottish philosophical and religious heritage had managed already to soften the harsher elements of utilitarianism; it seemed now set to engulf evolutionism and even social Darwinism; and in doing so it would provide the ground in Scotland for a positive response, in the later nineteenth century, to what we now call collectivism or state interventionism.

Unlike England, Scotland had long been used to state intervention in education. Acts of the seventeenth century Scottish parliament had regulated the provision of rural schooling and these acts remained as well-known, legal guidelines after 1707; in 1803 the British parliament was persuaded to legislate for Scottish schools, and as a result at intervals thereafter had to determine the levels of parochial schoolmasters' salaries. The Scottish experience of such governmental backing for national schooling meant that there was certainly less antagonism in principle to state 'interference' in education in Scotland than was the case in England, although in the earlier decades of the nineteenth century there would emerge in Scotland some of the same problems of sectarianism as occurred south of the border. But in Scotland there was not, in church organisation, in theology or in the system of church services, anything like the same divisions as there were in England between Anglicanism and Dissent.[25] The major churches in Scotland all shared the same theological 'standards', and claims that there were reasons of faith (rather than economic or social or political reasons) for forbidding children of one presbyterian church to go to the school of another, particularly to the parish school, were usually met by disbelief or disparagement. In the late 1840s and early 1850s, indeed, an influential group within the new Free Church was even willing to hand over all the Free Church's schools to a proposed national school system under the management of locally-elected boards, on the basis that any such representative parish council in Scotland, whatever the particular framework of church affiliation in any town or rural area, would be certain to secure an acceptable, protestant and generally non-sectarian religious schooling for its children.[26]

Yet successive attempts by government in the 1850s to legislate for a new national school system were to founder: but they foundered on the votes, not of Scots, but of English dissenter MPs who feared state intervention of any kind in English education—a successful Scottish bill, for them, seemed to offer a threatening and quite unacceptable precedent. The general belief in Scotland—that a national, state-supported schooling should have a readily agreed religious basis (presbyterian but not sectarian)—is assuredly one important reason for the apparent lack of concern in Scotland, in the succession of bills which preceded the Education Act of 1872, to introduce clauses which would enforce or institutionalise a period of 'religious observance' or religious instruction in each school day.[28] Yet these same years were marked out by a 'statistical war' among the Scottish presbyterian churches, from the results of which each hoped to claim some superiority in membership; there was also by then a determined campaign to disestablish the Church of Scotland. Nevertheless, the arguments surrounding the 1872 act in Scotland, in clear contrast to those which characterised the English act of 1870, demonstrated that in Scotland educational rather than specifically religious concerns were the most prominent: firstly, the need to provide *compulsory* schooling, sufficiently cheap or free, for all; secondly, the insistence on incorporating post-elementary instruction in the so-called higher subjects within a single system, along with and as an extension of schooling in the elements; and thirdly, the determination to achieve a unitary national system by putting a crushing economic pressure on the churches and other school-agencies to transfer their schools into the new national system—whereas in England the advantage had been firmly given to the various sects, and the state system there had been left, as it has been said, to 'those with little to pay and little to learn'.[29] In Scotland the value of an inclusive, tightly-organised, firmly supervised—and, above all, national—system was clear, not least since the school was still recognised as the prime and most hopeful weapon in the continuing war against crime and intemperance and other immoralities. Direct, divisive, sectarian influence was subordinated to national control, in due course to be placed firmly in the hands of the Scottish Education Department and its powerful inspectorate.

Crime, intemperance and immorality—for all the efforts of the churches—had remained, apparently unabated, to continue to perplex social reformers in the 1860s and 1870s. Intermittently the question was raised of reuniting the main presbyterian churches, in varying combinations, predominantly as a means to promoting a united and more potent front against social evils. In the 1880s there arrived an additional impetus to unite, in the need to provide a defence against attacks by secularist socialists who were openly taunting the churches for their ineffectiveness in social reforms. If they had not done so before, these attacks drove individual sects into a serious rethinking of their functions in a modern society and into a particularly keen examination of their internal organisations. Why did a portion of the population so happily remain outside the churches? What was it that was so apparently off-putting to so many? The churches' responses were to have a much wider impact than might at first be imagined.

The late 1860s and early 1870s were marked in the Established Church by a number of novel developments: for example, by new initiatives in home mission work, by a deliberate attempt to lessen clerical domination by better and wider use of lay-members in local church affairs, and by some quite radical moves to give a more prominent and a more publicly recognised place to women (e.g. through a new committee on Life and Work).[31] Many traditionalists and conservatives were upset by these and by other changes introduced by parish ministers who were determined to make the Sabbath ordinances more appealing and attractive, more 'customer-friendly'. They set about cutting the length of services, reduced extemporary prayers (even introducing read prayers and meddling with the introduction of service-books); they shortened sermons and at the same time worked to make their scriptural message more direct and accessible; they introduced 'sung praise', with instrumental music and hymns, often backed by a trained choir. There were also significant shifts of emphasis taking place in theology—a moving away from the wrathful God of the Old Testament and away from an older confessional doctrine to that of the 'saving' Christ and to the teaching of doctrines which emphasised the availability of grace to all sinners rather than its reservation to the predestined few.

Now by no means were all of these developments new, for many had been heralded earlier (e.g. in the atonement controversy of the 1830s) but they came together in the 1880s in an especially forceful way. In effect they represent part-answers to the underlying, constantly nagging questions about the role of the churches in a changed and changing society. The problem was to be posed in 1874 in a particularly direct and uncompromising way by the author of a grim and hard-hitting account of *The Ecclesiastical and Religious Statistics of Scotland*:

> Are the churches capable of dealing successfully with the great moral and social and religious evils which now threaten to sap the foundations of society? . . . Are the churches in Scotland mere conservative institutions existing for them-selves and for the salvation of individual souls, or do they exist for the salvation of society and for the sweetening and sanctifying of all relations: between man and man as well as between man and God?[32]

In 1880 Dr John Caird of Glasgow University, in the radical and revisionist book of *Scotch Sermons* that enraged conservative ministers of the time, offered this answer, simple and plain: he demanded that the churches first duty was to this world and in this world:

> The supreme aim of Christian endeavour is not to look away to an inconceivable heaven beyond the skies, or to spend our life preparing for it, but it is to realise that latent heaven, those possibilities of good, that underdeveloped kingdom of righteousness and truth, which human nature and human society contain.[33]

This was a view more sharply put here than that which had been put similarly but more hesitantly in earlier times, by John Lee and Norman Macleod in the Established Church or by Thomas Guthrie and James Begg in the Free Kirk.[34] What was important was that in 1880 Caird was a magisterial figure of great influence, the best-known, most renowned and most highly regarded preacher of his age: he hit a note that was to be sounded again and again. The churches' place was to be in society, among the people: if the churches were inhibited in their task of spiritualising the world by barriers to that world's being a decent place for its inhabitants, by de-humanising conditions which thwarted the good intentions of honest and moral people of all social classes, by barriers which made it impossible for them to live good lives in harmony together, then it was the churches' undoubted duty to cast these barriers down.

Donald Macleod, minister of Park Church in Glasgow and successor to his much more famous brother, Norman 'of the Barony', as editor of the popular religious magazine *Good Words*, was angered by traditionalists who objected to Caird's (and his) views and who asserted that the church had no place in meddling in politics, claiming that socialism and religion were necessarily antagonistic. In an article in 1881 he retorted that 'the spirit of Christianity is essentially socialistic—not the socialism of the Nihilist assassin or the Communist petroleuse, but the socialism of the New Testament'.[35] He was adamant that the churches should have no hesitation in joining in a crusade for moderate, reformist, community-welfare socialism, such as was attuned to older, Church-led and essentially *Scottish* social policies: the Scottish kind of socialism was something altogether different from the alien, atheistical and lawless socialism of continental Europe. Four years later, again in *Good Words*, Macleod was on the warpath once more, this time against those who, for any reason, opposed the principle of state intervention in matters of general social welfare: what he had to say demonstrates clearly the shift away from doctrinaire *laissez-faire* ideas and away too from the old Chalmers' standpoint—of antipathy to legislation for welfare purposes because it would dry up relief from voluntary and charitable giving and have no moralising effect. There is no doubt about the changed atmosphere in which Macleod's comments are made. We are here a long way away from earlier expectations that such evils as poverty and destitution would be best overcome by attacking personal sinfulness, particularly the sinfulness of those driven to drink: what Macleod and others were now concerned to uncover, and then to deal with, were those 'outside' and impersonal factors which drove even otherwise worthy folk into evil, into intemperance or impoverishment or immorality:

> Christians must be in sympathy with that state compulsion whose object is the prevention of what is cruel and demoralising, or the promotion of what is humanizing and elevating; limiting the hours of labour, granting protection to women and children, compulsory education, support of the poor, enforcement of sanitation and improvement of dwellings, public libraries, and such like. All these may be regarded as expressing a national feeling inspired by Christian principle.[36]

Caird and Macleod by their arguments were bringing the Established and the other churches, into the political foreground. Many churchmen, for example, found sympathy for Keir Hardie's plea in 1886 that the Liberal Party should offer a social reform programme to meet what he believed were particularly Scottish demands, namely, that the party should support 'the weak against the strong, the rights of the poor against the rich', on the assumption that these were things which in the 1880s would have to be accomplished by the state through parliamentary legislation. In political theory another change was taking place which would provide much backing for this motion.

The later 1870s had given birth to a novel political philosophy, which offered a secure intellectual base for those changing attitudes to government intervention in public welfare. The school of British Idealists, centred on T H Green in Balliol College, Oxford, which combined the philosophical and political teachings of ancient Greece with those of modern Germany, argued strongly for a 'common good' which would be realised by state intervention in the practical matters of social and community welfare. Recently scholars have begun to recognise the importance of the British Idealists in the construction of the welfare state, but two points which are highly relevant to this essay have entirely escaped the English and American writers who have turned their attention to the topic.[37] Firstly, they do not note that the general principles formulated and propagandised by Green and his followers were already inherent in much of the social idealism (traceable to the Reformation and kept alive by presbyterianism) which was part of the enduring heritage of Scotland—hence the ready acceptance of so much of the Idealist teaching north of the border. Secondly, they ignore the fact that a very large proportion of the Idealist school were themselves Scots—who were nearly all destined to be academics in Scotland and England; they formed a group who would dominate for decades the teaching of philosophy (and divinity) in most of the Scottish universities; they (and in time their former students) would occupy leading positions not only in the Scottish but also in the new English and Welsh universities. Thus Idealism had a surer base in Scotland than it might otherwise have had and, throughout Britain, no opportunity was lost publicly to diffuse the Idealist philosophy in a distinctive Scottish accent.

In order to gain a better perspective of the impact of Idealism in Scotland, however, we should glance again at the earlier reception given to Charles Darwin's writings. Writing about England, Dr John Kent has warned that we should not be surprised at 'the comparatively slight and slow effects that the Darwinian idea of evolution had on the popular imagination' and he underlines the fact that it hardly shook at all conservative attitudes, and older and ingrained religious beliefs. So it was, too, in Scotland where underlying religious convictions were not generally undermined, and where the pamphlets and books of secularist-evolutionists seem to have been peculiarly ineffective. The account of the creation in Genesis had been, after all, under severe attack in Scotland long before Darwin. In 1844 Robert Chambers, one of the famous Edinburgh publisher-brothers, had anonymously issued a remarkable book called *The Vestiges of Creation* which, drawing heavily on the researches in geology of another Scot, Charles Lyell, directly challenged the truth of the Genesis story. It soon drew a reply from that doyen of Free Church writers and brilliant amateur geologist, Hugh Miller, *In the Footprints of the Creator* (1849): in this book, which achieved very large sales (just as did *The Vestiges*) and was to be much reprinted, Miller aimed to prove that there was no necessary opposition between the implications of recent advances in man's geological understanding and the Biblical account of the creation. For Miller, what recent scientific research demonstrated was nothing more nor less than a hitherto unrevealed design in geological evolution; but that still depended, of course on there being a Great Designer.[39] *The Vestiges* and Miller's *Footprints* provided in Scotland a kind of geological prelude, with very extensive public discussion, to the similar arguments based on evolutionary biology which were set off by Darwin's *Origin of Species*: by 1859 indeed, when Darwin's book was published, much of the ground of the 'science *vs* religion' debate had been well worked over in Scotland and, while Darwin provided a valuable and very exciting extension to that debate, that indeed was in Scotland what it mainly was.[40] Nor did the Darwin's *Descent of Man* of 1871 find a Scottish public generally aghast at its novelty and bravery. The 1860s had seen much advance in Biblical criticism in Scotland (strongly influenced by recent German scholarship) and by 1871 there was an increasing readiness to accept the argument that theology itself was a changing and evolving 'science'. Older and stricter interpretations of confessional doctrine were being quietly altered, and the significant response to Darwin's second book (and soon after, to the works of Herbert Spencer) was for writers to accommodate the main elements of evolution within a redrawn interpretation of scriptural allegory. As we have seen, Henry Drummond warmly welcomed Darwin's views and he was at pains to publicise his contention that modern theological scholarship was actually in close accord with 'slow-growth or evolutionary theory'. Whether such an accommodation between the two was intellectually justifiable has since been much debated; but that matter is of much less importance to historians of the period than the knowledge of its very widespread acceptance by Drummond's extensive Scottish audience.[41] The general implications in Scotland were plain enough: Darwinism, happily, need not disturb the main framework of Christian belief and, indeed, it might even be adapted, with care, to its support. In the late 1870s and early 1880s, at least in the Free Church, the most vicious attack on traditional Biblical faith seemed to be coming from within, from a series of arrestingly novel commentaries and reinterpretations in the ninth edition of the *Encyclopaedia Britannica* written by a brilliant Hebrew scholar who was a professor in the Free Church College in Aberdeen. The trial for heresy of William Robertson Smith, and his condemnation in 1881, drove him south to a renowned academic career in Cambridge, and served also to loosen Free Church theological ties to an older puritanical evangelicalism—to respond more sympathetically, in Alexander Whyte's words, to 'the keen, restless, insatiable spirit of modern critical enquiry' and not to be frightened by it, to recognise that 'the mind of the world does not stand still' and that 'the theological mind will stand still at its peril'.[42] The place of the Free Church, as of the other churches, was in the realities—including the theological realities—of this world. We should remember that the case did not for a moment shake Robertson Smith's or his main supporters' belief in evangelical Christianity; it speeded up an agreeable liberalisation of theology which was in any event already well on its way. Nor was Robertson Smith's attachment to his presbyterian faith at all disturbed by other highly innovative studies in which he engaged, into the social anthropology of primitive religion and the comparative sociology of religions. Instead, such scholarship was seen to be positive and enhancing—the discoveries in biology and history and geology, it has been said, 'provided a guarantee of progress, where the utilitarians had only been able to hope they could engineer it'.[43] It also provided an intellectual atmosphere in which the Idealists' social and political philosophising, with its strong Christian and moral-religious backing, could flourish.

The Glasgow connection with Idealism was especially strong, no doubt aided by the existence of the Snell scholarships to Balliol College, Oxford, but mainly reflecting the long and powerful leadership of the brothers Caird, Edward (professor of Philosophy there from 1866 to 1893 before becoming master of Balliol) and John (professor of Divinity from 1862, and principal of the University from 1873). While John had been an undergraduate in Glasgow, Edward first studied in St Andrews in the days of Principal John Tulloch; it is remarkable how closely these two universities were associated with the burgeoning of Idealism in Scotland. It was to St Andrews that Henry Jones went as professor after being an undergraduate at Glasgow and then first holder of the chair of Philosophy in the University College of Bangor in his native Wales; from St Andrews in 1893 he went to Glasgow to succeed Edward Caird. It was to St Andrews that David G Ritchie came (more of him anon), to the chair of Logic, in 1893, to be succeeded there at his untimely death ten years later by Bernard Bosanquet, one of Green's most devoted disciples. William Wallace had also been an undergraduate at St Andrews before going to Balliol, then on to a fellowship of Merton College and from there to be successor to Green as Whyte's Professor of Moral Philosophy in 1882. Andrew Seth (later Seth Pringle-Patterson) breaks the mould a little: he was an undergraduate at Edinburgh before becoming the first professor of Philosophy in University College, Cardiff, in 1883–7, moving then to the chair of Logic in St Andrews before his translation to Edinburgh in 1891. Three other notable Idealists, all Scots, confirm the Glasgow connection with the academic leadership of the new philosophy. J H Muirhead was a student of Edward Caird's before going to Balliol, *en route* to a lectureship in Bedford College and Royal Holloway College in the University of London and then to the chair of Philosophy and Political Economy in Birmingham University. J S Mackenzie studied in Cambridge and Berlin after his undergraduate days in Glasgow, held fellowship-assistantships in Glasgow and Edinburgh and then a fellowship in Trinity College, Cambridge, before holding for twenty years the chair of Logic and Philosophy in the University College of South Wales and Monmouthshire. And John MacCunn, after studies in Glasgow and Balliol and having taught in Oxford for some years, was the founder-professor of Philosophy at Liverpool University. Of the many leading Idealists who were Scots, only R B Haldane—and Seth and Ritchie—avoided being taught in Glasgow and St Andrews, but even Haldane (after studying in Edinburgh and Gottingen) held a Ferguson scholarship in all four Scottish universities in the mid 1870s: he alone of the group avoided an academic career and was, from 1885 until 1911, in the Commons as MP for East Lothian. This listing of the Scots associated with the Idealist School is not intended to be exhaustive, but the major figures have been described; what it clearly shows is the exceptionally strong Scottish participation in (and leadership of) British Idealism. Let us now turn to one of them, comparatively unknown and unremembered now in Scotland, but a man and writer of some significance in the 1890s.

David Ritchie, son of the parish minister of Jedburgh in the Borders, was a student of classics and philosophy at Edinburgh University before winning an exhibition at Balliol. He became a convinced Fabian and 'practical socialist', and found in Idealism a vital intellectual support for his social reformism. He was seriously considering a career in the church when he was offered a fellowship at Jesus College, Oxford. Ritchie became a leading proponent of what came to be called 'evolutionary utilitarianism', both in Oxford and then in St Andrews from 1893 to 1903. What, for our purposes, is remarkable is the way in which Ritchie so revealingly brings together three strands of his philosophical heritage: older Scottish Enlightenment views of social development (drawn particularly from Adam Ferguson), the social idealism of Scottish presbyterianism (in its more liberated, post-Chalmers' variety), and the new idealism of Green and the Cairds. Like John Caird and Donald Macleod, Ritchie distanced himself from the utilitarianism of J S Mill and from doctrinaire *laissez-faire* ideas. Like nearly all of the Idealists, Ritchie was a Liberal in politics: for him Liberalism meant moving

> from the merely negative work of removing mischievous state action to the positive task of employing the power of government, which is now more or less the real representation of the 'general will', on behalf of the well-being of the community.[44]

In Ritchie's view, the old individualism had gone for good—literally, for the good of all; and the framing and the putting into practice of social policy for the good of all could be left to the new 'godly magistrate' of a truly representative government. His organic vision of society stressed cooperation rather than competition, and that would deal a last blow at policies of social welfare which were dependent on charity. It was a vision which in Scotland would eclipse at last the social conservatism of Thomas Chalmers and it dragged social philosophy away from the vestigial individualism of men like W G Blaikie in the 1860s; it allied social Darwinism to moderate socialism and saw no antagonism between ethics and the 'science of mind' then being developed into the new psychology; it was open to the implications of the new teaching in social psychology and comparative sociology—especially where these emphasised that feeling for community-interdependence and community-orientation which had, for centuries, been at the heart of Scottish social welfare. Ritchie and his fellow-Idealists applauded legislative action on behalf of the whole community and not for narrow or party interests, and also the development of community-controlled services by local government— something in which Glasgow took so striking a lead, supporting a 'municipal socialism' which was attracting much interest overseas.[45]

Ritchie, it seems to me, demonstrates neatly one characteristic shared by the leading Scottish Idealists: the social philosophy they developed drew quite heavily, wittingly or not, on their Scottish heritage. Society was evolving, and so their social ideals should be capable of evolving while having an assured core of basic principles; as the pattern of social need changed, for example, and as their understanding of society and of man's place in his society evolved (as researches in neurology or sociology or history or psychology offered new norms or other insights), so too should law be re-interpreted and revised and the duties of government reviewed. Their inheritance, the traditional values they had been heir to, were themselves rightly in process of change—'progressive', not stultifying; the problems facing society might be much the same, the approach to solve them need not be—indeed should not be in a changing and improving society.

Scotland in the nineteenth century had a lively political history, but it has been too often disregarded in studies of 'British' politics which deal only with England (and a side glance now and again at Ireland)—but Scottish politics is enlivened by Scottish issues and can be properly understood only as they are understood. Scotland's religious history is at once complex and fascinating: but it is not dominated by the Disruption as so many Free Kirk writers in the nineteenth century would have us believe; nor is it to be measured only by the mass of its supposed narrow-minded clergy or its burdensome respectability or its cheerless Sabbatarianism or even by the dutiful church-going which we are so often persuaded to expect. As with politics, there's more to it than that. Nor is Scottish education during the century to be written off merely as some kind of battle-ground between 'traditionalists' (which tradition? when?) and 'Anglicisers' (in the shifting sands of English education, which prescription is to be chosen and why?): again, there's more—much more—to it than that. And if we turn to the general assessment of 'the Scottish life-style' in the nineteenth century, what are we to choose in the grand living heritage of the nation at large? Just as Enlightened Scotland is not to be confined within the ridiculously narrow tableau of small groups of self-important, 'polite' gentlefolk in self-important, 'polite' Edinburgh, so too the riches of nineteenth-century living in Scotland are not to be defined by the simplicities of 'kailyard' or the brutalities of John Gourlay's Barbie. The 'real' Scotland lies, in part at least, in and behind some of the issues raised in this essay, to be glimpsed in the attempts throughout the century to elaborate, to revise and to implement particular social ideals. This plea for a more sensitive and better informed approach to nineteenth-century Scotland, by historians of literature as by others, has been energetically answered in one very recent study: as a parting comment, as a statement which gets to the essence of much of my argument, let me quote from Dr Willie Donaldson's summing-up in his assessment of *Popular Literature in Victorian Scotland*:

> Victorian Scotland . . . was a completely and lovingly imagined place, and a very different one from that visible through the narrow and distorting perspective of the printed book . . . Many of our conventional ideas about the period are at best only partly true, and some are quite false. On the whole popular fiction in Victorian Scotland is not overwhelmingly backward-looking; it is not obsessed by rural themes; it does not shrink from urbanisation or its problems; it is not idyllic in its approach; it does not treat the common people as comic or quaint. The second half of the nineteenth century is not a period of creative trauma or linguistic decline; it is one of the richest and most vital episodes in the history of Scottish popular culture.[46]

NOTES

1 Church of Scotland, *Chronicle of the General Assembly of 1870* (Edinburgh, 1870), pp 37–8.

2 William Ferguson, *Scotland, 1689 to the Present* (Edinburgh, 1968), p 291.

3 Iain G C Hutchison, *A Political History of Scotland, 1832–1924* (Edinburgh, 1986), p 132.

4 Michael Fry, *Patronage and Principle: a Political History of Modern Scotland* (Aberdeen, 1987), pp 109–10.

5 *Report of the Commissioners of Inquiry into the Condition of the Crofters and Cottars in the Highlands and Islands of Scotland*: PP 1884, pp xxxii, 23.

6 *First Report of the Congested Districts Board*: PP 1898, xxiii, p xix.

7 *Scottish Review*, (1914), p 32.

8 United Free Church of Scotland, *Proceedings of the General Assembly* (Edinburgh, 1900), p 97.

9 *Free Church of Scotland Monthly Record*, April 1871, p 69: quoted in Donald C Smith, *Passive Obedience and Prophetic Protest: Social Criticism in the Scottish Church, 1830–1945* (New York, 1987), p 222.

10 John Henshelwood, *Revival of Religion the Want of the Times* (Edinburgh, 1866), p 5 ff.

11 W H Gray, *Jubilee Jottings* (Edinburgh, 1897), p 265.

12 William Hanna (ed), *Memoirs of the Life and Writings of Thomas Chalmers, DD, LL D* (Edinburgh, 1850), ii, 257.

13 *See* D J Withrington, 'Non-church-going, *c.*1750–*c.*1850: a preliminary study' in *Records of the Scottish Church History Society*, xvii (1972), pp 99–113.

14 Hanna, *Thomas Chalmers*, ii, pp 238–46 (for this and following two extended quotations).

15 *See* the arguments used by the numerous 'Church Defence Associations' in the 1830s; and, in particular, for the state's duty to support schools as a means of increasing church-going, D J Withrington, '*Scotland a Half-Educated Nation* in 1834? Reliable critique or persuasive polemic?' in W M Humes and H M Paterson (eds), *Scottish Culture and Scottish Education 1800–1980* (Edinburgh, 1983), pp 55–74.

16 *Education Enquiry (Scotland). Abstract of Answers and Returns, 9 July 1834*: PP 1838, xlvii; *Answers made by Schoolmasters in Scotland to Queries circulated in 1838*: PP 1841, xix; *Reports, Commission on Religious Instruction, Scotland*: PP 1835–1839.

17 D J Withrington, 'The 1851 census of religious worship and education: with a note on church accommodation in mid-19th century Scotland' in *Records of the Scottish Church History Society*, xviii (1974), pp 135–55; for a close study of the census in one town, *see* A A McLaren, *Religion and Social Class: the Disruption Years in Aberdeen* (London, 1974).

18 *See* D J Withrington, 'Schooling, literacy and society' in T M Devine and Rosalind Mitchison (eds), *People and Society in Scotland, 1760–1830* (Edinburgh, 1988), pp 163–87.

19 Thomas Guthrie, *Plea on behalf of Drunkards and against Drunkenness* (Edinburgh, 1850); also *The City, its Sins and Sorrows* (London, 1857). Guthrie wrote that 'they drink to forget their poverty' and that 'they deserve succour rather than censure . . . it is justice not charity that the poor most need'.

20 Guthrie, like John Lee in the 1830s, was particularly well-informed about the destitution of those living in the Cowgate area of central Edinburgh; Begg was,

among many other things, a keen advocate of improved housing for the working classes; Hill was inspector of prisons for Scotland and a writer on education; Watson and Thomson initiated the industrial feeding school movement, as a means of reducing juvenile delinquency in Aberdeen.

21 D J Withrington, 'The churches in Scotland, c.1870–c.1900: towards a new social conscience?' in *Records of the Scottish Church History Society*, vol xix (1977), p 156.

22 *Chartist Circular*, 28 September 1839: they asserted that 'the liberty for which we contend is an emanation from the Deity . . . the omnipotent authority on which we rest the glorious charter of the people's liberties'; but were at the same time bitterly critical of 'the exorbitant livings of the reverend fathers'.

23 Quoted in Edward Boyle (ed), *The Infidel Tradition from Paine to Bradlaugh* (London, 1976), p 32.

24 *British Weekly*, 24 May 1900: the Free Church reported a decline from 285 in 1889 to 176 in 1899, while the United Presbyterians had not had so few candidates since 1826.

25 A C Cheyne, *The Transforming of the Kirk: Victorian Scotland's Religious Revolution* (Edinburgh, 1983), pp 66–7. (Professor Cheyne's book is without doubt the best introduction to nineteenth-century Scottish church history.)

26 D J Withrington, 'The Free Church Education Scheme, 1843–1850' in *Records of the Scottish Church History Society*, xv (1964), pp 103–15.

27 J D Myers, 'Scottish nationalism and the antecedents of the 1872 Education Act' in *Scottish Educational Studies*, iv, pp 73–92.

28 D J Withrington, 'Towards a national system, 1867–1872: the last years in the struggle for a Scottish Education Act', in ibid., pp 107–24.

29 For the contrasts with England, *see* Brian Simon, *Education and the Labour Movement, 1870–1920* (London, 1965) and J S Hurt, *Elementary Schooling and the Working Classes* (London, 1979).

30 Bruce Lenman and John Stocks, 'The beginnings of state education in Scotland, 1872–1885' in *Scottish Educational Studies*, iv, pp 93–106.

31 *Chronicle of the General Assembly of 1870*, p 31.

32 Cheyne, *Transforming of the Kirk*, p 132.

33 'Corporate Immortality' in *Scotch Sermons* (London, 1880), p 16.

34 *See* for example Norman Macleod's comment in his diary in 1851: 'The question in regard to elevating man is not so much what is good for him, as how the good is to be given to him. What he should have must correspond to what he needs.' (Donald Macleod (ed), *Memoir of Norman Macleod DD* (London, 1876, i, p 287.)

35 *Good Words*, February 1881, quoted in Smith, *Passive Obedience and Prophetic Protest*, p 301.

36 *Good Words*, December 1885, quoted in Smith, p 301.

37 For instance Andrew Vincent and Raymond Plant, *Philosophy, Politics and Citizenship: the life and thought of the British Idealists* (London, 1984); V Bogdanor, *Multi-Party Politics and the Constitution* (Cambridge, 1983); Michael Freeden, *The New Liberalism: an ideology of social reform* (Oxford, 1978); P Robbins, *The British Hegelians, 1875–1925* (New York, 1982).

38 John Kent, *From Darwin to Blatchford: the role of Darwin in Christian apologetic, 1875–1910* (London, 1966), *passim*: he suggests that in England 'by 1904 the process of absorbing the idea of Darwinism into Christian theology had not gone very far'—but in this respect there was a notable contrast with Scotland.

39 *See* two contrasting attitudes to Miller's book, one from a Scottish fellow-scientist, the other from an 'old guard' English aristocrat, in Peter Bayne, *Life*

and Letters of Hugh Miller (London, 1871), ii, pp 412, 415:

(a) Sir Roderick Murchison to Hugh Miller, 19 November 1849: 'I feel deeply indebted to you, on public as well as private grounds, for your vigorous defence of the noble cause of science, and for the enlightened manner in which you entwine it with Christianity. Such reasoning ought to put to shame the efforts of those who would put down science as antagonistic to religion'.

(b) Lord Ellesmere to Hugh Miller, 27 November 1849: 'I read the Vestiges with disbelief and detestation . . . in labouring for the benefit of such persons (i.e. non-scientists) to neutralize the emanations of a poisonous book, you have . . . done that which demands the gratitude of the Christian world'.

40 It has been said that Robert Chambers' *Vestiges* and George Combe's books on phrenology each sold many more copies than did Darwin's *Origin of Species*.
41 Cheyne, *Transformation of the Kirk*, pp 78–9.
42 Ibid., p 171.
43 Robert M Young, 'The impact of Darwin on conventional thought' in Anthony Symondson (ed), *The Victorian Crisis of Faith* (London, 1970), pp 21–2. Young states that 'the idea of opposing theology could not have been further from the mind of the main evolutionists. Their aim was to reconcile nature, God and man . . . The problem was not whether God governed the universe, but how? And the answer became, increasingly, "in the manner of law, not by meddling".'
44 Robert Latta (ed), *Philosophical Studies by David G Ritchie* (London, 1905), p 23.
45 *See* Bernard Aspinwall, *Portable Utopia: Glasgow and the United States, 1820–1920* (Aberdeen, 1984), chapter 5—'The Civic Ideal: efficiency and morality in local government'.
46 William Donaldson, *Popular Literature in Victorian Scotland: Language, Fiction and the Press* (Aberdeen, 1986), p 149.

FURTHER READING

William Ferguson, *Scotland, 1689 to the present* (Edinburgh, 1968) and T C Smout, *A Century of the Scottish People, 1830–1950* (London, 1986) are different but very recommendable general histories. A new three-volume social history of modern Scotland is in process of publication: the first volume—T M Devine, Rosalind Mitchison (eds), *People and Society in Scotland, 1760–1830* (Edinburgh, 1988)—has just appeared, aiming to 'establish the uniqueness of the Scottish route towards an industrial society'; it, and no doubt its sequel volumes, should be consulted. Two recent books at last give a due place to Scotland in modern British politics: Michael Fry, *Patronage and Principle: a political history of modern Scotland* (Aberdeen, 1987) and Iain G S Hutchison, *A Political History of Scotland, 1832–1924* (Edinburgh, 1986). The impact of religion on modern Scottish society and on Scottish social attitudes, and *vice versa*, is very well analysed in A C Cheyne, *The Transforming of the Kirk: Victorian Scotland's religious revolution* (Edinburgh, 1983): *see also* Callum Brown, *The Social History of Religion in Scotland since 1730* (London, 1987) and a still valuable contemporary commentary, Principal John Tulloch's *Movements of Religious Thought in Scotland during the 19th century* (1885), especially in the reprint edition (Leicester, 1971) with an introduction by A C Cheyne. Strange as it may seem, the best account I have found of Scottish philosophy in this period (evaluating German and other influences upon it) is A B McKillop, *A Disciplined Intelligence: critical enquiry and Canadian thought in the Victorian era* (Montreal, 1979): so strong, and indeed so immediate, was the Scottish contribution to Canadian intellectual movements that this offers a quite thorough account of political, religious and social idealisms in nineteenth-century Scotland. On some of the more particular issues raised in the foregoing essay, reference should be made to—Anand Chitnis, *The Scottish Enlightenment and Early Victorian English Society* (London, 1986); Edward Royle, *Radicals, Secularists and Republicans: popular freethought in Britain, 1866–1915* (Manchester, 1980); A D Gilbert, *The Making of Post-Christian Britain: a history of the secularization of modern society* (London, 1980); Anthony Symondson (ed), *The Victorian Crisis of Faith* (London, 1970). Such books as Robert M Young's *Mind, Brain and Adaptation* (Oxford, 1970) are worth consulting, for they comprise more general essays on innovations in science and medicine (and on attitudes to them) than may be apparent from their titles; two worthwhile, if from a Scottish point of view still disappointing, discussions of British Idealism are to be found in Melvin Richter, *The Problem of Conscience: T H Green and his age* (London, 1964) and Andrew Vincent, Raymond Plant (eds), *Philosophy, Politics and Citizenship: the life and thought of the British Idealists* (London, 1984).

Chapter 4

Walter Scott

DAVID HEWITT

For much of this century the work of Walter Scott has been ignored, or condescendingly noticed.[1] The fundamental reason for the decline in his reputation is common to most Scottish writers: too many people do not see why they should be interested in Scottish literature and history. Scotland no longer fascinates the world's imagination; it exercises little economic or political power; it has no 'troubles' to attract attention to the country, and become the subject of literature.

Yet Scott is still a controversial figure, particularly in Scotland. In volume II of this *History of Scottish Literature*, Andrew Hook argues that all the elements of Scottish literary romanticism were established before Scott, but that it was he who wove them together and brought them to a 'brilliant consummation' which moved Scotland 'squarely to the centre of the romantic map of Europe':

> Through Scott the aura of romance finally settled upon Scotland; Scotland's colourful and passionate history, her lochs and rivers and mountains, her loyal, valorous, and proud people, her tradition of poetry and song—all those aspects of Scotland that had already acquired considerable romantic appeal—now appeared in a new and totally irresistible form.[2]

Professor Hook believes Scott's success was 'critical for Scotland and Scottish culture', but others, from Scott's contemporary, Francis Jeffrey, editor of *The Edinburgh Review*, to David Craig in the twentieth century, have attacked the image Scott defined and propagated. His picture of Scottish history, scenery and traditional culture has been represented as profoundly irrelevant, and a distortion of the reality of Scotland both then and now.

Scott's very popularity, essential to the fixing of the image of Scotland, also generates widely divergent responses. Professor Hook argues that the establishment of Scotland's romantic identity was due to imaginative genius which reformed and recreated inherited materials, a view of the writer which is in splendid harmony with the poetic faith of the romantic period. On the other hand, the Scott phenomenon may be represented as the product of successful marketing, rather than authorial genius. Scott was the first author to be promoted in a modern way; a few months before the publication of *Waverley* in 1814, his Edinburgh publishers, Archibald Constable and Co., wrote to their London partners, Longman: 'the necessity of keeping up Mr

Scott's name by the greatest attention to the sale of his works increases every day'.[3] Constable's indubitably paid the greatest attention to the sale of his works. They offered them through a limited number of booksellers who had proven track-records in moving books. They advertised heavily, announcing new titles several months before their actual appearance. They sought to have his works extensively reviewed, the only kind of 'media appearance' that was then possible. They commissioned illustrations. They encouraged translation into other media, such as stage and opera. They offered Scott innumerable projects to try to keep him in the news. Without Constable's marketing flair, it may be argued, Scott's novels would not have been the first best-sellers. Few critics have been able to reconcile these two extreme positions with any comfort. Victorians like Carlyle who believed in the high-calling of the writer felt that Scott's achievement was tarnished by his involvement in the business of literature, the full extent of which was revealed in Lockhart's *Life of Scott* when it was published in 1837. In the nineteen thirties Q D Leavis found it hard to believe that popularity did not require unacceptable artistic compromises. Others have found Scott's declaration in the 'Introductory Epistle' to *The Fortunes of Nigel* (1822) that he wrote for 'general amusement' a brazen confession rather than a provocative tease, and the conclusive evidence that he fashioned what he wrote to satisfy public demand.

In addition, the wordly success which was the product of his popularity has always excited vigorous criticism. His response to his spectacular insolvency in 1826 was unquestionably both honourable and admirable. The debts for which he was legally liable exceeded £120,000; of these £20,000 were his private debts, £60,000 the debts of the printing business in which he was co-partner (but which were the equal responsibility of both men), and £40,000 the debts of his publisher but ranking against Scott because he had effectively guaranteed his publisher's borrowings. Instead of agreeing to the sequestration and sale of his assets and property for the benefit of his creditors (which would have left him free to enjoy what he could earn), he signed a deed of trust by which he committed all his future literary profits to repaying his debts, an end which was achieved some eight years after his death in 1832. But there is no agreement about Scott's moral responsibility for his insolvency; it is accepted that the lack of laws limiting liability, inadequate accounting, and an excessive reliance on bank borrowing to provide the working capital for the publishing and printing businesses were each factors, but was Scott too rapacious? At points Constable and his partner Robert Cadell complained bitterly about Scott's demands, and distrusted his agent John Ballantyne, but they usually accepted his terms. Was he honest with himself, even if he was devious in his commercial dealings? Was he worldly and venial as the Victorians believed? Was he wrong to use his wealth to build a house and purchase land? Is the Abbotsford he built a large house for the period, or is it not? Was his social ambition natural, or was it pretentious?

Such disagreements are not really about Scott but the politics of Scottish culture. They reflect critics' intellectual uncertainty about what makes for popularity and what it signifies; they show a healthy moral concern about the proper use of riches, and also some ambivalence about material success. All these matters are still enjoyably debated, but they are essentially irrelevant to the assessment of Scott's artistic achievement. Of course, they are often linked to criticism in the form of the question 'Did he misuse his artistic talents, and write too much too fast, to satisfy social and wordly ambitions?' It is an old issue which Scott himself felt constrained to discuss several times, but it cannot be resolved. There was no straightforward correlation between his material ambitions and his literary output; at no point, even after the financial crash, did the need for money directly affect the quality of his work.

Walter Scott's oeuvre is so very considerable that it is inevitably difficult to come to terms with his achievement. He was a poet and novelist. Between 1805 and 1817 he published seven long poems, and between 1814 and 1831 twenty-three works of prose fiction, some of which contain two or more tales. Although 'the Scotch novels' as they were known in the early nineteenth century are undoubtedly the best of these, many of the others are fascinating studies of political ethics. He wrote lyrics and other shorter pieces throughout his career. He was a historian who wrote a nine-volume *Life of Napoleon Buonaparte* (1827), and thereafter two histories of Scotland, and one of France (part of which has yet to be published). He was a formidable man of letters. His first major literary production was as editor; his collection of traditional ballads, *Minstrelsy of the Scottish Border*, was first published in 1802, and augmented and revised several times; he completed an edition of the mediaeval metrical romance *Sir Tristrem* in 1804, and major editions of the works of John Dryden in 1808 and Jonathan Swift in 1814; he edited various historical memoirs and collections of historical documents. His most sustained editorial endeavour was on the Magnum Opus (1829–33), the last edition of the Waverley Novels to be published in his lifetime, in which he annotated his own work, and illustrated the sources of his inspiration. His reviews, among the most intelligent and perceptive pieces of early-nineteenth-century criticism, occupy nearly five volumes of his collected prose. (Scott's review of *Emma* is the best study of an Austen novel by a contemporary, and his formulation of the relationship of Childe Harold to his creator has never been bettered: 'Childe Harold may not be, nor do we believe he is, Lord Byron's very self, but he is Lord Byron's picture, sketched by Lord Byron himself.'[4] From 1820 he wrote *Lives of the Novelists* which are modelled on and in effect complement Samuel Johnson's *Lives of the English Poets*, and he produced essays on chivalry, romance and drama for the *Encyclopaedia Britannica*. He was also what we would now call an ethnologist; most of his works are amply annotated with information about Scottish customs and beliefs, and he published *Letters on Demonology and Witchcraft* in 1830. He visited the continent after Napoleon's final defeat at Waterloo, and wrote up his observations on the state of Belgium and France in *Paul's Letters to his Kinsfolk* (1816). The extent of his journalism and controversial writing has not yet been fully established, but it includes such trenchant material as *The Letters of Malachi Malagrowther* (1826), in which he attacked a Government proposal to abridge the rights of the Scottish banks to issue their own banknotes. He wrote more than 10,000 letters. He was a most knowing and self-observant autobiographer. Although his short retrospective auto-biography is, like Gibbon's, more notable for its reserve than its openness (although knowing what to fence implies some knowledge of what is within), the journal which he kept in his last years is genuinely self-revelatory. As I have argued elsewhere,[5] it is a natural tragedy. It opens with Scott at the height of his fame and prosperity; within six months he was ruined and his wife was dead. The *Journal* records his strenuous efforts to be honest with himself but it also reveals how a heroic decision to do right and to repay his debts destroyed him physically and mentally. There is no greater diary in English than the *Journal* of Sir Walter Scott.

In common with many other writers of the nineteenth century, Scott was afflicted by 'that love of composition, which is perhaps the strongest of all instincts, driving the author to the pen',[6] or 'the rage of narration' as it is more memorably put in *Redgauntlet* (ch 3). Of course Scott wrote too much; all who survey his career will feel that it would have been prudent to have written less, and not to have written certain novels at all. But while there is no merit in quantity as such, it is impossible not to stand in awe of his industry. Walter Bagehot observed well that Scott 'shared abundantly in the love of administration and organization, common to all men of great active powers'[7] and although he was talking of Scott's political attitudes the com-ment can be justly applied to the literary life; it is a triumph of organisation to have completed so much, and we must recognise the amazing intellectual productivity. And in spite of the volume, Scott's output is not just task-work. Any familiarity with a range of his work reveals a wide curiosity, broad sympathies, a profusion of ideas, and an astonishing intellectual vigour. Furthermore, there can be few writers, if any, who have covered so many fields. Again, there is no particular merit in range, but Scott's ranging is a kind of exploration of the possibilities of literature; it is in itself a kind of intellectual enquiry. His output is marked by a literary restlessness which shows a creative exploration of the possibilities of different literary kinds.

It is often suggested that Scott's work as editor, historian and social anthropologist should be considered as the record of the research needed to write his poems and novels. For instance, the long 'Introduction' to *Minstrelsy of the Scottish Border* is a historical essay on life and politics in the Scottish Borders in the sixteenth century; *The Lay of the Last Minstrel* (1805) inhabits the same territory. But Scott did not believe in the hierarchy of literary kinds implied by this approach. The factor common to most of what Scott produced is his interest in history. Not only are most of his long poems and novels set in the past, but he was committed to making literature and historical evidence available by publishing editions, to facilitating a historical understanding of such material on a historical basis in his notes and introductions, to inter-preting literature in his essays and reviews, and to writing history in which a major concern is the way in which literature and learning create the climates of opinion which help to form political events. His alternation of kinds and his experimenting with forms are part of the process of exploring the past; the whole oeuvre is permeated by the interaction of historical and imaginative writing. In the 'Introduction' to *Minstrelsy of the Scottish Border* he says that through his 'Notes and occasional Dissertations' he wished to 'contribute somewhat to the history of my native country',[8] as though the songs were not themselves part of that history, but in the Magnum Opus the emphasis is reversed and historical notes are provided as commentary upon fiction. Literature illustrates history, and history illustrates literature; writing is laid down in layers, comment commenting on commentary. The provision of such varied evidence, presented in such a complex way, and in each case over many years, implies that he is never absolutely confident that truth can be captured in a particular form of words; it is as though he were constantly trying to work out the relationship of the literary artifact to what it conveys.

Exactly this issue is discussed in various novels. In *Redgauntlet* (1824) Darsie Latimer speculates on whether his understanding of his background could be affected by the literary form he uses. He writes to Alan Fairford:

> I repeat the little history now, as I have a hundred times done before, merely because I would wring some sense out of it. Turn, then, thy sharp, wire-drawing, lawyer-like ingenuity to the same task—make up my history as though thou wert shaping the blundering allegations of some blue-bonneted, hard-headed client, into a condescendence of facts and circumstances, and thou shalt be, not my Apollo—*quid tibi cum lyra?*—but my Lord Stair. (letter 1)

Darsie reports that he has told and retold his story to see if he can extract clues which would solve his mystery and now invites Alan to cast it in the form of a 'condescendence', a legal statement of fact produced by an advocate for use in a trial. Darsie suggests that the 'condescendence' is just another sort of fiction or faction: 'make up my history as though thou wert shaping the blundering allegations . . . '. Of course, story is a literary kind appropriate to Darsie who is the more imaginative of the two, and the condescendence to Alan who is about to undergo his final examination before becoming an advocate, but it is more than just finding a fitting literary form for the two different characters; Darsie expresses an awareness that a different way of writing might reveal a different aspect of the truth.

The same question is raised in a comic interchange in *The Antiquary* (1816) where Jonathan Oldbuck proposes that Lovel should attempt a Scottish epic:

> 'I'll supply you with a subject—The battle between the Caledonians and the Romans—The Caledoniad; or, Invasion Repelled—Let that be the title—It will suit the present taste, and you may throw in a touch of the times.'
>
> 'But the invasion of Agricola was *not* repelled.'
>
> 'No; but you are a poet—free of the corporation, and as little bound down to truth or probability as Virgil himself—You may defeat the Romans in spite of Tacitus.'
>
> 'And pitch Agricola's camp at the Kaim of—what do you call it,' answered Lovel, 'in defiance of Edie Ochiltree?'
>
> 'No more of that, an thou lovest me—And yet, I dare say, ye may unwittingly speak the most correct truth in both instances, in despite of the *toga* of the historian and the blue gown of the mendicant.'

'Gallantly counselled—Well, I will do my best—your kindness will assist me with local information.'

'Will I not, man?—why, I will write the critical and historical notes on each canto, and draw out the plan of the story myself. I pretend to some poetical genius, Mr Lovel, only I was never able to write verses. (ch 14)

Although the anonymous Author of Waverley makes fun of the famous poet Walter Scott who wrote Scottish epics, there is truth in jest; Oldbuck implies that although the poet may have made free with fact he perhaps produced a work more true to the spirit of Rome than the historian.

In many different contexts Scott suggests an awareness, sometimes even a distrust, of the way in which form may determine the message. Throughout his fiction he engages in literary 'fooling-around', and makes learned jokes which are just as serious as Swift's, or Sterne's, or Joyce's, and just as pertinent about the status of literature as those made by Alasdair Gray in *Lanark*. The finest of his essays on his own work, the 'Introductory Epistle' to *The Fortunes of Nigel*, is a provocative, knock-about dialogue with Captain Clutterbuck, whose name implies that he is a dashing fellow who makes a lot of noise. It is a marvellous discussion of Scott's aims, motives and practice as a novelist, but is so lively that in the 1831 'Introduction' Scott felt constrained to apologise for 'a species of "hoity toity, whisky frisky" pertness of manner, which, in his avowed character, the author would have considered as departing from the rules of civility and good taste.' The boisterous Author of Waverley is repudiated by a Scott who seems as inhibited and tightly-corseted as his most awkward hero. Jedediah Cleishbotham, Dr Dryasdust, and similar figures in other novels are literal-minded pedants with whom the Author of Waverley can argue about the ways in which imaginative literature can illuminate history, but he is just as liable to tease us into taking the opposing view. Nobody likes Miss Buskbody at the end of *Old Mortality* (1816), or Dr Dryasdust at the end of *Redgauntlet* but their desire to know what happened is a deliberate reminder of the artifice of fiction; Scott extracts himself from a conspiracy of reader and author to believe in the reality of that fictional world which concludes in tidy marriages and good fortune ever after, and implicitly suggests that what has been formed into a literary shape has somehow been falsified.

Scott was not fond of formal theorising; he has no work entitled 'A defence of fiction' and the nature of literature is seldom his overt subject. But in the innumerable incidental comments in reviews, in poems and in fiction readers become conscious of a man who is constantly investigating different kinds of writing, and in his practice as a writer recognises his active intelligence teasing and testing literature in the very act of creating it.

Although the layering of text in Scott's works can be intellectually justified, it alienates the readers of novels. Who is not put off by the sequence of introductory materials in the Magnum Opus edition of *Waverley*, which is the basis of all subsequent editions except one: Advertisement, General Preface, Appendix I, Appendix II, Appendix III, Introduction, Preface to the Third Edition? And then the first chapter is called 'introductory'. After this a Scott novel may seem a ramshackle structure, and if readers have any awareness of the repeated accusations of haste and carelessness that have been made ever since the novels were first published they may feel that in spite of Scott's inventiveness his work was ill-considered. Appearances and reputations are deceptive, however. The dreadful succession of preliminary essays are accretions, produced for a public avid to know more about the most popular writer of his day; the first edition of *Waverley* begins at chapter one. In spite of suggestions to the contrary, his work did not proceed uncorrected through the press, although it was frequently written under pressure and processed with haste; he used proofs as we should use typescripts now, as stages when he could revise and correct, and he had assistants read for inconsistencies, repetitions, verbiage, grammatical errors and so on. Extant proofs suggest that Scott's works were usually extensively revised and corrected. Even so, there is not a novel or a poem which has not some untidiness which might have been been obviated had more time been given to it, and critics have read these carelessnesses as evidence of deeper failures. In the 'Introductory Epistle' to *The Fortunes of Nigel* Clutterbuck voices the common criticisms and suggests that the Author of Waverley should take more trouble to plan; the latter replies that he does try but adds:

> I think there is a demon who seats himself on the feather of my pen when I begin to write, and leads it astray from the purpose. Characters expand under my hand; incidents are multiplied; the story lingers, while the materials increase; my regular mansion turns out a Gothic anomaly, and the work is closed long before I have attained the point I proposed. . . . When I light on such a character as Bailie Jarvie, or Dalgetty, my imagination brightens, and my conception becomes clearer at every step which I take in his company, although it leads me many a weary mile from the regular road, and forces me to leap hedge and ditch to get back into the route again. If I resist the temptation, as you advise me, my thoughts become prosy, flat and dull; I write painfully to myself, and under a consciousness of flagging which makes me flag still more; the sunshine with which fancy had invested the incidents, departs from them, and leaves everything dull and gloomy.

This passage is one of the finest pieces of romantic criticism, but it has been regarded as evidence of Scott's supposedly irresponsible attitude to writing. Perhaps the jocularity of the tone, and the apparent acceptance that there is a 'regular road' are misleading, but a point should not need the solemnity of Wordsworth, the intellectual ambition of Coleridge, or the insistence of Shelley before it can be taken seriously. As a description of practice, it confirms superbly the central tenet of romanticism, that literature is not the product of the rational mind, but of the imagination, which expresses itself in its own way and by its own rules. Scott declares that he is led by his imagination, and that his work seemingly develops at its own volition. When in the 'Introduction' to *Guy Mannering* he comments that 'in the progress of the work' the novel came to lose any resemblance to the story on which it was founded, and when in the 'Introduction' to *Redgauntlet* he says that 'various circumstances in the composition' induced him to alter the purport of his original conception, he is not providing evidence of shoddy writing but of the fact that a work of art develops organically. His confession of the surrender of planning controls should be cheered, for great art only comes from the unconscious development of literary ideas. Scott is a great explorer who works not according to formulated plans, but by allowing his imagination to develop literary situations and discover their emotional and intellectual implications.

However, critics have found it hard to recognise Scott's works as an expression of the imagination, or even to see in his work that interest in the life of the mind which characterises the poetry of Wordsworth, Coleridge, Keats and Shelley. For instance Ian Jack finds the novels repetitious, and dislikes both the improbable adventures of Scott's heroes and the abundance of romance elements such as witches, sybils, prophecies, smugglers or other banditti, villains, conspiracies, kidnappings, battles, miraculous rescues.[9] He is not alone in this response; the preference for nice moral and psychological discrimination and a probable plot, in which what happens arises naturally and inevitably from what has already taken place, has had a long critical ascendancy; for much of the twentieth century Jane Austen and Henry James were approved authors, while Dickens and Scott were not.

But Professor Jack's application of the standards of realistic fiction is inappropriate. In the 'Introductory Epistle' to *The Fortunes of Nigel* Scott objects to the application of the rules of artistic probability to his novels:

> [Fielding] challenges a comparison between the Novel and the Epic. Smollett, Le Sage, and others, emancipating themselves from the strictness of the rules he has laid down, have written rather a history of the miscellaneous adventures which befall an individual in the course of life, than the plot of a regular and connected epopoeia, where every step brings us a point nearer to the final catastrophe.

Although Scott overlooks the fact that every step in *The Bride of Lammermoor* brings us a point nearer to the final catastrophe, and although we are unlikely to consider *Tom Jones* a good example of the probable and the necessary in literature, the general point that that is not the only structural principle is correct. So too is the paradoxical observation that 'miscellaneous adventures' are more true to life than what is artistically probable. As historical events are not usually created by individuals but happen to them or around them, it is inevitable that the Waverley Novels should have romance plots, and that Scott's heroes should be (in Scott's words) 'never actors, but always acted upon'.[10] What should be at issue is not that Scott uses romance plots but whether he, like Coleridge in 'The Ancient Mariner' or Keats in 'Lamia', can transform tales of the marvellous into something enlightening and meaningful. Northrop Frye, who above all others has taught us how to discuss romance materials, tells us in *The Secular Scripture* that it was Scott who awoke his interest in romance, and he explains that there came a stage when

> ... I was ready to become fascinated once more by Scott's formulaic techniques. The same building blocks appeared every time: light and dark heroines, outlawed or secret societies, wild women chanting prophecies, heroes of mysterious and ultimately fortunate birth; but the variety with which they were disposed was now what impressed me.[11]

There is not just variety in his disposing of stock material; the basic patterns of romance as used by Scott have an organic and meaningful relationship with the history they interpret, and the trials and tribulations suffered by his characters exteriorise spiritual and psychological experiences that are not normally subjected to analysis and discussion, except in the unrealism of the realistic novel.

The romantic imagination works and expresses itself through romance. Coleridge and Keats use tales of the marvellous as a means by which they can describe the life of the mind, and they are inspired by traditional ballads, and by Spenser and Milton. Scott uses similar material but his great innovation is to naturalise romance in a social context; there is a happy marriage between his perception of history and the kind of literature he found most congenial. In *Waverley* Edward remarks after the creagh:

> It seemed like a dream to Waverley that these deeds of violence should be familiar to men's minds, and currently talked of, as falling within the common order of things, and happening daily in the immediate vicinity, without his having crossed the seas, and while he was yet in the otherwise well-ordered island of Great Britain. (ch 15)

It is long since critics thought it right to praise Scott for his treatment of social class and of the poorer members of society; it was recognised as revolutionary by his contemporaries, and it becomes wearisome to have to restate what is obvious but we do him a great injustice if we do not accept that this is indeed his greatest achievement. Of course poor people appear in earlier literature, but no writer before Scott was able to depict the structure of society in such a convincing way. In *The Gentle Shepherd* Allan Ramsay takes the conventions of pastoral literally, and presents actual shepherds instead of figures from a literary never-never land. In his novels Scott acts similarly; he takes the extraordinary galaxy of unreal people that are to be found in Ariosto and Spenser, and makes them real in Scotland. In Wordsworth the poor are figures to be contemplated, but in Scott they are individuals, with a life of their own.

He convinces the reader of the reality of his people by his use of physical detail and modes of speech that differentiate the social classes. He often emphasises the importance of detail; in a letter to Robert Surtees he explains that his plan in *The Lay of the Last Minstrel* and *Marmion* has rather been to exhibit 'ancient costume, diction, and manners, than to display my own ingenuity in making an ideal world, or dealing in general description, which may be as correct among the Iroquois as when the scene is laid in feudal Europe'.[12] In the novels he takes the process very much further and is much more skilful in insinuating detail that simultaneously suggests environment and behaviour. He describes the inside of the Mucklebackits' cottage in *The Antiquary* in a passage that tells us about their means of life, their possessions, the family ethic, and even the command structure: Maggie is clearly the dominant partner:

> there was confusion,—there was dilapidation,—there was dirt in good store. Yet, with all this, there was about the inmates ... an appearance of ease, plenty, and comfort, that seemed to warrant their old sluttish proverb, 'The clartier the cosier.' A huge fire, though the season was summer, occupied the hearth, and served at once for affording light, heat, and the means of preparing food. The fishing had been successful, and the family, with customary improvidence, had, since unlading the cargo, continued an unremitting operation of broiling and frying that part of the produce reserved for home consumption, and the bones and fragments lay on the wooden trenchers, mingled with morsels of broken bannocks and shattered mugs of half-drunk beer. The stout and athletic form of Maggie herself, bustling here and there among a pack of half-grown girls and younger children, of whom she chucked one now here and another now there with an exclamation of 'Get out o' the gate, ye little sorrow!' (ch 26)

Secondly, his language, particularly in the Scots novels, is a wholly convincing way of differentiating classes. The language question is contentious; even the evidence does not seem to be agreed, for it is usually maintained that the narration and the speech of the upper classes is English, while the speech of the middling and lower classes is Scots, when in fact the English is merely the standard written form of the language, and the Scots often uses the English forms of words that are common to both Scots and English. What Scott does is to represent the Scots-English speech of his upper class characters in standard written English, and to suggest the speech of the more old-fashioned, and of the other classes, in a language that is rather more dialectal. His language is not a phonetic transcription; it is a rhetorical mode that points the differences in the speech of the social classes. John Galt, learning from Scott, attempted to be very much more precise in rendering both social and geographical dialects, but it is the Burns-Scott compromise, which is more convincing than accurate, that was adopted by other novelists in the nineteenth century.

Although Scott successfully naturalises features of romance, they may seem repetitive. The heroes of *Waverley* (1814), *Rob Roy* (1817), and *Redgauntlet* (1824) are initially immature and, in one sense or another, fatherless; they undertake a journey into territory that is geographically and ideologically foreign to their experience, become involved in Jacobite plots and rebellions, suffer a loss of freedom and of social status, and risk death. Ultimately they are restored to their rightful place in society and the affections of their families. Similar figures crop up: outlaws like Donald Bean Lean, Rob Roy and the smugglers of *Redgauntlet*, outcasts who yet have a peculiar kind of wisdom like Davie Gellatley and Wandering Willie. Wild scenery plays a large part in each.

The repetitiveness is only appearance, a consequence of the novels being described in this particular way, for there is considerable variety in the way Scott develops stock material. For instance, although the heroes can be said to be fatherless, Scott makes quite different use of the motif in the three novels. In general, the father is the source of law and authority, and should steer the hero on his course in life. In *Waverley* Edward's real father has, from self-interest, resigned the role, and the alternate father, Sir Everard, is so gentle that Edward is freed from all discipline and permitted, in a great measure, 'to learn as he pleased, what he pleased, and when he pleased' (ch 3). The weakness of paternal authority allows Edward to choose substitute fathers in Fergus Mac-Ivor and Colonel Talbot, and one measure of his maturation is his ultimate choice of Talbot, who confirms his role by restoring Edward to society. But in *Rob Roy*, Frank Osbaldistone is a rebel against his father; he is turned out of paradise, he journeys north into a perilous country, is enmeshed by the enchanter Rashleigh, helped through increasing perils by the good angels Diana Vernon and Rob Roy, and eventually reconciled to his father through the teaching and guidance of Bailie Nicol Jarvie. Darsie Latimer in *Redgauntlet* has no father; Saunders Fairford and Hugh Redgauntlet propose themselves for the role but both are rejected by Darsie, who has to identify his real father, discover that he is dead and thus feel himself free to be himself. The choice of, or reconciliation with, or freedom from, the father is symptomatic of the hero's maturation, and has a political value in that the heroes choose the mode of life (not just the political party) which, in history, will predominate; but the lost father motif is treated in different ways in the three novels for the processes of choice, and reconciliation, are not the same. This is what we expect of literary romance. The implications of traditional stories change according to the teller, the audience, and the era in which the tale is retold. Scott develops the motif in different ways and is realising within different works the potentiality of romance to carry a variable cultural message.

Further, the situations are explored in different ways. *Waverley* is told by a narrator who has a complete command of the material he recounts; the first chapter is a discussion of what kind of novel *Waverley* is, while the final chapter removes the reader from the world of the fiction to discuss its relationship to 'life'. They read like Fielding in *Tom Jones*. The narrator is concerned to ensure that the reader appreciates the moral significance of what he recounts. His allusions identify him as a man of the early nineteenth century (Fergus and Flora are so alike that they might have played Sebastian and Viola 'with the same exquisite effect produced by the appearance of Mrs Henry Siddons and her brother, Mr William Murray, in these characters'; ch 21), and the irony with which he treats his hero establishes a knowing rapport with his readers. The narrator is prophet, teacher and the disposer of human events, suggesting the hero's fate, pointing its significance, and determining the outcome. When Flora wishes she could be a queen and command the ' "most amiable and worthy youth of my kingdom to accept happiness with the hand of Rose Bradwardine" ', Fergus remarks that he wished she could command Rose to accept him. The narrator comments:

> I don't know by what caprice it was that this wish, however jocularly expressed, rather jarred on Edward's feelings, notwithstanding his growing inclination to

> Flora, and his indifference to Miss Bradwardine. This is one of the inexplicabilities of human nature, which we leave without comment. (ch 23)

In his refusal to comment the narrator draws the reader's attention to Edward's lack of self-understanding and hints at the eventual outcome of the novel.

Rob Roy, on the other hand, is a first-person, retrospective narration, in which Scott experiments with trying to represent both the immediacy of personal experience, and the effect of this experience when recollected in tranquillity. Frank Osbaldistone tells his adventures and passes moral judgement on himself as a young man; he tries to impose a Providential pattern on the events of his life. At the same time he is reworking the earlier psychological experience of alienation from his father and the probable loss of Diana so that he can now come to terms with their final loss through death.

The difference in narrative method may not produce two works as sharply differentiated as we might expect, but then both novels were highly innovatory; for instance, although many first-person novels were written in the eighteenth century *Rob Roy* is the first fictional autobiography which attempts to realise both the experience as first perceived and as assessed later in the telling of the tale. Scott is striving to realise the potentialities of the forms. Because *Waverley* has a strongly *dirigiste* narrator, the romance materials are presented descriptively. When Edward is led to meet Flora by the waterfall to listen to her translation of Mac-Murrough's song, he is seduced sexually and ideologically. The narrator's comment is limited:

> Edward thought he had never, even in his wildest dreams, imagined a figure of such exquisite and interesting loveliness. The wild beauty of the retreat, bursting upon him as if by magic, augmented the mingled feeling of delight and awe with which he approached her, like a fair enchantress of Boiardo or Ariosto, by whose nod the scenery around him seemed to have been created, an Eden in the wilderness. (ch 22)

It is appropriate that Edward should understand an entirely new experience, indeed a kind of awakening, in the language of his favourite reading, but there is no further hint about the psychological import of the scene. In fact, Edward is in a sexual landscape. He enters Flora's retreat through a narrow pass guarded by a rapid and furious brook which issued 'from between precipices, like a maniac from his confinement, all foam and uproar', and by rocks that assume 'a thousand peculiar and varied forms' and which seem to 'forbid the passenger's farther progress'. When he gets through he finds himself in a 'sylvan ampitheatre', by a 'broken cataract' whose water is received in a 'large natural basin'. The sexual suggestiveness of the landscape is paralleled in Edward's movements; he comes from a barren scene through one that is unexpectedly exciting to find a kind of content. Of course Flora is inaccessible; she is on a bridge high above him and he can only look up and shudder at the vertical distance which separates them, but the features of the landscape suggest the underlying, and probably unrecognised, sexuality of her appeal to him.

The scene is described as though it was merely visual, and there is no attempt to explain its psychological significance, but in *Rob Roy*, as is appropriate in a restrospective autobiography, what is observed is interiorised. The climactic event is the murder of Morris who is hurled from the top of a cliff; Frank is horrified, but the incident is turned into a psychic metaphor which seems to express his deepest fears and anxieties. As he guards Diana and her father in the library of the Hall he dreams:

> I remember a strange agony, under which I conceived myself and Diana in the power of MacGregor's wife, and about to be precipitated from a rock into the lake; the signal was to be the discharge of a cannon, fired by Sir Frederick Vernon, who, in the dress of a cardinal, officiated at the ceremony. (ch 39)

The dream is psychologically appropriate: the most disturbing incident of the novel is the vehicle for the expression of Frank's immediate fear that the authority of the father and of the catholic church will kill his hopes of happiness and fulfilment. It is also an archetypal image; the deepest anxieties are expressed in dreams of falling, and here the fall reminds us that Frank has already been expelled from his patrimony, and it suggests a denial of another Paradise, union with Di. Of course, the dream has a reference not just to the events of the novel but to the telling of the tale; it is significant that the verb should be in the present tense ('I remember') for as he writes his father and Diana are both dead, and putting dream experience into words is one way of adjusting to the trauma.

There is no evidence to justify an argument that Scott was engaged in a systematic consideration of the implications of narrative stance, and yet one is forced to believe that imaginatively he was doing just that. He may never have said 'In *Waverley* I have viewed a young man's development in a detached way, let me now see what the hero can make of it himself' and then gone on to write *Rob Roy*, but his discussion of the interaction of literature and the self in *Redgauntlet*, in which literary creation is one of the means by which Darsie Latimer explores his quest for identity, suggests that he was consciously, but perhaps not systematically, exploring the significance of narrative mode.

Darsie tells his friend Alan Fairford that he is 'alone in the world' (letter I), and that his sense of loneliness is 'the more depressing, that it seems to me to be a solitude peculiarly my own.' The principal reason for his alienation is that he knows nothing of his background and parentage, and, as an eighteenth-century man, is thus without established status and identity; he tells Alan that his lack of a family is felt all the more acutely in a country 'where all the world have a circle of consanguinity, extending to sixth cousins at least.' He is independent, but this accentuates his loneliness, for although Alan is his only friend he feels that he has been repudiated because Alan will not regard 'our purses as common, as well as our sentiments'. He wishes he had a father, and he mourns his dead mother. He feels that he does not have

a secure social role; had he to work for his living the 'necessary communication of master and servant would be at least a tie which would attach
me to the rest of my kind'. Later in the novel it is suggested that his mixing
with a variety of people of widely different backgrounds is evidence of his
unsteadiness. He advises Alan that his father need not be afraid that Alan
will be influenced 'by such a reed shaken by the winds as I am', recalling the
words of the Gospel (Luke 7.24) and implying that he is a thing of no
substance at the mercy of whatever might blow. Thus Darsie suffers from
both an acute sense of social alienation and psychological insecurity.

He finds that he is unable to reconcile himself to the study of law and to
the professional ethos of Edinburgh. He believes he comes from England,
but having been forbidden to visit England until his twenty-fifth year expires
he goes on a 'wildgoose jaunt' to Dumfries-shire from whose coast he can
see the country of his birth. The journey involves him in improbable adventures, two narrow escapes from drowning, imprisonment, transformations
not into other creatures as would happen in the romances of Ariosto or
Spenser but into a person of a different name and family from what he
imagined. The journey is a typical romance plot; it is an exploration of his
family past and leads to the discovery of his own status in society, while his
writing up of his adventures becomes a mode of inner exploration through
which he comes to a mature understanding of who he is.

In telling his own story to Alan in his letters and journal Darsie observes
the interaction of the business of writing with his own mood. In the first letter
he tells Alan 'I have written myself out of my melancholy and blue-devils,
merely by prosing about them'. He later writes in his journal:

> the exercise of the pen seems to act as a sedative upon my own agitated thoughts
> and tumultuous passions. I never lay it down but I rise stronger in resolution,
> more ardent in hope. A thousand vague fears, wild expectations, and indigested
> schemes, hurry through one's thoughts in seasons of doubt and danger. But by
> arresting them as they flit across the mind, by throwing them on paper, and
> even by that mechanical act compelling ourselves to consider them with scrupu-
> lous and minute attention, we may perhaps escape becoming the dupes of
> our own excited imagination. (ch 9)

Just as Wordsworth writes *The Prelude* in the hope that he might fetch
'Invigorating thoughts from former years;/Might fix the wavering balance of
my mind',[13] so Darsie sees the act of writing as a restorative, self-defining
activity. Scott like Wordsworth recognises the therapeutic effect of creative
activity.

Redgauntlet consists partly of letters, partly of journal, partly of third-
person narrative. On the first occasion on which the letter form is replaced
by narrative, the narrator justifies the switch by suggesting that a genuine
correspondence can 'seldom be found to contain all in which it is necessary
to instruct the reader for his full comprehension of the story' (ch 1). Scott
thus recognises a need for an overview; but it is also implicit in his use of the
letter and journal forms that he was looking for forms which would allow

him to explore the dynamics of writing; the investigation of the psychological implications of the adventures of Darsie Latimer requires literary modes in which he can express his own consciousness. *Redgauntlet* is one of the most satisfying of the Waverley Novels because Scott fuses different kinds of fiction so as to illuminate the intellectual implications of each.

Redgauntlet shows that he was fully aware of the implications and possibilities of varying his narrative strategy. Indeed, when the sequence of long poems and novels is considered, Scott is seen as a writer who is continuously trying to realise the inner implications of romance by experimenting with form. In *Waverley* the controlling all-knowing narrator is detached; in *Guy Mannering* the astrologer, who is a type of the author, is placed within the novel, but because of the loss of oversight Scott uses journals, letters, and reports from other characters, which do not just vary the perspective but seem to indicate that he felt the past was too various to be controlled by the single voice. In *Tales of My Landlord*, first series, (*The Black Dwarf* and *Old Mortality*) he creates a fictitious narrator, Peter Pattieson, assistant schoolmaster of Gandercleugh. The next novel, *Rob Roy*, is a fictional retrospective autobiography; then he returns to Peter Pattieson, who is the nominal narrator of both the second and third series of *Tales of My Landlord* (*The Heart of Mid-Lothian; The Bride of Lammermoor* and *A Legend of Montrose*).

Many readers feel that the fictional narrators are irrelevant, but the frequency with which he adopts a persona suggests that he has to imagine a tale-telling role for himself. In *The Lay of the Last Minstrel* he even sets up the line of transmission for what purports to be a traditional story: Scott dedicates his poem to the Countess of Dalkeith, wife of the eldest son of the Duke of Buccleuch (who are Scotts), writes a poem in which a minstrel sings to the first Duchess at the end of the seventeenth century about the deeds of ancestors in the sixteenth. The Last Minstrel, and indeed all the other narrators, may only be a projection of a particular aspect of the author, but by imagining a new role he begins to explore new situations. His works could be said to be a series of dramatic fictions in which a created narrator, writer, speaker or singer presents a new story, or argues a position, or explores an experience. It is quite clear that he needs to role-play to get going, but it seems that the role is essential to allow him to escape from his own normality and explore experience, ideas, attitudes and feelings that he would not otherwise have discovered.

Peter Pattieson is one of his most important personae, the nominal narrator of three of his greatest works. In *Old Mortality* he is presented as a sensitive person, who after school wanders alone, and is mentally refreshed and disposed to write by solitude and quiet scenery. He is particularly fond of an old graveyard, which induces him to contemplate mortality:

> The daisy which sprinkles the sod, and the harebell which hangs over it, derive their pure nourishment from the dew of heaven, and their growth impresses us with no degrading or disgusting recollections. Death has indeed been here, and its traces are before us; but they are softened and deprived of their horror by our distance from the period when they have been first impressed. Those who

> sleep beneath are only connected with us by the reflection, that they have once
> been what we now are, and that, as their relics are now identified with their
> mother earth, ours shall, at some future period, undergo the same trans-
> formation. (ch 1)

The passage establishes Pattieson as a man concerned with last things, and
unswayed by earthly passions. But it is also profoundly ironic, for the tales
that Pattieson learns from Old Mortality of those buried in the graveyard
could generate deep and bitter controversy even in Scott's own day. So
the description of Pattieson's attitudes simultaneously establishes his moral
credentials for telling the tale, and proposes standards by which to judge the
events of the novel. Should we not understand the significance of this very
deliberate literary and religious placing of the narrator, Scott goes on to
describe Pattieson's methods of work. He gets his stories from Old Mortality,
but endeavours 'to correct or verify them from the most authentic sources
of tradition, afforded by the representatives of either party'. He consulted
moorland farmers 'from the western districts', travelling merchants, country
weavers and tailors. And to get the other side's version he approached
descendants of 'ancient and honourable families, . . . more than one non-
juring bishop, . . . a laird or two' and 'the gamekeepers of these gentlemen'
(ch 1). In *Old Mortality* Scott treats very controversial material; the drama-
tisation of Peter Pattieson helps him to disengage, and to present an unambiguous moral perspective, without imposing the single authoritative voice
as in *Waverley*.

Pattieson is a sensitive and thoughtful character, who is himself confront-
ing death, and the tenor of the tales he tells are dramatically appropriate. In
Old Mortality Henry Morton is revolted by

> the tyrannical and oppressive conduct of the government, the misrule, license,
> and brutality of the soldiery, the executions on the scaffold, the slaughters in
> the open field, the free quarters and exactions imposed by military law, which
> placed the lives and fortunes of a free people on a level with Asiatic slaves. (ch
> 13)

Having nearly become a victim of this tyranny Morton joins the Cameronian
insurgents, but discovers that they have as little idea of truth and justice as
the royal forces. He rejects the ideologies of the two contending parties and
asserts that human life is more valuable than political creeds: ' "God gives
every spark of life—that of the peasant as well as of the prince" ' (ch 35). To
ensure that at the end of the conflict this fundamental moral principle can be
made effective he proposes a constitutional settlement in which the rule of
law will secure the liberty and personal security of the subject. In spite of the
bigotry and cruelty of the world of 1679 as depicted by Scott, *Old Mortality*
is, intellectually, an optimistic novel; it concludes with the settlement of 1689,
and it implicitly asserts that the system of law and due legal processes can
attain and secure justice.

In *The Heart of Mid-Lothian* (1818) Pattieson is much less sanguine about the ability of men and society to save themselves. Butler argues with the rioters and he puts forward the position that seems to be established in *Old Mortality*, that justice is to be secured not by private action but in the operation of the legal system:

> 'You cannot have, by the laws of God or man, power to take away the life of a human creature, however deserving he may be of death. If it is murder even in a lawful magistrate to execute an offender otherwise than in the place, time, and manner which the judges' sentence prescribes, what must it be in you, who have no warrant for interference but your own wills?' (ch 7)

But in *The Heart of Mid-Lothian* the processes of law are not coincidental with justice. Effie is condemned to death for a crime she did not commit, and the Saddletrees highlight the issue when he, in the pride of his legal knowledge, says ' "The crime is rather a favourite of the law, this species of murther being one of its ain creation" ', to which she responds irrationally but superbly: ' "Then, if the law makes murders . . . the law should be hanged for them' " (ch 5). Justice is only attained in the exercise of the royal prerogative of mercy, which in turn is the earthly manifestation of divine grace. Jeanie regards God's law as the supreme determinant of human conduct, consistently acknowledges that truth and justice abide with God, and strives to reconcile herself and her conscience with God through scrupulous self-examination and through prayer. That she might do something for her sister comes to her as a revelation 'like a sun-blink on a stormy sea' (ch 18). The narrator has moved on from the position he arrived at in *Old Mortality* for he argues that ultimately justice is secured not by reference to the ideas of individuals, nor through the operation of the legal system, but is only attained in the love and mercy of God.

As there is no similar discussion of God, grace and mercy in the rest of Scott's work, and as the ideas of *The Heart of Mid-Lothian* do not form part of his normal thinking, we have to conclude that the process of being Pattieson and writing the novel has led him to discover and understand new experience. *The Bride of Lammermoor* (1819) is different yet again for here he seems to despair of human institutions, but does not find solace in the divine order of things. Edgar and Lucy are enlightened human beings, the Henry Morton and Jeanie Deans of the *Bride*, who for love overcome traditional family hatred and factional allegiance, who show themselves superior to the general superstition of the age, and who repudiate vengeance as a mode of justice when all around still practise it, but who are destroyed by the society in which they live.

It is obvious that Scott develops fictional narrators in poems such as *The Lay of the Last Minstrel* and novels like *Old Mortality*, but it is even more telling to explore the phenomenon in non-fiction because intellectual consistency is expected of it. In *The Letters of Malachi Malagrowther*, addressed to the Editor of *The Edinburgh Weekly Journal* Scott begins with a character sketch:

> I am by pedigree a discontented person, so that you may throw this letter into the fire, if you have any apprehensions of incurring the displeasure of your superiors. I am, in fact, the lineal descendant of Sir Mungo Malagrowther, who makes a figure in the *Fortunes of Nigel*, and have retained a reasonable proportion of his ill luck, and, in consequence, of his ill temper. If, therefore, I should chance to appear too warm and poignant in my observations, you must impute it to the hasty and peevish humour which I derive from my ancestor. But, at the same time, it often happens that this disposition leads me to speak useful, though unpleasant truths, when more prudent men hold their tongues and eat their pudding. (*Prose Works*, 21, p 269)

The creation of a naive fictional character who proceeds to utter political truths is a traditional device, used in the Bible and by writers like Swift, whom Scott had edited. Malachi Malagrowther is established as a truth-teller; the Christian name suggests that he is something of a prophet who is about to make unpalatable pronouncements, while the surname strongly implies that he is the voice of Scott. In pretending that his urgency is merely a rough-gruff manner, Scott courteously disclaims wisdom and covers up the passion, but by doing so he indicates that he believes he is wise, and reveals that there is a great force of emotion held in check by the careful exposition and articulation of his position; a simple observer can see clearly the real implications of Government actions, and feel that they are foolish and insulting.

Although the primary subject of *The Letters of Malachi Malagrowther* is the proposed curtailment of the rights of the Scottish banks to issue their own banknotes, the fundamental concern is the nature of the political conventions regulating the government of Scotland. Malagrowther at once states the central political theme of the *Letters*:

> I am old, sir, poor, and peevish, and therefore, I may be wrong; but when I look back on the last fifteen or twenty years, and more especially on the last ten, I think I see my native country of Scotland, if it is yet to be called by a title so discriminative, falling, so far as its national, or rather, perhaps, I ought now to say its *provincial*, interests are concerned, daily into more absolute contempt. Our ancestors were a people of some consideration in the councils of the empire. So late as my own younger days, an English minister would have paused, even in a favourite measure, if a reclamation of national rights had been made by a Member for Scotland, supported, as it uniformly then was, by the voice of her representatives and her people. Such ameliorations in our peculiar system as were thought necessary, in order that North Britain might keep pace with her sister in the advance of improvement, were suggested by our own countrymen, persons well acquainted with our peculiar system of laws (as different from those of England as from those of France), and who knew exactly how to adapt the desired alteration to the principle of our legislative enactments, so that the whole machine might, as mechanics say, work well and easily. For a long time this wholesome check upon innovation, which requires the assimilation of a proposed improvement with the general constitution of the country to which it has been recommended, and which ensures that important point, by stipulating that the measure shall originate with those to whom the spirit of the constitution is familiar, has been, so far as Scotland is concerned, considerably disused. (*Prose Works* 21, pp 270–1)

This is an important statement of political principle; there is no earlier work which provides a more coherent theory of Scotland's position under the Union, and it is as relevant now as it was in 1826. Scott's first argument concerns status; Scotland is a country, not a province. He argues, secondly, that government decisions should not be imposed on Scotland when they are opposed by its Members of Parliament, and, thirdly, that proposals for reform should come from Scotsmen because they can best make changes harmonise with the 'constitution', a word which seems to comprehend both the current body of law and the expectations of the electorate. His arguments represent these political ideas as established political conventions, unwisely and carelessly ignored by the Parliament and Government of the United Kingdom. It is not clear that these were accepted political conventions but Scott's rhetorical strategy is to construct an appeal to the past as a means of controlling the present.

In *Tales of a Grandfather*, on the other hand, Scott is pushed by the dramatic use of a particular persona to repudiate the past—to present it as a warning to the present—and he comes to a different perception of the significance of the Union. He presents himself as moral teacher; in the dedication to his grandson he says it would give him great pleasure if Hugh Littlejohn should grow 'wiser and better'[14] from reading the book. Of course Scott does not always remember that he is writing for his grandson, but the general purpose of imparting some knowledge of Scottish history, and of explaining such necessary concepts as the 'progress of civilisation in society', is apparent through the whole work.

The moral teacher is led by the logic of his argument to present the political reconciliation of Scotland and England as the culmination of Scottish history, and, by the momentum of telling Scotland's history, to repudiate war with a forthrightness that is without parallel elsewhere in Scott's work. The first chapter of the second series is entitled 'Progress of Civilisation in Society'.[15] He says man is distinguished from the animals by language, which is the means by which he can transmit and accumulate knowledge and experience, and he discusses the ways in which social structures and organisations both reflect and facilitate 'the capacity of amending our condition by increase in knowledge'. The chapter is a clear and succinct restatement of the kinds of idea which interested Scott's friends and teachers, and especially Adam Ferguson, but it leads Scott to present the Union of the Crowns in 1603 (the subject of the next chapter) as a necessary step in social and political evolution. In the 'Prefatory Letter' to the third series[16] Scott says that he aimed to give his grandson an opportunity of 'acquiring a knowledge of the past events of Scottish History', and he immediately comments 'and a bloody and tragic tale it has been'. The 'Prefatory Letter' was of course written last and is a statement of what Scott himself has learned from the systematic process of telling the history of Scotland: he explains that his generation has been the first not to witness 'either foreign or domestic war within their country'; he looks back at the experience of each preceding generation to a time when 'the blessings of peace were totally unknown'; he surveys the devastation of the continent in his own lifetime; he greets 'with sincere joy' the prospect that the rising generation may be 'less likely either to hear of, or to witness, the terrors of actual war'. As the 'Letter' comes between his account of the Union, and his discussion of the subsequent effect of the Union, the placing implies that the Union was a necessary step in securing the peace of the British Isles.

It is not impossible to reconcile intellectually the view of the Union taken in *The Letters of Malachi Malagrowther* with that in *Tales of a Grandfather*— it could be argued that *Waverley* constitutes that compromise—but the emotional implications of the two seem to be very different indeed. I would propose that the two works evolved as he wrote them, and that they led him to conclusions he did not foresee. His recreation of many different periods of the past, in different poems and novels, involves imaginative projection, and the successful creation of characters requires a dramatic imagination, but what is being discussed goes beyond this; in the process of writing his imagination explores moral and intellectual issues whose implications only seem to have come to him as the works grew.

A few years ago a critic said 'I am convinced that Scott wrote a number of books which deserve an enduring classic status. I am convinced that to see this it is necessary to discriminate very sharply.'[17] Scott may still be a controversial symbol in Scottish cultural life, but it is time that we stopped the grudging praise and accepted the greatness of his achievement. It is not necessary to discriminate sharply. The treatment of political ideas in *Woodstock* is as acute as in *Old Mortality*; the novels set in the middle ages, or the Elizabethan or Jacobean eras, or abroad, are no less alert to issues than the novels set in the eighteenth century, all of which are Scottish. What distinguishes the two groups is Scott's representation of 'life'. The more remote in time and place, the more the speech of characters seems artificial, and the more the concerns of the novel seem anachronistically located; history approaches allegory. In the Scottish novels, on the other hand, the evidence is thicker. Scott draws on a greater range of sources including his own personal observation, and provides more information about political and social conditions; his presentation of social structure, his treatment of social and political tensions and his representation of speech are more convincing. That is why the Scottish novels are better; it does not mean the others are bad, or even particularly weak.

Walter Scott is the most fertile and inventive of Scottish writers. He is a thinker about literature; he is a writer who transforms stock romance material into brilliant studies of social life, and acute analyses of psychological and spiritual conditions, and who strives to make these meaningful through his continuous experimentation with form. He exhibits a spiritual and intellectual versatility similar to Shakespeare's in *Lear* and *The Tempest*. He is of necessity a writer of the romantic period; it is time he was again recognised as one of the greatest of romantics.

NOTES

1   Quotations from Scott's novels are taken from the author's edition, *Waverley Novels*, 48 vols (Edinburgh, 1829–33); citations refer to introductions, chapters, etc. rather than page numbers to facilitate the use of other editions. Quotations from Scott's prose works are from *The Prose Works of Sir Walter Scott, Bart.*, 28 vols (Edinburgh, 1834–6), cited as *Prose Works*, and quotations from his poetry are from *The Poetical Works of Sir Walter Scott, Bart.*, J G Lockhart (ed), 12 vols (Edinburgh, 1833–4), cited as *PW*.

2   Andrew Hook, 'Scotland and Romanticism: The International Scene' in *The History of Scottish Literature*, vol 2 (1660–1800), Andrew Hook (ed) (Aberdeen, 1987), p 319.

3   National Library of Scotland, MS 789, f 21.

4   *Prose Works* 17, p 341.

5   David Hewitt (ed), *Scott on Himself* (Edinburgh, 1981), p xxiii.

6   'Introductory Epistle' to *The Fortunes of Nigel*.

7   In *Scott: the Critical Heritage*, John O Hayden (ed) (London, 1970), p 400.

8   *PW* 1, pp 237–8.

9   Ian Jack, *English Literature 1815–1832* being the Oxford History of English Literature, vol X, (Oxford, 1963), pp 187–94.

10   *Prose Works* 19, p 5.

11   Northrop Frye, *The Secular Scripture: A Study of the Structure of Romance* (Cambridge, Mass. and London, 1976), p 5.

12   *The Letters of Sir Walter Scott*, H J C Grierson (ed), 12 vols (1932–7), II, pp 53–4.

13   William Wordsworth, *The Prelude 1805*, bk 1, 649–50.

14   *Prose Works*, 22, p ix.

15   *Prose Works*, 23, pp 215–34.

16   *Prose Works*, 25, pp 109–14.

17   A O J Cockshut, *The Achievement of Walter Scott* (London, 1969), p 7.

FURTHER READING

SCOTT'S WORKS

Well-annotated editions of some of Scott's novels have been published by Penguin and the World's Classics in recent years, but only one has an authoritative text, namely *Waverley*, Claire Lamont (ed) (Oxford, 1981). There is as yet no critical edition of the Waverley Novels although this should be rectified as the Edinburgh Edition of the Waverley Novels appears during the nineties. There have been no critical editions of Scott's prose and poetry; those cited in note 1 above are closest to being authoritative.

The Journal of Sir Walter Scott, W E K Anderson (ed) (Oxford, 1972).
The Letters of Sir Walter Scott, H J C Grierson (ed), 12 vols (London, 1932–37).
James C Corson, *Notes and Index to Sir Herbert Grierson's Edition of the Letters of Sir Walter Scott* (Oxford, 1979).
Thomas Crawford (ed), *Sir Walter Scott: Selected Poems* (Oxford, 1972).

BIOGRAPHY

J G Lockhart, *Memoirs of the Life of Sir Walter Scott, Bart.*, 2nd edn, 10 vols (Edinburgh, 1839).
John Buchan, *Sir Walter Scott* (London, 1932).
Edgar Johnson, *Sir Walter Scott: The Great Unknown*, 2 vols (London, 1970).

CRITICISM

There is an immense volume of criticism. Comprehensive lists, covering publications to 1940 and 1978 respectively, can be found in:
James C Corson, *A Bibliography of Sir Walter Scott 1797–1940* (Edinburgh, 1943).
Jill Rubenstein, *Sir Walter Scott: A Reference Guide* (Boston, 1978).

The best of nineteenth century criticism, including the pieces by Carlyle and Bagehot mentioned in the essay, is anthologised in:
John O Hayden (ed), *Scott: The Critical Heritage* (London, 1970).

The following is a select list of contemporary criticism:
J H Alexander, *Marmion: Studies in Interpretation and Composition* (Salzburg, 1981).
A O J Cockshut, *The Achievement of Walter Scott* (London, 1969).
Daniel Cottom, *The Civilized Imagination* (Cambridge, 1985).
Thomas Crawford, *Scott*, 2nd edn (Edinburgh, 1982).
David Daiches, 'Scott's Achievement as a Novelist' in *Literary Essays* (Edinburgh, 1956), pp 88–121.
Avrom Fleishman, *The English Historical Novel* (Baltimore, 1971).
Robert C Gordon, *Under Which King?* (Edinburgh, 1969).
F R Hart, *Scott's Novels: The Plotting of Historic Survival* (Charlottesville, 1966).

Mary Lascelles, *The Story-Teller Retrieves the Past* (Oxford, 1980).
Georg Lukacs, *The Historical Novel*, trans H and S Mitchell (London, 1962).
Graham McMaster, *Scott and Society* (Cambridge, 1981).
Jane Millgate, *Walter Scott: the Making of the Novelist* (Toronto, 1984).
Judith Wilt, *Secret Leaves: The Novels of Walter Scott* (Chicago, 1985).

Chapter 5

James Hogg: The Play of Region and Nation

THOMAS CRAWFORD

Like Burns a decade before him, James Hogg (1770–1835) was born into a rural society in rapid economic and cultural transition.[1] Rich farmers were expanding and getting richer: lesser ones like Hogg's father were being driven to the wall while young people were under intense pressure to 'get on', either at home or, more usually, outwith Ettrick itself. The strongest cultural and literary influence was the authorised version of the Bible (for the young Hogg it was both a narrative and a lyrical influence, almost a folk one); the next oral tradition:

> He was remarkably fond of hearing stories, and our mother to keep us boys quiet would often tell us tales of kings, giants, knights, fairies, kelpies, brownies etc etc . . . She also often repeated to us the metre psalms, and accustomed us to repeat them after her; and I think it was the 122nd which Jamie . . . could have said. I think this was before he knew any of the letters. I am certain before he could spell a word. After he could read with fluency, *the historical part of the Bible was his chief delight* [my italics], and no person whom I have been acquainted with knew it so well. (William Hogg in Garden, p 13)

It is perhaps worth noting that the mood of the hundred and twenty second psalm ('I joy'd when to the house of God') is the antithesis of Calvinist gloom; its key words are 'peace', 'felicity', 'love', 'prosperity' and 'good'. Nevertheless, traditional balladry was in decline, and Elaine Petrie, the most recent investigator of this side of Hogg's heritage, has concluded that Hogg's mother was what folklorists call a 'passive informant' who 'provided her children with a good grounding in traditional lore but . . . it was one coloured by the weakened position of traditional belief in a transitional society', and that Hogg's older *male* relations were his main source for ballads as they were for traditionary tales about local history (Petrie, pp 49–50).[2] Hogg's earliest compositions were 'songs made up for the lasses to sing in chorus' (*Memoir*, p 10), but his first publication was a poem, not a song, on the folk theme of the swain who makes love to his girl's mother in the dark. Entitled 'The Mistakes of a Night', it appeared in *The Scots Magazine* for October 1794—and it was written in a form peculiarly associated with the eighteenth-century vernacular revival, the *Christ's Kirk on the Green* stanza as amended by Fergusson and Burns. He experimented with the pastoral, eclogue side of the revival in the decidedly uneven *Scottish Pastorals* of 1801, his first volume:[3] but it was in his lyrics, written generally to traditional tunes, but sometimes even to tunes of his own composition, that he first attained genuine quality.[4] Hogg wrote lyrics all his life. The best of them, like 'When the kye comes hame' or 'A Boy's Song', which Neil Gunn must surely have delighted in, are very fine indeed, but many others pander to popular sentimentality in the manner of the later kailyard school. There are patriotic songs (like 'Donald MacDonald'), satirical (like the 'New Christmas Carol'), Jacobite, and above all humorous, such as 'The Great Muckle Village of Balmaqhapple':

> D'ye ken the big village of Balmaquhapple,
> The great muckle village of Balmaquhapple?
> 'Tis steep'd in iniquity up to the thrapple,   [throat]
> And what's to become of poor Balmaquhapple?
> Fling a' off your bonnets, and kneel for your life, folks,
> And pray to Saint Andrew, the god o' the Fife folks . . .
>
> (lines 1–6)

As with Scott, it was balladry, expanding into ballad imitation, that was the greatest stimulus to his early writing; and—the parallel with Scott still holds—the next most significant step in his development was from ballad imitations to long verse-romances which evolved out of balladry, although he began to experiment in various forms of shorter prose fiction, in which he was later to excel, even before his longer poems began to appear. He used popular culture and oral tradition in all these genres, whether of verse or prose. The publication of Scott's *Minstrelsy of the Scottish Border* in 1802 greatly sharpened Hogg's conviction that selling the fruits of his brain on the Edinburgh literary market might be a lucrative substitute for shepherding or farming ventures—or, at the very least, a useful supplement.

At the very start of his literary career we observe in Hogg a tension between romance and anti-romance; a contrast already present in the thirteenth-century *Roman de la Rose* itself, between the love-allegory of the first part and the satire of the second. That tension does not appear in the ten traditional ballad texts, collected by him, which he sent to Scott for the 1803 edition of the *Minstrelsy*, although a certain grim irony is occasionally evident. But his ballad imitations in *The Mountain Bard* of four years later do incorporate some rough plebeian material. They fall into the same categories as the traditional texts he sent to Scott—the historical, the heroic, and the romantic-familial—with the addition of another, ballads about wraiths that tell how they came to die. If there is greater use of the supernatural, the superstition yet seems extraordinarily solid; it is part of the ideology of a world more concrete than that of pure romance, and it has, as Dr Petrie has pointed out, a predominantly ethical function—to reward, to illuminate, and to punish (Petrie, pp 127–74). The world of these ballad imitations has elements of the real Borders of tradition and history, as absorbed from oral informants, fused into what might be termed an ideal, metaphysical Borders forged in the smithy of the poet's imagination. They are above all ballads of *region*—of region as a literary construct, like Faulkner's Yoknapatawpha County or Hardy's Wessex, and which—like theirs—is related to a real geographical entity. As Dr Petrie says of 'The Laird of Lariston', 'he takes local figures and clothes them, as it were, in their own countryside'; while 'Thirlestane, a Fragment', when taken as a unity of the poetic text and the long prose notes inseparable from it, uses local tradition as 'the medium for an epic at local, if not national, level' (Petrie, pp 110, 112). *The Queen's Wake* (1813), which first established Hogg as a serious writer in England as well as Scotland, is made out of the lays sung by seventeen minstrels (to make a contrast with Scott, Hogg calls them 'Bards') at a song-contest held to celebrate the arrival of Mary Stuart as Queen in Edinburgh: the narrative sections frame and provide context for the seventeen songs, though only thirteen are given in full. Region and nation inform both the structure and texture of *The Queen's Wake*: it is a deliberate attempt to write not just about Ettrick, but about at least the majority of the regions that comprise the nation. There are not thirteen regions, however, for one song is given to the non-Scot, Rizzio, and certain bards sing more than once. The national dimension is heightened by the poem being set in a period when Scotland was independent and could be presumed to have a glittering court, and at the same time Hogg lends the poem solidity by disguising himself (the Bard of Ettrick) and some of his contemporaries as sixteenth-century Bards. Two of the 'Songs' (really, poems) are among the best things Hogg ever did: 'Kilmeny' and 'The Witch of Fife'.

The first is sung in the wilder (Highland) regions of Perthshire by a bard with the lowland name of Drummond; the second by the 'bard of Fife'. Drummond's study is not fairy lore but religion; his repertoire is 'the hymns of Heaven', and the lay he chants is a spiritual allegory (Mack, *Poems*, pp xxii–xxvi). The land Kilmeny is taken up into is not the highest Heaven, however, but 'the lowermost vales of the storied heaven . . . the land of *thought*' [my italics]; the way to it is through a rich natural landscape with associations of fertility and fruition, where the 'yorlin' (yellowhammer) sings and Kilmeny pulls

> The scarlet hypp and the hindberrye,   [wild raspberry]
> And the nut that hang frae the hazel tree.
> (lines 7–8)

When she returns, she has a 'joup [shirt] o' the lilly sheen', a 'bonny snood [maiden's headdress] of the birk [birch] sae green' and 'roses, the fairest that ever were seen' (lines 29–31). From her eminence in the land of thought she sees a panorama of the physical land of Scotland, and her heart cleaves to it (lines 181–201); a vision of future Scottish history—the troubled reigns of Mary Queen of Scots and James VI; and a second vision, the historical pageant of Europe during the revolutionary and Napoleonic eras, in which it appears that Scotland played a large part in the defeat of tyranny (lines 249, 255); and then a third vision still, of universal harmony (lines 260–3). Thus Kilmeny's secular visions move progressively from her region—the neighbourhood of Loch Earn in Perthshire—to her nation, Scotland; from

Scotland to Europe; from Europe to the kingdom of Heaven on earth (260–1) and beyond that to the end of the material universe, when 'the stars of heaven fell calmly away/Like the flakes of snaw on a winter day' (262–3). The allegory is profoundly Scottish, in the tradition of Ramsay's and Burns's *Vision* poems, but it also has affinities with Hogg's English contemporary, William Blake: one remembers 'To Mercy, Pity, Peace and Love/All pray in their distress', and 'The Little Girl Lost' and 'The Little Girl Found', in which the lost innocent sleeps in the desert while leopards and tigers play around her and she is tended by the lion and lioness.

The Bard of Fife in *The Wake* is wild-eyed, with haggard cheeks and thin grey locks. He is a 'wizard of the shore', full of spells and supernatural lore, an eldritch figure whose harp sounds trembling chords that echo 'romantic' passion in tune to his 'mad unearthly song' in a 'rugged northern tongue' ('The Eighth Bard' (lines 4–38). Hogg uses a deliberately archaic spelling to convey this 'rugged' quality. There is a fruitful contradiction between the Bard's zany frenzy (he is a prophetic, inspirational figure) and the comic energy of the ballad itself, which in the first edition ended with the auld man burnt to death in Carlisle. The comedy of mingled blood and wine is truly gruesome, and may even carry a religious irony:

> They nickit the auld man, and they prickit the auld man,
>   And they yerkit his limbis with twine,   [bound tightly]
> Quhill the reid blude ran in his hose and shoon,
>   But some cryit it was wyne.
>
> (lines 257–60)

Scott induced Hogg to write a new ending more in keeping with 'the most happy and splendid piece of humorous ballad poetry which I ever wrote,' and it is that ending which is almost universally printed today.[5] In the first text, the poem reminds us a little of the gruesome, savage humour of Dunbar; in the second, which is not inferior as poetry, the spirit is rather that of the more humane comedy of Henryson or Burns. For all its incidental laughter, the first version ends in tragedy of a sort, caused by the auld man's adventurous folly; the second, in his liberation, rendered in what is surely the funniest stanza in all lowland poetry:

> His armis war spred, and his heide was hiche,
>   And his feite stack out behynde;
> And the laibies of the auld manis cote   [skirts]
>   War wauffyng in the wynde,   [flapping]

to be immediately followed by four lines of sheer joy that miraculously manage to combine humour with pure poetry:

> And aye he neicherit, and aye he flew,   [snickered]
>   For he thought the ploy se raire;
> It was like the voice of the gainder blue,
>   Whan he flees throu the aire.

Perhaps it is not altogether fanciful to see 'The Witch of Fife' as a glorious series of variations on the theme of flight which fascinated Hogg throughout his career[6] and may go back to the young boy's delight in that Psalm 122 he learnt at his mother's knee. The child would surely imagine Jerusalem as a city in the sky:

> I joy'd when to the house of God,
>   *Go up* [my italics] they said to me.
> Jerusalem, within thy gates
>   Our feet shall standing be.
>   (Verse 1)

The key to all Hogg's work is that he was an inveterate, almost a compulsive mixer of genres—'pastoral-comical, historical-pastoral, tragical-comical-historical-pastoral' (*Hamlet*, II.ii.404–6)—and that the dominant one, though he almost always blended it with others, was Romance. Now the journey is a prime structural principle in Romance (witness *The Faerie Queene* and *The Pilgrim's Progress*), and Dr Groves has claimed the journey as a recurrent archetypal pattern in Hogg's poetry, both serious and comic: 'the mind discovers itself through motion, transition, and process, rather than through any static or idealised image of itself' (Groves, *Poems*, p xvii). Certainly 'Kilmeny' has a journey structure and psychological reference on a very compact scale; on a much larger scale *The Pilgrims of the Sun* has the same movement up and out of this world, and the same return. And its protagonist, Mary Lee of Carelha', journeys as a disembodied spirit through the sky under the guidance of a male angel. They fly past inhabited planets to the Sun itself, then back to Hogg's little country and his (and Mary's) little region within it—the 'metaphysical Borders'. Hogg's imitative skill is strained to its limits by the poem's successive metres; the ballad stanza in Part First to render Mary's innocent perfection in Carelha'; Miltonic blank verse for the space-travel of Part Second; Drydenesque couplets for the didactic narrative and explanations of Part Third; anapaestic and iambic tetrameters à la Walter Scott in Part Fourth for the heroine's return and the other events of the dénouement. Hogg's technique here is not unlike Joyce's more complex imitation of successive prose styles in the Oxen of the Sun section of *Ulysses*; only Joyce's intention is comic and Hogg's, in this work at least, serious. Dr Groves maintains we should read *The Pilgrims of the Sun* and indeed all Hogg's poems in the author's own spirit of 'openness and joy' (Groves, *Poems*, pp xxiv–xxv), and certainly if we do this we are carried along by his sheer energy and verve. But much the same can be said of Scott, and *The Pilgrims of the Sun* is not poetically so good as Scott's long narrative romances. Scott is a better *superficial* poet than Hogg, who has altogether too much bathos for the modern reader.

Nor can the inflated Spenserians of Hogg's next long poem, *Mador of the Moor* (1816) hold much for us today; Douglas Gifford is surely right to prefer its traditional sources—the Gaberlunzie Man legend of the king who goes about disguised as a beggar or a tramp, and the Cruel Mother whose mur-

dered child comes back to accuse her of infanticide; and he is equally correct
in condemning as sentimental Hogg's treatment of 'the unmarried mother's
ruin and wonderful redemption' (Gifford, *Hogg*, p 60). But if one is prepared
to forget poetic quality, then one can concentrate on how at the generic and
structural level the romance unites two parabolic paths and suggests the
possibility of reconciling opposites (Groves, *Poems*, pp xxvi–xxvii). There are
signs that critics are now prepared to look more kindly on Hogg's last
really long poem, *Queen Hynde* (1825), which once attracted almost universal
execration, even although, in Louis Simpson's words, 'on almost every page
there is ridiculous verse and action' (Simpson, p 93). Hogg sets his romance
in a distant and almost prehistoric Scotland which enables him to forget 'real'
regions and create his own nations, peoples and history; he 'plays about with'
cherished themes to produce a text which, if taken at speed, 'entertains and
is easy to read' (Gifford, *Hogg*, p 220). In an important analysis, Dr Petrie
has shown how its plot yields to the approach of structuralist folklorists like
Vladimir Propp (Petrie, pp 280–9), yet it is doubtful whether it will ever have
a place in the bedside reading even of specialists in the romantic period. But
things are quite otherwise with 'May of the Moril Glen',[7] first published in
Blackwood's Magazine in 1827, a 384-line poem where the beauty and terror
of the romantic supernatural are linked to a comedy even more eldritch than
that of 'The Witch of Fife'. Its central portion is a rollicking and exuberant
satire directed at male sexuality. When the King hears of the wondrous May,
whose beauty maddens every man who sees her, he hastens to 'prove' her,
accompanied by a train of eighty knights and the certainty that he will

> put her downe
> In grand polemyck waye . . .
>
> The vyrgin caste on him ane loke,
>   With gaye and gracefulle ayre,
> Als on some thynge belowe her notte,
>   That oughte not to have bene there.
>   (lines 191–2, 197–200)

This time the journey is inspired by the desire for a decidedly ambivalent
conquest. The knights chase after May on the king's orders, for he wants to
own her (Hogg's word), while the monarch himself

> in fitte of lofe,
> Lay spurrying on the le.   [spurring] [meadow]
>
> And aye he batterit with his feite.
>   And rowted with dispayre,   [bellowed]
> And pullit the gerse up by the rotis,   [grass]
>   And flang it on the ayre.
>   (lines 227–32)

May will not yield to the king or any of his lords and knights because they
are all married men; however, she promises to wed the first to become a

widower. Off they all go on another wild ride—to murder their spouses; the Queen and seventy-seven other wives were 'corpis before the morne'. Seven gilded chariots then come with a train of attendants to take May away, wrapped in a 'hailstone shroude' on a mysterious ship on the Firth of Forth. It is the last journey of the poem, modulating from the comic supernatural into a movement of wonder and awe:

> But ay the shyppe, the bonnye shyppe,
>   Outowre the greene waive flewe,
> Swyffte as the solan on the wyng,
>   Or terrifyit sea-mewe.
>
> No billowe breistit on her prowe,
>   Nor levellit on the lee;
> Sho semit to sayle upon the ayre,
>   And neuer touche the sea.

If Scott's connections with the early capitalist economy and his shift from poet to novelist were bound up with his financial and entrepreneurial involvement in printing and publishing, Hogg's corresponding linkage was largely by way of magazine publishing. First came the extraordinary episode of *The Spy*, which he began in September 1810 when he tried to take the Edinburgh literary public by storm, and ran it almost single-handed for a year. He modelled his weekly on the essay periodicals of the previous century (Addison, Steele, Johnson, Henry Mackenzie and others); the public he wished to attract, the educated middle classes, were well acquainted with the type, and what he hoped they would be looking for was 'amusing variations upon the same familiar themes.'[8] Yet the variations were sometimes quite revolutionary, and more innovative (and indelicate) than was altogether welcome to refined taste. Traditional rural tales, the story that later became 'The Love Adventures of Mr George Cochrane',[9] poems such as the kailyardish 'Auld Man's Farewell to his Little House' or the rousing Border song 'Lock the door, Lariston'—these are a far cry from *The Spectator* and *The Rambler*, and look forward to the innovations of *Blackwood's Edinburgh Magazine* seven years later. In some papers the theme is the unknown starveling author's struggle to sell his wares to commercial publishers—'a numerous race of beings in this world who feed themselves upon the brains of their own species'; and there is a very clear recognition that in the competitive jungle 'works of literature are become much like bank notes, they must be issued by certain firms, else they will not pass current.'[10] With the foundation of *Blackwood's Magazine* in 1817 and his establishment of a fruitful business relationship with its publisher, Hogg turned increasingly to prose. He himself, through his share in the 'The Chaldee Manuscript' at the very outset of the enterprise, his many writings in it, and the caricature figure of 'The Shepherd' in the 'Noctes Ambrosianae' (based on his real character but in many respects an embarrassingly condescending portrait), helped to set *Blackwood's* distinctive tone, which Carlyle characterised as 'a kind of wild, popular lower comedy' (*Journal*, 9 September 1830), and Hogg himself as 'intermixing all things

through other' (to Blackwood, 19 October 1817). Undoubtedly, the contra-
rieties and 'intermingledoms' of the magazine strengthened these same tendencies in Hogg's creative imagination, just as its leaning towards protestant
evangelicalism furthered his own use of oral traditions about the Covenanters
and chimed in with recollections of the simple presbyterian pieties of his
childhood.

Those pieties and traditions formed the groundwork of *The Brownie of
Bodsbeck* (1817), a historical romance of the Covenanting period based in
the first instance on oral history, and in the second on the pro-Covenanter
*History of the Sufferings of the Church of Scotland, from the Reformation to
the Revolution* (1721–2), by the Reverend Robert Wodrow. Its imaginative
field is the controlled interplay of superstition and covenanting heroism, and
its theme a unity of those opposites within the culture of the region as
part of the ambience of Hogg's 'Metaphysical Borders'. It tells how Walter
Laidlaw, a sheep farmer loyal to the Stuart religious establishment, discovers
that a band of westland whigs have taken refuge on the further hills of his
farm of Chapelhope. Out of compassion and ordinary human feeling he feeds
the starving refugees and allows them to stay, thus endangering his own life.
Quite unknown to Walter, his daughter Katherine is helping another group
of persecuted Covenanters who are hiding in an even more desolate spot, a
remote underground cavern. They are most of them wounded, sick, and
emaciated; their leader is so deformed and disfigured from his wounds that
those who see him from afar think he is a hideous supernatural 'Brownie' and
that his followers are also not of this world. Walter shares all his neighbours'
superstitions and is deeply disturbed by evidence that seems to show that his
favourite daughter is in league with the Brownie and perhaps with the Devil.
It clearly went against the grain with Hogg to end with everything rationally
accounted for: from a letter to Blackwood of 31 January 1818 it seems he
would have preferred to leave 'some mysterious incidents unexplained.'[11] But
for once Hogg was right to resist his natural bent; to have made the Brownie
a real hobgoblin would have weakened the emotional impact of Walter's
agonies and doubts, and even more that of his recognition of the truth. To
this end, his narrator is 'enlightened', though not subject to the sort of irony
that distances the narrator of the *Justified Sinner*. Hogg's openings are always
good, but this one would be a strong contender for the finest opening sentence
in Scottish fiction:

> 'It will be a bloody night in Gemsop this,' said Walter of Chapelhope, as he
> sat one evening by the side of his little parlour fire, and wrung the rim of his
> wet bonnet into the grate.

Equally good is the terrifying anagnorisis at the end of chapter 10. In an
age of political terror and religious martyrdom the oppressed cannot be too
careful about disclosing their views to those who might, or might not, be of
their cause. Katherine needs help from her old servant for her errands of
mercy, but wants a 'test' from her before she will trust her:

'Look at this for a test of *my* sincerity and truth.' So saying, she gave her
hand a wild brandish in the air, darted it at her throat, and snapping the tie of
her mutch that she had always worn over her face, she snatched it off, and
turning her cheek round to her young mistress, added, 'Look there for your
test, and if that is not enough, I will give you more!'
        Katherine was struck dumb with astonishment and horror. She saw that her
ears were cut out close to the skull, and a G indented on her cheek with a hot
iron, as deep as the jaw-bone. (p 99)

The positive values in the book are those of honesty and compassion—of
'human nature' itself, as Walter puts it; he is himself their male embodiment,
a development of the Burnsian 'honest man' and to that extent national, even
though he is so rooted in the Borders as to seem their very human essence.
Katherine is of course their female expression, a heroine of everyday life
like Scott's Jeanie Deans. The royalists, the dragoons, and the lecherous
episcopalian curate are the negation of these values, and their supreme antag-
onist is Claverhouse, 'who loathed the simplicity of nature' (p 63) and is thus
identified with the artificiality that Hogg detests. Claverhouse's oppression
was a *class* oppression: 'He seemed to regard all the commonalty in the south
and west of Scotland as things to be mocked and insulted at pleasure, as
being created only for the sport of him and his soldiers, while their mental
and bodily agonies were his delight' (p 105). There is much superb writing in
The Brownie: in Scots, Davie Tait's prayer (pp 127–9), which Douglas Mack
justly calls 'one of the comic masterpieces of Scottish literature' (p xix), Nanny
Elshinder's moving and deeply *serious* presbyterian eloquence (pp 218–19),
and some particularly vivid description in both English (p 91) and Scots
(p 147).
        Hogg's two longest works, *The Three Perils of Man* (1822) and *The Three
Perils of Woman* (1823), both feature the aesthetic interplay of region and
nation. In the first, the action is pushed back into the past—not into the far
distant mythical Scotland of *Queen Hynde*, where the nations and regions
provide a vague and idealised medium for the stylised action, but into a
'model' feudal Scotland (allegedly in the reign of Robert II) with 'model'
feudal magnates, princesses, marauding barons, and middle-grade squires—
a 'model' Scotland which forms the backdrop for a stylised metaphysical
Borders that seems almost the Platonic Idea of the Borders in Hogg's more
nearly contemporary stories. Man's three perils are War, Women and Witchcraft: the first and last are attributes of the metaphysical Borders (reivers,
moss-troopers, raids into and from England, and the paraphernalia of wizardry and the evil supernatural), while the middle one (decadent chivalric
love) is treated with all the satirical fantasy of 'May of the Moril Glen'. If
one dominating feature of European romanticism is sheer energy (Blake's
'Energy is eternal Delight', Beethoven's fifth symphony, the paintings of
Delacroix), and another is pure joy (the ninth symphony, the end of Shelley's
'Prometheus Unbound') then *Perils of Man*, for all its faults, is of a piece
with these masterpieces. Behind its apparently bewildering movements of
theme and plot lies the thematic conflict of chivalry versus necessity—the

very contradiction behind *Don Quixote*: in *Perils of Man*, a Cervantes-like parodying of romance and its ideals coexists with 'playing around with' romantic conventions for their own sakes. There is abundance of fantastic humour and linguistic virtuosity of the most breathtaking kind (above all in colloquial Scots), savage satire on war and its horrors, in which the masses are always the victims, and the attachment of positive value to the real hero of the novel, Charlie Yardbire—the Walter Laidlaw of the book.

The Three Perils of Woman, currently being revalued by Hogg specialists, has never been reprinted since the first edition in three volumes; a modern edition is urgently needed. Woman's perils are 'Love, Leasing [lying] and Jealousy', and the three are not shared evenly between the volumes: the first, Love, spreads over volumes one and two, while the third volume encompasses both of the other abstract themes. Hogg deliberately eschews any kind of linear or chronological structure; the work is subtitled 'A Series of Domestic Scottish Tales' (i.e., conventional unity is not claimed for it); the first takes place in Hogg's own day, the second and third eighty years before; and the subdivisions are not called parts or chapters but 'Circles'. The work has been consistently misunderstood because critics have been unaware of its complex allusiveness, and of its implicit polemic stance. That stance is a literary one, and the criticism is at the expense of the very man who liked to caricature Hogg in the *Noctes*—John Wilson (Christopher North). Blackwood had published Wilson's *Lights and Shadows of Scottish Life* in the previous year; and Hogg's book is in a sense an enormously extended gloss on it.[12] Hogg's intention, like Wilson's, is to cover both Highlands and Lowlands; and to follow 'nature itself', rather than 'nature abominably sophisticated', as he claimed Wilson had done (*Perils of Woman*, I, 65–6).

The First Peril deals with the Borders, not metaphysical this time, but contemporary and allegedly 'real', although the *pater familias*, Daniel Bell (a rich pastoral farmer of the early capitalist period, obsessed with the prices of sheep and wool and the breeding of 'toops'), has some of the Honest Man attributes of the Ideal Borderer. His son Josey is at College in Edinburgh, his daughter Gatty was educated at the schools of Hawick and the boarding-school of Carlisle before going to Edinburgh to perfect her ladylike accomplishments. She is in love with a Highlander, Diarmid McIon, but is afraid to show her feelings owing to false delicacy. McIon, in love with her, does not make a declaration, though she gives him three chances to do so; she then tries to deny her own feelings and puts on a great show of disliking him. His Highland pride will not then allow him to reveal his true feelings. Gatty's impoverished cousin Cherry is utterly straightforward, even naive: when Gatty tells her that she does not love McIon, and McIon tells her that he dos not love Gatty, Cherry believes them both. McIon proposes to Cherry on the rebound, and she accepts; when it is discovered that he is the heir to large properties in the Highlands, honest simple Cherry, having found that Gatty and McIon have never been out of love with each other, gives him up and the 'true' lovers are married; the three live together in what the uncharitable think is a *ménage à trois*, then Cherry falls ill and dies. It is a low mimetic variant of the folk *motif* of dying for love. Relations between the couple are now poisoned by mutual guilt, and perhaps—if Dr Groves is correct in his contention that Hogg means us to infer that all three had a venereal infection, which was in fact the cause of Cherry's death—by physical illness as well.[13] Gatty, afflicted by a form of religious mania, convinces herself that she will die at a particular moment. When the day and the hour arrive, she appears to die, though in reality she has merely sunk into a deep coma from which nothing can rouse her, during which she gives birth to a son. Three years from her 'death' she recovers completely (note how crucial the number there is for the plot: three refusals, love triangle, three years' purgatorial oblivion); Highlander and Lowlander, representatives of their cultures and their regions, are now united in a chastened harmony, not just of common sense, but of 'Mercy, Pity, Peace and Love'. There is no space for us even to glance at the rich incident of Peril First—the comic, almost comic-strip humour of the rich farmer from the southern side of the Border, Richard Rickleton, in his search for a wife, or the linguistic contrast between Mrs Bell's affectation of English and Daniel's rich Scots; or the ludicrous duel sequence, involving McIon, other Highlanders, and Rickleton. But one extraordinary subtlety should be mentioned. Dr Groves has recently contended that McIon gets his name from the *Ion* of Euripides, whose central character (like McIon) 'discovers his parentage, comes to be reunited with his mother, and is destined to become a national hero . . . just as McIon . . . will help to heal the divisions in Scottish society and rejuvenate the Highlands by reclaiming his estate and settling in the north with his Border wife Gatty';[14] and although Groves has only circumstantial and indirect evidence for the connection, he makes out an extremely plausible case. Parts Second and Third are both set in the Highlands at the time of the Forty-Five and its aftermath, and some of the characters overlap. We have space only to comment on the ending of Peril Third. Culloden has been fought, and the bloody pacification of the Highlands is in train. Plot complications founded on jealousy lead Alaster Mackenzie to fight Peter Gow, the former lover of his wife, Sally; both are badly wounded before they learn it is all a mistake. But they are betrayed by Peter's jealous wife to the redcoats, and killed. After wanderings, Sally is found on the grave of Alaster and Peter,

> sitting rocking and singing over the body of a dead female infant. He ventured to speak to her in Gaelic, for he had no other language; but she only looked wildly up to heaven, and sung louder. He hasted home; but the road was long and rough, and before his brothers reached the spot the mother and child were lying stretched together in the arms of death . . . (*Perils of Woman*, III. 371)

These selective comments fail to convey the enormous vitality and vigour of the work, as well as the uncertainties that beset one during the reading process; the blending of serious historical purpose and all the tragedy of the Jacobite experience with crudely presented humour characters and, in the character of Davie Duff the gravedigger, with an ill-conceived travesty of Highland English such as no modern linguist would concede was ever spoken by anybody. Hogg's statement about Region and Nation in this work—about the Borders, the Highlands, and Scotland—is put into a strangely distorted perspective by his reverse time-scale. We do not know whether he is saying—'look at the marvellous synthesis which it is now possible for us to have, symbolised by all that Gatty and McIon have achieved through *their* suffering; don't we come back to it with thankfulness when we see the horror and the brutality of the divisions of eighty years ago?' or whether what is being said is something else—'Gatty and McIon's chastened harmony, and the complacency of the Athens of the North, with people like John Wilson and Walter Scott at its centre (Scott even makes a brief appearance in Peril First!), are not so valuable, because their experience is not so intense, so universally human, as that of Sally as Jenny Nettles—the war-crazed woman with a dead baby in her arms.' Sally belongs in the world of Mother Courage in a way that Madge Wildfire does not. As David Groves has shown, one of the book's themes is the interweaving of human uncertainty and fellowship—a theme which he illustrates by quoting the words of the player in *Rosencrantz and Guildenstern are Dead*: 'Uncertainty is the normal state. You're nobody special' (*SSL* 21, p 194).

Uncertainty, ambivalence, and mystification prevail throughout Hogg's masterpiece, *The Private Memoirs and Confessions of a Justified Sinner* (1824). As the fictional 'editor' says in the brief coda allotted to him: 'With regard to the work itself, I dare not venture a judgment, for I do not understand it . . . I confess that I do not comprehend the writer's drift' (*Sinner*, pp 253–4). Neither, of course, did the writer—poor deluded Robert Wringhim; it is only towards the end of his memoir that he begins to realise the true identity of his distinguished friend, the incognito prince of a far country, who is so bound to him as to be almost a part of him, who urged and helped him to murder first, a blameless 'moderate' clergyman, then his own brother, his father, and his mother, and who made it possible for him to debauch young girls and be 'fou for weeks thegither' without his being aware of his orgies. And that identity is—the Devil himself. Or is it? Is the puzzled, rationalistic editor perhaps right after all? Were the 'Confessions' an 'allegory' produced by 'dreaming or madness', and was their deranged author Wringhim one 'who wrote and wrote about a deluded creature, till he arrived at that height of madness, that he believed himself the very object whom he had been all along describing'? (p 254). As Douglas Gifford has noted, it is this deliberate uncertainty which underlies the very structure of the book:

> The *parts* of the novel . . . and the arrangement of characters and incidents within the parts are designed so that they fit an overall pattern of rational/objective experience set against supernatural/subjective experience. This is not a total separation—but broadly one can argue that in part one the rational mind of reader *and* writer struggles to impose a logical explanation for the events therein; while in part two the reader tends, temporarily at least, to allow himself to be carried by the subjective account of supernatural events. Part three is a weighing-up of the two claims, with new evidence on both sides, which significantly comes to no final resolution of both or decision for either. (Gifford, *Hogg*, p 145)

The *Justified Sinner* has among other things been regarded as a satire on Calvinism in its antinomian distortion, as a profound exploration of moral evil, as the most 'appropriate' of 'all the impersonations of the Devil in art and literature' (André Gide), as primarily a book in the early nineteenth-century tradition of the Gothic novel, and as a doppelgänger presentation of an insane obsession. Its glory is that it is all these things, and more; and we should be aware that even although the 'phantasmagoria' of folk-devilry and Marlovian sensationalism 'takes possession of the circumstances' during Wringhim's flight and final agony, it still has a great deal of 'spiritual fabrication and emanation' about it (the phrasing is Gide's).[15] There is not and need not be any contradiction between the psychological interpretation and the demonological, for schizophrenia has traditionally been linked to the supernatural in our culture. Hogg's confusion, which one can only assume is deliberate, between an objective devil and subjective apparitions, far from being a blemish, is essential to the depth with which he renders Wringhim's psychosis. In his essay 'A Seventeenth-century Demonological Neurosis',[16] Freud examines the case of a painter called Christoph Haizmann who undertook, in his pact with Satan, 'to be his bounden son' (i.e., the Devil was to him a father-substitute; Gil-Martin, in view of his generally youthful appearance, was Big Brother to Wringhim); in the course of the neurosis there were visions of exultation and self-aggrandisement which may be compared to Wringhim's sensations of soaring and flight after he is assured of election, and a vision of a throne made up of gold pieces waiting for him to ascend, which is comparable with Wringhim's vision of the golden weapons pointing down from heaven (*Sinner*, p 138). Freud generalises: 'A dammed-up libido which cannot be satisfied in reality succeeds, with the help of a regression to old fixations, in finding discharge through the repressed subconscious' (Freud, p 105).

On the psychological interpretation, Wringhim can be regarded as a schizophrenic with paranoid tendencies, where paranoia is mental derangement marked by delusions of grandeur, these being intellectually systematised as antinomianism. The passage where Wringhim says 'I generally conceived myself to be two people' (*Sinner*, p 154) has been compared with the classic cases of dissociated personality, such as Miss Beauchamp, who split under hypnosis into three personalities, two of whom had no memories in common, and a third, 'Sally', who sometimes had control of the body when 'BI' and 'BIV' were absent, but existed co-consciously when either of these was dominant.[17] For the role of the Devil in abnormal psychology one can learn much from Wilhelm Reich's 'The Devil in the Schizophrenic Process'.[18] Reich quotes the case of a thirty-two year old female patient who felt herself at the mercy of mysterious 'forces' that urged her on to murder. When the forces were active she was a prey to the most intense anxiety, and she 'did not feel the forces as her own'. Her emotions towards 'the forces' were ambivalent, just as Wringhim's were for Gil-Martin; she 'felt both fear and love for the forces', as Wringhim did; and she became seriously ill for the first time when 'the forces' told her to poison the whole family with gas. (It will be remembered that Wringhim experienced various degrees of resistance to Gil-Martin's proposal to murder first Blanchard and then his own brother.) Reich's patient, then, had anxieties and conflicts which were hypostatised as 'forces' that did exactly the same thing as Gil-Martin when he urged Wringhim on to crime, and this case history, as well as other similar ones, enables us, as no amount of literary generalisation can, to gauge the profundity of Hogg's psychology.

In contrast to *Perils of Woman* and *Perils of Man, The Justified Sinner* is a work of great compression which shows the same creative deployment of language as in earlier works (e.g. the contrast between the hypocritical ecclesiastical English of Wringhim senior, and his servant's plain, honest Scots, pp 104–7), the same lodging of positives in *hommes moyens sensuels*, however many slips in conduct these may make (old Dalcastle; Robert's brother George), the same mastery of verbal dramatic irony, the same telling use of imagery, such as the symbolism of Robert caught in the weaver's web (pp 216–17), the same magnificent powers of description (e.g. the distortions produced by the mist on Arthur's Seat)—only all these occur at a much higher level, almost (dare one say it?) the level of perfection.

Region and nation are deployed in what is for Hogg a novel fashion. The location of Dalcastle is left vague, but it is probably in the western Borders, for it is a Glasgow heiress that 'old Dal' marries, and young Wringhim is brought up on the outskirts of Glasgow, where he first meets Gil-Martin and where the first murder is committed. But it is in the capital, at a time of great political and ecclesiastical conflict, that the second murder and the events leading up to it take place. And the 'enlightened editor' is of course an Edinburgh man. When Robert takes possession of the Dalcastle estate the action is naturally located there, poised and even relatively peaceful before the frenzied motion of the final pursuit. It is a zig-zag movement—first towards England, then to Edinburgh, where he writes his journal and has it printed in Watson's printing house, in which he has found a job; then south to Roxburghshire and finally to 'Ault-Righ'—the very Altrive of Hogg's farm. In the third part, where the narrator is again the editor, we are presented with Hogg's letter detailing the discovery of the Suicide's Grave, followed by the editor's visit to the locality, in which contemporaries like Lockhart, Laidlaw, actual farmers living in the vicinity, and Hogg himself, are mentioned—just as Scott is brought into the background of the Edinburgh sections of *The Three Perils of Woman*. The road is one of increasing narrowness—to Hogg's region, to his own farm, and to Hogg himself; and it is a journey in time as well as place. But the main journey is in the mind—Hogg's as well as Wringhim's.[19]

Depending on one's standpoint, this extraordinary work can be regarded as the least Scottish, or the most Scottish, of Hogg's works. On one interpretation, regionalism is subordinated to the European concern of romanticism, the Double, and the journey into the interior;[20] on the other, regionalism subserves the most profound exploration of national psychology in our literature, the extreme presentation of the extremes of 'the Caledonian antisyzygy'.

Those of us who are suspicious of much of the glib formalising which has been done under the antisyzygist banner will shrug our shoulders and remember that Hogg himself, however uncertain of his genius he may at times have been, was a man of remarkable balance and sanity. This is very apparent when he is put beside John Wilson. According to J H Millar, Wilson's judgement 'was liable to be distorted by sudden impulse' and his 'fits of boisterous elation were almost certain to be followed by periods of the most severe depression . . . He was a creature of moods, the sport of contending emotions, destitute of what is called ballast.'[21] Carlyle caught the essence of Hogg's personality and above all of his prodigious gift of storytelling; 'speaks Scotch, and mostly *narrative* [my italics] absurdity (or even obscenity) therewith. Appears in the mingled character of zany and raree show.' The impression is one of blending, not distortion. 'He has . . . two clear little beads of blue or grey eyes that sparkle, if not with thought, yet with animation.'[22] The *Noctes* creation was true to the extent that Hogg was a comic genius in life as well as in art, who appeared, when he first took Edinburgh by storm, 'to be engaged day after day, or rather night after night, in scraping on the fiddle, singing his own ballads, and with the help of Glenlivat, making himself and others uproariously merry!'[23] His thoughts 'flowed freely, and he gave them as they arose, with the energy of a man, and almost the *naiveté* of a child . . . to make him lose temper was utterly impracticable. If others got angry, he only "guffawed".' His physical vigour was extraordinary, and so was a corresponding exuberance and spontaneity—balanced, however, by controlled introspection. One is tempted to call him a Blake with comic vision that did not exclude a mystical and, on occasion, a tragic dimension. As Hogg himself once put it, 'the book of one's own mind and heart is inexhaustible, if it be properly studied';[24] without such study, he could never have made his journeys to the interior. He lacked Burns's powerful ratiocinative intellect, reported by almost everyone who had conversed with the poet, though he undoubtedly appreciated theological debate, and had the type of mind which when disciplined turns out good scholarly editing: witness his fascination with 'framing' and editorial commentary as narrative devices, as in the *Justified Sinner, Some Remarkable Passages in the Life of an Edinburgh Baillie*, and the notes to his ballad imitations in *The Mountain Bard*. If narrative skill is innate (and most field-workers who have specialised in folk-narrative would say that it is), then Hogg possessed it supremely, together with an uncanny ability to reproduce and caricature different linguistic registers. He belongs with those who have made creative use of the folk and popular literature of lowland Scotland, and who have ensured that the three great periods of Scottish Literature since 1700 have been ages in which imaginative writers have respected and borrowed from popular culture. He was the most Romantic Scottish author of the Romantic age.

NOTES

1 The account of Hogg in the *Dictionary of National Biography* gives an outline of his life. For fuller and more accurate detail, see the works of Gifford and Simpson in the following list of the short titles and abbreviations:

Brownie: Douglas Mack (ed), *The Brownie of Bodsbeck* (Edinburgh and London, 1976)
Garden: Mary Garden, *Memorials of James Hogg, the Ettrick Shepherd* (London, 1885)
Gifford, *Hogg*: Douglas Gifford, *James Hogg* (Edinburgh, 1976)
Groves, *Selected Poems and Songs of James Hogg*, David Groves (ed) (Edinburgh, 1986)
Mack, *Poems*: Douglas Mack (ed), *James Hogg: Selected Poems* (Oxford, 1970)
Perils of Man: Douglas Gifford (ed), James Hogg, *The Three Perils of Man* (Edinburgh and London, 1972)
Perils of Woman: James Hogg, *The Three Perils of Woman* (Edinburgh, 1823)
Petrie: Elaine Petrie, 'James Hogg: a study in the transition from Folk Tradition to Literature' (unpublished PhD dissertation, University of Stirling, 1980)
Simpson: Louis Simpson, *James Hogg: a Critical Study* (Edinburgh, 1962)
Sinner: John Carey (ed), James Hogg, *The Private Memoirs and Confessions of a Justified Sinner* (London, New York, Toronto, 1969)
SLJ: *Scottish Literary Journal*
SSL: *Studies in Scottish Literature*

2 *See also* Elaine Petrie, '"Odd Characters": Traditional Informants in James Hogg's Family', *SLJ* 10(1) (1983), pp 30–41.
3 Recently reprinted and edited by Elaine Petrie (Stirling University Press, 1988).
4 I am assuming with most Hogg scholars that songs such as 'Doctor Monroe' and 'Love is like a Dizziness', not published till much later, were in fact written around the turn of the century.
5 Hogg, *Familiar Anecdotes of Sir Walter Scott*, ed Douglas Mack (Edinburgh, 1972), p 123.
6 A point which has been made on more than one occasion by Dr Groves.
7 For the text see *Longer Scottish Poems Volume Two*, T Crawford, David Hewitt and A Law (eds) (Edinburgh, 1987), pp 329–40.
8 Gillian H Hughes, 'The Spy and Literary Edinburgh', *SLJ* 10 (1) (1983), p 47.
9 Reprinted in *Tales of Love and Mystery: James Hogg*, David Groves (ed) (Edinburgh, 1985), pp 48–145.
10 *The Spy*, 1 September 1810, p 4; and 17 November 1810, p 91.
11 Quoted in *Brownie*, p 195.
12 *See* Douglas Mack, 'Lights and Shadows of Scottish Life: James Hogg's "Three Perils of Woman"', *Studies in Scottish Fiction, Nineteenth Century*, H W Drescher and J Schwend (eds) (Frankfurt am Main, 1985), pp 15–28.
13 David Groves, 'James Hogg's *Confessions* and *Three Perils of Woman* and the Edinburgh Prostitution Scandal of 1823', *The Wordsworth Circle* 18 (1987), pp 127–31.
14 David Groves, 'Stepping Back to an Early Age: James Hogg's *Three Perils of Woman* and the *Ion* of Euripides', *SSL* 21 (1986), pp 176–96 (180).
15 *See* Gide's introduction to the [1947] edition, here cited from the New York reprint of 1959, pp xiv, xv–xvi.

16 Freud, *Complete Psychological Works*, James Strachey (ed) (London, 1950) vol 19, pp 72–105.
17 *See* Morton Prince, *The Dissociation of a Personality* (New York, 1906).
18 In his *Character Analysis* (London, 1950), pp 398–414 and ff.
19 For one interpretation of the book in terms of Hogg's inner conflicts, *see* Barbara Bloedé, 'James Hogg's *Private Memoirs and Confessions of a Justified Sinner: the genesis of the double, Études Anglaises* 26 (1973) pp 174–86. Further research is required into Hogg's interest in abnormal psychology and friendship with medical men. For example, there were three doctor members of the Forum debating club in Edinburgh during Hogg's period as secretary—Dr Andrew Duncan, Dr John Smith, and Dr Spence. Duncan is the best known of these (see *DNB*): he was president of the Royal College of Physicians in Edinburgh and obtained a charter for creating a private lunatic asylum in Edinburgh in 1807. Hogg was on good terms with Duncan, and visited the asylum in a serious spirit (information kindly supplied by Dr Gillian Hughes).
20 See, for example, Karl Miller, *Doubles* (Oxford and New York, 1987), pp 1–20.
21 J H Millar, *A Literary History of Scotland* (London, 1903), p 510.
22 'Extracts from Note Book' in J A Froude, *Thomas Carlyle* (London, 1882), II, pp 233–4.
23 R P Gillies, *Memoirs of a Literary Veteran* (London, 1851), II, p 134.
24 R P Gillies, 'Some Reflections on James Hogg', *Fraser's Magazine* 20 (October 1839), pp 414–30 (420, 421).

FURTHER READING

Hogg, James, *Selected Stories and Sketches*, Douglas Mack (ed) (Edinburgh, 1982).
——*A Shepherd's Delight: a James Hogg Anthology*, Judy Steel (ed) (Edinburgh, 1985).
——*Tales of Love and Mystery*, David Groves (ed) (Edinburgh, 1985).
——*The Works of the Ettrick Shepherd*, Rev Thomas Thomson (ed) (2 vols, London, 1865).

Batho, E C, *The Ettrick Shepherd* (London, 1927). Still useful for its bibliography, particularly of the poetry.
Kiely, Robert, *The Romantic Novel in England* (Cambridge, Mass., 1972).
Mack, Douglas, *Hogg's Prose: an Annotated Listing* (Stirling, 1985). Supersedes Batho for prose bibliography.
Miller, Karl, *Doubles: Studies in Literary History* (Oxford, New York, Toronto, 1987), pp 1–20.
Smith, Nelson C, *James Hogg* (Boston, 1982).

For recent specialist articles not cited in this chapter, *see The Bibliotheck*'s 'Annual Bibliography of Scottish Literature' and 'The Year's Work in Scottish Literary Studies' in *SLJ* Supplements, as well as the *Newsletter of the James Hogg Society* published at the University of Stirling.

Chapter 6

The Scottish Fiction of John Galt

KEITH M COSTAIN

Galt's debt to the thought of the Scottish Realist philosophers and philosophic historians of the eighteenth century has by now been well documented. In Galt's thinking, and therefore in his work, there is a tension caused by the mutual opposition of Realist and Romantic influences, a tension especially notable in Galt's attitude toward the imagination. The Realists encouraged him to regard it as a means to an end, subordinate to weightier concerns and mechanical in its operations. Romantic literature, on the other hand, and his own experience as a novelist writing in a Romantic age led Galt away from the naive mimetic theories of the Realists to an organic, expressive conception of the imagination. In practise he regarded the imagination, at least in fiction, not as a subordinate power but as omnipotent. This essay will examine the effects of this conflict of views upon Galt's understanding of the nature and function of the imagination. Such an examination helps to explain both Galt's theoretical pronouncements and the character of his fiction.

Galt's suspicion of the imagination could not but be encouraged by the writings of Thomas Reid, the principal epistemologist of the School of Scottish Realism.[1] Reid argued in favour of induction and against the radical subjectivity of Hume's theory of perception. He thought of the imagination not as a means but as a barrier to knowledge. His own 'objective' theory of perception insists that even the senses, the means by which we apprehend external objects, are 'judging faculties'. He suspected hypotheses because they were the products of the imagination and attacked metaphysics because he thought metaphysical thinkers content to remain in the realm of hypothesis. In Reid's opinion hypotheses are 'the reveries of vain and fanciful men whose pride makes them conceive themselves able to unfold the mysteries of nature by the force of their genius.'[2]

Galt adopted similar views. In his early 'Essay on Commercial Policy' (1805) he advocates the inductive method for the systematic study of phenomena.[3] Elsewhere he warns against giving 'to the metaphysical suggestion of the imagination, a credence and authority which history refuses to confirm.'[4] He thought Shelley the reverse of a reliable thinker and accused him, in language reminiscent of Reid, of 'metaphysical errors and reveries, and a singular incapacity of conceiving the existing state of things as it practically affects the nature and condition of man.'[5] He not only attacked Shelley for his 'reveries' but assailed Rousseau, Robert Owen, and Godwin as well for proposing schemes or advancing ideas that smacked of what in his treatise

Cursory Reflections (1812) he calls 'the heresies of liberty and equality'. The believers in such 'heresies', he asserts, are now 'ashamed of their dereliction from the maxims of experience.'[6]

Since the Scottish Realists diminished the significance of the imagination in those processes by means of which we attain knowledge it is not surprising to find that even in artistic expression they accorded it a humble role. The imagination, for Reid, was no 'esemplastic power'. It was not, as Coleridge defined it in the first volume of *Biographia Literaria*, 'the living Power and prime Agent of all human Perception.' Reid reduced the imagination to 'fancy' which, in Coleridge's view, is a 'mode of Memory' with 'no other counters to play with, but fixities and definites' (chapter 13). This was sufficient for Reid, if not for Coleridge, as the former indicates when he writes:

> Fancy may combine things that never were combined in reality. It may enlarge or diminish, multiply or divide, compound and fashion objects which Nature presents; but it cannot, by the utmost effort of that creative power which we ascribe to it, bring any one simple ingredient into its productions, which Nature has not framed, and brought to our knowledge by some other faculty. (*Essays*, II, 22)

That we perceive imaginatively and that therefore the imagination is creative in a primary sense is denied also by Dugald Stewart, in Galt's day the leading exponent of Reid's ideas. He observes that the poet's faculty 'is limited to combine and modify things which really exist, so as to produce new wholes of his own; so every exertion which he makes of his powers presupposes the exercise of abstraction in decomposing and separating actual combinations.'[7] When he writes in the abstract about the imagination Galt accepts Reid and Stewart's limited view of it as 'fancy', playing (as Coleridge puts it) with its 'fixities' and 'definites'. Galt echoes Reid and Stewart when he remarks in his *Literary Life* (1834) that 'no ingenuity can make an entirely new thing. Man can only combine the old together—only the forms of previously created things can be imitated.'[8] In his *Autobiography* (1833) he writes proudly of his own 'power of combination' which he thinks 'not very common' (II, 241).

Galt's published comments on his own works of fiction often, though not invariably, concur with such abstract pronouncements. He suggests that in the writing of his novels and stories his imagination played a subsidiary and mechanical part. In his *Literary Life* Galt observes that in producing his fictions 'I have but done as painters do,—made a composition by dovetailing different sketches together' (I, 146), thus leaving the false impression that he assembled his works like jigsaw puzzles. He admired the classical Greek sculptors for working 'from living forms and existing things',[9] seeking to follow their example by basing his novels on actual circumstances, and his characters on 'models' in real life. He often writes as if the result of this method were a simple transcription of factual reality, which is not more true of Galt than of the sculptors of Ancient Greece. Like other artists whose work has lasted, Galt did a great deal more than 'decompose', 'dovetail' and 'combine'.

Galt not only suggests that his imagination, at best, humbly re-orders what empirical observation has placed before it but that it is not to be appreciated for its own sake. It is a means to a higher end. In his *Autobiography* Galt claims that the novel is 'a vehicle of instruction, or philosophy teaching, by example, parables, in which the moral was more valuable than the incidents were impressive.' (II, 210). No one can doubt Galt's concern with values writing, as he did, when traditional moral views were challenged by revolutionary historical change. What Galt's readers must question, however, is the relative priority he assigns 'the moral' in relation to the imaginative 'vehicle' by which it is conveyed. Galt's priority order would have appealed to Hannah More but it is evident that his works would have been morally ineffective, and would have sunk without trace, had not his 'vehicle' with its 'impressive' incidents and characters in fact been of primary importance to him. This point will be developed later in this essay.

The Realists and Galt were inconsistent for they took an avid interest in theoretical history, a speculative form of historical writing which, in its attempts to reconstruct the stages of historical development, relies heavily upon hypothesis. An imaginative conception of how things 'might have been' before written records became available is essential to this kind of writing which Galt found sufficiently close to fiction to take as a formal model for his novels.

Galt went further in inconsistency than the Realists. In language reminiscent of many a romantic hero or heroine, he describes himself in his *Autobiography* as 'one who indulges so much in his imagination' (I, 280). He wrote to Blackwood to express his approval of the imaginative power of Lockhart's novel *Adam Blair*,[10] In his *Literary Life* he writes of Ann Radcliffe's *The Italian* 'I can recollect no work by which I have been more affected', he finds Schiller's *Robbers* 'a work of genius', and he indicates his enjoyment of Goethe's *Werther* (I, 24). He read Southey, Campbell, Shelley and Wordsworth but among Romantic poets he preferred Byron, as his *Life of Byron* (1830) attests. He though Byron's 'energy of expression' unequalled in his own time (chapter XLIX). The German poet Burger appealed to him, particularly for his rejection of 'what is called the conventual phraseology of regular poetry, in favour of popular forms of expression, gathered from the simple and energetic utterance of the common people.'[11]

Galt's private (and largely unpublished) correspondence is in tune with his obvious appreciation of the Romantic imagination. When he discusses his own imagination as it came into play in the creation of his fictions he does so in terms closer to Coleridge than to Reid. He writes in his letters not as if he were a mechanic 'separating actual combinations' in order to put them back together in a new way (changing horses into unicorns, so to speak) but as if he were the medium by whose means his characters made themselves known. His emphasis is upon irresistible, unconscious process, not upon conscious intent moral or otherwise.

Some way into the writing of *The Ayrshire Legatees* (1820–21) Galt seems to have been a little surprised to find his characters developing lives of their own. He informed Blackwood, his publisher, that his protagonist, Dr Pringle, 'I perceive is becoming an *individual* in the conversations where his family concerns are discussed' (MS 4005, f. 93. The emphasis is Galt's). When characters become individuals, whatever the author's initial intentions may have been, they assume a life as autonomous as any actual human life. While he was contemplating a later edition of *The Ayrshire Legatees* Galt confided to Blackwood that 'I am afraid to make alterations lest now that I cannot resume the characters, I should impair the metaphysical propriety of their modes of thinking and expression' (MS 4008, f. 175). In this case the imagination and the word 'metaphysical' are positively associated, as they are also when Galt writes to his publisher that one of his strengths as a novelist lies in 'the metaphysical anatomy of the characters' (MS 4017, f. 21). His ambivalent use of the word 'metaphysical' is, indeed, symptomatic of his theoretical ambivalence concerning the imagination generally.

Blackwood evidently did not appreciate Galt's point about the autonomy of character. Galt became angry with him for treating his characters as if in fact they were no more than the 'combinations' of elements he sometimes said they were—'combinations' which could be mechanically altered to suit a publisher's views. In response to Blackwood's criticisms of *The Last of the Lairds* (1826) Galt suggests that his publisher ought to know that 'nobody can help an author with the conception of a character nor in the evolution of a story' (MS 4017, f. 37) In another letter Galt informs Blackwood that he had resisted changes which the latter proposed for *Annals of the Parish* (1821) because the features that Blackwood advised should be altered 'are characteristic of the garrulous humour of the old doited author' (MS 4006, f. 223). Not even Galt could alter the way his characters thought, felt, or spoke. Again in connection with *The Last of the Lairds* Galt explained to Blackwood that 'the working out of character and the features of individuality are things which I cannot change. In fact the persons come to my imagination as actual persons, and I could no more change their mode of thinking than I could those of any living individual' (MS 4017, f. 44). These are not the words of an author who actually saw his task as the Frankensteinian piecing together of 'decomposed' parts.

In view of Galt's remarks to Blackwood quoted above it is not surprising that, on occasion, he should talk of his imagination and its productions in terms of *possession*. No one who has read *The Entail* (1822) cares whether or not it was based upon actual circumstances and real-life 'models' although in his autobiographical accounts of this novel Galt is careful to make the point that it was so based. He used a different language while he was writing the novel, enthusiastically informing Blackwood that 'It has taken full possession of my fancy & I always know that when I am myself interested I do not fail to the effort' (MS 4008, f. 182). Arguably, in spite of its flaws, *The Entail* is Galt's most powerful novel. He was similarly inspired when he began to write *Sir Andrew Wylie* (1822). He told Blackwood that Andrew 'has taken full possession of my imagination' (MS 4006, f. 223) and although the novel to which Andrew lends his name is inferior to Galt's best work, Andrew

Wylie is himself a vital, convincing, if not especially admirable character. The imagination as a possessive force whose dictates could not be resisted had, in fact, been Galt's experience from the time he began the first draft of *Annals of the Parish* for he acknowledges in the *Literary Life* that he conceived it 'as if the mantle of inspiration had suddenly dropped upon my shoulders' (I, 152). It must be added that such 'inspiration' descended only when Galt wrote about the Scotland he knew, as works such as *The Majolo* (1816) or *The Earthquake* (1820) demonstrate.

Galt's ambivalence concerning the imagination was shared by later nineteenth century realists. As artists they delighted in the exercise of their imagination but as moral and social realists rather than writers of 'romance' they felt obliged to under-estimate or denounce the very faculty which made their representations of reality memorable. In Galt's manner Charlotte Brontë refers the readers of *Shirley* to 'real life' for none of the 'originals' of her 'portraits', it is asserted, is 'a figment of imagination' (chapter 10). George Eliot, like Galt, draws a sharp distinction between the imagination of a character and of the author. Characters, like bad novelists, are likely to imagine 'things as they never have been and never will be' whereas the humble author who creates such characters must 'creep servilely after nature and fact' (*Adam Bede*, chapter 17). To what extent Galt crept in this 'servile' fashion remains to be examined.

'Fables are often a better way of illustrating philosophical truths than abstract reasoning', Galt wrote in his *Literary Life* (I, 155) with reference to his own work. In his Scottish novels and stories Galt attempted to interpret with the aid of the 'philosophical truths' he gained from the Scottish Realists, though not with their aid alone, such contemporary phenomena as the industrial revolution, the political effects in Britain of the great revolution in France, and the alterations in ways of thinking brought about by these momentous changes. He was ahead of his time among novelists in Britain in so doing, and in attempting this task he was, as he says he intended to be, 'instructive'. But he was not instructive in the *manner* he intimates. If 'fables' offer a 'better way of illustrating philosophical truths' than discursive argument it is not because they are another, more entertaining form of argument. If the novel is a 'vehicle of instruction' it is so not because the message is more important than its medium. The novel appeals first and most powerfully to the imagination and thus to the reader's moral sympathies. The appeal of the novel is strongest when, as is the case with Galt, the author lavishes his attention not upon instruction *per se* but upon the vehicle, the form. Thus, if primacy must be assigned to any single factor in Galt's work it must be attributed to the aesthetic. His works of fiction are artistic expressions of a vision which is neither exclusively derived from observation nor acquired solely from the ideas of his philosophical mentors. His novels express his vision in a manner which displays the kind of creative energy and skill which he admired in the Romantics.

Galt's interest in artistic form is well illustrated by the case of *The Last of the Lairds*. When he set out to write this novel he searched, as was his custom, for 'some novelty in the method of telling such a story as the Laird's' (MS 4017, f. 15). He had greater difficulty in writing the laird's story in the form of fictional autobiography than he had experienced with any of his previous novels in this, his preferred narrative mode. His laird was to be a semi-idiot whose observations, Galt realised, would not by themselves sustain the reader's interest. After throwing at least two attempts into the fire he hit upon a solution to his narrative problems which he eagerly explained in a letter to Blackwood:

> a self-told narrative will not give the effect I wish, and in consequence I am now engaged in drawing up a descriptive story, in which, though the Laird talks a great deal, the relief of description and explanation will lighten off and enliven the absurdity and weakness of his remarks and reflections. (MS 4017, f. 13)

Galt achieved the 'effect' he sought, a prime element of which was pathos, by having an observer of the laird's doings tell his story and 'frame' the laird's rambling bouts of self-revelation and ludicrous commentary. Here Galt's emphasis is upon point of view, form, and narrative technique for only by getting these right, he knew, could he hope to arouse the reader's moral sympathy.

Galt was equally concerned with form in his 'self-told' narratives, all of which are, of course, dramatic in narrative mode: in all of them, as he notes in his *Literary Life* with reference to *Ringan Gilhaize* (1823), everything 'was kept out of view . . . that might recall the separate existence of John Galt.' In these narratives he engaged in what he calls a 'transfusion of character'. That is to say, he had imaginatively to become someone very different from himself, see the world as they might see it, and speak in a voice not his own but appropriate to his supposed narrator. In *Ringan Gilhaize* he did this in order to show 'How a Reformer himself acted and felt in the opinion of a Covenanter' (I, 250–51). He explains in the introduction to his short story 'The Dean of Guild' (1833) that 'I try to see things as I conceive a Mr Wamle [the Dean of the story's title] may have looked upon them, and to describe certain public men as they might appear to such a person.'[12] He was anxious that his readers 'estimate the invention put forth' in the creation of *Ringan Gilhaize* as he was in the creation of his other fictional autobiographies. He found dramatic story-telling a stimulus to his imagination, to his intuitions about people, and a challenge to his artistic skill. He did not treat them as an excuse for moralising.

Galt's fictional narrators differ notably from each other as well as from their creator so that in Galt's hands the 'self-told' narrative assumes many shapes. Each is an experiment in literary form designed to express a unique character. *Annals of the Parish* is a mixture of fictional autobiography and historical chronicle because Mr Balwhidder, its narrator, permits the details of his own life to filter into his historical account of his parish. *The Ayrshire Legatees* is autobiographical in the primary sense for it is largely a novel in letters. Galt wanted to set his letter-writers in their cultural context and regard them from an ironic perspective so, in addition to letters, the novel consists of commentaries both of an 'editor' and of the recipients of the letters which 'frame' the epistolary observations of the Pringles. *The Provost* (1822) is more purely a fictional autobiography but because provost Pawkie depicts himself as if he were the ruler of a principality rather than the provost of a royal burgh the novel is also a satire on the 'great man' theory of history. Galt experiments with burlesque to establish the true moral stature of his 'hero'. *The Member* (1832) is in some ways a similar work but its satire is directed at the un-reformed House of Commons and was provoked by the debates over the First Reform Bill. It is thus connected with a specific issue and here one might expect didacticism but, as Ian Gordon reminds its readers, 'it is a novel, not a treatise in political science'.[13] As such it is notable for Galt's manipulation of viewpoint and for the subtle irony which pervades all of his best work rather more than for any 'message' it may have to offer. The scope of *Ringan Gilhaize* distinguishes it from all of Galt's other works of fictional autobiography. The action spans more than a century during which several generation of the Gilhaize family have been intimately involved in the great events of the Scottish Reformation and its bloody aftermath. The novel gives an epic character to the autobiographical form, though to accomplish his ends Galt asks his readers to suspend their disbelief in the prodigious feats of memory displayed by Ringan's very old grandfather who tells his story to Ringan when he is a very young child.

Galt did not limit his formal experimentation to his 'self-told' narratives. *The Entail*, written immediately before *Ringan Gilhaize* and also spanning a century (the eighteenth) is another study in obsession, this time of a secular kind. The novel is narrated not by its principal character but by an observer of the Walkinshaw family who is generally omniscient but, on occasion, captures the immediacy of the eye-witness owing to his supposed acquaintance with the characters. More important, however, is the fact that *The Entail* is a successful experiment in tragi-comedy, a mode Galt had first attempted without significant effect in his play 'Maddalen', published in his volume of *Tragedies* (1812). Galt thought that everyday life, conventionally the realm of the comic, could also produce instances of tragic heroism. There is a tragic undertone in his comic novels which in this novel is permitted to become more assertive and mingle inextricably with the comic to give this work its peculiar power.[14] This novel, and *Ringan Gilhaize* with its largely tragic vision, are reminders that although he was basically a comic writer Galt was not limited by or to comedy.

Galt was too interested in fictional technique, in the matching of vision, form and 'voice', to use his works merely as colourful containers for generalised instruction or philosophic truth. Their moral influence depends upon their aesthetic power. Had he been as exclusively pre-occupied with the didactic as he sometimes says that he is then he would have been content to adapt to his instructive purposes the forms of fiction as he found them. *Sir Andrew Wylie* is interesting in this respect for in this novel Galt in fact uses the conventions of the popular 'three decker', though not for the purpose of moral pedagogy. This work is a lengthy 'parable' about 'getting on' in the world and such lessons as we take from it—that crawling before one's social superiors pays dividends, or that native wit exercised in the appropriate company can bring one a gratifying position of power and influence—are hardly edifying. Galt is more concerned with the 'metaphysical anatomy' of Andrew Wylie, his most successful accomplishment in a work that ought to have been a 'self-told' tale, than with using him as a mouth-piece for any moral scheme.

Most of Galt's novels are set in a circumscribed locality which he enables his readers to imagine clearly and to see as a microcosm of a larger society. The sweep of Galt's imagination, however, can not be fully appreciated unless one reads his Scottish fictions as he meant them to be read—as parts of an inter-connected series. The series forms a complex tableau of a society which could not be encompassed within the limits of a single work, nor understood from a single point of view. By deliberately writing his works in this manner Galt anticipates such later writers as Trollope and Hardy.

Galt had the idea of a series in mind from the beginning of his career as a successful novelist. After the warm reception accorded *The Ayrshire Legatees* in *Blackwood's Edinburgh Magazine*, and when Blackwood was thinking of republishing it as a volume, Galt recommended to him that 'if you determine on republication perhaps it would be of some use to take the title of a general work and call it *Tales of the West*, the Parish annals would belong to the series and also Mr Duffle's travels' (i.e. *The Steamboat*[15] MS 4006, f. 225). Blackwood did not accept the recommendation but Galt thought of his works as parts of a series, one novel tending to beget another for the sake of balanced interpretation, historical depth and comprehensiveness of thematic development. He writes in his *Literary Life* of 'that series of fictions of manners, of which Annals of the Parish is the beginning' (I, 270), and he did not exclude his novels, novellas and stories of the 1830s, until relatively recently ignored by critics of Galt's work. His linkage of *The Ayrshire Legatees* with 'The Dean of Guild' in the introduction to the latter story suggests continuity and in fact the fictions of the 1830s are extensions or further explorations of the fictional world which Galt first depicted in his novels of the 1820s. Even *Lawrie Todd* (1830) and *Bogle Corbet* (1831), although their central characters leave Scotland for North America, may be read as extensions of the earlier *Tales of the West*.[16] In these novels, as in *Sir Andrew Wylie*, the central characters leave home to find an environment in which, unfettered by tradition or by current prejudice, social or political, they may put their talents freely to use.

Tales of the West as a series has been praised for its historical accuracy. In recent years, however, Galt's fidelity to fact has been questioned although, as Christopher Whatley points out in an essay which exposes some of the liberties Galt takes with facts, 'it is a mark of Galt's achievement that he has managed to create a world which people are prepared to believe in.'[17] Like Trollope's Barsetshire or Hardy's Wessex, Galt's 'West', though based upon an actual geographical region and its notable history, ultimately is a region of the mind. In this region (as in Shakespeare's *Histories*) historical fact is at the service of dramatic imperatives.

Just as Galt's characters transcend their 'models', and his appeal to the reader's moral sympathies is dependent upon his effective management of form, so in his fictional world myth transcends and helps to interpret history. Galt's portrait of his age and of the forces that helped to shape it strikes the reader as accurate not because of his strict adherence to observable fact but because the myths which order the world of his fiction are, we feel, faithful imaginative expressions of the antitheses of thought and feeling of a period of radical change.

Galt's fictional world is characterised by a tension between opposing myths, one a myth of progress and the other a pastoral myth.[18] The myth of progress, the basic terms of which he derived from the Scottish theoretical historians, expresses the aspirations of the commercial middle class—aspirations which Galt, a businessman as well as an author, himself shared. His pastoral myth, presented in Romantic terms, expresses the doubts which Galt the artist felt about the worthiness of these aspirations. The first of these myths is dynamic yet essentially amoral; the second moral but static. Galt suggests that it is possible to reconcile the two.

The basic premise of Galt's myth of progress, as of the theoretical history, is that history has an intelligible structure. Peoples, Galt and the theoretical historians hypothesised, by a process of 'improvement' move through a series of identifiable stages from simple, primitive origins to a complex, civilised and superior present, though not at the same pace. In the society which Galt depicts the pace is steady. *Tales of the West* dramatises the process whereby one form of what M H Abrams calls 'Christian prospectivism'[19] evolves into another—the process by means of which the religious idea of salvation turns into the secular idea of progress.

Ringan Gilhaize portrays the Reformation as a liberating series of events which begin the process of the secularisation of the modern world. The Reformation is shown to free the Scottish people from their bondage to a corrupt medieval church dependent upon arbitrary monarchical authority for its continued existence. Ringan and his immediate forebears are guided by the idea of salvation but when the state refuses to permit either the preaching or practice of Ringan's form of Covenanting Christianity he is forced to take political action. Remembering 'the hero-stirring times of the Wallace wight' (Vol I, Chapter VIII) he confronts the doctrine of 'the divine right of kings' with his fervent belief in 'the divine right of resistance'. Claud Walkinshaw of *The Entail*, who 'early preferred the history of Whittington and his Cat to the achievements of Sir William Wallace' (Vol I, Chapter I) is a more secular figure than Ringan. Ringan thinks in terms of martyrdom and self-sacrifice whereas Claud thinks of self-aggrandisement, and follows the path suggested by the Whittington story in raising himself, by his own efforts, from peddler to merchant to landowner. Claud, however, is descended from Covenanters and his conscience, though repressed, is not asleep. Ultimately it causes him to feel that the self-interested measures he has taken to fulfil his worldly ambitions have ensured his damnation. His son George, as avaricious as his father, has no such religious anxiety, and neither do the 'new men' of the novels which span the eighteenth and early nineteenth centuries, or which are set entirely in the latter. Mr Cayenne, the factory owner of *Annals of the Parish*, for example, is an unbeliever who, at a time of upheaval, merely feels it to be 'the duty of every good subject to die a Christian' (Chapter XLVII). The economic, social, and political effects of commercial, agricultural and industrial revolution, and of the revolutions in America and France had by this time induced men to work for salvation in this world rather than the next. Material reward for diligence in the exercise of individual talent became their goal, not spiritual recompense for a life lived virtuously in obedience to the will of God.

Galt writes in his *Autobiography* that his works of fiction 'would be more properly characterized . . . as theoretical histories, than either as novels or romances' (II, 219). He describes his works thus, it would seen, in order to minimise the part played in them by the imagination. But as we have seen, owing to its reliance upon hypothesis and speculation theoretical history is itself an imaginative form of writing and, for present purposes, one can take this point a step further. At base, theoretical history is mythic for, like the myths of imaginative literature, it imposes upon the confusing, often contradictory masses of historical detail an 'interpretation' not suggested by phenomena objectively observed and studied but by the heart's desire. William Robertson, for example, does not set out to enquire whether Europeans 'advanced from barbarism to refinement.'[20] He believes they did, and undertakes to explain how, with the considerable aid offered by hypothesis. Similarly, when under Realist influence, Galt assumes that the period from the Reformation to the First Reform Act was characterised by progress and *Tales of the West* reflects that assumption. One can read all the works in this series as inter-connected elements of an extended 'theoretical history' without denying the mythic nature of the whole.[21] The difference between the writer of fiction and the writer of theoretical history is largely one of procedure. From a basis in desire or belief the theoretical historian engages in discursive argument whereas the novelist expresses himself through the imagined lives of his many characters.

Myth and theoretical history focus not so much upon the events of history as upon underlying principles, essences, the imagined reality that lies behind the observable details—a reality coloured, to borrow Hartley Coleridge's words, by the writer's 'wants and yearnings'.[22] Galt was no radical but he did believe in liberty, the steady accession of which he saw as the principle that lay behind the progressive development he depicted. His myth of progress makes its appeal through its concentration upon freedom understood in a double sense: as freedom from the controls of traditions dating back to the feudal past and as freedom to celebrate a world of technological and political change with new ideas about every aspect of life. Among Galt's characters who rejoice in such freedoms is Mr Dipthong of *The Member* who avers that 'we are now a more refined nation than we were . . . and it is needful to our improved habits that . . . every thing we have of a public nature should correspond with our desires.' Rather like Galt in his essays directed against 'the country gentlemen'[23] he declares that

> the great properties have had their day: they are the relics of the feudal system, when the land bore all public burdens. That system is in principle overthrown, and is hastening to be so in fact. The system that it will be succeeded by is one that will give employment to the people—is one that will gradually bring on an equalisation of condition.
>
> (Chapter XXXIV)

Galt's fictional world is divided between those who do not favour the liberties he commemorates and vainly try to oppose improvement, and those who take the opposite course. The enemies of progress in the world of Galt's novels are reactionary feudal lairds who, to quote Mr Jobbry, the narrator of *The Member*, 'counted their descent from Adam's elder brother' (Chapter I). They cling to outmoded ideas and resent the growing power of the middle class whereas Galt's 'improvers' and 'new men' are members of that class. They are rural or urban capitalists who, at their best, increase production, profit, and employment by cleverly applying new ideas and technology to farming, commerce and industry. In doing so they hold out the promise of better times to those suffering Scotland's endemic poverty. In historical fact as distinct from mythical formulation, however, the lairds of the West were often themselves improvers and not the farcical reactionaries Galt portrays in his novels while many a capitalist bought an estate and a 'feudal' position with his accumulated capital.

From a moral point of view the 'new men' of Galt's novels are not always, nor even primarily, 'at their best' for they are interested in rising in the world and they estimate their success (their secular salvation) in terms of wealth and power rather than service to others. Mr Cayenne attempts to balance his interests with those of the community but his successor as director of the factory speculates to the point of backruptcy thus throwing all his employees out of work at once. Even Mr Balwhidder's second wife, the daughter of an agricultural improver, is so convinced that her main purpose in life is to increase her capital that she turns her husband's quiet manse into 'a factory of butter and cheese' (*Annals*, Chapter VI). Andrew Wylie offers sentimental reasons for his return to his native village once he has made a fortune and acquired power in London but the narrator of his story baldly declares that he returns 'with an honest pride to enjoy that superiority over his early companions, which, after all the glosses that may be put upon the feeling, is really the only reward of an adventurous spirit' (Chapter LXXXV). Much the same is true of Mr Jobbry, or of Mr Rupees, the nabob in *The Last of the Lairds*. Mr Rupees, like Wylie, grew up a cottar's son and, like Wylie, having made a fortune he returns to dispossess the local laird, the petty tyrant of the neighbourhood. He freely offers his opinion that 'every man of sense and talent seeks his fortune abroad, and leaves only the incapable and those who are conscious of their deficiencies at home' (Chapter XVII). Mr Pawkie of *The Provost*, a 'man of sense and talent' contrived, in every sense, to make his fortune at home, as the corrupt Provost of Gudetown. He presides (not always willingly) over various civic improvements without displaying any corresponding moral improvement himself.

Galt's novels and stories present many people of this type, and it may plausibly be argued that since, with the exception of Andrew Wylie (a significant exception since Wylie is Galt's archetypal 'new man'), he delineates them ironically he is taking a moral stand against them. Working against his irony, however, is the gusto with which Galt often portrays talented, manipulative, self-interested people. He enters with delight into their schemes and celebrates their sheer vitality. There was unquestionably something which attracted Galt in morally deficient but dynamic, successful characters. They are triumphantly themselves, warts and all, liberated not only from social repression but from moral imperatives, though none is a moral monster. Galt's attitude toward them is like that of the people of Hardy's Casterbridge toward Michael Henchard when they see 'how admirably he had used his one talent of energy to create a position of affluence out of absolutely nothing.'

Like many of his contemporaries, however, Galt was pulled in two ways. While he extolls progress and its liberating energies he did not, at least in his novels, have entire faith in the Realist view that although it was not the result of human design progress was Providentially the effect of human action. He did not always believe that Adam Smith's 'invisible hand' would somehow transform private vices into public benefits. While he celebrates the present he is not always sure that it is, in fact, an improvement upon the past. His pastoral myth, unambiguously expressive of Christian moral values, questions whether the myth of progress offers an adequate interpretation of historical events.

The myth of progress is centred in the city, and its exponents are those who have come under urban influence whether or not they actually live in an urban center. By contrast, the pastoral myth is focused upon the rural village. In turn, in Galt's fiction the village is association with childhood and thus with nostalgia and its idealising influence. When Galt is under the spell of nostalgia for a lost 'golden age'—the 'golden age' of childhood, dear also to the Romantic poets—he portrays the village as an unchanging *locus* for values, the opposite of those exalted by the myth of progress.

Unlike the latter myth, that of pastoral takes account of man's spiritual needs. The rural village is intimately associated with Nature, and in Nature there is a sympathetic principle as the narrator of *The Entail* intimates when he writes that 'there are few situations more congenial to the diffusion of tenderness and sensibility—the elements of affection—than the sunny hills and clear water of a rural neighbourhood' (Vol II, Chapter XXVII). In rural districts villages blend into their surrounding landscapes which, when pastorally depicted, are remarkable for their superlative beauty. In the pastoral region of Galt's fictional world natural beauty is an image of divine benevolence, an active image which causes men like Mr Balwhidder to write of Nature walking 'forth in her beauty to testify to the goodness of the Father of all mercies' (Chapter XI). The benevolence to which natural beauty testifies is essential for true community, which is enjoyed in the pastoral region. Its inhabitants have no need of worldly wealth, power, or success for they already live in paradise.

Galt, of course, was aware that myth is not history and historical facts which resist mythical interpretation are to be found in his works. He was fully aware of the exploitation of the worker both in town and country but chose not to dwell upon the fact. He knew that to be a laird and an improver was not a contradiction in terms, though he chose to represent Monkgreen, the 'improving laird' of *Sir Andrew Wylie*, as a notable exception to a general rule. He may have rejoiced that 'in principle' the 'relics of the feudal system' had had their day but he recognised that they still counted in fact. The point of this discussion of myth is not to suggest that Galt failed to observe what was going on around him. It is to draw attention to the fact that in the works of a writer accomplished in irony, especially in the analysis of character, there is also an expressive, imaginative element by means of which he communicates a subjective interpretation of his times. It is an interpretation which points to the uncertainty of a generation as to the true value of the great changes it witnessed.

The myth of progress makes a 'golden age' of the present in contrast to the past; pastoral myth seeks historical disengagement by a retreat into the innocent and timeless 'golden age' of childhood. It is left to the ministers in Galt's novels—a group of characters quite as large and important as his 'improvers'—to attempt to reconcile the values expressed by these myths.

Galt's ministers live both in the realm of myth and of historical fact. They live in pastoral villages, in touch with Nature and therefore with God, and they are the guardians of pastoral values. They are, however, to a greater or lesser extent, familiar with cities and they do not oppose 'improvement' outright because, unlike Galt's lairds, they care about the poverty which it is their daily duty to alleviate. What they try to do is to modify the self-interest of such capitalists as they are acquainted with, urging them to benevolent actions in the communal interest. Thus, with some success, Mr Balwhidder reminds Mr Cayenne, in *Annals of the Parish*, of his communal responsibilities; in *The Entail* Dr Denholm encourages Claud Walkinshaw to act according to the dictates of love and charity rather than avarice; the young Dr Lounlans, in *The Last of the Lairds*, mediates between the helpless laird and the rapacious nabob. Perhaps the best kind of synthesis between the values of the 'improvers' and pastoral values is suggested by Mr Balwhidder. He detects a connection between the rise of industry and urbanisation and the 'progress of book-learning and education' which, in his view, has produced 'a spirit of greater liberality than the world knew before, bringing men of adverse principles and doctrines into a more humane communion with each other' (Chapter LI) Perhaps the best values of pastoral may be retained in an industrial world by means of education and cultural enrichment. Such a possibility is tentatively expressed; it does not amount to a conviction but is more in the nature of a hope.

Now that Galt's Scottish heritage has been examined it is time to study him in a broader context. To modify what has been written of Housman, Galt's is 'a view of the universe' which happens to be set in Scotland.[24] Like every novelist of stature Galt is not narrowly regional even though his works are associated with a particular region. He bears comparison with the Victorian Realists who also focused their attention upon specific places so that they could write convincingly of man in the modern world. Their point of view, as George Levine has shown,[25] was influenced by Galt's contemporaries, the Romantics, who also, as I have argued, influenced Galt. It is important that Galt not become an icon of Scottish literary culture for nationalistic or any other reasons; he would then, like Burns or Scott, be celebrated and largely unread. Galt himself wanted the widest possible audience for his work.

To that end he created a literary language which is unmistakably Scottish but no mere imitation of the language he heard spoken in the Scottish lowlands. Like the language of Ramsay or Fergusson, Galt's is a subtle blend of English and Scots. He rejoiced that the writer in Scotland possessed 'the whole range of the English language' in addition to his own for this enabled him to 'enjoy an uncommonly rich vocabulary.'[26] Galt's style is the imaginative element upon which every other imaginative effect he achieves depends, and its subtlety can only be appreciated by detailed study.[27]

Galt's works are best studied as contributions to a substantial *oeuvre*. Until quite recently critics confined their attention to the novels of the 1820s. Now that Galt's creative work of the 1830s is recognised as significant[28] it is time to enquire into the relationship between his novels of the 1820s and the works which preceded them. These are usually written off as 'hack work' but it should be recalled that among them was an early draft of *Annals of the Parish* which would have been published in 1813 had not Constable turned it down. This is the novel by which Galt is best known and in which, with admirable economy, he sets out the fictional world which all his subsequent novels explore with the imaginative skill to which this essay seeks to draw attention.

NOTES

1   Reid's works and the works of others who shared his view of perception were available to Galt at the Greenock Library, which he patronised with enthusiasm. The ideas of the Realists were also 'in the air' at the time. *See The Autobiography of John Galt*, 2 vols (London, 1833), I, 17; 38; 54. (Further references to this work will be given in the text by volume and page number). *See also* Erik Frykman, *John Galt's Scottish Stories 1820–1823* (Upsala, 1959), pp 225–6.

2   Thomas Reid, *Essays on the Intellectual and Active Powers of Man*, 3 vols (Dublin, 1790), II, p 385; I, p 50. Other references to this work are given in the text of the essay by volume and page number.

3   'An Essay on Commercial Policy', *The Philosophical Magazine*, XXIII (November, 1805), pp 104–12.

4 'Transactions of the Dilettante Society of Edinburgh', *Blackwood's Edinburgh Magazine*, VI, No. xxxi (October, 1819), p 97.

5 *The Life of Lord Byron* (London, 1830), 255.

6 *Cursory Reflections of Political and Commercial Topics as Connected with the Regent's Accession to the Royal Authority* (London, 1812), p iv.

7 Dugald Stewart, *Elements of the Philosophy of the Human Mind*, 2 vols (Edinburgh and London, 1818 and 1821), I, p 481.

8 *The Literary Life and Miscellanies of John Galt*, 3 vols (Edinburgh and London, 1834), I, p 229. Further references to this work are given in the text of the essay by volume and page number.

9 John Galt, *Letters from the Levant* (London, 1813), p 218.

10 National Library of Scotland. MS 4008, f. 166. I should like to thank the Trustees of the National Library of Scotland for permission to quote from Galt's unpublished correspondence. All other references to it will be given in the text of the essay by manuscript and folio numbers.

11 *The Bachelor's Wife: A Selection of Curious and Interesting Extracts, with Cursory Observations* (Edinburgh, 1824), p 366.

12 *John Galt: Selected Short Stories*, Ian A Gordon (ed) (Edinburgh, 1978), p 49.

13 *The Member: An Autobiography*, Ian A Gordon (ed) (Edinburgh and London, 1975), X.

14 I have examined in detail the tragic-comic nature of this novel in 'Mind-Forg'd Manacles: The Entail as Romantic Tragicomedy' published in *John Galt 1779–1979*, Christopher A Whatley, (ed) (Edinburgh, 1979), 164–94.

15 This work, like *The Ayrshire Legatees*, was also published serially in *Blackwood's Edinburgh Magazine* (1821) and later republished in book form. It is a work in which the formula of the *Legatees* is limited and is an inferior novel.

16 *See* Elizabeth Waterston's introduction to her edition of the third volume of *Bogle Corbet* (Toronto, 1977), and Robert J Graham's article 'John Galt's *Bogle Corbet*: A Parable of Progress', *Scottish Literary Journal*, 13, No. 2 (November, 1986), 31–47.

17 'Annals of the Parish and History', *John Galt 1779–1979*, Christopher A Whatley (ed), pp 51–63.

18 I have examined these myths in detail, although in a different context, in 'Early Remembrances: Pastoral in the Fictional World of John Galt', University of Toronto Quarterly (Summer, 1978), pp 283–303; and in 'The Spirit of the Age and the Scottish Fiction of John Galt', The Wordsworth Circle, XI, No. 2 (Spring, 1980), 98–106.

19 M H Abrams, *Natural Supernaturalism: Tradition and Revolution in Romantic Literature* (New York, 1971), p 59.

20 *Dr Robertson's Works*, 8 vols (London, 1925), III, p 10.

21 I have argued elsewhere that the only individual novel Galt wrote that fulfils all the conditions of theoretical history is *Annals of the Parish*. It now seems to me more profitable, as I argue in the text of this essay, to regard *Tales of the West* as an extended theoretical history. *See* my article 'Theoretical History and the Novel: The Scottish Fiction of John Galt', *English Literary History*, 43 (1976), pp 342–65.

22 M H Abrahams, *The Mirror and the Lamp: Romantic Theory and the Critical Tradition* (New York, 1958), p 294, quoted.

23 Published in *Blackwood's Edinburgh Magazine*, XII (October, 1822), pp 482–91; XII (November, 1822), pp 624–32.

24 John W Stevenson, 'The Pastoral Setting in the Poetry of A E Housman', *Pastoral*

and Romance: Modern Essays in Criticism, Eleanor Terry Lincoln (ed) (Engle-wood Cliffs, New Jersey, 1969), p 2.

25 *See* George Levine, *The Realistic Imagination* (Chicago and London, 1981).
26 Galt makes these remarks in a brief introduction to his story 'The Seamstress', printed in *John Galt: Selected Short Stories*, p 21.
27 *See*, for instance, J D McClure's 'The language of *The Entail*', *Scottish Literary Journal*, 8, No. 1 (May, 1981), pp 30–50.
28 This recognition has been largely due to the work of Ian A Gordon, whose biographical study *John Galt: The Life of a Writer* (Edinburgh, 1972), and whose editions of the *Selected Short Stories* and of *The Member* have all urged the claims of Galt's work of the 1830s.

FURTHER READING

MODERN TEXTS OF GALT'S FICTION

Annals of the Parish, James Kinsley (ed), Oxford English Novels Series, 1967.
The Entail, Ian A Gordon (ed), Oxford English Novels Series, 1970.
The Provost, Ian A Gordon (ed), Oxford English Novels Series, 1973.
The Member, Ian A Gordon (ed), The Scottish Academic Press, Edinburgh, 1975.
The Last of the Lairds, Ian A Gordon (ed), The Scottish Academic Press, Edinburgh, 1976.
Selected Short Stories, Ian A Gordon (ed), The Scottish Academic Press, Edinburgh, 1978.
Ringan Gilhaize, Patricial J Wilson (ed), The Scottish Academic Press, Edinburgh, 1984.
The Ayrshire Legatees, The Mercat Press, Edinburgh, 1978.

BIOGRAPHY

Aberdein, J W, *John Galt* (London, 1936).
Gordon, Ian A, *John Galt: The Life of a Writer* (Edinburgh, 1972).
Timothy, H B, *The Galts: A Canadian Odyssey. John Galt 1779–1839* (Toronto, 1977).

CRITICAL STUDIES

Fyrkman, Erik, *John Galt's Scottish Stories 1820–23*, (Upsala, 1959).
Gibault, Henri, *John Galt: Romancier Ecossais* (Grenoble, 1979).
Hart, Francis Russell, *The Scottish Novel, From Smollett to Spark* (Cambridge, Mass. 1978).
Jack, Ian, *English Literature 1815–1832* (Oxford, 1963).
Scott, P H, *John Galt* (Edinburgh, 1985).
Waterston, Elizabeth (ed), *John Galt: Reappraisals* (Guelph, Ontario, 1985).
Whatley, Christopher A (ed), *John Galt 1779–1979* (Edinburgh, 1979).

ARTICLES

Apart from those articles mentioned already in the Notes the reader may find the following of interest:

Costain, K M, 'The Prince and The Provost', *Studies in Scottish Literature*, VI, No. 1 (July, 1968), pp 20–35.
McQueen, John, 'John Galt and the Analysis of Social History', in *Scott Bicentenary Essays*, Alan Bell (ed) (Edinburgh and London, 1973).
Swann, Charles, 'Past into Present, Galt and the Historical Novel', in *Literature and History*, No. 3, March, 1976.

The John Galt Number of the *Scottish Literary Journal*, 8, No. 1 (May, 1981) contains articles by Ian A Gordon, K M Costain, J D McClure and Patricia J Wilson.

Chapter 7

John Wilson (Christopher North) and the Tory Hegemony

ANDREW NOBLE

> Alas, Scotland—ay, well-educated, moral, religious, Scotland can show, in the bosom of her bonny banks and braes, cases worse than this; at which, if there be tears in heaven, the angels weep.
>
> John Wilson

> 'Before we are forgotten we will be turned into kitsch. Kitsch is the stopover between being and oblivion.'
>
> Milan Kundera

'I am,' wrote John Wilson to John Gibson Lockhart in 1834, 'at the Head of Scottish Literature. Pray then who is at the Tail? and who constitutes the Body? I think of the boy who was Dux of his class. On this side of the Border, of course, Mr Chairman, I rise to propose Professor Wilson and the Literature of Scotland.'[1] With Scott recently dead this assertion, in terms of public reputation, was no idle boast. With his old associate Lockhart now in London as editor of *The Quarterly Review*, Wilson was sufficiently modest not to extend his sway south of the Tweed. He did, however, tower physically and seemingly intellectually over the Scottish scene. Poet, novelist, a critical maker and breaker of British reputations as chief contributor to *Blackwood*'s and Professor of Moral Philosophy at Edinburgh, there was no apparent limit to his talents. Not only his fellow Scots prized him. If Edgar Allan Poe, with the Atlantic between himself and Wilson's intimidating presence, was profoundly sceptical of his critical acumen, Charles Dickens, visiting Edinburgh, was mightily impressed. Nor was Harriet Martineau's obituary of 1854 thought excessive:

> Such a presence is rarely seen; and more than one person has said that he reminded them of the first man, Adam; so full was that large frame of vitality, force and sentience. His tread seemed almost to shake the streets, his eyes almost saw through stone walls: and as for his voice there was no heart that could stand before it. No less striking was it to see him in a mood of repose, as when he steered the old packet-boat that used to pass between Bowness and Ambleside, before the steamers were put up on the Lake. Sitting motionless, with his hand upon the rudder, in the presence of journeymen and market-women, with his eye looking beyond everything into nothing, and his mouth

closed upon his beard, as if he meant never to speak again, he was quite as impressive and immortal an image as he could have been to his students of his class or the comrades of his jovial hours.[2]

If Wilson did not engender an audience of Byronic proportions, it has to be said that he was far harder to typecast; the variety of his roles was extraordinary. This enormous reputation scarcely outlived him. In the decade after his death, Ferrier, his son-in-law, completed a twelve volume edition of his works. Remnants of that edition, often uncut, are still to be found. The last publication of Wilson's writings was in 1876 when a selection from his finest work, *Noctes Ambrosianae*, appeared. The young Robert Louis Stevenson reviewed it thus:

> It was a fortunate idea to extricate from so much that was purely local, purely temporary, and often enough in ill humour, all that seemed permanently human in Wilson's *Noctes*. Few people nowadays would take the trouble to go through the fruit of these ten years of high-pressure literary action. Of the few who did so, most would feel a strange weariness and despair creep over them among these warfares of the dead. Bygone personalities have an odd smack of the grave; and we feel moved to turn the tables on the high-stepping satirist, and remind him, with something of the irony of country headstones, that not only they, but he—not only the rejected Whiglings, but the redoubtable Kit North— point the moral of dust to dust.[3]

Certainly much of Wilson's prose and verse is impregnated with the spirit of a Scottish graveyard on a wet Sunday. In such reiterated strains he is unbearable other than as a briefly observed symptom of nineteenth-century melancholic fine-feeling. The other side of his nature is, however, manic, animal high spirits and, at its best, *Noctes Ambrosianae* is charged with such crazy energies. Stevenson perfectly catches how Wilson's fissile personality was particularly suited to composing what might be described as bibulous intellectual farce. Himself increasingly restless under the sombre repressions of Victorian Scotland's middle-class gentility, Stevenson responded enthusiastically to a writer who seemed free of cant and honest about certain physical appetites.

> But of the more perennial part, picked skilfully from among this detritus of old literary and political convulsions, Mr Skelton has erected what is perhaps the most durable monument to Wilson's fame that we possess. In it we find the immortal trio at their best throughout. From beginning to end, their meetings are inspired and sanctified by Bacchus and Apollo. North can always lay aside his crutch; Tickler is always six feet high; and the Shepherd is always the Shepherd. For how is it possible to praise that adorable creation but in terms of himself? He is the last expression of sophisticated rusticity; at once a poet, a journalist, a Scotchman, and a shepherd; oscillating between Burns and the *Daily Telegraph* in things literary; and, in things moral, occupying all sorts of intermediate stations between a prize-fighter and Peden the Prophet. If it were lawful to marry words of so incongruous a strain we might classify him as a Presbyterian Faun.
> And this book is not only welcome because it takes us on a visit to Wilson

when he is in his best vein, but because Wilson in all his veins, is the antidote, or at least the antithesis, of much contemporary cant. Here is a book full of the salt of youth; a red-hot shell of animal spirits calculated, if anybody reads it, to set up a fine conflagration among the dry heather of present-day Phariseeism. Touch it as you will, it gives out shrewd galvanic shocks, which may perhaps brighten and shake up this smoke-dried and punctilious generation. Look at the profound and animal sensuality, which breaks out in the praise of all sorts of exercise and gloats, through near one-half the pages over the details of eating and drinking. 'O man,' says the Shepherd to Tickler, 'it would be a great pity to dee wi' sic an appetteet.'[4]

One cannot agree that in all his veins Wilson is the enemy of cant; in most of his veins he is, for nineteenth-century Scotland, a seminal source of it. The *Noctes* are different. This may have come from a more genuine symbiosis with Hogg's genius than Wilson would ever admit to. It certainly also derives from the salty vitality of the soaring flights of Scottish language used. Henry Cockburn believed the *Noctes* contains 'the best Scotch that has been written in modern times'.[5] Recourse to a traditional vocabulary, rhetoric and ambivalent wit seems to have given Wilson a fluency and honesty never elsewhere discernible. It may, in language and tone, have also limited the audience for his only fine work. Even the young Stevenson had doubts about the translatability of Scottish vernacular and, in this century, a critic as acute as John Gross has written the *Noctes* off as 'unreadable rigmarole'.[6]

While we will have cause to return to the *Noctes* in the light of Wilson's troubled relationship to the Scottish literary tradition, what can be immediately lamented is that Wilson's normal medium was an anglicised rhetoric, a deviant form of Scottish eighteenth-century genteel prose, that rendered it, largely and intentionally, beyond both fact and thought. As MacDiarmid has scathingly remarked of Wilson as exemplary orator of this virulent Scottish mode:

The main purpose of all verbiage is simply to batter the hearer into a pulpy state of vague acquiescence in which a sense of mutual enlightenment can at least exist as an illusion. The most important words in the language—"living experience", "passion", "beauty"—are the most effective for this purpose, and the clergy and the politicians in particular make great play with them. To such an extent has this gone that words have practically ceased to have any meaning; no wonder that Wyndham Lewis contends that a stiffening of satire or straight-speaking is needful in anything that wishes to survive the subtle misconstruings of the defensive reader or hearer . . . most of the words are *clichés*, headlines, a verbomania in which the expression of thought in any real sense of the term has practically ceased to be an element at all . . .

Scotland, in particular, is dominated in every direction by an abracadabra impervious to all sense—overriden by meaningless phrases. This is not surprising. 'Christopher North' was only the most extraordinary exponent of this sort of thing carried to the furthest degree, but it has long been not only general in Scotland but actually recognised and defended. It has been written, for example—and a similar tribute could be paid to the vast majority of Scottish 'philosophers', divines and public speakers generally—of the celebrated Dr

> Thomas Brown, co-professor with Dugald Stewart in Edinburgh University,
> that 'the fine poetical imagination of Dr Brown, the quickness of his apprehen-
> sion, and the acuteness and ingenuity of his argument, were qualities but little
> suited to that patient and continuous research which the phenomena of the
> mind so peculiarly demand.'[7]

Wishing to put his modernist scalpel to the tumour of post-Union rhetoric, MacDiarmid saw in Scottish church and academe florid eloquence masking intellectual paralysis. From his nationalistic point of view Scotland, detached from her roots, could produce not fruit but false verbal flowers. Left in a partial vacuum, anglicised literary intellectuals had, however, filled the void not only with mere rhetoric. Deprived of an authentic national identity they had assembled one from prefabricated English literary parts. Wilson, as the pivotal figure between the eighteenth and nineteenth centuries, is therefore of a cultural import far beyond his literary merits. How precisely his symptoms correspond to MacDiarmid's diagnosis of diseased Scottish rhetoric can be discerned from the following autobiographical piece:

> For having bidden farewell to our sweet native Scotland, kissed, ere we parted,
> the grass and the flowers with a show of filial tears—having bidden farewell to
> all her glens, now a-glimmer in the blended light of imagination and memory,
> with their cairns and kirks, their low-chimneyed huts and their high-turreted
> halls, their free-flowing rivers and lochs dashing like seas—we were all at once
> buried not in the Cimmerian gloom, but the cerulean glitter of Oxford's ancient
> academic groves. The genius of the place fell upon us. Yes! we hear now, in the
> renewed delight of the awe of our youthful spirit, the pealing organ in that
> chapel called the Beautiful; we see the saints on Calvary meekly bearing the
> cross! It seemed, then, that our hearts had no need even of the kindness of
> kindred—of the country where we were born, and that had received the con-
> tinued blessings of our enlarging love! Yet away went, even then, sometimes
> our thoughts to Scotland, like carrier-pigeons wafting love messages beneath
> their unwearied wings! They went and they returned, and still their going and
> coming was blessed. But ambition touched us, as with the wand of a magician
> from a vanished world and a vanished time. The Greek tongue—multitudinous
> as the sea—kept like the sea sounding in our ears, through the stillness of that
> world of towers and temples. Lo! Zeno, with his arguments hard and high,
> beneath the porch! Plato divinely discoursing in grove and garden! The Stagyrite
> voice of the smiling Socrates, cheering the cloister's shade and the court's
> sunshine! And when the thunders of Demosthenes ceased, we heard the harping
> of the old blind glorious Mendicant, whom, for the loss of eyes, Apollo
> rewarded with the gift of immortal song! And that was our companionship of
> the dead.[8]

At a stroke three national cultures are here rendered vacuous. Patriotism, pietism and philosophy are equally vulgarised. It was not classical learning (though he was a brilliant scholar) which attracted Wilson to England. Nor was it classical learning that he returned with; his lectures as Edinburgh's professor of moral philosophy were the antithesis of Greek clarity and rigour,

MacDiarmid is equally pertinent regarding these offerings to the aspiring democratic intellect:

> In the opinion of metaphysicians such as Sir William Hamilton and Professor Ferrier, he was trite, commonplace, limited, utterly unequal to clear and powerful thought; but these inferiorities were nothing against his sentimental eloquence and his fluent rhetoric, for these reached the Achilles' heel in the invincibility of the Scottish moral frame.[9]

Wilson's rhetorical eloquence and his life-long ability to make himself the focus of attention displayed themselves at an early age. Born in 1785, the child of a wealthy Paisley manufacturer, he was by the age of five using a chair as a pulpit and 'preaching' to an admiring domestic circle. This precocity in matters spiritual was outdone by his physical prowess. At the age of three he went fishing by himself to a distant stream. His subsequent career in field sports would have rendered Hemingway a poor second. The predator and preacher seemed to live separate lives.

Despite this absence of a childhood Wordsworthian conscience, Wilson before he left Glasgow University, read the newly published *Lyrical Ballads*. The eighteen year old undergraduate then wrote a long, and enthusiastic letter in 1802 to Wordsworth who, starved of responsive readers, was mainly impressed by the cogency of the young Scotsman's grasp of essential issues. Wilson, though apprehensive of the hurt he would be caused were the English poet not to respond, saw precisely the radical nature of Wordsworth's language and prosody; the dynamic interaction of creative mind and nature and the determining influence of environment on social and national character. He also saw the democratic impulse that lay at the heart of these early ballads as defined by their vision of an extended sense of loving community:

> But your poems may not be considered merely in philosophical light, or even as containing refined and natural feelings; they present us with a bond of morality of the purest kind. They represent the enjoyment resulting from the cultivation of the social affections of our nature; they inculcate a conscientious regard to the rights of our fellow-men; they show that every creature on the face of the earth is entitled, in every mind, *however* depraved, there exist some qualities deserving our esteem. They point out the proper way to happiness. They show that such a thing as perfect misery does not exist. They flash in our souls conviction of immortality. Considered therefore in this view, *Lyrical Ballads* is, to use your own words, the book which I value next to my Bible; and though I may, perhaps, never have the happiness of seeing you, yet I will always consider you as a friend, who has by his instructions done me a service which it can never be in my power to repay.[10]

How different from the outrage with which Jeffrey's *Edinburgh Review* had met the *Lyrical Ballads*.[11] Wilson had, however, a major reservation. Wordsworth, on occasion and especially in 'The Idiot Boy', had gone beyond the pleasure principle: 'No feeling, no state of mind ought, in my opinion, to become the subject of poetry that does not please.' Wilson then proceeds to draw a clear demarcation line in terms of the proper subjects of poetry:

> But we may lay this down as a general rule, that no description can please, where the sympathies of our soul are not excited, and no narration interest, where we do not enter into the feelings of some of the parties concerned. On this principle, many feelings which are undoubtedly natural, are improper subjects for poetry, and many situations, no less natural, incapable of being described so as to produce the grand effect of the poetical composition. This, sir, I would apprehend, is reasonable, and founded on the constitution of the human mind. There are a thousand occurrences happening every day, which do not in the least interest an unconcerned spectator, though they do no doubt occasion various emotions in the breast of those to whom they immediately relate. To describe these in poetry would be improper . . . This inability to receive pleasure from descriptions such as that of 'The Idiot Boy', is, I am convinced, founded upon established feelings of human nature, and the principle of it constitutes, as I daresay you recollect, the leading feature of Smith's Theory of Moral Sentiments. I therefore think that in the choice of this subject, you have committed an error. You never deviate from nature; in you that would be impossible; but in this case, you have delineated feelings which, though natural, do not please, but which create a certain degree of disgust and contempt . . . In reading 'The Idiot Boy', all persons who allow themselves to think, must admire your talents, but they regret that they have been so employed, and while they esteem the author, they cannot help being displeased with his performance. I have seen a most excellent painting of an idiot, but it created in me inexpressible disgust. I admired the talents of the artist, but I had no other source of pleasure. The poem of 'The Idiot Boy' produced upon me an effect in every respect similar.[12]

Wilson was not to know of Wordsworth's profound dislike of Smith's aesthetic theory. In his subsequent bitter quarrel with Jeffrey, Wordsworth, in fact, was to see Smith as progenitor of the whole Edinburgh critical school with its corrupt standard of restrictive gentility with regard to literature and its subject matter.[13] Certainly he could not accept Wilson's limiting sense of the domain of pleasure:

> I return then to the question, please whom? or what? I answer, human nature as it has been, and ever will be. But where are we to find the best measure of this? I answer, within by stripping our own heart's naked and by looking out of ourselves to men who lead the simplest lives and most according to nature, men who have never known false refinements, wayward and artificial desires, false criticisms, effeminate habits of thinking and feelings, or who, having known these things, have outgrown them. This latter class is the most to be depended upon, but it is very small in number. People in our rank of life are perpetually falling into one sad mistake, namely that of supposing that human nature and the persons they associate with are one and the same thing. Whom do we generally associate with? Gentlemen, persons of fortune, professional men, ladies, persons who can afford to buy or can easily procure books on half a guinea price, hot-pressed and printed on superfine paper. These persons are, it is true, a part of human nature but we err lamentably if we suppose them to

be fair representatives of the vast mass of human existence. And yet few ever consider books but with reference to their power of pleasing these persons and men of higher rank; few descend lower among cottages and fields and among children. A man must have done this habitually before his judgement upon the Idiot Boy would be in any way decisive with me. I *know* I have done this myself habitually; I wrote the poem with exceeding delight and pleasure, and whenever I read it I read it with pleasure. You have given me praise for having reflected faithfully in my poems the feelings of human nature; I would fain hope that I have done so. But a great poet ought to do more than this; he ought to a certain degree rectify men's feelings, to give them new compositions of feelings, to render their feelings more sane, pure and permanent, in short more consonant to nature, that is, to eternal nature and the great moving spirit of things. He ought to travel before men occasionally as well as at their sides.[14]

This early exchange with Wordsworth is seminal for understanding Wilson's subsequent career. By restricting the area of empathetic concern he found in Wordsworth's poetry, Wilson was making not only an aesthetic and moral decision but a political one. In the name of what was pleasurable to a certain class he emasculated Wordsworth's early poetry. This, as Crabb Robinson bitterly remarked, made his own poetry that of a 'female Wordsworth'.[15] In essence this effeminacy consisted of a mimicry of style while excluding disconcerting substance. It is also arguably a particularly acute manifestation of the conversion of the radical energy and intelligence of Romantic poetry into an imitative, melodramatic, Victorian high style; the purpose of which insidiously reversed the democratic impulse of the original romantic poets.

Wilson is, however, nothing if not a Scottish creature of paradox and contradiction. De Quincey who knew him best and longest saw him as having a 'versatility and ambidexterity of which we find such eminent models in Alcibiades, in Caesar, in Crichton, in that of Servan recorded by Sully, and in one or two Italians'.[16] Oxford, where he went after Glasgow, gave him a perfect theatre for his protean talents. Hyperactive, abnormally long-legged, he not only, academically and athletically, bestrode the place like a colossus, but, literally, assaulted the rigid, prevailing class barriers. De Quincey, ever eager to mythologise his friend and opposite, saw him as a latter day, pugilistic Robin Hood:

> Never indeed before, to judge from what I have since heard upon inquiry, did a man, by variety of talents and variety of humours, contrive to place himself as the connecting link between orders of men so essentially repulsive of each other, as Mr Wilson in this instance. From the learned president of his college, Dr Routh, the editor of parts of Plato, and of some Theological Selections, with whom Wilson enjoyed an unlimited favour—from this learned Academic Doctor, and many others of the same class, Wilson had an infinite gamut of friends and associates, running through every key, and the diapason closing full in groom, cobbler, stable-boy, barber's apprentice, with every shade of hue of blackguard and ruffian. In particular, amongst this latter kind of worshipful society, there was not many who had any talents—real or fancied—for thumping or being thumped, but had some *preeing* of his merits from Mr Wilson. All other pretensions in the gymnastic arts he took a pride in humbling or in

> honouring; but chiefly his examinations fell upon pugilism; and not a man who could either 'give' or 'take', but boasted to have punished or to have been punished by, *Wilson of Mallens.*[17]

With this hyper-democratic, aggressive athleticism went other usually incompatible talents and tastes:

> These features of his character, however, and these propensities which naturally belonged merely to the transitional state from boyhood to manhood, would have drawn little attention on their own account, had they not been relieved and emphatically contrasted by his passion for literature and fluent command which he showed over a rich and voluptuous poetic diction. In everything Mr Wilson showed himself an Athenian. Athenians were all lovers of the cockpit; and howsoever shocking to the sensibilities of modern refinement, we have no doubt that Plato was a frequent better at cock-fights; and Socrates is known to have bred cocks himself. If he were any Athenian, however, in particular, it was Alcibiades; for he had his marvellous versatility; and to the Windermere neighbourhood, in which he settled, this versatility came recommended by something of the very same position in society—the same wealth, the same social temper, the same jovial hospitality. No person was better fitted to win or to maintain a high place in social esteem; for he could adapt himself to all companies; and the wish to conciliate and to win his way by flattering the self-love and vanity
>
> > 'That he did in the general bosom reign
> > Of young and old.'[18]

Unlike the Greeks, however, Wilson does not seem to have been able to integrate his physical and intellectual drives. De Quincey never seems to have recognised the degree to which Wilson's 'rich and voluptuous poetic diction' was at odds with his aggressive proclivities and sociable impulses.

De Quincey met up with Wilson in the Lake District where Wilson, drawn by Wordsworth, had bought ground in 1805. As Wilson wrote to his friend Robert Findlay in 1805:

> . . . I have bought some ground in Windermere Lake, but whether in future years I may live there I know not. I think that a settled life will never do for me, and I often lament that I did not enter the Army or Navy, a thing which is now entirely impossible. While I keep moving, life goes on well enough, but whenever I pause the fever of the Soul begins and all enjoyment of earthly pleasure is at an end.[19]

Anyone less fit for the sessile, austere life prescribed by Wordsworth is hard to imagine. What he brought to Windermere were his near demonic energies and their accompanying need to create multiple forms of excitation. For example, De Quincey approaching Windermere in dawn light saw, as in a dream, three men with fourteen foot spears pursuing a bull. This was Wilson leading one of his routine nocturnal pursuits. In an age of legendary walkers his feats were gargantuan. He wanted to go to Africa with Mungo Park. He planned expeditions to Timbuctoo and Spain which had to be aborted. He established a sailing club at Windermere and owned a fleet of seven boats, some of them built at enormous expense by regular builders brought over from Whitehaven, besides a ten-oared Oxford barge. Again according to De Quincey, 'he had never less than three establishments going on concurrently for three years; one at the town or village of Bowness (the little port of Windermere), for his boatmen; one at his Ambleside hotel, about five miles distant, for himself; and a third at Elleray, for his servants, and the occasional resort of himself and his friends'.[20]

Nor did such expensive aquatic pursuits in the least dampen his energy or enthusiasm. As Malcolm Elwin has written:

> 'Mr Wilson of Elleray' was soon a local celebrity . . . As a sporting squire, his fame in the lakes endured as a tradition. 'It was a' life an' murth amang us, as lang as Professor Wilson was at Wastd'le Head,' an old innkeeper told Edwin Waugh many years later. He gave belts and prizes to the wrestling dalesmen, and though he never entered the ring himself, he once tackled the champion and succeeded in winning one of three falls. He could beat them all at the long jump or a foot race . . . The dalesmen loved him as a 'fine, gay, girt-hearted fellow, as strong as a lion, an' as lish as a trout', with 'sic antics as nivver man hed'.[21]

Whether he intended or not, his interaction with the highly responsive locals represented a practical refutation of all the pieties of rural life Wordsworth held most dear. He made one recorded attempt to involve Wordsworth in his activities. He invited him to join a fishing party numbering *thirty-two* persons. As Dorothy predicted, Wordsworth early absconded.[22]

In several respects Wilson on Windermere is like a later displaced Oxford man, Jay Gatsby. Extravagant wealth generates myths. Wilson built an innovative 'bungalow' with a seventy-foot room with an extraordinary mechanism of partitions so that he, the finest of amateur dancers, could have a ballroom. Before the floor was laid he covered it in turfs in order to hold cockfights. The house was all on ground level because he could not bear overhead noise. From his Oxford days came rumours of sexual intrigue. He had, it was alleged, lived in a gipsy encampment, because of admiration for a young 'Egyptian' beauty. Like Gatsby, the bubble burst. Whether due to the fraudulent activities of an uncle or his own excesses both Wilson's and his new wife's fortune vanished. Like Gatsby, too, there was a perhaps tragic flaw, which led them both to collude with forces which betrayed what was best in themselves.

Unlike Gatsby, however, Wilson betrayed what was best in others. He perverted Burns's achievement. He manipulated Hogg. He both flattered and insulted Scott. With regard to the English relationships he acquired in the Lake District, he subsequently, in the pages of *Blackwood*'s, made them the basis for quite unscrupulous *ad hominem* attacks. Wordsworth's coldness, Coleridge's addiction, Hazlitt's sexual imbroglios were all eventually made brutally public. By way of his notorious Irish collaborator MacGinn, even the loyal De Quincey's pre-marital activities were exposed. He played Scottish

Salieri to these English Mozarts. It is an unhappily recognisable pattern for a frustrated man of talent to compensate for his painful lack of genius by serving, usually at the sorry expense of his creative betters, an alternative source of authoritarian cultural power.

Some interpretations of Wilson's behaviour see it merely as the workings of a wayward, immature temperament. Scott, on being asked by his son-in-law, Lockhart, to support Wilson's Tory candidature for the Chair in Moral Philosophy saw him as his own worst enemy:

> You are aware that the only point of exception to Wilson may be, that, with the fire of genius, he has possessed some of its eccentricities . . . Recommend to Wilson great temper in his canvass—for wrath will do no good. After all, he must leave off sack, purge and live cleanly as a gentlemen ought to do; otherwise people will compare his present ambition to that of Sir Terry O'Fag when he wished to become a judge. 'Our pleasant follies are made the whips to scourge us', as Lear says; for otherwise what could possibly stand in the way of his nomination? I trust it will take place, and give him the consistency and steadiness which are all he wants to make him the first man of the age.[23]

Scott's politics seem to have blinded him both to the intractable problem of Wilson's personality and his gross unfitness for the post. De Quincey, with far more intimate knowledge, was driven to write that Wilson's character was a 'compound of cruelty and meanness, ambitious and domineering yet ready to crouch to those in powerful positions'.[24] Indeed Wilson's career is the story of the cost to both his talent and his friends on account of the public masters he sought to serve.

Ironically, it is De Quincey, his usually eulogistic supporter, who gives the clearest evidence of the sycophancy and authoritarianism in Wilson's nature. This derived from a trip they had planned to make to Spain which had to be cancelled because of Napoleon's invasion of that country. De Quincey, prone to fantasies of ultimate persecution, believed that execution at French hands would have been an almost acceptable price to pay in order to disabuse Wilson of his worship of Napoleon:

> You will suppose naturally that we rejoiced at our escape; and so undoubtedly we did. Yet for my part, I had, among nineteen-twentieths of joy, just one-twentieth in a lingering regret that we missed the picturesque fate that awaited us. The reason was this: it had been through life an infirmity of Mr Wilson's (at least in my judgement an infirmity) to think too indulgently of Bonaparte, not merely in an intellectual point of view, but even with his pretensions— hollower, one would think, than the wind—to moral elevation and magna-minity. Such a mistake about a man who could never in any one instance bring himself to speak generously, or even forbearingly of an enemy, rouses my indignation as often as I recur to it; and in Professor Wilson I have long satisfied myself it takes rise from a more comprehensive weakness, the greatest in fact which besets his mind, viz. a general tendency to bend to the prevailing opinion of the world, and a constitutional predisposition to sympathise with power and whatsoever is triumphant. Hence, I could not but regret most poignantly the

capital opportunity I had forfeited of throwing in a deep and stinging sarcasm at his idol, when we should have been waiting to be turned off.[25]

Given that Wilson's espousal of Toryism was as extreme as Walter Scott's, his advocacy of Napoleon seems absurd. Despite the anarchic, satirical tendencies in his own nature, it was not Napoleon, the revolutionary, with whom Wilson covertly kept faith. It was, rather, the authoritarian Wilson perceiving an ultimate master.

In another Scotland Wilson might have been a political demagogue. As it was, he had to settle for being a literary one. Such demagoguery inverts the relationship between artist and audience. The demagogue creates a mass response by articulating our darkest aspirations. Wilson's audience and the source of his power was the waxing middle-class, middle-brow audience of which Coleridge, our first literary sociologist, despaired.[26] The first third of the nineteenth-century saw Britain in the grip of a commercial, industrial class. The harsh ideologies of this class combined utilitarianism, mechanisation and fiscal ruthlessness. A by-product of industrialisation, particularly intense in nineteenth-century Scotland, the clergy and *literati* aesthetically disguised social reality under a sanctimonious gloss. As Czeslaw Milosz has written:

> Ethereal pastoral duets were sung at the rectory; the peace of books and flowers by the window protected the island of poetic fantasies from the world. However, close by, in the industrial city, human phantoms reeled and fell to the streets from hunger.[27]

In a world harshly transformed by economic forces Wilson, as 'conservative', provided a spurious legitimacy for these dominant forces. His main device was to present an ahistorical, apolitical image of a nation of pious, peasant communities where 'In some small kirk upon its sunny brae/Scotland lies asleep on the still Sabbath-day.'[28] Scotland, as recent economic and social history increasingly suggests, was arguably the European country most wracked by agrarian upheaval and with the consequent creation of the industrial slum.[29] It was the antithesis of the organic community beloved by conservative propaganda. Wilson usually preferred to remain silent about these new, terrible industrial realities. When he did, (as in the *Noctes*) discuss these new slum dwellers he treated them and their conditions only in terms of condemnatory contrast to their allegedly, rooted, contented rural brethren. He and Thomas Chalmers played variations of the same corrupt theme.[30]

Behind the dark coagulation of life in these new slums there lay an even deeper middle- and upper-class fear, so deep that it was rarely articulated. It was the fear, paranoid in its nature and intensity, of a revolutionary backlash. Only Carlyle was brave enough to voice it, and it is revealing that he could not stay in Edinburgh so to do. Carlyle's thought is almost entirely taken up with the causes and nature of the French Revolution and with what political reorganisation of Britain was necessary to prevent a similar insurrection. Wilson seems, in comparison, a far more literary figure, but almost everything he wrote is in varying degrees marked by an underlying anxiety about revolution. Like Walter Scott, he tended to keep his private fears apart from his public literary productions. Like Scott, too, he used historical analogies to discuss revolution which were simultaneously cautionary and comforting. This account of the dangers of mob unrest, from Wilson's review of Macaulay's *Lays of Ancient Rome*, is not, however, difficult to decode:

> No such mob-orator and poet, in our days, have our Tribunes of the People. Such spokesmen might do the state some mischief—haply some service. Thank Heaven, the history of our party feuds can show no comparable crime; yet there is not want of fuel in the annals of the poor, if there were fire to set it ablaze. What mean we by the mob? The rabble? No! no! The swinish multitude? No! no! no! Burke never in all his days called the lower orders of Parisians, at any period of the Revolution, '*the* swinish multitude.' His words are '*that* swinish multitude'—at one particular hour, a multitude of wild, two-legged animals, dancing, all drunk with blood, round a pole surmounted with the bright-haired head of a princess, who had all her life been a sister of charity for the poor. Mob is *mobile*. It matters not how much it is composed, provided it be only of the common run of men and women, and that they have, or think they have, wrongs to be redressed or avenged.[31]

Protesting too much, Wilson betrays the chronic, underlying anxiety of the new exploitative wealth. Implicit in his exclamatory denials is the possibility of the Roman mob being analogous to not only eighteenth-century France but early nineteenth-century Britain. Coleridge, attempting to define a conservatism of organic integrity, saw clearly that the sort of conservatism inspired by Burke was in lesser hands a wilful misinterpretation of the French situation in order to exploit and dominate the domestic situation. Writing in 1809 he defined the political current in which Wilson would increasingly immerse himself:

> But alas! the panic of property had been struck in the first instance for party purposes; and when it became general, its propagators caught it themselves and ended in believing their own lie; even as our bulls in Borrowdale sometimes run made with the echo of their own bellowing. The consequences were most injurious. Our attention was the convulsions in which it had been brought forth: even the enlightened Burke himself too often talking and reasoning as if a perpetual and organised anarchy had been a possible thing! Thus while we were warring against French doctrines, we took little heed whether the means by which we attempted to overthrow them were not likely to augment the far more formidable evil of French ambition. Like children, we ran away from the yelping of a cur, and took shelter at the heels of a vicious war-horse.[32]

The development of Wilson after 1816 as reviewer and public prosecutor of English Romantic poetry on behalf of his snobbish, semi-literate readership was preceded by a period of several years when he tried to establish himself as a poetic member of the Lake School. Not having been able to join them, he subsequently seems to have decided to beat them. He wrote a mass of poetry throughout his life. The best of it struggles toward mediocrity. It is interesting only in so far as he initiates certain themes which were to become kailyard stereotypes. Wilson can fairly claim to be the founding father of that sorry school. He also published two long poems. His most famous, *The Isle of Palms*, appeared in 1811. This was followed in 1816 by *The City of the Plague*.

Wilson had revealingly high expectations of *Isle of Palms*. Immediately prior to its appearance in Edinburgh he reported that:

> Walter Scott talks to me in great terms of what he has seen of the *Isle*. The elder Ballantyne is in raptures, and prophesies great popularity. Considerable expectations are formed here among the blues of both sexes and I am whirled into the vortex of fashion here in consequence . . . I think we shall attract some attention.[33]

Neither sales nor recognition lived up to Wilson's over-heated expectations. It did give him, however, a not insignificant reputation. It is now hard to see why. Wilson's method of composition was akin to painting by numbers; he wrote out a prose version of his poems and then 'translated' them into verse. There is also a plundering of English Romantic poetry which could be described at best as unconscious plagiarism. He was most often compared to Wordsworth; but in the *Isle of Palms* much stronger influences are Southey's exotic tales and Coleridge:

> But list! a low and moaning sound
> At distance heard, like a spirit's song,
> And now it reigns above, around,
> As if it called the Ship along.
> The Moon is sunk; and a clouded grey
> Declares that her course is run,
> And like a God who brings the day,
> Up mounts the glorious Sun.
> Soon as his light has warmed the seas,
> From the parting cloud fresh blows the Breeze;
> And that is the spirit whose well-known song
> Makes the vessel to sail in joy along.[34]

For the intertextually inclined, Wilson offers an embarrassment of riches. What is much more interesting, however, is the insight he offers us into incipient nineteenth-century middle-brow culture. What is obvious about *The Isle of Palms* is that its plot and the morality derived from that plot are seemingly incompatible. The story, a nineteenth-century ancestor of *The Blue Lagoon*, is about an engaged couple who are ship-wrecked on a tropical island on the Indian Ocean. They spend several years before being rescued and returned to Wales, where the girl's mother has stood looking lachrymosely seaward during the period of her daughter's absence. Wilson employed certain romantic themes, especially that of natural sexuality; but, having first titillated, he then imposes on his fantasy the strictest familial rectitude. As Elsie Swann has remarked:

Though profoundly influenced by pre-revolutionary thought, Wilson never allowed himself to be led away from the paths described by virtue and religion. The worship of liberty and the state of nature, led to such questionable results in Byron and Shelley, left him unharmed and impeccable—though it is true that rigid formalists have been found to object to the 'natural marriage' of the lovers in the poem (though celebrated on a Sabbath), and to deplore the absence of a clergyman on the island.[35]

For the modern reader such writing can provoke only irony. In his dilution of the linguistic rigour and the moral complexities of high Romantic poetry Wilson, to the satisfaction of his genteel audience, squared the circle between the demands of personal freedom and social convention. What he and subsequent now forgotten Scottish best-sellers like William Black were doing was to process the fissile stuff of repressed sexuality not only into escapist fantasy but also into endorsement of the church inspired domestic *status quo*.[36]

One major critic who celebrated *The Isles of Palms* was Jeffrey. As with the later *The City of the Plague* he was perhaps less enthused by Wilson's poetry for its own sake than for those not infrequent occasions when it provided him with a stick with which to beat Wordsworth. From Poe's creative point of view Jeffrey's favourable judgement seemed ludicrous. Writing in 1845, he defined Wilson as a poet making much impression 'upon the secondary or tertiary grades of the poetic comprehension. His *Isle of Palms* appeals effectively, to all those poetic intellects in which the poetic predominates greatly over the intellectual element.'[37] Crabb Robinson had been more acerbic:

> A Female Wordsworth is the designation of this author. A plentiful lack of thought, with great delicacy, and even elegance of taste, but with no riches with it, though the poetry is pretty. It is a libel on the great Philosophical Poet of the lakes to consider Wilson as his superior. This is one of the most scandalous insults upon Wordsworth by the Edinburgh reviewers.[38]

The City of the Plague is even more indigestible than the *Isle of Palms*. Taking as its historical occasion the Great Plague of London, it converts history into pure melodrama with imminent death provoking drunken and sexual licence; but a rural, virginal beauty loses neither her charity nor her maindenhead in this urban crisis and goes with her lover to a sentimental, pietistic death bed. Once again, potentially gross excitation, is conveniently packaged into cant. Jeffrey, however, saw this contradiction as neither manifest nor latent:

> There is something extremely amiable, at all events, in the character of Mr Wilson's genius:—a constant glow of kind and pure affection—a great sensibility to the charms of external nature, and the delights of a private, innocent and contemplative life—a fancy richly stored with images of natural beauty and simple enjoyments—great tenderness and pathos in the representation of sufferings and sorrow, though almost always calmed, and even brightened, by the healing influences of pitying love, confiding piety, and conscious innocence.

> Almost the only passions with which his poetry is conversant, are the gentler sympathies of our nature—tender compassion—confiding affection, and guilt-less sorrow.[39]

As we shall see, the literary treatment of suffering has in Wilson a cardinal metaphysical and political importance. For Jeffrey, however, the supreme virtue of poetry was in its capacity to engender quietistic pleasure. It was a literary form definably above the prose world's battles:

> We have often thought it unnatural to say, or to think, anything harsh of the innocent and irritable race of poets. Most other writers are apt, in a thousand ways, to excite our spleen, and mortify our vanity,—by pretending to instruct our ignorance, to refute our errors, or to expose our prejudices. They offend us, in short, by assuming notions, or at least showing us how much we still have to learn. The poet alone has none of this polemic and offensive spirit. His sole business is to give pleasure, and to gain praise from all descriptions of men. He contradicts nobody, and refutes nothing; but puts himself to a great deal of trouble for the sole purpose of raising delightful emotions in the breasts of the readers;—and asks no other reward than inward gratitude and approbation which, in such circumstances, it must be still more blessed to give than receive.[40]

This desire for poetry for poetry's sake, its reduction to harmonious vacuity, was the product of a war Jeffrey had waged with Wordsworth for over a decade. Wilson's talent was lauded because of the absence of Wordsworthian vices:

> Another and more intolerable fault, as more frequently attaching to superior talents, is that perversity or affectation which leads an author to distort or disfigure his compositions, either by a silly ambition of singularity, an unfortunate attempt to combine qualities that are truly irreconcilable, or an absurd predilection for some fantastic style or manner, in which no one but himself can perceive any fitness or beauty. In such cases, we are not merely offended by positive deformities which are thus produced, but by the feeling they are produced wilfully and with much effort, and by the humiliating spectacle they afford of the existence of paltry prejudices and despicable vanities in minds which we naturally love to consider as the dwelling place of noble sentiments and enchanting contemplations. Akin to this source of displeasure, but a more aggravated description, is that which arises from the visible indication of any great moral defect in those highly gifted spirits, whose natural office it seems to be, to purify and exalt the conceptions of ordinary men, by images more lofty and refined than can be suggested by the coarse realities of existence.[41]

This is such an inversion of what we now discern in Wordsworth as to border on absurdity. Worse confusion, however, was to follow. Complimenting Wilson on 'The Scholar's Funeral', where a consumptive Oxford death rehearsed many later images of blood-flecked phlegm behind native, bonny briar bushes, Jeffrey distinguished Wilson from and warned him against his ertswhile English associates:

We take our leave of it with an unfeigned regret, and very sincere admiration of the author's talents. He has undoubtedly both the heart and the fancy of a poet; and, with these great requisites, is almost sure of attaining the higher honours of his art, if he continues to cultivate it with the docility and diligence of which he has already given proof. Though his style is still too diffuse, and his range too limited, the present volume is greatly less objectionable on these grounds than the former. It has also less of the peculiarities of the Lake School; and, in particular, is honourably distinguished from the production of its founders, by being quite free from the paltry spite and fanatical reprobation with which, like other fierce and narrow minded sectaries, they think it necessary to abuse all whose tastes or opinions are not exactly conformable to their own. There is no shadow of this ludicrous insolence in the work before us; in consequence of which, we think it extremely likely, that he will be execrated and reviled, on the first good opportunity, by his late kind masters.[42]

Wilson, obviously perceiving the attention and authority Jeffrey had achieved as editor of *The Edinburgh Review* and seeking to write for it, payed court to Jeffrey on his return to Edinburgh. The most obvious act of homage was to throw his energies into Jeffrey's war against Wordsworth.[43] The immediate occasion for so doing was caused by the appearance in 1816 of Wordsworth's *Letter to a friend of Burns*, in which Wordsworth broke years of silent endurance of Jeffrey's critical assaults. Wordsworth not only attacked Jeffrey's critical acumen but related it to the dire lack of standards prevailing in genteel Edinburgh since the time of Smith and Hume. This provoked in (Blackwood's) *Edinburgh Monthly Magazine* (1817) a letter in Jeffrey's defence 'by a Friend of Robert Burns'. The friend was Wilson. There is some truth to his claim that Wordsworth was far more concerned with his own reputation than that of the dead Scottish poet. Wilson's tone, however, was extraordinary both in itself and due to the fact that it was to be the prevailing accent of *Blackwood's* for the next two decades:

> Wordsworth, in defending Burns, with the voice and countenance of a maniac, fixes his teeth in the blue cover of the Edinburgh. He growls over it—shakes it violently to and fro—and at last, wearied out with vain efforts at mastication, leaves it covered with the drivelling slaver of his impotent rage.
>   . . . Mr Wordsworth's friends should not allow him to expose himself in this way. He has unquestionably written some fine verses in his day; but with the exception of some poetical genius, he is, in all respects, immeasurably inferior, as an intellectual being, to the distinguished person whom he so foolishly libels.[44]

Whether such gross flattery failed to secure Wilson a position with Jeffrey or whether the *Blackwood's* opportunity intervened is not known. Wilson did not write for the Whig journal but carried his colours to its allegedly opposite Tory rival. There, his Wordsworthian responses became even more bizarre. In the first two years of the new magazine's life he pursued a violently pro and anti-Wordsworthian policy. Under the smoke-screen of the multiple aliases created by himself, Lockhart and Maginn, an extraordinary freedom was possible. Libels, challenges to duels and, on one occasion, death so caused, became a constant result of these malicious disguises. Wilson's critical responses often seemed to consist in sycophantically licking his victim before putting his teeth and claws into him. His treatment of Wordsworth was to model so much of his subsequent behaviour:

> He has brought about a *revolution* in Poetry; and a revolution can no more be brought about in Poetry than the Constitution, without the destruction or injury of many excellent and time-hallowed establishments. I have no doubt that, when all the rubbish is removed, and free and open space given to behold the structures which Mr Wordsworth has reared in all the grandeur of their proportions, that Posterity will see him as a regenerator and a creator.
> . . . Wordsworth is a poet distinguished for the originality of his genius,—for his profound knowledge of the human heart,—for his spiritual insight into all the grandeur and magnificence of the external world,—for the strain of the most serene, undisturbed, and lofty morality, within whose control no mind can come without being elevated, purified and enlightened,—for a Religion partaking at once of all the solemnity of faith, and all the enthusiasms of poetry . . .[45]

However much the older Wordsworth betrayed his radical, creative poetry by becoming a sentimental moralist in the service of the establishment, Wilson's whole policy was to deny that any reverence should be done to the earlier insurrectionary poetics. Poets who broke with Tory party politics were diseased public menaces with no reverence for tradition. The absurdity of Wilson's position is seen when, in the same year, he launched a furious attack on Coleridge who was already displaying himself as the seminal mind of nineteenth-century conservatism.

> We have not been speaking in the cause of Literature only, but, we conceive, in the cause of Morality and Religion. For it is not fitting that he should be held up as an example to the rising generation (but, on the contrary, it is most fitting that he should be exposed as a most dangerous model), who has alternately embraced, defended, and thrown aside all systems of Philosophy, and all creeds of Religion; who seem to have no power in retaining an opinion—no trust in the principles which he defends—but who fluctuates from theory to theory, according as he is impelled by vanity, envy, or diseased desire of change and who, while he would subvert and scatter into dust those structures of knowledge, reared by the wise men of this and other generations, has nothing to erect in their room but the baseless and air-built fabrics of a dreaming imagination.[46]

Unlike his virulent retaliation against the Whig *Edinburgh Review*'s assaults on himself and Wordsworth, Coleridge's fidelity to the conservative cause kept him not only silent under these attacks but, indeed, towards the end of his life to praise *Blackwood*'s as a vessel of traditional truth.[47] This is deeply unfortunate since Coleridge's analysis of Jeffrey and his circle is arguably even more applicable to Wilson and his. Despite the apparent opposition of party politics, *Blackwood*'s was, in fact, the continuance of the *Edinburgh* by even more extreme means. While titillating their middle-brow, middle-class audience, it emasculated the disruptive, progressive tendencies of the creative imagination. Critical extremism was no vice in pursuit of social rigidity. What John Gross has written of Jeffrey can be seen exaggerated to the point of caricature in Wilson:

> A well-drilled child of the Scottish Enlightenment, a debater trained to argue back to first principles, he was admirably equipped to play the schoolmaster to an audience looking for sound views and predigested information.
>   . . . Undoubtedly the chief use he made of his prestige was to uphold the conventional, the anaemic, the decorously second-rate, while trying to crush potential enthusiasm for Wordsworth and Coleridge. It could hardly have been otherwise. His whole success as an editor depended not only on his skill but on the positive zeal which he brought to his role of spokesman for the approved view of things, the polite consensus. He saw himself as public watch-dog sniffing out heretics, an official observer (his own phrase) representing traditional values which—or so he announced in the first number of the *Edinburgh*—it was 'no longer lawful to question'.[48]

By the time Wilson came to write his 'Apologia' for *Blackwood*'s in 1826 the role of the Edinburgh establishment as bulwark of church and burgeoning imperial state was polemically overt:

> As for our literary articles, knowing by whom they are written, and by what men they are valued, we leave them freely to be criticised by any petty *littérateur* that pleases. In our politics, we have been Tory through thick and thin, through good report and evil report; or as Mr Montgomery well expressed it, come wind, come sun; come fire, come flood. Honouring and venerating the churches established under divine Providence in these islands, we have to the utmost of our power supported their interests—not from any idle or obstinate bigotry, but because we conscientiously look upon them as the main stay of the constitution of England, as the bulwarks of the Protestant faith, as tending in the highest degree to promote Christianity, i.e. virtue and happiness. Finally, believing that a kingly government, checked and balanced by a proud aristocracy, and a due mixture of a popular representation, is the only one fit for these kingdoms (we meddle not with what may be fit under other circumstances in other lands or ages) we have always inculcated the maxim of honouring the King, and all put in authority under him, with the honours they deserve. *Their* enemies, Whig, Jacobin, Radical, Deist, Demagogue, or whatever other title they take, are *our* enemies, and with them we have no truce. Caring little for the newfangled and weathercock doctrines every day broached around us, and knowing, by long experience, that we have thriven under the old notions, we hold to them with a tenacity, which to some may appear obstinate, but which, as yet, we have seen no reason to repent. Intimately convinced that this country is a great instrument in the hands of God, we hope that it will not be turned to evil, and to the utmost of our ability shall resist all machinations for that purpose. And loving that country with a more than filial love, attached to all its interests, rejoicing in its prosperity, grieved to the soul in its adversity, delighted to see it victorious in war, still more delighted to see it tranquil at home, and honoured abroad during peace, we shall never cease to advocate the cause of those whose excursions we firmly believe have promoted, and will

promote, its happiness or its glory. Of the effect of our work in diffusing a healthy and manly tone throughout the empire, and of creating a proper spirit of courage and patriotism, it would be vanity to speak. It has had its effect and we are satisfied.[49]

If such as Coleridge were found lacking in terms of such stridently dogmatic loyalty, we should not wonder at the savagery of the assaults on the English radicals. Leigh Hunt and Hazlitt were the chief targets. They were also seen as the corrupters of Keats. In 1928 Wilson reviewed Keat's tragically short career with neither regret nor guilt for his and Lockhart's savage critical participation in it:

> Keats possessed from nature some 'fine powers', and that was the very expression we used in the first critique that ever mentioned his name. We saw, however, with mixed feelings of pity, sorrow, indignation, and contempt that he was on the road to ruin. He was a Cockney, and Cockneys claimed him for their own. Never was there a young man so encrusted with conceit. He added no new treasures to his mother-tongue—and what is worse, he outhunted Hunt in a species of emasculated pruriency, that, although invented in Little Britain, looks as if it were the product of some imaginative Eunuch's muse within the melancholy inspiration of the Harem. Besides, we know that the godless gang were flattering him into bad citizenship, and wheedling him out of his Christian faith. In truth, they themselves broke the boy's heart and blasted all his prospects. We tried to save him by wholesome severe discipline—they drove him to poverty, expatriation, and death.[50]

Radicalism, promiscuity and atheism formed an unholy triangle in Wilson's brain. No discipline could be severe enough in dealing with such sins. As John Gross has pointed out, for Wilson and Lockhart the 'Cockneys' were seen as new suburban men to be sneered at. Virginia Woolf, discussing Lockhart, thought that there were no snobs like the prosperous Anglo-Scottish.[51] Along with this, it may have been that Wilson was so sneeringly dismissive of the new London values because he wished to see Edinburgh the British literary capital.

Hazlitt, agonised by the blighting of his radical aspirations, saw in the Toryism of his day the activity of the mindless, merciless political victors of the early decades of the nineteenth century. For Hazlitt Scottish Toryism's alleged espousal of traditional values was a kind of ultimate bad faith since he believed that since the fall of the House of Stuart Scotsmen had been in a state of intense, exploitative self-interest. They were the mercenaries, bureaucrats, ideologues *par excellence* of an imperialism Hazlitt saw creating havoc abroad and repression at home. In varying degrees all the English Romantics, while devoted to Burns, shared Hazlitt's antipathy to the Scottish functional, respectable professional classes. Hazlitt perceived in them an innate authoritarianism:

> A Scotchman is generally a dealer in staple-propositions, and not in rarities and curiosities of the understanding. He does not like an idea the worse for its

coming to him from a reputable well-authenticated source, as I conceive he might feel more respect for a son of Burns than for Burns himself, on the same hereditary or genealogical principle. He swears (of course) by the Edinburgh Review, and thinks Blackwood not easily put down. He takes the word of a Professor in the University-chair in a point of philosophy as he formerly took the Laird's word in a matter of life and death; and has the names of the Says, the Benthams, the Mills, the Malthuses, in his mouth, instead of the Montroses, the Gordons, and the Macullamores.[52]

As well as its primitive roots and distorted political development, Hazlitt, a brilliantly sceptical product of the secular Enlightenment, saw clerical control of Scotland having created a fearful, repressed, dualistic, hypocritical state of mind. On the basis, however, that to every action there is an equal and opposite reaction, he deduced that a Scotsman escaping from his presbyterian chains of imposed morality would be a peculiarly monstrous phenomenon. Given the polemical, litigious battles that ranged between himself and *Blackwood*'s, it is hardly to be wondered at that he saw this group as the quintessence of all he loathed.[53]

They have been so long under interdict that they break out with double violence, and stop at nothing. Of all *blackguards* (I use the term for want of any other) a Scotsh blackguard is for this reason the worst. First, the character sits ill upon him for want of use, and is sure to be most outrageously caricatured. He is only just broke loose from the shackles of regularity and restraint, and is forced to play strange antics to be convinced that they are not still clinging to his heels. Secondly, formality, hypocrisy, and a deference to opinion, are the 'sins that most easily beset him.' When therefore he has once made up his mind to disregard appearances, he becomes totally reckless of character, and 'at one bound high overleaps all bounds' of decency and common sense. Again, there is perhaps a natural hardness and want of nervous sensibility about the Scotch, which renders them (rules and the consideration of consequences apart) not very nice or scrupulous in their proceedings. If they are not withheld by conscience or prudence, they have no *mauvaise honte*, no involuntary qualms or tremors, to qualify their effrontery and disregard of principle. Their impudence is extreme, their malice is cold-blooded, covert, crawling, deliberate, without the frailty or excuse of passion. They club their vices and their venality together, and by the help of both together are invincible. The choice spirits who have lately figured in a much-talked-of publication, with 'old Sylvanus at their head,'—
> 'Leaning on cypress stadle stout,'—
in their 'pious orgies' resemble a troop of Yahoos, or a herd of Satyrs—
> 'And with their horned feet they beat the ground!'—
that is to say, the floor of Mr Blackwood's shop![54]

For Hazlitt, then, the Scots with their duplicity and false eloquence were the chief propagandists for an alleged conservative order. At a time when Hazlitt felt that the people were being treated with an unprecedented rapacious hardness, Wilson and his ilk promulgated images of pastoral content caused by self-restraint and a proper respect for one's betters. The British state for

Wilson was not only hierarchical but organic. Unlike Burns, he did not wish The Tree of Liberty planted but put his trust on a native, ancient species. Thus he addresses Hogg in a *Noctes* episode:

> For we, James, the prime of the people of England, and Scotland, and Ireland— that is, of the Earth—*are Heretics*—that is we love the Tree of Freedom that is planted on earth, because it is a scion from the Tree of Life that grows in heaven 'fast by the Throne of God.' For centuries now have we flourished beneath its shade and been refreshed with its fruitage.[55]

The imagery and the concept of a transcendental sanction for traditional institutions is, of course, deeply Burkean. Admiring allusions to Burke's thought, eloquence, imagination are scattered through Wilson's writings: 'he had a soul that could rise up from languishment on Beauty's lap and aspire to the brows of the sublime.'[56] One could, indeed, almost define Wilson as a decadent Scottish mutation of the Irish genius where, genuine prudence quite vanished, criticism and creativity are put wholly at the service of ideology. To be fair to Wilson one can, however, also find in Burke a prescription for precisely the sort of social vision that Wilson promulgated. Thus Burke wrote:

> Good order is the foundation of all good things. To be enabled to acquire, the people, without being servile, must be tractable and obedient. The body of the people must not find the principles of natural subordination by art rooted out of their minds. They must respect that property of which they cannot partake. They must labour to obtain what by labour can be obtained; and when they find, as they commonly do, the success disproportioned to the endeavour, they must be taught their consolation in the final proportions of eternal justice. Of this consolation, whoever deprives them, deadens their industry, and strikes at the root of all acquisition as of all conservation. He that does this is the cruel oppressor, the merciless enemy of the poor and wretched; at the same time that by his wicked speculations he exposes the fruits of successful industry, and the accumulations of fortune, to the plunder of the negligent, the disappointed, and the unprosperous.[57]

Burke, seeing sinister manipulation solely in radical politics, placed faith in a spiritual underpinning of society. Christianity was the complete antidote to poverty and injustice. In Wilson, the Enlightenment's attempted secular impartiality wholly discarded, we find a regressive return to an older theocratic Scotland. Thinly disguised in fictional form, we hear slightly recast the old fear, discipline, and guilt inducing sermons. Wilson is in fact a creator of melodrama which is the true aesthetic form of the ideologue. Poetry was at the exclusive service of illusory consolation:

> We desire—not in wilful delusion, but in earnest hope, in devout trust—that poetry shall show that the paths of the peasant poor are paths of pleasantness and peace. If they should seem in that light even pleasanter and more peaceful than they even can be below the sun, think not that any evil can rise 'to mortal man who liveth here by toil' from such representations—for imagination and reality are not two different things—they blend in life; but there the darker

shadows do often, alas! prevail—and sometimes may be felt even by the hand; whereas in poetry the lights are triumphant—and gazing on the glory men's hearts burn within them—and they carry the joy in among their own griefs, till despondency gives way to exultation, and the day's darg of this worky world is lightened by a dawn of dreams.[58]

Wilson's most noted fictional achievement was *The Trials of Margaret Lyndsay*, the whole purpose of which is to demonstrate the spiritually submissive yet finally worldly successful soul. Walter and Alice marry in the shadow of their respective paternal deathbeds; the first of a series of death bed scenes which not only reflect the inherent morbidity of the popular fiction of the time but are the essential occasions for intensified guilt and hence repentance from sexual and radical sins. They have four children, a son and three daughters. As well as the demure, beautiful Margaret they have, icons of meek submission to the ways of God, a blind and an idiot daughter. Through song and psychic intuition these defective girls achieve compensation for their condition; they also die off conveniently early in the plot. Social conservatism is obsessed with the close-knit family group and, hence, this pastoral Eden is entered by a radical serpent. With no explanation, Walter Lyndsay goes over to the enemy. Walter becomes simultaneously adulterer and radical:

Perhaps there is a diseased pleasure in the troubled emotion of guilt that keeps the falling spirit so closely attached to it that it loses the power of a pure and reasonable happiness, and then adheres sullenly or fiercely to the error of its ways, although it knows they lead to infamy and death. It may have been so with this infatuated man. He loved his wife and his children, if not as he once loved them, yet better than all other objects on this earth. He could not lose the memory of so many smiles, tears, joys, griefs, tender words, and warm sighs of blameless delight, for so many long years. He remembered them all too, too well, when foolishly and wickedly absenting himself from Braehead. Yet still their power to recall him from destruction was dead and gone. It was gone never to return, till at the approach of that awful hour, when all the old sacred emotions of the soul, which guilt may have driven away from her sanctuary, will once more, and for the last time, appear, either to confound or to console, and when all low, foul, and earthly thoughts will moulder away into the damp and darkness of the grave.

Walter Lyndsay was not only a reformer in religion, but also in politics, and he had for some time been one of the Friends of the People. It was now a dark day over all Europe. Anarchy had taken the place of despotism, and Atheism trampled down superstition. The same thick and sullen atmosphere which preceded that dire earthquake in France, was spreading over this country. The poor caught the moral contagion; and there were thousands and tens of thousands that, in the sudden blindness of that frenzy, began to mock at Christianity and its blessed symbol—the Cross. Paine, a name doomed to everlasting infamy, undertook to extinguish the religion in the hearts and on the hearths of the poor; and the writings of the ignorant blasphemer were now read at Scottish ingles instead of the Big ha' Bible, ance their father's pride. Walter Lyndsay brought to Braehead a copy of the *Age of Reason*.[59]

Leaving aside for the moment this alleged antipathy between Burns and Paine, this exploitative use of guilt with death as its ultimate sanction permeates Wilson's fiction. The father's adultery leads inevitably to excruciating death bed scenes of remorse for both himself and his mistress. The family have to leave their pastoral cottage and take themselves to Edinburgh. This activates another recurrent theme in Wilson's work. He saw the growing urban Scotland as a cesspool of sin and was quite unwilling to see its inhabitants as victims of brutal economic pressures.

Unrealistically, however, certain social opportunities occur for Margaret. Having survived the sexual importunities of one of her father's radical associates, she falls in love with Harry Needham, an English sailor, who comes home on leave with her brother Laurence. Tempting fate they go to the theatre to see Home's *Douglas*. God and good taste will not, however, be so mocked. Again breaking strict morality this time by taking a Sunday sail, their boat capsises and Harry is drowned. Margaret's mother painfully dies while giving a stout negative to the question of 'shall I lift up my voice from the clay against my maker?'

Conveniently, Margaret is taken up by the middle-class Wedderburne sisters. The story then becomes a sort of moral and psychological inverted prelude to *Jane Eyre*. Inevitably, there is a Richard Wedderburne who falls desperately in love with Margaret. She realises that social class will never allow their heads 'to lie on the same pillow'. She flees to her mother's brother with enough education to start a small school and more than enough charm to make the old man very happy. Further suitors descend. Two attract her. One, Michael Graham, is a gentle consumptive; he is the missing link between Henry MacKenzie's heroes and those of the kailyard. She falls passionately in love with his opposite, the minister's prodigal son, Ludovic Oswald, recently returned from the army. They marry but, alas, it is a bigamous match. Hannah Blantyre and Ludovic's son return to the scene. Ludovic flees. Hannah clamorously dies. Ludovic, his health broken, returns to die. Richard Wedderburne and his sisters reappear. Ludovic recovers to 'live many years although never to enjoy strong health.' Despite her husband's lack of physical prowess we are finally told that 'God had not forgotten the orphan.'

Wilson, Elsie Swann tells us, 'aspired to the character of a prose Wordsworth, but had none of the noble plainness of his original. The work is stamped as an imitation, and artificiality, sentimentality, self-consciousness, and prettiness combine to mar the style'.[60] Wordsworth was even more acerbic in writing to Crabb Robinson of Wilson:

> He is a perverse mortal, not to say worse of him. Have you ever peeped into his *Trials of Margaret Lyndsay*? You will see there to what an extent he has played the plagiarist with the very tale of Margaret in *The Excursion* which he abuses; and you will also, with a glance, learn what passes with him for poetical Christianity. More mawkish stuff I never encountered.[61]

If *Trials* is mawkish it also contains a more covert vice. It is Wilson, not Keats, who is guilty of 'emasculated pruriency'. When, in an exchange of letters, Alexander Blair, the Birmingham intellectual (who actually supplied Wilson's university lectures with any philosophical coherence they had) accused Wilson's fiction as being voluptuous, Wilson's over-reaction was highly revealing:

> When I consider too, that the Volume I was inclined to think well of in some respects contains in your judgement passages of a voluptuous character which would have been unbecoming in any man, and are especially so in a man holding my station, I feel bitterly how my character breaks out unawares and pollutes and degrades my better aspirations, for till you told me of this, I believed that Tale to be a picture of purity and innocence. Oh! Lord! how years alter the nature of a man's soul! Would that I had ceased to be before I left Glasgow long ago, and now you would have thought of me as a boy of promise—now alas! grown into a man incapable of anything good.[62]

Ever self-dramatising, Wilson's self remorse is hard to credit. Carlyle, knowing him slightly in his last years, did, however, intuit in Wilson a vacuity and a consciousness of self-betrayal.[63]

In Wilson's life we can see self-betrayal and multiple betrayals of others. It is also possible to see him as a central figure in the betrayal of national literature and life. Tom Nairn in *The Break up of Britain* has written brilliantly on the troubling paradox of the fact that in the age of European romantic nationalism Scotland aspired to union.

> The new romantic *consciousness* of the past was in itself, irresistible. As a matter of fact, from Ossian to Sir Walter himself, Scotland played a large part in generating and diffusing it for the rest of Europe. What mattered in Scotland itself, however, was to render this awareness *politically* null—to make certain that it would not be felt that contemporary Scotland should be the independent continuation of the auld song. The whole emotional point of national*ism* was to feel just that: our future development must spring out of this, *our* inheritance from past generations, with its special values etc. Hence, what the new British-Scots middle class had to do was separate the inevitable new popular-national consciousness from action. One might say, very approximately: separate its heart from its head.[64]

Wilson was the clay-footed prophet of the British-Scots middle-class. He created a flatulent rhetoric of national feeling as an antidote to either true national consciousness or will. He exploited nationalism and religion in order to pursue class politics. He is the perfect example of Gramsci's analysis of the bourgeois intellectual. He betrayed his English Romantic acquaintances because their work, in both radical and conservative terms, was not only a critical dissent against the greedy, entrepreneurial middle-class but was committed to authentic nationalism.

Perhaps his greatest single achievement in this career of duplicity was his perversion of Burns's achievement. In one of his last major public appearances Wilson was principal speaker at a Burns Festival in 1844. Eighty thousand appeared and two thousand sat down in a marquee to lunch. Here Burns was put forward by Wilson not only as a placid, God-fearing peasant but upholder of British militarism and imperialism.[65] It is arguable that Wilson was significantly responsible for setting back Scottish literature by almost a century since he bears so much of the burden for inverting the discontented, radical, nationalist genius into the totem of a sentimental cult which worshipped almost everything Burns loathed. Seeing Wilson plain is part of demolishing that cult, recovering Burns and awakening Scotland from its condition of troubled, exploited torpor.

NOTES

1   Cited by Elsie Swann, *Christopher North* (Edinburgh, 1934), p 216.
2   Cited by Malcolm Elwin, *Victorian Wallflowers* (London, 1934), p 25.
3   *The Academy*, 22 July 1876, p 76.
4   Ibid.
5   *Memorials of his Own Time* (Edinburgh, 1945), pp 190–2.
6   *The Rise and Fall of the Man of Letters* (London, 1969), p 10.
7   *Scottish Eccentrics* (London, 1936), pp 99–100.
8   Cited by his daughter, Mrs Gordon, *Christopher North: A Memoir of John Wilson* (Edinburgh, 1879), pp 40–1.
9   *Scottish Eccentrics*, pp 103–4.
10   Whole letter cited by Mrs Gordon, pp 28–34.
11   *See* Andrew Noble, 'Versions of Scottish Pastoral: the Literati and the Tradition 1780–1830' in *Order in Space and Society: Architectural Form and its Context in the Scottish Enlightenment*, Markus (ed) (Edinburgh, 1982) pp 236–304.
12   Mrs Gordon, pp 31–3.
13   'A Letter to a Friend of Robert Burns', *William Wordsworth—Selected Prose*, J O Hayden (ed) (London, 1988), pp 414–30.
14   'Letter to John Wilson', *William Wordsworth—Selected Prose*, pp 311–12.
15   'Began Wilson's *Isle of Palms*. From the first canto, I believe, an *attenuation* of Wordsworth's poetry.' The three volumes of *Henry Crabb Robinson on Books and their Writers* Edith J Morley (ed) (London, 1938) is an unsurpassed source on the Wordsworth/Wilson controversy.
16   'Professor Wilson—Sketch in 1829', *De Quincey's Works*, Masson (ed) (London, 1897), vol V, p 260. For the fullest available account of the Wilson/De Quincey relationship see Grevel Lindop, *The Opium Eater: A Life of Thomas De Quincey* (Oxford, 1985).
17   Ibid., pp 274–5.
18   *Literary and Lake Reminiscences, De Quincey's Works*, vol II, pp 433–4.
19   Cited by Swann, pp 31–2.
20   'Professor Wilson—Sketch in 1829', pp 280–1.
21   *Victorian Wallflowers*, p 31.
22   For this and other of Dorothy Wordsworth's perceptive comments see Swann.
23   H J C Grierson, *Letters of Sir Walter Scott*, Vol. VI, p 162.
24   *The Opium Eater*, p 254.
25   'Professor Wilson—Sketch in 1829', pp 284–5.
26   See my 'Coleridge, Scottish "National" Literature and Walter Scott' in *Strathclyde Modern Language Studies*, Vol. V, pp 3–20 for an account of the Scottish dimension of this phenomenon.

27 *Visions from San Francisco Bay* (London, 1982), p 54.
28 J G Lockhart, 'Some Observations on the Poetry of the Agricultural and that of the Pastoral Districts of Scotland, illustrated by a comparative view of the Genius of Burns and the Ettrick Shepherd', *Blackwood's Magazine*, Vol. VI, February 1819, p 522.
29 See T C Smout *A Century of the Scottish People 1830–1950* (Glasgow, 1986) and *People and Society in Scotland*, vol I, 1760–1830, ed T M Devine and Rosalind Mitchison (Edinburgh, 1988).
30 Until the appearance of Donald C Smith's *Passive Obedience and Prophetic Protest* (New York, 1987) Chalmers and this whole strain of clerical pastoralism seems to have been far too sympathetically treated.
31 *The Works of Professor Wilson*, ed Professor Ferrier, Vol. VII, p 416.
32 *Biographia Literaria*, ed George Watson (London, 1976), p 120.
33 Mrs Gordon, p 171.
34 *Poems, Works*, Vol. XII, p 14.
35 Swann, p 48.
36 'Best Sellers of Yesterday: VI William Black', *Edwin Muir—Uncollected Scottish Criticism*, ed Noble (New York/London, 1982), pp 222–7.
37 Review of Wiley and Putnam's Library of Choice Reading, No. XXI. *Genius and Character of Burns* by Professor Wilson, *The Complete Works of Edgar Allan Poe*, ed J A Harrison (New York, 1965), pp 239–43.
38 *Henry Crabb Robinson on Books and Their Writers*, p 140.
39 'Art X *The City of the Plague and Other Poems*', *Edinburgh Review*, XXVI (June, 1816), pp 460–1.
40 Ibid., p 458.
41 Ibid., p 460.
42 Ibid., p 468.
43 The most complete account of the extraordinary convolutions of Wilson's response to Wordsworth is in A L Strout's 'John Wilson, "Champion" of Wordsworth', *Modern Philology*, May 1934, pp 383–94.
44 Cf. Strout, p 385.
45 *Blackwood's Magazine*, vol II, October 1817, p 73.
46 'Observations on Coleridge's *Biographia Literaria*', *Blackwood's Magazine*, vol II, October 1817, pp 3–18.
47 'Blackwood's Magazine is an unprecedented Phenomenon in the world of letters, and forms the golden—alas! the only—remaining link between the Periodical Press and the enduring literature of Great Britain.' *Letters of Samuel Taylor Coleridge*, Griggs (ed) (Oxford, 1971), vol VI, p 912. Such praise bespeaks the desperation of Coleridge's conservative cause. His organic hereditary order represented by 'enduring literature' was not essentially present in either middle-brow nineteenth-century consciousness nor in its social structure. In reality Wilson's sort of conservatism was a travesty of that for which Coleridge yearned.
48 *The Rise and Fall of the Man of Letters*, p 3.
49 *Contemporary Reviews of Romantic Poetry*, John Wain (ed) (London, 1953), pp 48–9.
50 Ibid., p 45.
51 'Lockhart's Criticism', *The Moment* (1947), pp 60–4.
52 'On the Scotch Character', *Collected Works of William Hazlitt*, Waller and Glover (eds) (London, 1904), vol XII, pp 255–6.
53 The most detailed account of Hazlitt and *Blackwood's* is to be found in Ralph M Wardle *Hazlitt* (New York, 1971).
54 'On the Scotch Character', p 258.

55   *Noctes Ambrosianae, Works*, vol II, p 164.
56   Ibid., p 237.
57   *Reflections on the Revolution in France*, O'Brien (ed) (London, 1969), pp 194–5.
58   'An Hour's Talk About Poetry', *Works*, vol IX, p 215.
59   *Tales, Works*, vol XI, p 205.
60   Swann, p 117.
61   Cited by Swann, p 117.
62   Cited by Swann, p 234.
63   'Christopher North', *Reminiscences* (London, 1972), pp 366–81. Arguably the best contemporary portrait of Wilson.
64   *The Break-Up of Britain* (London, 1981), p 150.
65   'Speech at the Burns Festival', *The Works of Professor Wilson*, vol VII, pp 212–29.

FURTHER READING

Clive, John, *Scotch Reviewers: The 'Edinburgh Review' 1802–1815* (London, 1957).

Daiches, David, *Literary Essays* (London, 1956).

Devine, T M and Mitchison, R (eds), *People and Society in Scotland Vol. I, 1760–1830* (Edinburgh, 1988).

Fontana, Biancamaria, *Rethinking the Politics of Commercial Society: The Edinburgh Review 1802–1832* (Cambridge, 1985).

Gordon, George (ed), *Perspectives of the Scottish City* (London, 1985).

Hobsbawm and Ranger (eds), *The Invention of Tradition* (Cambridge, 1983).

Oliphant, Margaret and Porter, M, *Annals of a Publishing House; William Blackwood and his Sons* (Edinburgh, 1897).

Wain, John, *Contemporary Reviews of Romantic Poetry* (London, 1953).

Chapter 8

Carlyle: The World as Text and the Text as Voice

RODERICK WATSON

Carlyle occupies a unique place in British cultural history. As a social historian, he was possessed by a vision of human fate which was essentially poetic. As a nineteenth-century intellectual, his impatient and iconoclastic mind created nothing less than an early version of modern semiotic study which claimed a role of crucial intellectual and social importance for what had hitherto been the rather less urgent avocation of essayist or 'man of letters'. As a 'Victorian sage', Carlyle speaks with Dostoevsky, Turner, Whitman, Nietzsche and Yeats as among the first of the Modernists, and indeed, many of the strengths—and the failings—of his vision were to become those of modernism itself. No doubt it was this potential that Walt Whitman glimpsed when his obituary for the old and 'altogether Gothic' Scotsman maintained that 'as a representative author, a literary figure, no man else will bequeath to the future more significant hints of our stormy era, its fierce paradoxes, its din and its struggling parturition periods . . .'[1]

It was *Sartor Resartus* which brought Carlyle to the stage of such potential and to his mature fame. Undoubtedly *The French Revolution* confirmed his public stature as spokesperson for the universe as a place of unseen forces—driven by ideas, and not by steam—a place newly revealed as the ever-changing locus of threat and excitement and dynamic change; but the special force of Carlyle's peculiar genius belongs to the earlier book. It is a difficult text to define, unique in its day for conflating philosophy, social satire, poetic insight and deeper truth-telling, all through the odd convention of a tongue-in-cheek fictionalised critical biography. Such an approach may be more familiar to post-modernist readers—in the spirit of Borges or Umberto Eco, perhaps—but even today it seems a rare and taxing book.

The title itself speaks for a certain wayward opacity: *Sartor Resartus*, (the tailor re-tailored, or, more properly, the old-clothes mender patched-up again) purports to be a nameless editor's summary, with the help of a German colleague, of the life and theories of Herr Dr Diogenes Teufelsdröckh (devil's dung), Professor of 'Things-in-General' at the University of Weissnichtwo. Teufelsdröckh's philosophy proposes that all human structures are merely 'clothes', or vestments of our animating minds, and like clothes, our ideas and symbols and institutions go out of fashion, or lose their usefulness, and must be remade. We need to 'see through' such conventions until they become 'transparent'. The main burden of Carlyle's argument is often taken to be an insistence—derived from German Idealism—that everything is fundamentally the product of mind or spirit; but in fact the intellectual wit and the social focus of his argument throws as much or more light on the nature of our dependence on 'clothes'. Our social and political conventions and symbols have no intrinsic value at all, he argues, for everything is extrinsic, acquired or constructed ('tailored') by us. In the early nineteenth century, in the pride of materialism, utilitarianism, imperial confidence and the 'railway age', such views were potentially upsetting, to say the least.

At least one early reviewer was sufficiently caught-up by the narrative's intellectual conviction and its various 'editorial' devices to spend some effort in doubting the literal existence of its scholarly hero. In fact such combinations of literary mystification and—apparent—facticity (Teufelsdrockh's autobiographical writings turn out to be six large paper bags filled with random jottings, philosophical memos and laundry lists), were a not uncommon device among Romantic writers at the time. (Carlyle admired Laurence Sterne's *Tristram Shandy*, while Henry Mackenzie's *The Man of Feeling* purported to be scattered fragments reclaimed by a rather reluctant editor. The German author E T A Hoffmann played similarly teasing games in the presentation of his tales of mystery and the supernatural,[2] while James Hogg set his *Confessions of a Justified Sinner*, 1824, within a similar framework of editorial comment and parallel 'documentary' narratives, just as R L Stevenson was to do for *Jekyll and Hyde* over sixty years later.) What *is* striking about Carlyle's book is that such a mock-ponderous fictive device should have been chosen as the vehicle for a passionately serious critical thesis, not to mention a thinly-veiled account of the author's own deepest and most painful moments of spiritual crisis. *Sartor Resartus* encompasses and prefigures so much of Carlyle's unique intellectual force that it makes the most appropriate focus for this chapter on one of the most original and controversial minds of the nineteenth century.

Widely famous in his own lifetime, Carlyle's popular reputation has wavered ever since between over-reverent accounts of him as 'the Sage of Chelsea' and denunciations of his work as wilfully iconoclastic or crypto-fascist. It is not our purpose to follow every trial and detail of this stormy career, and a brief summary will have to suffice. He had great difficulty, for example, in placing *Sartor*, which was completed in 1831, but *Fraser's Magazine* in London eventually published it in three parts, between 1833 and 1834. An American edition prefaced by Emerson (who had visited the Carlyles in Scotland) was published two years later, but the first British edition did not appear until 1838, a year after the success of *The French Revolution* on both sides of the Atlantic had made its author well known at last, and financially secure for the first time, at the age of 42. *The French Revolution* was written in Chelsea—then an unfashionable part of London—where Carlyle and his wife had moved in 1834. Public lectures were undertaken on a variety of subjects, and the publication of *Chartism* (1839), *On Heroes and Hero-Worship* (1841), and *Past and Present* (1843) soon followed. Carlyle became internationally known, and his many new friends and contacts included

Emerson, J S Mill, Lockhart, Dickens, Tennyson, Arthur Clough, Thomas
Arnold and Sir Robert Peel.

J A Froude (Carlyle's contemporary and first biographer) summarised his
friend's reputation at this time, and also something of his notoriety:

> *Past and Present* completes the cycle of writings which were in his first style,
> and by which he most influenced the thought of his time. He was a Bedouin,
> as he said of himself, a rough child of the desert. His hand had been against
> every man, and every man's hand against him. He had offended men of all
> political parties, and every professor of a recognised form of religion. He had
> offended Tories by his Radicalism, and Radicals by his scorn of their formulas.
> He had offended High Churchmen by his Protestantism, and Low Churchmen
> by his evident unorthodoxy. No sect or following could claim him as belonging
> to them; if they did some rough utterance would soon undeceive them. Yet all
> acknowledged that here was a man of extraordinary intellectual gifts and
> of inflexible veracity. If his style was anomalous, it was brilliant. No such
> humourist had been known in England since Swift . . .[3]

The analogy with Swift is a fitting one, for in *Sartor Resartus* Carlyle had
described the absurdities of war with his most savage ridicule:

> Straightway the world 'Fire!' is given: and they blow the souls out of one
> another; and in place of sixty brisk useful craftsmen, the world has sixty dead
> carcasses, which it must bury, and anew shed tears for. Had these men any
> quarrel? . . . not the smallest! . . . How then? Simpleton! Their Governors had
> fallen-out; and, instead of shooting one another, had the cunning to make these
> poor blockheads shoot.
>
> <div align="right">(<i>Sartor Resartus</i>, 'Centre of Indifference')</div>

In *Chartism* and *Past and Present* he had used an even darker Swiftean irony
to expose contemporary complacencies about the freedom of the individual
in a society where the labouring classes are condemned to work or not to
work (to eat or not to eat) according to capitalist laws of 'free' supply and
demand. By the 1850s, however, Carlyle's Calvinist penchant for excoriating
the worldly failings of his time had slipped into a harsher and narrower
preaching of the most misanthropic sort. Thus the would-be ironical tone of
many of the *Latter-Day Pamphlets* (1850) is in fact wildly unstable, as is his
notoriously racist defence of slavery as both a philosophical and an economic
concept in 'Occasional Discourse on the Nigger Question' from the previous
year.

It is as if Carlyle could no longer cope with his earlier and essentially
Romantic vision of the universe as a place in constant flux, redefining its
truths with every generation, and all under the final existential absurdity
implied by the surrounding infinitudes of space, time and extinction. Constant
striving, individual freedom of the most radically scathing sort and the passionate conviction of 'heroic' lives, had seemed to be the most valid response
to such a condition, and indeed his own stoutly puritan roots had early led
him to admire the unrelenting drive behind such figures as Mahomet, Luther,

Knox and Cromwell—unlikely heroes for sophisticated London. In later years, however, the arc described by such exceptional careers led Carlyle to conclusions about the rule of the fittest and the exercise of individual authority for its own sake, while the initial intensities of his visionary assurance slipped into a strained and raucous intolerance instead.

The Calvinistic elements in such a progression are not far to seek, and it will be necessary to return to Carlyle's early years in order to show how much both the genius and the failings of the vision behind *Sartor Resartus* can be derived from his particular Scottish roots.

Carlyle was brought up in Ecclefechan as a member of the 'New Licht' Burghers—a long standing sub-branch of the Seceders who had parted from the established Church of Scotland on the grounds that it was too little committed to the finely legalistic details of the old Covenant against patronage and state interference in matters religious. His father, James Carlyle, was a taciturn, irascible man, little read but given to absolute faith in the Bible and the virtues of manual labour at his trade as a stonemason, and later as a small farmer. Carlyle admired him greatly, and honoured his memory in the papers which were collected posthumously as his *Reminiscences*. But he confessed, too, that he 'was ever more or less awed or chilled before him', and that 'my heart and tongue played freely only with my mother.'[4] Like so many of their following, the family had hopes that Thomas would enter the Church, and indeed this was considered to be the ultimate aim when he left home in his fourteenth year (not unusual at the time) to study at Edinburgh University.

The son of a peasant, hard-up, shy and socially awkward, the young Carlyle was never to meet or mix in the literary circles of Burns and Scott. Despising all affectation, he was noted among fellow students for his impatient, impassioned seriousness and they learned to be wary of his caustic tongue. His best subject was mathematics, a field properly fitted for the total certainties which he seemed to crave. Having finished his course in the Arts, Carlyle had to support himself for the further years required of a student in Divinity. He took various teaching posts in mathematics, though he came to hate teaching, and busied himself, like his *alter ego* Teufelsdröckh, with intensive reading in a wide range of subjects.

Carlyle continued his studies in law, but by now a career in the Church did not appeal. He was entering 'the three most miserable years of my life'. Solitary, depressed, a martyr to dyspepsia and his own hypochondriac fears, he was suffering a crisis of faith in the religion of his childhood, and a crisis of self-confidence about his own vocation. Having early confessed to 'the wish of being known', he had yet to find a professional calling which seemed worthy of such an intensely cerebral nature. By the early 1820s, Carlyle seems to have come to something like the existential crux he later described in *Sartor Resartus*:

> . . . the net-result of my Workings amounted as yet to—Nothing. How then could I believe in my Strength, when there was as yet no mirror to see it in? . . . Invisible yet impenetrable walls, as of Enchantment, divided me from all

living . . . To me the Universe was all void of Life, of Purpose, of Volition, even of Hostility: it was one huge, dead, immeasurable Steam-engine, rolling on, in its dead indifference, to grind me limb from limb.

> (*Sartor*, 'The Everlasting No')

For eighteenth-century thinkers the universe as a well-made clock had seemed a cheerful argument for the existence of some divine Maker. On the other side of the industrial revolution, however, the metaphor has become a steam engine, and for Carlyle, like Dickens later,[5] that meant a 'Mill of Death'—powerful, mindless, insensate and automatic. The solution was to redefine the primacy of spirit and the power of mind, and that meant for him (as it was for Teufelsdröckh) a new conception of what his vocation was to be.

Carlyle described *Sartor* as 'symbolical *myth*', but he did attest to the personal authenticity, at least in essence, of the crisis he gave to Teufelsdrockh. This response was somewhere between a religious conversion to 'the light', and an existential leap of faith. Faced with universal nullity, he asserted a fundamental sense of individual freedom:

> The Everlasting No had said: 'Behold, thou are fatherless, outcast, and the Universe is mine (the Devil's)'; to which my whole Me now made answer: '*I am not thine, but Free, and forever hate thee!*'

Where before the world had seemed to be the grimmest of places, alien to the very possibility of any Ideal, now it could be a realm of endless potential, for eyes that could see it thus:

> . . . here in this poor, miserable, hampered, despicable Actual, wherein even now thou standest, here or nowhere is thy Ideal . . . Fool! the Ideal is in thyself, the impediment too is in thyself . . . O thou that pinest in the imprisonment of the Actual, and criest bitterly to the gods for a kingdom wherein to rule and create, know this of a truth: the thing thou seekest is already with thee, 'here or nowhere,' couldst thou only see!
>
> (*Sartor*, 'The Everlasting Yea')

What Carlyle saw was his vocation—a vocation which would allow his critical eye to decode the world itself, to read the text of the Actual now that he had turned from both the Bible and his books of law.

There are other factors in this renewal of confidence, of course, as there always are. He had begun courting Jane Welsh Carlyle, who was to become his devoted and life-long companion after their marriage in 1826; his finances were improving; and his studies in German had led to translations of Goethe and Schiller, and various critical articles and the beginnings of a reputation in literary circles.[6] Even so, Carlyle was still his father's son, and a modest literary fame was not quite enough for one brought up to believe 'that man was created to work, not to speculate, or feel, or dream'.[7] There had to be a further calling, more worthy perhaps of James Carlyle's Spartan ideal of meaningful labour and his horror of redundant words.

That labour took Carlyle out of Edinburgh to Craigenputtoch, an isolated farm-house from his wife's inheritance, where the couple managed a frugal life together for the six years before their move to London. Here Carlyle assembled his library and, surrounded by the bleakest of moors, did more than any individual in his day to introduce German literature to British readers. Key essays for his intellectual development also stem from this period, most especially 'Signs of the Times' (1829) and 'On History' (1830). Here too, wrestling with his health and his peace of mind, he set about the writing of *Sartor Resartus*, determined to 'speak out what is in me . . . I have no other trade, no other strength, or portion in this Earth.'[8]

In the 'symbolic myth' of *Sartor*, Teufelsdröckh's commitment to the Actual provides us with the model for his creator's discovery, or rather for his *invention* of his own vocation. Carlyle may have lost faith in the form of his father's Christianity, but, against the nullity of that 'Everlasting No', he had never doubted the *need* for faith nor the crucial importance to himself of a more than merely materialistic vision of the world. No Scottish Presbyterian divine would have quarrelled with the German professor's strictures on the need for work—existentially derived, perhaps—but also taken directly from Ecclesiastes:

> Up! Up! Whatsoever thy hand findeth to do, do it with thy whole might. Work while it is called Today; for the Night cometh, wherein no man can work.
>
> (*Sartor*, 'The Everlasting Yea')

> Whatsoever thy hand findeth to do, do it with thy might; for there is work, nor device, nor knowledge, nor wisdom, in the grave, whither thou goest.
>
> (Ecclesiastes 9:10)

Carlyle's philosophy has been called 'Calvinism without theology', and his friend and early admirer John Sterling was one of the first to note that although Teufelsdröckh retained an essentially religious vision of the universe, he lacked any conception of a personal God.[9] Even so, an Old Testament spirit abounds in *Sartor*, and this is more than just a matter of Carlyle's habitual use of Biblical allusions, or his rough but vividly oral style of writing, as if he truly were speaking from some pulpit. In fact the echoes from Ecclesiastes are revealing, for as a favoured text in the Scottish canon it is much given to reflections on the vanity of human affairs, with little to say about a personal God. Equally telling is its awareness of the endless cycle of life and the ever-present certainty of death, which is a vision very close to Carlyle's own, as is its account of a crisis of faith such as Teufelsdrockh had to undergo:

> Then I looked on all the works that my hands had wrought, and on the labour that I had laboured to do: and behold, all was vanity and vexation of spirit, and there was no profit under the sun.
>
> (Ecclesiastes 2:11)

The parallels can be taken much further, for the very spirit of *Chartism* is to be found in lines such as:

> The sleep of a labouring man is sweet, whether he eat little or much: but the abundance of the rich will not suffer him to sleep. There is a sore evil which I have seen under the sun, namely, riches kept for the owners thereof to their hurt.
>
> (Ecclesiastes 5: 12 and 13)

Teufelsdröckh knows that man is a prey to death when he reminds us that 'TIME, devours all his Children: only by incessant Running, by incessant Working, may you (for some threescore-and-ten years) escape him; and you too he devours at last' (*Sartor*, 'Getting Under Way'); and the Preacher, too, has much the same to say on the same theme:

> I returned, and saw under the sun, that the race is not to the swift, nor the battle to the strong, neither yet bread to the wise, nor yet riches to men of understanding, nor yet favour to men of skill; but time and chance happeneth to them all.
>
> (Ecclesiastes 9: 11)

Faced with such certainty, what can we hope for? The universe is a 'Sphinx-riddle' for Teufelsdröckh, and although Ecclesiastes believes that wisdom is good, he has to admit that we will never know the work of God under the sun 'because though a man labour to seek it out, yet he shall not find it.' (8: 17). Yet neither accept despair, and if their predicament cannot be escaped, at least it can be greatly eased by a clear-sighted recognition of it. Hence both the German professor and the Old Testament preacher accept 'light' as their salvation in the end, even if so few get the chance to see it, and its only achievement is to assure them of the ever-present darkness:

> Truly the light is sweet, and a pleasant thing it is for the eyes to behold the sun: But if a man live many years, and rejoice in them all; yet let him remember the days of darkness; for they shall be many. All that cometh is vanity.
>
> (Ecclesiastes 11: 7 and 8)

> . . . the thing thou seekest is already with thee, 'here or nowhere,' couldst thou only see! But it is with man's soul as it was with Nature: the beginning of Creation is—Light. Till the eye have vision, the whole members are in bonds.
>
> (*Sartor*, 'The Everlasting Yea')

> It is not because of his toils that I lament for the poor: we must all toil, or steal (howsoever we name our stealing) . . . But what I do mourn over is, that the lamp of his soul should go out; that no ray of heavenly, or even of earthly knowledge, should visit him . . . That there should one Man die ignorant who had capacity for Knowledge, this I call a tragedy . . .
>
> (*Sartor*, 'Helotage')

> Then said I, Wisdom is better than strength: nevertheless the poor man's
> wisdom is despised, and his words are not heard.
>
> (Ecclesiastes 9: 16)

Ecclesiastes' 'light' revealed the vanity of the world and the coming judgement
of God; what it showed to Teufelsdröckh was a much more complex and
sophisticated thing, fully illustrative of the originality and the striking modernity of Carlyle's thinking.

In 'Signs of the Times', the very first of his social essays, Carlyle had set
out to chastise the Victorian world for its complacent materialism and the
mechanistic implications of its love affair with Utilitarianism. He believed
that 'the great truth' is 'that our happiness depends on the mind which is
within us, and not on the circumstances which are without us.' As opposed
to this, he felt that thinkers such as Adam Smith and Jeremy Bentham
were set on redefining human nature along the materialistic (and hence
mechanically applicable) principles of enlightened self-interest. Thirty-five
years later, Dostoevsky was to make an identical attack on the 'mathematical
certainties' and 'the laws of nature' to which all such systems pretended,
noting that

> . . . a man, whoever he is, always and everywhere likes to act as he chooses,
> and not at all according to the dictates of reason and self-interest . . . where
> did all the sages get the idea that a man's desires must be normal and virtuous?
> Why did they imagine that he must inevitably will what is reasonable and
> profitable? What a man needs is simply and solely *independent* volition, what-
> ever that independence may cost and wherever it may lead.[10]

Notes from Underground championed the freedom of the spirit against all
would-be rational social controls and the limitations of easy definition, and,
as with Carlyle, Dostoevsky's creed leads to an essentially modernist account
of the universe as a place of restless and dynamic change. (In this respect
Carlyle's vision also prefigured much in the work of Hugh MacDiarmid.)

The Russian argued from the psychological standpoint of a perverse but
convincing individual, but Carlyle's essay takes a more abstract line based
on a subtle understanding of the importance of language. Thus in opposition
to the new fashion for speaking of society as a 'machine', the Scot sets up
the deliberately insubstantial metaphors of 'foam' and 'fire' and 'light' and
'sparks', (the very stuff of Turner's paintings—another great Romantic pre-
cursor of the modern sensibility), pointing out that 'man is not the creature
and product of Mechanism; but, in a far truer sense, its creator and producer.'
Well versed in German Idealism, Carlyle insists that mind and spirit are
primary: which is all the more reason to choose our social metaphors with
care, for if we speak too carelessly of 'the Machine of Society', then all too
easily ' "foam hardens itself into a shell" and the shadow we have wantonly
evoked stands terrible before us and will not depart at our bidding.' ('Signs
of the Times'). This is not high-flown idealism, but a real and subtle under-

standing of how human perception is controlled by the terms within which we choose to frame it.

For Carlyle, these terms are all we have. He needs no abstruse argument to prove that all is spirit, for *sub specie aeternitatis*, as he sees it, nothing else remains:

> . . . sweep away the illusion of Time; compress the threescore years into three minutes: what else was he, what else are we? Are we not Spirits, that are shaped into a body, into an Appearance; and that fade-away again into air and Invisibility? That is no metaphor, it is a simple scientific *fact*. . . .
>
> (*Sartor*, 'Natural Supernaturalism')

So history is the record of how that spirit passed, but like Ecclesiastes's works of God under the sun, it may never be possible to see it fully. This is what Carlyle understood in his essay 'On History', when he noted that 'Narrative is *linear*', but

> . . . actual events are nowise so simply related to each other . . . every single event is the offspring not of one, but of all other events, prior or contemporaneous, and will in its turn combine with all others to give birth to new: it is an everliving, everworking Chaos of Being, wherein shape after shape bodies itself forth from innumerable elements. And this Chaos, boundless as the habitation and duration of man, unfathomable as the soul and destiny of man, is what the historian will depict, and scientifically gauge, we may say, by threading it with single lines of a few ells in length!

Hence Carlyle concludes that 'History is a real Prophetic manuscript, and can be fully interpreted by no man.' Such a vision of simultaneity and flux places Carlyle once again among the precursors of modernism, as does his understanding of the relativity and the transience of all established opinion— 'Thus all things wax, and roll onwards; Arts, Establishments, Opinions, nothing is completed, but ever completing.' (*Sartor*, 'Organic Filaments'.)

Thus it follows that each age must recreate its own version of the truth, for systems and sacred texts and symbols, 'like all terrestrial Garments, wax old,' and 'the Solution of the last era has become obsolete, and is found unserviceable.' (*Sartor*, 'The Everlasting Yea'.) Such a point of view must have been a considerable comfort to Carlyle, as a young intellectual who had lost faith in his father's church, but had not lost the desire to put himself to some worthy and needful task. Thus was born the Professor of 'Things in General' and his Clothes-philosophy. Behind the droll facade of Diogenes Teufelsdröckh, we can see Carlyle struggling to define a valid role for himself—very much like Milton's search to find 'some graver subject'. Literature and literary criticism do not impinge enough on the world of affairs (and we recall that the elder Carlyle held a very low opinion of fiction and poetry— even the verse of Burns), while the conventions of university philosophy could scarcely satisfy the Romantic drive of Carlyle's poetic vision of the instability of the universe. What he did was to define the world itself as a text, and to appoint himself the critic (or prophet) uniquely suited to decode the 'celestial hieroglyphs', even if they can be discerned in only a line or two here and there.

The model is not exclusively literary, of course, for Biblical exegesis is the true forerunner of all such practice. Indeed, one of Carlyle's favourite metaphors is that history is a text 'whose Author and Writer is God . . . With its Words, Sentences, and grand descriptive Pages . . . spread out through Solar Systems and Thousands of Years . . .'[11] It was just this sense of scale which Carlyle found in his readings in German Idealism, along with his belief in an ultimate cosmic unity in which spirit is the only reality.

> . . . this so solid-seeming World, after all, were but an air-image, our ME the only reality: and Nature, with its thousand fold production and destruction, but the reflex of our own inward Force, the 'phantasy of our Dream' . . . *the living visible Garment of God.*
>
> (*Sartor*, 'The World Out of Clothes')

He did *not* believe, however, that man was created to 'dream' alone, and the key concept in his idealism lies in that phrase about the world also being 'the reflex of our own inward Force'. For him the spirit expresses itself through *work* and the world is no less than the fruits of our labour (spirit) made manifest. If the world is ultimately God's book, we too can still make books, we too can make history and create reality, we too can become critics or little Creators:

> So spiritual [*geistig*] is our whole daily life: all that we do springs out of Mystery, Spirit, invisible Force . . . Visible and tangible products of the Past, again, I reckon up to the extent of three: Cities, with their Cabinets and Arsenals; then tilled Fields . . . and thirdly—Books.
>
> (*Sartor*, 'Centre of Indifference')

Carlyle's insight can be compressed and summarised as follows: everything is spirit: the spirit manifests itself in mind and the mind expresses itself through work: work can be seen all around us: truly nothing is insignificant. Cities may crumble, but books—because they are the expression of mind— can last much longer, each with a different 'produce of leaves (Commentaries, Deductions, Philosophical, Political Systems; or were it only Sermons, Pamphlets, Journalistic Essays)' for each of the ages they pass through. Thus for Carlyle, thought never dies (though it may evolve) and the scholar can achieve a kind of immortality. Indeed 'the Wise man stands ever encompassed, and spiritually embraced, by a cloud of witnesses and brothers; and there is a living, literal *Communion of the Saints*, wide as the World itself, and as the History of the World.' (*Sartor*, 'Organic Filaments'.) The use of words such as 'witness' and 'communion', reveals how fully Carlyle has remodelled the calling of his father's faith to fit his vocation as a culture critic, a new kind of intellectual hero, a reader of the world and all its symbols—the first semiotician of Victorian Britain.

For such a man everything is symbolic, and nothing, however mean, is without illumination: 'Rightly viewed no meanest object is insignificant; all objects are as windows, through which the philosophic eye looks into Infinitude itself.' (*Sartor*, 'Prospective'.) Teufelsdröckh's task is to show that if the final reality is spirit and spirit alone, then everything else in this world is merely a matter of 'garments'. In the last analysis our clothes, houses and political institutions are merely how we 'dress' ourselves, and our bodies and our senses and even language itself are merely 'garments' of flesh and thought.[12] Yet this is not to dismiss such garments as trivial or beneath serious attention. On the contrary, the burden of Teufelsdröckh's whole philosophy—presented to us through an eccentric *persona*, and qualified by his 'biographer' as it may be—is to take the analysis of surface symbols very seriously indeed, and to use such subtle practice towards a cultural and political critique in an age otherwise wholly dedicated to stoutly practical, 'mechanistic', and materialistic ends. In other words, to invent semiotics.

This is not to say that Carlyle does not enjoy the fun of upsetting established priorities, and many of his propositions are as intellectually playful as anything written by Roland Barthes or Umberto Eco:

> 'Perhaps the most remarkable incident in Modern History,' says Teufelsdröckh, 'is not the Diet of Worms, still less the Battle of Austerlitz, Waterloo, Peterloo, or any other Battle; but an incident passed carelessly over by most Historians, and treated with some degree of ridicule by others: namely, George Fox's making to himself of a suit of Leather.'
>
> (*Sartor*, 'Incident in Modern History')

Teufelsdröckh's name and his strange origin, the autobiography in six paper bags, his Romantic 'Sorrows', and his 'editor's' asides and doubts about his 'sansculottism', all these speak for textual playfulness and perhaps a certain defensive irony in Carlyle's case. But there is no mistaking the intent behind his deconstruction of the nature of war, (in 'Centre of Indifference'); the passionate indignation behind his attack on the values of the landed classes (in 'Helotage'); nor the pointed satire of his vision of a naked House of Lords (in 'Adamitism'); nor his hatred for all the outworn ideas and dead symbols which continue to rule our lives—the 'old clothes' of an unexamined existence, '. . . with its wail and jubilee, mad loves and mad hatreds, church-bells and gallows-ropes, farce-tragedy, beast-godhood,—the Bedlam of Creation!' (in 'The Phoenix' and 'Old Clothes').

Carlyle's understanding of the power of symbols and how important it is to see through them, 'to look fixedly on Clothes . . . till they become *transparent*', goes further still, for he recognises the arbitrary nature of perception and even language itself—how we are governed by how we choose to see and to say things. If symbols 'have no intrinsic, necessary divineness, or even worth; but have acquired an extrinsic one', it follows that we should choose them with care, or look closely at those we have inherited to be sure that they are worthy of us. This is the first task of the culture-critic, for 'are not the tatters and rags of superannuated worn-out symbols (in this Rag-fair of a world) dropping off everywhere, to hoodwink, to halter, to tether you; nay if you shake them not aside, threatening to accumulate, and perhaps produce suffocation?' (*Sartor*, 'Symbols'.) The culture-critic's second task is to be alert to the emergence of *new* symbols, and these two terms go far towards defining Carlyle's approach to history, and most especially to his treatment of the French Revolution.

The point about the world of clothes is that fashions change and styles of dress go in and out of favour with great regularity. We have seen that this metaphor holds true for Carlyle's vision of the Universe as a place of constant flux, and of society, too, as a structure in 'perpetual metamorphosis'—phoenix-like—as new forces and new symbols within it rise and fall and rise again. Such is the text of the world which Teufelsdröckh has set himself to decipher for us. It is entirely fitting, then, that his own text should show something of that dynamic energy too, and it is here that the presumed identity between Carlyle and his German professor is most clearly demonstrated. '*Le style c'est l'homme*', and Carlyle's prose is unique. He was much criticised, even by admirers, for the self-assertive roughnesses, the repetitive insistence, the odd allusions, constant exclamations, and the generally unclassical lawlessness of his writing. But Carlyle defended himself, for surely this was not the time for 'Purism of Style', and after all, style is a product of 'all that lies under it . . . *not* to be plucked off without flaying and death.'[13]

Indeed, Carlyle's style is very much the mirror of the raw energy and the dynamic tensions within himself, which he identified as the condition of the world all around him. Carlyle had much admired the rough earnestness of his own father's speech, 'flowing free from the untutored Soul' (*Reminiscences*), and this *oral* insistence is central to his own written prose. True to his earliest experiences of exposition in the Burgher Church, Carlyle stands before the text of God (except that in his case the book is not the Bible, but History itself) and preaches the word.

Of course Carlyle's prose has long been recognised as an essentially (and sometimes exhausting) form of rhetorical address—full of sermon-like locutions, exclamations, and asides to the reader—while his punctuation and sentence structures make full use of dashes and sudden associative digressions.[14] Nevertheless, this is not simply the style of a self-appointed demagogue, despite its later decay into intolerance and insistence, for Carlyle was right to maintain that the mental set behind Johnsonian English was collapsing under the new apprehensions of the Romantic age, and right, too, in his conviction that his style, like the skin of an animal, is integral to 'the exact type of the nature of the beast'.[15]

Thus it is in his choice of metaphors, ('foam', 'fountains', 'sparks'), and in the very structure of his sentences, that Carlyle seeks to demonstrate his passionate apprehension of life as a fully dynamic state. Hence the turmoil of history is evoked at great length and by an extraordinary effort of the imagination in the recurring historical present tense of the prose in *The French Revolution*—a book that cost him the most desperate effort to write. It is fitting, too, that most of his sources were drawn from the memoirs of participants themselves, another recognition of Carlyle's commitment to the importance of lived experience and point of view in history. Again and again

Carlyle's prose seeks to engage us in the whirl of events as they evolve from the experience, the plans and the half-formed apprehensions of his protagonists:

> Still crueller was the fate of poor Bailly, First National President, First Mayor of Paris: doomed now for Royalism, Fayettism; for that Red-Flag Business of the Champ-de-Mars;—one may say in general, for leaving his Astronomy to meddle with Revolution. It is the 10th of November 1793, a cold bitter drizzling rain, as poor Bailly is led through the streets; howling Populace covering him with curses, with mud; waving over his face a burning or smoking mockery of a red Flag. Silent, unpitied, sits the innocent old man. Slow faring through the sleety drizzle, they have got to the Champ-de-Mars: Not there! vociferates the cursing Populace; such blood ought not to stain an Altar of the Fatherland: not there; but on that dung-heap by the River-side! So vociferates the cursing Populace; Officiality gives ear to them. The Guillotine is taken down, though with hands numbed by the sleety drizzle; is carried to the River-side; is there set up again, with slow numbness; pulse after pulse still counting itself out in the old man's weary heart. For hours long; amid curses and bitter frost-rain! 'Bailly, thou tremblest,' said one. '*Mon ami*, it is for cold,' said Bailly, '*c'est de froid.*' Crueller end had no mortal.
>
> (*The French Revolution*, Part III, Book V, 'Death')

Despite Carlyle's talent for dramatic recreation and his dependence on contemporary memoirs, later historians have verified the accuracy of much of this work. Furthermore, his sources have a different and more theoretical kind of validity as well, for however fallible and biased they may be, in their own way they are fully part of the flux of their times—immediate and, in a sense, oral too.

Carlyle's conviction about the spontaneity, the fluidity, and the power of human impulse as it operates, evolves and clothes itself in different ways within the flux of history, meets its proper correlative in his style. In so far as this prose is a 'voice' he can recognise the uniqueness and the relativity of all opinion, and yet at the same time he can also demonstrate its living, persuasive power across the centuries in that 'communion of saints' he longed to join. Carlyle's voice may be speaking to us from another century, yet, with all the force of literature—grammatically, rhetorically, ironically—his vision of lost times and the never-ending turbulence of human experience becomes immediately and palpably present. The closing lines of *The French Revolution* speak openly for the poignancy of this condition, but they also note its potential for endless growth and renewal:

> And so here, O Reader, has the time come for us two to part. Toilsome was our journeying together; not without offence, but it is done. To me thou wert as a beloved shade, the disembodied or not yet embodied spirit of a Brother. To thee I was but as a Voice. Yet was our relation a kind of sacred one; doubt not that! For whatsoever once sacred things become hollow jargons, yet while the Voice of Man speaks with Man, hast thou not there the living fountain out of which all sacredness sprang, and will yet spring? Man, by the nature of him,

is definable as 'an incarnated Word.' Ill stands it with me if I have spoken falsely: thine also it was to hear truly. Farewell.

—These words do not speak for the historian alone, for they recognise the fragility, and the intimacy, and the crucial importance of all discourse between all readers and all writers, when the world becomes text and the text becomes a voice.

NOTES

1   Walt Whitman, 'Death of Thomas Carlyle' (1881), in *Thomas Carlyle: The Critical Heritage*, J P Seigel (ed) (London, 1971), p 456.
2   Hoffmann was among a number of writers translated by Carlyle for his four volume book *Specimens of German Romance*, 1827.
3   *Froude's Life of Carlyle*, abridged and edited by J Clubbe (London, 1979), p 417.
4   From 'James Carlyle', in *Reminiscences* (1881).
5   *Hard Times* (1854), was dedicated to Carlyle.
6   His reading of Goethe had been very influential, especially *Wilhelm Meister's Lehrjahre*, as a semi-autobiographical development novel about a similarly ardent young spirit at large in banal society. (Carlyle's translation of it appeared in 1824.)
7   From 'James Carlyle', in *Reminiscences*.
8   Letter from Carlyle to his brother John, 17 July 1831.
9   John Sterling, letter to Carlyle, 29 May 1835, *The Critical Heritage*, pp 31–3.
10 Dostoevsky, *Notes from Underground* (1864), Chapter One. 'The Underground'.
11 *Sartor Resartus*, 'Natural Supernaturalism'; *see also* '. . . all history is a Bible. . .' a rejected MS quoted in *Froude's Life*, pp 224–6.
12 *Sartor*, 'The World out of Clothes' and 'Pure Reason'.
13 This debate is touched on in *Froude's Life*, pp 339–41; *see also Critical Heritage*, pp 26–33.
14 Recent research has shown that Carlyle's editors set out to regularise his punctuation in subsequent editions of his work. It is worth noting that the rather diffident delivery of his early lectures was much at odds with the considerable force of his written prose.
15 Letter to John Sterling, 9 June 1837.

FURTHER READING

Baumgarten, Murray, 'Carlyle: Mind as Muscle', in *Scottish Studies: Nationalism in Literature*, H W Drescher (ed) (Frankfurt, 1988).

Campbell, Ian, *Thomas Carlyle* (London, 1974).

Carlyle, Thomas, *Reminiscences*, C E Norton (ed) (London, 1972).

Clubb, J (ed) *Froude's Life of Carlyle* (London, 1979).

Ikeler, A Abbott, *Puritan Temper and Transcendental Faith. Carlyle's Literary Vision* (Ohio, 1972).

Waterston, Elizabeth, 'Past and Present Selves: Patterns in *Sartor Resartus*', in *Scottish Studies: Thomas Carlyle 1981*, ed H W Drescher (Frankfurt, 1983); also other essays in this collection.

Chapter 9

Nineteenth-Century Non-Fictional Prose

IAN CAMPBELL

In *Lothair* (1870) Benjamin Disraeli has a splendid if satirical vision of a Scotland rendered ungovernable. Monsignore Berwick, a Roman Catholic potentate and political schemer, sketches his plans to establish Roman Catholic power in Scotland.

> The original plan was to have established our hierarchy when the Kirk split up; but that would have been a mistake; it was not then ripe. There would have been a fanatical reaction. There is always a tendency that way in Scotland: as it is, at this moment, the Establishment and the Free Kirk are mutually sighing for some compromise which may bring them together again; and if the proprietors would give up their petty patronage, some flatter themselves it might be arranged. But we are thoroughly well-informed, and have provided for all this. We sent two of our best men into Scotland some time ago, and they have invented a new Church, called the United Presbyterians. John Knox himself was never more violent, or more mischievous. The United Presbyterians will do our business: they will render Scotland simply impossible to live in; and then, when the crisis arrives, the distracted and despairing millions will find refuge in the bosom of their only mother.[1]

The U.P. Church is no invention of fiction, of course: what is striking is the idea of religious faction making Scotland 'simply impossible to live in' during a century when faction and divisiveness are very evident. The pivotal date was 1843 which brought the Disruption of Established and Free Churches of Scotland but the divisiveness is as visible in the underpinning of *The Heart of Midlothian* (1818) as it is in the later view of religious Scotland in a Stevenson or a Crockett. Disraeli's view is that of a country which simply could not live with the multiplicity of ideas striving for mastery: an overview of the century's prose confirms the controversy, but also suggests the strong underlying continuing national life.

Some aspects of the continuity are easily identified. The nineteenth century was one during which Scottish speech and character were strongly prized, relics of a past age, memories of a greater Scotland. That they were prized is evident from the frequency with which they were described: evident, too, in the urgency felt by older writers to conserve and to preserve for posterity. E B Ramsay's *Reminiscences of Scottish Life and Character* (1857) is the most famous of many compendia of 'wisdom, knowledge of life, and good feeling' containing the proverbial and commonplace sayings of Scotland—though

Ramsay noted sadly in his introductory survey that 'No doubt, to many of my younger readers, proverbs are little known, and to all they are becoming more and more matters of reminiscence'.[2] Sir Archibald Geikie, looking back at the end of the nineteenth century, admitted that,'though no longer permanently resident in Scotland',

> I have been led by my official duties to revisit the country every year, even to its remotest bounds . . . These favourable opportunities have allowed me to mark the gradual decline of national peculiarities perhaps more distinctly than would have been possible to one continuously resident.[3]

This sentiment was to be echoed by numbers of returning Scots. William Black, returning after a successful London career in 1877 to the Highlands of his native Scotland, strongly impressed his travelling companion. 'I have never seen Black so frankly abandoned to the joy of living. All the way in the railway . . . his trained and vigilant eye was on the watch for every detail of form and colour . . .'[4] With many Scots forced to leave the country for shorter or longer periods, the return to a Scotland perhaps changed becomes a crucial moment, a moment splendidly caught and treated half-seriously, half-satirically in George Douglas Brown's *The House with the Green Shutters* with its description (chapter 16) of the uprooted Scot.

> That is why the heart of a Scot dies in flat Southern lands; he lives in a vacancy; at dawn there is no Ben Agray to nod recognition through the mists. And that is why when he gets north of Carlisle he shouts with glee as each remembered object sweeps on the sight.[5]

The danger of uncritical reminiscence is at the root of the satirical features in Douglas Brown's description of young Gourlay:

> With intellect little or none, he had a vast sensational experience, and each aspect of Barbie was working in his blood and brain.

In *The House with the Green Shutters* the results of uncritical nostalgia are strikingly, even horrifyingly underlined in a novel whose *rationale* was in part to combat the uncritically kailyard, and to invite a true analysis of Scotland and the experience of being Scots. Plainly the view is sharpened by a degree of absence: Cunninghame Graham's memorable 'Beattock for Moffat' concerns itself solely with the desperate wish to see the remembered country again before death, a bitter-sweet devotion to memory. Carlyle makes a striking point about that Scotland in his magnificent *Reminiscences*, in a detached fragment ('Christopher North') concerning that most boisterous of Edinburgh intellectuals, John Wilson. In a well-known description of Princes Street in 1814 Carlyle recalls a city pulsating with life and intellectual self-confidence, 'all that was brightest in Edinburgh . . . stept out to enjoy, in the fresh pure air, the finest city-prospect in the world and the sight of one another'. The cruellest of blows was the speed with which this intellectual coterie disappeared, the vigorous and self-confident world of John Wilson and William Hamilton, Francis Jeffrey and McVey Napier, editors, professors and lawyers. Already

> . . . in 1832, you in vain sought and inquired Where the general promenade, then, was? The general promenade was, and continues, nowhere.[6]

Carlyle's *Reminiscences* about that Scotland are striking for many reasons, for their extraordinary detailed recall and vividness of writing: even more striking, perhaps, is this acknowledgement that the Scotland being recalled has completely vanished, and there is no possibility of escaping the pressure of change to return to such a Scotland. The world of strong Ecclefechan piety embodied once and for all in his father, the genius of the world of Chalmers in Glasgow, Leslie, Christison, Jeffrey, Wilson, Brewster in Edinburgh, the ever-present influence of the Wizard of the North, are recalled for what they are—vanished picturesque detail.

Indeed the snapshot view Carlyle captured of Princes Street towards the close of the Napoleonic wars was a highpoint after which most reminiscence was to chart decline. Lockhart, one of the most bitingly gifted of prose writers, was soon to leave for London and the editorship of the *Quarterly Review*. Scott's wizardry was to begin its long decline in the 1820s, the gifted young were to feel more and more the attractions of a re-opened Europe and an ever-closer London. Small wonder that the general promenade of 1832 was hard to find: with one of the major works of nineteenth-century prose written but unpublished (*Sartor Resartus* was to have a long struggle to achieve book-length publication and recognition, first in the USA thanks to Emerson's untiring efforts) Carlyle was turning to London in his imagination, to the national capital with its ferment of Reform agitation, its publishers and its bright young writers: the loss of the Carlyles in 1834 for a new life in Chelsea was symptomatic of a century in which reminiscence of a Scotland left behind was so powerful a literary model.

The great Edinburgh years of 'Jupiter' Carlyle and Cockburn's reminiscences were over: while the Universities and the professions were to remain bastions of Scottishness and Scottish culture—bastions, admittedly, under powerful siege during the century as English-inspired reform and English-nationality teachers played a more and more significant part in the Universities—and while the Glasgow of Lockhart's *Peter's Letters to his Kinsfolk* and the Edinburgh of the *Noctes Ambrosianae* in *Blackwood's Magazine* were to remain in being for decades, the reality of Scotland increasingly approached the terse description by Geikie, 'the gradual decline of national peculiarities'. Already the tension was there which Christopher Harvie was to describe succinctly in a discussion of the 1920s in Scotland,

> A provincial culture, distinct from that of England for various reasons, rather than superior to it. An acute awareness among Scottish intellectuals of the power of parochialism and the mediocrity of its cultural values; a sense of attraction to and revulsion against the metropolis.[7]

To anyone familiar with the nineteenth century's own cultural historians the echoes are very clear. By 1853 Henry Cockburn clearly saw the decline of Scotland's heyday and, while losing no chance to chronicle it, admitted that 'it is useless and wrong to attempt to resist the general current'. To someone who could remember the first flash which was caused by the emergence of the *Edinburgh Review* at the end of the previous century, Scotland must indeed have seemed a quieter place.

> Its first flash electrified all the country; and for many years the excitement was renewed by every publication. Power awoke to alarm and indignation: the people, to knowledge and hope.

And yet: by 1852 only 600 copies of the *Edinburgh Review* were sold in the whole of Scotland, compared to 1813 when the figure was 12,000 subscribers—which meant, in Jeffrey's view, at least 50,000 readers at an epoch when the London *Times* had a daily circulation of only 8,000.[8] Writing at the later time Cockburn could fantasise: 'Restore [Sydney] Smith, Jeffrey, Brougham, and Macaulay, and its supremacy in the formation of public opinion would return'. The reality was harsher: the great names of the earlier part of the century were in London, or were dead, and London itself was seemingly moving closer with every year.

> In twenty years London will probably be within fifteen hours by land of Edinburgh, and every other place will be shaking hands, without making a long arm, with its neighbour of only a county or two off. This will add to our wealth, and in many respects to our ease. But is not seclusion often a blessing? Difficulty of being reached has its advantages. Our separate provincial characters will be lost in the general mass where London will predominate.[9]

Already London had claimed Lockhart and Carlyle: Cockburn's *Journal* increasingly reads like a litany of the old Scots who had remained to work in Scotland, and were now dying off. In 1850, Cockburn was to note the passing of the old Friday club, killed off it seemed by the final blow of Francis Jeffrey's death.

> Its continuance by the surviving members is scarcely possible; and with our recollections and habits, I do not see what new shoots could be engrafted on to the old stock. Let it go.

Cockburn's becomes a curious view of Scotland: as Karl Miller has noted, he is saying 'Come to Scotland . . . and he very nearly adds: but stay away from its industrial cities'.[10]

Selectivity becomes one of the most noticeable features of writing in the century, a selective vision from Carlyle's Chelsea, from Cockburn's citadel of memory, from the wonderfully chosen selective view of the *Noctes Ambrosianae*, from the politically motivated viewpoints of the writers who enlivened the *Edinburgh Review* and *Blackwood's Edinburgh Magazine* for decades. Selectivity makes generalisation about the century dangerous: George Elder

Davie has tellingly investigated a century where the philosophers were active, where it seemed a renaissance might come in that quarter even as the famous imaginative writers passed away: with Hamilton, E S Dallas, D F Gregory, James Clerk Maxwell and James Ferrier the country could hardly be called impoverished of exciting minds. What Dr Davie calls 'infectious intellectual confidence' brought debate and excitement: alas, it also brought controversy and eventually eclipse. The extent of that eclipse has led in the last decade to stimulating scholarship debating the extent to which a real democratic tradition in Scottish education, and a real Scottish philosophical school, did in fact perish or whether a selective portrait of the age can exaggerate what had survived as distinctive and still alive. What is undeniable is the general faltering of the period, the 'sudden provincialisation of the country' which Walter Elliot in *A Scotsman's Heritage* described in the 1840s and 1850s.[11] In this context there are areas of strength. Mrs Oliphant, for instance, defends *Blackwood's* from the charge of half-death just because the fireworks of the first years were no longer a feature of editorial policy. On the contrary, by mid-century

> there had never perhaps been a time when a band of contributors more active and productive surrounded the Editor of the Magazine. There was no onslaught upon the world, as in the old days when Wilson or Lockhart or Maginn was always in the act of couching a lance . . . [but] fiction was exceptionally strong in a cycle which had secured the three best novels of Bulwer and the new sensation of the 'Scenes of Clerical Life'. The old names had almost entirely disappeared.[12]

A point Mrs Oliphant makes strongly is the continuity of talent even if the old names have gone—and the internationalism and the open-ness of vision of the new names, '. . . almost all contemporaries of John Blackwood . . . keeping up from all corners of the earth a frequent correspondence, always with an eye open for "what would do for the Magazine" '[13] The names of the group of writers remains impressive: John Wilson, David Macbeth Moir ('Delta'), George Moir, Henry Stephens, De Quincey, W E Aytoun, Lord Neaves, 'all *habitués* of the house'—and not all in decline, either: 'Aytoun was in the heyday of his powers. Writing on almost every conceivable subject and winning success in widely different fields of literature . . . he exhibited a versatility that constituted him a veritable mine of talent'.[14] Reading Mrs Oliphant's *Annals of a Publishing House*, her history of Blackwood's, one is aware of the mine of talent throughout Scotland, in St Andrews, in Glasgow, in Aberdeen: J D Forbes, John Hill Burton, Principals Tulloch and Shairp in St Andrews. Archibald Geikie has already been mentioned, as well as 'perfervid Scot' of Aberdeen and Edinburgh,[15] John Stuart Blackie; a prominent part in public affairs was to be played by Sir Robert Christison, as it was by Lyon Playfair ('a true Scot, though most of his life was passed in England').[16] J D Forbes himself, a world-famous geologist and glaciologist who was professor in Edinburgh and Principal in St Andrews, was an example of a public figure of international reputation who maintained extraordinary links with foreign scholars[17] and who maintained a spirit of internationalism in Scotland for decades where he had influence. Forbes, naturally, regretted the loss of able Scots to London—Murchison, Lyell, Horner:

> of all the changes which have befallen Scottish science during the last half-century, that which I most deeply deplore, and at the same time wonder at, is the progressive decay of our once illustrious Geological School.[18]

Decay could take many forms: it could mean the departure of the talented young, it could mean the reshaping of Scottish intellectual and educational traditions to a model largely alien. Yet a strong continuity to Scottish intellectual life in the century comes from the Universities, from men of the calibre of Thomas Chalmers, whom Cockburn hailed as 'the greatest of living Scotchmen'—a man who had lectured in Chemistry, stood as a strong candidate for the Edinburgh mathematics chair, became Professor of both Moral Philosophy and Political Economy at St Andrews before assuming the chair of Divinity at Edinburgh—a formidable list of generalist accomplishments for a busy pastoral minister with a long list of publications, a vivid reputation as public orator, an astonishing record of benevolence to the poor through parish giving properly organised, and—for this alone he would be indispensable from this chapter—the distinction of being at the head of the Free Kirk when it left the Establishment at the Disruption of 1843.[19]

Non-specialism was a distinguished part of Scottish higher education, producing superb generalists, cross-disciplinary teachers and researchers. Blackie, for example, had an enormous reputation as a teacher and professor, to say nothing of his creative writing and political activities; 'Christopher North' himself was a formidable athlete and *bon viveur* without the fame brought by his bad eminence in *Blackwood's Magazine*, which itself was eclipsed by his long tenure of the chair of Moral Philosophy at Edinburgh University. That Wilson's appointment in 1820 was politically motivated (a superb candidate, Sir William Hamilton, had the misfortune to belong to the wrong political party, and was summarily passed over in favour of a disgracefully unqualified Wilson) did not prevent him from wielding enormous influence over generations of his students, along with the public who crowded to his lectures. Carlyle, as usual, trenchantly sums up the gains and losses of Wilson's lectures.

> 'Moral *Philosophy*', or 'Philosophy' of any kind, Wilson, I suppose, never taught, or much tried to teach: but he was a most eloquent, fervid, overpowering kind of man, alive to all high interests and noble objects, especially of the literary or spiritual sort, and prompt to foster any germ of talent or aspiration he might notice in that kind, among his pupils: and he did kindle several of them, to my after knowledge, into a certain generous, tho' *fuliginous* as well as flamy, fire and development of intellectual faculty—preferable, surely, to the logical frost which would otherwise have been their Academic portion, had Wilson *not* been there.[20]

Cockburn, too, notes in his *Journal* the unreliability of assuming that because a few world-famous names are dead, Scotland is necessarily dead. 'Chalmers, Sir William Hamilton, Christison, Alison, and Forbes . . . are all great names, and though, like our fathers, we have plenty drones, there are several excellent teachers besides these.'[21] The recent publication of *The Tounis College*, an anthology which rescues much half-forgotten student writing of the period, underlines the strong continuity of intellectual restlessness and enquiry of the period.

Another sampling point to suggest the continuity of enquiry would be an unpromising-looking compendium of biographical criticism, *I Can Remember RLS* by Rosaline Masson, which turns out on acquaintance to be a remarkable compilation of essays with, among the lightweight tributes, vivid recollections of student and professional circles in the Scottish cities, Stevenson's Dialectic Society, the D'Arcy Thompson Class Club which Stevenson helped found in the Edinburgh Academy, the Speculative Society, the Royal Society. Vigorous University theatricals are included, alongside intellectually lively circles of young lawyers such as those who met in 11 South Charlotte Street in Edinburgh where Charles Baxter received the likes of Sir Walter Simpson, James Walter Ferrier and W E Henley as regular visitors.[22] Privately and publicly, life obviously went on. As Carlyle was to admit in 1866 in his Rectorial address *On the Choice of Books* students could find their teachers and their set books boring: but the insatiable thirst for private reading could allow self-education on an exceptional scale in a country where University entrance was still relatively open to all. In 1828 William Edmonstoune Aytoun was similarly bored by his teachers, but found *his* stimulus in Shakespeare, Anderson's edition of the British Poets, in Hume, in Gibbon, while he should have been devoting himself to mathematics and metaphysics. Aytoun was to go his own way after University and return as an influential Professor of Rhetoric and Belles Lettres, which became in the 1860s the Chair of Rhetoric English Literature: Carlyle would have welcomed a chair in his lean years of the 1820s and early 1830s, but when fame came to him in the 1840s in London he shrank from offers of chairs in Scotland as from a living death.

That this was unfair—student numbers were rising dramatically in mid-century and able men were still very much in evidence—hardly matters in the context of this discussion. Selectivity of vision is something all those mentioned suffered from, a vision which saw rapid change and perhaps found it hard to appreciate the complexity and internal contradictions of that change. Individuals worked in their own way—the Chambers brothers, Robert and William, preserved and actively published Scottish history and tradition. They had served a hard apprenticeship of poverty in the outskirts of Edinburgh[23] and in the process mixed with a circle all but forgotten, that of George Gilfillan, Henry Scott Riddell, John C Denovan. In every city circles of young men faced the question of whether to stay or whether to go; a dilemma which has been revealed for the first time with the extraordinary early correspondence of Thomas and Jane Welsh Carlyle. The place and problem forms the subject of Aytoun's *Norman Sinclair* with its autobiography and its vision of a literary Edinburgh largely submerged by history. Hugh Miller, labouring as stonemason or editing the influential periodical *The*

Witness (as he did from 1840, impressively) exemplifies the semi-submerged nature of writing in the period. Editors, educators, booksellers, historians, librarians, clergymen, form a world tantalisingly mentioned, touching the edge of the *Noctes Ambrosianae* and the autobiographies of the era, interacting with the published and unpublished correspondence. Some figures of the period—Carlyle, Francis Jeffrey—were enormously visible and influential. Most were neither. Yet all are part of the rapidly evolving literary nature of nineteenth-century Scottish prose.

The nineteenth century, then, did have strong undercurrents in Scottish prose, and those undercurrents are not always immediately visible. Writers were affected by accidents of birth and class, education and political or religious conviction: above all, they tend to be grouped in classes or specialisms which makes a more systematic survey of nineteenth-century non-fictional prose more possible. Some categories yield a few highly visible names known for their writings: Patrick Geddes (1854–1932) and James Keir Hardie (1856–1915) indicate that politics had some impact in this way. Some categories yield dozens, indicating most clearly the survival of the professional classes which David Daiches has analysed (in *The Paradox of Scottish Culture*) as the basis of surviving institutions after the Unions of 1603 and 1707.

Historians, for instance, are a category of distinction in our survey, with names such as Archibald Alison (1792–1867), John Hill Burton (1809–81), Cosmo Innes (1798–1874), William Stirling-Maxwell (1818–78) and Patrick Fraser Tytler (1791–1849). In the tradition of William Robertson and Smollett, these professionals wrote in a country where historiography was a respected profession and where a career could be made. It is notable that a strong contribution is made by this group to *Scottish* history—though this does not detract from the importance of Alison's extraordinary *History of Europe* (1833–42). Noticeable, too, is the ability that people in this tradition have to make an impact on a wider reading public than those who read history as a specialised subject: it is just within our period to note the contribution that Sir Walter Scott (1771–1832) made to history, particularly when the later financial troubles of his life made him turn to a lifelong hobby interest for a source of profitable publication.

Men of business include historians, of course: a very considerable list of men of business wrote work of wide public impact in the century. The paradox of Scottish culture made lawyers and educators and clergymen likely to be professional authors as well as custodians, witting or otherwise, of much Scottish traditional culture. The *literati* outlived Robert Burns, and despite the often crude guying of that group constituted a body of educated and hard-working writers of varying talents. Lawyers form a class of men of business who distinguished themselves in writing. Some—like Charles Baxter (1845–1919) were to spend most of their time on law itself, while others, including Baxter's contemporary Robert Louis Stevenson (1850–94) possessed extraordinary talents which have found him a niche in a history of poetry, drama, fiction and non-fictional prose. The lawyers included some excellent minds, of the calibre of Henry Brougham (1778–1868), Henry Cockburn (1779–1854), Francis Jeffrey (1773–1850), John Gibson Lockhart (1794–1854) and Walter Scott himself. Practising legal professionals, they were many of them to rise slowly to literary fame while earning their living through law: some were to rise to legal fame more rapidly, and some rare talents like Jeffrey's were to rise to the top of their profession in both cases. To this list should be added that rogue talent of the period John Wilson ('Christopher North', 1785–1854) whose name, like those of most of the law figures mentioned, has already featured naturally in any preliminary survey of the prose of the period. Capable most of them of stupendous feats of sustained writing of articles and reviews for the major journals which happened to be in Scotland—in particular the *Edinburgh Review* and *Blackwood's Edinburgh Magazine*—the lawyers formed a coterie powerful and clever, wielding political power from the pages of the *Edinburgh Review* above all, where a rational Whig interest found a prestigious platform sufficiently enraging to their political opponents to lead to the launching of *Blackwood's* in 1817 in direct Tory competition. Exceptionally, Scott rose above considerations of political loyalty: respected throughout literary Scotland (to say nothing of the literary world) he would have been a welcome contributor to most periodicals and undoubtedly his ready pen could have risen to the challenge had not his own financial disaster of 1826 harnessed his energies to paying off his own terrible debts.

The law was a business; few proved it more than Scott, whose acumen raised income from all sources. Some lawyers left Scotland, like Brougham to find fortune in England; others remained in Scotland to join the other men of business. Some of these are almost too well known to mention, though it is forgotten that John Galt (1779–1839) and James Hogg (1770–1835) were both important writers of critical as well as imaginative prose, and both practised the art of autobiography in ways which critics of their fiction have had reason to thank. Other businessmen of the period had taken time to rise to fame: Alexander Smith (1830–67) had to work before he had leisure to write, as did Samuel Smiles (1812–94), and of course Hugh Miller (1802–56) had the distinction of being identified with his professional rather than his creative life, his stonemason activities acting in the popular imagination as Burns's agricultural ones had done. Yet Miller was to be a banker and influential editor for many years. Money had to be made: perhaps the most successful and famous exponent of that process, Andrew Carnegie (1835–1919) should be remembered more than he is for his own writing, as well as for endowing the funds which made, and still make, possible the appearance of the books of hundreds of less wealthy writers.

It would make dubious sense to read into this list of working writers anything distinctively and exclusively Scottish—John Stuart Mill, Anthony Trollope and William Morris all combined writing with professional activity in Victorian England in celebrated ways—but the high concentration of working-men-of-letters in Scotland in the nineteenth century had the effect of ensuring a degree of contact between the world of the contemporary everyday and those men who wrote about it.

It follows naturally that the category 'men of letters' does not lend itself to easy definition at this period. For one thing they were not all men by any means, and Elizabeth Grant of Rothiemurcus (1797–1885) is slowly emerging from undeserved obscurity as diarist and commentator, as Margaret Oliphant (1828–97) is at last being taken seriously as a hard-working literary professional whose copious (alas, too copious as she admitted) output includes essays and historical material, including a valuable history of the house of Blackwood to which reference has already been made. Another difficulty with 'men of letters' is the extraordinary diversity of occupations with which they combined writing. David Macbeth Moir is hard to define, though best known for *Mansie Wauch* (1828)—but his literary and writing life was diverse and copious and as hard to encapsulate as the career of R B Cunninghame Graham (1852–1936), traveller and writer, or R M Ballantyne (1825–94) who had to combine office work in Canada and in Edinburgh with writing both fiction and non-fictional prose. Well-known professional antiquarians and librarians such as David Laing (1793–1878) and David Irving (1778–1860) combined scholarship with very extensive publication: Andrew Lang (1844–1912) combined journalism with antiquarian research, professional writing with creative writing, and summers in England with winters in Scotland. Lang has been called the 'divine amateur', but, like Laing, he combined amateur interest with the real hard work of writing and getting writing published, a combination of hardness and almost obsessional interest in writing which characterises many of the writers-men-of-business here discussed. Poverty was to drive many, famous and not famous: some, like James ('B. V.') Thomson (1834–82) never escaped from poverty and their extensive writing is completely overshadowed by it. Thomson's *City of Dreadful Night* has recently been taken seriously after decades of neglect, and there are welcome signs that his prose criticism—strong, powerful and often original—is also undergoing long-postponed revaluation.

The list of writers who were also capable of earning a living is a long one, and no list would be inclusive: J Logie Robertson (1846–1922) wrote excellent essays as well as his more famous country poetry, and Dr John Brown (1810–82) was at the same time a busy doctor and professional author of essays and biography, best remembered for *Horae Subsecivae* (1858–61).

A separate category for *Academics* seems almost superfluous given the cross-fertilisation of specialisms in an age of generalists which has included so many academics already. William Edmonstoun Aytoun (1813–65) was to be a mainstay of *Blackwood's* and is remembered for fiction and poetry as well as for his critical and reviewing prose. In Aberdeen Alexander Bain (1818–93) and in Glasgow Edward Caird (1835–1908) were semi-legendary professors to their generations of students, and at the same time prolific prose writers, though neither approached in output nor in legend the incomparable white-haired and plaid-wearing John Stuart Blackie (1809–95), charismatic lecturer and classical scholar, activist for Scottish national politics and Gaelic culture—and prolific prose author. Blackie moved between Aberdeen and

Edinburgh Universities, Sir David Brewster (1781–1868) between Edinburgh and St Andrews—and both were highly visible public controversialists as well as successful academics. In St Andrews also, J F Ferrier (1808–64) was a public focal point for Scottish writing and aspirations as well as a very gifted philosopher whose ambitions unfortunately ran counter to the accident of birth which produced in William Hamilton (1788–1856) another highly gifted philosopher whose career and Ferrier's seemed fated to collide. St Andrews was to see circles of writers and essayists in summer particularly, and J C Shairp (1819–85) in St Andrews, and David Masson (1822–1907) in Edinburgh were to be long remembered as the centres of student circles of writers and essayists, as well as among their own professional peers. 'Christopher North' as teacher has already been much discussed: John Wilson (1785–1854) wrote prolifically in prose, fiction and poetry. Nor was he the only Wilson, for Daniel Wilson (1816–92), most of whose career was spent in Canada, was a well-known essayist particularly in the history of Edinburgh.

Churchmen naturally were involved in the production of a good deal of prose. Horatius Bonar (1808–89) was to become famous for his hymn-writing, but like many other ministers of the Church he wrote many prose works for the use of his flock. Thomas Chalmers (1780–1847), of course, was an exceptional writer as well as an exceptional public figure, and his prose was frequently reprinted—as was the more ephemerally-popular prose of a remarkable contemporary of Thomas Carlyle, Edward Irving (1792–1834). Irving came from Annan to the summit of popularity as a famous London preacher, but his heretical doctrine led to his expulsion from the Church of Scotland and to an early death. His prophetic sermons and essays still make remarkable reading. Alas, Irving's was not the only controversial trial of suspected heresy, and the historical work of A C Cheyne has recently illuminated the case of clergy whose prose writings earned them severe censure, or worse, from the ecclesiastical authorities in a century where controversy was rife, and feelings were easily outraged. The 'Leslie Affair' in which the controversial mathematician John Leslie had academic promotion blocked on the grounds that he had given approving mention of David Hume in passing illustrates the extent of popular high feeling.

The highest of feeling, of course, was reserved for the Disruption, when the Kirk split into two, a split which was to endure till 1929, though there remain to this day independent smaller bodies which declined to rejoin. The Disruption led to years of controversy and to the indubitable diversion of the writing energies of Churchmen: directing their energies to controversial literature meant less time and less wish to write poetry, fiction, non-controversial prose. This generalisation grossly oversimplifies a Scottish Church where the clergy remained active writers, and equally grossly overlooks the editing activities of such Churchmen as became celebrated literary editors, with extraordinary effect on the popular taste of their times.

Norman Macleod (1812–72) is a celebrated case, editor of *Good Words* and thus decisively influential on the reading of hundreds of thousands. Popular fiction owed editorial selection and taste formation to men such as Henry Drummond (1851–97) and, most crucially, William Robertson Nicoll (1851–

1923) who as editor of *The British Weekly* was indirectly responsible for the dissemination and popularisation of Barrie, Crockett and Maclaren. Nicoll was not responsible for the kailyard, of course, though he has had this sin laid at his door; but he did seek out and encourage the writing of short fiction of a retrospective kind, in a framework of ideas which would be acceptable to his readers, and it fell to the alertness of a youthful Barrie and a worldly-wise Rev John Watson ('Ian Maclaren') to respond to Nicoll's encouragement, and produce the sketches which grew to dominate their market and, for a long time, much popular perception of Scotland.

We return, inevitably, to E B Ramsay (1793–1872), 'Dean' Ramsay, whose *Reminiscences of Scottish Life and Character* have, with countless reprints, fixed the reminiscent tone and the idyllic character of much popular perception of Scotland and Scottish prose at this period. Where a George Douglas Brown would have foregrounded urban decay, industrial pressures, the emptying churches or the revolution of transport and local services, Ramsay was content to fix on the vanishing of a beautiful, essentially static Scotland and the need to preserve what one could. The paradox of a survey of active Scottish prose writers of the century is the quantity of energy and talent they displayed, along with the blurring of focus and uncertainty of attitude to their country with which they wrote.

How then can we sharpen the focus of the extraordinary gamut of talent in the nineteenth century prose writers? Plainly, some of the surviving institutions of a post-Union Scotland still functioned strongly. The Church, Disraeli's butt in *Lothario*, still functioned strongly, more positively than his satirical distortion would suggest. Ambiguity of attitude to that institution is strongly built into Scottish literature, as indeed it is to Victorian literature in England in much the same period. The reservations, the oblique and open criticisms of a Hogg or a Burns would lose much of their impact were they not representative of what must have been widespread and widely held attitudes in the readership of the time. Nor is it only the institution of the Church, in its various forms and schisms, which is the subject of ambiguous attitude: the personal beliefs and feelings of the reader and writer were also subject to change in the period, a change more likely to be described in coded message than in overt description. While *The City of Dreadful Night* is a superb example of open infidelity, it is remarkable in part for its isolation in a century of coded and indirect statements.

In this context George MacDonald (1824–1905) is all the more remarkable for the finesse with which he approaches questions of fragile belief and uncertain faith. His fantasy fiction has recently been re-assessed, rescued from a tendency to restrict it in genre to children's literature (an extraordinary fate which also befell Stevenson for many years) and to subject it to analysis revealing a deeply sophisticated inner structure and response to the working of the subconscious imagination. Influenced by early studies of natural philosophy and of German romanticism, MacDonald wrote much more than children's stories, excellent though these undoubtedly are: his essays on the fantastic imagination, his religious prose works, his criticism, his occasionally splendid realistic Scottish fiction all urgently demand reconsideration. Recently critical opinion of MacDonald still allowed for noticing a 'tendency to sermonize' which 'usually nullifies the virtues of [MacDonald's] Scots dialogue'[24]; a more remarkable artist in fiction, poetry and non-fictional prose is emerging into critical debate with wider reading and wider availability of MacDonald's copious and versatile output.

Here is a prose writer who is not hampered by schism in the Church, by Disruption nor indeed by dogmatic problems over Christ and the Church. Literature of a very high order is possible to an imagination splendidly responsive to nature, and to the problems of a complex human society, patiently seeking an original means of transmitting messages about life to that society. There is room for Disruption and theological debate: the Aberdeen University scenes in *Alec Forbes* and *Robert Falconer* reflect excellently the preoccupations and intellectual problems of the time, the hard-working austerity of Glamerton Church people, imagination-denying but dutiful, accurately depicting part of the Scottish inheritance. MacDonald expresses splendidly in Glamerton (his childhood Huntly thinly transformed) the embarrassment of the Scottish imagination faced by love, and by Love of a God acknowledged but not individually known or even considered. There is room in MacDonald for love, for a child's simplicity and an adult's sad love based on experience of suffering: there is room for 'good' books and dangerous life experience: there is room for retrospective imagination of a pastoral Scotland miles removed from kailyard and there is room for participation in a Scotland (indeed an England and a North America) where the new sweeps the old aside, where theological positions have to be re-interpreted (as MacDonald did in his life and his ministry) to cope with changing circumstances and changing belief. In short, MacDonald demonstrated in his prose that one could be part of the Scottish imagination in the nineteenth century—albeit living out of Scotland, as did Mrs Oliphant and (for most of his life) Stevenson—and still respond flexibly to the demands of a living literature.

In finding this balance and this possibility of active participation, MacDonald is reflecting in the circumstances of his life the activity of a century as we have surveyed it. While the Kirk was caught by controversy, its ministers were often active outside that cockpit in writing, in criticising, in encouraging writing, in collecting about the past and writing about the future. While the institutions of old Scotland seemed moribund or fast disappearing, many of the personalities in those institutions (the University professors, for instance) were teaching the next generation not to enbalm the past, but to respond to the challenge of the present and the future. Even as the kailyard grew, the newspapers of Scotland were full of reviews of new literature which contradicted the essentially static and retrospective values of that literature, and (like MacDonald) sought to find a new literature to depict a new life. This does much to explain the brooding power of *The House with the Green Shutters*: once it has achieved its opening aim of parodying kailyard, catching audience attention and satirising the values of a school of fiction the author despised, the book turns to the central question: what sort of Scotland are we writing about, a Scotland half a generation back in memory, balanced on the edge of an industrial upheaval for which it is unprepared, without public institutions or educational structures to guide or prepare it? In *The House with the Green Shutters*, we know, the result is tragedy. In much nineteenth-century prose the tone is one of facing an exciting future, and experimenting to find a literary language for that future.

The language, we have seen, already existed in a variety of forms partly explained by the variety of practitioners of writing: the professions; the wealthy independent writers; the Churchmen and University writers; the reviewers; the publishers and men of letters. Industry, trade, commercial activity all propelled men to write, and provided a living to those who could not make ends meet by writing in Scotland at the time. William Power has pointed (in *Literature and Oatmeal*) to the fact that 'overdeveloped trade and industry have been the chief enemy' of literature in Scotland,[25] but some trade and industry have been shown to be an indispensable part of the energy and the power which is reflected in the diversity of writing—springing from diversity of activity.

Sandy Mackaye in Charles Kingsley's *Alton Locke*, apart from being a parody of some features of Carlyle, is also a type of Scotsman intended to be recognisable to the audience—articulate, hardworking, working-class, passionate, over-verbal, thin-skinned, prodigiously gifted verbally, mal-adjusted to the society in which he made his living. Parody apart, Sandy Mackaye is a reminder of something this essay has tried to underline: the existence of a literate, hard-working, often self-made culture in Scotland in a nineteenth century whose prose writings have been obscured by the larger shadow of successful authors in the early decades, and kailyarders in the later. A splendid illustration of this underclass of Scottish writing is to be found in the magisterial correspondence of the two Carlyles, Thomas and Jane, whose *Collected Letters* are now appearing from Edinburgh and Duke, North Carolina. Not only are the expected men of letters there, the Jeffreys and the Christopher Norths, the John Stuart Mills and the Emersons writing from a distance—but Annandale, and student and post-student Edinburgh, are revealed as localities with their own strong writing circles. Annandale has, in an almost forgotten character like the Rev Henry Duncan of Ruthwell, not only a prodigious man of letters and amateur geologist, but a hard-working parish minister who founded and ran for a considerable time the *Dumfries and Galloway Courier*, keenly reflecting the literary activities of the surrounding parishes in letters, in reviewing recent publications, and in transcribing the literary meetings, the Burns meetings, the oratory Church and secular; Carlyle's earliest published writings are in the correspondence columns of the *Courier* and when he went to Edinburgh in 1809 to the University he was joining a clever Annandale writing circle (including Edward Irving) and joining the melting-pot of many other circles who met at University in the atmosphere of debating clubs, societies, student publication which flourished without leaving very permanent traces on literary history.[26]

Carlyle's is a case which illuminates this whole period and topic. When he married and settled in Edinburgh in 1826 it was as a self-made writer and translator who had written some fiction and poetry— happily forgotten in most cases—and a great deal of prose, biography, criticism, encyclopaedia writing, controversy. In addition he wrote, and received, extensive correspondence.

When Carlyle found Edinburgh too expensive he was to spend lonely years of exile in Craigenputtoch (1828–34) enlivened by occasional trips to Edinburgh and a superbly exciting taste of London during the Reform agitation of 1831. And he lived by writing prose, extensively, intensively, always waiting till he could write his own 'book', which turned out to be *Sartor Resartus*. If Jane in lonely Craigenputtoch recognised it as a work of genius, the world at large was slow to follow. But when the Carlyles had money to move to a city environment in the Spring of 1834 they barely hesitated: London was their destination, and Chelsea their home for the remainder of their married life.

But the important point is that when *The French Revolution* made Carlyle famous in 1837, he was not learning the craft of writing prose; he had come from a writing background in which he was only one of many besieging the editors' doors with unsolicited articles, jobbing for the Edinburgh and London publishers, working at commissioned articles for money and at creative writing for artistic satisfaction. While he was writing lives of Goethe and Schiller, and translating *Wilhelm Meister's Lehrjahre* and *Wanderjahre*, Carlyle was meditating his own work, and with *Sartor*, as we now see, he gave British literature a significant propulsion towards the modern period. Without the drudgery and the education of that drudgery, his mind would not have been marvellously stocked with British and European literature, his worldview not strongly shaped from the amalgamation of a strong and narrow Ecclefechan dogmatism, and a liberated city restless questioning. Carlyle did not spring new-minted to prominence in 1837: he was a man in his early forties extensively published, even more extensively trained in writing, reading and talking in a country which, till he left it in 1834, seemed able perfectly well to satisfy the demands of his reading and most of his writing. Only with the Reform agitation in the distance, and the decline of Scottish letters at the death of Scott, did the pull of London exert a definitive pressure.

The case of the Carlyles is a sharply-focused one not only in the extensive biographical attention they have received, but in the exceptional wealth of their correspondence which allows the reader today to see not only the emergent Carlyles, but the *milieu* from which they came. Clearly they came from exceptional homes, but equally clearly the little-recorded and little-published localities from which each emerged (Annandale and Haddington) were alive with literary activity.[27] The editing of other major surviving correspondences—Scott's, for instance, with its interplay between writers and practising lawyers—should reinforce this picture. So too do the extraordinary *Reminiscences* with which Carlyle, his memory sharp naturally and sharpened by the recent death of his wife, filled the empty winter of 1866–7. Carlyle's *Reminiscences* were partly the instrument of the downfall of his reputation on their publication—thin-skinned, nervy, indiscreet, unfair, but compulsively interesting and readable in their re-creation of a vanished Scotland in the early decades of the nineteenth century. Whether in the working-class circles of Annandale or in the uneasy contact Carlyle had with writing Edinburgh, there plainly was much activity in the early decades, and equally plainly the Edinburgh of Aytoun and Stevenson prolonged this activity. In all the University cities, in the regional newspaper centres of Scotland, in the Session minutes, the evidence suggests a strong and continuing tradition of reading, talking, writing. The long-lived Carlyles continued writing letters to that Scotland till the early 1880s, and the evidence (naturally narrowing as their families aged) suggests that the kailyard had not obliterated that Scotland. Far from it, the kailyard had picked on a feature which is not parodic but representative of a kind of reality, as was Mrs Gaskell's working-class circles in Manchester and Dickens's in Preston. Gregory Smith long ago sounded a warning against dismissing the notion of the hard-working, hard-writing Scot simply because the kailyarders had populated their novels with ridiculous numbers of the genre.

> Because that 'school' stood for Scotticism, and because its claims are now peremptorily dismissed, too many may conclude that there is nothing more to be looked for, that, in a word, the notion of northern idiosyncrasy, obvious and traditional, must be wiped off the critical slate.[28]

The critical debate between G E Davie and R D Anderson on the nature of popular education, and G E Davie's study of the effects of University reform; the extensive recent work (by S J Brown, notably) on Thomas Chalmers; the rescue of gifted but forgotten writers such as Hugh Miller from obscurity; the serious revaluation of the kailyard; the revival of interest in Mrs Oliphant and George MacDonald; and the *Duke-Edinburgh Carlyle Letters* are examples of the critical soundings that are being made in that vanished world of nineteenth-century prose.

The kailyard has threatened to obscure the reality of a Scotland which this paper has attempted to sketch: the newspapers, the publishing houses, the institutions of learning, the politicians and political parties, the Churches, the legal system, the amateurs and the professionals of Scotland contributed to a body of prose of a diversity to reflect the diversity of a country whose intellectual life continued while Thrums and Drumtochty dozed or concentrated on the politics of the parish pump. That it has taken patient research on local newspapers (such as William Donaldson's recent discoveries of serialised fiction in the popular press of the North-East) to unearth much prose, that superb correspondences have languished unedited and unpublished, that critical studies of politics or Church affairs have revealed much intelligent thinking and splendid writing among the minutiae of their subjects, that student journalism has been shown to have flourished despite almost total obscurity following publication, that an enormous number of working-class authors worked and achieved limited publication, alongside political thinkers and writers, suggests that the nineteenth century in Scottish prose is neither the waste land which, it has been suggested, followed the death of

Scott, nor the cosy backwater which lies behind the untroubled world of the essentially non-urban, non-industrialised kailyard. *The House with the Green Shutters* has been referred to already in this survey: its reflection of Scotland at the end of the century is of a country cruelly caught in rapid change and ill-equipped to deal with that change. Social institutions, public media of discussion and debate, the Churches, the educational system, are seen in Douglas Brown's satiric view as powerless to handle the speed of change: instead the older institutions crumble or ossify, the new commercial interests make a quick profit, and the human values of everyday are crushed. Bleak as *The House with the Green Shutters* is, it allows for a world where these values are not quite all: a world of rapid talk and some writing, a city world where the institutions are not quite dead and where public life is conducted at something above a stammer. While Barbie fills the foreground, Edinburgh (or in reality a scathingly reduced version of Brown's student days at Glasgow) is always there, where the abler young men go to be trained, to escape the paralysing boredom of Barbie, to lose that tongue-tied provinciality which makes Barbie helpless in the face of city businessmen like Gibson the speculative builder. The world of the Howff and the University, the glimpsed professional classes of Gourlay's Glasgow solicitors, the kindly attentions of MacCandlish the schoolmaster, the suggestion in the Baker of a well-read working class, all hint at a country where intellectual life continued, not in kailyard pastiche nor in endless reminiscence of a vanished bucolic Scotland, but continuing, planning, training, preparing for change. The despairing tone of *The House with the Green Shutters* arises from a lack of conviction that Scotland is ready to cope. The wealth of interest in the writing which this chapter has sketched suggests that a world of half-researched Scottish writing awaits discovery and critical discussion.

NOTES

1   B Disraeli, *Lothario*, B Vogdanor (ed) (London, 1975), p 32.
2   E B Ramsay, *Reminiscences of Scottish Life and Character* (New York, 1877 edn), p 147.
3   *Scottish Reminiscences* (Glasgow, 1904), p 7.
4   T W Reid, *William Black Novelist* (London, 1902), pp 184–5.
5   D Porter (ed) (Harmondsworth, 1985), p 144.
6   I Campbell (ed) (London, 1972), pp 366–7.
7   *No Gods and Precious Few Heroes* (London, 1981), p 129.
8   Cf. Bruce Lenman, *Integration, Englightenment and Industrialization, Scotland 1764–1832* (London, 1981), pp 111–12.
9   *Journals of Henry Cockburn 1831–54* (Edinburgh and London, 1874), 1: 116.
10 Quoted by A Bell, *Lord Cockburn: A Bicentenary Symposium 1779–1979* (Edinburgh, 1979), p 197; Karl Miller, *Cockburn's Millenium* (London, 1975), p 132.
11 Quoted by G E Davie, *The Democratic Intellect* (Edinburgh, 1961), p 287.
12 *Annals of a Publishing House: William Blackwood and his Sons* [third vol by Mrs G Porter] (Edinburgh and London, 1897), 2: 453.

13 Oliphant, 2: 454–5.
14 Oliphant [Porter], 3: 20.
15 A Geikie, *Scottish Reminiscences* (Glasgow, 1904), p 175.
16 Geikie, p 178.
17 Ian Campbell and David Hutchison, 'A Question of Priorities: Forbes, Agassiz, and their Disputes in Glacier Observations', *ISIS* 1978, 69 (248), pp 388–99: *see also* Ian Campbell,'Scotland and Switzerland', a study mainly devoted to the ninteenth century, in a forthcoming volume on Scotland and Nationalism H W Drescher (ed) (Frankfurt and Bern, 1988).
18 Quoted Geikie, pp 373–4.
19 *See* S J Brown, *Thomas Chalmers and the Godly Commonwealth* (Oxford, 1982) for a distinguished account.
20 Carlyle, *Reminiscences*, p 370.
21 Cockburn, *Journals*, 2: 51.
22 (Edinburgh and London, 1922), p 171.
23 Cf. William Chambers, *Memoir of Robert Chambers* (New York, 1872).
24 Quoted from M Lindsay, *History of Scottish Literature* (London, 1977), p 334.
25 William Power, *Literature and Oatmeal* (London, 1935), pp 16–17.
26 *The Collected Letters of Thomas and Jane Welsh Carlyle: Duke-Edinburgh Edition* K J Fielding and C DeL Ryals *et al.* (eds) (Durham, N.C.) 1 (1970): 91, 101, etc.
27 Details abound in the early volumes of the *Carlyle Letters*: see also *The Letters of Thomas Carlyle to his Brother Alexander with Related Family Letters* E W Marrs Jr (ed) (Harvard, 1968), and 'Letters from Home: The Carlyle Family Correspondence': *Prose Studies: Essays in Honour of K J Fielding* (10: 3: December, 1987), pp 307–16.
28 G Gregory Smith, *Scottish Literature: Character and Influence* (London, 1919), p 277.

FURTHER READING

The possibilities are immense; in the standard histories of Scottish Literature and English Literature (Saintsbury's writings on nineteenth-century Scottish authors are exceptionally interesting) and in the various recent histories of Scotland, the Edinburgh history and the New history. T C Smout's *A Century of the Scottish People 1830–1950* (1986), though not very full on literary matters, is indispensable as background to the period.

G E Davie established an authoritative view of nineteenth-century higher education in *The Democratic Intellect* (1971), which was the subject of detailed criticism in R D Anderson, *Education and Opportunity in Victorian Scotland* (1983). The debate continues: and Davie's most original and substantial recent contribution has been *The Crisis of the Democratic Intellect* (1986) in which much material is studied with relevance to the thinking, and the writing, of Scotland in the nineteenth century.

David Masson was an active participant in much of the period's writing and controversy: his *Edinburgh Sketches and Memories* (1892) and *Memories of Two Cities: Edinburgh and Aberdeen* (1911) are mines of information. Many other books could be cited with partial introductions to writing circles of the time: T H Darlow's *William Robertson Nicoll: Life and Letters* (1925) is unusually full. The present writer's *Kailyard: A New Assessment* (1981) attempts an introduction to the conflicting themes of the period.

For overall reference, the reader is commended to W R Aitken's magisterial *Scottish Literature in English and Scots* (Gale Research Information Guides: vol 37 of *American Literature, English Literature and World Literatures in English*: Detroit, 1982).

Chapter 10

Reviews and Magazines: Criticism and Polemic

JOAN MILNE and WILLIE SMITH

In England, the eighteenth century had seen the rise and subsequent disappearance of the periodical magazine devoted to literary criticism and essay writing. The abnormal success of *The Spectator* eclipsed in most people's minds the multi-variety of periodicals which enjoyed a may-fly existence. However, these early models did serve the purpose of fairly clearly delineating the two definitive genres of the periodical: the review and the magazine which became so popular in the nineteenth century. In essence the review was designed as a vehicle for criticism of new literature with the possibility of contemporary critics re-assessing the great writers of the past. The magazine was primarily concerned with the propagation of the new literature itself. It commissioned essays, poetry, short stories or serialised fiction from the ranks of aspiring young writers.

The popular demand for such publications was ravenous. Here for the first time, the intellectual and bourgeois community had access to an organ which allowed them to participate in the then rapidly moving world of ideas both passively, as readership, and actively, as contributors. Because these publications encapsulated all the excitement of a world in an age of change, they were necessarily force-fed with the latest literary and intellectual fads, whether exegesis of the 'new' economic theory, startling revelations of German philosophic thought, or even the 'science' of phrenology. All this was underpinned by a fundamental political bias, which D A Low refers to as a 'dynamic organicism'.[1] The periodical of the late eighteenth to mid nineteenth century, particularly in Scotland, demonstrates exactly a process, not just of commenting on the whole surge of change in society, but actively becoming a more and more important agent itself in that change.

In Scotland the true beginnings of the periodical lay with the publication in 1779 of *The Mirror*, soon to be followed by *The Lounger* (1785). This was an attempt on the part of Henry Mackenzie (1745–1831) (the 'Man of Feeling') to produce a suitably Augustan magazine which would lend literary cachet to the sense of intellectual confidence established by the Edinburgh Enlightenment. The magazine itself was never a healthy proposition and soon disappeared from circulation. However, in one respect, it interests us as a result of Mackenzie's now notorious review in 1786 of Burns's *Kilmarnock Edition*. The ecstatic praise of the Heaven-taught ploughman, together with the distinct plea to the readership to excuse lapses in 'taste', anticipates in many respects the dichotomy that was to dominate nineteenth century attitudes. Enthusiasm for new 'taste' and 'reason' came into conflict with a sentimental nostalgia for a Utopian past, a golden age, populated by philosopher peasants like Burns's cotter. In 1779 Mackenzie noted that the eventual failure of *The Mirror* was due to his basic inability to square the intellectual circle: 'We had not philosophy enough here for that paper [*The Mirror*]; it was too abstracted for most minor reading people, while others complained it wanted *depth*'.[2]

This paradox was to lie unresolved until Archibald Constable put together a brilliant team of writers and launched the *Edinburgh Review* in 1802. Constable felt that there should be an outlet for Whig views and that reform and revolution with their concomitant excitement must replace the old order. *The Review* hit literary Edinburgh like a thunderbolt. Constable was immensely influential, not just in the choice of his contributors, but in the manner in which he treated them. Now generally recognised as the first modern publisher, he was the first to pay regular stipends to his writers and to actively offer commissions. But even more vital, he understood that no periodical could survive without a strong hand at the helm over a substantial timescale. The editorship had to be a professional long-term post.

The post of editor was filled for almost a quarter of the new century by Francis Jeffrey (1773–1850), with the help of Francis Horner, Sidney Smith and Henry Brougham. Jeffrey had been called to the Scottish bar after a brilliant career at Edinburgh and Oxford Universities. He rose in time to the position of Lord Advocate and latterly became a judge. It was as a consequence of his legal training that his criticism of literature had an apparent formal clarity and philosophical depth rarely encountered previously.

It would be true also to say that *The Review* benefited considerably from its becoming in effect the mouthpiece of the Scottish Educational system. The Scottish Universities operated in a totally different way from Oxford and Cambridge in that the English colleges were specialist orientated, training students in the classics and mathematics. The Scottish student spent much of his time exploring the world of philosophy and logic. This strong adherence to philosophy and rhetoric aimed to produce a mind that was intellectually flexible, articulate and wide ranging. In Jeffrey's case it produced a man who could employ first philosophical principles to analyse literature. However, his readers did not always agree with his criticisms and his reputation as a reviewer was very mixed. Frequently Jeffrey's philosophical principles distorted the more intuitive and spontaneous art of criticism. Moreover many of Jeffrey's philosophical ideas were intrinsic to his Whig leanings and also coloured his writing. Politicisation and personalisation of criticism led to the alienation of Walter Scott who had been an early and enthusiastic reviewer. Not surprisingly he objected to such reviews as the following on *Marmion*:

> To write a modern romance of chivalry seems to be such a fantasy as to build a modern abbey or an English pagoda. For once, however, it may be excused as a pretty caprice of genius, but a second production of the same sort is entitled

to less indulgence and imposes a sort of duty to drive the author from so idle a task by a fair exposition of the faults that are in a manner inseparable from its execution.[3]

Jeffrey may have considered it his 'duty' to influence and change contemporary writing by pointing out the author's faults, but in Scott's case (as in many others) he did not succeed. A subsequent attack[4] on Scott's article on Spanish conditions in 1808[5] proved the final straw and Scott left for the London based *Quarterly Review*. This could not properly be a substitute for *The Review* and Scott had to wait until 1817 to find a more acceptable vehicle in William Blackwood's new magazine.

Political bias was also exercised by the bulk of the contributors, referred to acidly by Byron as 'The Bloodhounds of Arthur's Seat'.[6] Jeffrey, Brougham and Horner all cared passionately about politics and used *The Review* in much the same way as they used debating clubs. They took a stance and used the text to 'prove' their position, fighting tooth and claw to destroy the possibility of any alternative viewpoint. Byron lamented this in his 'English Bards and Scotch Reviewers' with his sigh '. . . it would indeed require an Hercules to crush the Hydra; but if the author succeeds in merely "bruising"one of the heads of the serpent, though his own hand should suffer in the encounter, he will be amply satisfied.'[7]

Jeffrey was often led into defending poetry that was ornate but essentially empty of feeling or intellect, simultaneously rejecting the simple language of the Lake poets as being essentially un-poetic, due to his Augustan sense of poetry as patterned, organised and depending for effect on a high poetic diction. His famous outburst of 'This will never do!' in his review of Wordsworth's *The Excursion* was a natural consequence of what he termed 'taste'. Yet Jeffrey's own lapses were frequent and comprehensive. To begin a review of an early Wordsworth piece with 'This is the very worst poem ever imprinted in a quarto volume',[8] is at best hyperbolic and at worst incompetent diatribe. Yet such was the enthusiasm by Edinburgh society for 'new rationalism', and a magazine to reflect it, that the *Review*'s being 'anti-romantic' served only to increase the sales, and under Jeffrey's rule the *Edinburgh Review* became the most influential periodical of the early nineteenth century. But the success of the *Review* resided mainly in its professional approach. Jeffrey and Constable were prepared to pay for excellence and that meant 20 guineas per *sheet* of a review and up to £1,000 for a single poem. Even two philosophic essays earned the author £1,000. The success of this policy was mirrored in the steady circulation: 7,000 in 1807, 13,000 in 1812 and rising to a peak of 14,000 in 1818.[9] The 'Blue and Yellow' as it was nicknamed, after its use of the Whig colours on its covers, swept all Tory opposition before it and became the voice of Edinburgh Rationalism, and very much the 'observer' of public taste; and with articles later commissioned from Carlyle and Cockburn, did display for a time at least 'the irrepressible passion for discussion which succeeded the fall of old systems on the French Revolution.'[10] It dominated literary life in Scotland, sweeping all rivals before it until, in a Tory backlash, William Blackwood (1776–1804) published *The Edinburgh Monthly Magazine* in April 1817. Blackwood soon realised that his first editors, James Cleghorn and Thomas Pringle, were not the men to challenge Jeffrey's hegemony. They were soon dismissed and replaced by the young advocates John Wilson (1785–1854) and John Gibson Lockhart (1794–1854).

These two men were, more than any others, to determine the fate of Scottish writing during the Victorian age. Their style was made plain in the very first edition of the new *Blackwood's Edinburgh Magazine* which appeared in October 1817. It contained three articles, all anonymous, that shook literary Edinburgh to its foundations. The first was a savage personal attack on Coleridge and his Hegelian principles.[11] Although masquerading as a review of *Biographia Literaria*, it spent most of its spleen in lashing Coleridge for his decadence, his corruption of the young and his libertarian idealism which was seen to be a flimsy cover for bloody revolution and anarchy—which would certainly have astounded Hegel as an interpretation of his thought. This failure on Wilson's part (since stylistically it appears to be his pen at work) to understand the function and purpose of Romanticism was to be a damning factor in his later development as a writer and critic.

It is strongly probable that the second article, signed 'Z', devoted to the discomfiting of the 'Cockneys', was written by Lockhart.[12] To say that being young and bursting to put thoughts into print is any excuse for his comments on the morals of Leigh Hunt, is to defend the indefensible. It was not polemic, but invective, made even more vicious by Lockhart's considerable rhetorical talent. Mrs Oliphant commented on the article that 'It can only arouse our astonishment and dismay that the hand of a gentleman could have produced it, let alone a critic.'[13]

James Hogg, having failed as editor of his *The Spy* (1810–1811) joined Lockhart and Wilson in assembling the third article.[14] Mrs Oliphant claimed that the three, joined by Blackwood and some of his Tory cronies, took only one uproarious night to write the infamous *Chaldee Manuscript*. This was a quasi-Biblical text filled with allegorical reference. It purported to be genuine, and an introduction tries to give it some kind of spurious provenance within the archives of 'the Great Library of Paris'. It undoubtedly seemed a great joke to its authors to turn intellectual Edinburgh into a complex bestiary peopled by priest-like beings supported or opposed by everything from the leopard, scorpion and wild boar (allusions to nicknames of Wilson, Lockhart and Hogg) to hyena and beagle. The 'man with the horn' was clearly Constable and all references to 'ebony' translated easily enough to Blackwood; while the 'magician' could only be the Wizard of the North, Scott himself, and Jeffrey the 'familiar spirit'. The conflict between the Whig and Tory publishers and their literary friends, although thinly disguised, was of course patently recognisable to those involved. The authors, in ignoring the limited size of the intellectual establishment, laid themselves open to the charge of personal libel. George Davie reckoned that the four Universities produced only about 120 graduates each year, of whom possibly a quarter lived in the Edinburgh area and participated in the life of the city;[15] which meant that *The Chaldee* was lampooning people who rubbed shoulders and wits with the authors on a daily basis in the small geographical area of the New Town.

As Scott himself commented 'Edinburgh is rather too narrow for satire so markedly personal'.[16]

The Chaldee Manuscript, however, inevitably achieved its purpose in offending the members of the Whig camp and delighting unscrupulous Tories. Cries of 'blasphemy' mingled with outraged shouts of 'libel'. Professors Sharpe and Playfair of Edinburgh University, both well-loved and respected figures in the town, and contributors to *The Review*, were perceived as being criticised unfairly in their religious belief; and one J G Dalyell went so far as to sue Blackwood for libel for being described as 'apelike'. As if this were not enough, Leigh Hunt (although himself 'a convicted libeller') issued a writ against Lockhart and refused to accept Blackwood's assertion that he had no idea who 'Z' was, and that he exercised no control over the content of the articles. The amount of protection Blackwood could offer was limited, and Wilson and Lockhart had no other option than to flee the city: Wilson to Elleray, his estate near Windermere, and Lockhart to darkest Lanarkshire. The affair was eventually settled, but left a lasting rift between Blackwood and his London agents, and an awareness that the political lines in Edinburgh had now been clearly drawn. As Professor J F Ferrier (later Wilson's son-in-law) remarked, 'The Chaldee Manuscript was the first trumpet-note which dissolved the truce of Edinburgh and broke the spell of Whig domination';[17] while Henry Mackenzie, still the doyen of Edinburgh letters, considered that the first edition contained several good articles, but mixed with some things so offensive that he would not wish it to be found lying on his table, and returned his copy to Blackwood.

Mrs Oliphant, in *Annals of a Publishing House, William Blackwood and his Sons* (1897) attempted to defend Blackwood's role in all this; but from the evidence available, Blackwood seemed more to advocate his 'Maga's' controversial role in order to succeed in its aims, and that essentially no publicity could be bad publicity. The best that can be argued for *Blackwood's* is that Wilson and Lockhart were only competing with the autocratic single-mindedness of 'the chief of critics', Jeffrey, and had to fight him with his own methods, but in greatly exaggerated form.

During the next few years there was yet another law-suit (on behalf of Professor Leslie); and a bitter wrangle ensued that almost ended in a duel between Lockhart and the anonymous writer of an article, 'Hypocrisy Unveiled and Calumny Detected in a review of "B.E.M."'. However, their attempts to uncover the gentleman's identity were foiled. Lockhart matured quickly, and turned from being the 'scorpion which delighteth to sting'[18] to the role of ruminative commentator in the vein of a latter-day Smollett, until his departure for London in 1825 to manage John Murray's *Quarterly Review*. He took to writing biographies (outstandingly of Burns and Napoleon); and his crowning achievement was his *Memoirs of the life of Scott* (1837–8). But, less fortunately for the development of Scottish culture and literary life in the century, John Wilson remained to succeed to the place left vacant by Mackenzie and Scott as 'uncrowned king' of Scottish social and intellectual life. He had come to *Blackwood's* with the Oxford Newdigate Prize for poetry and two volumes of poetry, *The Isle of Palms and Other Poems* (1812) and

The City of the Plague and Other Poems (1816), both of which are now seen as artificial and maudlin. He was physically very impressive; 'a young man of grand form and mien with the thews and sinews of an athlete, and a front like Jove to threaten and command. A genial giant, but not a mild one. Genius and fun and wit no less part of his nature than wrath and vehemence, and a power of swift and sudden slaughter corrected in turn by large radiance of gaiety and good humour'.[19] He was 'sudden' in all things.

These attributes were very much part of the ethos of 'Maga' as it developed under Wilson' editorship. To attract an audience it had to be always surprising, always unpredictable. At a time when *The Review* was entering the stasis of middle age, Wilson brought an excitement into popular publishing. His flaws, which were fundamentally linked to his emotional instability, rapidly became evident; yet were not only accepted by the public but were lauded by it. When in 1820 he was elected Professor of Moral Philosophy at Edinburgh University, as an unashamedly political appointee of Tory power, it was generally known that the subjects of his lectures arrived in note form, by letter, from his old friend Alexander Blair, Professor of Rhetoric at University College, London. Yet his lectures were packed by those who came to hear his marvellous voice and dramatic delivery.

This characterised his literary achievement also; strong on rhetoric and verbal pyrotechnics but weak on content, the quintessential 'hollow man', as MacDiarmid described him in his gallery of *Scots Eccentrics*.[20] But it must be said that the form of the magazine allowed his boisterous spirits an outlet they could find nowhere else. He was probably the first to write extensively and sucessfully about sports—walking, swimming, fishing and 'leaping'— and he had a genuine talent for weaving miscellanea into dialogue, nowhere better seen than when in 1823 he assumed the role of 'Christopher North' (an alter ego that increasingly became part of his true identity) in order to present his *Noctes Ambrosianae*.

In this series of imaginary dialogues set in Ambrose's, an Edinburgh tavern, North converses on a multi-variety of topics with his fellow tipplers: the 'Ettrick Shepherd' (James Hogg), 'Timothy Tickler' (Robert Sym) and 'The Opium-eater' (Thomas de Quincey). All of these helped to construct the series at first but gradually Wilson assumed sole authorship. The shepherd is portrayed as a hard-drinking salt-of-the-earth philosopher peasant. He is bibulously simplistic in his views of city life and shown as painfully grateful for the advice given and tolerance shown toward him by the 'gentlemen', especially the Professor.

It is surprising that Hogg, apart from occasional outbursts of anger, so good-humouredly accepted the betrayal of him as the simple 'country cousin' unable to cope with the sophistication of Edinburgh life represented by North and company. It may partly be due to the way in which, as the following extracts show, 'The Shepherd' is sometimes presented as more than equal to the taunting he receives from his friends. After a journey to Buchanan Lodge in a hackney coach, the satirising of a romantic response to nature by Tickler and North is juxtaposed with the Shepherd's genuine, if reductive, appreciation of the countryside.

Tickler: In vain Spring sought his Flora, in haunts beloved of old, on the banks
of the shaded rivulet . . .
North: Or in nooks among the rocky mountains . . .
Shepherd: Or oases among the heather . . .
Tickler: Or parterres of grove-guarded gardens . . .
North: Or within the shadow of veranda . . .
Shepherd: Or forest glade, where move the antlers of the unhunted red deer.—
In siccan bonny spats hae I often seen the Spring, like a doubtfu'
glimmer o' sunshine, appearing and disappearing fraw amang the
birk-trees, twenty times in the course o' an April day.—But, oh! sirs,
yon was just a maist detestable forenoon,—and as for the hackney-
cotch . . .[21]

The Shepherd then goes on to complain in very realistic terms about the
disadvantages of the hackney coach, preferring his own more simple means
of transport—the gig; 'but', he continues, 'when I happen to forgather wi' sic
scrubs as you, that grudge the expense o' a yeckipage o' their ain, I maun
submit to a glass-cotch and a' its abominations.'[22] The strength of the
Shepherd's character is underlined by the language in which he speaks. It has
a natural forcefulness lacking in the exaggeratedly elaborate and affected
'English' preferred by the more 'sophisticated' characters. The conflicting
feelings Wilson seems to have experienced about Hogg, both as a character
in the *Noctes*, and as actual person and author, are also evident in the way
he later swayed between lavishly praising Hogg's work in one edition of
Blackwood's, and bitterly condemning him a few editions later—but safely
under the protection of anonymity. Perhaps this instability of assessment
stems from Wilson's inability to reconcile his desire to conform to the 'new
rationalism' with his almost subconscious fascination with the romantic idea
of the superiority of 'natural man', almost a conflict between 'head' and
'heart', and a conflict Hogg himself would have recognised. Be that as it may,
there is no doubt that at the time the *Noctes*, through its energy, charm, and
humour, exerted considerable influence and fixed in the public mind a number
of important literary 'rules'.

First of all, despite Hogg's rich vernacular, it reinforced public attitudes
towards the use of Scots as an inferior language. Hogg, like Burns, wrote
largely in Lowland Scots. The Shepherd of the *Noctes* speaks his lines in a
less dense dialect. Wilson shares Jeffrey's point of view (expressed, for
example, when reviewing Burns) 'that to write in the Scots tongue was
anachronistic'. Any parochial language may for a time be accepted as a quaint
novelty, but for a poet to succeed, make money and establish a national
reputation he should necessarily write in English. Scots was permissible as a
comic vehicle or as a marker of social class, but was not the proper medium
for sophisticated comment.

The second main influence that Wilson's *Noctes* had was to force too many
Scottish writers to write in a way that was safely acceptable to 'polite' critics
and a new and genteel reading public, and to avoid radical ideas which would
upset the status quo of a British monarchy, aristocracy, established church
and populace in a strictly hierarchical order, set within a British Empire

which was clearly God approved. This influence combined with that of Scott's historical novels, with their sentimental nostalgia for a lost idyllic Britain, was, of course, perfectly in tune with current popular feeling, reaching an apogee with the beautiful stage-managing Scott did for the visit of George IV to Edinburgh in 1822. And while there is, of course, a realistic and socially satiric side to Scott's novels, to the contemporary reader this was all too easily lost in the timeless attraction of romance. Such was the attraction of this world that an attempt was actually made in 1839, by the Earl of Eglinton and his friends, to re-enact the tourney from *Ivanhoe*. This representation of a romantic myth in Victorian Scotland proved to be a disaster. It is, however, illuminating that a distinguished guest at this ill-fated Eglinton Tournament of 1839 was John Wilson, whose own prose and fiction so clearly shares the values of this reactionary mythology. A perverted 'cult' of feeling under-pinned Wilson's vision, permitting rural reality to shed its nastiness, becoming instead home to thoroughly unnatural 'natural' man. In his portrayals of Scottish rural life sturdy farmers, cottars and 'orra-men' are tearfully thin-skinned yet long-suffering, as is their Christian duty, in a way that young Harley in Mackenzie's book would have relished. Naturally, natural man was a Tory, espousing the sanctity of family, home and church and with a proper veneration for the ethos of the landed gentry.

Ian Campbell describes this phenomenon as 'a desire not to mirror reality, but to make possible the maximum sympathetic response, not according to verisimilitude, but by a calculated *distortion of verisimilitude* on lines tacitly agreed between author and audience'.[23] There is thus a fundamental differ-ence between English romantic 'suspension of disbelief' and nineteenth-cen-tury Scottish preference for nicely-calculated unreality. The reason for this is simple; nostalgia can be a semi-realistic and coherent method of generating philosophic 'sympathy' only if there is the established popular notion that the past had had its merits. English history reflected that country's essential economic and political success, whereas Scotland's story, except for a few bright defiant decades, had been one of economic failure and political and religious internecine squabbling. Nostalgia for the idyll was meaningless in a Scottish context.

All of this might have been relatively harmless whimsy were it not for the provincialisation of Edinburgh during the early years of Wilson's editorship. Lockhart had gone to London; Jeffrey relinquished the *Review* for a legal and political career in London; Carlyle, overcome by the strain of putting up with 'much that is spiritually *kleinstadtisch*,[24] had fled to London; Hogg and Galt were dead; Brougham and Cockburn increasingly devoted themselves to law. Wilson was left as the sole luminary of the periodical 'tradition' and he used both the powers of his editorship and the assumption of natural good taste of his stories to change the direction of writing towards the espousal of the values of the Tory rural classes through a sentimental nostalgia with little moral balance save that of the forms of Christianity. And with the *Review* emasculated, what balance there had been was lost.

As Wilson's health began to fail the reins of editorship were gradually taken up by one of the most politically and stylistically faithful of the contributors, David Macbeth Moir (1791–1857). He had written a number of stories in Wilson mode under the pseudonym 'Δ' ('Delta') for Blackwood. Indeed, it is possible that he was the author of the haunting 'Canadian Boat Song' published in 1829. But as a contributor, his most influential work was the serialisation from 1824 onwards, of *The Life of Mansie Waugh, Tailor of Dalkeith*. This is the account of the sayings and doings of a tradesman in what then was a small village. It was humorous and pawky and proved a considerable success, not just in Scotland, but in England, where it was regarded with delight as a portrait of 'couthy' Scots rural manners and peasant wisdom. It further expanded and allowed the legitimisation of pawky Scots humour where use of the vernacular became a marker of comic intention and the protagonists were 'kintra clowns'.

When Wilson retired from the editorship in the 1840s, his son-in-law, William Edmondstoune Aytoun (1813–65) gradually assumed Wilson's role. He had written some two hundred articles for Blackwood during the late 1830s and 1840s and openly associated himself with Wilson's ideas. His stories, from 'How we got up the Glemutchkin Railway' (October 1845) to 'How I stood for the Dreepdailly Burghs' (1847) show a nice sense of the ridiculous. His poetry was a mix of parody and satire on the one hand and the derivative historical ballad on the other. He virtually followed his father-in-law into the most influential professorship at Edinburgh University where he was appointed to the chair of Rhetoric and Belles Lettres in 1845. This, as Erik Frykman demonstrated, made him the first modern professor of English Literature as such.[25] His stance was very much that the Scots literary tradition lacked any obvious classical models and therefore had to be inferior to English writing. There is little doubt that this attitude was affected by the then current debate over the attempts to Anglicise the Scottish University curriculum and take it away from a general dependence on philosophy towards a narrower and classics-based education. He was a passionate supporter of the 'reformers', in line with his predecessors. He attempted to rediscover a different Scottish tradition, based on the later poetry of George Buchanan, and tried to find a continuity from the 1580s to the Victorians. Aytoun presupposed that Scottish writing was, and always had been, of two natures. On one hand, ancient Scots humanism blended with mediaeval classicism to create a certain poetic style that was typified by Burns's Augustan poetry in English. On the distaff side was what Aytoun had to regard as 'folk-poetry' written in dialect and owing little to classical form or allusion. It took as its model the long tradition of folk-lore for both its material and metaphors and a ballad-type structure for its form. This, to Aytoun, had the advantage of immediacy to and popularity with the vast bulk of the Scottish population, whether conventionally literate or not. Thus the *literati* could enjoy Milton and Dryden as a sign of their superiority, but could still be moved and amused by poetry in their native tongue and tradition. Aytoun saw his role, and that of *Blackwood*'s, as ensuring the survival of both traditions; but with the clear understanding that in writing for a mass audience, the 'superior' English classical path would be regarded as dominant and superior.

Scots language could be watered down and become a vehicle for comedy and plangent morbidity, in a land whose representation was being reconstructed in fiction to satisfy a growing British and American public and a growing tourist industry.

That the old impulse to confuse criticism with personal vendetta had not lost its bite over the years, is apparent in Aytoun's attack on what he called the 'Spasmodic' school of poetry. P J Bailey (1816–1902), Sydney Dobell (1824–74) and Alexander Smith (1830–67) were popular in the 1840s as writers of a poetry in which the poet takes on the *persona* of a Nietszchean adventurer concerned with discovering the secrets of the Universe through violent and frantic activity. With its high-flown utterances and turgid purple passages, it was wide open to parody; Aytoun published a mock review of a Spasmodic poem in the October 1854 edition. 'Firmillian: or the student of Badajoz, a Spasmodic Tragedy', purported to have been written by one T Percy Jones, and was the tragic story of a hero-poet who, in order to feel his way into the character of Cain, the subject of his latest *oeuvre*, commits a series of extravagant crimes, all of which end in disaster. Not content with that, in the next number Aytoun produced the poem itself. This spelt the doom of the Spasmodics. No-one could take them seriously after 'Firmillian', even although most readers were in on the joke and knew that Aytoun was the author.

But despite such amusing diversions, by the 1850s Edinburgh had lost all of its pre-eminence as a literary centre. The battle for the soul of the Universities and the 1843 Disruption in the church dominated intellectual debate. A concern for literature became less important to the readers of the *Magazine* and *Review*. At this same time, popular journalism had begun to take over the serialisation of fiction; with the 1855 repeal of the 'taxes on knowledge' which had restricted the development of local newspaper presses, there was a 'threefold increase in numbers of papers of all kinds in the period up to 1910'. William Donaldson has taken up the story of the movement of Scottish literary energy into the popular press in his *Popular Literature in Victorian Scotland*; meanwhile writers in the employ of *Blackwood*, like the young George Eliot and Margaret Oliphant increasingly concerned themselves with fiction centred around English and middle-class manners with a sententious morality, addressed to a wider English audience. Criticism was on the whole devoted to English publications, to suit a predominantly English readership. However much Mrs Oliphant with her two hundred or so contributions to *Blackwood*'s tried to resist the lure of the kailyard, her predecessors in the magazine had ensured that popular taste should embrace the sentimental and rural moralising story. There was little real enthusiasm for Mrs Oliphant's refusal to provide the conventional happy ending and despite her prolific energy and output, she never enjoyed the popular success that her work merited.

Other periodicals had indeed begun to cater to a popular audience earlier in the century. In February, 1832, the Edinburgh publishers William and Robert Chambers issued a 'Journal' designed to 'better' the reading public. William Chambers, as a philanthropic 'improver', saw a need to produce 'original and select' papers on literary and scientific objects including articles 'on the Formation and Arrangements of Society'.[26] The tone of the weekly $1\frac{1}{2}d$. magazine was educative but bright and readable. It soon achieved a circulation of 30,000. Robert Chambers had taken over as editor by 1836 and instituted a programme of 'encouraging literature' including support for Hugh Miller, and for James Gilfillan against Aytoun's attacks on him as one of the 'Spasmodics'. In later years, the *Journal* (now *Chamber's Journal*) published Stevenson, Conan Doyle, Buchan and Neil Gunn.

The *Journal*'s selling point (especially in the early part of its history) was its wealth of pawky anecdotes, stories, and easily digested items on Scottish history and biography, and all often written in a racy vernacular Scots. It was able to present itself thus because it was intended for a mass and indigenous readership and therefore did not face the 'identity crisis' of the two 'big' periodicals. However, almost in spite of itself, it became a success south of the Border by the 1840s, caught in the wave of enthusiasm among English middle-class readers for all things quaintly Scottish. But within a few years it too went the way of its companions, becoming progressively bland and anglicised.

It had, however, pointed up yet again the place which existed for literary journals which would satisfy a purely Scottish vernacular market. This was filled by the newspapers that proliferated towards the end of the 1860s and the popular literary journals, most famous of which was W D Latto's *The People's Journal*, which later developed into *The People's Friend*. Para-doxically enough, Latto's writing was vernacular but distinctly non-kailyard. There was little sentimentality and great good humour. Latto based his *persona*, Tammas Bodkin, on the tailor's apprentice in David Moir's *Mansie Waugh*. But this Bodkin developed differently from his cousin in *Blackwood*'s. It is true that he indulges in the usual capers of the Victorian hero urchin; but these exploits never descend into genteel moralising. When Bodkin grows up he becomes a successful tailor in Dundee, and even travels abroad, giving hilarious accounts of a continental breakfast:

> 'Tibbie' quo' I, 'this will never do. There's
> naething but hunger an' herschip here, I see.   [hardship]
> That's hoo the French folkies are sic wee
> ill-grown warrochs; they dinna get their meat.   [stunted fellows]
> An' they ca' *this* a breakfast, do they? Guid
> help them, puir bodies . . .'[27]

This works because the sentiments are entirely realistic and human and do not belong to the idyllic world, and in Scotland itself this kind of literature was more acceptable than the kailyard, which was almost an industry in exile. In addition, there was a certain didactic element coupled with social commitment in Latto's *Journal* that was latterly missing from the literary periodicals.

The most influential periodical by the end of the Victorian era stood right at the end of the line stretching from Jeffrey and Wilson through Moir and

Aytoun. This was in fact not a Scottish publication at all, but Sir William Robertson Nicoll's *British Weekly*. Nicoll, an Aberdeenshire minister, moved to London due to ill-health and was hired by the evangelical publishers, Hodder and Stoughton. They wanted a new magazine which would popularise non-conformist beliefs. Nicoll agreed to be editor of the magazine; the writers hired by Nicoll to propagate his faith were a mixture of ministers and teachers: S R Crockett, J M Barrie, 'Ian Maclaren' and Annie S Swan. These writers took the tradition that they had perceived as being the populist one in England, with its fascination for the sentimental and rural. In English writing this in fact had far less social and traditional moral basis, but Nicoll could look back to Wilson's example and the way it had triumphed in Scotland, and use that as a model. These writers became the doyens of the kailyard movement, distorting genuine sentiment and legitimate nostalgia to frame an imagined bucolic environment peopled by kindly, Christian folk who in their homely sanitised Scots propounded examplars of moral duty. They reflected a kind of Calvinistic Islam, submission to the will of the Laird, and his prophets; the factor, the dominie and the meenister. Although superficially sharing some common identity with Wilson's noble savage as seen in his philosopher-shepherd, they were even emptier. Yet for a generation the image of Scotland successfully propagated abroad was that created by Nicoll's debased kailyard mythology, despite alternative and far more valid images and ideals in both popular literature and serious fiction.

NOTES

1 D A Low, 'Periodicals in the Age of Scott', in *Scott Bicentenary Essays*, Alan Bell (ed) (Edinburgh, 1973), p 318.
2 H MacKenzie, Letter to W Craig in 1779 in Ian Campbell, *Kailyard* (Edinburgh, 1981), p 23.
3 F Jeffrey, *Edinburgh Review*, March 1808.
4 Ibid., April 1809.
5 W Scott, *Edinburgh Weekly Journal*, cited in Mrs Oliphant *Annals of a Publishing House: William Blackwood and his Sons* (London, 1897), vol I, p 180.
6 Byron, 'English Bards and Scotch Reviewers'.
7 Ibid.
8 Mrs Oliphant, *Annals*, vol I, p 278.
9 Roderick Watson, *The Literature of Scotland* (London, 1984), p 244.
10 Henry Cockburn, *Life of Lord Jeffrey* (London, 1852), Introduction.
11 *Blackwood's Edinburgh Magazine*, October 1817, pp 3–18.
12 Mrs Oliphant, *Annals*, vol I, p 173.
13 Mrs Oliphant, *Annals*, vol I, pp 133–5.
14 *Blackwood's Edinburgh Magazine*, October 1817, pp 89–97.
15 George Davie, *The Democratic Intellect* (Edinburgh, 1961), pp 19–20.
16 Mrs Oliphant, *Annals*, vol I, p 272.
17 Ibid., vol I, p 273.
18 *Blackwood's Edinburgh Magazine*, November 1817, p 205 ff.

19 M Gordon, *Christopher North: A Memoir of John Wilson* (Edinburgh, 1862).
20 Hugh MacDiarmid, *Scots Eccentrics* (London, 1936), p 99.
21 John Wilson, *Noctes Ambrosianae*, J Ferrier (ed) (Edinburgh, 1868) vol I, p 177.
22 Ibid., p 178.
23 Ian Campbell, *Kailyard*, p 40.
24 Carlyle in Campbell, *Kailyard*, p 30.
25 Erik Frykman, *W E Aytoun, Pioneer Professor of English at Edinburgh* (Gothenburg, 1963).
26 Trevor Royle, *The Macmillan Companion to Scottish Literature* (London, 1983), p 65.
27 W D Latto, *People's Journal* 1867, cited in William Donaldson, *Popular Literature in Victorian Scotland* (Aberdeen, 1986), p 48.

FURTHER READING

GENERAL

Daiches, David, *Edinburgh* (London, 1978).
Davie, George, *The Democratic Intellect* (Edinburgh, 1961).
Lockhart, J G, *Peter's Letters to his Kinsfolk*, W Ruddick (ed) (Aberdeen, 1977).
Royle, Trevor, *Precipitous City: A History of Literary Edinburgh* (Edinburgh, 1980).

REVIEWS AND MAGAZINES

Chambers, W, *Memoir of Robert Chambers* (Edinburgh, 1872)
Clive, John, *The Scotch Reviewers: The Edinburgh Review 1802–15* (London, 1957).
Cockburn, Henry, *Life of Lord Jeffrey* (London, 1852).
Donaldson, William, *Popular Literature in Victorian Scotland* (Aberdeen, 1986).
Douglas, Sir George, *The Blackwood Group* (Edinburgh, 1897)
Fontana, Biancamaria, *Rethinking the Politics of Commercial Society: The Edinburgh Review 1802–1832* (Cambridge, 1985)
Frykman, Erik, *W E Aytoun: Pioneer Professor of English in Edinburgh* (Gothenburg, 1963).
Gordon, M, *A Memoir of Christopher North* (Edinburgh, 1862).
Greig, J G, *Francis Jeffrey of the Edinburgh Review* (Edinburgh, 1948).
Oliphant, Margaret, *Annals of a Publishing House: William Blackwood and his Sons, Their Magazine and Friends*, 3 Volumes (Edinburgh, 1897–8). (The third volume was edited by Mrs Gerald Porter).
Tredrey, Frank, *The House of Blackwood 1804–1954* (Edinburgh, 1954).
Weinstein, M, *W E Aytoun and the Spasmodic Controversy* (New Haven & London, 1968).

Chapter 11

Popular Literature: The Press, the People, and the Vernacular Revival

WILLIAM DONALDSON

During the nineteenth century Scotland experienced a communications revolution. The automation of paper-making, mechanical typesetting, high-speed steam-driven rotary presses, and the growth of the railway network, combined to make cheap reading matter available on a hitherto undreamed-of scale. Major advances in popular literacy and increasing affluence in the rapidly expanding upper working and lower middle classes created a new reading public and a new mass popular literary market.[1]

The sheer cost of the case-bound book was often a major obstacle to ordinary people in search of recreational reading, and for much of the century book-buying was the preserve of the well-to-do. First-edition fiction appeared in a three-volume format retailing at a guinea-and-a-half, at a time when the average working man earned between 10 shillings to £1 a week. Even the middle classes tended to rent their novels from private subscription libraries rather than buy them outright, while such library services as were available to the ordinary reader like parish libraries and mechanics institutes tended to exclude fiction altogether on the grounds that it was frivolous or immoral. For most of this period, therefore, book-fiction represented the tastes and outlook of the upper middle classes conditioned by the London-dominated all-British bookmarket. What the great majority of Scots read tended to be very different in content and was not published in book form at all.

Chapbooks were the staple secular reading matter of the common people until well into the nineteenth century. They cost a penny and were published in pamphlet form on coarse paper, adorned with assorted, usually crude, illustrations. They contained a variety of tales, poems and songs and were sold in country districts by packmen and in the cities by professional chapbook 'patterers' using street-theatre techniques. The chapbooks mixed gritty social observation with slapstick humour and a lively strain of bawdry and their world-picture was dominated by the conventions of the old rural economy. As the century advanced, however, they became more diverse, merging with the popular literary miscellany at one end of the scale and the sensational novella at the other. Older titles like 'John Cheap the Chapman', and 'the Witty Sayings and Exploits of George Buchanan' were displaced by popular gothic material like 'Elizabeth, or The Exiles of Siberia', and 'The Iron Shroud; or, Italian Revenge'—the latter an intriguing story about the death of a nobleman in a horrible contracting cell, strongly reminiscent of Edgar Allan Poe. The chapbook reached the last phase of its development during the 1860s and 1870s when it became a vehicle for the early Western, carrying a whole series of pirated American tales like 'The Gold Digger of California, or The Mysterious Miner', 'The Stolen Beauty of the Rio Grande' and 'Romance of the Texan Pampas, or The Hermit of the Colorado Hills'.

As technical change affected work patterns and leisure became more widely available the Useful Knowledge movement came into being, dedicated to the idea of a cheap and moral literature, and it had a major impact on publishing and the availability of the printed word. Popular miscellanies like *The Selector* edited by Peter Buchan of Peterhead and the *Cheap Magazine* of George Miller of Haddington established a pattern that was to appear again and again during the century. Both men had come up through the chapbook trade—Miller had been a chapman himself, and Buchan trained as a printer at a leading chapbook house, the Randall Press in Stirling. Their publications owed obvious debts to the chap tradition. *The Selector* in particular was identical in appearance to a chapbook of the lower sort, an eight page pamphlet issued at roughly fortnightly intervals on coarse paper and very poorly printed. It contained short miscellaneous articles, occasional literary essays and serial fiction probably from the pen of the editor himself. Neither survived for very long. The limiting factor may have been their cost.

The first mass popular periodical was *Chambers' Edinburgh Journal*, the creation of William and Robert Chambers whose firm did more perhaps than any other to promote the spread of the printed word. The *Journal* was published weekly at a penny halfpence and began its long run in 1832. Although it was at the forefront of the Useful Knowledge movement, it was anything but dull. It carried stories and poems, jokes, anecdotes, popular Scottish history and biography and frequently used vernacular Scots. It was also one of the first periodicals to include women and children amongst its potential readers. Eventually the *Journal* became the victim of its own success. It sold well in England from the outset, and by the mid 1840s clearly found most of its readers there. It adopted a smooth 'Imperial' tone and much of its earlier vigour departed. Mounting business pressures reduced the Chambers's influence and the magazine passed into the hands of outside editors, most notably the English author James Payne. From the early 1860s onwards he edited the *Journal* from London, and it became for all practical purposes an English periodical.

But access to the printed word was not limited by the ability to buy the Chambers's magazine and its like. In the form of the religious tract it reached countless readers throughout Scotland unbought and unbidden. Tracts were scattered about on highways and in public places and thrust in millions into the unenraptured fingers of the poor. They bore a strong resemblance to the chapbook whose pernicious effects they were designed to counteract, and were printed on thin coarse paper with simple engravings and cuts. Later they switched to a smaller format illustrated with decorative capitals and floral borders and printed on stiffish pastel-coloured paper intended, no doubt, to discourage use for sanitary purposes. Early tracts were notable for their sternly admonitory tone and predilection for fierce texts, like 'Let the sinners be consumed' (Ps. *CIV*, 35) and 'After this, the Judgement' (Heb. *IX*, 27). Their unrelenting verbosity must sorely have taxed many of their intended readers. As the century advanced, however, vocabulary and idiom became more simple. Thus, for example, *Have You Signed God's Promise?* based on the text 'Who loved me, and gave Himself for me' (Gal. *II*, 20):

> What did she believe?
> That Jesus died for her;
> That Jesus died for all her sins;
> That Jesus died for all her sins, and so bore her punishment;
> That Jesus died in her stead, the reason being love.[2]

Many kinds of people wrote these things, from shock-haired pentecostalists to smooth DDs; but the new populism gradually prevailed. Tracts became more direct and more sensational, shipwrecks and shocking accidents being especially prominent. There were series based on incidents from the American Civil War and the careers of famous athletes. Vernacular Scots appeared in pieces like *Wull't Last,'Leez'beth? Wull't Last?* and *Diz ony o' You Chaps Ken Aboot Jesus?* being the last words of a rivetter depicted on the cover plunging to his death from a half-built ship. Various agencies sprang up to produce and distribute this material, most notably the Scottish Colportage Society which began in 1793 as the Religious Tract and Book Society of Scotland, and the famous Stirling Tract Enterprise founded in 1848 by the Stirlingshire seedsman Peter Drummond which grew into a massive world-wide concern. By the end of the century the Stirling Tract Enterprise alone was issuing twenty-five million tracts a year.

Subsidised publication was an obvious way of influencing public opinion and was used by various bodies, notably the Scottish Temperance League, which was based in Glasgow and published an extensive list of periodicals, tracts and books. The weekly *League Journal* combined news and features, literary extracts and fiction, and there was a children's magazine, *The Adviser* with a circulation approaching 100,000 copies a year. The League published temperance novels and ran fiction competitions with cash prizes of up to £250.

The most important of the popular media was the newspaper press which was to become the mainstay of Scottish popular culture during the second half of the century. At first the press was severely restricted by what contemporaries called 'the taxes on knowledge'—a series of Government impositions on advertising, raw materials and the means of circulation designed to control access to newspapers by making them too expensive for ordinary people to buy. When the most important of these was removed by the repeal of the Stamp Act in 1855, prices plummeted and the popular press began a period of explosive growth. By the end of the century there were more than 200 titles, many of them publishing daily, and the organisation of the press had been transformed. The most significant development was the new wave of working-class papers like the Dundee-based *People's Journal*. They were half newspaper, half popular miscellany and published original writing—

poetry, prose fiction, memoirs and reminiscences, biography, history, folklore and popular musicology in enormous quantities. Little of this ever found its way into book form.

The *People's Journal* was launched in 1858 as a weekly for the city of Dundee and its hinterland. By 1870 it covered the whole east coast. By 1890 it had broken into the west central lowlands and was claiming the biggest certified circulation in Scotland. By 1914 it had thirteen different editions and a circulation of a quarter of a million copies. It was the biggest weekly outside London and the first truly national newspaper in Scotland.

Like most of its rivals it took serial fiction very seriously. With books expensive and library provision patchy there was an obvious market for recreational reading-matter and the *Journal* proceeded assiduously to fill it. There were plenty of potential readers. Some three-quarters of the adult population were notionally literate and by the end of the century the ability to read had become all but universal.

This affected the literary market in a number of ways. The centre of gravity shifted from the upper middle classes with their circulating libraries and imported English novels towards a new reading public dominated by the upper working and lower middle classes who got their fiction in serial form in newspapers. Book-fiction had never sold particularly well in Scotland and by 1900 it probably comprised about 3 per cent of the British market. Scottish book novelists had to adapt to the fact that most of their readers lived in England, particularly those like J M Barrie and S R Crockett, who made their living wholly by the pen. As the latter remarked:

> We poor authors may get our fame and our inspiration from our homelands, but we have to get our money elsewhere than where the heather grows.[3]

During the second half of the century the press published several thousand original novels, and the newspaper replaced the book as the main source of imaginative writing. There was also a shift in the language of literature from English towards Scots and the press supported a vernacular prose revival of major proportions.

According to the conventional view, the Scots language ceased to be used as a discursive medium shortly after the Reformation, being confined to poetry as in Ramsay, Fergusson and Burns, or to the dialogue of novelists like Scott, Hogg and Stevenson whose main vehicle was standard English. But spoken Scots continued to be the language of the overwhelming majority of the lowland nation, and the new press used it freely. As soon as the technical means became available to do it, a radical new speech-based prose came into being reflecting the regional diversity of the spoken language and dealing with every aspect of contemporary life.

Its leading exponent was William D Latto, born in Ceres in Fife in 1823. He started life as a handloom weaver and combined a keen interest in radical politics with a driving urge towards self-improvement. Eventually he qualified as a teacher and became master of the Free Kirk school at Johnshaven in Kincardineshire. He wrote for a number of radical periodicals and this brought him to the attention of John Leng the proprietor of the *Dundee Advertiser*. He engaged Latto as a leader-writer and when the *People's Journal* started in 1858 invited him to become its editor.

Latto ran the paper for the next forty years and was the guiding spirit behind its success. His essays in Scots under the pseudonym, 'Tammas Bodkin' became a national institution and were several times re-issued in book form. Contemporaries acclaimed him as one of the leading writers of his generation and compared him with Walter Scott. Yet today he is completely forgotten. The decline in his reputation is highly significant and it springs from the gap which had developed between 'official' book-culture and the real world of Scottish letters. The collected essays, some sixty in number, were basically fresh compositions written expressly for the all-British market and possessing little of the vigour and originality of the newspaper material. The book Bodkin was a conventional figure descended from the Scotch mannerist school of John Galt and David MacBeth Moir. But in the newspaper, the persona was developed with much greater inventiveness and scope. The newspaper Bodkin had a different biography which included foreign travel and the inheritance of great wealth and he acted throughout as a vehicle for ideas. He dealt with international, national and local politics and commented penetratingly on every aspect of contemporary life. Here, for example, is a typically trenchant assessment of Ferdinand II of Naples, the famous 'King Bomba':

> Bomba is the very *beau ideal* —the maist perfect eemage an' exemplar o' absolutism an' oppression that we hae in Europe . . . The fact is, that Bomba is sae far convenient to the ither tyrants o' Christendom that he keeps them a' in coontenance, for, hoowever deeply they may sink into the mire o' depravity, he will be aye sure to keep a wee bit below them, sae that they can aye say in self-defence, 'We're no sae bad as his Majesty o' Naples at ony rate . . .'[4]

On electoral reform:

> Ane can scarcely be blamed for refusin' belief in Lord Derby's zeal for reform, seein' he disna profess to believe in't himsel' . . . Still, he is willin' to tak' the matter into consideration durin' the next recess, that is if the Hoose o' Commons disna tak' pity on him an' gie him a little mair leisure to consider aboot it, by relievin' him frae his office afore that time—a very probable contingency as I think . . . Sir Fitzroy Kelly may, if he likes, spout red-het Republicanism itsel 'to split the ears o' the groundlins' but Derby is the man wha drives the Dilly, and if Sir Fitz disna choose to gang the same gate wi' his Master Cabby, he maun joost 'seek aboot' as the sayin is, for some ither conveyance . . .[5]

And on agricultural housing:

> I've baith seen an' experienced a gude hantle o' the miseries an' inconveniences o' the filthy steys, erroneously styled hooses, wherein oor wealthy lairds an' money grubbin' farmers are wont to bestow their wark folk . . . ye'll see hovels that it wad beat onybody to tell, frae a cursory examination, whether they are

sheep-faulds, or tawtie pits, or human habitations . . . I've sometimes wondered what the Kamtchadale, the Bushman, or the Red Indian wad think were he set at large in the midst o' some rural district in oor ain land . . . where the cottarhooses are a' bigget wi' alternate layers o' divots an' stanes, an' where ye maun stap ower a stinkin' midden, flankit by a dirty deuk dub, eneuch to breed pestilence to poison a haill parish afore ye can secure a fittin' on the door stane. Wad the savage no be apt to regard us as a set o' puir degraded mortals, nae farther advanced in civilization than himsel? I question gin the Kaffir wad exchange his Kraal for the sma' comforts o' a ploughman's cottage.[6]

In Latto's hands vernacular Scots became a medium for dealing with the whole contemporary world. He was the first prose writer to be completely alive in the language since the seventeenth century.

His work had an enormous impact on the way Scots was used in the press. Its sheer ubiquity is probably the first thing a modern reader would notice. There was editorial comment in the vernacular, poetry and features writing in the vernacular, stories with vernacular dialogue including examples written entirely in demotic Scots, vernacular advertisements even. The language itself became more diverse. Following Latto a school of vernacular writers sprang up throughout the country using orthographically distinct local forms of Scots. The growth of phonetic systems of shorthand and the related movement in favour of spelling reform underlined the links between the sound oflanguage and its appearance on the page, and regional dialect variations began to be represented typographically. Here is an example from Shetland:

'An' da barns, an' da byres, an' da grice hoose, an' da fool hoose, an' a peerie stable for da horses i' da winter, an' da midden is a' behint da hoose wi a back door ta gaing ta dem. An' da rufes a' teckit sae clean an' trig lek, no' wi' flaas, an' strae an' simmons weighted doon wi' stanes, let wir teckin, min, bit a' clean an' smooth an' stoo'd awa' under da aizhins just as ye wi'd cut a peat wi' a tushker.'[7]

And from Buchan:

Aw'm thinkin wir progress is some lop-sidet. We mak great advances in mechanical science; but Aw'm nae sure 'at humane an' kindly feelin's grouin in proportion. It's a dangerous thing ti pit great pooer inti the han's o' bad men. Aw'm fair terrafee't ti see the wye 'at the pooers o' life an' death are bein' multiplie't on ilky han' . . . Muckle hooses an' muckle toons, weers owreheid in a' direckshins, weers oondergrun' in pipes, electrick messages fleein' throu the air, electrick cars and mottir cars rinnin throu the streets, tillyphones, tillygraphs, gramaphones catchin fat ye say, an' reelin't aff again as lang's the record laists—weel, it's a' terrable bewulderin . . .[8]

And from Renfrewshire:

'Weel,' Jean says tae me the Friday nicht afore last—ye man ken Friday's yane o' oor coortin nichts. She says, 'Can ye skytch, Jock?' I lucked at'er an' says, 'skitch! Mighty me, whits that?' 'Ye muckle gommerill,' says she, 'its scliden on the ice wi' yon airn things on yer buits.' 'Oh!' says I, 'skyten.' 'No,' says she, 'skytchen.' 'Aw weel,' says I, 'skyten or skytchen, its a' yin, an' we'll let that flee stick to the wa'; but if its me that can skyte, ye shood jist ocht tae see me, ma certi.[9]

All over Scotland standard literary Scots was replaced by speech-based usages reflecting the major dialectal varieties of the language.

The literary class grew enormously as the demand for original material increased and writing became a remunerative part-time occupation for thousands of people at every level of society. The *People's Journal* based its whole strategy upon this idea. As much of the paper as possible was written by its readers, from leading articles to poetry, short stories, serial fiction, and features of every kind. By the end of the century it was offering £100 (the equivalent of a year's income for a skilled artizan) for a 60–80,000 word serial. As journalism became a secure and well-paid occupation, a new kind of literary career became possible, that of the professional novelist working for the press. The most important of these was David Pae who wrote about fifty full length serial novels, only a handful of which were ever published as books. He wrote anonymously, took care to protect his privacy and was almost completely unknown. Yet he was probably the most widely read author of fiction in Victorian Scotland.

He was born in Perthshire in 1828 and brought up in the Borders. He served his apprenticeship as a bookseller and then worked as a journalist and theatre critic in Edinburgh. By the time he became editor of the *Dunfermline Press* in 1859 he already had a lucrative alternative career as a writer of serial fiction, and when he went to work for the *Dundee Advertiser* group in 1863 he had become the leading popular novelist in Scotland. The fact that there could be such a thing at all points not only to far reaching changes in the literary market but to a significant change in the moral climate in Scotland which made fiction and other forms of non-devotional reading matter increasingly acceptable for lower social classes. To the extreme evangelical fiction was simply a lie and as such intrinsically immoral. Indeed the form was regarded with varying degrees of distrust by religious activists of every hue. Fiction corrupted the reader. It inflamed the passions and made vice interesting. But the liberal wing of the movement became increasingly attracted by the possibilities of the new cheap press and a new kind of didactic book-length fiction came into being during the later 1850s and 1860s. Its leading exponent was David Pae. In novels like *Jessie Melville; or, the Double Sacrifice* and *Lucy the Factory Girl; or, the Secrets of the Tontine Close* he set to work upon his readers' moral sensibilities, declaring

It is the province of the novelist to instruct as well as to amuse; and when he neglects to aim at the fulfilment of his twofold duty, he fails to accomplish that good which the sphere and character of his labour are intended to effect. Should he strive only to amuse and excite, he may enlist the sympathy and fascinate the imagination of his readers, but he will teach them no new lesson, he will furnish them with no moral or intellectual nourishment. Nay, the great probability is, that his production will exert an unhealthy influence on the heart and mind. We deeply feel our own responsibility in this respect, and . . . have endeavoured to cast in the seeds of instruction and moral truth as occasion offered . . .[10]

The irony was that behind the moralist lurked a first rate thriller writer. In *Jessie Melville*, for example, the heroine, a high-born lady, has been swapped in infancy for the son of a serving man and brought up in poverty in the slums of Edinburgh. Later she meets and falls in love with her substitute, but cannot reveal her true identity because it would disinherit him. The complications are worked out in a fast moving narrative with plots and kidnaps, burglary and legal skulduggery, and it took the capital by storm when it was published in the *North Briton* in 1855. *Lucy the Factory Girl* pits its blonde blue-eyed heroine against the corrupt business world and the Glasgow gangland. Its labyrinthine plot is peopled with evil cotton lords, shady lawyers, gang bosses and crooked physicians, all hell bent on stealing her fortune (she is, naturally, an heiress) and then silencing her in the most abrupt and permanent fashion. The resulting desperate chase through Glasgow and its environs involves prostitutes, counterfeiters, body-snatchers, assassins, kidnappers and a professional torturer.

This was not perhaps the firmest foundation upon which to build a moral reformation. Despite his sincere desire to make evil serve the ends of good Pae was caught in an insoluble dilemma: the more deeply he entered the imaginative domain the more important fictional elements became. In engaging with fiction at all he tacitly endorsed the very things he wished to destroy. As the years went by the moral imperative progressively weakened and Pae treated fiction increasingly as an end in itself. His career reflects the growth during the second half of the century of a basically secular fiction free from external religious constraints. It also sheds light on the publishing practices which helped to make imaginative writing universally available, especially the techniques of syndication and serialisation.

Syndication was one of the chief means of promoting the distribution of non-book material. Anything from whole pages of standardised newsprint to individual columns of news, features, or fiction could be supplied by agencies or individuals servicing a number of papers simultaneously. Professional authors like David Pae used the technique widely. It greatly enhanced the financial rewards of authorship and significantly enlarged the potential audience. Pae's contract with Leng and Co meant that they had first call upon his material but outside their territory he retained control of his syndication rights and dealt with other papers throughout his career.

Serialisation involved the packaging of a basically expensive commodity—the novel—into cheap and affordable units, and it rapidly became the dominant mode of publishing fiction in Scotland. Books could have serialisation thrust upon them as the demand for fiction grew. In Edinburgh during the 1830s, novels were often broken up and re-stitched into separate portions rented out at 2*d.* a night. Alternatively, popular novels might achieve book form cumulatively after being issued in consecutive twopenny or threepenny weekly numbers. At least one Pae novel, *The Merchant's Daughter; or, Love and Mammon* (Edinburgh 1857) was produced in this way.

The serialisation of original novels in newspapers affected the form in several ways. Genuine book-length fiction—that is *c.* 80,000–120,000 words—immediately became the norm; but this was often exceeded. *Lucy the Factory Girl*, for example, which must be all of 150,000 words long, is a typical response to the virtually limitless column space now at the writer's disposal. The plot tended to grow in importance relative to other elements of the story and had to be managed with enormous resourcefulness and ingenuity if the reader was to be sustained through dozens of instalments spread over a period of six months or more. Most importantly, the imaginative world of the new fiction moved much closer to the readers' everyday lives, often using real communities and contemporary settings. The city was a legitimate part of the imaginative terrain and there was crime, poverty, disease, social injustice, factories, slums, strikes, in short the whole urban gamut almost wherever one cared to look—an interesting commentary on the notion that fiction in Victorian Scotland was wholly given over to sentimental, backward-looking rural fantasy and a further illustration of the distortions which have crept into our literary history as a result of too readily accepting as authentic the values of a narrowly commercial book-culture produced for export.

The strength of the Victorian press lay in its diversity. It catered for writers of every kind from exponents of the new mass fiction like David Pae, to the brilliantly able William Alexander, who was not only a distinguished author in his own right but a pioneer of the new professional journalism and for twenty years editor of a major Scottish paper. Alexander's reputation rests at present upon his classic novel of rural life *Johnny Gibb of Gushetneuk* (Aberdeen 1871), recently acclaimed as 'the masterpiece of Scottish Victorian fiction',[11] and the powerful short stories contained in *Life Among My Ain Folk* (Edinburgh 1875). Between 1852 and 1877 he published at least five other novels. But they appear in no bibliography or other work of scholarship. Until recently their existence was wholly unsuspected and their discovery is an illuminating commentary on the way in which the literary history of this period has hitherto been constructed.

The bookmarket would tolerate vernacular Scots only in a dilute and standardised form and would entertain fictional treatments of Scottish life only in so far as they satisfied basically English prejudices and expectations. If a writer wanted to treat contemporary life seriously, therefore, it was necessary to address a Scottish audience. The only way of reaching it was through the columns of the newspaper press, the major medium of communication still in Scottish hands. Alexander published all his fiction there and issued even *Johnny Gibb* in cased form reluctantly and at the insistence of friends. But the standard bibliography of his works produced in 1926 referred only to book and pamphlet material and so his long and productive career as a novelist was consigned to oblivion. He has been credited with a single brilliant success and denied the wider recognition he deserves. The more so because critics, not having access to the full range of his work, have often misinterpreted the little that was available to them.

Because of its country setting *Johnny Gibb* has been linked with the Kail-yard novel, from which it differs radically in outlook and technique, and treated as symptomatic of the backward-looking rural ethos which has so long, and so mistakenly, been considered the main preoccupation of Victorian Scottish fiction. Alexander's approach to language has also been misunderstood. He was one of the pioneers of the new vernacular revival, intimately acquainted with phonography and spelling reform and early forsaking literary Scots for an orthographically distinct speech-based standard. As a result his reputation has grown slowly and it has taken nearly a century for him to be acknowledged as a writer of national importance.

The man himself remains elusive; he shunned publicity and carefully guarded his private life so that we have to build up our picture of him almost entirely from published sources. He was born in Aberdeenshire in 1826 and abandoned his farming career in early manhood after losing a leg in an accident. The recuperation period was devoted to reading and study under the direction of the political economist William M'Combie who, amongst his many other activities, was editor of a struggling radical paper called the *Aberdeen Free Press*. Alexander joined the staff in 1853, succeeded M'Combie as editor, and built the paper into one of the leading dailies in Scotland. In addition to his journalistic work he led a hectic public life, being one of the main architects of Liberal supremacy in the North East. He also found time to create one of the most remarkable bodies of prose fiction in nineteenth century Scotland.

The lost novels are radically unlike anything we might have expected. They are predominantly urban in implication, uncompromisingly realistic in tone, and submit the most cherished Victorian social and political assumptions to searching examination.

Sketches of Rural Life in Aberdeenshire appeared in the *Free Press* during 1853 under the pseudonym 'Rusticus'. It takes a wide-ranging view of contemporary North-East society and tests ideas about social evolution and the perfectibility of institutions against the day-to-day life of the ordinary people of the region. *The Authentic History of Peter Grundie* which followed in 1855, is a study of social injustice and the plight of the urban poor. The main character is a working man—one of the earliest in British fiction—driven to the verge of destitution by economic forces beyond his control and the fierce competitiveness of city life. Alexander uses him to expose the sham of bourgeois 'philanthropy' and to attack the principles of self-help and *laissez faire*, insisting that poverty is produced not by moral inadequacy but by forces inherently present in the free market economy.

The contemporary equation of power with virtue and success with public morality provides the theme of *The Laird of Drammochdyle and his Contemporaries*, first issued in the *Free Press* in 1865 and now published in book form (Aberdeen University Press, 1986). The story is set in the North-East town of 'Strathaven' and deals with a ruthless struggle for power inside the local ruling class, resulting in the destruction of the laird and the minister, the traditional pillars of Scots rural society, by the rising urban bourgeoisie. These are represented by the Crabbice family, brewers and distillers flourishing within the new commercial ethos and cynically abusing the power that flows from their wealth. In *Drammochdyle* everything, including respectability, is for sale and the leading Crabbice ends the novel in the full flush of success, a prominent 'philanthropist', an elder of the kirk, and a leading and respected public figure. The novel is a grim reminder of the consequences of 'progress' and a bitter commentary on the naked economic individualism of the new industrial order.

His next work, *Ravenshowe and the Residenters Therein* (*Free Press* 1867–1868) is set in the pre-capitalist farming community of the Garioch at the beginning of the nineteenth century, and dwells on the harmonious and uncompetitive relations that exist between the tenants and their Scots-speaking laird. The underlying theme is the interaction of the environment with the individual and the shaping power of heredity over several generations. *Ravenshowe* marked the first stage of Alexander's epic fictional study of the agricultural revolution in the North East, covering almost a century of change. *Johnny Gibb of Gushetneuk* (originally published in the *Free Press* in 1869–1870) forms its central section and it reaches its conclusion in the later stories in *Life Among my Ain Folk* (originally published in the *Free Press* in 1872–3). *Johnny Gibb* shows the system a generation after *Ravenshowe* with the laird now an absentee and the farmer class divided into capitalistic muckle farmers and the smaller tenants of whom Johnny Gibb is the representative and spokesman. The short stories, 'Mary Malcolmson's Wee Maggie', 'Baubie Huie's Bastard Geet', 'Francie Herregerie's Sharger Laddie' and the brilliant 'Couper Sandy' show the triumph of rural capitalism and the harsh consequences for the cotters, labourers and smaller tenants. The central theme of the trilogy is the destruction of 'the poor man's country' and the fall of the small farmer class which Alexander saw as the last defence of traditional decencies and a human scale of values in the rural economy.

Alexander's last full-length novel, *My Uncle the Baillie* (*Weekly Free Press*, 1876–7) returns to the city of Greyness and the theme of the mercantile bourgeoisie. It deals with the rise to power of David Macnicol, the Baillie of the title. He starts life as a warehouse apprentice who marries the boss's daughter and climbs to the top of the power structure in the city, ending up with a string of company directorships and a substantial landed estate. Once again Alexander strips aside the respectable facade of Victorian public life. *The Baillie* is a withering exposure of the Chamberlainite ideal of civic virtue and the theory of enlightened self-interest, the idea that the pursuit of private gain automatically promotes the good of society and the cause of progress. The reality is woefully different. Greyness is riddled with political chicanery, business corruption, social injustice and the pursuit of private advantage all under pretence of altruism and the public good. Alexander's remarks in the introduction to *Life Among my Ain Folk* may stand as a fitting epigraph not only to *My Uncle the Baillie* but to the whole of his mature fiction: 'After all,' he said, 'who is it that has not, oftener than he wished, in his experience found loftiness of general sentiment and a profession of high principles set in the forefront, where the veritable life was guided by considerations as mean and sordid as well might be. Better, at any rate, have things in their real and undisguised forms then; and this merit we claim.'[12]

The cultural distortions of the British bookmarket have led to major misjudgements about central aspects of Scottish life during the second half of the nineteenth century. The spectacular growth of popular publishing created a new reading public. The book was displaced by the newspaper as the main source of recreational reading and serialisation became the dominant mode of publishing fiction in Scotland. There was an enormous rise in the value of literary property and a dramatic extension in the literary class, so that the reading and writing of fiction and other non-devotional material became an acceptable activity at every level of society with far reaching implications for the future cultural life of the country. There was a great outburst of creativity in the vernacular with the appearance of radical new speech-based varieties and a prose revival of unprecedented proportions supported by the national press. An independent Scottish literary market existed vigorously throughout the Victorian period, and an extensive popular literature dealing freely with contemporary social and political life, amongst which have lain unknown and unacknowledged for upwards of a century the novels of William Alexander. He is clearly a significant figure and our re-assessment of him and the movement he represents is a task of some urgency.

NOTES

1 For a fuller treatment of the subjects discussed in this chapter, *see* my recent study *Popular Literature in Victorian Scotland* (Aberdeen, 1986), and the intro-duction to my edition of William Alexander, *The Laird of Drammochdyle and his Contemporaries* (Aberdeen, 1986). Where accessible secondary sources are available I have cited them; otherwise references are to original source material.
2 National Library of Scotland, Stirling Tracts 1 (1.139.g).
3 M M Harper, *Crockett and Grey Galloway* (London, 1907), p 162.
4 For a fuller version of this example *see Popular Literature*, p 42. For difficulties in glossing this and other vernacular extracts the reader should consult *The Concise Scots Dictionary*, see General Bibliography, p 445.
5 *People's Journal*, 13 March 1858.
6 *People's Journal*, 15 May 1858.
7 *Shetland Journal*, 1837. I am indebted for this example to Mr John J Graham, compiler of *The Shetland Dictionary* (Stornoway, 1979).
8 *Peterhead Sentinel*, 7 May 1904.
9 *Seestu*, 30 November 1880.
10 Quoted in *Popular Literature*, p 94.
11 Francis Russell Hart, *The Scottish Novel* (London, 1978), p 88.
12 Quoted in *Popular Literature*, p 132.

FURTHER READING

CHAPBOOKS

William Harvey, *Scottish Chapbook Literature* (Paisley, 1903).
John Fraser, *The Humorous Chapbooks of Scotland* (New York, 1873).

CHEAP MISCELLANIES

William Chambers, *Historical Sketch of Popular Literature and its Influence on Society* (Edinburgh, 1863).
William Chambers, *Memoir of William and Robert Chambers* (Edinburgh, 1893).
R C Terry, *Victorian Popular Fiction* (London, 1983), pp 138–41.
Laurence J Saunders, *Scottish Democracy 1815–1840* (Edinburgh, 1950), pp 248–58.
Peter Buchan, *The Selector* (Peterhead, 1817).

TRACTS

The Third Annual Report of the Aberdeen Book Agent and Colporteur Society (Aberdeen, 1859).
The Story of the Stirling Tract Enterprise (Stirling, 1889).
'The Increase'. A Year's Record of Facts and Results in the Work of the Stirling Tract Enterprise (Stirling, 1890).

TEMPERANCE PUBLICATIONS

The Twentieth Annual Report of the Scottish Temperance League, (Glasgow, 1864).

NEWSPAPERS

R M W Cowan, *The Newspaper in Scotland a Study of its First Expansion 1815–1860*, (Glasgow, 1946).
Lionel Madden and Diana Dixon, *The Nineteenth-Century Periodical Press in Britain— a Bibliography of Modern Studies 1901–1971* (New York, 1976).
Joan P S Ferguson, *Directory of Scottish Newspapers* (Edinburgh, 1984).
William Donaldson, *Popular Literature . . .* op. cit., *passim.*
William Latto, David Pae and William Alexander: see William Donaldson, *Popular Literature . . .* op. cit., *passim.*

Chapter 12

Myth, Parody and Dissociation: Scottish Fiction 1814–1914

DOUGLAS GIFFORD

This essay does not attempt to give a comprehensive guide to the fictional range of the period. Millar and the histories, especially the pioneer work of Francis Hart in *The Scottish Novel*, must be the reader's next port of call.[1] What I argue is that the three main types of fiction in the period 1814 to 1914 generate themselves out of the prevailing confusion and regret regarding loss of national identity inherited from the eighteenth century and immeasurably deepened as a result of the failure of Scottish institutions like the church, the universities and the overall educational system to speak coherently for a Scottish *or* British set of traditions and values. Nevertheless, I argue that in the outstanding achievements (and there are far more than we used to think) the writers find vehicles for their longing for coherence within their own society; or alternatively express successfully their divided personal, social and political loyalties. At best, they make up a school of Scottish fiction as recognisably different in recurrent themes, symbols and settings as New England fiction is different from the English tradition from Austen to Eliot.

From the outset, it must be recognised that the new wave of Scottish novelists centred on Scott and *Blackwood's Magazine* were fully aware that their 'Scotch novels', part inspired as they were by Edgeworth's writings on Ireland or the cult of the local and picturesque as developed by Crabbe and Wordsworth, were an exciting new development. Scott had shown the way, and Hogg, Galt, Ferrier, Moir, Hamilton and many others seized the opportunity to portray local colour, eccentricity and old-fashioned ways before they and their language forms died out, in the face of urbanisation and the railways. But, in emphasising the novelty of content and the superficialities of 'Scotchness', we risk losing sight of the fiction's major attempt and the first of my three main themes; what I have elsewhere (in discussing Scott's major novels) referred to as the quest for a fiction of 'mythic regeneration', and what Roderick Watson recognised as the basis of the next century's distinctively Scottish school of 'mythopoeic realism', in the works of Muir, Gibbon, Gunn and Mackay Brown.[2] Throughout the century, writer after writer attempted to locate a source of revitalisation and spiritual renewal around a symbolic protagonist, operating within the framework of a historically confused, internecine community acting as paradigm or microcosm for a Scotland seen as internally divided, unsure of itself and the validity of its traditional communal relations. These protagonists and situations are clearly not based on English models. Henry Morton has functions and responsibilities within a national culture which none of Austen's or Dickens's or Thackeray's carry on behalf of their respective cultures. Morton (or Micah Balwhidder, or Jeanie Deans, or Wat of Chapelhope, or Charlie Scott of Yardbire, or Kirsteen Douglas, or Johnnie Gibb, or Alec Forbes, or Malcolm MacPhail, or David Balfour, or the four Black Brothers) carry the heaviest of responsibilities; in being themselves they are also 'being' Scotland, just as later Chris Guthrie and Finn MacHamish and Kirstie Haldane are 'being' Scotland in novels of the 'Scottish Renaissance'.

I am not saying the type is not found in English fiction; one thinks of Disraeli's Sybil singing the ancient song of England within the ruins of an ancient monastery (together with her faithful dog Harold, 'last of the Saxon kings'!). Her role is clearly similar to that of Jeanie Deans. She is given a pedigree of legendary authenticity, she too has a 'magic' which converts those she meets to her spiritual cause, she has to endure the same *Pilgrim's Progress* trials as Jeanie. But, significantly, Disraeli's roots for his 'New England' fiction (for example in *Sybil* (1845)) can be traced back through Carlyle (and particularly the vision of Abbot Samson in *Past and Present* (1843), with its allegation that modern sickness stems from the loss of English mediaeval authenticity and its ability to select leaders without ballot boxes) to Scott's similar sentimental Toryism or romantic conservatism in *Ivanhoe* (1819). The substantial Scottish contribution to English mythic fiction begins with Scott.

The novel of mythic regeneration which emerges in nineteenth-century Scotland esentially splits itself so that it has two main areas of interest. There is the (sick) society of Scotland, frequently set in a period of civil warfare, portrayed in terms of tension between classes, splits within family, representing the 'family' of Scotland; and there is the protagonist whose traditional virtue, rooted in ancient ways, refuses to accept expediential political settlement of chicanery, fights with a stubborn and unfashionable integrity, which often involves her or him in an almost legendary or fabulous quest throughout and furth of Scotland. The protagonist representing deep-rooted strengths of local community (threatened now by Anglicised or centralised Scottish or British power) is thus seen as antidote to social division and political injustice which threaten the survival of Scottish ways. This kind of novel is thus *both* a novel of social dissociation *and* something else. The affirmative, positive vision is the added, ambitious layer, although frequently the ambition fails, such are the colossal strains on naturalism and the psychological realism involved in presenting the mythic leader.

This is not the place to trace the mythic leader's cultural and literary pedigree, or the myth of organic and regenerative community which he evokes. Speculation may include the *Wallace* of Blind Harry, Henryson's presentation of Cresseid finding wisdom with her lepers, or Lindsay's reductive egalitarianism in his *Satire*'s John the Commonweal and the challenging populist voice of the poor man, temporarily usurping the King's throne. Gaberlunzie legends, visionary Scottish poetry from 'Rauf Coilyear' to Alan Ramsay 'Vision', and Burns with his Brechtian beggars, all suggest a tradition of social egalitarianism, if not quite a myth of a 'golden age', which haunts Scottish writers from Ramsay (in the *The Gentle Shepherd*) to Gibbon (in *A Scots Quair*). More close to Scott, if bathetic after such ambitious vision, lies *The Man of Feeling* (1771). While not Scottish, nor performing anything like the mythic function of explaining the origins and ends of a race to the race, Harley at least introduces the protagonist's innocence, a naivete which borders at times on that of some kind of 'holy fool.' Harley's relationship, too, with the Scottish 'common-sense' philosophy has certain seminal aspects; his spontaneous feeling is his guide, just as 'nature's voice' will be for Jeanie Deans. His example will also introduce a recurrent problem for the Scottish mythic novelist, however; the problem of overcoming the reader's scepticism concerning the portrayal of radical altruism. Too often, the realism of Mackenzie and Scott (in their portrayal of Harley and Jeanie respectively) borders on fabulism, as though the writer is forced to shift genres to handle the message involved. It is a shift which will indeed frequently move the mythic novel into the fable and the fantasy, as the work of MacDonald, Oliphant and Stevenson (and even Carlyle) will show.

But Scott is essentially the starting-point for all three of my main traditions. I have argued elsewhere that Scott in three novels moved towards his deepest and clearest feelings about Scotland, its sickness and its cure. In *Waverley* (1814), Scott took the first steps in fashioning an entirely new apparatus for the novel form which would allow him to express his unique vision of Scottish history. Scott's new use of history has been recognised; not so well recognised is the fact that he casts Edward Waverley's psychology in the mould of Harley's, as excessively imaginative, hyper-sensitive, disordered and self-indulgent. But where Harley was unbelievable other than as literary artefact, Waverley has to be a credible witness to the struggle for Scotland's soul. But Waverley is no mythic hero, rather the insipid pseudo-hero, rescued rather than rescuing. To this extent, his place is with the dreamers and failures of the second major and parodic tradition of Scottish fiction. The novel's importance for the mythic tradition is that it sets up the historical canvas of Scotland and places an anachronistic picaresque hero where later the mythic protagonist will stand. But *Waverley* also introduces a use of physical and landscape setting, together with first examples of that great, atmospheric symbolism which is so much the essence of the Scott-influenced novel from the Brontës to Melville. The eighteenth-century novel's pasteboard settings, coach journeys and inns, are transformed in *Waverley* to blue mountains and ravines which are symbolic barriers in Waverley's imagination as well as borders to the Highlands. Castles like Bradwardine's bleak fortress to the north, domestic house and garden to the south, with its shambling bear statuary crests representing Bradwardine's half comic, half dangerous character; rivers which divide into raging torrent and quite flowing, corresponding to the visions in Waverley's mind, just as his mind will light up lochs and caves and staghunts into mysterious waters, King's caverns, and highland grandeur—all prefigure the use of later symbols like 'the heart of Midlothian' (jail *and* Jeanie Deans), or Galt's use of the Scottish concept of entail, or Brown's use of the house with the green shutters.

Waverley had set the scene. The novel form and methodology was created, but not the protagonist for the setting and the job. Waverley is no Henry Morton or Jeanie Deans, but in *Old Mortality* (1816), Morton has a role as important as that of Jeanie Deans. Scott means him to stand as the suffering conscience of Scotland, struggling with opposing historical claims and yet instinctively maintaining wholeness of judgement. Scott makes Morton's movements towards joining rebellion as credible psychologically as Waverley's, with pique, political disenchantment, and Balfour's manipulation all factors in his final decision. As symbolic protagonist trapped by history he is much more convincing than as romantic lover. He comes close to fulfilling the role Scott wished him to play; but genuinely admirable as he is, mature beyond his years, Morton fails as a key figure in Scott's attempt to forge a new kind of mythic pattern for Scottish history, in which reasonable compromise is to replace perpetual polarisation. History defeats Morton, since nothing due to his efforts brings about the correction of Scotland's wrongs, but rather accidental effects of vastly larger political movements outside Scotland. The coming of William of Orange gives Scotland, as a by-product, the religious settlement it fought so bitterly about within itself.

But beyond Morton the satire is rich. Virtually all the other major characters are shown as the results of distorted and biased upbringing and conditioning. From Claverhouse's stoic unbelief in anything but a kind of arid chivalry (denied to the lower orders) to Balfour's ruthless, arid control of a fanatic disorder of mind; from Bothwell's frustrated pride in his royal descent to Mause Headrigg's whining bigotry; from Lady Bellenden's pedantic snobbery to Mucklewrath's appalling Old Testament madness, there is a clear illustration of a basic sickness in Scottish society. All represent dead ideas, codes, values; all are moved by devotion to corrupt and egotistical authority, whether Royalist or bigoted Presbyterian. Morton's journey is to discover that there is little to choose between either side, and his function, like Jeanie's, is to exemplify to both sides a healing compromise. Thus, he 'converts', on occasion, his enemies—Claverhouse, the Bellendens, Evandale, highlighting the converse, 'friends' proving disastrous to friends. Morton is sentenced to death by the Presbyterians for whom he has fought so valiantly. Civil division is tearing Scotland apart.

The setting echoes this division. The rich Lowland valleys are not only the bases of the Royalists; they are their metaphors, of order, improvement, and wealth. Gentler landscape goes with moderate religion and milder manners, whereas the wild and bare uplands of Lanarkshire, like the wild highlands of *Waverley*, are reserved for the Covenanters, metaphors for their stern enthusiasms and bleak outlook. When Morton makes his choice to help Balfour, it is, like Waverley's, made at a symbolic place, at a cross-roads, where old Bessie McLure (anticipating Jeanie Deans?) is the spirit of the older faith of Scotland as well as being archetype of the basic goodness of the Scottish peasantry.

Jeanie Deans is Morton's and Bessie McLure's descendant. But in *The Heart of Midlothian* (1818) Scott has changed his approach. Instead of writing a historical novel with a noble hero, he narrows his range to the Porteous Riots and to the central figure of a cowfeeder's daughter. She is 'nature's voice', speaking from the grass roots of the peasantry of Scotland, from where Scott believes moral regeneration will come, repudiating the social and moral corruption about her. She is based on a historical person, but her role is enacted (and Scott explicitly draws attention to this at several points) in terms of *The Pilgrim's Progress*. Scott is trying to create a myth of Scottish regeneration. The novel balances two situations and structures against each other. The first is a picture of decadent Scotland *and* Britain, expressed through a subtly woven 'pattern of pardons.' The second is Scott's tale of redemption, Jeanie's pilgrim's progress, in which she goes through her 'trials', her vales of despond, meeting monsters and nightmare demons and either surpassing or converting them through her instinctive sense of good. Scott, like Burns, is here following the 'sentimental school' of Francis Hutcheson, the philosophy whereby 'the heart ay's the part ay/that makes us right or wrang'; and the pattern which illustrates this is begun with Wilson and Robertson, smugglers who nevertheless (since most Scots see the calling as traditional and excusable) deserve pardon. The courts and government think otherwise, and without charity sentence them to death. In contrast, Captain Porteous, the English commander of the execution guard, fires into the crowd, killing several. For this the government not only forgives but mollycoddles him. An unforgivable crime has been wrongly pardoned, a forgivable crime ruthlessly punished. Lest we think this is coincidence, the pattern is repeated. Effie Deans is condemned to death by a court pressured by government, for supposedly killing her illegitimate child. Again, Scott's description of the courtroom scene leaves us in no doubt that he means us to sympathise—even the judge is moved by the harrowing scene before him. Yet 'King Rat', Ratcliffe the notorious robber and footpad, is not only pardoned by the Edinburgh magistracy but appointed, on the 'set a thief' principle, to act as chief warder of the Tolbooth in the which Effie is imprisoned! Again, the unpardonable has been pardoned and the pardonable refused mercy.

Scott builds up this pattern of events with a linking set of themes and images. It might appear that in the story of Jeanie and Effie Deans the Porteous Riots and the story of Wilson and Robertson are out of place, but if one reflects on the theme of the first chapter—that of the difference between the rate of crimes of passion between England and Scotland—one sees that Scott has opened the novel with a clear statement of one of his main structures. The Porteous Riots, the entire Scottish fabric beyond Jeanie, suffers from the 'Scottish disease' which Scott has shown in *Waverley* and *Old Mortality* and which Edwin Muir described as the Scottish 'dissociation of sensibility', the tendency to extreme and opposed reactions, the battle between the Head and the Heart.[3] Yet again the pattern of *Rob Roy* and the other great Scottish novels repeats itself. Outlaw figures ruled by their passions, like Wilson and Robertson (and Porteous), over-feeling Effie Deans, the rioting mob, are set against cold-hearted, expedient-minded authorities whose sole concern is order and material progress.

Scotland is shown in that very first chapter in microcosm. Dramatic incidents and lively discussion of its more barbaric nature and character are contrasted with the pedantic manuscript style of village schoolmaster Peter Pattieson, with all taking place in the Wallace Inn (a name meant to underline the argument's relevance to Scottish history). All the events of the first half of the book show imbalance and lack of compromise or charity. All the parties involved are either too strongly motivated by passion or, like Bartholomew Saddletree (Effie's uncle, who loves the processes of the law but falls asleep when his niece's fate is being decided), too little moved by the voice of the heart. Their symbol is the Tolbooth, that black and anachronistic Heart of Mid-Lothian.

Beyond the pattern of pardons, Scott's irony bites even more: in the picture of the Edinburgh gossips, especially Saddletree; in his description of the stolid, insensitive and too typical Laird of Dumbiedykes and his ferocious 'housekeeper', Mrs Balchristie; more gently in his picture of caring but ineffectual Reuben Butler; in the way in which honour is frequently found in the very places one least expects it, in especial amongst smugglers and thieves rather than amongst the great or pious. Two examples must show Scott at his most biting here. The first is summarised in the person of 'honest' David Deans, father to Effie and Jeanie. Deans is conventionally seen as a worthy if over-pious figure whose heart is nevertheless in the right place. I challenge this view and suggest that he is one of Scott's most trenchant satires. If one reads closely and objectively, banishing the thought that he ought to be sound because of his religion and station in life, then Scott's picture is acidly etched. His tender conscience is more concerned about whether Jeanie can give evidence in an 'Erastian' court, than with Effie's predicament. We are led by Scott to suspect that his actions in the Covenanting wars were not as courageous as David makes out. And triumphantly, Scott shows this paragon of Presbyterian virtue as an arch-compromiser of his ideals and beliefs in the magnificent Chapter 43, in which David finds that he can square his conscience with the idea of having Reuben Butler as a son-in-law. This is a superb piece of extended satire as David turns somersaults of belief and rationalises his good fortune. He stands in direct contrast to Jeanie. Scott explicitly contrasts this picture of one of the 'unco guid' inventing 'God's voice' with Jeanie's reliance on 'commonsense' and the voice of nature.

If Scott undermines Presbyterianism's excesses here, he manages some bitter comment on the hypocrisies of aristocracy and power. Jeanie gets her pardon, but only through the agencies of the King's mistress. That is to say that Scott deliberately shows that the 'crime' of his central situation is paralleled completely by the expediency of the royal situation. Effie had an illicit lover. The King has an illicit lover. Effie at least married her lover eventually, there being real love in her affair. But Scott is not saying that one is better than the other, simply that it is ironic that the two should co-exist but be seen by society in such utterly different lights. Most ironic of all, where is Robertson/Staunton to be found with his paramour in the closing stages of the book? Where else but walking the very cobblestones of his former atrocities in the Royal Mile, representing the Crown at the opening of that most august of ceremonies, the General Assembly. But the ultimate fate of their child shows up their union as a prolonged spiritual waste, which they disguised with social pretence.

In all this the major theme has emerged as that of expediency set against integrity. Jeanie is, of course, the integrity, and her role is to show that the end never justifies the means, as well as showing from where will come a Scottish and British regeneration. With Madge Wildfire as her doppelganger, her gypsy and outlaw opposite (Madge's garb and fragmented dignity and beauty reflect the broken traditions of Scotland), she walks the length of the country seeking, like David Balfour in *Kidnapped* and *Catriona*, a moral source, unaware that the source is within herself. Others realise it; it is part of her (and David Balfour's) strange integrity that she converts villains and enemies into helpful friends or harmless opponents. She is the one person in the book who will not adopt the expedient—and the one person who achieves balance, integration and peace.

Scott has been attacked for his Roseneath ending in which Jeanie is given her reward and her husband his ministry. Whatever the arguments that Scott was spinning out his material, it seems to me that symbolically at least the Roseneath section has it place. Not only is it Jeanie's reward, it is the new Scotland over which she and her like will preside. Roseneath is to Scott (although not in fact) an island, which in miniature shows Jeanie's way of living 'paying off'. Consider the character of Roseneath. It is poised between savage Highlands and more peaceful Lowlands. Duncan of Knocktarlitie, clad half as a Highlander and half as a Lowlander, is its presiding and anachronistic mafioso genius. Jeanie and Reuben civilise him and unite these wild and divided regions. Scott's meaning is clear. Thus can Scotland regenerate itself.[4]

Following Scott, the other major novelists who work consciously within the regenerative tradition include Hogg, Galt, MacDonald, Alexander, Oliphant and Stevenson. Not all of the novels by these writers follow Scott's *Heart of Midlothian*, and many add to the elements, or vary them; but there emerges a clear line of descent in which the overriding aim is to envisage a symbolic figure of traditional and Scottish integrity (often of integrity in linguistic terms, in so far as local and authentic Scots is held to by that figure, against cultural and political threats couched in forms of intrusive English). Bearing in mind Jeanie Deans's peasant origins, her continuity of language and values, her 'magical' abilities to convert enemies and reassert what she feels as inherited community values, Hogg's *The Brownie of Bodsbeck* (1818) and *The Three Perils of Man* (1822), together with the shorter tales of *Winter Evening Tales* (1820) and *The Shepherd's Calendar* (1829) provide a kind of complementary assertion of native Scots values and traditions. In a way, Hogg could be placed *before* Scott's mythic efforts, since his tolerant, community-minded, yet dangerous-to-meddle-with Border giant, Wat of Chapelhope, hero of *The Brownie*, represents an older and hitherto unbroken peasant tradition; Wat's role throughout is to represent essential folk strength. The prickly native spirit of 'nemo me impune lacessit' surrounds him, and his outburst before the Privy Council in Edinburgh on behalf of peasant commonsense anticipates rather than echoes Hutchesonian formalisation of instinctive and heart-felt natural behaviour. His links with Lindsay's John the Commonweal, and with the 'reductive idiom' of vernacular poetry, seem clear, like those of Charlie Scott of Yardbire in the *Three Perils of Man*. This Hogg called 'a Border romance', and it and *The Brownie* share similar protagonists, with their outstanding features of likeability, simplicity, and earthy 'rightness'. But they are different in genre; and here a significant problem is revealed for the writer who wishes to create a fiction of symbolic national revitalisation. There comes a point (as Scott found with Jeanie on her travels and later in Roseneath) where 'realism' is strained beyond credibility by symbolism and legendary invocation. When this occurs *during* the development of the novel, the result is a dangerous strain of modes; conventions of naturalism render the mythopoetic role of the central figure incredible. Hogg is better than any of the other novelists (with the exception of William Alexander) in avoiding this strain. His novels are very different from each other; but they are (with the exception of the *Three Perils of Woman*), currently the subject of debate as to the direction and meaning of its many, often conflicting modes[5] generally consistent within themselves. There is historical fiction, there is legendary folklore, there is Defoe-esque burlesque autobiography (particularly in *Basil Lee* (1820) and *An Edinburgh Bailie* (1832)) which belong to our second and parodic tradition. Even in the apparent mixture of modes in *The Justified Sinner* (1824) there is, I have contended, a consistent ambivalence as underlying organising principle.[6] It is interesting, nevertheless, to note that Hogg's strongest statement of national heritage and identity, *The Three Perils of Man*, moves deliberately into folk-history and romance; as though Hogg realised that the fable allowed more scope. His comic embassy to Sir Michael Scott presents a gallery of Scottish types (from over-sensitive poet to reductively insensitive peasants) presided over by essentially genial and tolerant humanity, Charlie Scott. It would have been impossible for Hogg to convey the wealth of lore, cultural attitudes, defiant rural Scottishness, without recourse to a solution which would allow fantasy, fable, comedy and folk-history to emulsify.

Efforts in the mythic regenerative tradition tend to belong to a writer's earlier period. Just as one can see Hogg moving away from it even before 1822, so with John Galt, whose *Annals of the Parish* (1821), *Sir Andrew Wylie* (1822) and perhaps *Ringan Gilhaize* (1823) represent his more affirmative statements about Scottish cultural identity and tradition, contrasting with the less flattering light in which these are seen in *The Provost* (1822), *The Last of the Lairds* (1826), *The Member* (1832), and *The Radical* (1832). What enables Micah Balwhidder, the unpopular new minister of Dalmailing, to win over his enemies, is clearly his instinctive and 'commonsense' (in the meaning of the school of Scottish philosophy which carries the name) qualities, since Galt mildly satirises his intellect, conservatism and occasional gentle selfishness. It is by being of his flock that Micah leads them, ushering them through the gates of improvement and political change. He may not be a giant mythic figure, but Galt makes us wonder who else could have maintained continuity in Dalmailing; and more, Galt suggests that it is this type, rather that the Anglicised and too often absent lairds and gentlefolk or the new entrepreneurial gentry like Nabob Cayenne, who are the essence of the community. Galt's success is to make Balwhidder an eccentric, totally credible historical and local individual as well as a type and symbol of the way in which Scottish community can change and retain identity. His day may be well over when he retires, but he has enabled transition, in a manner not unlike that of the later *Johnny Gibb of Gushetneuk* (1871).

Andrew Wylie was a protagonist whose 'Scottishness' was exemplary to outsiders. The audience for this novel, and its didactic purpose that humble Scots worth and sense should be seen as vital to British moral development, was clearly not that sought by *Ringan Gilhaize*, the dark and complex portrait of a 'justified murderer', an Ayrshire peasant-farmer whose family are wiped out in one of the atrocities of Claverhouse's Royalist troops during 'the killing time.' Ringan's 'destiny' is to kill Claverhouse at Killiecrankie and change Scottish religious history; and at first sight he seems to carry a weight of collective historical responsibility, a kind of 'great memory' of wrongs done not just to himself but to Scotland. I leave it to the reader to decide if this apparent mythic role is in the end sanctioned; there is the possibility, contained in Ringan's Hebraic monologue and austere obsessive attitudes, that Galt's deeper purpose is parodic, and that the novel ultimately satirises the self-deluding vengefulness of 'God's chosen.' So interpreted, it would of course belong to our second tradition. But, as we shall see, such ambiguity of purpose becomes a dominating feature of all three traditions.

Sir Andrew Wylie clearly continues much of the moral and aesthetic intention of Mackenzie. Andrew and Harley, while contrasting in many respects, share a common sense of intuitive goodness. But Galt has with Balwhidder and Wylie conceived beyond the pedigree of Addison and Goldsmith. An assertion is being made that the origin of social worth lies *necessarily* outwith polite breeding and English conventional manners. It is precisely the pawky and wily sentimentality of these protagonists which contrasts with their genteel and aristocratic encounters, so that the nobility of Ayrshire and London are forced to recognise an integrity greater than their own. Unfortunately, the dwarf-like, comically naive Wylie strains our credibility in his dealings with and conversion of sophisticated and decadent Lords and Ladies in London to the point where this giant novel—one of Galt's longest and clearly conceived as a kind of sentimental epic—collapses into a kind of unintentionally grotesque fable, the problem of control being similar to that encountered by Scott with Jeanie Deans, and a problem to be encountered in turn in this tradition by MacDonald and Stevenson.

Handling the figure of exemplary ordinariness, of Scottish rudimentary worth, calls for rare balance of respect for the reality of social type, togther with skill in capturing native idiosyncracy. If the controlling attitude is one of condescension or exploitative manipulation, the mythic role is jeopardised, as happens with Wylie and later with George MacDonald's Malcolm. The other risk is that of *Ringan Gilhaize*, the risk of unsureness as to final attitude towards one's creation, stemming perhaps from divided allegiances and value systems within the writer. But this is not the same as the *conscious* playing off of Scottish 'quaintness' and manners against a norm which the writer has located *outside* Scottish social shared ideologies and codes. To simplify this consideration, I suggest that an 'inside' and 'outside' way of seeing the subject matter are the two usefully significant and different approaches. When Galt is 'inside' his Scottish value structure he allows convincing complexities of awareness and subtleties of judgement for his Balwhidder, Pawkie, and Gilhaize. Their identity is respected and celebrated, their motivation sympathetically analysed, as Scott with Fergus Mac-Ivor, Morton, or Reuben Butler.

It is extremely hard to pinpoint the cross-over from sympathetic identification of author and subject to authorial exhibition of subject to outside amusement. Are Cosmo Bradwardine or Cuddie Headrigg shown off for amused and polite laughter? Or does sufficient empathy redress the exploitation? Much of *Annals* is a balancing act of both, with the overriding mythic level of the minister's action finally in control. Wylie lacks that depth and authenticity of background which convinces us that Balwhidder believes in the right of the patrons to appoint him to his charge, but believes also in his parishioners' worth. Wylie's saintly oddity, his holy foolishness, comes from nowhere in Scotland, however much Galt strives to boast the worth of this Scottish simpleton. The failure is measured by comparison with a later and quieter mythic masterpiece, William Alexander's *Johnny Gibb of Gushetneuk* (1871). One is first struck by the rich and intensely localised Aberdeenshire dialect, which concedes little to audience; even more than Galt, Alexander allows his characters their own expression and integrity. As with language, so with subject matter. Like Galt, Alexander *feels* from the inside the validity of the patronage controversy. The novel deals with events in the parish of Pyketillim before and after the disruption of 1843, and it has a fairness and a detached sympathy nowhere else found in the Scottish novel. The local quarrels of laird and tenant, factor and village, are given in rancorous detail— Dawvid Hadden the factor being a particularly fine sleekit sycophant. But Alexander recognises what Fergusson had seen in his depiction of community quarrels in his poem 'The Election'—that closed and impoverished communities must absorb and forgive their internal offences, or destroy themselves. Even Hogg cannot match Alexander's persuasive rendering of a community in day-to-day action, and beside it much of Barrie and even Gibbon's depiction of rural life shows up as contrived and over-heated. Johnny Gibb (the name harking back to peasant roots similar to those of Jeanie Deans?) is the personification of this principle of implosive absorption of daily offence and betrayal. Solid, undramatically effective in everything he does, whether it be building a home for the new Free Church or taking in an orphan girl, Johnny's independence, homeliness and worth are solid in ways Andrew Wylie never achieves. Through him Alexander sums up and recommends the enduring qualities he sees in his small farmers; he is the type of Gibbon's John Guthrie in *Sunset Song*, without the bigotry. Significantly, too, Alexander asserts his right to defy the established Church of Scotland without appearing contumacious and bigoted. Like Balwhidder, Johnny is a presence of authority, for all his foibles, who is necessary for social and historical continuity and peaceful change. This is the type of man who holds society and community together, argues Alexander. It is sad to see how Gibbon presents his type as both doomed and prejudiced by the time he writes *Sunset Song* (1932).

The nineteenth century novel of mythic regeneration is taken furthest in the work of George MacDonald, whose strange mingling of social realism and symbolic fantasy cannot fully be understood without reference to this Scottish tradition. Elsewhere, David Robb has dealt far more fully than I can with his realistic and fantastic works,[7] but in the context of my essay I select a few of his works as major and, until recently, misunderstood examples of deliberate attempts to argue a Scottish-based moral regeneration for Victorian Britain; a regeneration all the more striking in that it was carried in the vehicle of a system of theology both dedicated to attacking narrow-minded Presbyterianism and religiosity of whatever description and yet, in itself, often over-rigorous, excessively mystical, and tinged with sado-masochism.

MacDonald is unusual amongst Scottish novelists in that his tendency to fable and fantasy is both deliberate and prior to his social realism, where most of the others tend to slide inexorably towards the supernatural fable in the course of working within realism, and often as a result of realism's failure to contain their mythic symbolism. *Phantastes* (1858) is his first novel and most ambitious and achieved fantasy. I begin, however, with later work which is naturalistic (although there is no discontinuity between fantasy and 'social realism' for MacDonald). Several of his novels are within the mainstream of the mythic traditions; from *David Elginbrod* (1863), *Alec Forbes of Howglen* (1865), *Robert Falconer* (1868), to *Sir Gibbie* (1879) and the two volume *Malcolm* epic, *Malcolm* (1875) and *The Marquis of Lossie* (1877). Within a wide range of MacDonald's fiction, three distinct modes can be seen: straightforward social realism, a highly unusual blending of realism and fantasy, and out-and-out moral fable or fantasy. Significantly, however, the essential core of all these is the same: the presentation of an exemplary quest undertaken by a protagonist who learns to reject narrow formality of religion or rational materialism.

MacDonald's orientation towards his fiction is not unlike that of Alexander. Both are from the North-East (though MacDonald was to leave in his twenties, to remember and recreate the north in a more nostalgic and idealised manner than the resident Alexander). Both are aware at first hand of Presbyterian division and rigour, though MacDonald rejects his 'Missionar'[8] background and the claims of Calvinism in idealistic disgust with its narrowness of imaginative and aesthetic tolerance where Alexander's realism allows him to accept differences of belief as inevitable. Both define as essential to their communities the strong, independent, and historically rooted figure whose ideas are normative—and who is described in terms which show the author to identify, as it were, from the inside of community, and then outwards to acceptance of a wider British scale of polite values. Just as with Scott and the Galt of *Andrew Wylie*, both tend to a divided relationship with their material, so that while both endorse the values of Johnnie or David Elginbrod, for example, sharing their attitudes towards affectation, pretension, and hypocrisy, there is nevertheless a tendency to 'frame' this identification within a superior authorial awareness of what sophistication in the larger outside world can offer. Thus there is created a paradox in which the humble and mythic type (Jeanie, Malcolm or Johnny) is held up as all-worthy by an author who simultaneously contradicts domestic values through use of a contrastingly middle-class Anglicised background language with which the author clearly identifies and which endorses the views of the very society with whom the national hero is designed to conflict.

It is this flaw which increasingly destroys the consistency of the later Victorian-Scottish mythic novel. *David Elginbrod* lacks a clear moral cynosure, in that David, simple, devout grieve of Turriepuffit, disappears from the novel early on, only his influence and memory persisting through the sophisticated love-adventures in England of the young Scots tutor, Hugh Sutherland, and the wilfully deceitful Lady Euphrasia. As with *Andrew Wylie*, the desire to use a nostalgically perceived Scottish simplicity amidst sophisticated, fashionable, and commercially viable settings pulls the 'inside' orientation outside Scottish values and community, so that the reader's memory of David becomes increasingly fabulous and unreal, and his sentiments, stripped of convincing provenance and piously declaimed by Hugh in standard English, stereotypical instead of archetypal.

Alec Forbes is better, the action being contained within Aberdeen and its rural environs. Instead of the gulf opening up between exemplar and protagonist, as with David and Hugh, Alec Forbes combines both roles, an authentic, cheerfully vernacular local hero who relates convincingly to a community of characters who symbolise nineteenth century Scotland in much the same way as John Spiers saw Douglas Brown presenting his view of the nineteenth century in allegory.[9] The local miserly merchant, Bruce, is quite explicitly so-called to indicate a Scottish Fall since the great King of Bannockburn, fantasising inappropriately that he *is* the king, 'digging the pits for the English cavalry . . . plotting still, but in his own shop.' Malison, the violent schoolteacher, is a powerful condemnation of the negative destruction MacDonald saw in so much Scottish pedagogy, as well as a moving picture of the final redemption of the man. Thomas Cram, the Missionar mason, is similarly a picture of strength and weakness, feeling and bigoted theory, combining in a strange mixture of value and distortion which MacDonald saw as typical of nineteenth century Scotland. It is a novel which is defiantly assertive of dialect, of Scottish integrity; and the Jeanie Deans-like figure of Annie Anderson, the 'pearl of price' to whom Alec Forbes at last attains, is a link between Scott's heroine and the Kirsteens, Sandies and Chrisses of the later fiction.

One figure, Cosmo Cupples, cantankerous poetic librarian and guiding spirit to Alec, is especially significant. His role as mentor calls for a ubiquitous social movement which becomes incredible; but here is the reason for MacDonald's tendency to move from realism to fantasy. For in *Sir Gibbie*, with its central figure of the mute Aberdeen slum child who is actually Sir Gilbert Galbraith, titled, but heir to nothing in terms of land, MacDonald again creates a symbolic figure whose function is hardly acceptable within the confines of social realism. Gibbie is virtually a Christ-child, as he wanders innocently away from Aberdeen into the green fields, converting those he meets to his vision of life. And in *Malcolm*, Malcolm Macphail, in reality rightful heir to the Marquis of Lossie, continues the symbolism of the simple Scottish protagonist whose worth is hidden from the eyes of the sophisticated world by its cataracts of false gentility and linguistic affectation. Language is a major concern of the two important, continuous and undervalued novels which make up MacDonald's most ambitious work. Malcolm's regaining of his rightful position is treated in a manner totally different from conventional handling of the same theme in English fiction. His ideas on language are striking; he vows to retain his Scots, even as Marquis (although he will acquire English in order to communicate furth of Lossie). The position of Marquis is forced to come to him on *his* terms, thus asserting the validity of his experience as adopted son of the Highland piper, blind Duncan Macphail, and authentic member of the fishing village of Portlossie. His fulfilment comes after his traditional quest, which takes him to London and the redemption of his London-corrupted sister Florimel, and the assumption of responsibility in Lossie for harbours and farms, a kind of 'primus inter pares' return to chieftainship in Scottish terms. And his redemptive historical Scottish presence is constantly emphasised—for example, in the way he chastens his foster-father Duncan's obsessive and hate-filled memory of the Glencoe massacre.

The novel has become fable somewhere through this epic. Weird symbolism, at times verging on the surreal (as with the hump-backed mad Laird who runs from humanity throughout crying 'I dinna ken whaur I cam frae,' or the cat-demon, black witch-woman Mrs Cattanach, sluggishly and profoundly evil, or Malcolm's prolonged battle to defeat the demon-will of his aptly and traditionally named mare, Kelpie), lends a fantastic resonance to the realism, so that the volumes move elusively between recognisable Victorian worlds and those of fabulous imagination. As with *Sir Gibbie*, this is quite deliberate, and necessitates to my mind a reconsideration of these works as requiring new terms of criticism and reference which won't condemn them as failed realism or failed romance. They link up easily with his quest novels which are more explicitly in the fantastic mode, as do other tales such as *The Portent*, or short stories like 'The Grey Wolf' or 'The Wow o' Rivven'. These stories anticipate MacDiarmid's early lyrics in their original and forceful combination of traditional supernatural with transcendental symbolism; they cannot be fully understood outwith the Scottish tradition.

Phantastes, Lilith (1895), and the long-short story 'The Golden Key' (1867), are the major fantasy works, although it is wrong to separate them from the so-called children's fantasies, *At the Back of the North Wind* (1871), and the Curdie stories. Indeed, it is crucial to an understanding of Macdonald to see his work as containing the child-like as a major part of significant adult experience. Only then can the strangely adult elements of the child stories be seen as the natural converse. Reading the closing passages of *The Princess and Curdie* (1888), with its appalling black ending for the city of Gwyntestorm (Curdie's city, of which he became King), one perceives that MacDonald's mind did not finally distinguish between myth and reality, or child and adult insight. Thus, *Phantastes* and 'The Golden Key' can be read alongside

Malcolm and *Sir Gibbie* as quest novels not so unlike in essentials. In a sense, Anodos is Malcolm's spiritual mind seeking identity; and *Phantastes* successfully allegorises the more earthly predicaments of the journey before inheritance. To the extent that fable speaks more directly of qualities which the writer prefers to conventional moral values, representing them in figures which do not strain credibility to breaking point, MacDonald's fantasies (growing increasingly dark until the baleful grave-worship of *Lilith*) belong to a mythic mode strongly favoured by Scottish poets and novelists since Hogg's *Pilgrims of the Sun* and *Kilmeny*, as well as the more traditional folk-fantasies like *The Witches of Eildon* and *the Three Perils of Man*. MacDonald's work is far less idiosyncratic if one sees it as the outstanding point of a consistent movement from realism to fantasy in the work of Scottish writers of prose or poetry from Carlyle's *Sartor Resartus* (1833) on throughout the century. In *Dr Jekyll and Mr Hyde* (1886), 'Markheim', or Oliphant's *Beleaguered City* (1880), or even Thomson's *The City of Dreadful Night* (1874), one recognises the recurrent need to find allegoric, fantastic and fabulous symbols for metaphysical ideas incompatible with social realism. And, later in the century, Davidson, Barrie and 'Fiona McLeod' follow the same movement.

Stevenson's major efforts in the fiction of mythic regeneration are not, however, in the allegoric mode. I have written more extensively on this elsewhere;[10] suffice it to sum up my argument by claiming that the two David Balfour stories, like the Malcolm novels, are his main effort in the genre. Stevenson in this extended work moved from portrayals of the adolescent as victim of Chance (*The New Arabian Nights* (1882), *The Dynamiter* (1885)) to protagonist as conscious moral agent. He had begun this movement with the superb novella, *The Merry Men* (1887), in which Charles Darnaway, in search of Spanish gold in a Scottish Hebridean bay, discovered and exemplified a higher truth which contrasted with the bigoted Calvinist deformation of his uncle, Gordon Darnaway, the wrecker. In miniature, Stevenson portrayed an islanded version of a peculiarly Scottish struggle between a negative and ultimately God-defying theology and an intuitive common-sense based morality which honours the dead and desires reconciliation with the past. Scott's Roseneath, microcosm of Scotland's internecine struggle, is echoed in several respects, although the briefness of canvas, while allowing for remarkable amounts of Highland-Lowland contrast, and tremendous interaction of landscape and action, does not permit a broad historical framework. *Kidnapped* (1886) follows Scott more fully in creating a situation where the sick forces of Scottish history are confronted with the protagonist who speaks with nature's voice—here, David's growing awareness that he has a political and moral duty which will lead him on a quest as exemplary as that of Jeanie Deans. The problem is that the major political theme which makes this into a novel of mythic regeneration does not occur till far too late in the book; and the continuation of the political theme of the need to bear national witness continues only part way through the sequel, *Catriona* (1893). But within these two novels lies Stevenson's main effort to write affirmatively and symbolically about the need for traditional Scottish virtue to oppose expediency, the expediency of the powers which would send James of the

Glens to the gallows for a murder he did not commit. David journeys all round Scotland; he wins over those most hostile to what he stands for; he bridges the Lowland-Highland division in his relationship with Alan Breck; he asserts the validity of humble and rural Scottish judgement; and he fails.

This failure is highly significant. David's farewell to politics in *Catriona* sums up the mythic quest. 'Till the end of time young folk (who are not yet used with the duplicity of life and men) will struggle as I did, and make heroical resolves . . . and the course of events will push them upon one side,' laments David (and, I think, Stevenson).[11] In this light the final inevitable failure of *Weir of Hermiston* can be foreseen. I have argued that the novel (like the last third of *Catriona*) was moving fatally towards false sentiment of the kind Stevenson was picking up from Crockett and the school of Robertson Nicoll,[12] but there is a more serious genre confusion within the novel than that of realism and sentimentality. On one hand the novel arranges itself in the classic manner of the *House with the Green Shutters*, in the form of what we discuss later as 'the novel of dissociation', in which the brutal father figure clashes in polar opposition with the sensitive son, the theme thus symbolising the opposition of Scottish archetypes of excessive materialism (with its consequent emotional repression) against self-indulgent hyper-sensitivity (lacking in formal discipline and traditional control). *Weir* could well have partnered *The Master of Ballantrae* as a superb analysis of the conflict of generations, values and types of Scottish life, the author from detachment describing peculiarly Scottish social polarities. But Stevenson raised dragons which would have torn the book apart when he introduced the anachronistic four black brothers. 'The old Elliot spirit awoke with a shout in the four sons', says Stevenson; their function was to represent the slumbering strengths of Scottish peasantry, radicalism and religious tradition, and poetic genius in Hob, Gib, and David respectively.[13] But Stevenson was stretching too far. In addition to the three brothers above, the fourth, Clem, was clearly there to represent peasantry urbanised, a mechanised countryman, somewhere between Bailie Nicol and Buchan's Dickson McCunn, post-industrial genius of the new Scotland.[14] Stevenson clearly had difficulties in reconciling the four symbolic roles with reality of psychological presentation, and would have had immense trouble persuading us that they would regress or revert to ancestral type and heroically rediscover the slumbering lion heart of Scotland in bursting open the jail in which Archie lay condemned. Stevenson lacked historical awareness, and by the time of writing was detached and perhaps alienated from any credible perspective on modern Scotland. His heroic assertion in this novel called for such perspective, but the black brothers are not up to the task of being at once real and mythic; at least not so in the manner of a Chris Guthrie or a Finn MacHamish.[15]

The strength of the mythic affirmative tradition lies in its unity of vision; its protagonist sits at the heart of a radiant and poetic imagery, the quest allowing us to see Scotland whole, as MacDiarmid's drunk man saw and felt it, as a sort of map of his own and his country's nervous system and of the heart of Scotland and its sickness or health. The weakness of the tradition lies in the ease with which such a form can be exploited by writers unsure of their response to their country (or countries) or, more simply, less able in their ability to create structure and symbol. John Wilson, Tory editor of *Blackwood's Magazine* and dominant figure in Scottish literature after Scott, is elsewhere in this volume taken to task by Andrew Noble. His influence must be seen as enormous; and in his two novels and volume of short stories (*The Trials of Margaret Lyndsay* (1822), *The Foresters* (1825) and *Lights and Shadows of Scottish Life* (1822)), the unhealthy manipulation of sentimental episodes typical of Mackenzie, combined with a representational Scottish bucolicism inherited from Burns, to produce what would look like a deliberate parody of *The Heart of Midlothian* or *Malcolm* or *Johnny Gibb* were it not for the fact that Wilson's political and reactionary propogandistic purpose is so hysterically strong that there is no question of any comic or burlesque aim. Margaret Lyndsay is, in the traditional sense, the soul of the peasantry of Scotland; but that soul is now being admonished and reformed, rather than celebrated for its enduring and instinctive rightness, so that the poetic wholeness of, say, Jeanie and her surrounding narrative, is here fragmented, the family systematically destroyed because her father dared to exceed his weaver's station in reading Thomas Paine's *The Rights of Man*. Wilson distorts wilfully thereafter, contriving a horrendous symbolic admonitory end for Walter; his radical weaver's indulgence of dangerous ideas leads (of course) to a love of drink and scarlet women, and his disturbing of the feudal hierarchy of Braehead village leads to the ritual extirpation of virtually all his relatives with Margaret alone surviving, the chastened symbol of peasantry adopting the path of a patient Griselda. Wilson is, however, only the extreme example of a degenerative mythic fiction in which the genuine mythic novel's archetypes are distorted and exploited. Sometimes Galt was guilty of gross exploitation and manipulation, especially in *Sir Andrew Wylie*, and also Hogg; despite recent special pleading for *Three Perils of Woman* to be seen as more subtle and parodic, I remain as yet unconvinced, and continue to see it as an example of how easily even the major writer can succumb to the temptation to exploit conventional stock figures, here taken from melodrama and conventional literary ruralism.

We now have to be careful. It would be too easy to apply the conventional term 'kailyard' to this emerging tendency to sentimentalise rural life and restrict Scottish character depiction to a foreshortened range of complexity and type. I suggest a moratorium on the overused general term 'kailyard', other than in the quite specific sense employed by Gillian Shepherd in her essay in this volume, in which she limits the term to description of a few specific novelists in a particular decade. Within the blanket area of typical usage of the general term lie too many differing, if related, types. Distortive ruralism can be politically directed, as Wilson showed; it can be directed towards the endorsement of religious organisations; it can be escapist, not so much into the cabbage-patch, but, as in the 'escape to Scotland' identified by Edwin Muir, into colourful history; and it can be allied to a romanticised Celtic pseudo-mythology. Nearly all variations involve an 'outside-in' authorial orientation, in the sense that new English and American markets were encouraging the explanatory and comfortably patronising attitude of the author, who (like MacDonald in the more English orientated of his fictions like *Ranald Bannerman's Boyhood* (1871) or Barrie *via* his schoolmaster of Glenquarity in *A Window in Thrums* (1889), could 'sit on the fence' and observe curious native habits, but when it suited him, drop off on to the side of identification with the peasantry, or cross the fence to assure his non-Scottish audience that he recognised the quaint narrowness of language and behaviour of his erstwhile associates.

It could be argued that even the major fiction of the period of Scott frequently suffers from this dual identification. The author of *Waverley* or 'The Two Drovers' constantly glosses and stands above his highlanders and lowlanders, acting as go-between and guide. It is a question of the degree of exploitation, and the lengths to which the author will go in distorting the material. The post-regenerative fiction, on the other hand, *appears* to celebrate the mythic status of Scotland's history, society and peasantry especially; but in reality, by performing an authorial distancing of perspective, relocates lowland and highland communities in an anachronistic never-never land. The types of this escapist and reductive fiction include the politico-religious, the historical, the Celtic-elegaic and the 'urban kailyard'. Following Wilson and *Blackwood's Magazine* in method and often in Tory orthodoxy of belief, and Galt in peasant archetypology, writers down the century include D M Moir and his *Mansie Waugh, Tailor of Dalkeith* (1828) and a host of lesser figures like Andrew Picken, Robert Pollock and Andrew Cunningham. In the later part of the century, Norman Macleod, chaplain to Queen Victoria in 1857, editor of *Good Words* from 1860 to 1872, and Moderator of the General Assembly in 1869, exemplifies the type. Liberal in his theology, a supporter of abstinence and foreign missions, immensely popular at home, throughout Britain, and abroad, Macleod's fiction nevertheless reduces his Scottish communities. *The Starling* (1867) can stand as example; here is the exemplary hero, ex-sergeant of Waterloo, Adam Menzies, likeably wayward as a youth, heroic as a man, and in retirement the model of humane charity in his village, Drumsylie. Ex-poacher, but a lover of country and sport, he is contrasted with the rigid orthodoxy of his local church, minister and zealous elders; he is 'nature's voice', the true and instinctive kindness of spontaneous feeling, of the 'common sense', set against overly rigid authoritarianism. The starling symbolises natural song, offending against the Sabbath from its cage outside Adam's house, causing the confrontation of minister and Adam in the novel, Adam refusing to have the bird destroyed because of its link with his dead boy Charlie, his 'young chevalier'. 'I'm Charlie's bairn', piteously pipes the bird. Such obvious artifice recalls the stock stageprops of Mackenzie's sentimentality, and artifice will be put to use in the work of S R Crockett, like *The Lilac Sunbonnet* (1894), in Barrie's *A Window in Thrums* (1894) and *The Little Minister* (1891), and in the work of 'Ian McLaren', in *Beside the Bonnie Briar Bush* (1894) and *The Young Barbarians* (1901). And a paradox should be noted here. This kind of fiction works by asserting the remote virtues of Scottish community untouched by complex political questions, or socio-economic subleties, or satanic mills and industrialisation, or sexual debates. Its function is thus apparently one of reassurance that such blighting modern problems have not spoiled all of the Western world, yet in sense it asserts at the same time the primacy of centralised political and military power in Victorian Britain. Adam Menzies had won Waterloo, in his way; just as in McLaren's *Young Barbarians* the most mischievous boy, Speug the rough horsedealer's son, was inevitably destined to win the VC, holding a pass in Africa against hordes of howling Masai. Thus, these villages, Muirtown and Thrums and Drumsylie and the rest, are simultaneously never-never land *and* part of Victoria's vision of the simple strengths of imperialist Britain. The modesty of canvas and authorial presentation belies a complacently chauvinistic assumption that in Andrew Wylie, Adam Menzies, and their ilk, the Scots hold the key to fundamental moral rightness; yet the fear of appearing actually to identify with the quaintness of their protagonists forces their authors to write through a *persona* far superior to them in sophistication of register.

The element of military symbolism in these basically political assertions of the superiority of simply social conformity in Victorian Britain forms an overlap with the historical fiction, which runs from Scott, of course, through work like Thomas Dick Lauder's *The Wolf of Badenoch* (1827), G R Gleig's *The Subaltern* (1825), Michael Scott's *Tom Cringle's Log* (1836), reaching its height in the robust celebrations of regimental manliness in James Grant's *The Romance of War or The Highlanders in Spain* (1845), or Norman Macleod's *The Old Lieutenant and His Son* (1862). But boundaries between apparently very different kinds of fiction are in reality vague; so that aspects of 'kailyard' abound in the novels of Grant, Crockett and the young John Buchan. Indeed, Crockett illustrates the ease of crossover outstandingly, being author of the sickly and coy *The Lilac Sunbonnet* (1894) *and* the vigorous period tales of Galloway like *The Raiders* (1894) and *The Men of the Moss Haggs* (1895). The last of these is a most impressive historical novel which owes much to Hogg's *Brownie of Bodsbeck*; but, however entertaining, both are retreats from modern Scotland and the by now pressing debates over industrialisation, Highland Clearance, Crofter's rights, or mass politicisation. 'Mythic regeneration' here has descended into stereotype, so that dim repetitions of the forceful social patternings of *Redgauntlet* or, more frequently, *Kidnapped*, are detectable, as in the frequent character oppositions of Crockett and Buchan, feeble echoes, devoid of the symbolic meaning which Scott and Stevenson gave to their mythic prototypes. When one compares Buchan's *John Burnet of Barns* (1898) with *Ringan Gilhaize* or *Old Mortality* one sees how much has been lost. Buchan's is a pasteboard use of scenery, his confrontations of Scottish protagonists mere conventional melodrama, owing more to *Lorna Doone* than traditions of Scott. Admittedly Buchan was young, and admittedly he went on to develop a deeper vision—but even at best, as in the eerie stories of *A Watcher by the Threshold* (1902), that deeper vision belongs to that pseudo-elegaic and self-indulgent strand, mainly Celtic in ambience, already present in Scott and Galt's *Entail*, found in Grant's highlanders, and developed by William Black in novels like *Macleod of Dare* (1878), with its ridiculous love affair of noble Highland chief and London actress, which exploited clichés from both cultural sides and literally drowned chief and lady in melodrama at the end. Comparison of this contrived and fashionable nineteenth century version of soap opera with Gunn's powerfully symbolic drowning at the end of *The Lost Glen* (1932) reveals the historically irrelevant posturing of Black, who nevertheless had real talent, as occasional pieces like 'The Penance of John Logan' (1889) show. He had the intelligence and insight to perceive genuine difference in Gaelic perception; but obviously market forces conquered integrity, and 'the darling of the lending libraries' went on to write about forty novels which moved between fashionable London and 'Thule', 'Far Lochaber', 'Green Pastures' and Picadilly, 'Mincing Lane' and Inverness.

In all these types we can chart the fall of a myth, the desire to present a serious historical-metaphysical synthesis which can do justice to the writer's conception of Scotland. Gone is the attempt to locate the protagonist within a framework of credible social and historical forces. Saddest of all is the end-of-century 'Celtic Twilight' luxuriant nostalgia and death-wish which follows Black's portrayal of 'tragic dignity', the literary equivalent of Landseer's 'The Monarch of the Glen' (1851) or Horatio McCulloch's moody, history-ruined, brooding and broken majestic landscapes, painted between 1845 and 1870. Most telling, too, is the dual persona of the monarch of the Twilighters, William Sharp (with 'Fiona MacLeod', his female soul). Sharp was the English man of letters, the critic; Fiona was the priestess of 'the Celtic Gloom,' the mood of feyness which accompanied the death-throes of Gaeldom. To read Sharp/McLeod now infuriates, such is the sado-masochistic luxuriance in vague and Ossianic cloudiness. Dimly, for example, in *Pharais, A Romance of the Isles* (1894), one can detect symbolic and mythic elements in the tragedy of Alastair and Lora. Young, recently married, expecting a family, there is however a doom which hangs over them. Alastair is brainsick, and tries to hide from Lora to spare her. This is all, with ornate and pseudo-Gaelic moodiness wrapped like mountain mist around it. Here, as in *The Mountain Lovers* (1895), Gaeldom is seen as decaying, but not from Clearance or political relegation, absentee landlord or cultural neglect; rather from an inner flaw, an inherent decadence, which was a more politically acceptable diagnosis for the period. The novel is the result of marrying Scottish fictional traditions with conventions and imagery drawn from the pre-Raphaelites and the Irish revival of the 'eighties, so that second sight, dreamy atmospheric richness and morbid sensitivity derived from overlong communion with mountain flood and nature herself luxuriate. What Ossian was to Duncan Ban Macintyre in the eighteenth century, this is to the authentic Gaelic poetic tradition of John Smith and Mary Macpherson in the nineteenth. It is the triumph of images of death and decay over those of regeneration and affirmation. 'Fiona Macleod' created morbid artefacts for the consumption of the non-Gaelic market. Unfortunately and all too often it is this aspect of morbidity and literary cliché which blights the work of good writers like Neil Munro or John MacDougall Hay in *Gillespie* (1914).

William Donaldson has rightly drawn our attention to the huge amount of fiction which was published in local newspapers all over Scotland. He suggests that we should take this vast non-book fiction into account. How far he is justified in suggesting that the 'canon' of Scottish fiction will be altered can only be answered when these texts are available to the general reader. Where Donaldson does give examples, in the cases of William Latto, editor from 1860 of *The People's Journal* of Dundee, William Alexander (of *Johnny Gibb*), and David Pae, prolific producer of serialised fiction, I feel that on the quality of samples and outlines (and these I accept cannot be final evidence), while vernacular writing may have boomed, and the range of subject matter extended to include factory and mill, the achievement of novels and sketches usually remains below the level of the accepted best. Latto's 'Jock Clodpole' follows a long tradition from Hogg and his 'John Miller', the Nithsdale shepherd, or Galt and his persona of Mr Duffle in *The Steamboat* (1822), of inventing a homely persona who can comment on the doings of the big world in a way which generates comic tension out of the discrepancies between the viewed and the viewer. Clodpole and the American persona of 'Ezekiel Twentyman' also follow the episodic and rumbustious set-pieces of the 'Noctes Ambrosianae' of *Blackwood's Magazine* in the 1820's. To argue that there is 'much memorable writing' among the pieces, does not make the case for overall unified achievement and, given the models cited, it is hardly fair to argue that there is nothing else quite like this in Scottish letters.[16] The case for Alexander is, however, excellently made; I am (see below) convinced of the importance of *The Laird of Drammochdyle* (1865) and look forward to further publication of Alexander. Donaldson's account suggests that the third example, David Pae, extends what is usually considered the material of the 'kailyard' novel into the city. There are indeed extended descriptions of city life, which recall the vivid imagery of Alexander Smith in his poem 'Glasgow' (1857); but on his own admission Donaldson allows that it is over-didactic, suffers from implausibility of plot, and appeals to the lowest instincts of the reader.[17] 'Urban fairytale' is how he describes what was regarded as Pae's best, *The Factory Girl; or, the Dark Places of Glasgow* (1863),[18] although his claim that it is 'an unrelenting attack on the commercial ethos, the devouring materialism which the author saw as threatening to engulf Scotland in the first great wave of capitalist expansion' is a challenging one and deserves serious consideration. The extent to which Pae deserves a place superior to 'urban kailyard' pictures like that of Sarah Tytler in *St Mungo's City* (1892) remains to be seen.[19]

So far, I have considered what can generally be described as a tradition of mythic affirmation which, from its inception, contained the seeds of its own decadence. Inability to sustain serious political and convincing serious projections of Scottish heroic identity led to debased and falsified versions addressed to increasingly non-Scottish quaint or reassuring images of noble savages or simplistic communities. One could almost describe these later fictions as novels of mythic degeneration.

Such failure of national creativity and sense of shared identity meant that the most responsible fiction, accepting the historic impossibility of heroic assertion, adopted strategies which were all varieties of ironic treatment of national character, in ways comparative, parodic, and reflective of national dissociation.

It may seem artificial to separate the women writers from the Scott, Hogg, and Galt group; but the detached quality of their irony and their singular and much more precise detached observation of middle-class and affected manners, as Jenni Calder points out in her essay in this volume, makes them different in their handling of Scottish life and attitudes; and to isolate them helps stress their continuity and their significant achievement, too often unperceived because they are seen as minor individuals and variations on the major male theme. Thus, Susan Ferrier usually gets tagged on at the end of the Scott era; Oliphant after Stevenson and Douglas Brown. The tradition of female Scottish irony begins with Elizabeth Hamilton's *The Cottagers of Glenburnie* (1808) and Mary Brunton's *Self-Control* (1811), *Discipline* (1814) and *Emmeline* (1819). These and Susan Ferrier's three, *Marriage* (1818), *Inheritance* (1826) and *Destiny* (1832), and perhaps Catherine Sinclair's *Modern Accomplishments* (1836), are the main examples of the first wave of women 'improver-satirists'; and something of the contradiction at the heart of their work can be discerned in my description. Their strength is their acid edge and their accurate and clear perception of social folly, class pretension, and most of all, their ear and eye for vernacular detail. There is throughout a comparative technique which exhibits local Scottish habits alongside those of polished and Anglicised society, and by no means always to the credit of the southern side. London society in *Marriage* lacks the human warmth, the rough honesty, of Edinburgh and Scotland, and apparently unattractive characters like gruff, misanthropic Mr Ramsay in *The Inheritance* turn out to have a peculiarly Scottish dry humanity against which English polite relations are found cold and wanting. But it has to be admitted that the foibles of native Scotland are more mocked than endorsed. Hamilton's presentation of scruffy Glenburnie, with its ducks and dungheaps, next to its filthy houses and lazy lubberly girls, with their hairy butter and clarty towels, may allow its presiding genius Mrs McLarty to be filthy *and* handsome, a kind of homely Madge Wildfire, but the nett effect is to firmly place the subject matter well outside the author's sympathies and identification. Hamilton's caustic description of Glenburnie prepared the way for Ferrier's presentation of dreary Highlands and Glenfern castle in *Marriage*, with its sullen servants and the grotesque sisters Nicky, Grizzy and Jacky (and, perhaps, Scott's Tullyveolan in *Waverley*); the mode is exhibitory, and the audience meant to compare their own implied superiority with the inferiority of the subjects described. Mrs McLarty, like the sisters of Glencairn, or the laird of Glenroy in *Destiny*, may carry some symbolic representational national virtue of a residual sort, but the 'improving' mind of the authoress— and this is true right through until Catherine Carswell's *Open the Door!* (1920)—ultimately denies the survival worth of the symbol. The authoresses do not identify with much of the Scotland described.

There are other contradictions. Social climbers are amongst the most satisfying of their satirical topics, from the Flinders family of *Cottagers* to

Ferrier's Miss Pratt and the Reverend McDow.[20] Hamilton argues that the Flinders are not despised for their want of birth, 'but on account of their paltry attempts of concealing the meanness of their origin by parade and ostentation. It is they . . . who . . . have undermined our national virtues, and destroyed our national character'.[21] Yet the gusto with which such are revealed, the obvious relish in their vulgarity, undermines the Christian persona which invariably in these novels expresses the author's own pious standpoint. Mrs Mason in *Cottagers*, Mrs Douglas in *Marriage*, and a host of other pompous men and women who act as wooden struts for their story's heavy bourgeois respectability are never the voices allowed to talk of the purple arms and awkward gait of rural girls. There is an acidic voice and a respectable voice; and the author reveals in the discrepancy between them the unsureness of moral and social values so typical of the century. These women may be detached; but they lack a consistent point of view, so that their work is no real and coherent social critique, and all that remains is the nostalgic love of old Scots songs and of old-fashioned couthiness. Mrs Violet McShake, the ancient Edinburgh tenement dweller of *Inheritance*, represents the strengths and weaknesses of such writing. Grotesque and vividly of the past, there is an unintentional ambiguity in the way she commands our respect yet shocks our sense of good manners which captures the woman writer's dilemma; the impossibility of synthesising the didactic, improving message with the fascinated, affectionate description of the grotesque aspects of Scottish society which are seen as anachronisms.

Margaret Oliphant's work succeeds at best on a higher level, but she too shares this contradictory approach. She evades the problem by often locating her fiction outside Scotland, for example, in her *Chronicles of Carlingford*,[22] outstanding amongst which is her vivid picture of a Scottish doctor's head-strong, restless social climber, *Miss Marjoribanks* (1866). But even here, as in the Scottish-set *Kirsteen* (1890), we still find her predicament to be that of being trapped somewhere between love of Scottish traditional characteristics and desire for Anglicised social improvement. *Kirsteen* especially shows this. A fine novel in many important ways, its inconsistency of portrayal of Kirsteen's social evaluations—for example, in her at first sympathetic but finally snobbish assessment of her sister and her hardworking doctor husband as 'lowering' the blood of her Douglas ancestors—seriously damages the reader's expected identification with the heroine. But one important development takes place in Oliphant's fiction which helps to change the character of later women's fiction in Scotland. *Kirsteen, Hester* (1883) and, to a lesser extent, *Miss Marjoribanks* present heroines who defy social conventions and insist, with varying success, on opening doors hitherto closed to women; doors which, like Catherine Carswell's in her novel of 1920, significantly entitled *Open the Door!*, are seen as Victorian restrictions on personal development sexually, aesthetically, and professionally. Oliphant only tackled the last two. All her women's efforts modestly assert rights in these areas, *Miss Marjoribanks* even satirising the very limited self-assertion of its heroine, Lucilla. But from such tentative starts as these and novels like *Crossriggs* (1901) by Jane and Mary Findlater, the restricted field of women's place in

Scotland is sufficiently reploughed for later novelists like Carswell, Willa Muir, Nancy Brysson Morrison, Nan Shepherd, Naomi Mitchison, and Jessie Kesson to develop a major branch of Scottish fiction. *Crossriggs* implies in its title the cross-grained unnatural forces which trap Alexandra's sexuality, in Oliphant-like bonds of family duty, the ties of children of a less able sister, a gormless saint of a father, an impossible love for a married man. Like Oliphant, the Findlaters do not permit triumphant assertion of self or more than very limited fulfilment or escape; but, like Oliphant, the atmosphere of repressive, unjust limitation of outstanding vitality and talent is claustrophobic. Much more depth study of women's writing in Scotland is urgently required.

It is significant that the women's fiction rarely attempts the mythic regenerative or its converse, the parody of the mythic. They are content to remain in an ironic and comparative tradition, unconsciously mirroring the tensions within Scotland between a sense of traditional manners and language and a growing sense of the worth of aspiration to 'North British' (and eventually downright 'English') identity. *Blackwood's Magazine* also encouraged and developed a fiction based on this implicit measuring process, in which the author's eye moves back and forward between the polite and the vulgar, the exotic and the familiar, the English and the Scottish, in ways which present Scottish types, like Smollett's soldier Lismahagow, as parodies of the native. Indeed, Smollett's *Humphry Clinker* (1771), and its tour around Scottish manners, was the forerunner of the parodic type. *Peter's Letters to His Kinsfolk* (1819), by John Gibson Lockhart, is to an extent a novel of this kind, as is *The Youth and Manhood of Cyril Thornton* (1824) by Thomas Hamilton; probably the outstanding example of the type, with its English hero coming like Waverley to give a commentary on Scotland; here, on Glasgow College life, city manners, quaint old-fashioned customs of Scotland (such as the comic burial of the country laird). W E Aytoun will later make excellent short story comedy out of such idiosyncracies; his ponderous *Blackwood's* novel, *Norman Sinclair* (1861) lacks the comedy and real social commentary of stories like his 'How we got up the Glenmutchkin Railway and How we got out of it' (1853), which works through a yoking together of roguish British-oriented sophistication with comic grotesque extravaganza in traditional Scottish vein worked up from oddities of past outlandish Scottish and highland life and character. *Blackwood's* was to remain the vehicle for the flourishing survival of the Anglo-Scottish novel of comparison till the end of the century.

But there was lurking within Thomas Hamilton's poorly structured, rambling Anglo-Scottish novel a darker theme which was to be developed into one of the Scottish novel's most powerful aspects of the century's fiction. Cyril Thornton was not Smollett's touring gentleman or a version of Waverley; a more profound protagonist, he carried the guilt of his brother's death, a black mark which haunted his life. Hamilton made, in the end, too little of this, just as John Gibson Lockhart made not enough of excellent materials in *Adam Blair* (1822) and *Matthew Wald; The Story of a Lunatic* (1824). The first is the Hawthorne-like story of a minister who sins sexually, whose mind collapses under the guilty strain, and whose Calvinist village and parishioners, after insisting on years of exile and atonement, allow him to return to his ministry; the second is an even more disturbing study of recurrent morbidity and eventual madness, marred by its Gothic excesses and sub-romantic agonies. But there comes a point where the fiction of the nineteenth century becomes aware of its own posturing; matures, as it were, into a parodic and ironic sense of the *degeneration* of national archetype, and produces a new rhetoric, new narrative strategies and perspectives, to express its detached evaluation. This maturation of ironic vision we are familiar with in poetry. It underlines Ramsay's disguises of authorial stance in 'Lucky Spence's Last Advice' or 'The Vision', Burns's dramatic monologues of Holy Willie and devil, together with their 'built-in' ambivalence of interpretation in much of their greatest poetry. Is 'Tam o' Shanter' straightforward folk-tale with supernatural pyrotechnics, or is there an alternative reading which permits it to be sub-titled 'the Presbyterian's nightmare'? Techniques of creative ambiguity are well-known in Scottish literature, from Henryson's *Testament of Cresseid* and *Fables* to Montgomerie's *The Cherrie and the Slae*; perhaps the social dynamics of a small country with an even smaller, incestuous cultural circle eventually insist on stratagems of ironic double meaning.

Whatever the traditional and conventional background, the basic grammar of this fiction of Scottish social degeneration (and eventual dissociation) is clear enough. From Scott onwards it operates at two basic levels (that of parody of the 'insipid hero',[23] and that of the contrast of two sets of cultural values, embodied in the confrontations of a traditional with a modern and alienated protagonist, the two entangled in positions of mutual moral and social destruction. The author selects from three available relationships with his material. He can work through the 'discovery' of a manuscript, or records (thus enabling the author to slip away from authorial identification with his creation); through the autobiographical/dramatic monologue; or through authorial omniscience. All three present material which is not susceptible to single and straightforward interpretation, and which indeed often permits of 'mirror-image' *reversal* of interpretation. These authorial approaches are often mixed together. *The Provost* has a 'superior' introduction to the 'manu-script' which is Pawkie's account, is dramatic monologue, and is irresolvably enigmatic, a methodology close to that of *The Justified Sinner* and *The Master of Ballantrae*. But recognition of an underlying similarity of theme enables us to link what at first reading seem to be unrelated constructions. For example, Scott's *Waverley*, Barrie's *Sentimental Tommy* (1896) and *Tommy and Grizel* (1900), and Munro's *Gilian the Dreamer* (1899) can thus be seen as descendants of morbid or insipid anti-heroic and downright anti-social protagonists in Scott, Hogg, and Galt, and progenitors of such in Brown and MacDougall Hay.

What these fictions have in common is an ambivalent attitude towards their central figures, linked to a parodic purpose. Worth and deficiency are curiously juxtaposed. Waverley is a sensitive dreamer whose tendency to create a surrounding of pathetic fallacy comes close to destroying him; sen-timental Tommy is presented as destroying himself through an excess of self-dramatising imagination; and Gilian, the dreamer, likewise exists more in a world of self-projection and idealisation than reality. Significantly, all three novelists have indicated that the protagonist of their novels holds a particularly personal claim on them; yet all are treated with an ironic distancing and equivocation which frequently suggest an unsureness of authorial identification and value location. One is reminded of the difficulty of locating authorial endorsement in *Provost* and *Annals*, and the apparent mutual exclusivity of opposing interpretations in *The Justified Sinner* and *The Master of Ballantrae*.

But *Waverley, Redgauntlet*, the *Tommy* novels, and *Gilian* particularly, deserve to be reconsidered as sophisticated and Scottish versions of a nineteenth century theme, that of the confusion of Romantic delusion with external reality. The problem of Emma and Dorothea in *Emma* and *Middlemarch*, and of the central women of *Madame Bovary* and, say, *On the Eve*, is here intensified and much more narrowly focused in these Scottish 'heroes'. And from Hogg's *Basil Lee* (1820) and Archibald Sydeserf in *An Edinburgh Bailie* (1832) and Galt's *Provost* and related studies, to the much later treatment of enigmatic, self-deluding protagonists of morbid sensitivity in Douglas Brown, MacDougall Hay and the novels of John Davidson, especially *Ninian Jamieson* (1890), we have the development and culmination of a tradition of deliberate mockery of the attempt to create a Scottish heroic mythology. Not with a bang but with anticlimax went Waverley and Redgauntlet from their worlds of idealism and romance; so too Hogg's even pettier time-servers and changers of sides and loyalties, Basil Lee and Archibald Sydeserf. For all his glorious dreams, Tommy ends up hanging ignominiously from a high wall, strangled by the clothes of a Scottish stereotype, the country doctor; while Ninian is the provost of and a lunatic, who believes he is the direct descendant of the Royal Stewart line, and legitimate claimant to the British throne.

With the exceptions of *The Provost* and *Edinburgh Bailie*, an unwillingness to accept historical change and progress has been the hallmark of the protagonists of this tradition. Nostalgia, preference of the past and the manufacture of an illusory present are their characteristic. All are social misfits, physically dislocated from their families, communities, and nation. Thus any glimpse of heroism and symbolic leadership is reduced and parodied, to the point that Davidson's wandering pilgrim-child, Strongsoul, and Barrie's elf in Peter Pan, become logical heirs to this dismembered kingdom, where the co-ordinates of reality give way to those of consciously chosen never-never land. Redgauntlet has become Captain Hook (it is worth remembering that Barrie emphasised Hook's raffish Stuart looks and descent!),[25] and the pilgrimage of Jeanie Deans has been reduced to the childish, if seriously undertaken, *Pilgrimage of Strongsoul*, in which the quests of Henry Morton, of Jeanie, of David Balfour, of Anados, and Sir Gibbie, are reduced to a quite explicit parody of Bunyan. The boy is 'knighted' for his saving of Pansy, the Duke's daughter, by a lady who turns out to be Victoria herself, and who 'knew *The Pilgrim's Progress* quite well',[26] he becomes 'my Lord Strongsoul of Dunmyatt'—again, conscious irony on Davidson's part, since he knows full well that Dunmyatt is the not-quite mountain standing beside Wallace's monument and near Bannockburn. Like the later reduced and mocking echoes sounded so often by Robin Jenkins which parody former Scottish glories by diminishing them to misquoted Burns and squalid street names, Davidson consciously and ironically plays with what he sees as outmoded conceptions of Scottish destiny and significance. Shortly after this (1922–1935) John Buchan carries forward the form without the ironic detachment in an unintentional gallimaufry of stereotypes in his adventures of the Gorbals Diehards, slum boys under the benign care of Dickson McCunn, Glasgow philanthropist grocer;[27] S R Crockett creates his street arab, *Cleg Kelly* (1896), and *Wee MacGreegor*, J J Bell's 1903 roguish 'street arab', and forerunner of 'Oor Wullie', captures the national imagination entirely. The focus on a sort of inverted national hero thus descends through the period 1814–1914 to the point where unheroic parodic symbolism (consciously and unconsciously presented) dominates national culture. Even the most 'realistic' novels centre much of their focus on the bewildered adolescent.

Two novels indicate what has happened to the affirmative *and* parodic type by the early 1900s; Buchan's early but typical *John Burnet of Barns* (1898) and Violet Jacob's much better, but neglected, *Flemington* (1911). The first has lost any movement in history as meaningful context. 'History' is now merely an excuse for a *Lorna Doone* exploration of the Southern Uplands, and melodrama involving colourful gypsies and wild action. We search in vain for the metaphysical struggles of a Morton, even of a David Balfour. On the other hand, *Flemington* tightly and effectively manages to show, through the sensitive, grandmother-dominated figure of Archie Flemington, a real sense of the problematics of Scottish loyalties and idealism in a way clearly inherited from Stevenson and David Balfour, but distilled and matured to a parodic historical bitterness. Archie's dilemmas are set, traditionally, within the contradictory influences of Scotland in the immediate pre- and post-Jacobite period. His formidable grandmother, ironically called Christian Flemington, has been slighted by the chevalier, and has changed sides, raising the boy in her new allegiance. Archie becomes a Hanoverian spy, with no clear-cut heroism being allowed, brave and resourceful though he is. His loyalty becomes increasingly dubious as he begins to see the corruption about him (marvellously embodied in 'Skirlin' Wattie', the legless, bloated gaberlunzie who is drawn in a cart by five dogs, whose evil is belied by the sweetness of his folksinging voice.) Archie is painfully drawn across all his Hanoverian loyalties to a friendship with the man he's spying on, James Logie of Montrose, a leading Jacobite. He betrays James, tearing himself apart in so doing. Archie's torn identity is Scotland's, his pains those of the riven land. The description of Scotland after Culloden is deliberately low-key, dreary and unromantic—just as much of the novel's setting, around the dreich mudflat basin of Montrose, has been also. This is a novel which despises the myths of Scottish history, seeing instead poisoned principles, tortuous self-destruction, political storms in teacups. The sensitive are destroyed, says Jacob; Archie finally saves James, but thus brings about his own death; while the insensitive and power-dealing survive relatively unscathed. One remembers David Balfour's disillusion in *Catriona*.

In many ways, *Flemington* could be considered with the last and finest tradition of Scottish fiction, that which contrives to achieve a detached portrayal of a dissociated and self-warring Scotland. It shares with this group the focus on divided self, within a broken and divided family and nation. It has a version of the recurrent theme of the brutal parent whose unfeeling egotism and material calculations destroy a sensitive, indeed hyper-sensitive, child. Its major themes involve confrontation of Past and Present, Disorder and Order, and a cause of passionate personal involvement and a 'cause' of calculating and arid expediency. It comes at the end of virtually a hundred years of fiction, from *Waverley* in 1814 to *Gillespie* in 1914. We come with it to the major tradition of Scottish fiction; a tradition which, apparently unconcerned with details of social change, is in fact deeply preoccupied with the exploration of Scottish *psyche*. This major tradition examines deeply embedded dualism and divided loyalties as inherent in the Scottish mind.

Scott's 'unified design', his preference for periods of civil war within Scotland as background, have long been recognised. Critics have long discussed Scott's dualisms. Essentially Scott's patterning of opposites symbolises a divided Scotland, in which the outlawed romantic claim of the past represents an over-emotional, imaginative and destructive throwback to an older national identity, expressed through figures like Rob Roy, Fergus Mac-Ivor and Balfour of Burley. Conversely, figures such as Bailie Nicol Jarvie, Richard Waverley, Colonel Gardiner and the Duke of Argyll, stand for a prudential, if unromantic, progressive realism. Scott's recurrent and symbolic patterning is surely now recognised as located within particularly Scottish co-ordinates, particularly in *Waverley, Old Mortality, The Heart of Midlothian, Redgauntlet* and *The Bride of Lammermoor*. It can be argued endlessly how far Scott rightly diagnosed Scottish history as the opposition of the principles of conservatism and progress (as Coleridge saw it), and how far, as Hart suggests, he instead projected aesthetic patterns of division between barbarity and civility onto external creations.[28] What matters for the tradition of Scottish fiction is that Scott, from 'The Two Drovers' to *The Heart of Midlothian*, set down a model of arrangement of types and situations for later novelists to develop. For example, Scott's Redgauntlet as a figure anticipated in many ways the archetypal dominating, demonic, Past-oriented symbol to be found in Galt's *Entail*, Stevenson's *Weir of Hermiston* and *The Merry Men* (in hanging judge Weir and Gordon Darnaway respectively), Brown's *House with the Green Shutters* and MacDougall Hay's *Gillespie*—not to mention Barrie's 'magerfu' Tam' (and perhaps even his Stuart Captain Hook!) and Jacobs's formidable grandmother, Christian Flemington. It is worth recalling the jingle applied to *Green Shutters*, describing its aim as to

> Paint village hell where sadist monster mutters
> Till Scotland's one mad house with its Green Shutters
> Depict the lust that lurks in hall and hovel
> And build thereon a Scottish national novel.[29]

What identifies this third fiction of dissociation of self, family and society, and of authorial stance, is the notion of dualism. Dualism is, as Karl Miller has demonstrated in *Doubles* (1986), an international preoccupation of literature. But the extent to which it obsesses writer and subject matter of the serious Scottish fiction of our period is far more intense and ubiquitous than anywhere else barring the related American Puritan tradition. What this Scottish dualism presents is a commentary on what is seen as a divided and unhealthy society. Through recurrent patterns of relationship such as father versus son, brother versus brother, or variants, a recurrent and shared symbolism states overwhelmingly the same theme; that in lowland Scotland, aridity of repressive orthodoxy, religious and behavioural, tied to an exaggerated work ethic and distorted notions of social respectability, have stifled and repressed vital creative processes of imaginative and emotional expression, to the point where it too often has become, individually *and* collectively, self-indulgent, morbid, and unbalanced.

The closeness to Muir's diagnosis of a Scottish 'dissociation of sensibility and intellect' is enticing, but dangerous, since Muir's thesis based itself essentially on linguistic division, arguing a separation of 'feeling' Scots from 'thinking' English.[30] Ironically enough, Muir failed entirely to perceive the nineteenth century Scottish novel's thematic demonstration of the validity of his argument concerning the dangers of separating emotion and thought into mutually exclusive expessive areas. The very attack he mounted on Scott, for withdrawing from engagement with 'real' Scotland, can be stood on its head so that Scott is seen as expressing consciously and successfully the polarisations of passion and calculation which since Covenanting-Episcopalian and Jacobite-Hanoverian periods of civil war have warped Scotland. But Muir's identification of the polarisation of heart and head remains a stimulating one, closely linked to the fundamental perception of the major novelists that history forced Scottish family and community development into deformation following Reformation and constant internecine warfare. To view Scott thus clearly contradicts accepted ways of seeing Scott as bringing 'all the earlier strands in Scottish literary romanticism . . . to a brilliant consummation'.[31] Andrew Hook concluded the foregoing volume 1 of this series by arguing that Scott created an aura of romance for Scotland, and recently David Groves has argued the romanticism of Scottish writing of this period, and tried to make us see, for example, the poetry and fiction of Hogg in romantic contexts.[32] I think Scott offers a model for accommodation of these approaches *and* those of opposing ambiences within a single work. As I suggested with *The Heart of Midlothian* and much more strongly in *Waverley* and *Old Mortality*, the romantic impulse sets up a texture of landscape and symbolism and *apparent* transcendent value (the ideals of Flora, the self-destructive courage of Bothwell, the passionate loyalties of Rob Roy), only to have their world of high imagination and noble feeling undercut by the ironic discovery of hard-headed selfish calculation on the part of many of the most romantic characters, (Fergus wants an earldom, and even thinks of changing to the English side when he cannot have it), or considerations of expediency which finally dominate romantic considerations (Jeanie gets her pardon for her sister from the King's mistress; heart-felt sympathy must be translated into shrewd manipulation, just as Scott's continual message underneath his enticing landscapes and heroic action is that dreams must give way to reality.) Scott sends out dual messages.

Seen in the context of Scott's models of ambivalent romance-realism, the achievement of the best fiction of the century can be seen as development of the technique of detached balancing of opposed interpretations of life. At their best, both Hogg and Galt continue the essential statement of dissociated response. Hogg's *The Private Memoirs and Confessions of a Justified Sinner* indeed develops further Scott's model of handling contradictory readings which later writers from Stevenson down to Linklater, Robin Jenkins, Muriel Spark and Alasdair Gray have exploited. Working up Scott's ambivalence of attitude towards *Waverley*, or more recently Galt's use of dramatic mono-logue to enigmatic effect in *The Provost*, Hogg took the notions of dual perspective to its logical conclusion, an Escher-style depiction of reversible readings. Thus subjective idealism could be presented from within *and* without, with the further subtlety that the 'rules' of the readings could *either* be those of modern psychological materialism *or* those of traditional religious, folk, and supernatural belief. I have argued this more fully elsewhere, as also with the other great achievement in this mode, Stevenson's *The Master of Ballantrae*.[33] The reader should note that the debate as to my rightness of interpretation of the latter as sharing Hogg's reversible perspectives is an ongoing one, reflected in this volume in the commentary of Francis Hart on that novel. With the greatest admiration for the distinguished work of Hart, I hold to my view that the figure of MacKellar shows Stevenson exploiting the 'Holy Willie' tradition, of self-condemning dramatic monologue, which runs down to him through Galt and Hogg (perhaps with help from the Puritan tradition of Hawthorne and Melville); that the 'old wife' MacKellar is presented with the possibility of a reading which sees him as prejudiced. I stress that it is a *possibility*. The essence of this ambivalent mode is that *either* way of reading is valid; thus romantic *and* mundane perspectives are allowed to move ambiguously together, till our sense of confusion as to who is hero, what is right, as with Hogg's *Sinner*, dominates. I think the Stevenson of *Jekyll and Hyde*, the Stevenson who had oscillated all his life between triumph or guilt in his rejection of his respectable family's bourgeois values, finally resolved his dilemma as did Hogg, by retreating into concealing detachment (so reminiscent of *The Scarlet Letter*, 'Young Goodman Brown', or 'The Minister's Veil'), which allowed either value structure and either interpret-ation, to exist, side by side. These two novels, *Sinner* and *Master*, are the most subtle expressions of a peculiarly Scottish dissociation of sensibility in which the writer through creative ambiguity simply 'floats' the values being satirised, so that, from Hogg's or Stevenson's point of view, the final comment is 'plague on both houses', with responsibility passed onto the reader.

But, in addition to this complex and double dualism, in which *both* sets of value structures contend unsuccessfully for domination in the mind of the reader (a battle deliberately presented not in terms of a good side versus a reader (a battle deliberately presented not in terms of a good side versus a bad, but as types of behaviour, extremes of 'average' humanity), there are simpler and more direct statements of dissociation within author *and* Scottish society. In these novels, values are clearer altogether in their deployment of their major symbols, and 'dissociation' exists in the sick society, *not* in the author. For example, what Coleman Parsons called the 'demonology of characterisation', the demonic symbolism so frequently employed by the Scottish novelist,[34] is now clearly attached to the materialistic, arid aspects of Scottish society. In Scott, Galt, Hogg and Stevenson, the devil metaphor 'wavered' from one extreme to the other, here locating passionate extremity, there identifying unfeeling materialism. It is fascinating to see how the demonic metaphor changes, from Scott's usual deployment of it as locating the excessive romantic passionate man, or the idealist (Fergus, Balfour, Staunton, even Rob Roy and Redgauntlet), to its diametrically opposite location in Galt's *The Entail*, where both Claud Walkinshaw and his son George are shown as Providence-defiers and touched with demonism precisely because their Nicol Jarvie qualities have become with them an obsession. *The Entail* seems to me the first of the 'sadist monster' line, beginning a long descent from the recurrent figure of the brutal male repressor to twentieth century respresentation of matriarchal domination. Its brutal father destroys his firstborn Charles because the boy values decisions based on feeling and heart rather than those based on commercial expediency. (Note, however, the subtle mockery by Galt of 'polite' sensibility, in Charles's tendency to purple self-indulgence, associated with his priggish standard English.) Claud ignores all the earthly and unearthly warnings given by coincidental events and his Bible. His family grows increasingly deformed, with wonderful irony in the trial of his 'natural' son Wattie to establish whether he is fit to own and run his estate. As so often in Scottish fiction, the 'natural' turns out to have more natural virtues than the so-called 'normal' brothers and sisters. And Galt clinches his symbolism portraying the rise and fall of a greedy, deformed, and male-dominated society by allowing the family matriarch, the wonderful tenacious and rich Scots-speaking Leddie Grippy, to emerge from her total oppression in the beginning to total triumph at the end. The theme is that the dislocation of heart from head, the preference of materialism to community of feeling and family, is anti-providential and self-destructive. Claud is punished by a stroke which leaves him struggling but powerless to express the agony of remorse he feels too late. There are intrusive elements which flaw the grand simplicity of family destiny; Mrs Eadie, the Highland lady who has second sight, is related to Galt's debased, fashionable fiction such as *The Omen* (1825); as with *Sir Andrew Wylie*, he is playing to the taste of fashion, now posturing in the vein of the new kind of post-Gothic supernatural now favoured by Scott.[35] But, Galt's 'Russian realism'[36] and the sweep of generations in this novel, make it his greatest work.

This clear-cut fiction describing sickness and dissociation in Scottish society is not handled on the same scale till *The House with the Green Shutters*. Stevenson, I have suggested, presented a more complex union of authorial and thematic dualism. But this detachment came hard, and late. Most of the earlier fiction swings from extremes of respect for the father-figure and what he stands for to defiant assertions of the worth of the rebel. His novels change their co-ordinates continually, so that *Treasure Island* (1883) or *John Nicholson* (1884) present father-figures of respectability as valid, where the fable folktale *The Merry Men* (1887) portrays him (an uncle, but father-surrogate) as made monstrous through bilious bigotry. *The Merry Men* is the best of his simpler novels of dissociation, in which the boy discovers the superiority of feeling humanitarianism over his heaven-offending plans for material self-advancement. His uncle's terrible fate is gross parody, in Stevenson's island microcosm, of nineteenth century Scottish blending of religious piety and personal profit. Perhaps the unfinished *Weir of Hermiston* would have emerged as one of the strongest statements of father-son alien-ation as metaphor for Scottish dissociation, with its 'arid' master of law, the cruelly jesting hanging judge, and his over-sensitive son, both of the same name, each the other's opposite in temperament and values, and (like James and Henry Ballantrae) two halves of a total personality. Certainly what appeared as 'An Unfinished Romance' in 1896 influenced the novel which in 1901 seemed to sum up 'the nineteenth century in allegory'. This is how John Spiers saw George Douglas Brown's *The House with the Green Shutters*,[37] the very name of which I discover to be taken directly from Stevensonian suggestion.[38] The aridity of both dominating protagonists is stressed; the same description (with regional difference) is given of the excess of the 'splurg-ing' or 'splairging' of their hyper-sensitive sons; both share their father's Christian name.[39] The demonic metaphor is employed in both to denote grimly unattractive sides to the father-figure, Weir jesting in crimson robes in the place he holds sway, his unholy joy in sending Duncan Jopp to the gallows markedly un-Christian, just as Gourlay's 'offence against the holy ghost' is stressed as diabolic at the end of *Green Shutters*.

I need not labour the common symbolic patterning and recurrent themes of these and their successors, endless variations on the same theme, from *Gillespie, Flemington* and *The Justice of the Peace* (Frederick Niven, 1926) or A J Cronin's *Hatter's Castle* (1931), to Jenkins's *Happy for the Child* (1953) or Crichton Smith's *Consider the Lilies* (1968). In all these, the pairing of contrasting protagaonists has specifically and socially satiric purpose. Wal-kinshaw, Weir and Gourlay Senior, Gillespie Strang, all represent a fusion of power, authority, orthodox social respectability, and repression of attitudes incompatible with or critical of what they stand for. The identification of such versions of Holy Willie, David Deans, Reverend Wringhim and Provost Pawkie with a dominating and all-powerful church may have been lost toward the end of the century; but social standing and the status one holds amongst one's peers has replaced this explicit religiosity with a kind of orthodoxy which pays homage to Mammon disguised in various Scottish institutional forms, from kirk to university, laird to town council. Keir Hardie called this 'churchianity', and Willa Muir examined it in *Mrs Grundy in Scotland* (1936) as 'MacGrundyism'.[40] The common diagnosis is that social attitudes of the century up to the First World War and beyond, have preferred superficial orthodoxy, respectability and visible signs of material or snobbish success to wish for the 'whole man alive.' In *The Entail*, this reductive materialism is seen in Walkinshaw's sneer at the fact that Charles has actually used the middle class education he has been given to make genuine personal and moral choices involving aesthetic and immaterial considerations, enlightened by his 'college' education. Such paradoxical parental attitudes are endlessly repeated. The arid and socially expediential parent drives the son into education to acquire social status, only to find that education has an effect the opposite of that desired. Charles, Archie Hermiston, John Gourlay, and Eoghan Strang are merely a handful of Scottish progeny whose fathers sneer at art and the education they have worked to provide. 'Signor Feedeleerie!', Judge Weir's summing up of the worth of his son's excitement at living art, also sums up the sneer implicit in all.[41]

The social attitudes described by these novelists have been commented on by historians from William Ferguson to Checkland, by cultural and social commentators from Willa Muir to George Davie. The century's protagonist is identified at his worst as 'the unspeakable Scot',[42] whose blend of 'hypertrophication' of conscience (to borrow David Craig's notion)[43] with social ambition, transform concepts of religious authenticity and social worth into expediential social behaviour, in which manners matter as markers of status and material worth. Instead of synthesising religious fundamentalism with social behaviour, the new Scottish materialist individualism of the nineteenth century exploits integrated belief and behaviour for what is useful in consolidating and advancing family position. Thus Claud Walkinshaw employs his family Bible and the ritual of family prayer with servants to enhance his authority; thus, he rejected the warning his randomly opened Bible clearly gave him against his rampant materialism and untraditional, anti-family and community behaviour when it did not suit him. The very title, *The Entail*, is a symbolic indicator of the way in decisions based on wrong values corrupt the future. Thus these *nouveau riche* merchants, landowners, or unnaturally reactionary institutional figures like Judge Weir, or the many brutal schoolmasters like Miles Malison in MacDonald's *Alec Forbes*, warp and force rebellion on the next generations, thus entailing (using the colloquial sense of 'resulting in' *and* the sense of a willed enforcement) a result which paradoxically is the direct opposite of that which the entailer intended. Galt's 'theoretical histories' of minister, provost, radical, member of parliament, and laird are, in this context, doubly important as signs of the transition from a traditional consensus within community and religion in harness with social behaviour, to a post-revolutionary and early industrial individualism and opportunism. Scott's recurrent patterning of 'Rob Roy' figures against 'Bailie Nicol' figures, and confrontations of past loyalties with present pragmatic 'progress', likewise mirrors this transition and predicts the triumph of the values and goals of the pragmatic, 'prudent', present and future. Stevenson's *Master of Ballantrae* may be more complex in terms of ambivalent readings; but like the rest of the fiction of dissociation it portrays (beyond all questions of guilt or blame) a tragedy of familial self-destruction. The Duries of Durrisdeer, masters of Ballantrae, long a power in Scotland, are destroyed by their polarisation into extremes of dour materialism and repression on stay-at-home Henry's (and MacKellar's side), and artful, self-indulgent imaginative freedom on that of James. They lose their birthright, their land, and are separated from their traditional community, responsibilities and inheritance, and exiled to a howling wilderness and a 'common' grave; 'common' too, in the sense that Stevenson intends the re-unification in death to signify that what has been dissociated by warping Scottish experience is now once again whole—if, ironically, only in death. *Weir* presumably was to restate the familiar dislocation; the aridity of the father's lack of spontaneous affections and authoritarianism feelings entailing the dangerously indulgent relationship of insipid mother (full of 'sad little mutinies') and excessively feeling son. When that which is whole is broken into parts, say these novels, then the parts are differently but equally malformed. In eliminating spontaneous feeling, creative imagination, artistic and aesthetic sensibility from its value-structure, nineteenth century Scotland breaks up its wholeness of psyche, divides its communities and families.

Beyond Scott, Hogg, Galt and Stevenson, four novels from the second half of our period are worth special consideration as variant treatments of the essentially recurrent theme. They are *The Laird of Drammochdyle* (serialised in the Aberdeen Free Press, 1865), Margaret Oliphant's *Kirsteen* (1890), Douglas Brown's *The House with the Green Shutters* (1901), and MacDougall Hay's *Gillespie* (1914). Each is different in emphasis from the others, but there is in each a foregrounding of the notion of destructive and mutually exclusive polarisations of social and family types; types explicitly drawn from Scottish religious, economic and cultural history.

We owe William Donaldson a great debt for recovering Alexander's lost work for us. More that Latto and Pae, it seems that Alexander balances the claims of literary art with those of social responsibility. Anticipating Gibbon and Gunn he takes on the twin task of recording *and* evaluating his social tradition. To quote Donaldson: 'in works like Ravenshowe and the Residenters' (1867–8), Johnny Gibb (1869), and the studies of *Life Amang My Ain Folk* (1872–3), we have his epic fictional study of the agricultural revolution in Aberdeenshire spanning almost a hundred years of change.'[44] *The Laird of Drammochdyle* shows Alexander in grimly sardonic mood, and directly anticipates *Green Shutters*. Here, argues Donaldson, is the 'destruction of the traditional elite by the rising capitalist bourgeoisie'[45] in the decline of Edward Boyce, the Laird, from his position as lynchpin of his community to that of despised wife beater, suspected murderer, and terminal alcoholic. The parish minister too, educated and sensitive Dr Graham, is likewise brought to alcoholic ruin; and lesser rural figures like Ross the hotel owner are echoes of this decadence. The strengths of the writing lie in Alexander's detachment from his tragedy. Like Brown, he portrays a real community (with perhaps greater fairness of assessment) and juxtaposes the gossipy and trivial with the significant and tragic. A lesser writer like Pae would have succumbed to the temptation to melodramatise, to overstate; Alexander allows the reader to perceive the dangers beginning to threaten the laird from within and without, or to perceive gradually that the reverend Graham is *not* a stock kindly figure of eccentric worthiness who will lead the book's 'hero', crippled Robert

Morris, out of darkness into literary light, but a weak man all too vulnerable to hypocritically neighbourly predators, the Crabbices, unpleasant types of the new entrepreneurial rich with their brewing, property and shady interests. Once plain Peter Craib the carter, Peter Crabbice is now Strathaven's centre of power and 'respectability', exactly the type of MacGrundyism Willa Muir identifies as the nineteenth century Scottish disease. But I can not quite agree with Donaldson that Alexander explicitly intended to show the destruction of laird and minister and the like by 'the rising capitalist bourgeoisie.' Indeed, as with Pae, the echoes of Dickensian type and situation mar the authenticity, Crabbice alternating between being drawn as convincing local specimen and drawn as a derivation from Bounderby, just as his son resembles James Harthouse. Perhaps the reason the novel finally lacks the power and totally integrated effect of *Green Shutters* stems from a central authorial confusion as to exactly what his targets are. Alexander's temperance sympathies make the anti-drink argument dominate overmuch, even if the picture of the decline of laird and minister is bleakly convincing. And the tone of the novel, with its frequent set discussions between worthies on drink or marriage, anticipates that of Tressell's *The Ragged Trousered Philanthropists* (1914); we are too conscious of the educational machinery to accept the whole. Indeed, in some ways the novel could be considered as a weaker version of the mythic and regenerative *Johnny Gibb*, in that Robert Morris, self-improved and dependable in his traditional virtues, survives to prosper out of initial tragedy. What makes it fit more appropriately in the dissociative grouping is, however, the sense of social dislocation, and of the decline of the community's mutually supportive tradition. Robert's success is a small thing beside the total triumph of the Crabbices. No sentimental Dickensian coincidence and comeuppance here! Instead, a grimly believable ending where a way of life is seen being lost, and community degraded.

Kirsteen approaches the matter of Scottish social decay from an angle that can only be seen as strikingly early feminist. It is one of Oliphant's small group of mature, deeply ironic studies of complex women in 'difficult' settings. Kirsteen's is that of Argyllshire at the time of the Napoleonic wars, seen as social backwater (Oliphant has little or no concern with peasant Highlanders and folk tradition). Central to her difficulties is her autocratic and brutal father, a dark and decayed Highland aristocrat whose money was made out of the slave trade, a figure mid-way between Redgauntlet and Gourlay. Her sumph-like mother, neglected and whining, similarly lies midway between Mrs Hermiston and Mrs Gourlay. Kirsteen is the sensitive child, a touch too wilful, too fond of her own perspective on society and morals. Once again, the novel hovers between the mythic redemptive and the dissociative modes, finally settling in the latter as its pattern reveals no transformation of central protagonist and society, but instead of kind of compact made out of necessity between Kirsteen and her murderous father, and a rejection of sentimental dreams by Kirsteen for her business enterprise as doyenne of dressmakers in nineteenth century Edinburgh. As with Alexander, the importance of the book's fundamental realism and irony is betrayed by irrelevant pre-occupations—in this case, Oliphant's perpetual tendency to pious sentimentalism (Kirsteen may possess gumption and drive to a surprising degree for a nineteenth century heroine, but she stays virgin all her life, obsessively clutching the bloodstained handkerchief given by to, and found on the body of, her first adolescent love Ronald.) Mrs Oliphant—and Kirsteen—should have known better.

These variants only underline the achievement of Douglas Brown in *The House with the Green Shutters*, the archetypal statement of the theme. Behind the obvious divisions of father-son, father-family, father-merchant and community lies a rich background of symbolism which links this novel to Greek tragedy, to Hardy's *The Mayor of Casterbridge* (1886), to Ibsen's *Pillars of Society* (1877) and *The Master Builder* (1892) as well as to *Weir* and *Drammochdyle*, *Kirsteen*, *Entail* and *Redgauntlet*. Gourlay is the town carrier; spider at the heart of his web, and source of energy, shown at the start at the zenith of his powers, as his massed horses lumber out of the square, symbolising (as later bull metaphors do also) his heavy dominance and power. He is the traditional Scottish male totem figure, a Black Bull 'worshipped', like Milton's Satan, with the town's hate and perversion of all natural human feeling. His house stands (where the church, perhaps, should dominate) at the centre of the town. From the outside, it looks splendid, but inside it is untidy and dirty, mortgaged up to the hilt, and its position blocks a supply of natural spring water to the town. Inside the house, the wife is weak and slatternly, cancer rotting her breast, just as Janet rots internally from consumption. Beyond the house, the minister is a hollow pedant, living outside the town, his charge; the laird is a drunken weakling, the schoolmaster perceptive (it is his analysis of young John which discovers John's fatal flaw) but hopelessly and irresponsibly detached to the point of ironic mockery of kailyard dominies and Scottish education; he prefers his arid study of Adam Smith's *Wealth of Nations* to human involvement. And, following their leaders like black sheep, the local worthies; deacon, merchants, 'bodies' with hearts 'black rotten', malicious gossip their only occupation. Ian Campbell has shown us how accurately Brown parodies the MacLaren-Barrie type,[46] but, beyond parody, the symbolism portrays a village of the damned, in which the very absence of kailyard church matters or ministers holds the key to the symbolism. The church *is* there and commented on, bitterly, but subtly and by ironic implication. Consider Gourlay when we first meet damning his men, whose 'black look' unnaturally terrifies and whose sneer is a black frost; whose black power is so great it can psychologically 'down' strong men, and whose physical strength is awesome and incredible (witness the hurling of Gibson through the window of the Red Lion); who will drive no other horse than his black stepper, and whose Tamberlaine-like challenges to God are so vividly evoked by Johnny Coe. The thunder and lightning at young John Gourlay's birth is crucially important, in that it both suggests omens of heavenly wrath, and associates Gourlay with lightning, just as John will do when truanting, and later, when he is tormented by the hellish imagery of lightning fused with the eyes of his dead father. Consider also the extent to which Gourlay's unnatural distortion of family and social relations is emphasised through demonic metaphor. He will see the town 'damned' before he will support them in railway development; unable to express genuine emotion, he 'damns' old Peter Riney, his oldest servant, in taking leave of him; and most of all, in the climatic and hell-dominated chapter 25, his satanic offences are shown as culminating not just in his intention to destroy his son physically, but in his worse intention, which Brown describes as a 'sin against the Holy Ghost', the rendering of his son 'animo castrato' (powerful ideology indeed for Victorian Scottish fiction!), drained of manhood and self, in short, robbed of his soul. Gourlay's downfall holds an 'unholy' fascination for his neighbours; and throughout (in a manner reminiscent of Hogg's sinister use of colloquialism) the casual use of words like 'sinister', 'damn', 'malevolent', as well as the invocation of 'God' carries a further and dark irony. Gourlay in chapter 25 is explicitly revealed as devil; his wrath 'brings the hell on which man is built to the surface. Gourlay was transformed.' John escapes to the 'benignness of the darkened heavens', haunted by the demonic eyes of his father; the end not far removed from that of Robert Wringhim's nightmare self-destruction. Brown has gone far beyond describing MacGrundyism in his portrayal of the outward social respectability of Gourlay in contrast to his inward rottenness. Social orthodoxy and the Presbyterian inheritance have decayed in Barbie far beyond Craig's 'hypertrophication' to the point of sickness Hogg diagnosed in the Auchtermuchty parable in *The Sinner*. The townspeople are possessed, but now, later in history, not by Satan, but his replacement, as Brown sees it, in Mammon and what Gibbon will later describe as the mythical wolf-beast and gryphons of malice, hypocrisy, envy and gossip. These possess minister and laird, deacon and merchant; religion has warped to the point where Deadly Sins gallivant through the town, festering beneath its 'God'; John Gourlay, merchant, town carrier, awesome bully, demonic presence. To this extent the novel operates as parody of religious parable, or as a fable of social degeneration; once again we note the potential of much of the fiction for shift of categorisation, whereby we could consider this with *The Provost* or as parodic mockery of the fiction of mythic regeneration. Where Hogg mocked the pretensions of the Elect, Brown mocks their fallen descendants, their self-righteousness; there is even mockery of their ancient core of Calvinism, its belief in predestination, in the way the tragedy at the centre of Barbie seems pre-ordained. Brown deliberately uses Biblical language to evoke the horror of the 'bodies' at the climax; 'their loins were loosed beneath them', as they invoke their misused God's name in their cries of fear.

But Brown has another layer of meaning beyond the ironic exploitation of religious and demonic metaphor. There is the other John Gourlay, son of the 'sadist monster', and he is clearly intended to contrast at every point with his father. There is, in the patterning of the novel, a dominating and contrasting pairing of the two Gourlays; and the reader is directed beyond the levels of the supernatural and its symbolism with its specifically religious satire, to Brown's diagnosis of the Gourlay (and lowland Scottish) dissociation of sensibility. John Gourlay senior is shrewd (if not actually intelligent) hard-working and self-disciplined, the representative of a tradition of canny merchants going back through Galt and Scott at least as far as Allan Ramsay's

'Wealth or the Wuddy'. In *this* reading, Gourlay is not to be seen as totally degenerate. He has some integrity, and some respect from the better 'bodies', who admit he is 'the only gentleman in Barbie.' Representative of solid material worth, he is the only gentleman in Barbie, according to Johnnie Coe; he keeps his promises and the outside of his house scrupulously tidy; and his tool box is the finest and best kept in Barbie. But his son is his polar opposite at all points, feckless, lazy, undisciplined and shallow. Hyper-sensitive, the smell of new varnish vividly evokes school, to the point of acute depression. He reads penny dreadfuls in the attic, hidden by his mother from his father's disapproval, he's devoid of 'smeddum', and, like Archie Hermiston, 'splurges.' But he has an extraordinary strength of imagination and a morbid sensitivity to imagery, language and physical detail, even of weather; where to his father, 'dead to the fairness of the scene', 'a fine morning . . . was one that burned the back of your neck.' The dominie succinctly says that the boy's curse is to possess 'a sensory perceptiveness in gross excess of his intellectuality.'

Here, Brown is approaching an argument close to that of Edwin Muir's hypothesis concerning the Scottish separation of emotion and thought. I have often wondered why Muir, in his essay on Brown in *Latitudes* (1924) failed to see how uncannily Brown bore testimony to his central theme, that 'when emotion and thought are separated, emotion becomes irresponsible and thought becomes arid.' Is not this exactly Brown's presentation? Are not father and son living examples of such fatal dissociation? Neither can flourish, lacking the qualities of the other. Indeed, in familiar fashion, each destroys the other, and the father virtually prophecies this (Brown ironically indicating the predestinated clash) when he tells the boy to put down the poker of the new kitchen range before he kills someone with it.

Brown redeems young John continually from his initial feckless description. His hayloft reading of the silly story of Dick Turpin and Black Bess, allows Brown to suggest that 'perhaps he was not altogether the wrong sort of boy, if he liked that sort of thing!' If the boy's fancy is as fertile as this, then some worth and character must yet be present. And this is developed to allow John to impress the Jock Allan circle in Edinburgh, when he goes to university, with his understanding of the Scot's gift for the vivid phrase, and then to gain the Raeburn prize for his essay on 'An Arctic Night.' The Edinburgh passages can be read as satirical pictures of a decadent Enlightenment, as John Spiers sees them.[47] Certainly Jock Allen, toping lawyer, sentimental indulger (and tempter) of young men, represents that hardheaded yet hard-drinking, worldly yet sentimental combination so familiar in Scotland since Henry Mackenzie himself. But to count the Professor and the passages describing the Raeburn prize announcement as satirical also is to Miss Brown's intention that John should be offered true enlightenment by the Professor here, together with encouragement and a warning against his fatal flaw. The Professor stresses *wholeness* of imagination, describing 'a radiant fulness' which is clearly Shakespearian, in its empathetic and creative powers; and he clearly separates this from the sort of vivid and overwrought sensibility, the morbid self-dramatisation, possessed by young John. With discipline, he advises, the secondary gift could be developed into the primary; without discipline, it can only be a curse. John decides, celebrating the Raeburn in the pub, to ignore the Professor—'him and his advice!' closes the chapter ominously. The closing sequences of the novel show John descending into a world of horrific fragments, dissociated from reality, self-destroying. He cannot live with the part of self he is left with after he is killed his father; and when he is dead, Brown fuses together the religious parable and the dissociation theme by transforming Mrs Gourlay into the voice of God, of wholeness, of judgement on Barbie and what has happened to Scotland. Reading from Corinthians, her text (found much as Walkinshaw 'chose' his divine messages in *The Entail*) is concerned with lack of charity. Brown's point is that charity, the quality Scott gave to Jeanie Deans above all others, and the quality which enabled her to move regeneratively through a broken landscape, is a fusion of qualities of heart *and* head. Thus he stresses the need of Scotland for a reconciliation of emotion and empathy on one hand and shrewdness and sense on the other.

The House with the Green Shutters was the outstanding example of its type of Scottish fiction, artistically successful *and* socially relevant. *Gillespie* followed in 1914. For all its dangerous closeness to the atmosphere of Celtic gloom found in 'Fiona MacLeod', *Gillespie* belongs firmly in the tradition of Scottish fiction of dissociation. Bob Tait and Isobel Murray gave an excellent introduction to the 1979 edition of the novel; but they tried too much to separate it from *Green Shutters*, though they accepted that it fits in 'a Scottish tradition stemming from Hogg and Stevenson.'[48] To my mind there is no doubt that Hay found therein his inspiration—although I agree that *Weir of Hermiston*, as part of the same tradition, may also have stimulated him. But the parallels between *Green Shutters* and *Gillespie* are too frequent for chance. Both have a tyrant ruling a small town (is there not an echo of 'Barbie' in Brieston?); both have a necessary and symbolic connection between tyrant and House as symbol of pride and destiny; both set a sensitive son against his brutal father, with the attendant weak and son-indulging mother; both portray the sons at university trapped in a vivid and gloomy subjectivity; both use the surrounding characters as tragic chorus. But why not accept the tradition? The pattern of division is inherited, and is the central symbolic strength of the Scottish novel. Hay used his predecessor's dark vision and moved it into the western highlands, enriching the landscape of Brown's lowland situation with the added dimension of romantically portrayed land and sea-scape. He made the central figure more subtle—Gillespie has vision, as he looks forward to trawling and the revolution it will bring to Scottish fishing. Hay makes us admire his epic plans, as do the locals as they witness 'progress' changing their lives. Brown's tyrant was a victim of economic change and limited by his past, where Gillespie creates a new future. Hay's supporting characters have more range than Brown's—his angel of revenge, the widow whose husband Gillespie has ruined and destroyed, Mrs Galbraith; Topsail Janet, his equivalent of Madge Wildfire, the innocent who endures all and cleanses the tragedy with her pity and wonder; more important than all Brown's relics of community decency, the doctor, tirelessly working to redeem the spiritual and physical infection that Gourlay has brought to Brieston. And over all this impessive range of characterisation Hay attempts something more than Brown again, in his symbolism of the 'angels' wings', seen in the imagery of the wings of the great bird which Janet rescues, in the wings of a fate and providence Mrs Galbraith sees beating behind the superficial events of Brieston and Gourlay's ambition, and seen even in the suggestion that the cage birds that Gillespie has sneaked from the plague-vessel may also be the birds of Death, God's punishment on a fallen people.

Brown's novel is perhaps the more successful because it avoids such dangerous tensions between opposing positive and negative interpretations. It is significant in considering Hay's work at the end of our period to realise that his commitment to Christian belief (he was a Glasgow minister) was at odds with his growing pessimism regarding the decay of city values and rural community. His angelic disturbance, high above the squalid affairs of men, comes close to a melodrama which is only redeemed by the novel's colossal sense of tragic destiny in the destruction of family by its opposing parts.

There are later versions of the same pattern, to be found amongst others in the works of Frederick Niven, Lewis Grassic Gibbon, A J Cronin and Robin Jenkins. The dissociative theme continues to recur in modern works like Crichton Smith's *Consider the Lilies* and William McIlvanney's *Docherty* (1975). These, however, are post-war variants of a tradition and recurrent symbolism most clearly expressed in the century between *Waverley* and *Gillespie*.

NOTES

1   J H Millar, *A Literary History of Scotland* (London, 1903) and Francis Hart, *The Scottish Novel* (London, 1978). *See also* Further Reading.

2   Roderick Watson, *The Literature of Scotland* (1984), p 313 and p 373.

3   Edwin Muir, *Scott and Scotland* (London, 1936), *passim: see* further discussion below.

4   A fuller version of this discussion of Scott appears in Douglas Gifford, 'Scott's fiction and the Search for Mythic Regeneration' in *Scott and his Influence*, J H Alexander and David Hewitt (eds) (Aberdeen, 1983) pp 180–9.

5   Cf. Douglas Mack, 'Lights and Shadows of Scottish Life: James Hogg's *The Three Perils of Woman*', in *Studies in Scottish Fiction: Nineteenth Century*, Horst W Drescher and Joachim Schwend (eds) (Frankfurt am Main, 1985) pp 15–28, for a fascinating argument that the novel parodies John Wilson's *Lights and Shadows of Scottish Life* (1822).

6   Douglas Gifford, *James Hogg* (Edinburgh, 1976) pp 138–84.

7   Cf. Robb's essay in this volume and his study *George MacDonald* (Edinburgh, 1987).

8   'The Missionar Kirk in Huntly (Macdonald's birthplace) was . . . an Anti-burgher Secession church . . . a product of the secession from the established Kirk of Scotland by the Erskine brothers and their adherents in 1733 . . . its Scottishness was due to the independent, democratic insistence on a non-pragmatic, idealistic

faith, fiercely felt within the individual. Despite his subsequent rejection of some of his theological inheritance, MacDonald's spirit always had the . . . absoluteness of the Covenanters whose distant heir he was. He was one of Scotland's many religious outsiders . . .' (*Robb*, pp 5–6).

9 John Spiers, 'Nineteenth-century Scotland in Allegory', *The Scots Literary Tradition*, 2nd edn (London, 1962) pp 142–51.

10 Douglas Gifford, 'Stevenson and Scottish fiction: The importance of *The Master of Ballantrae*', in *Stevenson and Victorian Scotland*, Jenni Calder (ed) (Edinburgh, 1981) pp 62–87.

11 *Catriona*, Emma Letley (ed) (World's Classics, London, 1986), ch XX, pp 382–3.

12 'Stevenson and Scottish fiction', in *Calder*, p 64. William Robertson Nicoll was editor of *The British Weekly*, the popular evangelical periodical which published the 'Kailyard' writers, especially Crockett, Barrie and 'Ian Maclaren'.

13 *Dr Jekyll and Mr Hyde: and Weir of Hermiston*, Emma Letley (ed) (World's Classics, London, 1987), ch V, p 134.

14 Dickson McCunn's adventures and of his adopted Glasgow keelies, the 'Gorbals Die-hards' are recounted in *Huntingtower* (1922), *Castle Gay* (1930) and *The House of the Four Winds* (1935).

15 Chris Guthrie and Finn MacHamish are heroine and hero of Lewis Grassic Gibbon's *A Scots Quair* (1932–34) and Neil Gunn's *The Silver Darlings* (1941) respectively.

16 William Donaldson, *Popular fiction in Victorian Scotland* (Aberdeen, 1986) p 53.

17 *Donaldson* p 85.

18 *Donaldson* p 91. It is significant, that despite the claims made for Pae's 'realism', Donaldson says that 'Pae seems to have had little first-hand knowledge of the Scottish underworld, or its language', importing his criminal slang from and W H Ainsworth, overwhelmingly London-centred in language and style. He quotes remarks of thieves like 'Bustay Bill, Little Tip, Heavy Ben and the Swaggerer', like 'now, old covey, you must be quiet. I say, Bob, shall I take the mitten from his cheese-trap . . . we grabbed him and mittened him near the Green but we didn't know what chink he has . . .'. Donaldson argues that this set back the development of a plausible crime fiction in Scotland by at least a generation. Surely this admission of fundamental implausibility in language and style of Victorian Glasgow low-life elements drastically sets back the case for Pae as a major moralist, especially when Donaldson adds that the novel 'includes a substantial element of fantasy and wish-fulfilment'?

19 The most thorough study of Glasgow fiction, Moira Burgess's *The Glasgow Novel*, 2nd edn (Glasgow, 1986) knows of the novel, but does not value it highly. Entry 54, p 75 presents '*The Factory Girl, or, The Dark Places of Glasgow. Showing evil over-ruled for good, iniquity punished, and virtue rewarded . . .*' and comments; 'a long and eventful tale of crime, bodysnatching, religion and romance, perhaps summed up in its title!'

20 Miss Pratt is from *The Inheritance*, McDow from *Destiny*.

21 Elizabeth Hamilton; *The Cottagers of Glenburnie* (Edinburgh, 1888 edn) p 188. The passage occurs at the end of Ch 16.

22 The Chronicles are 'set in an imaginery English country town' and 'resemble Trollope in having clergymen among their central characters . . . and show her serious interest in the problems of women (Merryn Williams, preface to *The Curate in Charge* (Gloucester, 1987) p ix). In addition to *Miss Marjoribanks* and *The Curate* (1875) the series included *Salem Chapel* (1863) *The Perpetual Curate* (1864) *The Rector* (1863) *The Doctor's Family* (1863) and *Phoebe Junior* (1876).

23 Scott's description of his heroes made in his 1817 anonymous review of the first

series of his *Tales of my Landlord*. Cf. D D Devlin, *Walter Scott* (London, 1968), p 11.

24   Cf. Tom Hubbard, 'The fiction of John Davidson', *Studies in Scottish fiction*, Drescher & Schwend (ed), pp 273–90.

25   Chapter five of *Peter Pan* clearly locates Hook in the Scottish-British line of the Stuarts. 'In dress he somewhat aped the attire associated with the name of Charles II, having heard it said . . . that he bore a strange resemblance to the ill-fated Stuarts! Barrie also links the novel with Stevenson in the same chapter; Hook is the only man the Sea-Cook (Long John Silver) feared.

26   John Davidson, *The Pilgrimage of Strongsoul* (London, 1896) p 128.

27   *See* note 14.

28   Francis Hart, *The Scottish Novel*, p 19.

29   Quoted by Angus MacDonald in *Edinburgh Essays in Scottish Literature* (Preface H J C Grierson) (Edinburgh and London, 1933) p 165.

30   Edwin Muir, *Scott and Scotland*: The Predicament of the Scottish Writer (London, 1936) p 20ff and p 115ff.

31   Andrew Hook (ed), *The History of Scottish Literature: volume 2, 1660–1800* (Aberdeen, 1987) pp 318–21.

32   The work of David Groves has recently emphasised this; *see* the introduction to his edition of *James Hogg: Selected Poems and Songs* (Edinburgh, 1986) and his review of the year's work (1984) in Scottish Literature in *Scottish Literary Journal; The Year's Work* J H Alexander (ed) (Aberdeen, 1987).

33   *See* note 10.

34   Coleman Parsons, *Witchcraft and Demonology in Scott's Fiction* (Edinburgh and London, 1964) p 203.

35   Cf. Scott's view of Galt's novel in *Blackwood's*, vol XX, July, 1826 pp 52–9, where he condemned 'the superstition of the olden time . . . spectres, fairies, and other supernatural apparitions . . . banished to the cottage and the nursery'. For further discussion of this important watershed in attitudes towards the supernatural, *see* Gifford, *James Hogg*, pp 124–5.

36   George Kitchin, 'John Galt', in *Edinburgh Essays*, p 115.

37   John Spiers, *The Scots Literary Tradition*, p 142.

38   Stevenson's 'A Gossip on Romance' (*Memories and Portraits*, 1887) supplied the title suggestion. Certain spots await their particular drama, he argues; the inn at Burford Bridge 'seems to wait the coming of the appropriate legend. Within these ivied walls, behind these old green shutters, some further business smoulders . . .'. He goes on to suggest that the old Hawes Inn at the Queen's ferry similarly awaits its meaning to be told in story. But 'the man or the hour had not yet come; but some day, I think, a boat shall put off from the Queen's ferry . . . and some frosty night a horseman, on a tragic errand, rattle with his whip upon the green shutters of the inn at Burford.' And he tells in a footnote how *Kidnapped* represents his Hawes story; 'some day, perhaps, I may try a rattle at the shutters'. Brown took up the challenge and the title.

39   Weir of Hermiston says to his son 'you're splairging: you're running at lairge in life like a wild nowt'. Archie is 'a splairger', and 'there's no room for splairgers under the fower quarters of John Calvin'. The term is used five times in chapter three; while Brown constantly links young Gourlay with 'splurging', showing him frequently 'on the splurge' (drinking excessively). 'Young John Gourlay's death maun make a splurge, ye know', sneers Gourlay senior towards the end.

40   Willa Muir, *Mrs Grundy in Scotland* (London, 1936).

41   *Weir of Hermiston* Emma Letley (ed).

42   Cf. T W H Crossland's satirical attack on the Scot in *The Unspeakable Scot* (London, 1902).

43   David Craig, introduction to his edition of Lockhart's *Adam Blair* (Edinburgh, 1963) p xxi.

44   *See* William Donaldson's edition of Alexander's *The Laird of Drammochdyle* (Aberdeen, 1986) p xiii.

45   Donaldson (ed), *The Laird of Drammochdyle*, p xiii.

46   Ian Campbell, *Kailyard: A New Assessment* (Edinburgh, 1981), p 92ff.

47   Spiers, *The Scots Literary Tradition*, pp 148–9.

48   *See* Bob Tait and Isobel Murray's edition of Hay's *Gillespie* (Edinbugh and Vancouver, 1979), pp xv–xvi.

FURTHER READING

It is impossible to give details of all the books mentioned. The articles on specific novelists and fiction generally will give further information; thereafter *Millar*, *Hart*, and other works cited in the notes will help. In addition, the reader should check recent new editions from Aberdeen University Press, Canongate, Penguin, Scottish Academic Press and Virago especially; Virago have recently done much to make Scottish women writers available. Information on critical work and first editions can be found in the following:

Aitken, W R, *Scottish Literature in English and Scots: a Guide to Information Sources* (Detroit, 1982).

Burgess, Moira, *The Glasgow Novel; a survey and bibliography*, 2nd edn, (Glasgow, 1986).

Campbell, Ian, *Nineteenth Century Scottish fiction: a critical Anthology* (Manchester, 1979).

Craig, David, *Scottish Literature and the Scottish People 1680–1830* (London, 1961).

Daiches, David (ed) *A companion to Scottish Culture* (London, 1981).

—— *Literature and Gentility in Scotland* (Edinburgh, 1982).

Drescher, Horst and Schwend, Joachim (eds) *Studies in Scottish Fiction: Nineteenth Century* (Frankfurt am Main, 1985).

Gifford, Douglas (ed) *Scottish Short Stories 1800–1900* (London and New York, 1981).

Lindsay, Maurice, *History of Scottish Literature* (London, 1977).

Royle, Trevor, *The Macmillan Companion to Scottish Literature* (London, 1983).

Watson, Roderick, *The Literature of Scotland* (London, 1984).

Wittig, Kurt, *The Scottish Tradition in Literature* (Edinburgh and London, 1958).

Finally, connections should be made with volume 4 of this *History*; in particular, with the essays of Beth Dickson ('Foundations of the Modern Scottish Novel'), Isobel Murray ('Novelists of the Renaissance'), Joy Hendry (whose account of Violet Jacob in 'Twentieth century Women's Writing: The Nest of Singing Birds' introduced me to *Flemington*), and Gavin Wallace ('Compton Mackenzie and the Scottish Popular Novel'). All overlap with and develop arguments in this volume.

Chapter 13

Heroes and Hero-makers: Women in Nineteenth-Century Scottish Fiction

JENNI CALDER

In Margaret Oliphant's novel *Hester* (1883) the crisis comes when the central character confronts her exclusion from the male world of business and finance. The man who seems to love her bluntly announces, on the dance floor, that he does not want her help or an understanding of the difficulties he faces. He wants only her sympathy, ' "to know that you sympathise, and think of me, and feel for me, and believe in me, and that you will share whatever comes" '.[1]

It comes as no surprise that in a Victorian novel about middle-class life a woman is being asked to 'feel for' and 'believe in' a man. In so far as the supportive role of women was practical it tended to lie in the maintenance of an appropriately soothing environment for the father, husband or son whose life of action and achievement lay outside the home. The emotional role is very often passive. Oliphant's Hester is indignant at such assumptions.

> Many people no doubt have waltzed with very little inclination for it, people who were both sad and sorry, disappointed, heartbroken; but few more reluctant than Hester, who felt her position intolerable, and by whom the complacent injustice of it, the calm assertion that such blind adherence was all that was to be looked for from a woman, was more irritating and offensive than can be described. Was it possible that he thought so? that this was what she would have to encounter in the life she should spend with him? Her advice, her intelligent help, her understanding, all ignored and nothing wanted but a kind of doggish fidelity, and unreasoning belief? Hester felt it cruel to be made to dance even, to be spun through the crowd as if in the merest caprice of gaiety while at such a crisis of her fate.[2]

In Hester's world it is accepted by men and women alike that not only should women be excluded from business and money-making; it is hardly desirable for them to be aware that money has to be made.

Margaret Oliphant is a major figure in nineteenth-century Scottish fiction, though her stature is only beginning to be acknowledged. Her output was enormous, of varied quality, but always expressive of an intelligent woman's experience of a world that did not treat her gently. Her chronicling of mainly middle-class provincial life over nearly half a century of Victoria's reign illuminates many aspects of women's lives, as well as being of great documentary value.

The predicament of Hester is instructive. She is a striking character, though not an entirely attractive personality. She is limited in education and experience, impatient of conventional constraints, independent of mind but financially dependent. She longs to do something that ' "that no one can tell you or require you to do . . . Something voluntary, even dangerous . . ." '[3] When she articulates this yearning to another of her admirers she is firmly told that it is a woman's function to inspire men. ' "There is nothing a man might not do, with you to encourage him. You make me wish to be a hero." '[4] Hester's reply sums up her frustration. ' "Do you really think . . . that the charm of inspiring . . . is what any reasonable creature would prefer to doing? To make someone else a hero rather than be a hero yourself?" '[5]

Most women in European fiction of the period in which Oliphant was writing were contained within the role of hero-maker. Many accepted this containment passively; a few, like Hester, with rebelliously bad grace. A few challenged it to some purpose. In many ways Scottish attitudes and Scottish fiction reflect this pattern. Yet it could be argued that women associated with Scottish fiction have a substantiality, robust rather than dramatic, which is closely linked with environment, social as well as physical.

Both Oliphant as a novelist and Hester as a character are examples of this robustness. Oliphant, whose first fiction was published in 1849, had always peopled her novels with independently-minded women (though not all her women are independent) and often with helpless men. This reflected her own experience. For most of her adult life she was breadwinner and chief prop not only of her own children, but of her husband, until his death, and of her brother and his children. The men she knew best were not strong, nor capable, nor decisive, and her male characters tended to take the line of least resistance. The consequences are sometimes disastrous, sometimes relentlessly unhappy. Her women often avert disaster, less often unhappiness.

Hester is trapped between a need for action, which alarms men and women alike, and the comforts offered by marriage, which seems the only escape from a minimal existence. The only encouragement lies in the example of an older relative, Catherine Vernon. Catherine has broken the mould. She had a moment of glory when she saved the family fortunes by calm and incisive action. She earned respect and gratitude, but she paid for it: she never married. As Hester herself recognises, men don't like women who 'step out of their sphere'.[6] Closer to Hester are more conventional influences. Her mother, for example, 'represented all the timid opinions and obstinate prejudices of weakness; all that is gently conventional and stereotyped in that creature, conventionally talked about as woman from the beginning of time'.[7] Her friend Emma 'represented that vulgarer type of feminine character which, without being either strong enough or generous enough to strike out a new belief, makes a practical and cynical commentary upon the old one, and considers man as the natural provider of woman's comfort, and, therefore, indispensable, to be secured as any other source of income and ease ought to be secured'.[8]

Hester recognises something of herself in both these, and is appalled. The novel is, in fact, about self-discovery, and about how self-discovery does not necessarily offer solutions. The book ends on a note of irony. Hester is left with 'two men whom she may choose between, and marry either if she pleases'. 'What can a young woman desire more than to have such a possibility of choice?'[9] The choice between marriage and marriage offers no promise of happiness: Hester, of course, does want more.

By the 1880s women were questioning traditional views of marriage and beginning to construct a rather different picture of the possibilities of women's lives. Oliphant was not a feminist in the political sense, but her fiction illustrates her responsiveness to the need for change. The patterns of human relationships that Oliphant goes back to over and over again tell us a great deal about Victorian society and attitudes. It seems likely that the grittiness, the irony and the no-nonsense approach of Oliphant herself is a direct result of her Scottish background. Most of her adult life was spent outwith Scotland, but she wrote a number of novels set in Scotland or about Scots. Her best-known fiction, for example her *Chronicles of Carlingford* stories, which came out in the 1860s, explore the quality of particularly English areas of provincial life. But in her examination of the character, influence and rivalry of ministers of the church she was almost certainly affected not only by Scottish experience but by what is arguably a very Scottish alertness to subtle differences in the content and style of belief.

Scotland of course shared with England the main currents of nineteenth century life. But there were features of the impact of industrialisation, of urban expansion and rural decline, and of the main movements for reform that had particular prominence in Scotland. Harsher circumstances and a more rigorous, more uncompromising attitude contributed. The effect on women—this is to generalise, but I hope helpfully—was contradictory. As the century progressed women were both more constrained and more vigorous than further south. Oliphant herself ventures on a direct contrast in her novel *Effie Ogilvie* (1886). Effie is both dismayed and tempted by the easy-going attitudes of her English neighbours in a small community clearly located in Galloway. Effie is reserved, serious, described as 'insipid' by the English father of the man who wants to marry her.[10] But she is also a young woman of high principles and high hopes and, naively it might be said, never doubts but that her actions should obey the logic of those principles and hopes. Like Hester Effie experiences the shock of disillusion and opens her eyes on 'a disenchanted world':[11] in both cases the disenchantment is caused by men failing totally to understand the strength and nature of women's needs and convictions.

Like *Hester, Effie Ogilvie* could not end on a note of promise. Both novels reflect Oliphant's ironic and forthright view of the hypocrisies so deeply rooted in the nineteenth century idealisation and limitation of women. And in the Scottish context this idealisation did have a particularly ironic resonance. The historian T C Smout has described Scotland as 'an exceptionally male-dominated society'.[12] Few could argue with that. With some exceptions and some significant anomalies life in Scotland has through most of the last two hundred years and in most sections of society revolved around the needs, comforts, ambitions and self-images of men. The achievements of women have come largely as a result of women detaching themselves from the impositions of men, or of accepting them as a necessary preliminary to getting on with their own lives.

Margaret Oliphant might be seen as an example of a woman who did both. As a wife and mother she did a great deal more than was conventionally expected of her. Her husband, weak in health and in purpose, contributed little. But it was through her writing that she felt herself substantiated. 'I remember walking along the street with delightful elation,' she wrote of the publication of her first novel *Passages in the Life of Margaret Maitland* (1849), 'thinking that, after all, I was worth something, and not to be hustled about.'[13] Many of her female characters are equally desirous of not being 'hustled about'. In *Margaret Maitland* the reflections on the limitations of women's lives are quietly ironic. For example, Margaret says of her education, 'I just learned my lesson, and sewed my seam like other bairns'[14] and later, at a 'genteel school for young ladies' in Edinburgh she learned 'divers things that were thought needful'.[15] The irony itself is genteel, but nonetheless present. It is gently underlined when attention is drawn to the fact that 'men are honoured in all ranks for labouring in an honest avocation'[16] while women are scorned and condemned for doing exactly that. Thirty years later Oliphant was much more direct in her exposure of double standards.

Hester longs to work, but although she and her mother are living in reduced circumstances any suggestion that she might earn the means of increased comfort is greeted with horror. By the time *Hester* was written this issue, whether middle-class women should earn, and therefore be equipped to earn, was being hotly discussed. It was of course very much a part of the movement towards opening up education and professional training to women, which in the Scotland of the 1870s was beginning to have some impact. But attitudes in Scotland were strongly coloured by a characterisation of women that is often seen as peculiarly Scottish. The function of women was presented primarily in terms of supporting their menfolk. Women in Scotland seemed less likely to be regarded as not robust enough, morally or physically, to enter the world of work than as having a role that was incompatible with earning a living. What was manifested in Oliphant's life, though less so in her work, was the need to earn in order to support her menfolk.

Both Oliphant's life and her work emphasise the role of women as mother and helpmate, though without undermining the need for independence. One commentator has said of her that 'the greatest source of whatever happiness she had . . . was her children . . . Motherhood was her passion. Any other human relationship, any intellectual pursuit, was secondary to it'.[17] Motherhood and surrogate motherhood feature profoundly in her novels. But it is not a 'Madonna and infant' portrait she paints. There is nothing either reverential or sentimental about her treatment; on the contrary, her depictions are gritty with the practicalities and the economics of care. She is scornful of passive mothers. A typical juxtaposition of passive and active maternity can be seen in *The Doctor's Family* (1863). Nettie Underwood takes over the practical, day-to-day care of her sister's children, as her sister is helpless and incapable and her sister's husband an alcoholic. Interestingly Nettie, spunky and independent, is a colonial girl, having grown up in Australia. Her forthright nature and brisk commonsense seem to owe much to her detachment from English manners. Equally interesting is the fact that Nettie sees the care of her nieces and nephews as a vocation. She *chooses* to be a surrogate mother; motherhood is not foisted on her by social expectations or by marriage. ' "I have my work to do," ' she says, referring to her maternal responsibilities, ' "and I must do it as best I can. I cannot keep considering you all, and losing my life." '[18] It is a striking reversal of the more usual attitude.

Nettie has a quality that is present throughout nineteenth-century Scottish fiction. Although resentful of the demands others are making on her, she sees all her purpose and reward in life in the care of children. The Scottish mother, channelling all her hopes and energies into the lives of particularly her sons, is a commanding if often a curtailed figure. In Oliphant she appears in more recognisable guise in the characterisation of Mrs Campbell in *A Son of the Soil* (1866). Colin Campbell is a crofter's son, destined for Glasgow University and great things. His mother's tender concern is a foil for his restless ambition, and also an inspiration. There are two dominant features of her characterisation: her intimate, rhythmic involvement with the necessary and unceasing domestic and rural tasks, and her virtually unarticulated support for her son.

This near passive concern is expressed in glimpses such as this: 'His mother was sitting by the fire without even her knitting, with her hands crossed in her lap, and clouds of troubled, tender thought veiling her soft eyes'.[19] It is reinforced by her husband's view of her.

> 'Your mother's an innocent woman . . . she kens nae mair of the world than the bairn on her knee. When you're a man you'll ken the benefit of taking your first notions from a woman like that. No an imagination in her mind but what's good and true. It's hard work fechting through this world without marks o' battle . . . but a man wi' the likes o' *her* by his side maun be ill indeed if he gangs very far wrang . . .'[20]

The implication is, of course, that a good woman exists as a support for husband and sons. There is no irony in Oliphant's projections here, although irony does come into play when she explores Colin's inadequate relations with women and his assumption that they need to be protected and looked after.

Oliphant knew better. Her portrayals of motherhood go hand in hand with her experience of men as weak and vulnerable. The few strong male characters in her fiction tend to be prone to villainy. They are not heroes. There are tensions here that are never fully worked out, but nevertheless reflect the uneasiness in the face of the role of women that was at the heart of so much Victorian rationalisation and hypocrisy. Oliphant portrays women who are resilient and courageous, often determined. The point about Nettie Underwood is that she exercises a choice; there is no self-suppression in order to accommodate the needs of men. Yet Oliphant's attitude to Catherine Vernon, and to Hester, is ambivalent. Catherine's life is ultimately sterile; she is not allowed to be either likeable or fulfilled. There is little indication that Hester will do better. The ironic ambiguity of the novel's ending is entirely appropriate, yet it also reflects a problem. To create a character like Hester, passionate, unconventional, full of longing (there is more than a touch of George Eliot's Dorothea in her) only to package her up in an acceptable marriage would have been a let-down. To have suggested that such a woman might go on to success in business or a professional career would have taken Oliphant further than she wanted to go.

Oliphant's career took her from the years when the attitudes we usually think of as 'Victorian' were hardening into the period when they were under attack. This, and the fact that she wrote constantly for nearly fifty years, mean that she inevitably dominates any discussion of women and fiction in nineteenth-century Scotland. Yet though her own life demonstrates the inadequacy of the conventional mid-Victorian view of women and her novels are so often about women who reject it, to give the impression that there was any radical change either in social attitudes or in Scottish fiction by the end of the century would be misleading. Equally misleading would be to suggest that earlier in the century things were very different.

To say that in the early decades of the nineteenth century Scotland's fictional women were preoccupied with money, marriage and property is almost to be tautological. It is very difficult to disentangle any of these centres of fascination from the other two. The intimacy of the relationship can be seen strikingly in two very different novelists, Susan Ferrier and John Galt. Ferrier wrote two substantial explorations of the marriage theme, *Marriage* (1818) and *The Inheritance* (1824). (Her third novel, *Destiny* (1831) has a rather different tone and emphasis.) Of the two the former is as much about family and proprietorship as it is about marriage, and the latter as much about marriage as it is about the inheritance of money and property. The use of the world 'marriage' in this context does not imply an emotionally rewarding personal relationship so much as a social and economic nexus which may or may not be supported by some warmth and affection.

There is perhaps more of both these latter qualities in the novels of John Galt, who was writing at the same time. Yet Galt too is pre-eminently concerned with the social and economic consequences of marriage. Hester feels excluded from the adventurous, and dangerous, world of business. Yet her friend Emma sees marriage as essentially a financial arrangement, and the relationships between men and women examined in many Scottish novels of the nineteenth century, those concerned with the contemporary scene at least, are, precisely, business relationships. And, not surprisingly, the success or failure of many fictional females depends on their business acumen. There are the temptations of romance, of course, and sometimes women, and men, succumb to them. But on the whole the rewards are few, and they are few because, although throughout the long history of story telling the expectations of love have been high, the preparation for sustaining an intimate and mutually supportive emotional relationship was virtually non-existent.

When the novelist Matthew Lewis heard that Susan Ferrier was writing a novel he commented, ' . . . I have an aversion, a pity, a contempt for all female scribblers. The needle, not the pen, is the instrument they should handle, and the only one they ever use dexterously'.[21] The attitudes of such as 'Monk' Lewis may have sharpened the pen of Ferrier. *Marriage* is acute, spirited and caustic. She examines marriage in the context of a range of social and economic aspirations. She employs a device, the separation of twin girls and their upbringing in very different circumstances, which enables her to present telling contrasts in character and social and physical environment. Her heroine is Mary, exempt from satire as is Mrs Douglas, whose example and influence shape Mary's views and expectations. This exemption from satire, and the selflessness and modesty of both these women, tend to place Mary on a level of piety and virtue beyond the abrasive realities of life in both the Highlands and London, the two main arenas of action. But Mary is a girl of spirit, intelligence and sensitivity, and thus retains our interest. She is not, however, a hero (as surely many of Oliphant's women are), but unequivocally a heroine.

Life in both environments is limited, and limited for similar reasons, although these reasons operate in a different way and on a different scale in the two localities. In the Highlands Mary is surrounded by aunts whose moral ambitions are 'to knit stockings, scold servants, cement china, trim bonnets, lecture the poor'.[22] If in London society the vehicles of morality are social accomplishments—the arts of dress, adornment, singing, playing, conversation—the effects are equally constraining and equally tyrannous. When Mary goes to London to join her estranged mother and sister the assumption is that she is hoping for a husband. To acquire one it seems she must accept the brittle laws of London society. Mary escapes from one narrow environment only to be expected to adapt to the regulations of another.

Mary's virtue and commonsense, partly native, partly the result of Mrs Douglas's benign influence, enable her to detach herself, though not without pain, from what she recognises as social requirements masquerading as moral imperatives. She marries a worthy and serious man, they make their home in the Highlands: the approving phrase is 'virtue joined to prosperity'.[23] The Highlands, though not unscathed by satire, are a more appropriate context than London for such harmonious decency.

The Inheritance is a less evenly modulated book and in some respects the satire is harsher, in that the effects of materialist actions and aspirations are more uncompromising. The heroine, Gertrude, is both more challenging and more gullible, more threatened and more passionate. Ferrier takes her narrative to the borders of Gothic melodrama, but never away from the love-and-property theme that is at the novel's core. Only when the two are separated does Gertrude get her reward.

The bewildering glare of romantic passion no longer shed its fair but perishable lustre on the horizon of her existence; but the calm radiance of piety and virtue rose with a steady ray, and brightened the future course of a happy and useful life; and Gertrude, as the wife of Edward Lyndsay, lived to bless the day that had deprived her of her earthly Inheritance.[24]

But there is a twist to the story. Ferrier cannot resist, having established her heroine's moral re-education, rewarding her with more than a good and affectionate marriage. The novel's last sentence tells us that ultimately Gertrude gains the inheritance she thought she had lost.

The lesson seems to be that it *is* possible to have both love and property; indeed, that if you are virtuous and sensible, rather than selfish and ambitious, you will gain both. In Galt's hands the dimensions of love and property are more tortuous, more suggestive of comedy and, in many ways, more challenging. In *The Inheritance* Ferrier examines a small segment of Scottish society, the landed upper class and its margins. There is little scope for experiment, particularly for women. Galt looks at a broader territory, in which social and economic relations are both more entrenched and more precarious, where the place of women seems if anything more narrowly defined, but which in fact allows the possibility of sheer force of personality taking over.

This last phenomenon is seen at its most impressive in *The Entail* (1822), perhaps Galt's most substantial and commanding novel. The fact that the character who takes over is female is itself a major current in the novel's achievement. *The Entail* is a story of sheer greed, with the goal of ownership of property overriding all else. Women and marriage are important, in the eyes of the pivotal figure Claud Walkinshaw, only in so far as they enhance property or lead to the acquisition of more. The novel is a magnificently intricate web of intrigue and manipulation, and there is a highly appropriate as well as comic irony in the triumphant emergence from it all of the Leddy Grippy.

When we first meet Miss Girzy Hypel it is made clear that she is lacking in conventional feminine charms—'she did not make quite so tender an impression on the heart of her resolved lover as he himself could have wished'.[25] Equally, it is clear that this is secondary. The proposed marriage is a move in Claud Walkinshaw's extension of property, a business proposition between the intending bridegroom and the bride's father. Both men are astute bargainers. Girzy's father, the Laird of Plealands, puts his case:

> Is na she a coothy and kind creature?—She'll make you a capital wife.—There's no another in the parish that kens better how to manage a house—Man, it would do your heart gude to hear how she rants among the servan' lasses, lazy sluts, that would like nothing better than to live at heck and manger ['heck'—'hayrack': to live with everything provided], and bring their master to a morsel; but I trow Girzy gars them keep a trig [neat] house and a birring wheel [active spinning wheel].[26]

All these are significant qualities, especially to such as Claud, jealous of unnecessary expense. They are important in other ways. This celebration of the practical and frugal habits of the Laird's daughter is a bargaining ploy, but it also underlines a particularly Scottish quality which emerges in fiction in different contexts and with different connotations. This is the characterisation of women, and not necessarily working-class women, as having an energetic and creative practicality. As Girzy rises in the world and becomes 'Leddy' of a large estate she never loses this. She does not lose touch with the activities that are for her part of the essential rhythm of life. Even when she is taking an active and initiatory role in business and legal matters and out-manoeuvring rival manipulations she can be found at her spinning wheel.

Once Leddy Grippy's children are grown the dimensions of her character deepen and strengthen. Once her husband is dead there is nothing to hold her back, and she proves more than a match for all the scheming that is going on, which itself reflects a totally dismissive attitude towards women. The entail itself is all to do with male heirs. Women are significant only in so far as they assist or impede a man's prospects as an heir. The implications of Leddy Grippy's triumph are both ironic and moral, in that in a story of an entail a woman should feature with such significance and such success.

She does not achieve a state of worthy virtue, like Ferrier's Mary and Gertrude. Indeed, she proves herself not so much virtuous as more astute, cunning and clever than all the others who are playing the game of manipulation. What is particularly striking is that Galt does not suggest any incongruity in the Leddy's defeat of the men at their own game. In fact, her activities are represented as an extension of those indulged in by many of the other female characters. Almost everyone is scheming for money and property.

Galt's fiction contains more conventional portraits of women, including characterisations of dedicated Scottish mothers. Mrs Malcolm in *Annals of the Parish* (1821), a neat and industrious widow whose main pleasure, concern and hope for the future is centred on her children, is an example of all that might be considered most praiseworthy in Scottish womanhood.

> She was a genty body, calm and methodical. From morning to night she sat at her wheel, spinning the finest lint, which suited well with her pale hands. She never changed her widow's weeds, and she was aye as if she had just been ta'en out of a bandbox. The tear was aften in her e'e when the bairns were at school; but when they came home, her spirit was lighted up with gladness, although, poor woman, she had many a time very little to give them.[27]

Such a picture of honest poverty combined with the vocation of motherhood was one the Victorians would find hard to resist. Galt's portrait is a pre-Victorian characterisation that can also be seen as a tool of Calvinism, which reinforced the Victorian curtailment of women. It was in the nature of Calvinism to be particularly wary of the wiles of women. They were seen both as dangerous temptresses and as vulnerable, weak links in the chain of moral probity. Scottish fiction found ways of circumscribing or distancing the disturbing aspects of this view of women. Those like Mrs Malcolm are both restricted and in a sense supported by work and poverty. At no time does it occur to the narrating minister that his parisioner might have needs and wants other than those bound up with the welfare and prospects of her children. We have already looked at women who play their parts on the social and economic scene for stakes that have little to do with love (in a modern sense) or sexual fulfilment. Money, property and social status are the consuming passions. (There are suggestions of the temptress in Ferrier's work, but she is successfully contained.) In other words, women's sexual energies are either suppressed, subsumed by a devotion to children, or channelled into other kinds of strongly-felt activity.

Robert Louis Stevenson focused the problem neatly in his essay 'Some Portraits by Raeburn'. Raeburn's approach to his female subjects, Stevenson argued, differed from his approach to the men.

> The younger women do not seem to be made of good flesh and blood. . . . In all these pretty faces you miss character, you miss fire, you miss that spice of the devil which is worth all the prettiness in the world; and what is worst of all, you miss sex. His young ladies are not womanly to nearly the same degree as his men are masculine; they are so in a negative sense; in short, they are the typical young ladies of the male novelist.[28]

Stevenson himself was haunted by the problem of the 'negative' characterisation of women. But in fact, however many examples of negative definitions of what is 'womanly' we can find, there are equal numbers of more positive projections. They are not confined to women of rustic strength, or to the businesswomen, or to those who yearn for a wider sphere of action. There are also women of commitment and passion, if not of overt sexuality. We find them in Scott, for instance. They are not the women who marry his heroes, but are impressively heroic in themselves. They range from Flora MacIvor (*Waverley*, 1814) to Meg Merrilies (*Guy Mannering*, 1815) and Madge Wildfire (*The Heart of Midlothian*, 1818). These are all women whose passion sets them outside conventional society. Another kind of heroic nature is seen in *The Heart of Midlothian*'s Jeanie Deans, whose dignified independence is not passionately expressive but is nonetheless rooted in commitment.

Jeanie Deans shows us woman as hero, yet her legacy is limiting. She is a good woman, obedient to moral imperatives which have been shaped by her father's convictions, although she appears to challenge him. Her actions do not take her so far out of the conventions imposed by her class and her sex as to make it impossible to return. Unlike some of Scott's women she is neither rebel nor outcast, and offers no encouragement in the search for an acceptable means of expression for female sexuality. Male sexuality can often be expressed through heroic action. This is less likely to be true of women.

Oliphant showed how narrow was the scope for heroic womanhood. But the nineteenth century Scottish novel offers a wealth of female characters with enduring substantiality. The physical delineations of this substantiality have more to do with work than with sex, which is what one would expect in a literature that could not escape the burdens of Calvinism. Courage and action is generally represented in terms of the shouldering of responsibilities;

expressiveness is more likely to emerge in the encouragement of a son than in the love of a husband. Stevenson himself was not able to find space for womanly women until towards the end of his career. He created only two major female characters that have the resonance he finds lacking in Raeburn: the older Kirstie in *Weir of Hermiston* (1894) and Uma in *The Beach at Falesá* (1893).

The logical, though extreme, extension of the Raeburn tendency can be found in George Douglas Brown's *The House with the Green Shutters* (1901) where Mrs Gourlay and her daughter Janet are not just tyrannised into the margins of an overwhelmingly male territory but are physically debased and abused. What makes *The House with the Green Shutters* so mean-spirited an example of Scottish Victorian fiction is this uncompromising relegation of women which, however satirical, is almost inevitable in the grossly male dominated society that Brown depicts. The sluttish, unattractive, insignificant Mrs Gourlay and her ailing daughter are characterised entirely in terms of their failure to service and support their menfolk. Not only do they have no rights, they have no personalities beyond what is interpreted by husband, father and son. With the two men dead they have no alternative but to die also.

This might be seen as the summation of Smout's 'exceptionally male dominated society'. But of course the other side of the picture, which we have been looking at, was also being painted in stronger colours in the closing years of the century. The growing awareness amongst women that their lives had infinitely greater potential than had been acknowledged had imaginative as well as practical implications. Amongst the few women writing were the sisters Jane and Mary Findlater who began their careers as novelists in the 1890s. Daughters of a Free Church minister, neither their background nor the environment of their girlhood were particularly conducive to writing. (Indeed the powerful alliance of Calvinist and Victorian values laid a discouraging hand on all of Scottish imaginative literature, as the struggles of Stevenson's life and career demonstrate.) Yet both the Findlater sisters became highly respected authors, singly and together. They collaborated on three novels, all written and published well into the twentieth century, yet reflecting the repressions and containments of the nineteenth.

Crossriggs (1908) has at its centre a woman who shares something of the predicament of Oliphant's Hester, and also has many of the qualities that we have noticed as typical of female characterisation. Alexandra Hope is the mainstay of a household which consists of a charming, eccentric and somewhat feckless father and a widowed sister with numerous children. It is Alex who cares for the children, organises meals, stretches the financial resources and, when they will stretch no further, seeks work to support the family. The circumstances are not unfamiliar. Yet there are significant differences from the treatment such a woman and such a situation would have received earlier. In the hands of the Findlaters Alex has dimensions of which Hester is only dimly aware. But Alex's awareness elevates her not to self-realisation but to an understanding and a necessary self-denial that have tragic currents. It is true that she has the opportunity to earn and, although her father and sister are uneasy they do not obstruct her efforts. But there is little satisfaction in the work itself, for Alex has neither the education nor the training for a career.

A more complex factor in her frustrating existence is that she loves a married man and is loved by an engaging, eager and (she feels) sexually dominating younger man. She is appalled by the implications of this emotional tangle and makes every effort to suppress her own sexuality. Yet it is undeniably there on the page, in her personality and in the pain of her situation. There is no responsibility that she shirks, yet she has an angry sense that she is wasting her life. It is an anger akin to Hester's, expressed a quarter of a century earlier. In a sense Alex has her reward: unexpected money and the unexpected opportunity to travel. The final paragraph leaves her looking forward to a world 'rich in beauty and in new experience'[29] yet such hopefulness as there is is the result of sheer effort of the will. That effort might fairly be seen as another manifestation of Scottish robustness, of a strength that grows out of a closeness to certain kinds of practical and physical reality. Yet however present these are scarcely a comfort. It is the tensions of the novel that linger, and the hunger of Alex herself for a great deal more than life has allowed her or can promise.

Crossriggs is a novel that opens the doors to the twentieth century but sees little that is encouraging in prospect. It seems a fair reflection of women's position in Scotland at the turn of the century, with a few battles won and many yet to be engaged. Yet there was encouragement in the very fact that Jane and Mary Findlater were examining female character with confidence and sensitivity. This is significant in the contexts both of the development of fiction and of the growing assertiveness of women. The two writers must have looked back on the nineteenth century with the knowledge that there was much about women in Scotland that was not being said by Scotland's novelists. Their contribution is all the more important in view of the fact that in the decades that followed there was little change. The story of the portrayal of women in nineteenth-century Scottish fiction is a story of exceptions. There would continue to be exceptions, but fiction maintained its tendency to lag behind the realities of women's lives.

NOTES

1   Mrs Oliphant, *Hester* (London, 1984), p 400.
2   Ibid., pp 401–2.
3   Ibid., p 330.
4   Ibid.
5   Ibid., p 331.
6   Ibid.
7   Ibid., p 331.
8   Ibid., p 332.
9   Ibid., p 495.

10 Mrs Oliphant, *Effie Ogilvie. The Story of a Young Life*. (London and Glasgow, 1886) I, p 188.
11 Ibid., II, p 247.
12 T C Smout, *A Century of the Scottish People 1830–1950* (London, 1986).
13 Mrs Oliphant, *Autobiography and Letters* ed Mrs Harry Coghill (1898) (repr Leicester, 1974, intro Q D Leavis).
14 Mrs Oliphant, *Passages in the Life of Margaret Maitland* (London, 1849), I, p 10.
15 Ibid.
16 Ibid., I, p 97.
17 Vineta and Robert A Colby, *The Equivocal Virtue* (1966), p 29.
18 Mrs Oliphant, *The Doctor's Family* (London, 1986), p 171.
19 Mrs Oliphant, *A Son of the Soil* (London and Glasgow, 1866), I, p 36.
20 Ibid., I, pp 38–9.
21 Quoted in Rosemary Ashton, Introduction, Susan Ferrier, *Marriage* (London, 1986), p xv.
22 Susan Ferrier, *Marriage* (London, 1986), p 168.
23 Ibid., p 513.
24 Susan Ferrier, *The Inheritance* (Bampton, 1984) p 894.
25 John Galt, *The Entail* (Oxford, 1984), pp 19–20.
26 Ibid., p 22.
27 John Galt, *Annals of the Parish* (Edinburgh, 1980), p 8.
28 R L Stevenson, 'Some Portraits by Raeburn', *Virginibus Puerisque* (London, 1909), p 149.
29 Jane and Mary Findlater, *Crossriggs* (London, 1986), p 379.

FURTHER READING

Ashton, Rosemary, Introduction, Susan Ferrier, *Marriage* (London, 1986).

Binding, Paul, Introduction, Jane and Mary Findlater, *Crossriggs* (London, 1986).

Coghill, Mrs Harry (ed) *Autobiography and letters of Mrs Margaret Oliphant*, with an introduction by Q D Leavis (Leicester, 1974).

Colby, Vineta and Robert A, *The Equivocal Virtue: Mrs Oliphant and the Victorian Literary Market Place* (New York, 1966).

Gordon, Ian A, *John Galt: The Life of a Writer* (London, 1972).

Terry, R C, *Victorian Popular Fiction 1860–80* (London, 1984).

Uglow, Jennifer, Introduction, Margaret Oliphant, *Hester* (London, 1986).

Williams, Merryn, *Women in the English Novel, 1800–1900* (London, 1984).

——*Margaret Oliphant: A Critical Biography* (London, 1986).

Chapter 14

Realism and Fantasy in the Fiction of George MacDonald

DAVID S ROBB

Despite a lifetime's wide-ranging literary activity which included the writing of poetry, essays, stories for children, sermons, the editing of a children's periodical, the creation of several anthologies and the editing of *Hamlet*, George MacDonald (1824–1905) was best-known in his own day as a prolific writer of novels. From *David Elginbrod* (1863) to *Salted With Fire* (1897) he published twenty-nine works which, despite their variety of length and strangeness of nature, it is convenient to call 'novels'—a count which does not include *Phantastes* (1858) and *Lilith* (1895), works of fantasy which strain even that copious term. In such a hectic career with a vast output designed to keep the wolf from the door of himself and his large family, unevenness is to be expected. Most who know MacDonald's writing, however, would agree that his best novels are among the dozen set wholly or in large part in Scotland, his 'Scottish novels', written throughout his long life as a writer— *David Elginbrod* and *Salted With Fire* both belong to this group. By the end of the novelist's life, when J H Millar was writing his *A Literary History of Scotland* (1903), most readers would have regarded MacDonald as essentially belonging to an earlier era—he had his greatest reputation in the 1860s and 1870s—and would have agreed with Millar that MacDonald's main claim on posterity is the fact that he 'has given us many admirable pictures of north-country life and character'.[1] For long, MacDonald has been thought of as, simply, a regional novelist who spoiled a lot of potentially good work in that vein by 'preaching'. Even when the preaching is not overt (though he steps forward as a direct commentator in his own novels with increasing frequency), his novels were easily recognised from the first as marked by a tendency towards idealism. In the Victorian critical debates over realism and romance, MacDonald seemed clearly in the latter camp.

Miller, however, thought *Phantastes* and *Lilith* 'tedious and unintelligible', a view which most of MacDonald's contemporaries would have shared. These dreamlike fantasies, specifically designed to lead the reader out of the world of the everyday, stood little chance of general popularity in MacDonald's lifetime and it has been left to the later twentieth century for them to achieve the reputation which is their due. That said, they have not become widely familiar to today's readers and remain a somewhat eccentric enthusiasm. Nevertheless, it is on them, and on his authorship of works which reveal the same capacity for creative fantasy (some short stories and children's fairy-stories, including three novels—*The Princess and the Goblin* (1872), *The Princess and Curdie* (1883) and *At the Back of the North Wind* (1871)—which have become children's classics) that his present-day reputation depends.

A case could be made for seeing the works for children as the ideal introduction to MacDonald as a writer. They are not only of patently high quality, but express with clarity so many of the themes and values which are central to him: the fundamental principle of moral growth as a human instinct and imperative; the value—and, indeed, the necessity—of seeing the world in a childlike way; the hatred of materialism—a notion which includes not only acquisitiveness but also the limiting commitment to the world of the senses and to philosophies which are merely the products of sense and reason; the requirements of obedience, faith and courage; the necessity, and goodness, of death. Being explicit written for children, they enable the reader to experience and accept most easily that tactic which is fundamental to Mac-Donald's writing—to turn his reader, imaginatively, into a child once again, or, rather, to bring out the child in each of us. The two *Princess* books are thoroughly and accessibly fairy-tale in nature; *At the Back of the North Wind*, part fairy-tale and part realistic novel, makes clear, perhaps better than anything else he wrote, MacDonald's commitment to bringing the two domains of the everyday world and the larger reality beyond into a true and visible relationship. Whether he is telling the tale of the little princess who is threatened by the goblins in the caverns below her castle and who is saved by—and who saves—the plebeian miner's boy Curdie, or whether he is making the slow illness and death of the son of a London cab-driver seem, by its modulation into the tale of the child's adventures with North Wind, a positive, enhancing thing, MacDonald is capable of holding children and adults alike by the scope and vigour of his imagination, by the depth of his seriousness and by the resonance of his symbolism.

By contrast, the two great adult fantasies can worry and baffle many readers who are introduced to them, because their meaning is as unclear, at first encounter, as their genre and method. Even readers who recognise swiftly the various literary roots of *Phantastes* (in Novalis and Hoffmann, in Spenser and Bunyan, in Dante, Coleridge and Shelley—to name only the greatest and most obvious) must still grapple with the dream-like discontinuity, of narrative and of theme, with which MacDonald has created his fairyland world and its denizens. A brief summary would suggest to anyone who had not read it that the work is, like countless other tales, merely an account of a journey from the everyday to the marvellous and back again but even in the everyday portions the hero is called, strangely, Anodos, fantastic things occur, and the distinction between dream and reality is hopelessly blurred. The tale of Anodos's journey through Fairy Land, too, is strikingly episodic, not only in locations and characters but in atmosphere and in degree of moral urgency. Control over structure is not overt and MacDonald is either, here, only half competent or particularly subtle in a flexible evocation of dream and apparent inconsequence. I believe it is the latter which is true, and regard his quelling of the instinct towards linearity and structure in narrative to be one of the work's peculiar distinctions. It is a work, also, rare in MacDonald's output in that it is not overtly Christian in its concerns: even *Lilith*, restrained and oblique as it is in thoughts about God, Man and ultimate things, is more outward than *Phantastes*.

If explicit Christian doctrine is absent, however, a concern with moral growth is certainly not: at the outset, Anodos is a moral *tabula rasa* while at the end he is, like Coleridge's Wedding Guest, a sadder and a wiser man. Yet despite the natural temptation to depict moral growth—that core-concern of countless of the world's stories (and quite a few of his own)—MacDonald, I believe, has the peculiar distinction here of showing his hero as still fallible, still capable of immersement in self, even at the end as, in his dream-death, he glories in the good which he will do for mankind. Some read this passage, just before his final plummet back into his waking world, as a sign of his achieved moral status. I suggest, rather, that it undercuts the complacency of exactly that kind of notion. Just as the work is open-ended and deliberately non-conclusive in narrative terms (Anodos's life back at his home is, at best, a half-life of yearning for the dream-world he has left), so is it in moral terms, also: by the end, Anodos has achieved a glimpse of the moral issues of existence but his mastery of them is still far from concluded. Here in particular, MacDonald's originality and independence of mind is striking, imposing.

He achieves a similar open-endedness in *Lilith* though by more structured means. The hero of the later work, Mr Vane, eventually finds himself, like his predecessor of 1858, trapped in the commonplace world which separates him from the more awful, more unpredictable world which contains what he nevertheless longs for. Yet where Anodos had stumbled into a dream-universe, Vane discovers that the reality which he did not know he was inhabiting is, in fact, a riddle. The difference in metaphor points to the different ways in which the world of *Lilith* is imagined and the book containing it structured. For *Lilith* is not merely a bleak re-run of *Phantastes*, despite their broad identity of literary kind. *Phantastes* is designed as an experience for the reader—it is a wonderland for our imaginations and despite the frequent clarity of its moral concerns (so that we regularly find ourselves thinking allegorically) it is achieving its design when in reading it we surrender, simply, to magic and curiosity. *Lilith*, on the other hand, has a message—about Self, Evil, and Death—which we must consciously decode. Consequently, the work is, unlike its stable-mate, explicitly designed. It depicts a world which, unlike the dreamscapes which may just be the contents of Anodos's dreaming mind, is apparently actually there, and the shifts to and fro between the everyday world and the frightening terrain of the evil princess of the title, of the much metamorphosed Adam and Eve and their offspring, of the Peter Pan-like Little Ones, and of assorted monsters and terrors, are handled so as to suggest that they have a rationale and could be controlled by Vane if only the key to the riddle could be found. *Lilith* lacks most of the exuberant spontaneity of *Phantastes*: in its stead it offers profound seriousness and insight into some of life's deepest problems, as well as a striking technical competence and assurance which suggests that the long years between his first great book and his last were far from wasted.

Most readers and critics, however, agree with C S Lewis who, in an influential essay which served as the preface to an anthology of religious quotations from MacDonald's writing, insisted that MacDonald was not so much a writer—a craftsman in words—as a myth-maker, an inventor of resonantly meaningful images, situations and stories.[2] Lewis's dictum that MacDonald was 'seduced into writing novels' by necessity and by the prestige of the form has become a habitual lament.[3] Richard Reis, for example, sees those twenty-nine novels as regrettable attempts by MacDonald to write against the grain in '*trying* to write conventional realistic novels' instead of concentrating on myth-making.[4] His genius, we are told, was incapable of expression through the medium of Victorian fictional realism and his many attempts in that way are, apparently, failures.

Yet any remotely sympathetic reader of his non-fantasy works will find grounds for doubting the wisdom of complete rejection of this large proportion of MacDonald's life-work. For one thing, there are so many good things in them: characters who stick in the memory; vivid descriptions of childhood adventures and activities; scenes of high, and sometimes gripping, melodrama; extensive, convincing, pithy and eloquent passages of Aberdeenshire Scots; intimately drawn, detailed renderings of various facets of nineteenth-century Scottish society; an occasional, enriching seam of comedy; an ability to evoke the variety of nature's features, from the most gentle to the most terrifying; a natural and profound ability in symbolic resonances; an extraordinary seriousness which, on occasion, can infuse even the most trite material with conviction. Nor is MacDonald's success in these works always merely in episodes: however uneven and wilfully various these novels appear to be, the best of them, such as *Alec Forbes of Howglen* (1865), *Robert Falconer* (1868) and the two Portlossie novels, *Malcolm* (1875) and *The Marquis of Lossie* (1877), all have a powerful sense of controlled, underlying movement—a secure structural purpose lying within the superabundance of episode—which suggests an architectonic strength with which MacDonald is seldom credited. Above all, the novels simply have an instantly recognisable personality, a queerness (it is surprising how often the word is used—approvingly—of MacDonald's work) which at least gives it distinctiveness and which can be appealing. In their very nature, too, the novels are more explicit in their treatments of MacDonald's characteristic preoccupations: to know MacDonald, it is necessary to know them.

It is true that these virtues are constantly balanced against the imminence of failure. MacDonald consciously eschews the received wisdom of the art of the novel—a wisdom which, then as now, elevates mimetic illusion, and the minimalising of anything which works against that illusion, as its ultimate goal and inevitable method. His claim of another and better concept of art, as not so much an end in itself as a means to divine ends, has not aided his universal acceptance for it apparently involves—in his hands at least—the flouting of many accepted, seemingly inevitable canons of form, taste and judgement in fiction. Hence his notorious 'preaching', which can take the form either of direct address to the reader or of the manifest manipulation of the fates of characters to express his belief in a just and loving god. Hence, too, his ready use of the stock formulae of melodrama—aristocratic villains, virtuous (and triumphant) scions of the lower classes, heroines perfect in beauty and nature, seductive flirts who come to bad ends, sage old men and women, etc. Much of his writing is artificial in ways which sophisticated readers find hard to forgive: the only mistake they make is in assuming, often, that MacDonald writes thus because he does not know what he is doing. So his critics are right when they describe him as going against the grain, not only of majority taste but also of the literary medium of the novel. His true failures, however, come in *The Elect Lady* (1888) and in many pages of the other Scottish novels of the 1880s and 1890s, when, simply, his idiosyncratic imagination fails to light and one is left with merely the precious and perverse formulae which require his unique imaginative vitality to bring them to life. The amazing thing is that there are so many pages—and books—in which that vitality is present and in which his success, as I see it, is apparently bound up with the very perversities for which he has been condemned.

I have argued elsewhere that the so-called realistic novels are much more nearly akin to the fantasy works than most critics suggest, and that the chasm of kind which is now habitually believed to exist within MacDonald's fiction is not, in fact, very wide—or deep—at all.[5] In particular, there are powerful structural, episodic and archetypal features in the novels which bring them, like the fantasies, close to the world of the fairy-tale. In both types of writing, MacDonald's basic aim is the same: to follow the example of Novalis in romanticising the commonplace.[6] Both kinds are patently the products of a unique imagination with its own special and very private way of working; both, too, come from a writer who is prepared, even when apparently writing in the literary form of greatest mass appeal, to be at odds with conventional expectations and to persistently revel, apparently, in the eccentricity and isolation which is thereby entailed. For the remainder of this essay, I shall explore in some detail one particularly important facet of his imagination and also consider one aspect of the likely influence on him of his Scottish origins.

In addition to the fairy-tale writing, a reader wishing to do justice to MacDonald as a novelist must also come to terms with *David Elginbrod* (1863), *Sir Gibbie* (1879) and the four other novels mentioned above. Apart from portions of *David Elginbrod*, *Robert Falconer* and *The Marquis of Lossie*, these works are set in the North-East of Scotland, in places with which MacDonald was familiar from the first phase of his life, before he graduated with an MA degree from King's College, Aberdeen in 1845 and moved south to London. Aberdeen is an important location in three of these (*Alec Forbes*, *Robert Falconer* and *Sir Gibbie*), while Huntly, where MacDonald was born and brought up, is central in *Alec Forbes* and *Robert Falconer*. The 'Portlossie' of *Malcolm* and *The Marquis of Lossie* is Cullen, on the Banffshire coast. Throughout these novels (and, indeed, several of the other weaker but nevertheless characteristic novels), the sense of the landscape, seasons, climate and way of life of the North-East is powerful and appealing.

These are not only regional novels, however: they are to a considerable, if varying, degree autobiographical as well. Several are clearly modelled on the broad outlines of MacDonald's early life, with its boyhood in a small town and farm environment followed by a move to Aberdeen University, with the pleasures and disappointments of the first years of adulthood. Cullen was one of the seaside villages which provided the MacDonalds with summer holidays. Many of the anecdotes which make the renderings of childhood so vivid in *Alec Forbes* and *Robert Falconer*—and in, for example, *Ranald Bannerman's Boyhood* (1871), probably the best of his non-fairy writing for children—clearly derive from memories of his own early years. Family history, too, finds its way into his pages, especially those of *Robert Falconer*. Autobiography, a common enough resource in the works of many novelists, is clearly of especial importance in MacDonald's novels.[7]

It has long been obvious, to those who know and respond to MacDonald's fantasy works, that their author was gifted with a special kind of imagination. This is implicit in Lewis's vision of MacDonald's mythopoeic genius, and in Auden's brief but enthusiastic essay along the same lines.[8] Contemplation of the fantasy writing, with its immense symbolic suggestiveness, encourages the reader to see MacDonald's imaginative uniqueness in terms of a profound openness to religious truths and imagery, and also, perhaps, in terms of an intuitive apprehension of psychological archetypes. Either way, MacDonald seems to have access to mental regions far beyond the familiar or explicable. Consideration of the best of the novels, however, enriches this notion by suggesting that MacDonald's imagination is also fed, vitally and powerfully, by memory. His greatest imaginative and literary gifts have to do with his capacity to reach into the depths of his own being and to use what he finds there to charge his tales with religious meaning and archetypal significance. But his own past life also, with its experiences both great and small, was obviously a major part of what was deepest within him: to MacDonald, with his capacity for faith and also with his instinct to find meaning, pattern and divine significance even in the meanest flower that blows, the details of his own life-story provided him with a vocabulary to express his deepest beliefs. For his contemporaries were right: these novels are, among other things, important and effective regional novels and contain much that is accurately documentary and anecdotal. As I have argued elsewhere, their realism serves a romance purpose by offering what is strange, distant and alien to the vast majority of their readers—the world of rural North-East Scotland.[9] And to this clear distancing of place and culture there is added the more subtle distancing of time. The products of the memory are useful to MacDonald because what they provide both is and is not reality: they help in that deep and fruitful confusion of realism and romance which makes his best Scottish novels so memorable.

Furthermore, his past life provided significant memories of not one but two broad kinds. Obviously, the outward shape and circumstances of a boyhood in Huntly, the early loss of his mother, the deeply loving relationship with his father, the companionship of friends and the intimate encounter with a wide variety of nature's faces, the restrictive Calvinist ethos of the nonconformist Congregational church of which the MacDonalds were stalwart members, emotional and intellectual growth during adolescence and undergraduate days at King's College, Aberdeen, his increasing radical questioning of Calvinist doctrine—these constitute the large, bare bones of an early life from which MacDonald could also recollect a myriad of smaller details. In addition to this outward autobiography, however, MacDonald was acutely aware of his own past inner life, which was significant not only for its emotional dimension but also, in his eyes, for its intellectual and literary landmarks as well. His own past reading, from the imaginative delights of Hogg's tales and the *Arabian Nights* (both of which young Alec Forbes delights in), through Byron and Shelley to the literary enthusiasms of his maturity (Shakespeare, the poetry and drama of the English renaissance, Wordsworth and Coleridge, the poetry and fiction of German Romanticism, the great poets of his own day)—all this can not only be seen deeply influencing his writing, but it is explicitly referred to with great frequency in the course of his fiction. MacDonald clearly regarded what a person reads as both a sign of, and immense influence upon, character and moral stature.

In both the realistic fiction and the fantasy writing, memories form a rich and central resource for his imagination to work on: the balance between memories from life and memories from literature is worked out anew in each case but, broadly, we can say that the realistic fiction draws particularly from MacDonald's outer life while the fantasy and fairy writings depend particularly on memories of literature. Nevertheless, there is no completeness of division between the two sorts of memory, any more than there is between the two areas of MacDonald's fiction. The world of the realistic fiction is thoroughly impregnated by the archetypes, the symbolism, the idealism of the fantasy writing: it is the commonplace deliberately romanticised. Conversely, the dreamscapes and fairy settings of the fantasies contain many echoes and indirect references to the world in which MacDonald lived and breathed and had his being. Similarly, the experiences of reading (and of listening, for who having read *Ranald Bannerman's Boyhood* can doubt that listening to oral folk-tales and legends was one of the formative aspects of MacDonald's childhood in Huntly?) have a status equal to the outward landmarks of MacDonald's life. In work after work, MacDonald painstakingly catalogues the discoveries made by his characters between the boards of the books they read: the best characters have the surest literary taste, and an encounter with Shakespeare, or Spenser, or Milton, or Wordsworth always constitutes an epoch in their lives. Hence, too, the frequency, in MacDonald's pages, of poems and interpolated stories: he takes the formal freedom provided by the models he found in the fiction of the German Romantics to insert songs, tales and snatches in a joyous chaos. His writing overflows with a sense of God's presence, in the abundance of literature as in the richness of life experience.

A sign of how conscious MacDonald was of the importance of memory in the activity of his own imaginative life is to be found in the source from which he derived that curious title, *Phantastes*. By way of explanation of the word, he quotes (with alterations) two lines from 'The Purple Island' by Phineas Fletcher, an imitator of Spenser. The lines are the first two in the following stanza:

> *Phantastes* from the first all shapes deriving,
> In new abiliments can quickly dight;
> Of all materiall and grosse parts depriving,
> Fits them unto the noble Princes sight;
> Which soon as he hath view'd with searching eye,
> He straight commits them to his Treasurie,
> Which old *Eumnestes* keeps, Father of memorie.
>
> (Canto 6, st. 48)

In this allegory, the 'noble Prince' is the Intellect or Understanding, served by three chief counsellors of whom Phantastes and Eumnestes are the second and third. Phantastes is a version of the Imagination, acting by freshening 'all shapes' (romanticising the commonplace?) and by making them presentable for the noble Prince. This process seems to be not so much an act of basic censorship but rather an idealising of the everyday. Once Phantastes has performed his treatment and the noble Prince, the Understanding, has sanctioned the result, the transformed data is stored in the memory, to be available when the Understanding wishes to use it. The memory stands very close indeed to the Fantastic Imagination (a phrase MacDonald used as a title for his key essay on fairy-tales): this allegory suggests that it is an essential resource enabling the 'noble Prince' to work properly, as in the creation of works of art.[10]

What MacDonald finds lying in his memory, therefore, is truth—it is what the 'noble prince' has stored away: hence its suitability as material for fictional art which MacDonald always saw as valuable chiefly because of the divine truth it contained. Hence, too, the many repetitions (of character-types, situations, themes) which have seemed to many readers to be a sign of his incapacity as a writer.

Phantastes as a whole suggests the essential role of memory in MacDonald's art, for not only is the entire tale, which is told retrospectively as most stories are, apparently dependent on it, but time and time again a memory seems to be the vital means whereby the doors into wonder are opened. At the beginning, for example, Anodos's adventures begin with the appearance of the beautiful fairy grandmother while he is trying to penetrate the memories embodied and hidden in his father's secretaire. Then he is precipitated into Fairy Land by the act of remembering the astonishing incidents of the evening before. On several occasions, Anodos reflects that there is comfort in memories of the past. At one point, he compares memory to a mirror: both are agents of 'reflection', just like thought itself. MacDonald clearly associates mirror/memory/thought together as means whereby everyday reality is reproduced yet subtly altered so as to give pleasure:

> Why are all reflections lovelier than what we call the reality?—not so grand or so strong, it may be, but always lovelier? Fair as is the gliding sloop on the shining sea, the wavering, trembling, unresting sail below is fairer still . . . All mirrors are magic mirrors. The commonest room is a room in a poem when I turn to the glass . . . There must be a truth involved in it, though we may but in part lay hold of the meaning. Even the memories of past pain are beautiful.
>
> (*Phantastes*, Chap. 10)

Phantastes, therefore, is both the attempt of its central character to reproduce from memory, and thereby re-enter, the wonderful world of Fairy Land
from which, at the end, he is cut off, and a synthesis from MacDonald's
memories of his own wide and idiosyncratic reading.

It is not merely that MacDonald was at his best while striving to directly
reproduce, on the page, things that he remembered: his creative mind was
not just a mirror, however prized by him that device might have been.
It is as if, rather, the consciousness of distant memories provided a helpful
element within the mental and emotional environment in which invention
and verbal creativity could flourish. We can perhaps see this process with
some clarity in a narrative poem of his entitled, 'A Story of the Sea-Shore'.
The tale is of a young woman in a Scottish fishing community whose be-
trothed is lost at sea and who, maddened by grief, dwells by the rocky
shore by a ruined cliff-top castle until she is found drowned in a pool.
This gloomy tale is the occasion for declarations of faith by MacDonald
as narrator, who hints that he too has known earth's pain. It is possible
that he is recalling moments of anguish in his student days when, in
depression due, perhaps, to disappointments in love as well as to growing doubts about the Calvinist vision of god, he would wander by the
shore at Aberdeen.[11]

The tale is presented as a local legend from the vicinity of Cullen, for it is
preceded by a lengthy introductory section (136 lines in a poem of around
500) in which MacDonald tells how the tale was told to him by an old friend
during an adult visit made by the poet to one of the scenes of his youth.
Already, memory is piled on memory: MacDonald as he writes is remembering the tale-telling and its happy associations which, in turn, are enriched
by more youthful recollections of the tale-teller,

> a girl, on whose kind face
> I had not looked for many a youthful year,
> But the old friendship straightway blossomed new.
> (31–3)

But the visit has been more than a matter of picking up old friendships: it
has been a multiple confirmation that this land of past happiness is still there,
can still be returned to, and that his memory, that bodiless vision, has been
a reliable medium of contact with it:

> I found my home in homeliness unchanged:
> The love that made it home, unchangeable,
> Received me as a child, and all was well.
> My ancient summer-heaven, borne on the hills,
> Once more embraced me; and once more the vale,
> So often sighed for in the far-off nights,
> Rose on my bodily vision, and, behold,
> In nothing had the fancy mocked the fact!
> (7–14)

As he writes, MacDonald recalls with loving minuteness the scene in which old friendship is renewed:

> The heavens were sunny, and the earth was green;
> The large harebells in families stood along
> The grassy borders, of a tender blue
> Transparent as the sky, haunted with wings
> Of many butterflies, as blue as they.
>
> (34–8)

Memories provide the environment in which loving happiness is renewed, for they are a means of transcending time and asserting eternity:

> Brought near by memories of days that were,
> And therefore are for ever;
>
> (40–1)

And he precedes his gloomy story of the demented girl, not only with this laden account of how he heard the tale, but with an over-flow of his own dearest memories of Cullen where he used to explore within the policies of Cullen House. That garden, he says, 'was my childish Eden', not only because of the natural beauties of the place but because of

> a little room,
> Half-hollowed in the side of a steep hill,
> Which rose, with columned, windy temple crowned,
> A landmark to far seas.
>
> (72–5)

He had never entered this room but had merely gazed through its locked door 'half-filled with rainbow hues of coloured glass'. Nevertheless, this cool, secluded chamber had possessed his imagination: he had longed 'to dream there through hot summer days' and

> To find half-hidden in the hollowed wall,
> A nest of tales, old volumes such as dreams
> Hoard up in bookshops dim in tortuous streets!
>
> (102–4)

And the hidden room had an ultimate attraction to his imagination:

> Still in the midst, the *ever more* of all,
> On a low column stood, white, cold, dim-clear,
> A marble woman. Who she was I know not—
> A Psyche, or a Silence, or an Echo:
> Pale, undefined, a silvery shadow, still,
> In one lone chamber of my memory,
> She is a power upon me as of old.
>
> (92–8)

He finds confirmation that what had once been a power upon him can still be so—and he is referring, not just to people and places, tangible things, but also to dreams, emotions, longings, fantasies. The past may be another country where things are done differently but its strangely attractive customs are always accessible. Visits there confirm for him the message of his own happy childhood—that happiness is a basic, despite the pains of experience; that his sense of 'home', of that intimate divine love of which a child's experience of happy domesticity is a simulacrum, is well founded.

Here, I think, is the reason why, throughout his career he returned again and again to Scotland in his fiction. Although it is not obvious, the Scotland to which his imagination turns is usually the Scotland of his childhood in the 1820s and 1830s: not just in the sense that the geography of his fictions is the landscape of his own early acquaintance but also in the few hints of dating which the novels offer. The Scotland of *Alec Forbes* and *Robert Falconer*—let alone that of later novels such as *Castle Warlock* and *Donal Grant*—is a place where transport consists of stage-coaches, steamers between Aberdeen and London, horseback, and (for students) Shanks's pony. The railway which the adult MacDonald used so often to travel between Huntly and the south of England makes no appearance in the best of the novels: it is absent until *The Elect Lady*, which is weak, in large part, because it lacks the memory-based density of its predecessors. In the riot in *Alec Forbes*, in which the hero, while a medical student, is chased by a mob enflamed by the thought that he has perhaps been grave-robbing, MacDonald is clearly recollecting an incident in Aberdeen in 1831 in which an anatomy theatre was burned down in the wake of the Burke and Hare case.[12] The fictional disturbance is set on by Alec's enemy Beauchamp, an aristocratic fellow-student who would have been born during the Regency, that period on which MacDonald, along with many Victorians, looked back with considerable moral distaste—a feeling amplified in MacDonald's case by his partisan support for Lady Byron, his first major benefactor and one who, in her marriage, must have seemed a major victim of the evil of Regency *mores*. Many of MacDonald's aristocratic villains have Regency associations and they become, in his work, symbols of human pride, materialism, licence and worldly selfishness. This is particularly clear in the paste-board Baron Rothie, in *Robert Falconer*, a novel notably rich in period memories, local economic history and MacDonald family history. Less obviously located in a particular past is *Sir Gibbie*, for long one of the most enduringly popular of the novels, with its fantasy of the mute street-arab who, miraculously, ends heir to a family fortune and puts it to challengingly Christ-like uses. Yet even here he looks back to distant memories of the terrible floods in Moray and Nairn in 1829—a natural disaster which had also provided a model for incidents in *Alec Forbes*. In the later novel, a footnote acknowledges that his direct memories are being pleasurably reinforced by his return to the classic account of the catastrophe, written by Sir Thomas Dick Lauder.[13] 'Known to me from childhood, it wakes in me far more wonder and pleasure now, than it did even in the days when the marvel of things came more to the surface.' (*Sir Gibbie*, Chap. 36) Memories of past experience and past reading mix and emerge, in MacDonald's writing, perpetually.

Yet it was not just as a fructifying medium that the memory of his past life in Scotland influenced MacDonald as a writer. As the author of two of the earliest and best fantasy novels ever written, as well as of a large number of acclaimed fairy-tales, MacDonald was clearly committed to literary values which exalted the artificial, the imaginative and imaginery, the aesthetic. He clearly loved the sheer literariness of his art, and it was this instinct for its artifice which helped him reject the overwhelming priority of mimesis in the novel. His novels, and, indeed, his entire life's output, proclaim him to be a willing outsider, a conscious and gleeful contradictor of the received and the commonplace, a provider of the alternative. Mysterious as the origins of any writer's artistic personality always are, it seems likely that this attitude to art and its relationship with society was formed, at least partially, by his sense of the attitudes held in that childhood society to which he returned, in memory and imagination, so often throughout his life.

If there is one scene from the Scottish novels which imprints itself on the reader's mind (and it was a scene which struck many contemporary readers) it is that in *Robert Falconer* (Chap. 23, 'An Auto da fé') in which Robert returns home to find his grandmother in the act of burning the violin which he had been secretly treasuring and mastering. As in so much else that is effective in his fiction, recollection is involved here. MacDonald is not remembering an experience of his own yet the incident had actually occurred in the family past and he had known the model for Mrs Falconer, his redoubtable grandmother Mrs Charles Edward MacDonald, well—she died in 1848.[14] Beyond these personal considerations, however, is the fact that the incident is simply a powerful natural symbol of the fierce, destructive mistrust of art and imagination in the world of Scottish Calvinism in which Mac-Donald was brought up. The scene crystallises one of the important themes of *Robert Falconer*, which is much concerned with the growth of Robert's artistic instincts and with the necessity of their finding an outlet despite the opposition which surrounds them: the book makes clear the belief which underlies much of MacDonald's life work, that art provides a route to God. The suppression of the artist in Robert takes its place among the still larger themes of man's need to find his heavenly father and of the need to confront the opposition to this impulse from the world of matter.

Had MacDonald written only this book on this theme, it would still have been clear that his concern with art as a means to God, and his consequent prizing of the artistic life, was of great importance. It is not, however, the only instance. There is a particularly interesting and explicit return to the theme in a later novel, *The Marquis of Lossie*. The fisher boy, Malcolm MacPhail (who now knows he is the marquis of the title but has not yet claimed his rights openly) has gone to London with a loyal fisher friend, nicknamed Blue Peter, to guard over Malcolm's errant half-sister Florimel, who is in danger of falling prey to London worldliness. Exploring the streets of the capital, Malcolm stumbles upon what he has never seen before—a theatre with a performance about to start. Going in under the impression that it is a church, he is soon undeceived and finds himself, to his delight, at a production of *The Tempest*, which he had known from his reading.

MacDonald's detailing of the reaction of his naive but intelligent playgoer is fascinating, because it confirms that he regarded art as addressing itself to our individual, inner worlds, in the form of memory and our capacity to recognise the familiar. Malcolm thinks that Prospero's sea-shore is an actualisation (not even an imitation) of what is dearest to him:

> But surely he had seen the vision before? One long moment its effect upon him was as real as if he had been actually deceived as to its nature: was it not the shore between Scaurnose and Portlossie, betwixt the Boar's Tail and the sea? and was not that the marquis, his father, in his dressing-gown, pacing to and fro upon the sands? He yielded himself to illusion—abandoned himself to the wonderful, and looked only for what would come next.
>
> (*The Marquis of Lossie*, Chap. 10, 'The Tempest')

Just as interesting, however, is the account of Malcolm's return to the production a few days later. He contrives to get Peter into the theatre—the devout fisherman also assumes that 'this'll be ane o' the Lon'on kirks' and there is a little gentle satire at the expense both of his simplicity and also of the worldliness of the London audience—the two are played off equally against each other. The right-hearted Peter, off his guard, responds at first with open fascination, caught by the interest of the nautical opening and, like Malcolm, by the belief that the island-shore is Portlossie. Then the penny drops: 'I'm jaloosin'—it canna be—it's no a playhouse, this?' When he discovers not only that it is indeed a playhouse and, worse, that Malcolm had known it to be such all along, it causes a major breach of trust—a tempest—between the two. MacDonald understands Peter's feelings, but nevertheless appears to favour Malcolm's conduct and we are encouraged to blame Peter for his lack of openness and trust in the goodness of intention (and also, we feel, the superior taste and knowledge) of his aristocratic friend. Malcolm discovers that theatre is not only a blameless convention in itself, at least at its best, but that it has the function, always vital in MacDonald's thinking, of leading us beyond earthly limitations: 'The play-hoose is whaur ye gang to see what comes o' things 'at ye canna follow oot in ordinar' life.' (Chap. 17, 'A Difference') Peter, however, rejects the theatre and its onward-leading function, just as he rejects the new, more variously experienced Malcolm who is developing before his eyes: 'There's a sair cheenge past upo' you, but I'm gauin' hame to the auld w'y o' things.' (Chap. 20, 'Blue Peter') Peter's conservatism is not just his own but can be felt as representative of a central part of the entire ethos of Scottish Calvinism. As Henry Grey Graham comments:

> It is the peculiarity of Scottish dissent that it never arose from love of change, from any breaking forth of new views and opinions. It was rather a determination to preserve more purely the creed and habits of their fathers. In fact, radical as Scottish temperament is called, it was then not the radicalism of those who uproot old institutions and seek out new paths; it was really a conservatism as keen as that of the Jacobite in resistance to change, whether in dress, in farming, and in social customs, or in theology and worship.[17]

MacDonald rejected the Calvinist rejection of art as powerfully as he rejected Calvinist theology. Indeed, one would be hard put to it to be certain that the theological issue had priority in him. Despite his love for the family which nurtured him, and for the society in which his early years were spent, MacDonald found himself at odds with the world he first knew and his life work is a massive assertion that values, both theological and artistic, other than those first offered him are true. The contradictions visible in his written output are merely echoes of the contradictions he found in himself as he contemplated where he came from.

NOTES

1   J H Millar, *A Literary History of Scotland* (London, 1903), p 618.
2   C S Lewis, *George MacDonald: An Anthology* (London, 1946), pp 14–18.
3   C S Lewis, *The Allegory of Love: A Study in Medieval Tradition* (Oxford, 1936), p 232.
4   Richard H Reis, *George MacDonald*, Twayne's Engish Authors Series 119 (New York, 1972), p 115.
5   David S Robb, 'George MacDonald's Aberdeenshire Fairytale' in *Studies in Scottish Fiction: Nineteenth Century*, Horst W Drescher and Joachim Schwend (eds) (Frankfurt am Main, Bern, New York, 1985), pp 205–16.
6   Novalis, *Fragmente des Jahres 1798, Gesammelte Werke*, No. 879, vol III, p 38; repr in *European Romanticism: Self-Definition*, Lilian R Furst (ed) (London & New York, 1980), p 3.
7   The standard biography is by the novelist's son Greville MacDonald, *George MacDonald and his Wife* (London, 1924).
8   W H Auden, Introduction to *The Visionary Novels of George MacDonald*, Anne Fremantle (ed) (New York, 1954); repr in W H Auden, *Forewords and Afterwords*, selected by Edward Mendelson (London, 1973), pp 268–73.
9   David S Robb, 'The Fiction of George MacDonald' in *Literature of the North*, David Hewitt and Michael Spiller (eds) (Aberdeen, 1983), pp 70–81 (p 79).
10 George MacDonald, 'The Fantastic Imagination' in *A Dish of Orts* (London, 1893), pp 313–22.
11 Greville MacDonald, p 80.
12 Fenton Wyness, *City by the Grey North Sea: Aberdeen*, 2nd edn, (Aberdeen, 1972), pp 236–7.
13 Sir Thomas Dick Lauder, *An Account of the Great Floods of August 1829, in the Province of Moray and Adjoining Districts* (Edinburgh, 1830).
14 Greville MacDonald, pp 26–9.
15 Henry Grey Graham, *The Social Life of Scotland in the Eighteenth Century*, 4th edn, (London, 1937), pp 374–5.

FURTHER READING

WORKS BY MACDONALD

A Dish of Orts (London, 1893).
Alec Forbes of Howglen (London, 1865).
At the Back of the North Wind (London, 1871; repr New York, 1950).
Castle Warlock (London, 1882).
David Elginbrod (London, 1863).
Donal Grant (London, 1883).
The Elect Lady (London, 1888).
Heather and Snow (London, 1893).
Lilith: A Romance (London, 1895; repr, with *Phantastes*, and intro by C S Lewis,
    London, 1962).
Malcolm (London, 1875).
The Marquis of Lossie (London, 1877).
Phantastes: A Faerie Romance for Men and Women (London, 1858; repr in Everyman's
    Library, London, 1915; repr, with *Lilith*, and intro by C S Lewis, London, 1962;
    repr as Everyman Paperback with intro by David Holbrook, London, 1983).
Poetical Works, 2 vols (London, 1893).
The Princess and Curdie (London, 1883; repr Harmondsworth, 1966).
The Princess and the Goblin (London, 1872; repr Harmondsworth, 1964).
Ranald Bannerman's Boyhood (London, 1871; repr London & Glasgow, 1911).
Robert Falconer (London, 1868).
Salted With Fire: A Tale (London, 1897).
Sir Gibbie (London, 1879).
What's Mine's Mine (London, 1886).
Wilfrid Cumbermede (London, 1872).
Works of Fancy and Imagination, 10 vols (London, 1871).
    In recent years, there have appeared in American paperback editions heavily
abbreviated versions of MacDonald's novels under such titles as *The Tutor's First
Love [David Elginbrod]* and *The Maiden's Bequest [Alec Forbes of Howglen]*. Need-
less to say, these have no value to the serious reader of MacDonald.

BIOGRAPHICAL STUDIES

MacDonald, Greville, *George MacDonald and his Wife* (London, 1924).
MacDonald, Greville, *Reminiscences of a Specialist* (London, 1932).
MacDonald, Ronald, 'George MacDonald: A Personal Note' in *From a Northern
    Window*, Frederick Watson (ed) (London, 1911), pp 55–113.
Raeper, William, *George MacDonald* (Tring, 1987).

BOOKS ON MACDONALD

Hein, Rolland, *The Harmony Within: The Spiritual Vision of George MacDonald*
    (Grand Rapids, 1982).

Reis, Richard H, *George MacDonald*, Twayne's English Authors Series 119 (New York, 1972).
Robb, David S, *George MacDonald*, Scottish Writers Series 11 (Edinburgh, 1987).
Wolff, Robert Lee, *The Golden Key: A Study of the Fiction of George MacDonald* (New Haven, 1961).

SHORTER STUDIES

Grierson, H J C, 'George MacDonald' in *The Aberdeen University Review*, 12 (1924–1925), no. 34, November 1924, pp 1–13.
Lewis, C S, Preface to *George MacDonald: An Anthology* (London, 1946), pp 10–22.
McGillis, Roderick F, 'George MacDonald—The *Lilith* Manuscripts', *Scottish Literary Journal*, 4, 2, December 1977, pp 40–57.
——'George MacDonald and the Lilith Legend in the Nineteenth Century', *Mythlore*, 6, 1979, pp 3–11.
Manlove, Colin N, *Modern Fantasy: Five Studies* (Cambridge, 1975), pp 55–98.
——'George MacDonald's Early Scottish Novels' in *Nineteenth-Century Scottish Fiction: Critical Essays*, Ian M Campbell (ed) (Manchester, 1979), pp 68–88.
——*The Impulse of Fantasy Literature* (London, 1983), pp 70–92.
Prickett, Stephen, *Romanticism and Religion: The Tradition of Coleridge and Wordsworth in the Victorian Church* (Cambridge, 1976), pp 211–48.
——*Victorian Fantasy* (Hassocks, 1979), pp 150–97.

Chapter 15

Robert Louis Stevenson in Prose

FRANCIS R HART

In the best study of Stevenson, Jenni Calder singles out a passage from a later essay, 'The Coast of Fife',[1] which depicts a scene and a figure to which Louis's imagination often returned. The place is Magus Muir; the scene, the murder of Archbishop Sharpe; the figure, the Covenanter who remained in the coach, hiding his face with his cloak, Hackston of Rathillet. The passage epitomises much. It contains one of the most vivid recollections of Louis's Scottish youth, yet it comes in one of his latest essays, written far away. It recalls his earliest writings: 'incomplete romances' of Hackston 'lumbered' in desk drawers, then were destroyed, hidden forever like Hackston's face. Aspects of the Scottish past of central interest to Louis's imagination were recovered only near the end of life. His literary models were anything but Scottish; he never felt he could belong to Scotland, was always having to leave it, could repossess it only at a final distance.

The passage epitomises his 'genius of place'.[2] Even his sense of history was topographical. It suggests his episodic focus: the 'perdurable power' of an incident 'at once awakes the judgment and makes a picture for the eye'. His is an art of episode, of tale and novella; the established long novel presented problems he seldom solved, and need not have tried to. The adventure story,[3] which had been relegated to low generic status, is essentially episodic. Adventure is a form and an aesthetic of experience, a mixture *par excellence* of reality and artifice; hence, the passage's stress on 'artifices', on 'picturesque effects', its typical down-playing of his art. Finally, there is the figure of Hackston himself, whom Calder sees as an example of Louis's lifelong fascination with moral ambiguity. Is he a hero of conscience, a fanatic, or an enigmatic adventurer?

Enigmas and paradoxes abound, and as a result, the critical study of Stevenson is pock-marked with pitfalls and traps of bias. My business here is to use such traps and enigmas toward an understanding of what he was trying to do. And, given my focus on the actual process of writing, I will date works, not by publication, but according to time of composing. This writer who disparaged his 'trade' is the same for whom learning to write was *the* vocation; the same who carried on the first serious correspondence in English on the nature of fiction;[4] the same who started many works, lost momentum, and left too many diverse fragments to be explained wholly in terms of illness or early death; the same who did not trust himself to carry the long novel to a fitting end, and finished *Treasure Island* and *The Master of Ballantrae* only because he was committed to serialisation. What was the problem?

It might be defined in three dimensions. In form, it is a problem of scale, which could be dramatised by placing *Prince Otto* next to 'Thrawn Janet', *St Ives* next to *Jekyll and Hyde*. In mode, it is a problem of consistency. Noble lays the old charge most severely:

> He, the most sensitive of stylists, is capable of crudely changing genre . . . disconcertingly and self-destructively changes type, a change usually made in the direction of an escape into the 'safe' form of the adventure story and away from the moral and metaphysical difficulties which he has initiated.[5]

Alistair Fowler's is the best corrective to such extravagance.[6] Generic and modal mixtures are familiar to us in a time of post-modernist fabulation; we no longer denigrate the adventure story *à priori*. But there remains the puzzle of Louis's uncertainty about the relation of art to reality, his ambivalence as a romancer. 'With all my romance,' he wrote Colvin, 'I am a realist and a prosaist, and a most fanatical lover of plain physical sensations plainly and expressly rendered; hence my perils.'[7]

Third, in intention, the problem is a lasting ambivalence over morality in art. There is the man who wrote:

> Here, in England, too many painters and writers dwell dispersed, unshielded, among the intelligent bourgeois. These, when they are not merely indifferent, prate to him about the lofty aims and moral influence of art. And this is the lad's ruin. For art is, first of all and last of all, a trade . . . The arabesque, properly speaking, and even in literature, is the first fancy of the artist; he first plays with his material as a child plays with a kaleidoscope.[8]

There is also the man W E Henley described:

> A deal of Ariel, just a streak of Puck,
> Much Antony, of Hamlet most of all,
> And something of the Shorter-Catechist.[9]

Somewhere, Calder says, 'Stevenson always hoped, was a Holy Grail that represented a true fusion of art and morality.' But what is the morality? On one hand is the man who told Archer that 'one dank, disspirited word is harmful' and it is 'the business of art' to send the reader rejoicing; on the other, the believer that 'a profound underlying pessimism' is 'the last word of the Stevensons . . . their sense of the tragedy of life is acute and unbroken.'[10]

Can one account for so many fundamental divisions in one author? The biographers must decide if they can to what extent they were temperamental, to what extent they were created by his cultural situation. Whatever the causes, Louis was an intensely social being, an essentially impersonative man, histrionic in imagination. His close friend and keen admirer Henry James wrote that his 'costume' is part of his 'character', a 'writer with a style—a model with a complexity of curious and picturesque garments.'[11] His responses were chameleontic, and he was extraordinarily susceptible to the aggressive influences of friends. In the dedication to *Travels with a Donkey*, he says, 'Every book is, in an intimate sense, a circular letter to the friends of him who writes it.'[12] This is definitively true of Stevenson, for friendship was his idea of grace. The friends he then had in mind were a London literary coterie who, in the 1870s, were eagerly seeking a New Author to assume the status of departed Victorian greats and thought they had found him. They of the Savile Club gave the expatriate Bohemian Scot a status and a living remote from the respectable Edinburgh he could not belong to. They imposed their ideas of what and how he should write, and on occasion he rebelled at the demands to 'do nothing but refined, high-toned bejay-bedamned master-pieces.' The early Stevenson belonged to this late age of belle-lettristic Men of Letters,[13] and his essays and travel books reflect their demands.

The travel-essayist of 1871–6 was a fugitive in search of a place and a subject. His essays and travel books display a romantic personality exper-imenting with styles of impersonality, an aesthete with the voices of a lay moralist. The mixture of late-Romantic passion for style and a 'nostalgia for eighteenth-century proprieties'[14] is peculiar, but not to Stevenson—rather, to a cult of stylism looking for its spokesman. In his personal essays, per-sonality is a curious phenonemon. The tradition from Montaigne to Hazlitt and beyond had been definitively personal, but for Stevenson personality is less to be explored than to be created. Moreover, he was a child as well of Bunyan and the sermon, for whom the value of personality lies in its parabolic potential. Thus, in 'Ordered South' and later 'A Chapter on Dreams' he first makes his impersonal parable and only then enters personally. The aesthete mixes strangely with the preacher, but Louis always had the preacher in him, as did other Victorian agnostics. The Victorian Sage[15] had not vanished with aesthetic reaction or Darwinian iconoclasm. What changed was the authority he could claim and the morality he could teach. The morality of aestheticism, following Walter Pater, is a strange blend of Stoicism and Hedonism: Stoicism sees man spiritually alone in an indifferent universe; the Higher Epicureanism elevates aesthetic experience to spirituality and (the heritage of Dandyism from Brummell to Wilde) makes style itself a morality.

Louis preached a lay morality for the young, and the dedication of *Virginibus Puerisque* (1876–9) indicates his problem.[16] He was to be spokesman for youth; hence, the strident representativeness, the 'we' posture, the forced texture of aphorisms based on slender experience. 'Crabbed Youth and Age' is a good specimen. It attacks 'catchwords' of prudential morality, yet speaks of old age as if he knew about it, in general certainties. And through the neo-Augustan assurance peers the Paterian for whom the world of knowledge is perpetual flux, and our 'most elaborate view is no more than an impression.' The difference between such early essays and the finer, later ones of *Memories and Portraits* (1882–7) is not that the writer is older, but that the persona is younger, moving toward authentic memoir. It is not that he was avoiding personality but that he didn't have material to create it. A later note to 'Ordered South' explains: 'A youth delights in generalities, and keeps loose from particular obligations'; the older man 'has acquired humility, but also a stronger sense of self.'

Nine of the early essays deal with travel and strange places, and the first three books are all 'travels'. All reflect the new Victorian cult of tourism with its uneasy exercises of public personality.[17] Its travel aims are complex: escapism and discovery mix strangely; to go 'out of oneself' is to fulfill or create oneself. The paradoxes, we will see, are central to adventure. Meanwhile, the kind and degree of personality in travel narrative are matters of decorum, and Stevenson's travel books are governed by decorum. This, rather than a development toward 'personality',[18] may explain basic differences. *An Inland Voyage* (written 1876–7) is lightest and most distanced; travel by barge makes for ease and distance, for a playful egoism of mirror-images where people exist to look and be looked at. The picturesque of *Edinburgh* (1878) is different as it must be; playful aesthetic distance gives way to strongly textured ironic contrast. The 'I' is involved and knowledgeable. The 'I' of *Travels with a Donkey* (1879) is an omnipresent critical ego, a Scottish protestant in Catholic country, who finds the tolerant community he seeks to replace old divisions. After a radical break in his life came the fourth and best of his travel books. In *The Amateur Emigrant* (written 1879), he indeed found 'his own, authentic voice', with a remarkable fusion of Augustan decorum and a 'brilliance of . . . powers as a social realist.'[19] The book's partial suppression and the hostility to it of his 'little Sanhedrin' of London friends[20] are first signs of the ominous power of friendship over Louis's imagination.

London wanted a new novelist. His route from travel-essay to novel led through short story. Our constructing of Louis's imaginative history runs here into a problem. Is it sound or fair to suggest a developmental logic? His dual impulses as a writer—to strike out repeatedly in new directions; to return repeatedly to unfinished work—make this tricky. Critics look for developmental integrity, and where they fail, their subject is blamed for incoherence or a loss of nerve. At least we can insist on original dates. Thus, the 'New Arabian Nights' were written the year of travel books (1878). First Scottish stories such as 'The Merry Men' and 'Thrawn Janet' belong in composition to the Braemar summer (1881) of *Treasure Island*. Complex fables such as 'Markheim' and 'Olalla' belong to the Bournemouth period (1883–5) of four early novels and the Henry James conversations. An entire volume could be given to this uniquely creative time, but no simple linearity could do it justice.

We know that the 'Nights' were written in haste and playful collaboration, but they do not deserve the usual prejudices of genre critics: e.g. that RLS began in parody, that he lost his comic distance, retreated from satire to fantasy, and 'blundered' into 'the protective excesses of farce and melodrama.'[21] Shall we say the same of Dickens? Whatever the modal mix of the stories, their motive and their problem is adventure, Louis's major fictional idea. The foolish adventurers are saved by the miraculous interventions of Prince Florizel, himself the embodiment of the perilous obsession of quixotic adventure in the modern world. Poor Harry, progenitor of Henry Durie and other divided heroes, is caught in a Kafkaesque 'sad imbroglio' of which he understands nothing. Rev Rolles learns that a mild young cleric has a secret talent for crime. Scrymgeour discovers that adventures into evil are less desirable than mundane life as an Edinburgh bank clerk and the company of his dull father.

The Braemar summer opened up new matter, but criticism bogs down still in disputes over genre and mode. 'The Merry Men' is not folk ballad, romance, or allegory.[22] It is what Louis said: a 'fantastic sonata' about sea and wrecks.[23] The musical analogy suggests his typical aim to fuse moral fable with Paterian aesthetic. Its morality is unambiguous. The evil of greed drives old Gordon to murder and madness. The nephew gives up the treasure hunt, prays for the souls of all at sea, and chooses to help the poor survivor rather than pursue his 'dismal lunatic' uncle. There are real evil and real redemption, but they are natural and human.

While a complex narrative method envelopes it in ambiguity, the morality of 'Thrawn Janet' is similarly humanistic. But the end of tragic. A superstitious diabolism turns the enlightened but naive minister into a devil-ridden fanatic. This idea will generate Louis's major Scottish theme, to be variously developed in *The Master, Ebb-Tide, The Beach at Falesá*, and *Weir*. And the alternation of endings, between uncertain salvation and tragic defeat, will become an unsettled rhythm of his imagination.

In 'Olalla' and 'Markheim', conflict is internalised. The time of composing is the months of *Jekyll and Hyde*; 'Olalla'[24] is almost as long as the novella, and together they suggest a scale Louis might have done well to adhere to. Their linkage in theme is pronounced, and it turns on the key term 'link'—a linkage of body that belies a division of soul. Watching the degenerate Spanish family of 'Olalla', the idealist Scots narrator is obsessed with a paradox: the son's innocent energy of body; the mother's sensual sloth. Of the daughter Olalla, his extravagant imagination makes a 'peerless unity', a 'link' both 'brutal and divine'. He insists on oneness of body and soul; she insists otherwise, for linkage is her tragedy. She orders him away, and he sees her at last as 'an emblem of sad and noble truths; that pleasure is not an end, but an accident; that pain is the choice of the magnanimous; that it is best to suffer all things and do well.'[25] A vision of unity has been dashed by the 'profound underlying pessimism' of the Stevensons. No wonder Louis found the tale 'unreal' and preferred 'Markheim', where the horror-stricken murderer rejects the mysterious stranger's fatalism, surrenders himself, and the stranger, no devil but a guardian angel, 'undergoes a wonderful and lovely change'.[26] A spurious diabolism is defeated by human conscience. An acceptance of moral duality need not be destructive, as it is in 'Olalla' and *Jekyll and Hyde*.

But to trace such development in longer forms, we must back up to the Braemar summer.

Writing *Treasure Island* provided liberation from the demands for 'bejay-bedamned masterpieces'; writing 'for boys' relieved the need for 'psychology and fine writing'. But critical condescension to 'adventure as boy's daydream' is misled. More acceptable but also extreme is critical over-emphasis on the insinuated sly moralist, or on archetypes of the mutilated antifather. The book can be heavily thematised as a 'series of contests for power . . . conflicts of authority, loyalty, obedience and duty.'[27] But to do so distorts the book's mood and proportions. More truly suggestive is a fact of its genesis: Louis wrote his installments for friendly listeners, and the most enthusiastic was his father, whose 'kind of picturesque' it was, an adventure for engineers, a tribute to a cramped but childlike imagination.[28] I gave the book to a tough Boston cabbie once, and it changed his life.

Treasure Island is indeed a 'parable of adventure' (Fowler). But I wonder whether the disputes over 'kind' that so dominate—I would say distract—Stevenson criticisms are productive. True, Louis himself thought about fiction categorically. He frustrated unity critics and himself by mixing categories. And generic expectations do operate in any reading. But every text plays against generic conventions to make its own code, and this is the case with *Treasure Island*. The opening chapters—the mood masterpiece of the inn's environs, the mystery of Captain Bones, old Pew's nightmarish death—are darkly romantic. But the message soon is clear. Daydreams about sea travel, islands, and treasure (held here by men, not boys) will be deflated by real adventure. The word 'strange' (essentially adventuristic) echoes throughout, and it is tied to actuality. The linked word is 'tragic', but the tragic is rejected. The squire is a fool, and the doctor begins as one. In this foolish quest many are slaughtered, and the men who ultimately split the treasure use it foolishly or wisely according to their natures. Jim goes along willingly, but once in his apple barrel, he loses all romantic feeling for the adventure. The adventure will live in his mind as a nightmare of Long John Silver.

With Silver, we meet that central phantom of Stevenson criticism, the Glittering Scoundrel. Scoundrel he is, but he glitters only in the clouded eye of critical thesis. He is a confidence man, a fortune-hunting impostor with dreams of gentility, an able commander who handles his handicap with skill. As for the putative bond with Jim, it is mostly on Silver's side. Silver is a 'better man' than the pirates, but they are a drunken lot. He saves Jim to save his own neck. Jim admits to a sore heart at the thought of the 'shameful gibbet' awaiting Silver, and when Silver escapes, Jim hopes he is comfortable somewhere. But that is all.

To remember the book in terms of the Jim-Silver bond is to forget its proportions. Jim is bound to Silver only while he is held hostage. The definitive chanciness of the adventure turns on Jim's role alone: 'There is a kind of fate in this,' says Livesey; 'every step, it's you that saves our lives.'[29] The long major episodes have Jim off on his own, and in them his developing qualities stand out: he is impulsive, acting out of 'notions'; he is, as Savater says,[30] 'audacious'; he is resourceful—all an adventurer should be. The emphasis is not on romantic atmosphere but on logistics. We are reminded of Louis's interest in military tactics and of his eighteenth-century master Defoe. The island is a diagrammatic plan for action—as Chesterton noticed, like an eighteenth-century woodcut.[31] The RLS of romantic place and moral dilemma is not borne here, but in the sequel.

The Black Arrow (written 1883) is an odd book 'for boys', but boys preferred it to *Treasure Island*, and critics as astute as Leslie Stephen and R H Hutton thought it his best book so far. Louis said that a child should be given 'some perception of what the world is really like—its baseness, its treacheries, its thinly veiled brutalities.'[32] Brutalities are not veiled at all in *The Black Arrow*; the England of Wars of the Roses is a maze of treacheries. The 'tushery' dialogue should not conceal the moral complexity. Young Dick is no Hamlet, but he is no mindless activist either. Caught in a world where 'all that care for me be blood-guilty of my father's death', he becomes a bloody fighter, believing in neither side. But he outgrows violence when he sees 'the cruel consequences of his own behaviour' in war's carnage. The image of Arlblaster, the old skipper he has ruined, haunts him: 'He saw, through tears, the poor old man, bemused with liquor and sorrow, go shambling away, with bowed head, across the snow, and the unnoticed dog whimpering at his heels, and for the first time began to understand the desperate game we play in life.'[33] No boy's day-dream, real adventure is a desperate game.

In its desperate game, its political cynicism, its horror of war, its parodic Hamlet allusions, its 'babes in the woods', its Meredithian heroine Alicia, *Black Arrow* looks ahead to *Prince Otto*. In other ways, it is a bridge from *Treasure Island* to *Kidnapped* and beyond. The figure of Brackley, the real-politician, will take various forms. The episodes of flight, pursuit, hiding are the kind that make adventures in *Kidnapped*. The pair of friends are like David and Alan, but also (when Joanna is disguised as a boy) like David and Catriona. They are a pre-sexual friendship safe for juveniles; they are also an idea of friendship that was, for Stevenson, the only stability in a world of moral chaos.

Prince Otto (written 1883–4) establishes this theme as central to Louis's moral code. The code, neo-calvinist, holds that 'nobody does right'; some attempt it for amoral reasons; others have great difficulty learning to do it; the hero's surface charm and frivolity are masks for his incapacity—grounded in self-distrust and distrust of any action—to do anything. Daiches calls this the 'profound pessimism' that is masked by all of Stevenson's comedies.[34] Stevenson calls it cynicism: 'So much of cynicism to recognize that nobody does right is the best equipment for those who do not wish to be cynics in good earnest.'[35] What it equips for is a self-forgiveness that is basic to mutual forgiveness. Otto learns this in his climactic talk with his last friend, Gotthold. The issue (as with David and Alan) is whether the friends can forgive each other. Gotthold realises 'it is ourselves that we cannot forgive, when we refuse forgiveness to our friend.' Otto concludes, 'What matters is how bad we are, if others can still love us, and we can still love others?' This, Gotthold declares, 'is the true answer to the pessimist, and the standing miracle of mankind.'[36] And so it is.

Otto is also Stevenson's satire of political activism. Eigner[37] has thoughtful pages arguing a kinship with Trollope's Palliser books, and the novel, especially in its feminism, recalls the political Meredith as well. But Harvie demonstrates the book's and Louis's conservative retreat from politics: 'The move within *Prince Otto* is a move away from politics toward personal authenticity'—and authenticity Louis found only in friendship. Harvie's is a good corrective to the view of the book 'as an "out-of-character" mistake,' but *Otto* is likely to remain the freak in the show. The true Stevensonian's test, Furnas says, is 'the ability to admire *Otto*.' The test of one who would understand what Stevenson wanted to write is to realise his 'inordinate' ambition for this modern pastoral satire. He worked on it for years; he gave it more labour than any other book, and, save for *The Master* and *Weir*, it was 'closest to his heart'. It may well be that 'last gasp' of his 'sedulous ape' style, but somewhere, Calder tells us, 'Stevenson always hoped, was a Holy Grail that represented a true fusion of art and morality.' The joining of stylist aesthete and lay moralist may explain why in *Otto* he thought he had found it.

Fittingly, in an extraordinary friendship of the Bournemouth years after *Otto*, Louis engaged in his most serious thinking about fiction and wrote his most perfectly executed book. The mysterious interplay of personality, theory, and art can only be guessed at. The exchange with Henry James, his most pluralistic admirer, began in print and extended through many armchair evenings. The two were the 'most conscious novelists of their time in England,' and they 'thought more profoundly about their art, and cared more intensely for it, than any of their contemporaries.'[38] This is not to say that *Kidnapped* (1885–6) was a logical application of the principles in 'A Gossip on Romance' (1882) or 'A Humble Remonstrance' (1884), but it comes closest of his novels.

The theory is paradoxical, like much about Stevenson. The consistency is in its separation of art from life, its deviation from psychological and ethical norms in current fiction. Its basic paradoxes are that the 'neat, finite, self-contained, rational' alternative of romance appeals to the sensual and illogical; the half-shutting of eyes against 'the dazzle and confusion of reality' bathes us in immediate experience.[39] These paradoxes, with the stress on circumstance, incident, and the 'fitness' of place, are definitive—not of what *we* call 'romance', but of what we call adventure. It is no accident that Stevenson's most perfected novel is also his most complete realisation of the idea of adventure, for this was his central idea in life and art. Its centrality has posed a major obstacle to critics. Adventure is misunderstood as a 'genre'. It is ideologically suspect; in Stevenson's time it is associated with late imperialism.[40] The link can be seen in David's complicated feelings as 'civilised' visitor to a 'primitive' culture, his shame at departing from his own cultural code, his shame at the superiority of the 'primitive'. The idea is also aesthetically suspect: moral-seriousness critics think it incapable of mature thematic interest and argue that Stevenson must go beyond 'mere adventure' to be taken seriously. This is to miss the essence of the idea and its profound congeniality to Stevenson. Adventure is an aesthetic approach to experience. Its ethical code is one with its aesthetic: style and form are ethical values. The code centres on the imperatives of friendship, of male bonding as a key to survival.

The bond is between Highlander and Lowlander, but this is not essential. It matters less that the places are Scottish than that they are places of adventure. Every place, from roundhouse to Lettermore and beyond, is where a new happening tests the bond of friendship. This (to use Louis's later terms)[41] is the 'bildende', the 'philosophy'. It is the ultimate pathos, too, for the one place the adventurous bond cannot survive is at home. It belongs to adventure, and adventure happens away from home, from the conventional code. David is forced to live for a time outside of his home code—such is always the case in adventure—but he cannot forget his home, his conventional self, and so he feels that peculiarly social emotion, shame. But he has discovered powers and values more vital and compelling, and once he is 'home' again he is haunted by the memory of that other self, feels homeless, and again feels shame. Thus, the ending of Kidnapped is profoundly fitting in its ambivalence, its irresolution. Adventures end this way. Louis's later desire for closure violated this idea.

This ambivalence is related to another paradox of adventure. Adventure is aboriginally narrative, story, told from memory by the survivor. Nothing (as Louis had written in the 'Hugo' essay) is 'reproduced to our senses directly'; everything has 'been through the crucible of another man's mind'[42] and yet is the more intense for its vicariousness. The style of Kidnapped perfectly embodies this paradox. The secret of its vivid economy—it stays in memory as a texture of scenic impressions—is its memoiristic mode. The vivid and the memorable fuse; the immediate and the dream-like overlap. Place is one with happening and person, and every element is fitting, every impression is unified in mood. David and Alan are two divided moods; I associate them with what Louis saw as the divided moods of that 'Celt', his father.[43] They are brought into a vital but unstable unity. They become friends.

The unity is illusory. In the tale Louis wrote in the same months, the division is illusory. The two books, so different, so central to Stevenson's achievement, belong to a single imaginative impulse and moral concern. Dr Jekyll and Mr Hyde (written 1885) was inspired by a nightmare, and some of its horror spills over inexplicably into David. In both, the painful ambivalence of friendship is central, and in both, the feeling critically examined is shame.

The key to Dr Jekyll is not in his conventional sins, but in what he calls his 'almost morbid sense of shame'—the word echoes through his account.[44] The archetypal act of shame is to hide, and he creates Mr Hyde, but it is not Hyde who hides, it is Jekyll. His instrument of hiding is intended to divide his moral duality into separate beings and thus 'free' both. This fails dreadfully, for Jekyll the scientist has made a dreadful error of judgement. His moral error follows: rather than use his discovery in a 'noble spirit', he uses it simply to hide. But he has failed to create separate identities. What hides behind Hyde is as before, 'the only Henry Jekyll, that incongruous compound'. The 'war among my members' goes on. This—not some 'voluptuary' immorality (Stevenson mocked such a reading)—is Jekyll's evil. Some critics object to the mechanism of the 'powders', but this is irrelevant, for the powders do not work. 'The drug had no discriminating action; it was neither diabolical nor divine'. It was impure; it made no separate identities. The two remain bound, linked, to each other, for Jekyll is the person, while Hyde is only a part. Here is the horror: not to discover that one has an evil part, but that the part has taken over.

Because he is only a part, other characters respond strangely to the 'sight' of Hyde.[45] One of the main motives of the long preparatory narrative is to portray this strange response. No one can describe it other than vaguely, just as no one can visualise his face; the denial of image takes on thematic importance, for all else is vividly imaged. All we see is an abstract 'sneer', for that is all Hyde is. His 'sins' are correspondingly vague, but we know two instances of his evil: colliding with and trampling over the girl; killing Carew and 'trampling his victim under foot'. Both are acts of utter indifference. This is all we know or need to know. It is not a tactic of indeterminacy on Louis's part. It is not Victorian censorship. Hyde is no 'ordinary secret sinner', for Stevenson has no interest in such sins. Hyde is 'inorganic', 'indifferent', unreal in that he is a total denial of the 'bonds of obligation'. This is what Jekyll has sought. When first he 'is' Hyde, he feels a light, youthful sweetness that is the 'solution of the bonds of obligation'. It is an illusion.

The narrative evolves through others who do feel an obligation to Jekyll. They are his friends, care for him, take risks for him; Lanyon dies; Utterson faces great danger. Utterson overcomes his inclination to 'Cain's heresy . . . [to] let my brother go to the devil in his own way'.[46] He keeps 'faith to his dead friend', desires 'the society of his surviving friend'. But friends cannot know Jekyll—this is the tale's suspense—for shame keeps him hidden. The final meaning is embedded perfectly in the final narrative method. Jekyll lives on in his 'full statement'; he can make a full statement as Hyde cannot, for he remains a full person. But it is only in death that shame frees him to reveal himself to his friends. Like *Otto* and *Kidnapped*, *Jekyll and Hyde* is a parable of friendship.

We do not know in what sense his wife Fanny made Louis transform his original 'bogey tale' into a 'moral allegory',[47] but its allegorical thrust has had potent offspring. It has been adopted as the myth of Scottish consciousness, and my reading is not meant to question the adoption. Like *The Master of Ballantrae*, with which it is often compared, the tale is Louis's admonition to a culture obsessed with the myth of separation, with diabolism, with secret sins. Hyde is no more real a devil than James Durie. But *The Master*, while thought about earlier, grows in a different context, and belongs to a time when Louis went through the deepest trauma of his life.

The disaster of the W E Henley friendship stretches through the Saranac period to the sailing of the Casco for the South Seas (1888). The whys and wherefores of the quarrel, and its nasty posthumous aftermath, are matters for biography.[48] What matters here is the profound impact on Louis: he went off to the Pacific deeply depressed, never wanted to see home again, felt it as well that the ship sink, and so on. Nothing in his painful, uncertain life, nothing since his early conflicts with his father, had had such an impact. His sense of life was altered. We can understand only if we realise what friendship had come to mean; in his residual Calvinism, it was the hope of grace. The essay 'Old Mortality' says it best:

> The first step for all is to learn to the dregs our own ignoble fallibility. When we have fallen through storey after storey of our vanity and aspiration, and sit rueful among the ruins, then it is that we begin to measure the stature of our friends: how they stand between us and our own contempt, believing in our best; how, linking us with others, and still spreading wide the influential circle, they weave us in and in with the fabric of contemporary life . . . The powers and the ground of friendship is a mystery.[49]

When, at Saranac, Louis's idol of friendship was dashed, his linkage to self and world was irrevocably changed.

The novel that he laboured at from Saranac in 1887 to its (for him) unsatisfactory end in Honolulu in 1889, belongs to this crisis. In its sense of helpless goodness betrayed, misrepresented, poisoned into obsessive hatred, *The Master* reveals much of his state of mind. *The Master* has emerged as the pivotal text in Stevenson reassessment; there is neither room nor occasion here for adding another full salvo to the battle. I can only identify some major issues, state my own reasoned views based on a careful rereading, and invite the reader to form his own. The reader must also select among critical orientations: mythic with Eigner and Fiedler; generic with Kiely and Mills; psycho-political with Harvie; rhetorical with Douglas Gifford. I find Gifford's general scheme most congenial, but (with apologies) separate it from his brilliant special-pleadings.[50]

The book is not romance, not adventure, though its strange final parts partake superficially of both. It is a tragic psychological novel, and throughout, its centre is Henry Durie, whom only a reader already deluded by brother James's lies or infatuated with the romantic diabolism the book satirises could find 'dull and uninteresting'. The titular 'master' is master only of spite, deceit, and blackmail—or, in the ironic epitaph, of 'the arts and graces'. The book's Scottish duality is the division of aesthetic and moral.

Stevenson subtitles the book *A Winter's Tale*—a tragic satire. It is a tragedy of shame and blackmail. The satire is aimed at those who idolise reputation, fear shame and scandal more than evil, and are therefore primed for blackmail. Henry begins as a strong and kind figure who is maliciously misrepresented not just by his brother, but by his family and community as well. His critical episode is the duel. Once he believes he has killed James, he begins his complex and turbulent descent into evasion, obsession, ultimately madness. His tragic flaw is that he allows himself to be shamed and blackmailed by what he knows to be false. The triumph of evil arises from the failure of goodness to believe in itself; this is Stevenson's moral vision from its inception in *Prince Otto* and its biographical genesis in his sense of his father's morbid religious shame. James, the greedy and indifferent confidence man, becomes a devil only when the good man believes him to be. He is a devil of deceit and false conception, the true Calvinist's conception of the devil as father of lies, deceiver of the mind. Those who glamorise James's diabolism, including some romantic critics, are victims of his ingenious deceits.

If the book's evil of division is grounded in lies and falseness, then the truthfulness of the narrator becomes a central issue, moral and aesthetic. As the duel is critical for Henry's tragedy, so the Nonesuch voyage, one of Louis's greatest episodes, is the crucial test of Mackellar's truthfulness. Gifford pleads for a view of Mackellar as the ironically unreliable, self-satiric, self-righteous and duplicitous monologuist of Scottish satire.[51] On this he bases his view of the book as a crafty duplicity with no definitive value-structure, which sustains contradictory readings: one (for the naive) a conventional providential view; the other, a view of (in Fowler's words) an 'Ur-Existential World of Chance'. The thesis is fascinating; my rereading will not support it.

Mackellar is a reflective, perplexed, and sympathetic MA, with an abiding sense of fairness and a willingness to admit his partialities and the reasons for them. His sympathies swither and he knows it. Who else would include the Chevalier's memoir of James? Who else could either undergo or narrate the deeply disturbing experience alone with James on the Nonesuch? Only here does Mackellar almost give in to the fatalism that has paralysed the family. As the ship pitches wildly and James rides high and low, Mackellar slips into dangerous extremes of vision. James gives him full warning in the story of the Count and the Baron, and Mackellar is almost duped into believing himself a mere slave to customary bias. If we believe James here, we too are duped. This is the truth behind Gifford's claim of two contradictory meanings. Mackellar recovers, and his blunt rejoinder is the reality. At the end, he is deeply caring, honestly troubled, loyal but balanced; he rejects the idol reputation that has deluded the rest including his obsessed master. He views the deaths with tragic choral resignation; he feels sad compassion for all the sons of man. It is Stevenson's final word on the idolatry of reputation and the divisiveness of shame. The division is both aesthetic and moral. As Fiedler says, 'The question about single motivating force in Stevenson's work is a double question really . . . a question of technique and a question of morality.'[52] In Ballantrae, the double question is answered with resounding if incomplete success, perhaps for the last time.

What remained were new starts and old themes revisited. South Sea fictions such as 'The Beach at Falesa' (1892) and The Ebb-Tide (1889, 1893) well deserve the positive reassessment they have received.[53] London friends might disapprove of a new concern with island derelicts, men adrift, but they were far away and friendship had lost its innocence. Louis had become involved with and realistic about the politics of late imperialist adventures, and the results confirm Fowler's claim (and this essay's thesis) that 'the whole adventure form served a revelatory or exploratory purpose, ever disclosing deeper, less suspected and more surprising insights'.[54] To Calder they suggest that Louis might have become 'an explorer of alienation and isolation, an analyst of values, akin to Joseph Conrad'.[55]

But just as interesting are the continuities. The devil of 'Falesa' turns out to be the fraud of the local confidence-man, and he is killed by the hero in a weird violence of child's play. This is Stevensonian and Scottish in a folkloric way: the dousing of devil-worship with mockery; the tragic-satiric theme of *Ballantrae* in miniature. Herrick, the hero-derelict of *Ebb-Tide*, is a variation of Henry Durie, the good man crippled by self-distrust. The powerful menace to which he submits himself in despair and then withdraws from in a final clutch of autonomy, is an extraordinary creation, more interesting than James Durie. Attwater embodies a complex moment in cultural history and a fusing of all that Stevenson was drawn to and repelled by: the spiritual tyrant, the rigid calvinist, the selfish sybaritic aesthete, all subsumed under the colonialist racist despot. Herrick finally realises the problem of conceiving him adequately in order to resist him. It is Stevenson's problem and the reader's. It will be the problem of David with Prestongrange and Lovat. Indeed, the interesting final phenomenon of Louis's imaginative history was the way such new fictions led him back to Scotland. The return had begun with late essays and *Ballantrae*. But it required, as Calder says, the 'break-through' of stories like *Ebb-Tide* and 'Falesa' to end 'entrapment' in 'Scotland's past'.[56] And so it is revealing to read *Catriona* (better called *David Balfour*) as following those stories directly.

Catriona comes at a moment in Louis's life when he is responding directly to Polynesian reality. Reality wins out over texture and image; structure ('philosophy, destiny, *bildende*') over episode. Recall his recent dissatisfaction with *The Master*'s structure. A new structuralism came with the discovery of *realpolitik*, a critical distance from Scotland, the nostalgia of permanent exile. The novel is highly structured. David has two moral dilemmas to deal with; like Henry Durie, he is trapped in false positions, and the falseness is of principle and of appearance. Each dilemma mixes falseness with innocence; each links an exploitative father with an innocent daughter. Each expresses a frankly dual moral vision: political corruption and innocent friendship. There is nothing David can do to resolve the political dilemma; the 'course of events' will roll on and destroy innocents, like Hyde trampling his victims. He can only withdraw to a private role where he will protect innocence and be loyal to friendship. Readers seeking erotics are turned off by the brief brother-sister episodes in Holland. But the urgent concern of both lovers with friendship is no evasion, but a fundamental Stevenson issue: can one be a true friend in a corrupt world of appearances?

Paradoxically, the post-Henley preoccupation with appearances requires what Henry James complained of: the starving of the visual imagination.[57] No longer a visual texture, appearance has become a moral problem. While every episode is carefully localised, its appearance has little importance compared with its moral and political significance. David's ride from Clack-mannan to Inveraray is realised only in time, and Inveraray serves only as a setting for the meeting of defence lawers, who seek to exploit his appearance as a witness. The novel's texture is dialogic; David is placed in situations where he plays the skilful debater. He is less the observer of *Kidnapped*, more the moral and intellectual protagonist. His adventure is now moral, and visual texture would be a distraction.

The change in adventure shows in Louis's long, frustrating work on *St Ives* (1893–4). The fragment is his longest book, and he struggled with it for over a year, resented it, but was convinced at life's end that he could make something of it. The Stevensonian must decide of this rich gallimaufry whether (1) it is the same kind as *Kidnapped* but Louis no longer liked the kind, or (2) he could no longer do it, or (3) it is a new kind he couldn't yet understand. I suspect the third. *David Balfour* splits off from *Kidnapped* in one direction; *St Ives* in another. In James More and Simon Grant we have had Stevenson's new sense of adventurer in the imperialist context; St Ives is the adventurer telling his own story, a discontinuous character changing personae with place and attire. David has shown the 'singular aptitude for getting into false positions' of Louis's heroes; it is hard to say what is true or false about St Ives. David is ashamed of borrowed clothes; St Ives is all borrowed clothes. His delight is in disguise and impersonation. The potential is for a *Felix Krull* before its modernist time. Not surprisingly, Louis wasn't prepared for the moral or aesthetic implications; the once 'sedulous ape' is uneasy with his most impersonative hero, the histrionic writer with his best actor, the Francophile with his Frenchman. So, intermittently he imbues St Ives with the moral consciousness of David, anxious about his masks and ploys, disturbed by adventurism. Louis now wanted moral coherence—'philosophy, destiny, *bildende*,' a continuous character.

Likewise, *St Ives* is his novel of greatest particularity and amplification. Selection, simplification, compression had been his stylistic norms; no 'large, loose, baggy monsters' for him. But in the final novels he was working for amplification. Those who think his form was tale or novella may say he was doomed to failure. *St Ives* cannot prove this, nor can the fragmentary *Weir of Hermiston*, but both testify to the magnitude of the struggle.

Renaissance critics a generation or two ago found in *Weir* (1893–4) Stevenson's final breakthrough to tragic Scottish realism.[58] Their heirs are more cautious. Calder can now suggest that '*Weir of Hermiston* is perhaps a red herring, best left out of the final assessment, certainly if it is only to be used to indicate what Stevenson *might* have done.'[59] Gifford courageously argues *Weir*'s decline from splendid beginnings to the incipient 'Kailyard' of the church scene and the lovers' tryst.[60] What can be added? The marvellous language and characterology of early parts have been detailed often. The shortcomings of later parts needn't be belaboured. Speculation on what Louis might have done, while inevitable, is speculation. More useful might be some attempt to understand why he had such trouble with a book to which he was so attached.

The mother is a masterpiece of ironic pathos, seen chorally as a prisoner of her own heredity and weakness. The father is a force of brutal grandeur whose nature simply excludes some human elements. No judgement is allowed. Indeed, just as judgement is the story's moral crux, so too it is the formative problem of its technique. When Archie asks Glenalmond for judgement, the reply is also the narrator's: 'I decline jurisdiction.'[61] Uncertainty of form and perspective enters with Archie's abrupt surrender and retirement to country lairdship. For a while, the sheer stylistic force of old Kirstie sustains us. But her powerful legend of the four brothers gives way, as Gifford complains, to the artifice of social types.[62] Archie, the divided, tormented rebel, fades into an onlooker, then a Wertherian swain. The lovers' meetings are rendered in an uneasy sentimentality. The narrative voice has become so different that Simpson can plausibly argue it is not the author's.[63] This voice, rather than the putative 'Kailyard' mode, seems the key to the book's diminishing. *This* reader is balked not by the idyllic, but by the fatalistic. The narrator's talk of Fate (like Hardy's and Conrad's is forced and repetitive. 'Fate played his game artfully . . . The generations were prepared, the pangs were made ready, before the curtain rose on this dark drama.' And romantic Archie is too fanciful and elegaic to be convincing in his 'sense of the tragedy of life.'[64]

However 'acute and unbroken' was the Stevensons' tragic sense, Louis was always distractedly ill at ease with tragic fatality. Plot and place have become traps for both Archie and his author. Perhaps Louis had been too long and too far away from Scotland to imagine another escape. Yet, there is no reason why—as he wrote Barrie[65]—Archie should not escape this place, this doom, no reasson save in modal and philosophical assumption. A sadder, more fitting end would be for Archie to flee and survive as a fugitive, homeless and longing for home, the perpetual exile like Louis himself, the Lord Jim figure. Such an end would be open, picaresque, haunting, as is the end of *Ebb-Tide*, or the end of *Kidnapped*. But this was the alternative of adventure, and Louis had lost faith in it, as his feelings about *St Ives* show. He now felt a strong imaginative need for closure, and closure demanded unacceptable options: a specious salvation or an exaggerated fatality. Catastrophe too can be melodramatic—as sometimes in Hardy, as in Brown and Hay—if the fatality is forced. A writer committed to the idea of adventure is committed to Chance as governor of events, and Chance as William James has explained, is anti-fatalistic.[66] But Louis had lost faith in adventure.

Adventure is by nature episodic, open, discontinuous—its element picaresque. It tends always toward ambiguous survival and is hostile to closure. Adventure is not merely a late imperialist ideology, though it was exploited by that ideology, and though his new awareness of that exploitation may have poisoned Louis's adventurism as it would T E Lawrence's. Adventure is not simply a form of evasion, a juvenile fad, but a universal form of experience and narrative. It is not something 'simple' to be transcended into mature seriousness, the assumption that underlies and distorts the long-lived Evasive Child school of Stevenson criticism. The sad fact is that Louis came to anticipate their biases, and then he wrote in a trap. The happy fact for Scottish literary history is that he sometimes did not, and then he felt free to live and write for his idea.

NOTES AND FURTHER READING

1 *Robert Louis Stevenson: A Life Study.* (Hereinafter, 'Calder, *LS*.') (New York, 1980), p 48. For the essay, *see The Works of Robert Louis Stevenson*, South

Seas Edition (New York, 1925), vol XIII. I cite this edition throughout unless otherwise indicated.

2   David Daiches, *Robert Louis Stevenson and His World* (London, 1973), p 16.

3   My idea of adventure is based on the following: Georg Simmel, 'The Adventurer', trans D Kettler, in *On Individuality and Social Forms* (Chicago, 1971); Paul Zweig, *The Adventurer* (New York, 1979); Walker Percy, *The Message in the Bottle* (New York, 1975); Jacques Riviere, 'The Adventure Novel', in *The Ideal Reader*, trans B A Price (New York, 1960); J -P Sartre, *La Nausee*; Hannah Arendt, *Origins of Totalitarianism* (New York, 1958); Martin Green, *Dreams of Adventure, Deeds of Empire* (New York, 1979). *See* my essay, 'Scott and the Idea of Adventure', in *Sir Walter Scott*, A Bold (ed) (London, 1983).

4   *Henry James and Robert Louis Stevenson*, J A Smith (ed) (London, 1948).

5   Andrew Noble, in *Robert Louis Stevenson*, Noble (ed) (London, 1983), pp 171–2.

6   Alistair Fowler, 'Parables of Adventure', in *Nineteenth-Century Scottish Fiction*, Ian Campbell (ed) (Manchester, 1979).

7   Quoted in Edwin M Eigner, *Robert Louis Stevenson and Romantic Tradition* (Princeton, 1966), p 96n.

8   'Fontainebleau', in *Works*, XIII, 252.

9   Quoted in James Pope Hennessy, *Robert Louis Stevenson* (New York, 1974), p 96.

10   Calder, *LS*, p 186. Archer quote in Calder, p 214; tragedy quote in J C Furnas, *Voyage to Windward* (New York, 1951), p 231.

11   *James and Stevenson*, Smith (ed), p 126.

12   *Works*, I, 149.

13   John Gross, *The Rise and Fall of the Man of Letters* (New York, 1969), especially Chapter Five.

14   Travis R Merritt, 'Taste, Opinion, and Theory in the Rise of Victorian Prose Stylism', in *The Art of Victorian Prose*, G Levine and W Madden (eds) (New York, 1968), pp 23–7.

15   John Holloway, *The Victorian Sage* (New York, 1953).

16   *Works*, II, 3. 'Crabbed Youth and Age', pp 50–1; 'Ordered South', p 81.

17   Richard Sennett, *The Fall of Public Man* (New York, 1977), especially Chapters Three and Eight.

18   Calder (*LS*, p 79) argues that there is a deliberate distancing of self from experience, and a gradual development of personality.

19   Noble, pp 14, 179.

20   Robert Louis Stevenson, *From Scotland to Silverado*, J D Hart (ed) (Cambridge, 1966), p xxxviii, quoting Richard Aldington.

21   Robert Kiely, *Robert Louis Stevenson and the Fiction of Adventure* (Cambridge, 1965), p 120. Even though I differ, I have learned much from this pioneering study.

22   Honor Mulholland, 'Robert Louis Stevenson and the Romance Form', in Noble. Cf. Calder, *LS*, p 165.

23   Quoted from a letter to Henley, by Mulholland, p 106.

24   *See* the sensitive reading by Kenneth Graham in Noble, pp 38–44.

25   *Works*, XII, 179, 195.

26   *Works*, XII, 123.

27   Fowler, pp 108, 111.

28   Calder, *LS*, pp 167–8.

29   *Novels and Tales of Robert Louis Stevenson* (New York, 1900), II, 233.

30   Fernando Savater, *Childhood Regained: The Art of the Storyteller*, trans F M

Lopez-Morillos (New York, 1982). Chapter Two is on 'the purest piece of storytelling I know'.

31   Quoted by Fowler, p 108.
32   Quoted by Pope Hennessy, p 171, re: bringing up Lloyd Osbourne.
33   *Works*, XVII, 85, 244–5.
34   Quoted by Eigner, p 62.
35   Ibid.
36   *Works*, VII, 199–203.
37   Eigner, pp 53–9; Christopher Harvie, 'The Politics of Stevenson', in Calder (ed), *Stevenson and Victorian Scotland* (Edinburgh, 1981), pp 116–18; Furnas, p 217; *Works*, VII, xv; Calder, *LS*, p 186.
38   Smith, in *James and Stevenson*, p 24.
39   ·*Works*, XIII, 150–1, 133–4.
40   Cf. Arendt and Green (note 3 above).
41   Letter to Colvin re: *St Ives*, *Works*, XXV, 2.
42   *Works*, V, 22.
43   *Works*, XIII, 76–7.
44   *Dr Jekyll and Mr Hyde and Other Stories*, Calder (ed) (Harmondsworth, 1979), pp 81, 85.
45   Ibid., pp 96, 77. See Andrew Jefford, 'Dr Jekyll and Professor Nabokov', in Noble, pp 47–66.
46   *Dr Jekyll and Mr Hyde*, pp 29, 59.
47   Pope Hennessy, p 207.
48   Furnas, pp 281–99; Daiches, pp 77–80; Calder, *LS*, pp 237–42; *Stevenson's Letters to Charles Baxter*, D Ferguson and M Waingrow (eds) (New Haven, 1956), pp 182–235.
49   *Works*, XIII, 29–30 (published May, 1884).
50   Eigner, pp 171–94; Leslie Fiedler, 'The Master of Ballantrae', repr in *Victorian Literature*, A Wright (ed) (New York, 1961), pp 284–94; Kiely, pp 197–229; Carol Mills, '*The Master of Ballantrae*: An Experiment with Genre', in Noble, pp 118–33; Harvie, in Calder (ed), *Victorian Scotland*, p 119; Douglas Gifford, 'Stevenson and Scottish Fiction', in Calder (ed), *Victorian Scotland*, especially pp 73–85. (My kind editor is accustomed to our friendly disagreements.)
51   Gifford, pp 73–80.
52   Fiedler, p 285.
53   ·*See* Calder intro to *Jekyll and Hyde and Other Stories*, pp 115–26; Fowler, pp 115–26; for the other side, *see* the significantly titled 'Robert Louis Stevenson: Forms of Evasion', by Peter Gilmour, in Noble, pp 188–201.
54   Fowler, p 121.
55   Calder, *LS*, p 316.
56   Calder, intro to *Jekyll and Hyde*, p 19.
57   James and Stevenson, p 239.
58   *See*, e.g., Kurt Wittig, *The Scottish Tradition in Literature* (Edinburgh, 1958), p 262: 'Achievement came to Stevenson only in *Weir of Hermiston*'; S G Smith, *A Short Introduction to Scottish Literature* (Edinburgh, 1951), p 25; Foreword by Hugh MacDiarmid to S G Smith's *Carotid Cornucopius* (Edinburgh, 1964), p 14.
59   Calder, *LS*, p 316.
60   Having disputed Gifford on *The Master*, I express admiration for his candor and sense on *Weir*!
61   *Works*, XXVIII, 47.
62   Gifford, in Calder (ed), *Victorian Scotland*.
63   K G Simpson, 'Author and Narrator in *Weir of Hermiston*', in Noble, pp 202–27.

64 *Works*, XXVIII, 106, 105.
65 *Works*, XXVIII, 149.
66 'The Dilemma of Determinism', in *Writings*, J J McDermott (ed) (New York, 1967).

Chapter 16

The Kailyard

GILLIAN SHEPHERD

The classification of a genre or school of any type or art, visual, musical, or literary, usually relates to a recognisable medium or attitude common to all of its practitioners. In the case of the Kailyard School of Scottish fiction, the description originates in the prefatory couplet of one collection of anecdotes by one of the writers identified with the school. Ian Maclaren (the pseudonym of John Watson) chose for a motto for his first novel, *Beside the Bonnie Brier Bush* (1894), two lines from Burns:

> There grows a bonnie brier bush in our kail-yard,
> And white are the blossoms on't in our kail-yard.[1]

It was one of the school's earliest critics, J H Millar, who first attached the epithet to it in a caustic article in W E Henley's *New Review* in 1895, although Millar later gave credit for the tag to Henley himself.[2] A later, equally caustic critic, George Blake, analysed the aptness of the term:

> It is an interesting fact that the literatures of domesticity and rustic humour in the States and in Scotland, relatively primitive communities, are classified according to the same symbol. For a kailyard is a cabbage-patch, even if the kail, or kale, of Scotland are the curly greens of England, the humblest of domestic vegetables. The term suggests immediately the rural cottage and its modest kitchen garden, a sort of inner shrine of decent living in pious poverty; it admirably suggests the limited range of this school of fiction.[3]

Blake's brief analysis itself admirably suggests the essential elements— domesticity, rusticity, humour, humility, modesty, decency, piety, and poverty—which characterised some of the works of the three Victorian writers who came to be synonymous with the Kailyard: Ian Maclaren (1850–1907), S R Crockett (1860–1914), and J M Barrie (1860–1937).

It may be argued that the novels themselves—more accurately described as collections of anecdotes—are slight enough, and similar enough, to merit little close critical attention, although some critics have discovered in them evidence of literary craft and narrative skill. It is noteworthy that some of the Kailyard's most thoughtful admirers are those of today, some of them going so far as to call up in favourable comparison Hardy, Ibsen and D H Lawrence.

What is most interesting about the Kailyard novels is not their content *per se* but their continuing impact. For almost a century the handful of novels known collectively as the Kailyard School of Scottish fiction have attracted opprobrium, opposition, and charges of opportunism. What is most curious about the sustained criticism they have endured is the mere fact of its existence. Why should a dozen books or so written by three Scotsmen in a single distant decade[4] continue to attract critical attention and arouse at one extreme contempt and at the other whole-hearted admiration? These extremes are not a reflection of changes in taste or fashion from Victorian sentiment to late twentieth-century stringency. Contrast an early comment on Crockett's *The Lilac Sunbonnet* (written half way through the Kailyard decade) with a more recent judgement. J H Millar described it in 1895 as ' . . . an irresistible flood of nauseous and nasty philandering . . . a perpetual flow of bad breeding . . . a slough of knowing archness, of bottomless vulgarity';[5] while Islay Murray Donaldson, in 1985, praised it as ' . . . no pastoral idyll but a real unidealised rural society where men are rough and wash in tin basins by the stable door and women knit stockings and speak their mind forcibly', a society evoked, for her, by a technique equal to that of D H Lawrence.[6]

In her unqualified approval Murray Donaldson is, so far at least, outnumbered by critics who have found little good to say of the Kailyard over the last hundred years. Much of the onslaught makes entertaining reading in the late twentieth century, distanced by years and possibly by the tolerance born of understanding. 'Slop' and 'sludge' are among the epithets applied to the Kailyard; but many novels before and after could have been so described and have not survived to merit even passing mention in literary histories. What keeps these novels controversial?

Two factors—or perhaps two facets of the same factor—appear to distinguish the Kailyard novels from other inherently unmemorable works of fiction: their extraordinary commercial success and their apparent irrelevance to the community from which they came. Before looking at the reasons for these factors, more precise definition of the Kailyard itself is necessary.

First, not all writers of Scottish fiction during the late nineteenth and early twentieth century were of the Kailyard School. Robert Louis Stevenson, George MacDonald, William Alexander, George Douglas Brown, 'Fiona Macleod' (William Sharp), Margaret Oliphant, the Findlater sisters, Sarah Tytler (Henrietta Keddie), John MacDougall Hay, Frederick Niven, and many others (not to mention the host of fiction writers in the Scottish popular press) belonged to no school but reflected a range of literary skills and a diversity of Scottishness which—at least in the case of the first three or four— have stood the test of time on both counts rather better than those of the Kailyard writers.

Second, not all of the work of these three Kailyarders was written to the Kailyard 'formula', which required an omniscient narrator, an episodic format, a rural setting, an imprecise chronology, a Free Church minister and/or a lonely schoolmaster, both frequently 'stickit' or failed and one or other usually assuming the narrator's role. Children usually represented original sin or original innocence, and in the latter case frequently died young;

and women tended to be either fey, strange, glamorous young women or fey, strange, blind but far-seeing old women. Thomas Knowles, author of what is probably the most exhaustive critique of the Kailyard School, *Ideology, Art and Commerce: Aspects of Literary Sociology in the Late Victorian Scottish Kailyard* (1983), describes it thus:

> In its 'classic' form, the Kailyard is characterized by the sentimental and nostalgic treatment of parochial Scottish scenes, often centred on the church community, often on individual careers which move from childhood innocence to urban awakening (and contamination), and back again to the comfort and security of the native hearth. Typically thematic is the 'lad o' pairts', the poor Scottish boy making good within the 'democratic' Scottish system of education, and dying young as a graduated minister in his mother's arms with the assembled parish looking on. The parishioners themselves, their dialect sometimes translated for an English audience, sprinkle their exchanges with native wit, and slip easily from the pettiness of village gossip to the profundities of rustic philosophizing.[7]

Knowles, though, goes on to suggest that such a uniform description fails to do justice to the heterogeneity of Kailyard fiction, citing Barrie's and Crockett's 'Street Arab' stories; but these are not, by strict definition, Kailyard novels despite being the work of the definitive Kailyard authors.

What ultimately characterises a Kailyard novel goes further than the superficial analyses above or the formulae which dictated its contents, to a holistic situation involving both novel and the personal characteristics of the men who wrote them, for profit, for a particular market; and it extends to the social, religious, and economic characteristics of that market. For while the Kailyard novels may have been written by Barrie, Crockett, and Maclaren, it is not far-fetched to claim that they were in a sense dictated by their readers. They are the product not only of three individuals but also of an era.

The Kailyard School has been attacked on grounds of both bad art and bad patriotism. Despite the claims of such critics as William Power, who described all three writers as 'first-rate literary craftsmen',[8] it is hard to find much literary merit in their work other than a superficial fluency of narrative and an abundance of evocative imagery: there is no doubt that they were competent wordsmiths. There is also an arch but dry humour whose power to amuse will vary with the disposition, and possibly nationality, of the reader. Apart from these attributes, however, the novels are notable for negative qualities. There is neither delineation nor development of character; the dimensions of time and location are left flat, featureless, and vague; the social mores that are portrayed are isolated from cause and effect, except when they are manipulated to make an authorial point. They are the equivalent in photographic terms of an album of miscellaneous snapshots compared to a full-length feature film.

Nor is there any linguistic consistency in the Kailyard novels, rather a mixture of non-accented narrative containing quoted vernacular in either parentheses or glosses and of unwieldy phonetic transcriptions of dialect speech and correspondence. The latter in particular produces some awkward passages, typified by the following extract from *Beside the Bonnie Brier Bush*:

> My dear lassie
> Ye ken that I wes aye yir freend, and I am writing this tae say that yir father luves ye mair than ever, and is wearing oot his hert for the sicht o' yir face. Come back, or he'll dee thro' want o' his bairn. The glen is bright and bonny noo, for the purple heather is on the hills, and doon below the gowden corn, wi' bluebell and poppy flowers between. Naebody 'ill ask ye where ye've been, or onything else; there's no a bairn in the place that's no wearying tae see ye; and, Flora, lassie, if there will be sic gledness in oor wee glen when ye come hame, what think ye o' the joy in the Father's Hoose?[9]

Here Maclaren, sacrificing plausibility to plangency, ignores the probability that such a letter, had it been written by a Scots peasant, would have been written in standard English and not in spoken (synthetic) Scots; he infuses his poetic periods with strong pastoral (in both senses) images, culminating in an explicit biblical echo which establishes the anecdote as a parable in Scots.

This, in essence, is what the Kailyard stories are on one level: parables—brief, vivid tales designed to make a universally comprehensible, morally improving point—or fairy tales, which, for children, are the same thing. Consider the opening words of Barrie's *The Little Minister*: 'Long ago, in the days when our caged black-birds never saw a king's soldier without whistling . . .'[10] The rhythms are unmistakably those of the fairy or folk tale, and herein lies the second reason for critical animosity towards the Kailyard writers: they wrote about their chosen Scottish scenes not as if they were true but as if they were fable; and they wrote not for their fellow Scots but for other markets to whom the Scots voice was literally foreign, requiring translation. There was, of course, no intrinsic betrayal in the writing of fairy tales; George MacDonald was doing so in a manner beyond reproach. What stuck in the craws of the contemporary as well as later critics was that the Kailyarders presented their characters and settings as real, but contrived a distorted, perverted, negative reality which bore little resemblance to the Scotland of the late nineteenth century.

In the Kailyard Eden the only serpents were the implicit threat of distant, urban squalor, poverty, riot and unrest, industrialisation and secularisation. In Thrums and Drumtochty, squalor was illusory and poverty ennobling: 'It had been the ordinary dwelling room of the unknown poor, the mean "little end"—ah, no, no, the noblest chamber in the annals of the Scottish nation!'[11] The slums of Victorian Glasgow and Dundee bore far from silent testimony to the ignoble meanness of the little end, but Barrie rose above it. And not only Barrie; in George Blake's bitter words:

> The bulk of the Scottish people were . . . condemned to a purely urban, sophisticated, and mainly ugly sort of life during the nineteenth century. A really dramatic, often beastly, revolution was taking place. And what had the Scottish novelists to say about it? The answer is—nothing, or as nearly nothing

as makes no matter. They might as well have been living in Illyria as the agonized country of their birth![12]

Blake goes on to argue that these errors of omission and commission suggest a sort of 'national infantilism'. But this diagnosis suggests in turn that the Kailyard writers did not know what they were doing, whereas the circumstantial evidence makes it likely that they knew only too well.

The obvious parallels in their own circumstances argue for the existence of a common philosophy. Barrie, Maclaren, and Crockett were all born in the same decade (1850–60) and published the bulk of the kailyard canon in another ten-year span (1888–98); all had rural backgrounds; all were graduates of Edinburgh University; all subscribed to a greater or lesser degree to the doctrines of the Free Church of Scotland; all were uncommonly prolific in their writing and phenomenally successful at home and abroad; all came into fiction writing via journalism and flourished under the aegis of William Robertson Nicoll, himself a Free Church minister whose background was remarkably similar to theirs and who in his heyday was editor of *The British Weekly* and literary adviser to Hodder & Stoughton (publishers of both Barrie and Maclaren).

Nicoll's advice to journalists was to the point:

> Count the number of your words, and adapt them to the usual requirements of the periodical. See that your subject is in line with the subjects in the paper. Above all things, be sure that what the editor prints is what the editor likes, that originality, unless of a very compelling nature, is not required, and that there is a fashion in journalism as well as in other things.[13]

These injunctions demanded writing to order, not to express but to impress. The readers of *The British Weekly* who were to be impressed were '. . . the vast number of educated Nonconformists in Scotland and England who take no Christian paper, and despise the Nonconformist religious papers for their want of culture . . .'[14]

The Kailyarders were therefore writing in the main for people like themselves. They were not writing for the lower-class market, whose needs were served by the popular press.[15]

Knowles suggests in his sociological study[16] that an increased emphasis on education following the implementation of the Education Acts in 1870 and 1872, coupled with technical advances in printing and improved delivery by rail, stimulated discussion on methods of refining literary taste and especially of refining working-class literary taste. Knowles makes a case for an anxious awareness of the general need for 'recommendable reading', in a context not dissimilar to present-day concern about home videos.

Barrie's own view was unequivocal:

> The professional realists of these times, who wear a giant's robe and stumble in it [the reference is to Hardy], see only the seamy side of life, reproducing it with merciless detail, holding the mirror up to the unnatural instead of to nature, and photographing by the light of a policeman's lantern. The difference

> between them and the man whose name they borrow is that they only see the
> crack in the cup, while he sees the cup with the crack in it.[17]

Maclaren too was 'perfectly aware that people swear and do other things
which are worse, but without being Pharisees [he objected] to books which
swear on every page and do the other things on the page between being our
companions for the hour when the light is lit and the streets are quiet'.[18]

From this position, then, the Kailyarders wrote to restore the balance; but,
almost inevitably, the reaction became reactionary, and refusal to reflect only
the seamy side became refusal to reflect it at all.

The Kailyarders created for their comfort a world of romantic illusion, a
cottage Garden of Eden. William Power seems to suggest that the regression
was born of despair at prevailing social conditions:

> The fact of the matter is that social conditions in industrial Scotland at that
> time were somewhat beyond the scope of idealism. It was better to help to keep
> alive the native faith and virtues and idyllic memories of the people than
> to remind them of the scorching fires of Moloch through which they were
> passing.[19]

This view ignores the fact that those who were passing through the fires were
not those who had idyllic folk-memories. The myth of an earlier time of pre-
lapsarian innocence and uncontaminated goodness was the creation not of
peasants, weavers, or even village school-masters but of the ruling class whose
personal remoteness from poverty combined with ideological remoteness
from responsibility for social reform to produce an attitude that was, in many
respects, colonial. The natives, in other words, liked to live as noble savages
in mean little ends and would be as ill-equipped to cope with the benefits of
an advanced civilisation as they would be to withstand its disadvantages.
America might have been lost as a colony but the Scots remained (and indeed
through the Kailyard were to become objects of bemused contemplation by
the Americans).

The untrammelled innocence of the Scots peasant was, perhaps, perceived
by the Kailyard novelists as redemptive. Ian Maclaren's tale, 'Domsie', from
Beside the Bonnie Brier Bush, contains an illuminating passage:

> The six elders—three small farmers, a tailor, a stonemason, and a shepherd—
> were standing beneath the lamp, and the light fell like a halo on their bent
> heads. That poor little vestry had disappeared, and this present world was
> forgotten. The sons of God had come into their heritage, 'for the things which
> are seen are temporal, but the things which are not seen are spiritual'.[20]

Such a vision is consistent with the theological doctrines of the Free Church
after the Disruption of 1843, which as Alan Bold suggests[21] stood for presbyterian fundamentalism and the rejection of state interference. High priest
of these doctrines was Thomas Chalmers, who believed devoutly that the
salvation of Scotland was to be found not just in the preservation of rural
values but in their re-introduction to the towns.[22] He compared the urban,

working-class Scot unfavourably with a mythological peasant, in whose obedience, humility, and willingness to be directed was found the cement of society.

Chalmers too was indulging in fantasy and illusion. Nonchurchgoing in the 1880s and 1890s was a growing rural phenomenon and was not countered or replaced as it was in towns by the zeal of other agencies, particularly the labour movement. The influence of church and state—embodied in minister and dominie—was waning; the increase in numbers of textile workers and weavers and the accompanying decline in numbers of agricultural workers focused rural discontent on changing conditions. The small towns and villages of Scotland were microcosms of dissent, manifested in riots, social division and secularisation.

The churches could do, or did, little to counter the unrest. Most of the radical changes of the late nineteenth century—the Crofters Act of 1886, the medical inspection of children, council housing, municipally owned utilities, old age pensions—were promoted by the labour movement.

These manifestations of positive change were equally ignored by the Kail-yarders. Their preferred solution to social division was the same as that of Chalmers—a benevolent, church-led paternalism. The symbol of this paternalism was the omnipresent, omniscient, male narrator—the minister or school-master who existed apart—metaphorically and often physically—from his flock and who observed their comings and goings and shortcomings with confidence in ultimate redemption here or hereafter.

The kailyard writers might have salvaged from this approach some integrity as national representatives had their aim been solely to reflect, if not reconcile, division in society. David Daiches sees this aim as fundamental, for instance, to Scott's greatness:

> Scott's problem was the problem of every Scottish writer after Scotland ceased to have an independent culture of her own: how to reconcile his country's traditions with what appeared to be its interest . . . This conflict within Scott gave life and passion to his Scottish novels, for it led him to construct plots and invent characters which, far from being devices in an adventure story or means to make history look picturesque, illustrated to him what was the central paradox of modern life.[23]

Scott was not diverted from his pursuit of resolution by his need to be commercially successful. Ironically, it seems likely that it was commercialism that perverted any sense of moral purpose that the Kailyarders might have had. The immediate and startling success of their rustic stories with the English and American markets must have convinced them, encouraged by Robertson Nicoll, that they had hit upon a formula which bore repeated testing. This adherence to and dependence on a formula of proven success insulated them against any external influences which might have caused them to revise their ideas; and it increased the distance between observers and observed. The result was that Barrie, Crockett, and Maclaren ceased to write as Scots within a Scottish nation, despite their recurrent device of narrator.

Instead they wrote with increasing detachment and cruelty and decreasing plausibility. The common voice used a reductive idiom which was patronising rather than paternal. Its manifestations included bathos, mockery, sadism, and downright falsity, as may be easily demonstrated from one text, Barrie's *Auld Licht Idylls*. Four brief quotations will suffice.

> The friendliest thing I have seen today is the well-smoked ham suspended from my kitchen rafters.[24]

> The only really tender thing I ever heard an Auld Licht lover say to his sweetheart was when Gowrie's brother looked softly into Easie Tamson's eyes and whispered, 'Do you swite (sweat)?' Even then the effect was produced more by the loving cast in Gowrie's eye than by the tenderness of the words themselves.[25]

> In one week three of the children died, and on the Sabbath following it rained. Mr Dishart preached, twice breaking down altogether and gaping strangely round the Kirk (there was no dust flying that day), and spoke of the rain as angels' tears for three little girls. The Auld Lichts let it pass, but, as Lang Tammas said in private (for, of course, the thing was much discussed at the looms), if you materialise angels in that way, where are you going to stop?[26]

> Tammy, who died a bachelor, had been soured in his youth by a disappointment in love, of which he spoke but seldom. She lived far away in a town to which he had wandered in the days when his blood ran hot, and they became engaged. Unfortunately, however, Tammy forgot her name, and he did not know her address; so there the affair ended, to his silent grief.[27]

The tone is unpleasant; the situations are unlikely; the effect is not one of mythic regeneration in country simplicity hoped for by the fundamentalists but one of mythic degeneration. Barrie and his peers dismantled their characters in stereotypical characteristics and having held them up to ridicule failed to restore them to wholeness; and thereby they sacrificed their own integrity.

There was little substance to their retailing of the rural way of life, despite their shared personal experience of it. Small, trivial details of everyday life were magnified beyond reasonable proportions and distorted for easy effect, and the tone of lighthearted amusement was often spiced with malice and condescension. Maclaren's *Beyond the Bonnie Brier Bush* is full of examples:

> It was good manners in Drumtochty to feign amazement at the sight of a letter, and to insist that it must be intended for some other person. When it was finally forced upon one, you examined the handwriting at various angles and speculated about the writer. Some felt emboldened, after these precautions, to open the letter, but this haste was considered indecent . . . Ordinary letters were read in leisurely retirement, and, in the case of urgency, answered within the week.[28]

And Barrie, too, employed caricature rather than characterisation:

> At first, it appears, they limited their comments to 'losh, losh,' 'keeps a','

'it cows,' 'ma certie,' 'ay, ay,' 'sal, tal,' 'dagont' (the meaning of which is obvious).[29]

The culture represented here is far from organic; it is synthetic—manufactured and mass-produced. The idyllic village is home only to the village idiot, capering to his creator's tune.

The divided self is a recurrent theme in Scottish literature, and many writers and critics have attempted to explain the Scots obsession with internal and social division; Gregory Smith's 'Caledonian antisyzygy', Edwin Muir's 'dissociation of sensibility' and David Craig's 'swithering of modes', all go some way to make sense of the complexities of a national character which is in many respects contradictory. Willa Muir made her contribution by inventing Mrs MacGrundy, who 'officially took over the control of Scottish passion, throwing Scottish intelligence behind her'. Willa Muir saw her creation as a 'negative thwarted perversion of what might have been . . . a national consciousness'.[30]

Perhaps her male counterparts were the Kailyard novelists. For one brief but crucial span of Scottish history they, in their own small way, sought to thwart a national consciousness that might have been, and to divert attention from the appalling problems of an emerging and maturing industrial nation. It was not national infantilism; it was attempted national infanticide.

NOTES

1   I Maclaren, *Beside the Bonnie Brier Bush* (London, 1895).
2   J H Millar, 'The literature of the Kailyard' in *New Review*, vol 12, Jan–June 1895, pp 384–94.
3   J H Millar, *A Literary History of Scotland* (London, 1903).
4   The Kailyard works which conform most closely to the criteria identified in this essay are as follows: Barrie's *Auld Licht Idylls* (1888), *A Window in Thrums* (1889), *The Little Minister* (1891), *Sentimental Tommy* (1896), *Margaret Ogilvy* (1896); Crockett's *The Stickit Minister* (1893), *The Lilac Sunbonnet* (1894); Maclaren's *Beside the Bonnie Brier Bush* (1894), *The Days of Auld Lang Syne* (1895), *Kate Carnegie and Those Ministers* (1896), *Afterwards and Other Stories* (1898). The other works of these prolific writers escape the genre, it is argued, by virtue of some manifestation of individuality which allows them to stand on their own.
5   Millar, 'The Literature of the Kailyard'.
6   Islay Murray Donaldson, 'S R Crockett and the fabric of *The Lilac Sunbonnet*' in *Studies in Scottish Fiction: Nineteenth Century*, Horst W Drescher and Joachim Schwend (eds) (Frankfurt, 1985), pp 291–305.
7   Thomas D Knowles, *Ideology, Art and Commerce: Aspects of Literary Sociology in the Late Victorian Scottish Kailyard* (Gothenburg, 1983).
8   William Power, *Literature and Oatmeal* (London, 1935).
9   Maclaren, *Beside the Bonnie Brier Bush*, 'The Transformation of Lachlan Campbell'.
10 J M Barrie, *The Little Minister* (London, 1891).

11   J M Barrie, *Sentimental Tommy* (London, 1896).
12   George Blake, *Barrie and the Kailyard School* (London, 1951).
13   William Robertson Nicoll, *People and Books* (London, 1926).
14   Quoted in Knowles, op. cit.
15   For an extended analysis of this topic, *see* William Donaldson, *Popular Literature in Victorian Scotland: language, fiction and the press* (Aberdeen, 1986).
16   Knowles, chapter 2.6.
17   J M Barrie, 'Thomas Hardy: The Historian of Wessex' in *The Contemporary Review*, 56, July 1889, pp 57–66.
18   I Maclaren, 'Among my Books: Ugliness in Fiction' in *Literature*, vol 1, 6 Nov 1897, p 80.
19   Power, *Literature and Oatmeal*.
20   Maclaren, *Beside the Bonnie Brier Bush*, 'Domsie'.
21   Alan Bold, *Modern Scottish Literature* (London, 1983).
22   An illuminating account of Chalmers's attitudes and impact is given in T C Smout, *A Century of the Scottish People 1830–1950* (London, 1986).
23   David Daiches, *Literary Essays* (Edinburgh, 1966).
24   J M Barrie, *Auld Licht Idylls* (London, 1988), chapter 1.
25   Barrie, *Auld Licht Idylls*, chapter 4.
26   Ibid., chapter 3.
27   Ibid., chapter 2.
28   Maclaren, *Beside the Bonnie Brier Bush*, 'Domsie'.
29   Barrie, *Sentimental Tommy*, chapter 7.
30   Willa Muir, *Mrs Grundy in Scotland* (London, 1936).

FURTHER READING

Blake, George, *Barrie and the Kailyard School* (London, 1951). A brief, tetchy evaluation of the kailyard writers written from the point of view of a man associated with industrial Scotland and the people of its cities in his novels; it remains one of the most readable and convincing criticisms.

Brown, Callum, *The Social History of Religion in Scotland since 1730* (London, 1987). A useful background to the social changes which caused, accompanied and arose from the schisms of the Church in Scotland in the 1800s.

Campbell, Ian, *Kailyard: A New Assessment* (Edinburgh, 1981). The definitive recent study on the topic.

Craig, David, *Scottish Literature and the Scottish People 1680–1830* (London, 1961). Despite its title, Craig's book contains a lengthy analysis of the literary culture of Scotland in the second half of the ninteenth century, linking the absence of writing 'worth attention' from 1825 till 1880 with the increase in emigration of Scots from Scotland and the development of nostalgia as a 'cult-emotion'.

Crosland, T W H, *The Unspeakable Scot* (London: Grant Richards, 1902). Crosland's diatribe represents a reaction against Scots and Scotland which was probably fairly wide-spread. There is more than a grain of truth in many of his observations, however extreme; and it is still very, very funny.

Drescher, Horst W, and Schwend, Joachim, (eds) *Studies in Scottish Fiction*: Nineteenth Century (Frankfurt, 1985). Contains several articles on the kailyard, including one on Crockett's *The Lilac Sunbonnet* by Islay Murray Donaldson, which shares some of the qualities of kailyard writing, in its curious mixture of attention to detail and sentimentality. The most interesting aspect of the study is Donaldson's suggestion that *The Lilac Sunbonnet* was Crockett's 'farewell to a ministry he had outgrown' in the Free Church of Scotland. She sees the influence of George MacDonald in both the matter and the manner of the novel.

Hart, Francis Russell, *The Scottish Novel: A Critical Survey* (London, 1978). Hart's survey is the most detailed and in many ways the most comprehensive by any critic. He shares with Islay Murray Donaldson an unaffected admiration for *The Lilac Sunbonnet*, which he sees as 'drenched in . . . the imagery of Eden'. Hart identifies as a characteristic of Crockett and the kailyard writers 'a terrible yearning for old Eden', an 'idyllic focus'; but the suspicion that he is seeing vision where none exists is hard to withstand, especially in the light of claims that *A Window on* [sic] *Thrums* is 'sentimental only insofar as a quiet, somewhat grim domestic heroism might be named sentimental' and that *Beside the Bonnie Brier Bush* has the same 'pathetic resonance' as *Old Mortality*. Scepticism regarding his views on kailyard is fuelled by the fact that he devotes no fewer than nine pages elsewhere in his study to an evaluation of Jane Duncan's *Reachfar* novels, referring to them as 'studies in the pain of demythlogizing one's lost past [and] in the profound need for compensatory myth'.

Knowles, Thomas D, *Ideology, Art and Commerce: Aspects of Literary Sociology in the Late Victorian Scottish Kailyard* (Gothenburg, 1983). Knowles provides a social and sociological context for the kailyard which is unlikely to be improved on. His textual analysis is consistent and convincing; and in many ways he is the most balanced of the critics of the genre.

Millar, J H, *A Literary History of Scotland* (London, 1903). One of the earliest anti-kailyard critics, whose personal outrage is evident in all of his debunking. For a sound, contemporary view of the kailyard novels and their impact on Victorian society he remains unsurpassed.

Muir, Edwin, *Scott and Scotland* (London, 1936). Muir sees the dichotomy between the language of Scottish thought and writing and the language of Scottish feeling and talking as leading to a 'dissociation of sensibility'. His conclusion that 'when emotion and thought are separated, emotion becomes irresponsible and thought arid' may reasonably be applied to the linguistic and thematic characteristics of the kailyard writers.

Muir, Willa, *Mrs Grundy in Scotland* (London, 1936). Willa Muir's companion volume to her husband's *Scott and Scotland* develops the thesis that Victorian gentility took different form in Scotland, largely because of the influence of the Kirk. She sees the principal victim of that gentility as the 'vigorous Rabelaisian life of the countryside'.

Power, William, *Literature and Oatmeal* (London, 1935). Power takes an early socio-logical view of the kailyard, going so far as to blame not the writers but their market for any shortcomings in the former. He sees the kailyarders not as some kind of literary oppressors but as victims of social conditions which were more awful than could be legitimately described in fiction.

Smith, G Gregory, *Scottish Literature: Character and Influence* (London, 1919). Gre-gory Smith was one of the first critics to develop a satisfactory explanation of many of the idiosyncrasies of Scottish fiction with his theory of the Caledonian Antisyzygy—the combination of opposite attributes that make up the Scottish character.

Watson, R, *Literature of Scotland* (London, 1984). As a general survey of Scottish writing, Watson's study provides few startling insights; but he is strong on the writers who were contemporary with the kailyarders. He too subscribes to the notion that Thrums and Drumtochty represented a lost Eden.

Chapter 17

Language and Nineteenth-Century Scottish Fiction

EMMA LETLEY

> ... her accent and language drew down on her so many jests and gibes, couched
> in a worse *patois* by far than her own, that she soon found it was her interest
> to talk as little and as seldom as possible.

This is the linguistic plight of Jeanie Deans in Scott's *Heart of Midlothian*
(ch. xxviii) as she travels south of the border. Her situation is similar to that
encountered by the Scots writer at the outset of the nineteenth century. Such
a writer had inherited some very restrictive attitudes from the eighteenth
century; books of Scoticisms, such as those compiled by James Beattie, and
grammars, aimed at a market of aspiring Scots continued to be reprinted and
published well into the century: Augustan linguistic gentility was still a serious
literary force to be reckoned with.

An essential part of the animus towards and anxiety about Lowland Scots
was the lack of enthusiasm about regional literature; in 1813, the publisher
Constable, told the writer John Galt that Scots novels would not sell; and
Galt's rejected manuscript, later to become *Annals of the Parish*, was not
published until 1821. Scots novels written at the end of the eighteenth century
or earlier in the nineteenth that had a regional setting, such as Smollett's
Humphry Clinker (1771) or Elizabeth Hamilton's *The Cottagers of Glenburnie*
(1808), tended to combine this with a very reduced place for Scots language,
which featured in a very attenuated form often in association with some kind
of defect on the part of the speaker.

The situation changed with the publication of Scott's *Waverley* in 1814
heralding the rise of the regional novel; this, in turn, meant that there was
now a form of fiction available to the writer that did not simply tolerate the
presence of Scots; it required it. Gradually, too, the rise of Edinburgh-based
periodicals came to provide a hospitable market for regional texts with Scots
language. The *Edinburgh Review* was founded in 1802, the *Quarterly* in 1809,
and, in 1817, *Blackwood's Edinburgh Magazine*. Moreover Edinburgh was an
important centre for the newly-industrialised publishing business, boasting
two of Britain's leading houses, namely Blackwood and Constable.

The coincidental development of print culture, with the rise of the northern
periodicals, and the advent of the regional novel, all combined to influence

the climate for Scots language in literature. Scott's work was very successful indeed; David Craig has shown that he made approximately £10,000 per annum from his first four novels;[1] and they prepared the market for Scots in the novel. Scott was firm about the use of the native tongue: 'It has been my object to describe these persons, not by a caricatured and exaggerated use of the national dialect, but by their habits, manners, and feelings,' he wrote in *Waverley*'s Postscript. *Waverley* paved the way for a much more engaged use of Scots in literary discourse than had hitherto been possible: it did so by making the language as accessible as possible to a non-Scots readership. Edward Waverley, a stranger to Scotland and an Englishman, is as unfamiliar with the language as he is with the locale. Explanation can thus be integrated dramatically into his experience of the country:

> The first greetings passed, Edward learned from her that the *dark hag*, which had somewhat puzzled him in the butler's account of his master's avocations, had nothing to do either with a black cat or a broomstick, but was simply a portion of oak copse which was to be felled that day. (Chapter x)

This is Scott's usual method in the Waverley Novels; his heroes are not, in the main, Scots-speakers, but either outsiders or Scots who speak English. Scots is most generally reserved for dialogue and English for exposition and narrative, a division that remains prominent throughout nineteenth-century Scots literature. The kind of Lowland Scots employed is what is most usually called Standard Scots and it derives from the Lothians.

Redgauntlet (1824), dealing with the imaginary return of the Young Pretender after the 1745 Rising, provides a good focus for looking at issues and debates around Scots in the period. With its double hero, Alan Fairford, Edinburgh lawyer, and Darsie Latimer, Jacobite scion, Scott shows his reader a younger generation whose language is mainly Anglicised; In this, they are distinguished, as are a number of other fictive characters of the earlier nineteenth century in Ferrier, Galt and Hogg, from the older generation, such as Alan's father: his language is a mannered, legal Scots, combined with Lowland Scots and, on occasion, a mixed Scots-English blend. In the main, Scots is associated with the older generation irrespective of political allegiance; and the novel itself mirrors mimetically a process whereby Scots is gradually displaced by English (in this it can be compared with Galt's *The Entail*).[2] The displacement of Scots by English is reflected in the text by the fact that the younger members of the upper classes do not speak Scots apart from the most occasional of Scotticisms; as they are an important part of the story-telling voice, we have also to note that the narrative voice overall is decidedly Anglicised (Darsie is in fact English, although educated in Scotland). We have to recognise, however, that the instability of Scots orthography, the exigencies of printers, and the difficulties of reproducing Scots accentual features in the text mean that we should not be absolutely confident of knowing a speaker's exact accentual habits.

In showing English ascendancy the novel reflects an actual situation; but, on occasion, a writer may deny a real social-linguistic situation. In *Red-*

gauntlet Scott incorporates a letter written by Alan Fairford's father (often thought to be modelled on Scott's own father). Graham Tulloch comments: '. . . generally by the 1760s (when *Redgauntlet* is set) educated people tried to avoid them [Scots words] in letters . . . In short he is made to write as he speaks.'[3] Saunders Fairford would not have written like this to Darsie Latimer: '. . . God forbid that you should be in any manner disaffected to the Protestant Hanoverian line, yet ye have ever loved to hear the blawing, bleezing stories which the Hieland gentlemen tell of those troublous times . . .' (Letter ix).

Redgauntlet, in dealing with the process of historical change, continually sets past against present, and romance against modernity, and presents an outmoded feudal order. In this context, Scots is associated with the past and with a balladic and folkloric memory, an association which comes to the fore in the story told by the blind fiddler in Chapter x, 'Wandering Willie's Tale', a story of diablerie, a 'supernatural legend', as the romantically-inclined, light-headed Darsie calls it. Its presence in the text of the novel raises the controversial issue of 'display' Scots, Scots show-cased for the reader's appreciation. Such a use of Scots language is sometimes considered reductive (a similar use is found in another very powerful Scots story of duality and the supernatural, the interpolated 'Tale of Tod Lapraik' in Stevenson's *Catriona*). David Craig comments justly on *Redgauntlet* as a text 'showing something like the complete variety of Scots which Scott used': on the set piece of the Jacobite, Summertrees, he remarks:

> In such usage, then, we have not rendering of shades of real speech, consistently carried out, but a literary habit in which Scots may be taken up for favourite effects but is not felt to be feasible as the language of the hero or moral centre of a book.
>
> (Craig, p 258)

The charge of using Scots for special effects, or reductivism, can be partly answered however, by thinking about how the story (and this applies to other Scots interludes in nineteenth-century texts) is linked with the narrative as a whole, its themes and concerns, its moral centre, with, for instance, its investigation of change and its ambivalence about change. The reader must make up his or her own mind about whether show-cased Scots is as undesirable in a literary text as it might well be in a real situation. Advantages on a literary level, or on an aesthetic level, may well outweigh the charges of linguistic reductivism which, perhaps, belong to a nationalistic, rather than to a literary debate (and this is not to deny the important connection that there has been historically between language and national identity).

In any case, Scots in *Redgauntlet*, as in the majority of cases in the Waverley novels, is not used as the voice for heroes, but is confined to the past, to the older generation, to a number of 'characters', to the old and, in certain senses, to the marginal. Standard English is employed for heroes, for the main narrative voice, exposition, historical background and discussion (ch. viii on the current status of existing Jacobites and Jacobitism is a case in point).

Scott's practice was not the only linguistic course open to the writer in the early nineteenth century. Scots, and Scots of an alternative variety, could be made part of the characterisation of the hero. This was the path taken by John Galt, who in his local histories, such as *Annals of the Parish* (1821) and *The Provost* (1822) makes Scots of the Ayrshire/Renfrewshire kind the language of his protagonists. His broad comic tone and his less standard language (than Scott's) made Galt a somewhat difficult proposition for the Edinburgh literary establishment, whom he characterised iconoclastically as those 'wasps and clegs' [clegs: horse flies] who 'make their living by tormenting poor authors' (*The Steamboat*, ch. xvi). Dismissed as a man of questionable taste whose humour was a little risqué for a fastidious audience, Galt made a courageous stand about the use of Scots for tragic matter, in particular, in his novel *The Entail* (1823); whilst in *Ringan Gilhaize; or the Covenanters* he insisted that Scots could be employed for important historical concerns, in both narrative and in dialogue.

The Scots writer did not use the vernacular with critical impunity; Scott was judged 'unintelligible to four-fifths of the reading population of the country' as Francis Jeffrey expressed it; Galt was castigated for employing 'Clydesdale jargon' and for vulgarity, both thematic and linguistic; whilst James Hogg came in for some harsh words about his 'bad taste' and his 'bad Scotch'.[4] Awkwardly for the writer, compromise itself was problematic. Galt commented on the reception of his novel *The Provost*: '. . . some objection has been made to the style, as being neither Scotch nor English,—not Scotch, because the words are English,—and not English, because the forms of speech are Scottish.'[5] This hybrid style was part of Galt's compromise; his other, and more interesting compromise, was to create a persona, himself subject to anglicising pressures, into whose mouth he could put either Scots or an anglicised language blend; the narrators of *Annals*, *The Provost* and the more obviously anglophone persona in *The Last of the Lairds* (1826) are examples.

The standard authorial attitude in the early part of the century is that Scots should be supported by the Scots novelist; and the use of Scots itself becomes an issue within the text, calling forth explanation and comment:

> Besides the beautiful inflexions which help to make the idiomatic differences between the languages of Scotland and England, the former possesses many words which have a particular signification of their own, as well as what may be called the local meaning which they derive from the juxta-position in which they happen to be placed with respect to other.
>
> (Galt, 'The Seamstress')

Less overt was the support given in Scots in fiction as certain writers reclaimed its position in those centres of authority traditionally subject to the control of Standard English, notably law court and Kirk. An implicit aim of the Scots novelist of the 1820s was to give Scots back its voice in these contexts. Scott had done this at Jeanie Deans's trial in *Heart of Midlothian*; whilst James Hogg brings his native tongue into dramatic tension with English in lively courtroom interchanges, as in the following from *Confessions of a*

Justified Sinner (1824) in which Bessie McLure responds to the questions of the depute advocate:

> 'But you say that gown is *very like* one your mistress used to wear.'
>
> 'I never said sic a thing. It is like one I hae seen her hae out airing on the hay raip [washing line] i' the back green. It is very like ane I hae seen Mrs Butler in the Grass Market wearing too; I rather think it is the same. Bless you, sir, I wadna swear to my ain fore finger, if it had been as lang out o' my sight, an' brought in an' laid on that table.'
>
> 'Perhaps you are not aware, girl, that this scrupulousness of yours is likely to thwart the purposes of justice, and bereave your mistress of property to the amount of a thousand merks?'
>
> ('The Editor's Narrative')

The Scots here is the mark not only of resistance through prevarication but also of an alternative to the public, Standard English view. It is part of Bessie's strategy of defence, as it is also of other characters in Hogg's work who are forced into confrontation with anglicised authority: the Border characters in *The Brownie of Bodsbeck* (1818) in conflict with the Royalist forces are a dramatic example; so too, is Tibby Hyslop in the story 'Tibby Hyslop's Dream'.

A number of writers, and Hogg is among the greatest, make strategic use of Scots language so that it emerges as part of a linguistic plot; in *Confessions*, for example, a split narrative, employing Scots to rich effect, insists on at least the possibility of a non-rational, alternative, non-standard interpretation of the events narrated as opposed to the safer, reasoned explanations offered by the editor. In this, as in its role in political contexts, the strength of Scots, in tension with English, makes its own contribution to the overthrow of a dominant Standard English.

By the time of Scott's death in 1832, considerable strides had been made in this process leading towards the greater acceptance of Scots in literary discourse. The reductive associations of Scots and defect (i.e. as impure and imperfect expression), so prevalent in the late eighteenth and early nineteenth centuries, had been effectively countered (although there were still decidedly demarcated spheres of influence for Scots and English); advances had been made in getting Scots back into tragic and historical literature, and into fictive scenes of courtroom and Kirk. From 1830 until *c*.1860 there is, arguably, little of interest in literary texts that can properly be called seminal in terms of the developing acceptance of Scots language; but there are significant social and cultural changes and shifts that inform the use of Scots later in the century.

Of all the events or changes that could be chosen to demonstrate the way that written discourse can require Scots and English (and it can be said that the most challenging uses of Scots in fiction, if not in poetry, are those which maintain a tension with Standard English), the Disruption of 1843, is one of the most important; its literary spokesman was William Alexander in *Johnny Gibb of Gushetneuk* (1871). The Disruption, the schism in the Church of

Scotland leading to the formation of the Free Church, affords maximum literary possibilities for a writer who wishes to use Scots and English. The situation itself, with its inherent divisions and dualities and tensions between Church and State, can be articulated dramatically using both language varieties without injuring the Scots; furthermore, the different groups in the conflict are, to some extent, naturally delimited by language difference: because of its established structure the Moderate Party is associated with Standard English, the language of political control, whilst the non-Intrusionist group, without an existing structure, is connected with the dialectal Scots of the North-East. In confrontation with anglicised ministers, landowners and churchmen, Johnny Gibb employs a vigorous dialectal Scots which makes both literary and political points. In this text, as in many others of the period, English tends to be associated with dishonour and dissembling and is spoken by characters such as the minister Sleekaboot [to sleek: to slink or sneak; to flatter, wheedle], whose name would have been self-explanatory, and the absentee landlord Sir Simon Frissal whose position in Gushetneuk is anomalous from the outset.

Johnny Gibb draws attention to the importance of the North-East and its language in the later part of the century. The Highlands, too, came to be part of a fashion and style that had wide repercussions in literature. The movement and visits of English people to Scotland had found a literary voice from 1822 onwards: George IV's visit to Edinburgh in that year was orchestrated by Scott and celebrated with some irony by Galt in *The Gathering of the West*. With Queen Victoria's purchase of Balmoral in 1848, the cult of the Highlands got underway in earnest; in literature, it exploded towards the end of the century with the much-maligned Kailyard School and its emphasis on Scotland as an exotic, foreign place with a quaint, foreign tongue. Increased railway communications, most significantly in the 1860s, further effected the interchanges, both of persons and in print, between Scotland and the South. Further developments in print culture led to the rise of local newspapers, an obvious and encouraging outlet for writing with a local bias and localised language, as well as Edinburgh and Glasgow-based daily papers which were often very hospitable to Scots writing.

As the acceptability of Scots in literature increased so, too, did the literary choices open to the writers of the North. There had been and continued to be a significant number of Scottish writers from Byron to Carlyle who chose not to take up the challenge of writing in or with Scots—Byron perhaps the most notable; despite the Scottish overtones identified by T S Eliot in his work, he chose to write in English.[6] Of those who did employ Scots, George MacDonald, like William Alexander, exercised his choice in favour of a variety of Scots other than the central Scots made popular by Walter Scott. MacDonald used the Aberdonian dialect, although in a less aggressively orthographic form than his compatriot, Alexander. Extension is a key issue in the language debate in this period and MacDonald is one of the mid-century writers who can be singled out for extending the written uses of Scots into contexts where the constraints of a narrow realism might demand otherwise; notably, he uses Scots for prayer in his fiction. Historically, religious matter has been associated in Scotland with Standard English, or, at least, with an Anglicised Scots. 'Their religion . . . came to them in English garb', as one late nineteenth century reviewer put it in *Macmillan's Magazine* of June 1897. The comment is only just: the Bible in its Authorised Version, the Psalms and the Shorter Catechism all came to a Scots audience in un-mediated English. In the following passage MacDonald defies a strict realism in the interests of a greater spiritual reality:

> I am well aware that most Scotch people of that date tried to say their prayers in English, but not so Janet or Robert, and not so had they taught their children. I fancy not a little unreality was thus in their case avoided.
>
> (*Sir Gibbie*, III, Ch. vii)

Thus, MacDonald has his heroes, and all his admirable characters deploy Scots as a mark of value and, at the same time, he contrives to extend the fictional use of Scots language.

It is an implicit assumption in the work of various writers of the time, MacDonald included, that Scots is dying; it is an assumption or, more harshly, an affectation that continues today. The idea appears in print as early as 1838 when Cockburn states roundly that Scots is 'going out as a spoken tongue every year';[7] it hardens into a cliché by the period following the Education Acts of the 1870s and by the end of the century has become a truism. In 1887, Stevenson published this in the first poem, entitled 'The Maker to Posterity' in *Underwoods*:

> *'What tongue does your auld bookie speak?'*
> He'll spier; an' I, his mou to steik: [ask] [mouth] [stop, shut]
> *'No bein' fit to write in Greek,*
>   *I wrote in Lallan,*
> *Dear to my heart as the peat reek,* [peat-smoke]
>   *Auld as Tantallon.*
>
> *'Few spak it than, an' noo there's nane.*
> *My puir auld sangs lie a' their lane,* [all alone]
> *Their sense, that aince was braw an' plain,*
>   *Tint a'thegither,* [lost altogether]
> *Like runes upon a standin' stane*
>   *Amang the heather.'*

These verses can be read as a *bona fide*, straightforward regret about the decline of Scots following, for instance, the Education Acts. Such a reading is wholly inadequate however; Stevenson is here using a well-tried technique amongst Scots writers who use Lowland Scots; he is making Scots (and he does this also in his private discourse, in his correspondence, in particular, with Charles Baxter) part of his persona: in this case, his mask of the man who loves to have his 'hour as a native Maker' as he phrases it in his Note to *Underwoods*. As the critic, William Sharp, noted at the time of publication, 'When we turn from the English to the Scottish poems we have to reckon, as it were, with a new author.'[8]

The vernacular mask assumed by Stevenson in *Underwoods* has pre-decessors in, for example, the Burns of some of the Verse Epistles or James Hogg in his *Memoir of the Author's Life*, where the writers make use of the native tongue as part of a very carefully and self-consciously constructed persona. In fiction a variant is found in the narrators of John Galt's *The Provost* and *The Member*. Later writers who use such a mask include poets such as James Logie Robertson who from 1881 produced his Scotticised versions of Horace entitled *Horace in Homespun: a Series of Scottish Pastorals* purportedly written by one Hughie Haliburton, as 'Sketches of Scottish Life among the Ochils':

> He lives among the people whom he describes—wears their dress, speaks their language, shares their joys and sorrows. He is, in short, one of themselves. He counts himself, and is counted, no better than his neighbours—except only that he is allowed to lay special claim to a gift of graphic expression, which on occasion takes a metrical form.
> His Pastorals reveal all about himself that he cares to make known. They represent him as a veritable shepherd living in healthy solitude with social instincts. (Preface)

The use of this kind of Scotticised linguistic mask can be a very useful artistic device both in self-presentation and in the portrayal of literary character. In both cases it gives the writer a certain critical immunity, and effectively circumvents the quibbles of the linguistically fastidious, quibbles summed up in De Quincey's much-quoted carp:

> such a style [the Greek Doric] is picturesque, no doubt. So is the Scottish dialect of low life as first employed in novels by Sir Walter Scott; that dialect greatly assisted the characteristic expression; it furnished the benefit of a Doric dialect: but what man in his senses would employ it in a grave work, and speaking in his own person?

In poetry, as opposed to prose, the contrast and divisions between Scots and English are sometimes thought to be less acute for the writer because in the context of a single poem the writer can avoid, to quote Colin Milton, 'the usually invidious contrast between English narrative voice and Scots dia-logue.'[10] It can be argued (and my suggestion in this essay that certain texts have quite discernible linguistic plots takes this stand) that it is precisely the mixture of Scots and English in a narrative that makes for some of the most interesting literary uses of Scots; on this basis it cannot be denied that the poetry of the period does not provide the most challenging locus for consider-ing language choice. There are exceptions, though, where the interplay of the two languages, what has been called the 'linguistic dichotomy' of the Scots writer,[11] makes crucial points of literary and sociological import; Hogg's poem 'Kilmeny' with its more anglicised style for scenes in Heaven, and Scots for earth, is a telling example.[12] Nevertheless, the general tendency is for the poetry of the period to be either in Scots or in English although, of course, individual authors (MacDonald and Stevenson, among others) published poems in both Scots and English.

Language choice, too, involved a distinction not simply between Scots and English, but also, as has been suggested above, between different kinds of Scots. Margaret Oliphant, herself a prolific novelist, makes the case clear in a comment about John Galt's literary uses of Scots which were, so she thought:

> . . . usually (except when a peasant of the rudest order was speaking) fine, old-fashioned Scotch, the Scotch of the old ministers, and the old ladies, full of idiom and curious construction, not dialect at all.

This is a variation on those comments by writers themselves, as well as commentators on language who refer, with some condescension to the 'Doric' and its superiority to 'Broad Scots'. In the course of the century, this becomes an attitude that is assimilated into literature as a fictional topic within the text. Thus, in the novel we find comments such as this:

> There were still to be found in Scotland old-fashioned gentlefolk speaking the language of the country with purity and refinement; but Florimel had never met any of them, or she might possibly have been a little less repelled by Malcolm's speech.
>
> (*Malcolm*, III, Ch. iii)

Similarly, the writers of the Kailyard School make a special point of commenting upon Scots within the text both in general terms and in the way they give rather irritating parenthetic glosses to the words employed. Of course, there were sentimental uses of Scots, Kailyard-like linguistic habits, well before the official so-called Kailyard novels of the 1880s and 1890s; John Galt's *Sir Andrew Wylie* (1822) has unfortunate moments of both that sentimentality and that linguistic over-persuasion that have come to be associated with Barrie, Crockett and Maclaren; the high-water mark of Kailyard uses of Scots, however, can be seen in Barrie's somewhat regrettable portrayal of his mother, *Margaret Ogilvy* (1897) where Scots is used as a vital part of the portrayal of a very sickly filial relationship, and Ian Maclaren's novel, *Beside the Bonnie Brier Bush* and, in particular, the sketch therein called 'The Cunning Speech of Drumtochty'.

With the Kailyard writers as a group, Scots in literature becomes an exoticism tailored to meet market demands to appeal to an audience that had, for a time at least, an apparently insatiable appetite for engaging in a recreation of Scotland-as-a-foreign-place. It must be said, though, that there are Kailyard texts which are much more than simply defensible in their uses of Scots: Barrie's *Sentimental Tommy* (1896) makes a brilliant imaginative use of Scots as the register of fantasy and the boy-hero's inner life in tension with a mundane English of displacement and poverty. Scots becomes an integral part of Tommy's relationship with his mother and of the mental images of the place she has never been—the Scottish village of Thrums. It is a moving picture in which his disillusion when he finally visits the magic place in Chapter ten of the novel is expressed in a mixture of Scots and Cockney, with each variety helping to make the point about his situation and feelings.

Barrie's fictional village of Thrums and Maclaren's Drumtochty became so popular that one contemporary critic, writing in the *Academy* of 27 June 1896, was prompted to remark that even 'Dickens and Thackeray lacked the support of the grandest advertising agency the world has yet seen. Caledonia, stern and wild.' Despite their popularity, however, there were some dissatisfactions about the work of the Kailyard writers and, in particular, with the very attenuated version of reality that they offered. Not only were their books sentimental, indulgent and backward-looking, they also tended to omit anything to do with city experience. In the later part of the century, one of the most striking features is the increasingly strong 'distinction between traditional, usually equated with rural, dialects of Scots, which were widely approved, and "slovenly perversions of dialect", usually equated with urban dialects, which were not.'[14] In literature, Scots is influenced by city experience, a fact which calls forth some harsh comments from critics. George Douglas Brown in his great novel *The House with The Green Shutters* (1901), with its powerful portrayal of smalltown life and its fiercely unsentimental tone, is one text where city experience affects the language. The *Glasgow Herald* of 17 October 1901 said, '. . . the dialect spoken by the characters is an offence to the ear, and one shivers, even if Glasgow born, to the harsh vulgarity of the "A' wull nut" [I will not] variety of Scots.' Just as city Scots tended to be censured whilst rural-based Scots did not, so also was there a distinction in the eyes of critics between Lowland Scots, on the one hand, and Highland English (or Gaelicised-English) on the other. Lowland Scots in different forms, whether literary versions of Aberdonian, Lothian or Ayrshire/Renfrewshire, aroused negative comments throughout the nineteenth century; this other dialect did not.

The literary dialect intended to represent English as spoken by a native speaker of Gaelic has two aspects, and for purposes of convenience and clarity, it is convenient to distinguish between Gaelicised-English and Highland English. The first, employed for the most part by male, rather than female, characters, in the fiction of Scott, Hogg, Galt and Stevenson, among others, is a synthetic form and looks like this:

> 'I could fery well wish, Malcolm, my son,' said the old man, 'tat you would be learnin' to speak your own lancuach [language]. It is all fery well for ta Sassenach [Saxon, i.e., non-Celtic] podies [bodies, people] to read ta Piple [Bible] in English, for it will be pleasing ta Maker not to make tem cawpable of ta Gaelic, no more tan monkeys; but for all tat it's not ta vord of God.'
>
> (*Malcolm*, I, Ch. vi)

The other variety of language is that which can be termed Highland English and, in the main, in fiction is found spoken by women and girls and is often singled out by its creators for its charm and picturesque qualities. The hero of William Black's *A Princess of Thule* (1873), Frank Lavender, turns his

Highland heroine into 'a wonderful creature of romance' and, in so doing, comes to view her language as the register of this romance:

> The second impression which Lavender gathered from her was, that nowhere in the world was English pronounced so beautifully as in the island of Lewis. The gentle intonation with which she spoke was so tender and touching—the slight dwelling on the *e* in 'very', and 'well' seemed to have such a sound of sincerity about it, that he could have fancied he had been a friend of hers for a lifetime. (Ch. ii)

Highland English tends to avoid the more aggressive orthographic features of Gaelicised-English and to concentrate on one or two features or on syntactic peculiarities. Stevenson's Catriona in the novel of that title is one character who employs this kind of language in contrast to David Balfour's Lowland linguistic habits.

The relatively widespread acceptance of Highland English and Gaelicised-English as opposed to Lowland Scots is underlined by its reception in that very conservative sub-genre, the Scottish children's book. In contemporary reviews, and within texts themselves, there is appreciably less evidence of anxiety about these varieties than there is about the 'rougher tongue', to use George MacDonald's phrase for Lowland Scots. Whilst Celticisms and Highland language are sometimes approved, often overlooked, Scots as such is not seen as at all acceptable. The editor of *Young Folks* warned Stevenson firmly about having too much Scots in *Kidnapped* on the grounds that the young reader would baulk at more than a sparse use of Scots. In the same year, 1886, George MacDonald included some very heavy-handed apologies for those occasions when he does include Scots in his boys' story *Ranald Bannerman's Boyhood* which are all too typical of the practice of the children's writer of the day. The growth of periodicals and magazines for young readers during the last decades of the nineteenth century provided some outlet for writing with a regional bias; but this often tended, as in *Young Folks* and *Good Words* to be severely restricted as regards non-Standard language; thus, the place for Scots was often much reduced, often to the farmyard or to some other marginal place, such as the sea-bed.

S R Crockett's comment on his reductions of Scott's novels for a young, familial audience, is linguistically typical of the attitude to Scots in fiction for a juvenile audience: in *Red Cap Tales* (1908) he notes that

> These were Scottish children to whom the stories were retold, and they understood the Scottish tongue. So the dialect parts were originally told in that speech. Now, however, in pity for children who have had the misfortune to inherit only English, I have translated all the hard words and phrases as best I could. But the old is infinitely better . . .
>
> ('The First Tale from Waverley')

The stated aim is translation into 'pure' Standard English, and this is only partly undermined or subverted by a contrary and more creative linguistic strategy within the texts. Stevenson's *Kidnapped*, as I have argued elsewhere, stands almost alone as a book for children which has comparable uses of Scots, and comparably subtle uses at that, to those found in adult fiction.[15] It is, nevertheless, when we look at juvenile fiction of the period that we can most strongly see, set in relief, the movement in adult fiction from Scots and defect, to Scots and integrity, which is combined in the period with a greater acceptance of Scots in literature than had previously been the case.

It must be said, however, that the Scots concerned is a synthetic form that is constructed for literary use, and may bear little exact relation to actual spoken Scots. The fact of this syntheticism becomes an issue with the Scottish Renaissance in the earlier part of the twentieth century and in discussions of the work of Hugh MacDiarmid, and is part of a debate that is mainly outside the scope of this essay. It is relevant, though, to note that considerable scholarly effort has been devoted to comment on the nature of certain writers' Scots: J Derrick McClure's work on Galt's language and Graham Tulloch's on Scott's are excellent examples.

It can also be argued that linguistic accuracy or the provenance of particular words is not necessarily the main issue when thinking about Scots in literature since Scots in fiction, for example, has what is often primarily a symbolic rather than a realistic or linguistic function. Writers themselves become increasingly aware of this in the twentieth century; Lewis Grassic Gibbon's heroine Chris Guthrie in *A Scots Quair* (1946) makes this clear as she shows how she associates Scots with certain feelings and experiences and English with a quite contrary mental set. For her, as for the Scots writer, the native tongue is a symbolic matter:

> You saw their faces in firelight, father's and mother's and the neighbours', before the lamps lit up, tired and kind, faces dear and close to you, you wanted the words they'd known and used, forgotten in the far-off youngness of their lives, Scots words to tell to your heart, how they wrung it and held it, the toil of their days and unendingly their fight.
>
> (*Sunset Song*, Ch. i)

English, by contrast, is the language in which nothing 'worth saying' can be expressed.

Within a text, too, a writer can have his characters revert to Scots for moments of intense emotion, happiness, or sorrow, or to show special affection for someone. Characters can be made well aware of the association of Scots and friendliness, and, on occasion, they make much use of it for purposes of manipulation: 'Thus, with a coaxing mixture of her vernacular speech, which our heroine always used when she had a point to carry, did Mrs Mark Luke address her husband.' This is the heroine in chapter two of 'Mrs Mark Luke; or West Country Exclusives' (1834), a novella by Mrs Johnstone. Similar linguistic manipulators include Lady Margaret Bellenden in Scott's *Old Mortality*, James Durie in Stevenson's *The Master of Ballantrae* and James More in *Catriona*.

In recognising that the use of Scots is a symbolic matter we, perhaps, see the debate about 'lifeless English and living Scots' take a different turn;[16] it is not simply the case that many writers have felt forced into writing in a constraining and unnatural tongue (Standard English) as opposed to a more natural and thus liberating one (Scots) but rather that the two language varieties are of the greatest possible use to the writer. A writer can, for example, show a character drawing on assumptions about living, warm, affectionate Scots in contrast to cold, antipathetic English as part of his or her strategies: Stevenson's James Durie is a past master at this: 'He had laid aside even his cutting English accent, and spoke with the kindly Scots tongue, that set a value on affectionate words' (Chapter iv). Similarly, I would suggest that the argument against occasional, or 'intermittent' Scots, to use Stevenson's term, becomes beside the point when we see how the writer can use Scots in tension with a controlling Standard English to the greatest artistic effect. In fiction, a writer can stage an imaginative defeat of Standard English as Stevenson does in 'Thrawn Janet':

> 'Will you,' says Mr Soulis, 'in the name of God, and before me, His unworthy minister, renounce the devil and his works?'
> Weel, it wad appear that when he askit that, she gave a girn that fairly frichtit them that saw her, an' they could hear her teeth play dirl [chatter] thegither in her chafts [mouths]; but there was naething for't but the ae way or the ither; an' Janet lifted up her hand an' renounced the de'il before them a'.

The contrast between the minister's English and the Scots expresses a strong tension; but the formal English cannot contain the visual and oral power of the Scots, with its terrifying physical description of Janet with her *girn* and her teeth *playing dirl*. The inadequacy of the minister's efforts and of his language is underlined when, the next day, Janet appears transformed, with 'her neck thrawn [twisted], an' her heid on ae side, like a body that has been hangit, an' a girn on her face like an unstreakit corp [not laid out for burial].' English, like its speaker, has emerged defeated by a strong and imaginatively-achieved use of Scots.

It could be argued today that it may well be preferable to think about the 'unexplored possibilities of vernacular expression', to use MacDiarmid's idea, than to castigate a writer for using insufficient or a dilute form of Scots: to invoke MacDiarmid again: 'Any language, real or artificial, serves if a creative artist finds his medium in it.'[17]

NOTES

1   David Craig, *Scottish Literature and the Scottish People 1680–1830* (London, 1961), Appendix B, p 297.
2   J D McClure, 'The Language of The Entail' in *Scottish Literary Journal*, VIII (May 1981), 30–53.
3   Graham Tulloch, *The Language of Walter Scott* (London, 1980), p 330.
4   Francis Jeffrey, 'Waverley', *Edinburgh Review*, XXIV (November 1814), 208; 'The Entail; or the Lairds of Grippy', *The Literary Gazette* (21 December 1822),

p 800; 'The Brownie of Bodsbeck', *British Critic*, n.s. X (October 1818), 403–18; 'The Private Memoirs and Confessions of a Justified Sinner', *New Monthly Magazine and Literary Journal*, XII (1814), 506.

5 John Galt, *Ringan Gilhaize; or the Covenanters*, Patricia J Wilson (ed) (Edinburgh, 1984), p 323.

6 T S Eliot 'Byron' in *From Anne to Victoria: Essays by Various Hands*, Bonamy Dobree (ed) (London, 1937), pp 601–19.

7 As quoted in Introduction, *The Concise Scots Dictionary*, Editor-in-Chief Mairi Robinson (Aberdeen, 1985), p xii.

8 William Sharp, 'From a Review, "Academy"', xxxii, 212–14 (1 October 1887) in *Robert Louis Stevenson: The Critical Heritage*, Paul Maixner (ed) (London, 1981), p 269.

9 'On Style', *The Collected Writings of Thomas De Quincey*, David Masson (ed) 15 vols (Edinburgh, 1889–90), X, 188.

10 Colin Milton, 'From Charles Murray to Hugh MacDiarmid: Vernacular Revival and Scottish Renaissance' in *Literature of the North*, David Hewitt and Michael Spiller (eds) (Aberdeen, 1983), p 90.

11 James Kinsley, 'Burns and the Peasantry, 1785', *Proceedings of the British Academy*, LX (1974), p 4.

12 Douglas Mack comments also on this in his introduction to *James Hogg: Selected Poems* (Oxford, 1970), p xviii.

13 M Oliphant, *Annals of a Publishing House: William Blackwood and His Sons. Their Magazine and Friends*, 3 vols (Edinburgh, 1897), I, 450.

14 Mairi Robinson, *CSD* op. cit., p xii.

15 R L Stevenson, *Kidnapped* and *Catriona*, Emma Letley (ed) (Oxford, 1986), Introduction.

16 A O J Cockshut, *The Achievement of Walter Scott* (London, 1969), p 27.

17 Roderick Watson, *MacDiarmid* (Milton Keynes, 1983), p 16; Hugh MacDiarmid, *At the Sign of the Thistle* (London, 1934), p 189.

TEXTS CITED/FURTHER READING

Modern editions and reprints of the main texts cited above are as follows:

Alexander, William, *Johnny Gibb of Gushetneuk*, intro Ian Carter (Aberdeen, 1979).
Brown, George Douglas, *The House with the Green Shutters*, Dorothy Porter (ed) (Harmondsworth, 1985).
Galt, John, *Annals of the Parish*, James Kinsley (ed) (Oxford, 1986).
—— *The Entail*, Ian A Gordon (ed) (Oxford, 1984).
—— *The Last of the Lairds* (Edinburgh, 1976).
—— *The Member* (Edinburgh, 1978).
—— *The Provost*, Ian A Gordon (ed) (Oxford, 1982).
—— *Ringan Gilhaize; or the Covenanters*, Patricia J Wilson (ed) (Edinburgh, 1984).
—— *Selected Short Stories*, Ian A Gordon (ed) (Edinburgh, 1978).
Hogg, James, *The Brownie of Bodsbeck*, Douglas S Mack (ed) (Edinburgh, 1976).
—— *Memoir of the Author's Life and Familiar Anecdotes of Sir Walter Scott*, Douglas S Mack (ed) (Edinburgh, 1972).
—— *The Private Memoirs and Confessions of a Justified Sinner*, John Carey (ed) (Oxford, 1981).
—— *Selected Poems*, Douglas S Mack (ed) (Oxford, 1970).
—— *Selected Poems and Songs*, David Groves (ed) (Edinburgh, 1986).
—— *Selected Stories and Sketches*, Douglas S Mack (ed) (Edinburgh, 1982).
Scott, Walter, *The Heart of Midlothian*, Claire Lamont (ed) (Oxford, 1982).
—— *Redgauntlet*, preface W M Parker (London, 1958).
—— *Waverley*, Andrew Hook (ed) (Harmondsworth, 1972).
Stevenson, R L, *Kidnapped* and *Catriona*, Emma Letley (ed) (Oxford, 1985).
—— *The Master of Ballantrae*, Emma Letley (ed) (Oxford, 1983).

In cases where texts have not been re-edited or issued in modern editions, the following have been used:

Barrie, J M, *The Kirriemuir Edition of the Works of J M Barrie* (London, 1913).
Black, William, *A Princess of Thule* (London, 1873).
Crockett, S R, *Red Cap Tales* (London, 1904).
Galt, John, *Sir Andrew Wylie* (Edinburgh, 1822).
Johnstone, C I, *The Edinburgh Tales* (Edinburgh, 1845–46).
MacDonald, George, *Malcolm* (London, 1875).
—— *Ranald Bannerman's Boyhood* (London, 1871).
—— *Sir Gibbie* (London, 1879).
Robertson, James Logie, *Horace in Homespun* (Edinburgh, 1886).
Stevenson, R L, *The Swanston Edition of the Works of R L Stevenson* (London, ????).

In addition to the works of individual writers, the following anthologies may be of interest:

Buchan, John, *The Northern Muse* (London, 1924).
—— *The Oxford Book of Scottish Verse*, chosen by John MacQueen and Tom Scott (Oxford, 1866 repr with corrections, 1975).

—— *The Penguin Book of Scottish Verse*, Tom Scott (ed) (Harmondsworth, 1970).

Of specific interest to scholars and students in Lowland Scots are:

Aitken, A J, McIntosh, Angus, Pálson, Hermann (eds), *Edinburgh Studies in English and Scots* (London, 1971).
Aitken, A J (ed), *Lowland Scots: Papers Presented to an Edinburgh Conference* (Edinburgh, 1973).
Aitken, A J, and MacArthur, Tom (eds), *Languages of Scotland* (Edinburgh, 1979).
McClure, J D (ed) *Scotland and the Lowland Tongue* (Aberdeen, 1983).
Scottish Language no. 5, 1986: Proceedings of the First International Conference on the Languages of Scotland, Guest Editors MacAulay, Donald, and McClure, J D.

Studies with a more literary bias include:

Craig, David, *Scottish Literature and the Scottish People 1680–1830* (London, 1961).
Daiches, David, *Literature and Gentility in Scotland* (Edinburgh, 1984).
Hewitt, David, and Spiller, Michael (eds), *Literature of the North* (Aberdeen, 1983).
Letley, Emma, *From Galt to Douglas Brown: Nineteenth-Century Fiction and Scots Language* (Edinburgh, 1988).
Muir, Edwin, *Scott and Scotland* (London, 1936, new edn, intro Allan Massie, 1982).
Young, Douglas, *The Use of Scots for Prose* (Greenock, 1949).

The following are relevant to the use of Scots in individual authors:

McClure, J D, 'The Language of *the Entail*', *Scottish Literary Journal*, VIII, pp 50–51 (Aberdeen, May 1981).
Murison, David,'The Two Languages in Scott' in Jeffares, A N, *Scott's Mind and Art* (Edinburgh, 1969). Tulloch, Graham, *The Language of Walter Scott* (London, 1980).

Chapter 18

Scottish Poetry in the Nineteenth Century

EDWIN MORGAN

It has never been the easiest of tasks to get nineteenth-century Scottish poetry into focus, and much of it resists order and categorisation, to an uncomfortable degree. The absence of commanding creative figures in Scotland to whom other poets could relate themselves, even by way of opposition; the lack of good critics who might have stopped, at various points, a slide into sentimentality or derivativeness or mediocrity; the decline of the famously sharp literary journals like the *Edinburgh Review* and *Blackwood's Magazine* which tended to be replaced by family magazines such as *Chambers's Journal* and *The People's Friend*; a rapid downturn in the intellectual and cultural sprightliness of Edinburgh, leaving a vacuum not yet convincingly filled by the struggling giant of Glasgow, and presenting therefore a country without a true national centre; add to that a diaspora—Byron, William Bell Scott, George MacDonald, David Gray, Robert Buchanan, James (B V) Thomson, Robert Louis Stevenson, John Davidson—which leaves endless and largely unanswerable questions about a poet's 'Scottishness': and it is not hard to understand why Hugh MacDiarmid was so determined that the twentieth century should deliver, if he had anything to do with it, a more solidly based and recognisable Scottish poetry than the nineteenth had done. However, the present task is to see what was actually there.

At the beginning of the century, the poetry of Walter Scott and James Hogg enjoyed a popularity it has never been able to regain, and although it met (and largely created) the contemporary taste for historical romance it did not prove greatly seminal for later poets, and much of it seems to look beguilingly back rather than proddingly forward. When Lord Cockburn said in his *Memorials* that the 'eighteenth century was the final Scotch century' we do not necessarily agree with him but we can see what he means. Scott, in writing *The Lay of the Last Minstrel* (1805), prepares the way for statements like Cockburn's. In this creaky yet sombrely effective narrative, the old minstrel who tells the story, who chants it as Scott in fact had chanted it to the Wordsworths when they visited him in Jedburgh, is supposed to be living towards the end of the seventeenth century, having survived what to him were the hard and dangerous times of the Commonwealth and Civil War, and the events he relates are supposed to have taken place a long time before, in the Borders, at the middle of the sixteenth century, and even involving (with intentional anachronism) the wizard or early scientist Michael Scott who lived in the thirteenth century; and all this, of course, projected by the author to a nineteenth-century audience. It is a many-layered poem about Scotland, about the Scottish experience or spirit, with a great deal of nostalgia coming through the figure of the old 'last minstrel' himself and also through the suggested identification of Scott with him; he too is the last minstrel of the old history of Scotland which moves him so much. Similar qualities are found in *The Lady of the Lake* (1810), which deals with the clash between the centralising and unifying values of King James V and the admired but wild and uncontrolled values of the Highland chieftain Roderick Dhu, and which again presents a past that can be recreated, whatever its angers and follies at the time, in terms of drama, charm, and high romance. The fact that the long narrative poems of Scott do not on the whole stand up well to line-by-line analysis, the verse being filled out with expletives, sown with clichés, and propped up by fairly coarse-textured rhetorical devices, has told against him in modern times, but there is a case to be made, as one makes it with Edmund Spenser, for the large-scale cumulative effects a long poem can sustain, and Scott keeps some powerful and unexpected passages for those who can yield to his storytelling. Anyone who finds this difficult can still enjoy the more intimate style of the attractive autobiographical introductions to the six cantos of *Marmion* (1808), written as verse letters to different friends and talking in an easy familiar style about friendship and art and life and memory:

> Heap on more wood!—the wind is chill;
> But let it whistle as it will,
> We'll keep our Christmas merry still.

James Hogg, friend and colleague of Scott's, and a co-collector of ballads and folk-songs, described the difference between them as being that Scott was king of the 'school o' chivalry' whereas Hogg was 'king o' the mountain an' fairy school which is a far higher ane nor yours'. In spite of this claim, he actually does himself an injustice, since his remarkably varied work holds many surprises, as recent editions have made clear.[1] Legend and folklore and the supernatural do certainly feed into such successful and well-known poems as 'Kilmeny', with its mysterious brooding atmosphere and many critical interpretations, and 'The Witch of Fife' with its grotesque humour and alternative endings, but it is limiting to think of Hogg only in these terms. He was willing to try anything, and although he wrote too much, and often badly, his resolute belief in spontaneity and freshness of attack was coupled with a tantalising sophistication that led him into areas where Scott had no entry. There is an astonishing contrast between the rollicking, traditional, satirical Scots of 'The Great Muckle Village of Balmaquhapple' and the quiet straight lyrical English and almost timeless magic of 'A Boy's Song'. English is also used to wickedly lively effect in *The Poetic Mirror* (1816–31), with its parodies of Wordsworth, Coleridge, Scott, Byron, and others, including the author himself; their complex mixture of mockery and tribute shows a kind of literary insight that is different from his more regularly credited insight into folk-song and folklore and oral poetry. In other poems like 'A True Story of a Glasgow Tailor', 'The Dominie', and 'Disagreeables', he developed a rough, bold, colloquial blank verse, in English but with snatches of Scots dialogue, which is racy and readable and entertaining—and not a mountain or fairy in sight. One of his 'disagreeables' is a creditor:

> I do remember once.—'Tis long agone,
> Of stripping to the waist to wade the Tyne—
> The English Tyne, dark, sluggish, broad, and deep;
> And just when middle-way, there caught mine eye,
> A lamprey of enormous size pursuing me!
> Lord what a fright! I bobb'd, I splashed, I flew!
> He had a creditor's keen ominous look,
> I never saw an uglier—but a real one.

Byron's claim to be considered as a Scottish poet depends partly on his maternal parentage and his early upbringing in Aberdeen, partly on Scottish qualities of temperament which he claimed to have, and partly on the sheer problematics of regarding such a European, mercurial, and in many ways anti-English figure as an English poet. (The pros and cons of this are usefully rehearsed in recent essays by Tom Scott and Philip Hobsbaum.[2]) T S Eliot, comparing the busts of Byron and Scott, thought he saw 'a certain resemblance in the shape of the head'. The huge popularity of Byron's verse narratives, from *Childe Harold's Pilgrimage* onwards, rolled on a wave that Scott had started, but quickly extended itself into exotic settings, contemporary history, and heroic identification of new *zeitgeist* and new individual, in ways that soon began to give Scott's narratives a distinctly dusty look. 'So much for chivalry,' says Byron in his *Childe Harold* preface, and 'these monstrous mummeries of the middle ages'. And as Scott's narrative poems became worse and worse, being naturally displaced by his prose fiction, so Byron's became better and better, culminating in the sustained brilliance of *Don Juan*. Rapidity and insouciance of composition link Byron to Scott and Hogg, but Byron had access to technical virtuosity that far surpassed theirs. Hogg, in a dedicatory poem to Byron which was far from sycophantic, put his finger on the spot in praising him for

> thy bold and native energy;
> Thy soul that dares each bound to overfly,
> Ranging thro' Nature on erratic wing—
> These do I honour.

'Bold', 'energy', 'dares', 'overfly', 'erratic'—these are the right words, and sometimes Hogg is uncannily perceptive. What is interesting is that Hogg adds 'native'; he still claims the mould-breaking energies as Scottish. The splendid digressionism of *Don Juan*, its many voices and tangents and recoveries, its daring shifts of tone, do seem to have something of that Scottish quality which so disconcerted and irritated Dr Johnson when Boswell left him to converse with those master printers the Foulis brothers at the Saracen's Head Inn in Glasgow: they were 'good and ingenious men', Boswell reports, but they had an 'unsettled speculative mode of conversation' and they 'teazed him with questions and doubtful disputations'. Also, what one might call the encyclopedism of *Don Juan*—and Byron shares this with Scott—its lists, its informativeness, its use of many languages, is a recurring Scottish pre-occupation. When Byron looked back (in *Don Juan*, X.19) at *English Bards and Scotch Reviewers* (1809), his early squib against Francis Jeffrey and the *Edinburgh Review* and most other things Caledonian ('it being well known', as he says in a note, 'there is no Genius to be found from Clackmannan to Caithness'), he frankly admitted a necessary callowness, 'to show my wrath and wit', but 'I "*scotched* not killed" the Scotchman in my blood.' It is interesting that the admission quotes from an English writer's most Scottish play.

Although Byron, by leaving Scotland and never returning to it, ruled out any potential he might have had for providing a personal focus for other poets in the country, he did prove to be one of the influences (others were Shelley, Poe, and Whitman) taken up by writers who resisted the sentimental sub-Burnsian blandishments of the popular *Whistle-Binkie* anthologies (1832 and many later editions). Not that Scottish traditions were useless or exhausted: there is much charm in the songs and local epistles of Robert Tannahill the Paisley weaver-poet, and individual poems like William Tennant's lively fantasy of rustic merrymaking, *Anster Fair*, and William Bell Scott's smilingly, dancingly sinister 'The Witch's Ballad', still deserve anthology space. *Anster Fair*, written in English in near-Spenserian stanzas, offers an unexpected link between Byron, who favoured similar metres, and the seventeenth-century Scots song, 'Maggie Lauder', on which the poem is based. If 'Scottish traditions' include the eighteenth-century James Thomson, we can add the author of 'The Luggie' to the list, since the rather formal, latinate, and by Victorian times distinctly old-fashioned descriptive diction of that poem, praising the countryside north of Glasgow, shows his strong influence; but the unfortunate David Gray, dead of tuberculosis at the age of twenty-one, did not live long enough to write underivatively, and his best poems are a group of personal sonnets owing much to Keats and Shakespeare, but delicate and moving within their limitations.

But for sixty years *Whistle-Binkie* must have thought it ruled the roost. Victorian morality took strong root in Scotland, and these tightly packed, assiduously produced, biographically annotated, and constantly revised anthologies, in which you would be hard put to find a dozen really good poems, but which seemed so innocuously comic and sentimental, were carefully devised as instruments of social control, as was made clear in the 'new and enlarged edition' of 1890. After lauding 'this broad, fresh, living stream of healthy Scottish song', the preface continues: 'When the first portion of *Whistle-Binkie* was issued from the press, our Scottish firesides were still greatly under the influence of the old chap-books, which, while they embodied much genuine poetic feeling, expressed in terse and graphic language, were yet permeated and marred by much that was coarse and indecent,—these last two characteristics being, indeed, the chief features of many of them. It was the purpose and glory of *Whistle-Binkie* to exhibit, to cherish, and to preserve all the tenderness, the refinement, and the genius of the national muse, without the coarseness and licentiousness by which it had been debased.'

During this period the real poets, minor though they may have been, had to look elsewhere. Those of them, like Alexander Rodger and William Thom, who contributed to *Whistle-Binkie*, kept their strongest verses for other pages. Life as it really was, and as it appeared to thinking and feeling spirits, comes to us fitfully but sometimes powerfully, sometimes with great pathos, sometimes with irony and wit, in the often imperfect work of half a dozen poets whose names ought not to be forgotten. Alexander Rodger, the 'Glasgow radical' mentioned above, gained notoriety from the anti-monarchist ballad he wrote at the time of George IV's visit to Edinburgh in 1822. Walter Scott, who helped to stage-manage the royal progress, produced a celebratory version of an old song, 'Carle, now the King's come', and Rodger promptly published his anti-celebratory 'Sawney, now the King's come', advising ambitious Scots to 'kneel, and kiss his gracious bum'. He made a spirited attack on time-serving clergy in 'Black Coats, and Gravats sae White'. He wrote an incisively epigrammatic elegy for Thomas Paine, one of his heroes. And in the particularly interesting longer poem, 'Shaving Banks', he uses the Burns stanza with much skill to warn the ordinary working public that the grand new invention of Savings Banks, ostensibly a rainy-day protective device, is really just one more devious method of enslaving working people, of 'shaving' them of their hard-earned cash. Rather like Holy Willie, the speaker of Rodger's poem (a minister) is brashly and brutally self-condemnatory:

> Come, come, my lads, this is nae hoax,
> Here are our books—and here's our box,
> We'll put your siller in the stocks;
>   and when it's there,
> Confound you for a set o' blocks,
>   Gin ye see't mair;
>
> What then?—Ye tim'rous, backward set,
> The interest ye'll be sure to get,
> The stock will help to pay some debt
>   John Bull is awn,   [owed]
> Or creesh the sair-worn wheels o' State,   [grease]
>   To keep them gaun.   [going]
>
> For look ye, it is our intent
> To cleek you firm to Government . . .   [hook]

Also associated with Glasgow were Alexander Smith and James Macfarlan. Smith tends to be remembered as the author of one very fine and resonant poem, 'Glasgow', which was among the earliest attempts to bring positive and powerful images of the industrial city environment so resolutely avoided by the Whistle-Binkians. A poet in the Romantic tradition, he extended romanticism into the machine age and found 'Another beauty, sad and stern' in the furnaces and foundries and shrieking trains which seem to thrill, terrify, and exalt the watcher in a strong and new transfusion of emotions. The city is the growing point, and the conservative somnolent countryside must learn to deal with 'The roar and flap of foundry fires,/That shake with light the sleeping shires'. And the whole country must learn that close-knit rural communities are not necessarily the ideal:

> A sacredness of love and death
> Dwells in thy noise and smoky breath.

Smith's ambitious and overblown longer poems, 'A Life-Drama' and 'Edwin of Deira', scarcely survive, but 'A Boy's Poem', though somewhat laboured and over-descriptive in a Tennysonian manner, has some excellent passages reflecting love and loneliness in Glasgow and the Firth of Clyde.[4]

Smith, in his preface to *Golden Leaves from American Poets* (ed J W S Hows, 1866), was able to praise Edgar Allan Poe's poetry while deploring the man ('the most disreputable of poets'). Smith's Glasgow contemporaries might have felt the same way about the pedlar-poet, James Macfarlan. If alcohol, ingrained vagrancy, and general unreliability tended to make Macfarlan's death at the age of thirty another Victorian morality-story, the poet himself, autodidact as he was, used all his miseries to project something general and almost mythical about the individual, and especially the creative individual, in industrial society. Byron, he said, set him off into poetry; Poe, it is clear from the echoes, sustained him; and his work looks forward in some respects to James (B V) Thomson's *The City of Dreadful Night*. He enjoyed a measure of fame, particularly for his rousing march-song, 'The Lords of Labour', where the workers are Titans drawing their 'steam steeds' through the 'triumphal arch' of tunnel-builders' skill; 'heroes who wield no sabre', their sweat-drops turned to jewels 'in the crown of toil'. His city poems, especially 'The Street' and 'The Midnight Train', resemble and rival Smith's 'Glasgow' (plagiarism, if any, could go either way). 'The Ruined City' is a powerful, Poe-like vision, in almost science-fiction terms, of a 'city's blasted heap' under a 'fierce, relentless sky', abandoned to reptiles and wild beasts. It ends:

> The sunset's wild and wandering hair
>   Streams backward like a comet's mane,
> And from the deep and sullen glare
>   The shuddering columns crouch in vain,
> While through the wreck of wrathful years
> The grim hyena stalks and sneers.

His most ambitious poem, 'The Wanderer of the West' (1856), constructed in ten sections with different metres, combines a Byronic wanderer-hero with the autobiographical story of a young poet trying to break out of poverty into art and fame. Here, 'The Lords of Labour' is turned over to reveal the dark side of the struggle, where 'the poor Boy-Poet grimes within a dismal den,/Piles the fire and wields the hammer, jostled on by savage men', where the forges are 'like great burning cities' (an astonishing image-reversal) and

where 'the soul is dwarfed within him that was cast in Titan mould'. For all
its imperfections, there is something very moving about Macfarlan's poetry.[5]

Janet Hamilton, a shoemaker's daughter from North Lanarkshire, was
a remarkable woman who overcame many disadvantages—no education,
marriage at fourteen and a large family to raise, blindness in middle age—in
order to write poetry which would have a social function within communities
in Scotland, especially outside the main cities, and which she dedicated to
'her Brothers, the Men of the Working Classes'. She wrote in both English
and Scots (the earliest poems she came across were volumes of Allan Ramsay
and John Milton, lying on a weaver's loom), but most of her best work is in
Scots, and in a poem called 'A Plea for the Doric' she laid her finger on at
least one of the Scottish poet's problems:

> I'm wae for Auld-Reekie; her big men o' print
> To Lunnon ha'e gane, to be nearer the mint;
> But the coinage o' brain looks no a'e haet better,   [not a bit]
> Though Doric is banish'd frae sang, tale, and letter.

Her subjects range from Garibaldi and Poland to *Uncle Tom's Cabin* and the
Crimean War, but cluster strongly about the immediate and familiar issues
of the family, work, education, and the place of women in society. Her
Victorian earnestness is lightened by a humorous direct appeal that shows
she really would like people to listen; working men, she says, don't respect
themselves enough, and live in a dangerous ignorance:

> Ye've means, but want the wull to use them,
> Ye whiles neglec', an' whiles abuse them;
> Ye hae nae time for e'enin' classes;
> Ye've time to drink, an' see the lasses—
> Staun at hoose-en', or change-hoose door,
> An' smoke an' swear, an' raise a splore,   [uproar]
> An' play at cards, or fecht wi' dougs,
> An' whiles to clout ilk ither's lugs;   [ears]
> O wad ye no be muckle better   [much]
> To read a book, or write a letter?
> Had ye the wull, wi' book an' pen
> Ye'd fin' the way to mak' ye men.
> ('Rhymes for the Times—I')

She complemented her poems with essays on social subjects, which are also
worth reading.[6]

Like Hamilton and Macfarlan, the Aberdeenshire weaver-poet William
Thom enjoyed some contemporary fame, but in a life of general poverty and
hardship. Among much mediocre sentimental work, which he placed in
Whistle-Binkie, he also wrote some powerful satirical and grotesque poetry,
a mode which unfortunately no critic encouraged him to develop. At least
two poems, both in Scots (one modulating towards English), leave the
impression of a fiery indignation, and an original cast of expression, that

never spread themselves into what might have been an *oeuvre*. In 'Whisperings
for the Unwashed', the early morning town drummer drums loud enough to
physically waken the weavers in their hovels but never loud enough to waken
them spiritually and shake them from their apathy; they are such craven
nonentities to society that when they die 'They grudge the grave wherein to
drap ye,/An' grudge the very *muck* to hap ye.' 'Chaunts for Churls' is a wild
reel of rhythm and rhyme where Sawtan (Satan) and Sin have a dialogue
about the gains they expect from the Disruption in the Church of Scotland
in 1843. Thom ended his touching prose *Recollections*[7] with a strange image
which sums up much of the desperate yet buoyant commitment to art which
kept the self-taught poets going:

> Now, amid the giant waves of monopoly, the *solitary* loom is fast sinking. Thus
> must the Lyre, like a hencoop, be thrown on the wrecking waters, to float its
> owner ashore.

Contemporary subjects are treated with a more ironic and detached intelligence by the elusive James Young Geddes of Dundee and Alyth, of whom
little seems to be known beyond his books.[8] A favourite theme is art versus
the machine. In 'A Work of Art' he praises a grocer's almanack on his wall,
showing a Hartz mountain scene, a 'brilliant, glowing chromograph' which
Ruskin and Whistler would despise but which he prefers to his 8-day kitchen
clock protesting 'with prosaic knock'; yet both have their place, and 'Clock
and picture argue on'. The machine makes a comeback in 'The Man and the
Engine', where a mechanic feels he has become 'a part/Of the mill machinery'
but

> I think I could find a poem here,
> Were I only blessed by a little wit,
> And my engine should be the theme of it.

Another nicely contrasting pair of poems is 'The People's Theatre' and
'Glendale & Co.' In the former, a mobile theatre arrives in Alyth, apparently
ramshackle and dubious:

> It came within the bitter winter time,
> Thick was the ground with snow, the air with rime—
> It came in ruins on an ambulance,
> And we, the townsmen, looked at it askance.

(Anyone who could write that third line is no negligible poet!) But the poem
comes round to see values in the temporary changeable art of the theatre
which can be set against everyday material money-making. The long lines of
Whitmanian free verse which characterise the remarkable 'Glendale & Co.'
are devoted to demolishing, with sharp perceptiveness, step by step, the
credentials of this *Metropolis*-like weaving conglomeration.

Glendale is methodical—
The works an enlargement of the man;
There nothing imperfect; no repairing, no patching—
The imperfect machine cast into the furnace;
Every machine with its duplicate prepared, ready to be put in its place.
Imperfect men and women cannot be recast—cannot be rejuvenated—
They could not endure the fiery furnace;
They must be discharged—
To do otherwise would be to break down the system:
The works are for workers;
The workhouses and benevolent institutions are for the old and infirm.
Why regret the harshness of the system?

If Poe made Macfarlan, Whitman certainly made Geddes. It becomes clear that three strands of influence are at work on nineteenth-century Scottish poetry: a minor one from America, in addition to the more important ones from the English Romantics and from the native Scottish tradition, whether in English (Thomson) or in Scots (Ramsay, Fergusson, Burns, Hogg).

During the last quarter of the century, more familiar names come on the scene, all exiles from Scotland: Robert Louis Stevenson, James (B V) Thomson, John Davidson. Even more familiar is the name of an 'internal exile' who outlived Thomson and Stevenson: William McGonagall. McGonagall has never been long out of print; the other three poets are not easy to obtain, and are probably, despite critical opinion in their favour, not very widely read. What can be said about this apparently unedifying situation? It is usually assumed that McGonagall is enjoyed because he is unintentionally amusing, and everyone likes a good laugh. True, if dubiously defensible. But we know, from tested public performance, that an actor with a good voice can read the best of McGonagall (e.g. 'The Little Match Girl') quite straight and with some pathos, as doubtless Dickens would have done. If voice seems to be the key, we perhaps direct ourselves to Hamish Henderson's argument[9] that the clumsy ametricality of the lines (on the page) can be related to McGonagall's Irish family background of 'Come-all-ye' folk-song, the value of his poems being no more than that of their originality in uniquely and consistently forming their style out of the detritus of folk poetry. Perhaps anything carried to an extreme is attractive, as William Blake claimed. The obvious 'badness' of McGonagall also does not cancel the genuine popular appeal of someone who, unlike many of his poetic contemporaries, gave himself the function of commenting on the noted public events of the time.

McGonagall may seem a natural product of a Scotland which had so little sense of aesthetic, to say nothing of political, direction. The number of uprooted or exiled poets who went to England or elsewhere, with mixed fortunes of popular success and mixed posthumous reputations, can also appear a natural development in the latter part of the century—not helping the poetic situation in Scotland itself, yet showing, almost as in a scientific experiment, how much could or could not be made of the uprooting in terms of new poetic strength stimulated by new living environment. Robert Buchanan allowed his prickly combativeness to embroil him in endless literary controversies, to the detriment of his own literary art, which remained unexamined, derivative, turgid and repetitive. Fatally lured towards religious and philosophical heights which he could not command, he succeeded in only a handful of the poems of his voluminous output: some London genre sketches, one or two tragic ('The Scaith o' Bartle') and comic ('The Widow Mysie') idylls set in Scotland, and a few passages of light satire which one would have liked to see more of:

> Far is the cry from Byron's brandy
> To Pater's gods of sugar-candy!
> Lost the Homeric swing and trot,
>   Jingle of spur and beam of blade,
> Of that moss-trooper, Walter Scott,
>   Riding upon his border raid . . .
> And troubadours devoid of gristle
> Play the French flute and Cockney whistle.
>   ('The Outcast', Canto II, 1891).

Buchanan's Scottish experience was sandwiched between being born in England and returning to England as a young man, so the Scottish connection, although he felt it and acknowledged it, could hardly be paramount in his work. With Robert Louis Stevenson that connection goes much deeper into the fibre of the man, and he relished and experimented with Scots as well as English, and had thoughts about Scottish poetry as something that might still be distinct from English or 'British' poetry. The limitation of what he actually achieved goes with his having been more essentially novelist than poet, but the variety and range of his verse are impressive nevertheless. When he uses Scots, he is aware that he is doing what he can with a thinned-out literary medium, and in the well-known note in *Underwoods* (1887) he makes it clear how sceptical he is that the mushrooming scientific study of dialects in his own time will help Scots to survive: he puts his faith neither in a close use of local speech ('Let the precisians call my speech that of the Lothians. And if it be not pure, alas! what matters it?') nor in a proleptic Mac-Diarmidism which would deliberately revive obsolete words as well as show no geographical favouritism (the latter he would go along with up to a point, in an easygoing sort of way). Perhaps the result of this is that many of his Scots poems are fairly conventional, some of them leaning to the kailyard ('Ille Terrarum') or once more rehearsing well-known religious objects of attack ('The Scotsman's Return from Abroad') or doing both together ('A Lowden Sabbath Morn'); but then we have also the delightfully nostalgic portrait of youth in 'A Mile an' a Bittock', the folkishly sinister ballad of 'The Spaewife', and the perfectly poised gentlemanly complaint of 'The Counterblast Ironical'. And in the famous valediction 'To S R Crockett' he achieves excellence by using only three Scottish words, but each one (whaups, howes, peewees) carefully placed in each of the three stanzas, to maximum effect. Stevenson was bolder in English than in Scots, and followed his mentors, Matthew Arnold and Walt Whitman, into convincing experiments in free verse.

The narrow lanes are vacant and wet;
The rough wind bullies and blusters about the township.
And spins the vane on the tower
And chases the scurrying leaves,
And the straw in the damp innyard.
See—a girl passes
Tripping gingerly over the pools,
And under her lifted dress
I catch the gleam of a comely, stockinged leg.
Pah! the room stifles me,
Reeking of stale tobacco—
With the four black mealy horrible prints
After Landseer's pictures.
I will go out.

('Storm')

Stevenson had his depths and darknesses, and although these received more extensive embodiment in his prose fiction, his verse too has some sombre moments, often coming out of the theme of exile which his own life exhibited in extreme form. To write firmly and strongly on that subject, avoiding the various kinds of sentimentality that lie in wait, is a good achievement for a Scottish poet, and Stevenson in his verse letter 'To S.C.' (his friend Sidney Colvin) sent a South Seas message guaranteed to make the recipient think. He asked Colvin, the next time he visited the British Museum, to have a long look at the huge Easter Island statues at the entrance—they too are exiles. Stevenson identifies himself with the displaced Pacific monoliths; they too must have known blood and violence, like the graves of the martyrs on the Scottish moors, and the Standing Stones behind that, in his poem 'To S R Crockett'.

So far, so foreign your divided friends
Wander, estranged in body, not in mind.

James (B V) Thomson and John Davidson were exiles nearer home, and produced between them the last and strongest phase of the furth-of-Scotland poetry before Hugh MacDiarmid with his heroic heave turned the lever north again. Both have singular powers, but exercised in very different ways: Thomson the author of one great poem, *The City of Dreadful Night* (1874), Davidson a prolific writer of lyrics, dramatic monologues, eclogues, 'testaments', verse dramas, and poems of contemporary social and political comment, in styles ranging from the colloquial to the latinate sublime. Both were examples of the Scottish type of religious atheist or religious materialist; they were both interested in science and evolution; they both took up themes from the struggles of ordinary people in industrialised society; and both had psychological problems that in Thomson's case led him virtually to drink himself to death, and in Davidson's fostered a frustrated megalomania that led to suicide. They attracted much admiration from modern poets like T S Eliot and Hugh MacDiarmid, who saw them as forerunners or prophets of a modern awareness, a modern sensibility. Eliot, another exile, brought something of them into English poetry; MacDiarmid in his poems brought Davidson at least back to Scotland.

The City of Dreadful Night is partly the reaction of an uprooted Scottish poet to Victorian London at the height of its expansion, but partly also it is a poem with a mental landscape, an attempt to exteriorise, through powerful nightmarish images, the inner struggles of a man's life. Passages of general comment alternate with passages describing action as the insomniac speaker wanders through the city and has various meetings and encounters. The city, doubtless based on London, and probably also using Thomson's early memories of Glasgow, is not to be identified: it becomes simply 'the city', any city that is very large and very old, it has huge buildings, great bridges, squares, cathedrals, mansions, slums, endless streetlamps. The night inhabitants, and the actors of the poem, are the outcasts of daytime society, the tramps, the drunks, the drug-addicts, the half-crazed, the homeless, the sleepless, the lonely. The speaker, the 'I' of the poem, is both a familiar and an intimate of this night world, who can align himself with its sufferings, and yet also an observer, an artist, a reporter, an imaginative reconstructor, who is able to stand apart and build up a poem, an art object, in organised sections, for an audience. Abstract and particular passages move in alternation towards an extremely powerful conclusion. The last section (XXI) takes us to the north of the city, where there is a bleak ridge or plateau looking over this metropolis, and on the ridge is a colossal bronze statue of a winged woman based on Albrecht Dürer's *Melencolia*. She is the embodiment of whatever it is that makes the night city dreadful, an image of alienation, lethargy, and apathy, frozen in brooding inward thought, but also suggesting great endurance and latent power—power under a spell which no one can yet break.

> The moving moon and stars from east to west
>   Circle before her in the sea of air;
> Shadows and gleams glide round her solemn rest.
>   Her subjects often gaze up to her there:
> The strong to drink new strength of iron endurance,
> The weak new terrors; all, renewed assurance
>   And confirmation of the old despair.

In so far as Thomson's city is London, the companion-piece by John Davidson which T S Eliot yoked with it in his mind is 'Thirty Bob a Week', the dramatic monologue of a London clerk with wife and family to support on that amount—not absolute poverty, but near it—who comes across as a heroic figure on the edge of despair:

> It's walking on a string across a gulf
>   With millstones fore and aft about your neck;
> But the thing is daily done by many and many a one;
>   And we fall, face forward, fighting, on the deck.

But Davidson was no Cockney himself, arriving in London only in his early thirties, and he remained a more markedly Scottish writer than Thomson. Although a contributor to the *Yellow Book* in the 1890s, and a co-member of the Rhymers Club with W B Yeats, he brought something from outside, from the north, a hardness and roughness, a hammering quality, an obsessiveness with certain themes, especially some dealing with science and religion, which literary Londoners commented on and sometimes criticised. Yeats thought Davidson had too much 'violent energy, which is like a fire of straw . . . and is useless in the arts'. Perhaps so, but Davidson produced, among a mass of over-ambitiously grandiose writing, some very fine poetry: 'The Crystal Palace' with its brilliantly crisp and detailed mockery of the building and its visitors, 'The Wasp' with its nice imaginative projection into the feelings of a wasp trapped in a railway carriage, 'Snow' with a fusion of science and art worthy of MacDiarmid's later ideals; the wonderfully evocative urban landscapes of 'The Thames Embankment' and 'In the Isle of Dogs', the touchingly autobiographical 'The Last Journey' (Epilogue to 'The Testament of John Davidson'):

> Farewell the hope that mocked, farewell despair
> That went before me still and made the pace.
> The earth is full of graves, and mine was there
> Before my life began, my resting-place.

Much of his later work, the long blank-verse 'Testaments', which involve a search for a modern system of thought and a search for a hero, can be regarded as a surrogate world piled up by a desperate man; some of this poetry, dedicated to a Nietzschean 'will to live', is turgid and labyrinthine, some of it has great power both of image and of incident. It is a strange paradox in Davidson that one can turn from this darkly and brutally exalted arrogance to a moving awareness of the reverberations of the ordinary and everyday:

> An unseen roadman breaking flint,
> If echo and the winds conspire
> To dedicate his morning's stint,
> May beat a tune out, dew and fire
> So wrought that heaven might lend an ear,
> And Ariel hush his harp to hear.
>
> ('Matinée')

Davidson was not the only Scottish poet writing at the end of the century, and other writers and other styles would also feed into the new developments of the twentieth century, but with Davidson we can at least understand Hugh MacDiarmid's intense reaction to that

> small black shape by the edge of the sea,
> —A bullet-hole through a great scene's beauty,
> God through the wrong end of a telescope.
>
> ('Of John Davidson')

NOTES

1   Hogg, James, *Selected Poems*, Douglas S Mack (ed) (Oxford, 1970); Hogg, James, *Selected Poems and Songs*, David Groves (ed) (Edinburgh, 1986).
2   Bold, Alan (ed) *Byron: Wrath and Rhyme* (London, 1983) pp 17–56.
3   Rodger, Alexander, *Poems and Songs, Humorous, Serious, and Satirical*, Robert Ford (ed) (Paisley, 1897).
4   Smith, Alexander, *Poetical Works*, William Sinclair (ed) (Edinburgh, 1909).
5   Macfarlan, James, *Poetical Works* (with Memoir by Colin Rae-Brown) (Glasgow, 1882).
6   Hamilton, Janet, *Poems Sketches and Essays*, James Hamilton (ed) (Glasgow, 1885).
7   Thom, William, *Rhymes and Recollections of a Hand-loom Weaver*, W Skinner (ed) (Paisley, 1880). *See also* Bruce, Robert, *William Thom, the Inverurie Poet—A New Look* (Aberdeen, 1970).
8   Geddes, James Young, *The Spectre Clock of Alyth and Other Selections* (Alyth, n. d., c. 1885); *In the Valhalla* (Dundee, 1891).
9   Henderson, Hamish, 'William McGonagall and the Folk Scene', in *Chapbook* Vol 2 No 5 (Aberdeen, 1965), pp 3–10, 23–34.

FURTHER READING

Buchanan, Robert, *Complete Poetical Works* (2 vols) (London, 1901).

Cockburn, Henry, *Memorials of His Time* (Edinburgh, 1856).

Craig, David, *Scottish Literature and the Scottish People 1680–1830* (London, 1961).

Davidson, John, *The Poems*, Andrew Turnbull (ed) (2 vols) (Edinburgh, 1973).

Gray, David, *Poetical Works*, Henry Glassford Bell (ed) (Glasgow, 1874).

Kinsley, James (ed) *Scottish Poetry: A Critical Survey*, especially John W Oliver, 'Scottish Poetry in the Earlier Nineteenth Century', and Douglas Young, 'Scottish Poetry in the Later Nineteenth Century' (London, 1955).

Scott, Sir Walter, *Poetical Works*, J Logie Robertson (ed) (Oxford, 1894); *Selected Poems*, Thomas Crawford (ed) (Oxford, 1972). *See also* John O Hayden (ed) *Scott: The Critical Heritage* (London, 1970).

Stevenson, Robert Louis, *Collected Poems*, Janet Adam Smith (ed) (London, 1950, 1971).

Thomson, James, *Poems and Some Letters*, Anne Ridler (ed) (London, 1963).

Young, Douglas (ed) *Scottish Verse 1851–1951* (Edinburgh, 1952).

Chapter 19

Reclaiming Local Literature:
William Thom and Janet Hamilton

WILLIAM FINDLAY

Twentieth century critical surveys of nineteenth century Scottish literature have been so relatively consistent in their judgements, one with another, that a critical orthodoxy has arisen regarding assessment of the general literary output of the period, and of poetry in particular. With the exception of a few novelists such as Scott, Galt and Stevenson, a few prose writers such as Thomas Carlyle and Hugh Miller, a few poets such as Alexander Smith, James Thomson and John Davidson, and a few local versifiers who produced the odd half-acceptable set of rhymes, the vast bulk of nineteenth century Scottish literature has been condemned as balefully mediocre and obsessed with the themes of 'whisky and weaver bodies and bairnies and nostalgia and sentimentality' (to quote Kurt Wittig's neat summation).[1] From J H Millar's *A Literary History of Scotland* (1903), through the work of subsequent literary historians such as William Power, George Blake, Kurt Wittig, David Craig and Maurice Lindsay, and down to Roderick Watson's *The Literature of Scotland* (1984), a critical consensus of this kind has by and large prevailed.[2] J H Millar was the first critic to denounce the sickly sentimentality of the Kailyard writers,[3] and his criticism finds a complement in George Douglas Brown's contemporaneous novel *The House with the Green Shutters* (1901), which Brown wrote out of antagonism to what he described as 'the sentimental slop'[4] produced by Kailyard writers such as Barrie, Crockett and Maclaren. However, Brown came to feel that his personal animus against the Kailyard had led him to 'embitter the blackness' too much in his novel and that 'there was too much black for the white' in his depiction of small-town Scottish life.[5] There is growing reason to believe that, equally, literary historians, taking their lead from J H Millar, have allowed too much black in their evaluation of Scottish literature produced in the Victorian period. In saying this, I by no means wish to suggest that they have not had good reason to take the grue at so much of what they have read, nor am I especially concerned to suggest that writing they have read and found wanting needs to be reassessed (though there has been some such reassessment in recent years of Kailyard fiction). But I do wish to suggest that perhaps their animus, albeit understandable, against so much which is depressingly bad has dulled their curiosity about the possible existence outside mainstream book-culture of a body of work reflecting themes and values of a quite different kind to the Victorian writer's prevailing obsession with 'whisky and weaver bodies and bairnies and nostalgia and sentimentality'.

In the case of fiction the existence of just such a body of work has recently been tellingly revealed by William Donaldson in his book *Popular Literature in Victorian Scotland*. This pioneering study, which discloses for the first time the abundance of fiction to be found in the popular newspapers and journals of the period, challenges many established views and has potentially profound implications for our perspective on nineteenth-century Scottish literature. For example, of the critical orthodoxy that fiction in Victorian Scotland concerned itself exclusively with an idealised rural past and ignored industrialisation and the urban experience of the mass of the people, the fruits of Dr Donaldson's research lead him to conclude that this view cannot be sustained because:

> It is based solely on an interpretation of bourgeois book-culture which assumes the Kailyard to be typical and considers further enquiry unnecessary, while even middle-class fiction during the period is largely unexplored and the real popular literature of Victorian Scotland is practically *terra incognita*. Even in the fairly modest sample taken for the present study, there are cities and slums, factories, workers, capitalists, crime, poverty, disease, in short the whole urban gamut almost wherever one cares to look. The point is an important one. A number of conclusions have been drawn from this apparent failure to deal with the fact of urbanisation highly unfavourable to the Scots as a civilised and culture-producing people. If it is not true—and it is not—then our ignorance of the real range and complexity of the imaginative experience in Victorian Scotland has led to serious misjudgements not merely in criticism or creative writing, but in the whole contemporary intellectual and cultural milieu.[6]

The serious misjudgements to which William Donaldson refers can be seen in the assessments of literary historians who have taken little or no interest in the rich miscellany of popular literature to be found in the weekly press of the period which catered for a working- and lower middle-class popular readership. Little of this material found its way into book-form, which is an important reason why literary historians, whose criticism has been centred on book-culture, and a book-culture produced in the main for an all-UK literary market, have tended to ignore it. In fairness, it has to be said that, as William Donaldson acknowledges, 'on the whole Scottish Victorian press exists in a bibliographical wilderness',[7] and this has helped discourage the exploration of original source material. In addition, the sheer quantity of material is daunting, with more than 200 newspapers titles in existence in Scotland by the end of the nineteenth century. One can understand therefore why, where any literary historian has dipped into this 'alternative' culture, he has hastily withdrawn from the sea of print which has threatened to engulf him, and has preferred to rely in drawing his generalisations, in the case of local poetry, on a handful of Victorian verse anthologies.

As Dr Donaldson's research has concentrated on the fiction to be found in the Victorian press, the extent and nature of the poetry published in the same popular medium has still to examined. Also awaiting thorough investigation are the many small books of locally published local poetry. However, there are tentative signs that such an examination, or reclamation, of popular or local poetry is getting under way. Most notably, the poet Tom Leonard has prepared for publication in 1988 an anthology, *Renfrewshire Poetry from the French Revolution to the First World War*, which will contain much nineteenth-century poetry he has unearthed. This poetry stands in direct contrast to the kind of poetry that has till now been seen as characterising Victorian poetry in Scotland. In Leonard's words, the local poetry he has found is often

> committed, anticlerical, republican; descriptive or work and poverty, with no separation between writer and persona, no 'distancing' of emotion; much of it is about drink, people who enjoyed getting drunk and people who saw the suffering it caused and wrote bitterly of it, with or without satire, and with no Salvation Army tambourine jingling at the end.[8]

Tom Leonard describes this poetry as having 'no separation between writer and persona' because for him the particular value of local poetry, and why it needs to be reclaimed, is precisely that it is written out of *local* experience by *local* poets and thereby carries an immediacy and authenticity of voice. With the local poet there is none of the distantiation and objectification which characterises the traditional image of the poet as a kind of patriarch who looks down, judge-like, on 'them'—'them' being here the locals of a community and, more often than not, the local labouring classes. The poet as detached diagnostic judge makes an implicit separation between himself and the local world described and assumes that those whom he describes do not read the literature that supposedly describes them. This separation of the judging mind from those who are being judged perpetuates a dominant value-system which patronises and marginalises the lives and experience of those who do not conform to it. In such poetry, the local is judged to represent in some sense a deviation from an implicit norm, and the patriarchal poet, in the literary version of a nudge and a wink, signals this deviation to his readership, with whom he is in a kind of collusion.

Notwithstanding these remarks, it should be noted that Tom Leonard's prizing of local literature is not confined to poetry which is anti-establishment, but extends to an eclectic range of work encompassing a variety of writers and themes. Indeed, it is the rich diversity of the local Renfrewshire poetry which he has unearthed that has convinced him that, as far as nineteenth-century local poetry in Scotland generally is concerned, 'Locality by locality, A to Z of behind-the-counter library stock, old newspaper by old newspaper, people must go on with the work of release.'[9]

Tom Leonard's Renfrewshire anthology provides, appropriately, a modern day complement to *The Harp of Renfrewshire*, one of the best-known nineteenth-century anthologies of local poetry. Other such anthologies include *Harp of Perthshire, The Bards of Angus and the Mearns, The Bards of Galloway, The Glasgow Poets, One Hundred Modern Scottish Poets, Whistle-Binkie*, and others.[10] Literary historians have acknowledged the lamentable existence of anthologies such as these and have reserved their strongest criticism for the last-named collection, whose full title is *Whistle-Binkie or the Piper of the Party, Being a Collection of Songs for the Social Circle*. As Roderick Watson has put it, 'the title [*Whistle-Binkie*] has provided a generic label for all such milk-and-water vernacular verse, in a sentimental, complacent, and utterly trivalised notion of what poetry might be'.[11] Such criticism, which is admittedly justified, has been repeated by literary historians many times. It reaches its apotheosis in the assessment of Ian A Gordon, who saw the publication of *Whistle-Binkie* and *One Hundred Modern Scottish Poets* as representing 'one of the two blackest places in Scots letters'. Of the multi-volume *One Hundred Modern Scottish Poets* he bemoaned that 'every provincial newspaper was systematically ransacked' and that 'anything showing even rudimentary versification was admissable—and was generally admitted'.[12]

Despite the justification of condemning the sentimental banality of the vast bulk of the poetry in such anthologies, it seems to me that such condemnation should be qualified and not over-step into blanket condemnation of all local poetry produced in the period. The preferences or, at worst, prejudices of editors have to be borne in mind. For example, even supposing every provincial newspaper was ransacked by the editor of One Hundred Modern Scottish Poets, would his selection criteria be ours? Some account must be taken, too, of the readership for whom an editor had an anthology in mind; or, to put it a different way, did an anthology set out to serve an expressed function which the poetry chosen had to fit? *Whistle-Binkie*, for example, was, as its sub-title indicates, *A Collection of Songs for the Socal Circle*. Most of the 'poetry' in the collection actually takes the form of either lyrics written to airs indicated by the poet, or verse obviously intended to be recited publicly. In this last regard, as Douglas Young has noted, 'this collection was the great stand-by of reciters at family parties, kirk *soirees*, Volunteer picnics', and so on.[13] We may despair today at the predominance of the mawkish and the pawkie in such a work, but the great success of *Whistle-Binkie* in its own day testifies to a popular demand for material to be sung and recited in social circles. In *Whistle-Binkie* itself we are told disarmingly that 'the songs are of different degrees of merit' but that the object is to display 'that peculiar talent for song-writing for which Scotland has always been distinguished',[14] and to supply a 'collection of Comic and Sentimental Songs . . . excluding all pieces of an indelicate or immoral description'[15] for ladies and gentlemen wishing to entertain their friends at domestic social gatherings. Since the material chosen for the kind of social circle envisaged clearly had to be inoffensive and undemanding if it were to prove acceptable for an agreeable and decorous evening's entertainment, we should not go on to conclude from anthologies such as *Whistle-Binkie* that they represent the whole truth about local poetry.

One critic who has condemned *Whistle-Binkie* and the kind of poetry which characterises it, but yet appreciates (albeit disparagingly) that it has a function as 'verse designed to be sung or declaimed before a sociable gathering in a mood of relaxation',[16] is the afore-mentioned Douglas Young. In his own anthology, *Scottish Verse 1851–1951*, Young included examples of Victorian verse which also showed him aware of the existence of a quite different kind of local verse to that found in Victorian anthologies such as *Whistle-Binkie*. There are poems such as Edward L Sloan's 'The Weaver's Triumph' which relates a weaver's triumph over a merchant and his lackey who try to cheat him out of the real worth of the cloth he has woven; John Mitchell's 'The St Rollox Lum's Address to his Brethren' which proclaims the values of Liberal industrialism; Moses Peerie's 'The Goodly Ironmaster' which satirises its subject and his supposed Christian-minded charity; and 'The Last Sark' by Ellen Johnston, who died in the Barony Poorshouse of Glasgow, and whose social criticism can be sampled from the opening stanza of her poem:

> Gude guide me, are ye hame again, and hae ye got mae wark?
> We've naething noo tae pit awa, unless your auld blue sark.   [shirt]
> My heid is rinnin roond aboot, far lichter nor a flee: [fly]
> What care some gentry if they're weel though a' the puir wad dee?[17]

But despite his exceptions in drawing attention to such verse, Douglas Young remained sceptical of the value of further enquiry. In an article on Scottish poetry of the later nineteenth century, he said, after quoting from Ellen Johnston's 'The Last Sark':

> For this and similar pieces see *The Bards of Angus and the Mearns, The Harp of Renfrewshire*, Mr Edwards of Brechin's seventeen volumes of *Modern Scottish Poets*, and other regional or temporal collections usually to be picked up on street-barrows or second-hand stalls. With the current craze for Victoriana . . . it may be that some will relish odd items of versification extractable from 'wee buikies' printed at Kirkintilloch or Duns, Lesmahagow or Auchtermuchty . . . There are hundreds of volumes, comparatively few of which I have scanned, through which the quest for period-flavour pieces may be agreeably pursued at odd moments; and the poets' corners of local newspapers would yield certain gleanings among the advertisements for ferrets, tomb-stones and secondhand pianos.[18]

Notwithstanding the dismissive tone of these comments, Douglas Young is one of the few critics who seems to have looked beyond mainstream book-culture and actually scanned some 'wee buikies' and newspapers. On his own admission, though, even he did scarce more than attempt a superficial sampling. As a consequence, like other critics before him and since, he placed heavy reliance on the supposed representativeness of that handful of verse anthologies named earlier. Nevertheless, if there can be discerned beginning to stir today a mood of dissatisfaction with that over-reliance—and it is the purpose of this essay both to call attention to that nascent mood and to contribute to it—it must be acknowledged that the inclusion of poems such as those mentioned above in Young's *Scottish Verse 1851–1951* has, at least in this writer's case, added to the seeds of doubt which have been sown regarding acceptance of the established critical view of local poetry produced in the Victorian period. That such seeds of scepticism have now started to germinate and put down roots, however, is, it must be owned, in large part due to the work of William Donaldson and Tom Leonard, as referred to earlier. But it also owes something to my own exploration of the kind of 'wee buikies' dismissed by Douglas Young. Whilst it would be ill-advised at this provisional stage of investigation to attempt generalised conclusions regarding nineteenth century local poetry, there is sufficient evidence coming forward to suggest that established critical views should in the meantime be regarded more circumspectly than has hitherto been the case. In illustration of why this is so, I would like to draw attention to the work of two poets, William Thom and Janet Hamilton.

I have chosen Thom and Hamilton as representative local writers for a number of reasons. One is a man and one woman; and one is from the North-East and the other from the industrial West Central Belt. Both were closely identified in their time with particular localities—Thom with Inverurie and Hamilton with Coatbridge—and both were self-taught poets who remained close to working-class life throughout their lives. Both wrote not just poetry but recollections, and their prose and poetry share something of a symbiotic relationship which allows us better to understand the local context—that is, the social and cultural milieu—out of which they wrote their verse. In addition, much of their work is blighted by the kind of baleful qualities which critics have found in so much of the literature of the period, yet they both wrote other work possessing qualities more attractive to our age and of more enduring value. The apparent prevalence of the former kind of qualities in their writing might dissuade any reader scanning their work from enquiring more conscientiously; and the inclusion of Thom in *Whistle-Binkie* might alone be thought to damn him irredeemably and put him beyond the pale of further enquiry. However, if further enquiry can and does reveal a quite different side to such poets' work than a superficial acquaintance might suggest, it begs the question of how many other local poets need to be reassessed and how much other local writing awaits reclamation.

William Thom (1798/99?–1848) and Janet Hamilton (1795–1873) were of the same generation, and both were writing in that mid century period which has been seen as constituting a literary hiatus between the death of Scott and his generation of writers and the arrival of Robert Louis Stevenson. Thom and Hamilton also wrote in both Scots and English, and they shared a keen sense of Scottish literary tradition. Both experienced privation and observed at first-hand the evils attendant on industrialisation. Bearing these facts in mind, the necessarily brief discussion of their work which follows will not only keep in mind the more general critical orthodoxy outlined at the outset, but will implicitly address a particular set of oft-repeated critical views. It has been held, for example, that 'the less said about the two generations after Scott the better' (Kurt Wittig),[19] and that 'from 1825 to 1880 there is next to nothing worth attention' (David Craig).[20] Similarly, in mid century Maurice Lindsay finds nothing but 'a hiccuping re-tasting of long since digested vernacular flavours'.[21] For most critics the strongest vernacular flavour being thus re-tasted was the poetry of Robert Burns. The Victorian period produced a scunnersome abundance of pallid limitations of Burns, with the imitators holding a distorted view of the national bard as 'an inspired ploughman, alternating between drink and sentimentality' (Ian A Gordon).[22] As Kurt

Wittig concluded, 'Burns had summed up a tradition, but since little was added to it, it rapidly became an exhausted stereotype'.[23] This exhaustion extended to the use of the vernacular, as 'the sentimental rustification of Scots had left it frozen in time and place as a language apparently reserved for the "poetry corners" of local newspapers and hundreds of talentless imitators of Burns' (Roderick Watson).[24] This same sentimental rustification was seen to characterise the content as well as the medium of Scots poetry, and 'the industrial fret' (to use George Blake's phrase),[25] was completely ignored. Hence, there was, as David Craig diagnosed it, 'a lacking sense of the contemporary'.[26] No-one has defined this supposed lack in the literature of the period more clearly than William Power:

> . . . though Scotland had been severely industrialized, though the number of miners, artisans, and textile workers was possibly greater than that of all agricultural workers, and though Glasgow was one of the largest of British cities, it was still assumed, for literary purposes, that the majority of Scots people lived in rustic villages . . . The fact of the matter is that social conditions in industrial Scotland at that time were somewhat beyond the scope of realism. It was better to help to keep alive the native faith and virtues and idyllic memories of the people than to remind them of the scorching fires of Moloch through which they were passing. Not until these fires had been largely quenched was Scots literature able to face *la vraie vérité* of Scots life.[27]

To read William Thom's 'wee buikie', *Rhymes and Recollections of a Handloom Weaver* (first published Aberdeen 1844),[28] is to learn that few writers were better acquainted with *la vraie vérieté* of Scottish life than him. Thom's essay of recollections is a valuable document, not least because it bears witness to 'the scorching fires of Moloch' of which William Power speaks and serves as typical of the experience of many. Thom was aware of this last aspect and said of his 'Recollections': 'The self-portraiture herein attempted is not altogether Egotism . . . , inasmuch as the main lineaments of the sketch are to be found in the separate histories of a thousand families in Scotland within these last ten years' (xi). The main lineaments, as we shall see, speak of poverty and interminable toil, social injustice and the destitution caused workers by fluctuations in trade.

William Thom was an Aberdonian. At the age of ten he was apprenticed to a local firm of cotton manufacturers; and at the age of fourteen he entered a large weaving-factory known locally in Aberdeen as the 'School Hill Factory'. He was to work in this factory as a weaver for some seventeen years, and in his 'Recollections' he offers a bitter exposé of the conditions which prevailed in what he describes as this 'prime nursery of vice and sorrow' (1):

> It is a duty, do it who may—and it shall be done—to expose the factory system of that day, as it stood in our 'moral North.' Fairly to put the knife into the dead monster, lay bare its dark core, dissect it in broad day, that the world may see who had the fat and who the famine portion of that heartless trading.

For Thom, the School Hill Factory was characterised by 'wheels, and din, and dust, . . . naked hunger, sin, and withering misery' (3); and he speaks of how 'At every turning of my native city I meet the shadow of a former shopmate, haggard, and prematurely old, worn beyond the pale of usefulness on earth, sunken, perishing' (2). There were three to four hundred men and women working in the odious '*rickles*' which constituted the factory, and in addition to exposing the appalling working conditions they endured in the factory, Thom is not afraid to admit that many of his fellow workers compounded their predicament through dissipation. However, in admitting the high incidence of sexual promiscuity and alcoholism, Thom is not concerned to censor but to seek causes. For example, of the prostitution some of the young women resorted to, he explains how this arose as a result of an iniquitous system of fines for lateness or non-attendance imposed by the factory owners. Ordinarily, wages barely afforded basic sustenance, so if fines were applied, workers found themselves owing the company and working weeks and sometimes months for nothing. Destitution thus drove many to desperate measures; yet, comments Thom, 'the wise and well provided will often condemn, without one pitying look, nor seek to see that strong link between crime and cause' (7).

Though ill-fed, ill-clothed, ill-housed and exhausted by long working-hours, remarkably, some of the workers who had a 'turn for reading' would meet, Thom tells us, to 'gossip over all we knew of books and the outer world':

> Then came glimpses,—the only glimpses afforded us of true, and natural, and rational existence. . . . The Wizard of Waverley had roused the world to wonders, and we wondered too. Byron was flinging around the terrible and beautiful of a distracted greatness. Moore was doing all he could for love-sick boys and girls,—yet they had never enough! Nearer and dearer to hearts like ours was the Ettrick Shepherd, then in his full tide of song and story; but nearer and dearer still than he, or any living songster—to us dearer—was our ill-fated fellow-craftsman, Tannahill, who had just then taken himself from a neglecting world, while yet that world waxed mellow in his lay. Poor weaver chiel! What we owe to thee! Your 'Braes o' Balquidder,' and 'Yon Burnside,' and 'Gloomy Winter,' and the 'Minstrel's' wailing ditty, and the noble 'Gleniffer.' Oh! how they did ring above the rattling of a hundred shuttles! Let me again proclaim the debt we owe to those Song Spirits, as they walked in melody from loom to loom, ministering to the low-hearted; and when the breast was filled with everything but hope and happiness, and all but seared, let only break forth the healthy and vigorous chorus 'A man's a man for a' that,' the fagged weaver brightens up. His very shuttle *skytes* boldly along, and clatters through in faithful time to the tune of his merrier shopmates!
>
> Who dare measure in doubt the restraining influences of these very Songs? To us they were all instead of sermons. Had one of us been bold enough to enter a church, he must have been ejected for the sake of decency. His forlorn and curiously patched habiliments would have contested the point of attraction with the ordinary eloquence of that period. So for all parties it was better that he kept to his garret, or wandered far 'in the deep green wood.' Church bells rang not for us. Poets were indeed our Priests. But for those, the last relic of our moral existence would have surely passed away! (7–8).

In claiming that but for songs 'the last relic of our moral existence would have surely passed away', Thom is attaching a primacy to song, based on the reality of his factory experience, which casts important light on the special appeal of songs and song-writing for a local working-class poet such as him. Organised religion is clearly regarded with disaffection, its emphasis on visible respectability communicating debarment to the impoverished factory-workers in their 'curiously patched habiliments'. In consequence, as Thom puts it, songs took on the power of sermons and poets were priests. Poetry and song had a cathartic power to uplift and give hope to the toil-worn and dispirited; in the slough of despond which was factory life, song, we are told, 'walked in melody from loom, ministering to the low-hearted', and a song such as Burns's defiant and rallying anthem of universal brotherhood, 'A man's a man for a' that', took on immediate significance. The function to be fulfilled by songs contributed to *Whistle-Binkie*, of supplying material for the entertainment of genteel social circles, is therefore clearly at a far remove from the function which song performed in offering temporary respite from the toil and hardship endured by factory operatives such as Thom and his workmates.

One notes, too, the special appeal of self-taught poets and song-writers from the Scottish folk/literary tradition such as Burns, Hogg and Tannahill. In songs by such writers the native vernacular tradition spoke directly to the likes of Thom and his fellow-workers, and inspired some to emulate the work of their folk idols. That Burns, Hogg and Tannahill were of the people at once bred a warmth of familiarity and demonstrated that being uneducated and of humble social station was no barrier to creative endeavour. The Scottish vernacular tradition in literature was regarded as inherently democratic and all-including; it was seen as a common possession of all the Scottish people, and anyone, no matter how lowly, could contribute to it.

After seventeen years in the unspeakable School Hill Factory, Thom spent nine years in the Dundee area before a trade crash in 1837 silenced in one week upwards of six thousand looms. Thom was then living in Newtyle, a village of weaving-shops which had sprung up following the completion of the Dundee Railway a few years before, and in his 'Recollections' he conveys an idea of the friction which could develop when industrialisation was imported into a small, long-settled community. Neither employers nor locals offered the incomers any relief or sympathy in their distress, and employment and hunger gradually drove them away from Newtyle. Eventually, Thom, his wife and four children were forced to take to the road, too. The hardship of their wanderings in the Carse of Gowrie makes for moving reading. Starving and exposed to the elements, they sought shelter as and where they could and sunk ever deeper into distress. Thom was driven to comtemplate suicide, and to compound his despair, the exposure and privation led to the death of his infant daughter as they lay in an almost roofless farm out-house one night:

> I think it must have been between three and four o'clock when Jean wakened me. Oh, that scream!—I think I can hear it now. The other children, startled

from sleep, joined in frightful wail over their dead sister. Our poor Jeanie had, unobserved by us, sunk during the night under the effects of the exposure of the preceding evening, following, as it did, a long course of hardship, too great to be borne by a young frame. Such a visitation could only be sustained by one hardened to misery and wearied of existence. I sat a while and looked on them; comfort I had none to give—none to take; I spake not—what could be said— words? Oh, no! the worst is over when words can serve us. And yet it is not just when the wound is given that pain is felt. How comes it, I wonder, that minor evils will affect even to agony, while paramount sorrow overdoes itself, and stands in stultified calmness? Strange to say, on first becoming aware of the bereavement of that terrible night, I sat for some minutes gazing upwards at the fluttering and wheeling movements of a party of swallows, our fellow-lodgers, which had been disturbed by our unearthly outcry. (19–20)

In time Thom won back to Aberdeen and recommenced factory-weaving, and after a year he was offered more profitable work in Inverurie. But Thom had scarce settled in Inverurie when his wife died in childbirth. Soon after, Thom suffered enforced unemployment and, unable to feed himself and his three children, he resolved to throw himself and them on the mercy of the House of Refuge in Aberdeen. Rather that, says Thom bitterly, than 'worm through all the creeping intricacies that lie between starvation and parish charities . . . how preferable, surely, the unseen, silent sadness in a House of Refuge to the thousand and one heartless queries, taunts, and grumblings, that accompany the Elder's "eighteenpence"' (32). To ease the weight of his grief and the weariness of this unemployment Thom had taken to composing poems. He had succeeded in having one of these published in the *Aberdeen Herald* under the telling anonymous signature of 'Serf'. The poem attracted such interest that on the eve, literally, of his removal to the House of Refuge, Thom received by post the then substantial sum of five pounds from a would-be patron. Of his patron's timely intervention, Thom wrote: 'Lately I looked to nothing but increasing labour and decreasing strength—interminable toil and ultimate starvation—such is the fate of nine-tenths of my brethren—but now daylight breaks on my destiny' (39). The 'daylight' this patron brought extended to having a book of Thom's poems published and to taking Thom to London to meet many of the literary lions of the day. At this point 'Recollections' ends.

Of the dozen poems by Thom published in *Whistle-Binkie*, all would deserve the damning epithet 'whistle-binkie-ish', and none would give an unsuspecting reader any indication of the harsh experiences Thom endured in his life as described in his 'Recollections'. Whilst poems such as 'Dreamings of the Bereaved', 'Jeanie's Grave' and 'The Mitherless Bairn' relate to the death of his wife, the sentiments he expresses, though obviously sincerely meant, come across in poetic terms as conventional and cloying. However, in turning to the poems in *Rhymes and Recollections of a Handloom Weaver* a truer impression of Thom is gained. In these poems, most of which are in Scots, the two broad themes which predominate are love (many of the 'poems' here being songs), and what might be loosely termed 'social injustice'. The appeal of songs for Thom and his fellows has already been commented on. Sadly,

most of Thom's poems and songs dealing with love are decidedly undis-
tinguished. Some are admirable in parts, but there is only one of the love
poems which I believe is rescuable in its entirety and worthy of inclusion in
an anthology today. It is 'Whisper Low', which I give in full:

> Slowly, slowly the cauld moon creeps
>   Wi' a licht unlo'esome to see;   [unlovely]
> It dwalls on the window whaur my love sleeps,
>   An' she winna wauken to me.
>   Wearie, wearie the hours and slow,
>   Wauken, my lovie, an' whisper low!
>
> There's nae ae sang in heaven's hicht,
>   Nor on the green earth doun,
> Like soun's that kind love kens at nicht,
>   When whispers hap the soun';
>   Hearin'—fearin'—sichin' so—
>   Whisper, my bonnie lovie, whisper low!
>
> They lack nae licht wha weel can speak
>   In love's ain wordless wile;
> Her ee-bree creepin' on my cheek   [eye-brow]
>   Betrays her pawkie smile;
>   Happy—happy—silent so—
>   Breathin'—bonnie lovie, whisper low!
>
> Was yon a waft o' her wee white han',
>   Wi' a warnin' "wheesht"to me?
> Or was it a gleam o' that fause moon fa'in
>   On my puir misguided e'e?
>   Wearie—wearie—wearie O—
>   Wauken, my lovie, an' whisper low!
>
>   75–76

Whilst this cannot be claimed a perfect lyric, somehow it overcomes its
deficiencies. At points it threatens to teeter into sentimentality but it just
manages to hold its balance, and the tension this generates is part of the
poem's attraction. There is an eerieness, in the Scots sense of ghostly or
strange, which also contributes to the appeal. The moon casts a cauld gla-
mourie over the poem which fits the eerie mood of uncertainty as to whether
the loved-one the poet is addressing is alive or dead. There is a hint of the
carnal in the poem, too, and this, along with its eerieness, is reminiscent of
love lyrics by the twentieth century Scots poets William Soutar and Hugh
MacDiarmid.

Of the other poems in the volume, a note Thom supplied to one of them
suggests their concerns:

> Who are they that beat about in the substanceless regions of fancy for material
> to move a tear? Who but the silken bandaged sons of comfort?—ink-bleeders
> whose sorrows are stereotyped—they who see life only through the hazy

medium of theory, and do at farthest obtain but a mellow blink of those sickening realities that settle about the poor man's hearth. (66)

These comments are appended to a poem addressed to one of his motherless children who is in the Aberdeen infirmary following a serious operation. The poem is prefaced with the angry quotation: 'Hospital charities for devastated homes! Faugh! Give me my wages; have I not laboured?' (65) Moved by the sad sight of his son in this '*cauldrife* lonely lair', he rages:

> Has God disown'd them, the children of toil?
> Is the promise of Heaven no more?
> Shall Industry weep?—shall the pamper'd suppress
> The sweat-earned bread of the poor?

'Monitor's Song' was similarly called forth as a result of a visit to the Aberdeen School of Industry which housed the children of poverty-stricken parents and destitute orphans who had been rounded up from lanes and entries. Behind the 'cold grey granite walls' of this grim building, a monitor sings of how, '. . . aft unkent we greet and sing,/And ply the warp and netting string' (81). Another poem, 'The overgate Orphan', was written in response to a woman in Dundee being found dead of starvation with her seven year old boy asleep beside her. In a prefatory note Thom comments:

> Starvation to death is not uncommon amongst us; yet we are in the nineteenth century—the pearl age of benevolent societies, charity-schools, and 'useful knowledge'. Would benevolence be perverted, charity made colder, or the knowledge *useless*, that made us timeously acquainted with catastrophes like these? . . . That the 'Murder of Neglect' is perpetrated in this land is one terrible fact, and it is as true, though, alas! not so terrifying, that he who is ignorant of it, or, knowing it, feels it only as an incident per course, bestowing upon it a *fushionless* shrug, and a 'woe's me,'—*that man has blood upon his head!* (45–46)

That Thom's own children suffered poverty and the loss of their mother obviously gave an edge to his anger at the plight of orphans and deprived children.

Of the charitable agencies Thom criticises, the Church is singled out on more than one occasion (doubtless reflecting his experience of its attitude to impoverished factory-workers, as alluded to earlier). In 'Justice—A Reverie', a spokesman for the poor recounts to the goddess Justice how 'Our kirk . . . endures a spot/Upon her fair repute,/An water winna wash the blot,/Nor Gospel wring it out. . . .'

> Our fa'en guides hae racht an' wrung   [fallen ministers]
> An' pouch'd the slave-won pack;   [pocketed]
> In very kernal conscience flung,
> An' wail'd, 'Fie! send it back!'

Justice, in turn, mocks the passivity of the complainants:

'What slave' quo' she, 'tholes ha'f sic whackin'   [endures]
As whacks dealt down on you,
        Aye silent syne?
  (95–6)

A particularly interesting poem is 'Chants for Churls', which takes for its subject the 1843 Disruption in the Church of Scotland and satirises both factions equally. The opening two stanzas give a taste:

Ken ye carls howkin' out,   [digging]
Wha darena howk within,
  Holy wark gies your sark,   [shirt]
  Yer siller, an' yer sheen.   [shoes]
Gae mak' a fyke to feed the kirk,   [make a fuss]
Although ye starve yer kin,
  An' ye'll be lauchin' lairdies yet,   [laughing]
  Youplin in yer yardies yet,   [howling]
Heich ayont the moon.

We've kirks in ilka corner,
An' wow but we can preach;
  Timmer tap, little sap,   [timber]
  Onything for bread.
Their sermons in the draw well,
Drink till ye stretch
  We're clean sairt sookin' at it,
  The Deil's dazed lookin' at it;
Daud him on the head.   [strike]
    (98–99)

The Establishment, whether local or national, does not escape Thom's rage, either. 'The Stricken Branch' is an allegorical satire on what a note describes as 'the Sympathy, Justice, and Liberality of our enlightened, Free-trade-loving, Universal-brotherhood-advocating, fellow Burgher, Bailie *Thinclaith*'. Thom, as an incomer, obviously fell foul of a local closed-shop to be found at work amongst the guildry of a small town such as Inverurie: 'In every small community there is a vehement working of the *Keep-out* system, which is only changed for the *Keep-down*. A stranger is never welcome beyond the role of "*buy and come again*"' (81–83). Looking beyond the clearly far from cosy parish of Inverurie, 'A Chieftain Unknown to the Queen', written in 1843, concerns a visit to Edinburgh of Queen Victoria, on which occasion the poor were cleared from the streets so as not to offend the royal gaze:

Then mony a chieftain's heart
  Beat high'neath its proud tartan screen;
But one sullen chief stood afar and apart,
  Nor recked he the smile o' a Queen.

> 'Wha's he winna blink on our Queen,
>   Wi' his haffets sae lyart and lean?'   [locks] [grizzled]
> O ho! it is Want, wi' his gathering gaunt,
>   An' his millions of mourners unseen.
>
> Proud Scotland cried 'Hide them; oh, hide!
>   An' lat nae them licht on her een;
> Wi' their bairnies bare, it would sorrow her sair;
>   For a mither's heart moves in our Queen.'
>   (50–51)

Thom's longest and strongest poem raging against social injustice is 'Whisperings for the Unwashed'. We are told that the scene is a town in the north, that the time is six o'clock in the morning and that the town drummer is going about his business rousing the sleeping inhabitants. This is the opening half of the poem:

> RUBADUB, rubadub, row-dow-dow!
> The sun is glinting on hill and knowe,
> An' saft the pillow to the fat man's pow—   [head]
> Sae fleecy an' warm the guid 'hame-made,'   [blanket]
> An' cozie the happin o' the farmer's bed.   [cover]
> The feast o' yestreen how it oozes through,   [yesterday]
> In bell an' blab on his burly brow.   [sweat drop]
> Nought recks he o' drum an' bell,
> The girnal's fou an' sure the "sale";   [meal bin]
> The laird an' he can crap an keep—   [crop]
> Weel, weel may be laugh in his gowden sleep.
> His dream abounds in stots, or full   [young cattle]
> Of cow an' corn, calf an' bull;
> Of cattle shows, of dinner speaks—
> Toom, torn, and patch'd like weavers' breeks;   [empty]
> An' sic like meaning hae, I trow,   [am sure]
> As rubadub, rubadub, row-dow-dow.
>
> Rubadub, rubadub, row-dow-dow!
> Hark, how he waukens the Weavers now!
> Wha lie belair'd in a dreamy steep—   [stuck fast]
> A mental swither 'tween death an' sleep—   [hesitation]
> Wi' hungry wame and hopeless breast,
> Their food no feeding, their sleep no rest,
> Arouse ye, ye sunken, unravel your rags,
> No coin in your coffers, no meal in your bags;
> Yet cart, barge, and waggon, with load after load,
> Creak mockfully, passing your breadless abode.
> The stately stalk of Ceres bears,
> But not for you, the bursting ears;
> In vain to you the lark's lov'd note,
> For you no summer breezes float,
> Grim winter through your hovel pours—
> Dull, din, and healthless vapour yours.
> The noble Spider weaves alone,

And feels the little web his own,
His hame, his fortress, foul or fair,
Nor factory whipper swaggers there.
Should ruffian wasp, or flaunting fly
Touch his lov'd lair, 'T IS TOUCH AND DIE!
Supreme in rags, ye weave, in tears,
The shining robe your murderer wears;
Till worn, at last, to very "waste,"   [in weaver's language, broken threads]
A hole to die in, at the best;
And, dead, the session saints begrudge ye   [elders]
The twa-three deals in death to lodge ye;   [boards to make a coffin]
They grudge the grave wherein to drap ye,
An' grudge the very *muck* to hap ye.

(16–18)

These last four lines are worthy of Burns. Unfortunately, however, it has to be said that little else of Thom's output achieves this quality, and here lies a problem for someone, like me, urging the recovery of work by local writers such as Thom. A few of his poems, such as 'Whisperings for the Unwashed', 'Chants for Churls' and 'Whisper Low', are of acceptable quality and interest to us today and are worthy of being anthologised, but the bulk of his verse would leave us indifferent. But the importance of a writer like Thom in contributing to a reassessment of our Victorian literary inheritance lies in the inimical circumstances he struggled against in achieving his writing and the witness his work bears to the reality of life lived under those circumstances. If that witness is not, in literary terms, of the highest quality, that is little surprising given the privations Thom endured. What is remarkable is that Thom found the wherewithal to bear witness at all, and I believe that due appreciation should be given to this in assessing the work of someone like him. If a local writer such as Thom can be approached in a spirit of open-minded and sympathetic enquiry, and consideration is taken of the hostile conditions he laboured under in producing his work, a quite different view can emerge from that gleaned by, for example, the lamentable poetry he is represented by in *Whistle-Binkie*.

Janet Hamilton was quintessentially a local poet in that in her whole life she never travelled further than twenty miles from her home in industrial Lanarkshire. From the age of seven till her death at the age of seventy-eight she lived in Langloan, Coatbridge. Her father was a shoemaker, and at the age of thirteen she married his journeyman, by whom she had ten children, seven of whom survived. She was thus, as she herself put it, 'the daughter, wife and mother of working-men' (456),[29] and as such she had little leisure or inducement to pursue her life-long passion for self-improvement. She had no formal education but her mother taught her to read at an early age and she proved a precocious reader with a voracious appetite for books of all kinds. At the age of eight, to her great joy she found in a neighbouring weaver's house a copy of Milton's *Paradise Lost* and a volume of Allan Ramsay's poems. Of the Ramsay she said that she was at home at once, and she went on to read other Scots poets such as Burns, Fergusson, M'Neil and

Tannahill. In her adult years she always tried to keep abreast of the times and was deeply interested in all that pertained to 'the march of the mind'. She took a keen interest in national issues and was especially interested in foreign affairs. For example, such was her enthusiasm for the cause of Italian freedom that she sent Garibaldi a gold nugget a friend had sent her from the gold diggings. Garibaldi sent her a gracious letter of thanks which she had framed and hung on her wall, and his son later paid her a visit specially to thank her on behalf of his father. Janet Hamilton, then, may have lived a life which in geographic and social terms was severely circumscribed, but her mind was far from fettered by local boundaries.

In view of her precocity as a reader it is remarkable that she was over fifty before she learned to write, and that it was not until she was fifty-four that she began composing the poems and essays which she contributed to Cassell's *Working Man's Friend*, and which were eventually to appear in book form in a number of editions. Remarks by her son give some idea of the difficulties she had to work against in achieving her writing: 'My mother's pieces were mostly all composed amid the bustle and noise incident to the affairs of a family being conducted in a small house, or while she was engaged in conversation with her family or friends' (viii). One of her friends and biographers, who also lived in Coatbridge, added that whe also wrote at night when the house had gone to bed but that even then she had to contend with 'the thud of the ponderous hammers smashing the molten metal in the works close by . . . the shrill screaming of whistles, and the never-ending rattle of machinery'.[30] It is the fact that she lived amongst, and often wrote out of the immediacy of, this kind of industrial experience—that is, 'the industrial fret' which George Blake and others have seen as being ignored in our Victorian literature, as was noted earlier—which makes Janet Hamilton's life and writing so relevant to our discussion here. It is relevant, too, that, in common with William Thom, she produced her work under conditions far from conducive to literary composition.

In her childhood Langloan was a small weaving village comprising two rows of thatched *but and bens* with fine, well-kept gardens, and situated in a rural location. But in her lifetime she saw it change beyond recognition as it became engulfed by industrialisation and merged into Coatbridge. It was doubtless her experience of this dramatic change that inspired her to write her many sketches of reminiscence about village life and character as she had known them before they were swept away. For example, one of her essays, 'Local Changes,' finds her comparing the Langloan of the past with that of her present. If her description of the past inclines to the lyrically sentimental, it nonetheless graphically illustrates the radical changes which have occurred in her parish:

> . . . the weird fires of spunkie [Will o' the Wisp or marsh fires] glimmer and dance no more on the marsh, which is now lighted up by the lurid flames of iron smelting furnaces, and the sweet breath of the gowany and white clover lea is now exchanged for the stifling and sulphurous fumes arising from smouldering heaps of hot cinders and burning slag; and in place of the pale, indolent

artizan basking on the green brae, and chanting some favourite Scotch ditty, we see crowds of black begrimed, sweating, and toiling mortals at the fires high and low, making the air vocal with "the frequent curse and the cheek-distending oath,"and for the song of the birds and the music of the stream, we have the scream of the locomotive and the never-ending clank of machinery and grinding of wheels. Great, indeed, is the change which has passed over thee, erst green "Bergens-howm," for within thy once lonely bounds the so-named "Langloan Ironworks" now stand, with the dwelling of those who are attendant on labouring at them.

. . .In our locality, where now is the flowery blossoms of the cottage garden so lone and sequestered that a pair of cuckoo lovers might undisturbed tell their tender tale? Where now are the unsmirched, unsmoked hawthorn blossoms that once shaded the ebon wing of the blackbird, and the hazels tha sheltered the callow young of the thrush? Coal, smoke, and the deleterious fumes of charcoal fires have blackened and poisoned them, and my own lovely little flowery dell, alas! is desecrated by the hob-nailed hoofs of the navvy. Mounds of clay and debris now cover it, and the lover of nature has exchanged the whistle of the blackbird and the song of the thrush for the shrieking, hissing, and whistling of steam, and the once clear waters of the Luggie for a sink of stench and pollution; ah! these roaring, blazing, smoking furnace-fires, these hammering, grinding, grating, jarring noises . . .

(386, 388–89)[31]

Such changes she also described in rhyme, as in her longish poem 'A Wheen Aul' Memories', where she contrasts the Langloan and environs she knew as a child with how they were sixty years on. One of the places she visits on her imaginary walk around the locality is Simmerlee:

> Oot-owre the auld brig, up to sweet Simmerlee,
> Sweet, said ye?—hech, whaur?—for nae sweetness I see;
> Big lums spewin' reek an' red lowe on the air,   [glow]
> Steam snoring' an' squeelin', and whiles muckle mair!
>
> Explodin' an' smashin' an' crashin', an' then
> the wailin' o' women an' groanin' o' men,
> A' scowther't an' mangle't, sae painfu' to see—   [scorched]
> The sweetness is gane, noo it's black Simmerlee.

(167)

Her imaginary visit to Gartsherrie perhaps best suggests how thoroughgoing the process of industrialisation has been, in that it has not only wrought great visual—and aural—transformation of the landscape, but has supplanted a long-settled traditional way of life:

> Noo I'll dauner awa' up by Carlincraft Burn,
> An' roun' by auld Hornock I'll tak' a bit turn,
> Sae lown an' sae lanely that wee cosie neuk,   [sheltered]
> To think what they've made o't I canna weel bruck.   [approve]
>
> The auld warl' dwallin' had a muckle clay brace,   [fireplace]
> An' a lum whaur the stars glintit doun i' yer face

As ye sat by the fire; to the blue licht abune
Ye micht glower through the reek at the bonny hairst mune.   [harvest]

There was Carlincraft Jock an' his queer tittie Meg,   [sister]
Wha caretna the warl' nor its fashions a feg,
Jock's hoose had nae door but a stane prappit broad,   [propped up board]
Roun' whilk would come snokin' slee Lowrie the tod.   [sly][fox]

Noo the bodies are gane an' their dwallin's awa'
An' the place whaur they stood I scarce ken noo ava,
For there's roarin' o' steam an' there's reengin' o' wheels,   [crashing]
Men workin', an' sweatin', an' swearin' like deils.

An' the flame-tappit furnaces staun' in a raw,
A' bleezin' an' blawin' an' smeekin' awa',   [smoking]
Their eerie licht brichtenin' the laigh hingin' cluds,   [low][clouds]
Gleamin' far ower the loch an' the mirk lanely wuds.   [dark][woods]
                                              (168)

It would be wrong to conclude from her poems and sketches of reminiscence that Janet Hamilton deplored change and wallowed in nostalgia for the traditional life of the rural peasantry as sentimentally depicted by, for example, Burns in 'The Cotter's Saturday Night'. Part of her interest for us today is that she actually lived a traditional way of life in her early years and experienced at first hand how it abruptly gave way in her locality under the pressure of industrialisation. The sense of loss which she communicates is therefore real and, in human terms, understandable. But, importantly, she balances what has been lost against the benefits which have accrued from the changes wrought. Dubbed in her time 'a poetess of social progress' (22), she saw the nineteenth century and industrialisation as bringing 'cheap bread, cheap clothing, cheap education, [and] cheap literature' (396) to the working class, thereby providing the means for their material and mental advancement. She always identified with her class (her books carry dedications 'to her brothers and sisters of the working classes'), and she wanted her writing to contribute to assisting their advancement. She saw intemperance as the greatest barrier to the social progress of the working class and she wrote many poems and essays attacking the vice. Most of these poems and essays are of little interest to us today, but of those poems which are still of interest—largely because they are written out of the immediate experience of industrialisation—a number incorporate attacks on social evils such as intemperance which she saw as impediments to the advancement she so earnestly desired for her class. One of her best poems which exemplifies this, and which presents a vivid impression of local industrial life, is 'Oor Location':

A hunner funnels bleezin', reekin',
Coal an' ironstane, charrin', smeekin';   [smoking]
Navvies, miners, keepers, fillers,
Puddlers, rollers, iron millers;
Reestit, reekit, raggit laddies,   [roasted]
Firemen, enginemen, an' Paddies;

Boatmen, banksmen, rough and rattlin',
'Bout the wecht wi' colliers battlin',
Sweatin', swearin', fechtin', drinkin',
Change-house bells an' gill-stoups clinkin',   [drinking measures]
Police—ready men and willin'—
Aye at han' when stoups are fillin',
Clerks, an' counter-loupers plenty,   [shopmen]
Wi' trim moustache and whiskers dainty—
Chaps that winna staun at trifles
Min' ye they can han'le rifles.
'Bout the wives in oor location,
An' the lasses' botheration,
Some are decent, some are dandies,
An' a gey wheen drucken randies,   [a good number][drunken]
Aye to neebors' hooses sailin',
Greetin' bairns ahint them trailin',
Gaun for nouther bread nor butter,
Just to drink an' rin the cutter.   [carry out liquor from a public house unobserved]
Oh, the dreadfu' curse o' drinkin'!
Men are ill, but tae my thinkin',
Leukin' through the drucken fock,
There's a Jenny for ilk Jock,   [each]
Oh, the dool an' desolation,   [distress]
An' the havoc in the nation,
Wrocht by dirty, drucken wives!
Oh, hoo mony bairnies' lives
Lost ilk year through their neglec'!
Like a millstane roun' the neck
O' the strugglin', toilin' masses
Hing drucken wives and wanton lassies.
To see sae mony unwed mithers
Is sure a shame that taps a' ithers.
    An' noo I'm fairly set a-gaun,
On baith the whisky-shop and pawn;
I'll speak my min'—and whatfor no?
Frae whence cums misery, want, an' wo,
The ruin, crime, disgrace an' shame,
That quenches a' the lichts o' hame?
Ye needna speer, the feck ot's drawn   [ask][the most]
Out o' the change-house an' the pawn.
    Sin and death, as poets tell,
On ilk side the doors o' hell
Wait to haurl mortals in;   [pull]
Death gets a' that's catcht by sin:
There are doors where death an' sin
Draw their tens o' thoosan's in;
Thick and thrang we see them gaun,   [closely-packed]
First the dram-shop, then the pawn;
Owre a' kin's o' ruination,
Drink's the kind in oor location.
        (59–60)

The evils against which Mrs Hamilton raged were real enough, yet her moral earnestness may be little to our taste today. Nevertheless, her indignation helps energise her verse and conveys an urgency which complements her description of the 'industrial fret' which characterises her locality. Another of her best poems which achieves this has the ironic title, 'Our Local Scenery'. I give the opening section:

Smoorin' wi' reek an' blackened wi' soot,	[suffocating]
Lowin' like Etna an' Hecla to boot,	[blazing]
Ought o' our malleables want ye to learn?—	[anything] [ironworks]
There's chappin' an' clippin' an' sawin' o' airn;	[iron]
Burnin' an' sotterin', reengin' an' knockin';	[boiling][crashing]
Scores o' puir mortals roastin' and chokin'.	
Gizzen'd an' dry ilka thrapple and mouth,	[cracked][throat]
Like cracks in the yird in a het simmer drouth;	[earth]
They're prayin', puir chiels, for what do you think?	
It's no daily bread, it's drink, 'Gi'e us drink!'	
'Callan.' quo' I, 'ye maun rin like a hatter,	[lad]
Bring up twa pails fu' o' clear caller water;	[fresh]
Be aff, noo, ye imp! come back at a canter,	
Keep oot o' the store, or I'll fell ye *instanter!*'	
Wae on the store an' the publican's bar,	
It's no a haet better—sometimes it's waur;	[not a bit]
Men, when they're het, hoo they sweat an' they swear,	
Coup up the whisky and toom down the beer.	[throw over][empty]
While droonin' their brains an' toomin' their purses	
The verra air rings wi' oaths an' wi' curses.	
It's no juist a pay or an orra bit fuddle—	[now and then]
Aft in a day they guzzle an' muddle.	
The puir wifie says there's little comes till her	
It's the drink, it's the drink that licks up the siller.	

(157)

The same confident use of a fluid Scots in describing industrial experience can be found in other poems by her. Interestingly, some of these deal with wider issues beyond the local, yet make use of industrial imagery. Here, for example, is part of 'Rhymes for the Times. IV.—1865':

Juist noo there are mony wha rin to an' fro,	
An' knowledge increases, abune an' below;	
The yird's like a riddle, pits, tunnels an' bores;	[earth]
Whaur bodies, like mowdies, by hunners an' scores,	[moles]
Are houkin', an' holin', an' blastin the rocks,	
An' droonin's an' burnin's, explosions an' shocks,	
An' a' ither meagries, amang us are rife:	[troubles]
Oh, mony's the slain in the battle o' life!	
It's Mammon we worship, wi' graspin' an' greed,	
Wi' sailin' an' railin' at telegraph speed,	
Get gowd oot the ironstane, an' siller frae coal,	[gold]
An' thoosan's on thoosan's draw oot o' a'e hole.	

> Wi' oil shale aneath us, an' fire-warks abune,
> I think we'll tak' lowe, an bleeze up to the mune.   [catch fire]
>
> (225)

Poems such as these by Janet Hamilton (and there are more in this vein by her) call for the modification of established views that, mid century, 'the sentimental rustification of Scots had left it frozen in time and place',[32] and that there was 'a lacking sense of the contemporary'[33] in the literature of the period. As was noted at the outset, William Donaldson has argued in *Popular Literature in Victorian Scotland* that such critical orthodoxies are based on mainstream book-culture, and on books produced mostly in London with an all-UK literary market in mind. Interestingly, comments by Janet Hamilton in her poem 'A Plea for the Doric' help confirm the truth of the skewed effect this London market orientation and its commercial considerations had on mainstream Scottish writing mid century:

> I'm wae for Auld Reekie; her big men o' print
> To Lunnon ha'e gane, to be nearer the mint;
> But the coinage o' brain looks no a'e haet better,   [not one bit]
> Though Doric is banish'd frae sang, tale, and letter.
>
> (162)

What is at issue, then, is whether writing by 'the big men o' print' can be taken to represent the whole truth about Scottish writing in the Victorian era. William Donaldson argues that it does not and that our 'ignorance of the real range and complexity of the imaginative experience in Victorian Scotland has led to serious subsequent misjudgements not merely in criticism or creative writing, but in the whole contemporary intellectual and cultural milieu'.[34] My contention in this essay is complementary to Dr Donaldson's, in that my exploration of 'wee buikies' of local writing, as illustrated by the work of Janet Hamilton and William Thom, inclines me to believe that similar misjudgements mark established views of the work of local writers. For example, of the oft-stated view that nineteenth-century writers recoiled from *la vraie vérité* of Scottish life and retreated into the safety of 'whistle-binkie-ism', we have seen how the realities of social and industrial change inescapably affected the lives and influenced the work of William Thom and Janet Hamilton. Whilst it must be said that much of the work of local writers such as Thom and Hamilton *is* sentimental and pallid in the manner of so much of the writing of their time, allowance must be made for both the influence of period taste and, in their case, the fact that they were entirely self-taught and had to struggle to find their own authentic poetic voices in circumstances inimical to literary endeavour. The testimony we find in their prose and poetry to *la vraie vérité* of working class life in Victorian Scotland, and the fact that they apparently saw no contradiction between the vigour of that testimony and the sentimental conventionality of much of their work, suggest that local writing has a wider range and more complex background than has hitherto been appreciated (just as William Donaldson found was the case with popular fiction). Local writing awaits thorough investigation and assessment, in a spirit of open-minded enquiry free from preconceptions fostered by well-known anthologies such as *Whistle-Binkie*. Whilst I would not wish to suggest that writing of the highest quality is lying neglected, I believe a sufficient body of valuable poetry and prose awaits reclamation, and that such reclamation will contribute to that more general reassessment of nineteenth-century Scottish literature already being undertaken.

NOTES

1   Kurt Wittig, *The Scottish Tradition in Literature* (Edinburgh & London, 1958), p 253.
2   J H Millar, *A Literary History of Scotland* (London, 1903); William Power, *Literature and Oatmeal: What Literature Has Meant to Scotland* (London, 1935); George Blake, *Barrie and the Kailyard School* (London, 1951); Kurt Wittig, op. cit.; David Craig, *Scottish Literature and the Scottish People 1680–1830* (London, 1961); Maurice Lindsay, *History of Scottish Literature* (London, 1977); Roderick Watson, *The Literature of Scotland* (London, 1984).
3   J H Millar, 'The Literature of the Kailyard', in *New Review* vol 12, (January-June 1895), pp 384–94.
4   James Veitch, *George Douglas Brown* (London, 1952), p 153.
5   Ibid.
6   William Donaldson, *Popular Literature in Victorian Scotland* (Aberdeen, 1986), p 87.
7   Ibid., p x.
8   Tom Leonard, 'On Reclaiming the Local and the Theory of the Magic Thing', in *Edinburgh Review* No. 77 (May 1987), p 45.
9   Ibid., p 46.
10 *The Harp of Renfrewshire*, Second Series, William Motherwell (ed) (Paisley, 1872); *Harp of Perthshire*, R Ford (ed) (Paisley, 1893); *The Bards of Angus and the Mearns*, Alan Reid (ed) (Paisley, 1897); *The Bards of Galloway* M M Harper (ed) (Dalbeattie, 1889); *The Glasgow Poets*, George Eyre-Todd (ed) (Glasgow, 1903); *One Hundred Modern Scottish Poets*, 16 vols, David Herschell Edwards (ed) (Brechin, 1880–97); *Whistle-Binkie or The Piper of the Party: Being a Collection of Songs for the Social Circle*, 2 vols (Glasgow, 1878). The latter was first published in 1832 and issued in many series with material added throughout most of the century.
11 Roderick Watson, op. cit., pp 281–2.
12 Ian A Gordon, 'Modern Scots Poetry', in *Edinburgh Essays in Scots Literature* (Edinburgh & London, 1933), p 126.
13 Douglas Young, 'Scottish Poetry in the Later Nineteenth Century', in *Scottish Poetry: A Critical Survey*, James Kinsley (ed) (London, 1955), pp 236–7.
14 From the Preface to *Whistle-Binkie*, op. cit., vol 1.
15 Ibid., p 74.
16 From the Foreword to *Scottish Verse 1851–1951*, Douglas Young (ed) (London & Edinburgh, 1952), p xxiii.
17 Ibid., p 65.
18 Douglas Young, op. cit., pp 251–2.

19   Kurt Wittig, op. cit., p 253.
20   David Craig, op. cit., p 273.
21   Maurice Lindsay, op. cit., p 296.
22   Ian A Gordon, op. cit., p 126.
23   Kirt Wittig, op. cit., p 253.
24   Roderick Watson, op. cit., p 346.
25   George Blake, op. cit., p 13.
26   David Craig, op. cit., p 146.
27   William Power, op. cit., pp 163–64.
28   Although the first edition was published in 1844, all references will be to a more complete later edition: William Thom, *Rhymes and Recollections of A Hand-Loom Weaver* (Paisley, 1880). It should be noted that the separate sections 'Recollections' and 'Rhymes' *each* have a pagination commencing p 1.
29   Her work appeared in a number of editions. The most comprehensive is the Memorial Volume, to which all references here are made, except where indicated otherwise: Janet Hamilton, *Poems, Sketches and Essays* (Glasgow, 1885).
30   Joseph Wright, *Janet Hamilton and Other Papers* (Edinburgh, 1889), pp 27–8.
31   The essay 'Local Changes' is to be found in a different edition of her work: Janet Hamilton, *Poems, Essays, and Sketches* (Glasgow, 1870), pp 385–9.
32   Roderick Watson, op. cit., p 346.
33   David Craig, op. cit., p 146.
34   William Donaldson, op. cit., p 87.

FURTHER READING

Donaldson, William, *Popular Literature in Victorian Scotland* (Aberdeen, 1986).

Leonard, Tom, 'On Reclaiming the Local and the Theory of the Magic Thing', in *Edinburgh Review* No. 77, (May 1987), pp 40–6.

——(ed), *Renfrewshire Poetry from the French Revolution to the First World War* (Paisley, due 1988).

Young, Douglas, 'Scottish Poetry in the Later Nineteenth Century', in *Scottish Poetry: A Critical Survey*, James Kinsley (ed) (London, 1955), pp 236–55.

——(ed), *Scottish Verse 1851–1951* (London & Edinburgh, 1952).

Chapter 20

Gaelic Poetry in the Nineteenth Century

JOHN MACINNES

The poets of the nineteenth century inherited a broken world. A new world was meantime emerging, often with cataclysmic effect, all around them. They composed poetry, of course, as individuals, out of individual sensibilities, and the Gaelic reader will evaluate them individually, poets and poems alike. But in such a study as this we have to pay attention also to the sociology of the poetry, where failure is as interesting as success. We must ask what structures these poets inherited from the past; which among these was adaptable, and which had already reached an unrepeatable perfection. What strategies could Gaelic poets now adopt if they were to cope with the demands of their age?

Literacy in vernacular Gaelic—the adaptation, in the eighteenth century, of Classical Gaelic orthography—is obviously a very important factor. In the nineteenth century there is a dramatic increase in the number of books of Gaelic poetry in print. But even literate poets may use traditional styles, and Gaelic poets certainly did so. There were still current, particularly before the Clearances, vast repertoires of oral song-poetry, aristocratic as well as plebeian, much of it exhibiting stylistic features that worked semiotically, revealing the ancient landmarks of the Gaelic cosmos. The forces that shaped Gaelic society had also ordained that poets came to occupy a role as the acknowledged spokesmen of society—custodians of its identity—sustaining and celebrating a conservative social order through the development of bardic praise-poetry. In the eighteenth century that order was destroyed; its bardic conventions, expressing the customary expectations of Gaelic society, were now anachronistic; yet the panegyric code of the bards had long since become a pervasive style in Gaelic poetry. The result was that the more nineteenth century poets confined themselves to the security of established practice, the less likely were they to be able to cope realistically with the problems of their contemporary situation. The farther they moved away, on the other hand, from these stylistic codes that gave Gaelic poetry such a distinctive flavour, the less likely was their acceptance as poets in what was still, in the main, a traditional society. Those who did experiment were first and foremost those who had been formally educated in English or who had educated themselves. It is important to remember that the 'university of art'—*univers na h-ealadhna*: the courses of instruction in colleges of poetry and rhetoric—was long gone. In the nineteenth century there was no rounded, let alone liberal, education possible in Gaelic. It is very much the century of the Gaelic autodidact.

Writing in 1918, W J Watson, with characteristic clarity and directness, has this to say:

> The poetry of the nineteenth century, with some exceptions . . . shows increasing English influence in style, thought, and metre. Much of this later poetry is pretty and witty, but it has little of the old fire and virility; often, not without reason, it expresses the wail of a dejected and harassed people. It is at this stage, and at no other, that the famous 'Celtic Gloom' is to be found in the literature, when the Gaelic people were left dependent, intellectually and economically, on what was to them a foreign and distasteful culture. The poetry that was inspired by the infamies of Culloden and the Clearances could not be other than gloomy . . .

Watson's own criteria are clear. As a classicist, he notes that in the older Gaelic world the qualities which go to make Gaelic poets *Gaelic*

> are very different from what English-speaking people of the present day are accustomed to. In fact, the poets' outlook on things and the qualities that appealed to them—race, physical beauty, manly accomplishments, free-handed generosity, wisdom in council—are more akin to what is found in Homer and Pindar.[1]

If such are our criteria, these judgements are perfectly defensible. Later writers, as one might expect, have not all taken such an unequivocal stance. None the less, in what literary criticism we have (most of it written in English and perhaps subtly conditioned by that) the main thrust of Watson's argument has not been turned. We still measure nineteenth century poetry against the great triumphs of our past. We still agree, however reluctantly, that the social conditions of the age and the poetry that reflects them mark our lowest point. We find the poetry nostalgic and anachronistic, still limited by the stereotype of panegyric or going off in false directions that could lead to nothing but sentimentality, as when it borrows from English or Scots and reproduces weak and prettified aspects of Romanticism.

Yet the fact of the matter is that this poetry is much less dull and trivial than that would suggest. Watson himself noted, in his sweeping judgement, that there were 'exceptions': they are the poets whose imaginative world is still that of heroic society and its praise-singers. Their poetry is still instinct with the old, splendid craftsmanship; and they are not alone in that respect. But equally conspicuous to the historian are the writers of 'Heroic' poetry which even in its own time was held by some to be bogus. The question of authenticity has been decided long since in favour of the sceptics, but the poetry is none the less nineteenth century Gaelic poetry; and its acceptance by Gaels—partial acceptance, it may be, by a minority of readers—demands our consideration accordingly. Under the influence of Romanticism and other movements, some of them in religion (and there is a vast corpus of religious poetry deriving from this century) sensibilities were being extended. There is a palpable widening and deepening of human sympathies. We may deplore dependence on 'a foreign and distasteful culture' and deprecate the 'increasing

English influence in style, thought, and metre.' More trenchantly, we have to go on to ask whether it is these influences, in themselves, that are to be deplored; or is it the circumstances, the denial of cultural opportunity, that prevented poets from drawing upon an even wider range of influences, from absorbing them, from turning them to their own advantage, in the creation of a contemporary poetry? A similar question must arise in a political context. There are some poets who are realistic enough in their political observations without apparently being able to place these observations in a sufficiently wide frame of reference. We may, of course, if we wish, see the poetry of the century as a strange amalgam: the unsettled complex of a transitional age. But if we view it, as indeed we must, from within Gaelic society itself, we shall find it at least as rich and rewarding as that of any other period in Gaelic history. In geographical distribution it spans the Gaidhealtachd, literally 'between Perth and St Kilda,' as the traditional phrase has it, from Aberdeenshire to Dunbartonshire, from Sutherland to Argyll, and south to the Island of Arran. In its diversity of aims and levels of writing, it serves to remind us that we are dealing not with one simple tradition but with what is still the art of a nation. Parochial limitations there may be but there are also European dimensions.

From the events that cluster round the end of the eighteenth century and the beginning of the nineteenth, we can without difficulty select a number that signal for us some of the activities that characterise the history of the century and the themes we shall encounter in the poetry. In 1785, the first large-scale Clearances were carried out on the Glengarry estates; the following year there were extensive emigrations to Canada, from the same lands. In 1800, the first Clearances occurred in Sutherland. In 1807, publication of the Gaelic Bible (New Testament, 1767; Old Testament, completed in 1801) concluded a process that leads back into the seventeenth century; although only from 1767 onwards was the sacred text made linguistically accessible to all. In 1807 also there appeared the 'official text' of 'The Poems of Ossian in the original Gaelic.' (The 1818 'Ossian' was published 'for the general good of the people of the Gaidhealtachd'; it was distributed free throughout the Highlands and a copy sent to every parish school where Gaelic was taught.) In 1804, the brothers Alexander and Donald Stewart published a celebrated anthology of poems 'collected in the Highlands and Isles': one of the primary sources for the study of Gaelic poetry, it continues a cultural campaign which began in the eighteenth century and goes on throughout the nineteenth. Finally, in 1801 the British Expeditionary Force under General Sir Ralph Abercromby landed at Abukir Bay in Egypt and won a decisive victory, although Abercromby himself was killed, at Alexandria. The loyalty of his Highland Regiments and Abercromby's appreciation of their gallantry are duly recorded: 'My brave Highlanders, remember your country, remember your forefathers.'[2]

All of these events, one way or another, are diagnostic. The themes they suggest: military glory in the service of the expanding British Empire; celebration of the religious life, set in the context of a Protestant Evangelicalism; emigration and concern with conditions of life in the New World, its attractions or its hardships; are all woven into the fabric of the verse. There also runs through it, as a terrible *leitmotif*, the theme of dispossession. And almost everywhere, variously expressed, we can sense a continuing Gaelic identity. Poets are still the spokesmen of society.

Initially at any rate the Gaelic response to military service was direct, naive, and enthusiastic. As in other parts of the Empire, a warrior tradition was given a new setting, with enough in the way of military trappings and emblems to maintain a feeling of continuity. The kilt and the bagpipes, both allowed in the Army after they were otherwise proscribed, in 1747, were of course the egregious symbols. An anonymous song, composed apparently between 1747 and the rescinding of the 'Disclothing' Act, in 1782, makes a vivid and revealing comment. A young Gael complains that since the tartan dress has been taken away, no girl will look at him. He has put on the grey trousers, like the Lowlander who lives on the far side of the Clyde. Then he continues:

> Tha mi màrach dol dhan Arm
> Gheibh me eibhleadh 's còta dearg
> Bonaid bhiorach mholach ghorm
> Slat de ribein stoirm mam chluais[3]

(Tomorrow I am going to the army/I shall get a kilt and a red coat/A shaggy, cocked, blue bonnet/A yard of ribbon storming about my ears.)

That new identity was securely established by 1800. The Cameron Highlanders, for instance, were raised in 1793, the Gordon Highlanders, the 92nd Regiment, in 1794.

Alexander MacKinnon from Arisaig (1770–1814) enlisted in the 92nd Regiment when he was twenty-four years of age. He fought with Abercromby in Egypt in 1801 (where he was severely wounded and left for dead on the field) as previously he had fought with Abercromby and Moore in the Netherlands campaign in 1779. He celebrated both experiences in songs entitled *The Battle of Holland* and *The Battle of Egypt*; these paeans earned him lasting fame. MacKinnon is one of two exceptional poets who W J Watson singles out as being unaffected by increasing English influence in style, thought and metre. In spirit at least his war-songs are the celebrations of a Gaelic warrior in a British imperial setting. In *The Battle of Egypt* he retails the tactical moves of the action in detail: this is description by an involved professional observer. But he has his bardic models to guide him and the campaign 'well deserved a bard to sing it.' Abercromby is *ar n-ard cheann-feadhna*, 'our high chief'; 'commander-in-chief' but, more precisely, the leader of band of picked warriors, a *comitatus*: this is a commander 'who could inspire us to action like Fionn rousing the host.'

Such songs run like a continuous thread through the nineteenth century, as campaign follows campaign, to the Crimean and Boer Wars. (They are found, indeed, as late as the Second World War.) In their realism of observation they have a strong and authentic voice. They also carry, and modify, the traditional formulas of panegyric: these signals that give the poets, and us, our bearings. To a foreign reader they are probably on the whole tedious, their value lying in their historical testimony to a successful transference of loyalties and the forging of identity in a novel setting. But from within Gaelic society they are charters that reflect and endorse a new security. Their aesthetic power is inextricably bound up with the assertions they make.

They exist, however, on a different literary level from certain other songs that touch on war and service in the British Army. From an anonymous song, probably by a woman, come these verses about the same 'Battle of Egypt.'

> Och, alas, brown-haired lad
> Handsome brown-haired lad
> Och, alas, brown-haired lad
>
> That battle they fought in Egypt
> (After it) they did not rise together . . .
>
> Stretched out in the rushes
> Blood pouring about their shoulders
>
> Stretched out without a pillow
> And gold will not ransom them
>
> Many a gentleman's daughter
> Will now lie alone . . . [3]

or this, from *Oran an t-Saighdeir*, 'The Soldier's Song':

> One day when I was out strolling
> High on the Brae of Edinburgh
> Who did I meet but a soldier
> And he asked me what was my news.
>
> He said: 'Enlist in the Army
> It's the best profession under the sun
> You'll have silver in your pockets
> And gold you'll never need![3]

The young man is talked into enlisting and given a musket (feminine in Gaelic)

> They gave me to carry
> A grey-faced female who won't wash my shirt for me
> One they call Janet,
> Daughter of King George,
> And little do I care for her.
> A pity they haven't got her locked up
> In the great Castle of Edinburgh
> Long might she live there
> Before I'd ask how she was.

Songs of this type, however, are practically non-existent in the collections of the nineteenth century although that 'Soldier's Song', for example, is one of the most popular in oral tradition to the present day.

But absence from the written record of soldier's protest songs should not delude us into thinking there was a strong underground anti-military tradition.

At any rate, the songs that have survived to be collected in the twentieth century express no more than the common soldier's complaint the world over with his lot. From 'The Soldier's Song' again:

> My curse upon the French
> Mustering their camps
> And my curse upon the Colonel
> He didn't even give us furlough
> The girls all getting married
> And I can't have one of them.

At least as common, even in oral tradition, are statements such as this, from a song with the refrain:

> O light we thought the journey, leaving happily
> with little sorrow, going to meet Bonaparte,
> because he threatens King George.
>
> Though only the Gaels should be there,
> and they manly, handsome, strong, they would put the fear of death
> into every enemy alive . . .
>
> Hearty lads, let us be merry, let
> us uphold our country's honour . . .
> Scotland, Ireland and England, at present
> joined together: they are of one mind,
> like the sound between flint and hammer.[4]

The modern reader may well feel there is an ironic ring to that neat metaphor that expresses British unanimity but none is intended. Neither is there any emotion but pride in the words of the Skye soldier who hopes to return to the 'Land of MacLeod'—even if the last phrase might suggest otherwise.

> Nuair a chuir iad sinn air bord
> Anns an ordugh bu ghrinne
> Bha gach fear is bean a' ràdh
> 'Cha dean pàirt aca tilleadh' . . .
>
> Nuair a chuir iad sinn air tìr
> Am measg sìoban is muran
> Thug sinn batal air an tràigh
> Is gun d'rinn pàirt againn fuireach . . .
>
> Thainig esan, mac an Righ,
> Is mer aon dhinn 'sa chuideachd:
> 'An iad seo Gàidheil an Taobh Tuath?
> Bha iad bhuam is fhuair mi uil' iad.'

When they put us on board/in finest order/every man and woman was saying/'Some of them will never return'.

When they put us ashore/amongst the spume and the bent-grass/we fought a battle on the shore/and some of us stayed there.

He came himself—the King's son/—he was as one of ourselves in the company:/'Are these the Gaels of the north?/I needed them, and I have got them all.'[5]

If it is true to say that the British Empire and the Highland Regiments re-created the Gaelic view of the world, so that now the enemies of the Empire were the enemies of the Gael also, it is even truer that religion brought a new identity. The mediating process here is what is sometimes known as the 'Evangelical Movement', sometimes as the 'Evangelical Revival.' It was a Protestant movement (the greater part of the Highlands and Islands had been Protestant since the Reformation) manifesting itself among Presbyterians, Baptists, Congregationalists, etc, and bound up with social protest. Evangelicalism was a highly complex, asymmetrical movement which did not affect all communities equally, and certainly not all individuals in any community. Nevertheless, it is not an exaggeration to say that overall it produced something like a cosmological revolution in Gaelic society. For that reason it is necessary to look in some detail at the background to the religious poetry of the nineteenth century. The immediate setting is that of Gaelic society midway through the first period of major Clearances (1782–1846). Chiefs and Tacksmen had turned against their own tenantry: the tenants were by now developing their own hostility against landlords. In a traditional, hierarchical society, in which there were no social mechanisms to organise expression of 'untraditional' emotions, the hostility demanded formulation by a circuituous route. Religion provided just that. The process had began in the eighteenth century when religious poets were the first to protest against the tyrannical exactions of landlordism; when Dugald Buchanan, for instance, in his poem *An Gaisgeach* ('hero, warrior', etc) displaces the hero of tradition and bardic praise with the hero of Christian life and belief. And in *An Claigeann*, 'The Skull', his attack on contemporary rack-renting is charged with anger and contempt. Buchanan's influence was enormous; his poetry, printed, but very soon also circulating orally (controlled by the written text), set and sung to traditional secular melodies, spread throughout the Gaidhealtachd. His own conversion, from what he and his kind would call nominal Christianity, to an austere and passionate faith, occurred when the Gaelic world, a relatively fixed social order, had already been shattered in the aftermath of the Forty-Five, and the ancient cultural landmarks were being uprooted. These changes of course continued; the exactions of the landlords intensified; the attitudes of the tenantry changed in reaction to them. Even those who did not personally experience a radical conversion could hardly fail to be affected by a religious movement which so unflinchingly acknowledged the misery of human existence. It squared only too well with contemporary Gaelic experience. The world was essentially a place of suffering, a vale of tears. Nor was there any comfort to be found, if people were realistic, in nostalgia. A Golden Age was mere sentimentality. In a poem that opens with a traditional formula *Mìle marbhphaisg ort a shaoghail*, 'World, a thousand shrouds upon you!' ('plague', 'malison', etc. are conventional renderings), Mrs Mary Clark, 'Bean Thorra Dhamh', in Badenoch (*c*.1740–*c*.1815), is one of the earliest poets to comment on that. The formulaic opening would be immediately recognisable; the reference to the pre-Forty-Five law of pit and gallows and the rule of chiefs is startlingly new:

> Chuir iad cas air reachd na fìrinn
> Is ghluais iad dìchiollach 'san droch-bheart
> Claoidh nam bochd 's 'gan lot le mìorun
> Banntraich 's dìlleachdain gun choiseachd
> B'uamhasach an cleachdadh tìre
> Croich is binn air aird gach cnocain
> Cuirt nan spleadh gun lagh gun fhìrinn
> Is tric a dhìt an tì bha neo-chiont'.

They placed their foot on the rule of truth/and they proceeded diligently in mischief/harassing the poor and wounding them with malice/—widows and orphans without the power of walking:/fearful was the custom of the country/—a gallows and sentence on the summit of every hillock:/the court of make-believe, without law, without truth—/often did it condemn the innocent.[6]

The Gaels now had the Bible in Gaelic. It is true the translation was in a 'high' register of the language (derived, though at one or two removes, from Classical Gaelic), but as Gaelic literacy was founded on Bible reading, through the narrow, religious curriculum of the Gaelic schools, and at home through the innovation of family worship, this soon ceased to be a barrier to understanding. Biblical diction presently became an important part of the fabric of spiritual songs, creating a new rhetoric of exposition, providing a new reservoir of imagery; and used with the same ease, and to much the same good effect, as Marxist jargon elsewhere in political argumentation. An even more alarming consequence was that the laity were now able to interpret the Scriptures for themselves, without relying on the clergy: worst still, they began to judge the faith and works of their ministers in the light of Biblical standards. What one landlord described as 'the peasant religion' had clearly arrived. To the ordinary people it was *An Creideamh Mór*, 'The Great Faith', from whose subversive influence, according to Skye tradition, ministers prayed to be delivered.

The popular conception of the Calvinist minister is that of a man of levity, given to hunting and shooting, highly convivial ('as good a drinker . . . as the laird'—a severe standard), violinist and piper, the best dancer in the parish, a fine judge of horseflesh, and much concerned with good husbandry and agricultural development. Some of the descriptions may be slightly exaggerated but there is plenty of contemporary evidence to make it plain they are on the whole true. The Rev Roderick MacLeod of Skye (1794–1868)—the famous Mgr Ruairi, who himself later became one of the leaders of the

Evangelicals—confessed that at the beginning of his ministry 'his mind was occupied with his barge, and steed, and gun, and such-like amusements': he was frequently the violinist who played at the dances that followed upon funerals. When MacLeod was settled in Skye in 1823, one of his first duties was to assist his fellow-presbyters in finding their beds after a clerical gathering. 'Presbyteries are for the most part held at public houses . . .', another writer comments, and 'The holy fathers stand in no need of Paul's advice to Timothy respecting his weak stomach.'[7]

It was against these 'Moderates', as they were called, that the Evangelical 'Men' (*na daoine*, that is to say, the laymen) and an emergent clergy, drawn from the lower classes of society, set their faces and the poets their songs. Traditionally the clergy of the Established Church in the Highlands were drawn from the upper classes; in addition to aristocratic lineage, which many of them could claim, they formed an 'aristocracy of learning'—as the learned orders of mediaeval and later Gaelic society have been described. The Presbyterian ministers in fact continued the significant role and function of the earlier Gaelic literati: throughout the nineteenth century they are among the foremost collectors of the song-poetry of oral tradition. Highly educated, well-versed in the Classics, they were gentlemen farmers, sometimes on a very large scale. In the 1840s, John Matheson of Uist in his *Oran na h-Eaglais*, 'The Song of the Church', expresses the Evangelical view of them in a parody of the Creed:

> Creideam an crodh is an caoraich
> Creideam an stìopainibh mór
> Creideam 'san duais tha mi faotainn
> An t-airgead, an glìob, is an t-òr
> Creideam san uachdaran thimeil
> An aghaidh an nì a deir Pol.
>
> Creideam an cumhnanta gnìomha
> Creideam am dhèanadas féin
> Creideam sa Phatronage bhreugaich
> A dh'èalaidh a stigh air a' chléir
> A dh'fhògar na teachdairean diadhaidh
> Nuair chunnaic iad iomhaigh na béist.

I believe in cattle and sheep/I believe in great stipends/I believe in the rewards I receive/silver and glebe and gold/I believe in the temporal lord/In the face of what Paul declares.

I believe in the covenant of works/I believe in my own achievement/I believe in the lying Patronage/that has crept in upon the clergy/and drove out the godly messengers/when they saw the image of the beast.[8]

Matheson is said to have 'made a bolt for freedom' and deserted the Evangelicals—but he made his mark while he was there. The new faith had allowed him to express the common opinion, shared by converted and unconverted alike. It is well to emphasise again the grass-roots nature of this social and religious upheaval. The ordinary tenantry, turning against their landlords, turned also against their clergy, who belonged to the same social stratum. The clergy, for their part, regarded religious Enthusiasm with grave suspicion as a parochial variety of a wider subversive movement, which threatened Church and State alike. They themselves were loyal members of a State church and their sermons were often said to contain news of British imperial victories. In some instances, indeed, these topics apparently formed the staple of the address. By such means, the role of the Gael in a military context would have been bolstered. The Evangelicals, ironically, did not extend their opposition to that aspect of clerical instruction. Instead, they tended to align themselves with the view that British imperialism was a civilising influence in the world. Foxe's *Book of Martyrs*, with its sense of England's divine mission, was known; it was an acceptable document in certain Evangelical circles and contributed still further to security within a universal social order. Very occasionally, we may find a hint of another view:

> Is fhad on thòisich an aimhreit
> Is an ainneart tha mór
> Dhùisg an cogadh an Cain
> Mharbh e bhràthair gu h-òg
> Bha an claidheamh 's gach linn
> A' cur nam mìltean fo'n fhòid
> Dhòirteadh aibhnichean fala
> Tre shannt, an-iochd is pròis.[9]

Long ago did disagreement begin/and excessive force/warfare awoke in Cain/he killed his brother when he was young/the sword in every age/has put thousands beneath the sod/spilling rivers of blood/through greed, cruelty and pride.[9]

But these statements from John MacLean's *An Cogadh Naomh*, 'The Holy War', even if that 'War' is spiritual, do not actually recommend pacifism. Such poems draw on the bardic images of the warrior, still asserting cultural continuities. Side by side with them, we have poems in tribute to colonial missionaries, such as Peter Grant's *Oran nam Misionaraidh*, 'The Song of the Missionaries' or another of MacLean's poems *Craobh-sgaoileadh an t-Soisgeil*, 'The spreading of the Gospel':

> Luchd-teagaisg diadhaidh truacant
> Tha dol thar na stuadhan ard
> Tha sluagh cur cùl ri iomhaighean
> 'S a' tighinn gu Ios le gràdh.

Compassionate, godly instructors/who go across the high billows/the people turn their backs on images/and come to Jesus with love.

This is simply the standard British view expressed in Gaelic. The poetry that carries it is often pedestrian but it is not parochial. Behind it lies a coherent theory of history: God's will is at work in the historical process; the Gaels have their own place in that scheme; and finally, at the end of time, universal peace will descend upon all. Psychologically, the price the Gaels paid for this world-view was that they came to regard the Gaidhealtachd itself as a heathen mission-field. It was not, of course, an entirely new attitude: Alcuin's famous question with regard to the singing of English heroic ballads: 'What has Ingeld to do with Christ?' had been echoed by clergymen who regarded the Gaelic heroic ballads as myths of a competing faith. But while Gaelic society was relatively whole, the clergy in general gave the secular arts encouragement and respect. Now, however, when so much of the distinctive social order lay in ruins, anything that symbolised the traditional Gaelic arts came under attack as 'vanity.'

> Chan noimheachd air Oisean nam Fiann
> No gaisgeach bha riamh am feachd
> Cha noimheachd air creachadh nan Gall
> Le ceatharn nan gleann 's nan stùchd
> No idir air siubhal nan gleann
> An éideadh nach ceangladh glùn.
> Chan noimheachd air fineachan treun
> A chogadh 's nach géilleadh beò
> Clann Ghriogair bha aineolach treun
> Clann Domhnaill le'm b'aiteas làmh dhearg
> Clann Chamshroin bha calma gun chéill
> Ach noimheachd air soisgeul nan gràs
> Bhi sgaoileadh 's gach aird mu'n cuairt.

Not a tale of Ossian of the Fian/nor any hero in a host/not a tale of plundering the Lowlanders/by the caterans of the glens and the mountains/nor any tale of roaming the glens in the dress that does not impede the knees/nor a tale of brave clans/who would fight and never surrender till death/Clan Gregor who were strong, and ignorant/Clan Donald whose delight was the Red Hand/Clan Cameron who were bold, without sense/none of these but the news of the gospel of grace/spreading in every airt all around.

So James MacGregor, in 1825. Peter Grant (1783–1867), a Baptist minister and one of the most renowned writers of Gaelic spiritual songs, attacks the singing of secular songs, gatherings in houses of music, and levity in general; and lists them beside Sabbath-breaking, drunkenness, swearing, and all manner of superstition. Peter Grant of Strathspey is the type of one kind of Evangelical; The Rev Dr John MacDonald (1779–1849), minister of Ferintosh, and known as the Apostle of the North, is of another, and very different, kind. MacDonald was not an ascetic at all: he was robust and convivial, a piper all his life, and interested enough in Gaelic secular poetry to have made a valuable collection from oral tradition of Fenian ballads. His own poetry, all of it religious, consists for the most part of versified exposition and exhortation but without the extraordinary eloquence which is said to have marked his extempore preaching. The elegy on his father, the saintly catechist of Reay, presenting him as an ideal of Christian life, contains some of his vivider remarks: he stresses how he hated hypocrisy:

> 'S an eudan mhùgach, bhalbh
> 'S na h-osnaidh chneadach, chiùchranach
> Gun sùgh annt' ach an dealbh.

and a sullen, dumb face/groans and plaintive sighings/that have no substance in them beyond the appearance.

We shall see how another poet applied these lines later. In the same poem, he takes a palpable hit at some of the assertive laymen who moved from parish to parish, as itinerant preachers, sometimes sporting a distinctive, eccentric style of dress, and were fast becoming so anti-clerical that even the Evangelical ministers grew uneasy. The poet's father, he says, would not perplex and weary his listeners 'with hard, high questions'. This is precisely one of the charges levelled in the seventeenth century at the wandering poets, the 'inferior rhymers' who moved from place to place, quartering themselves on their unwilling hosts. It is one example of the many continuities that run beneath the surface of Gaelic cultural history.

A very great deal of the religious poetry of the nineteenth century can be characterised by a remark made by a Mull poet in 1850. He thinks his poems 'may be defective in poetry but is confident [they] are founded on the Scriptures.' Within a considerable section of Gaelic society, however, and over a very wide area of the Gaidhealtachd, they clearly had an aesthetic power. Sung to traditional melodies, dignified with formulaic passages that sometimes echoed secular poetry but more often embodied Biblical imagery, they had much the same effect in creating the sense of solidarity that bardic poetry, classical and vernacular, had in earlier ages. We can sense in the traditions of last century not only bewilderment with the loss of a way of life, with Clearance and emigration, but also an intellectual and spiritual hunger accompanying the physical hunger of economic poverty. Theological exposition in verse, carried by traditional music, supplied some of the needed pabulum. But this must be seen in context. Lacking alternative sources of liberal and philosophical learning, lacking, too, political and social institutions which an autonomous community would have provided, this movement developed what was essentially a recluse religion, practised in open society and seeking to dominate it. It had neither the resources nor the strategies to cope with more than a limited range of human experience. Yet it was a movement which was full of intellectual passion and dissenting fervour and which attracted men and women of powerful mind and personality. It helped to create a spirit which was anti-authority in general, anti-ecclesiastical in particular. Rather remarkably, the energies thus engendered were spent more in theological and denominational dispute, on the one hand, and in direct action (during the years of the Land Agitation campaign), on the other, than in the creation of what detached critics would call 'memorable' poetry. Religious poems of the nineteenth century stand primarily as endorsements of a state of grace—charters of Gaelic identity within that context— and their aesthetic and spiritual power derive from an undivided substance. As a matter of fact, traditional Gaelic verse, still closely tied to the recurrent melody of its stanzaic organisation, was formally too rigid to contain the passionate eloquence that found a place in the extempore prayer and the extempore sermon. They are the real art-forms of the Evangelical Revival.

There is one poet, however, whose work displays the originality and eloquence of direct experience: Iain Gobha na Hearadh (1790–1852), John Morrison, the Harris blacksmith. His most often quoted poem is the subtle psychological study of the Old Man and the New Man—the old Adam and the regenerate Christian. But there is much of the same freshness running through all of his poetry.

> 'I am drowned in the "old" man's sea
> in sharp cold dew and winter's coldness
> the glorious "new" man comes to his temple
> and he sets my feet a-dancing
> It is the "old" man who has made me gloomy
> the "new" man is my blazing lantern.'[10]

Earlier than our period (but not published until 1816) Donald Matheson (1719–1782) in Sutherland recognised the disintegration of the old Gaelic social order and realised that God had ordained a deliverance from the hand of the oppressor.

> 'I see a wonder/happening at this time;/we have but to listen/to what He is telling us.
>
> I see a reflection/of what happened long ago,/when the Israelites were/in Egypt in distress./He brought them with a strong hand/away from Pharaoh, himself/ when he pursued them.
>
> I see a wonder happening at this time;/it is the fulfillment of a truth/revealed to us long since./There would be a vacant land,/and people would be sent there;/there they would settle/with their cattle and their children.'[11]

In the apportionment of blame for eviction and emigration, this Evangelical vision of the Promised Land—a promise of a new earthly world rather than a spiritual other world—has apparently escaped censure. Most of the enticements to emigrate were put in more mundane terms and the poems composed by emigrants in the New World, Nova Scotia in particular, show sharp contrasts between acceptance or optimism and a sense of loss and betrayal. This Christian hope, a novel variation on the old messianic theme of Gaelic tradition, was undoubtedly diffused throughout society and cannot have failed to exercise an influence.

In the poetry of Clearance and Land Agitation, landlords are the main targets. Even when we find references to ill-gotten gains, as in 'A Song for Sportsmen' by John Smith (1848–1881)—'Some of them trafficked in opium/they gathered a great deal of riches . . .'—and the rapacity is clearly seen in a context of imperialism, there is still no suggestion that the Empire, under which the Gaels lived, was, in itself, an alien polity. In the work of other poets, there is a recurrent plea which can be summed up in the formula: 'Do not replace people with sheep for sheep will not defend Britain in the face of the enemy.' These poets were political realists but their strain of realism does not make for great, or even stirring, poetry.

There are no more than a handful of statements that overtly criticise the clergy on the specific issue of eviction: nothing comparable for instance, with the denominational violence expressed against the Established Church. Nor does the composite portrait of the 'Calvinist minister' of popular, English-language accounts ever make an appearance: the grim, pro-landlord ascetic, opposed to music and song, who at best acquiesced, preaching that such suffering was sent in retribution for the sins of the people. This last doctrine, straight or distorted in growth, has of course its roots in universal Christian teaching; but there is nothing in Scottish Gaelic verse that parallels an Irish Catholic poet's expression of it at the time of the Plantation of Ulster. Moreover, the 'Calvinist' label, equally applicable as it is (with different sets of reservations) to both main groups, Evangelicals and Moderates, simply obscures the divisive social and cultural hostilities of the age. In actual fact, many ministers, especially among the Evangelicals—most of whom became Free Churchmen at the Disruption of 1843—supported the crofters. One of the two greatest champions of the crofters' cause, the Rev Roderick Macleod, Mgr Ruairi, was Free Church, and a notorious ascetic; the other, decidedly not puritanical, was the Rev Donald MacCallum. MacCallum was arrested and imprisoned for inciting the lieges to subversion. There are many paradoxes in all this. One of the most greatly loved clergymen of the entire Gaidhealtachd was Dr John MacDonald, mentioned above, who was certainly not a grim ascetic. Yet, whatever he may have said in his sermons, he never refers to Clearances in his poetry.

Mary MacPherson (1821–1898), *Mairi Mhór nan Oran*, 'Big Mary of the songs', often invokes the name of Mgr Ruairi poignantly in her poetry and is eloquent in celebration of the Rev Donald MacCallum. She is also the most eloquent opponent of the clergy who remained aloof.

> Preachers have so little concern
> Seeing the plight of my people—
> As dumb on the subject in the pulpit
> As though their listeners were of the brute creation.

John Smith's analysis of the issues of the time is much more intellectual than Mary MacPherson's; Smith was a university educated writer, Mary an oral poet. Each of them attacks the pharisaic aspect of Evangelicalism, each characteristically, in modes that make a fine stylistic contrast. The attack is very conspicuous in two of Smith's major poems ('The Spirit of Pride' and 'The Spirit of Kindliness'); e.g. this from the former:

> 'I'm certain I'm a child of grace,
> numbered forever with the elect;
> my belief is firm and strong,
> and I loathe the name of pride.
> I am conscious of that love;
> my new nature's Spirit-given,
> I praise the One who quenched my hauteur
> I'll find favour, being a lamb.'[12]

Then Mary MacPherson:

> The people have become so strange/that sorrow to them is wheat/and if you don't go into a whelk-shell for them/you cannot stay alive.

> We will not go into a whelk-shell for them/and we can stay alive/although we shall not put on long faces/or wear a look of gloom/with groans and plaintive sighing/that have no substance in them but vapour/so the world may believe/ that a Change has come upon us.

The poem ends with an eloquent rejection of the Evangelical attitude to the vanity of earthly life—including music and song: 'But because vanity is a plant/that satisfies the flesh/it clings to me as firmly/as the thong does to the shoe.'

The gloomy, long-faced hypocrisy which she rejects, however, is the gloomy hypocrisy that the Rev Dr John MacDonald also inveighs against, almost in identical words, in the lines quoted above from the elegy on his own father. Given the fame of the 'Apostle of the North', and the people's familiarity with his spiritual songs, the connection is no doubt consciously and deliberately made.

In that climate of opinion, Mairi Mhór could hardly escape conscience-searching. But she had come to terms with herself and elected to remain robustly of this world, albeit with a strong religious sense of ultimate justice. Her introspection borrows from religion but never turns morbid. She had herself undergone a harrowing experience of unjust conviction and imprisonment for theft; it was this 'that brought my poetry into being', and the anguish of it remained ardent in her until the end of her life. But it also gave authority to her words of comfort to the Skyemen who were imprisoned in Edinburgh in 1883: 'A good college is prison/I myself got to know that, long ago.' Mary had an intense, passionate affection for her native Skye, its community and its way of life in her own youth. All these elements combine in her work, resolved and integrated and given a major dimension by being set in the context of nineteenth-century radicalism. She is representative of many traditional strains of Gaelic poetry, and sometimes limited by them, but her best work gives the sharp feel of immediate experience while at the same time conveying the pressure of contemporary events. Because she possesses such abundant emotional vitality and because she is not a self-conscious analyst of historical processes, the Gaelic world of the later nineteenth century, with its varied and sometimes antipathetic movements, is more vividly and intimately realised in her poetry than in that of any other poet of the age.

Among the hundreds of poets who deal with similar—and different—themes, Neil MacLeod (1843–1924) and Dr John MacLachlan (1804–1874), for example, William Livingstone (1808–1870) stands out as the self-taught man of learning, with the strengths and weaknesses of autodidactism. (In passing, one may contrast John Smith again: the formally educated writer who can construct a successful modern heroic ballad, taking some details from 'Ossian', but is never in danger of being overwhelmed by the influence of his sources or led astray by them.) Livingstone's *Fios thun a'Bhaird*, 'A Message to the Poet', is dignified but full of anger at the desolation brought about in Islay. It is a beautiful and moving poem, in its marriage of craftsmanship and artistic sincerity.

But what a literary historian must find astonishing, especially in a writer who was so aware of contemporary issues, are his long poems: for instance, the poems set in the days of the Norsemen (two poems each running to over a thousand lines) and during the Wars of Independence. None of Livingstone's longer poems can be said to lack energy; what they are singularly lacking in is architectonic power, and for the most part they simply do not succeed. But it is the grand ambition more than the false directions that concerns us here. Livingstone, a Nationalist, Gaelic as well as Scottish, self-taught in Latin, French and Welsh, with some Greek and Hebrew, and well-read in the history of his country, is a failed epic poet. In his attempts to write 'heroic' verse, the influence of Sir Walter Scott is faintly detectable. Within Gaelic, and easily accessible as a source of malign influences, there was 'Ossian', especially the Gaelic verse translations of James Macpherson's 'translation' from Gaelic. It is at such points as these that a vagueness of conception in design and imagery can be seen entering Gaelic poetry. This is largely a phenomenon of acculturation. Emigration to the cities, which increased in volume throughout the century, brought Gaels more and more in contact with Scots and English, and with the popular, rather than the learned, cultures of these languages. Gaelic poets in their new milieu naturally tried to 'modernise' their tradition; what they produced all too often are song-poems, sometimes composed to Lowland melodies, on sentimental subjects, where pathos is produced to order, as in poems on the death of children or other tragic losses, e.g. Neil MacLeod's 'The Death of the Widow's Child' or 'The Death of Mairi' by Evan MacColl (1808–1898):

> She died at the beginning of her beauty;/Heaven would not spare its own;/she died, oh Mairi died, like the sun quenched at its rising.[13]

Many of these compositions are by no means lacking in tenderness and compassion but the expression of the emotion often strikes us as facile. The same defects of sentimentality and simulated emotion are also conspicuous in the numerous songs that gaze nostalgically back at the lost homeland of the Highlands. But here a note of caution is necessary and the observation is applicable also to what may seem to be romantic evocations, of a lost Golden Age, in the poetry of the Clearances. There are recurrent formulas of the type of 'Land of Bens and Glens and Heroes' to be met with almost in every poem. These are not mere romantic clichés but semiotic markers drawn from the established panegyric code of Gaelic poetry and still functioning as such. The signal they give is that the Gaidhealtachd is still, culturally and geographically, a 'territorial' unity.

By the later nineteenth century, cheap Gaelic books, anthologies and individual poetry collections among them, were easily available and a variety of periodicals which included Gaelic verse enjoyed wide circulation. Among the poems which appear in these sources and which illustrate the effects of 'Twilight', 'pathetic fallacy' and contrived sentiment, few can have been more popular than 'MacCrimmon's Lament', published in 1836. As has recently been shown, it is in fact based on Sir Walter Scott's English 'MacKrimmon's Lament' of 1818.[14]

But in all these movements, William Livingstone stands out from the common run of his contemporaries. For one thing, his longer works are poems, not songs: they have no musical component, actual or potential. What he is apparently trying to do, in successive efforts, is to provide the Gaelic nation with its own Heroic Poem, that uniquely European literary institution, without which a European nation has not really achieved maturity. That any poet in a culture so reduced as Gaelic was by the mid-nineteenth century should even think of such a scheme is remarkable. But the Gaelic sense of identity was still strong enough, in spite of the appearances. There is a perverse, if not downright lunatic, expenditure of energy in the venture, but it is, of course, perfectly understandable. For if we seek to isolate one unifying principle in the poetry of the nineteenth century, it is to be found in a continuing consciousness of a Gaelic cosmos which tries to assert, and reclaim, an identity in non-parochial terms, and in spiritual as well as temporal contexts. To modern critics, it seems that what is 'parochial' in the poetry of that age is by the same token not only more immediate and realistic but also more successful in achieving universality than the poetry which was consciously designed to enlarge Gaelic horizons. But clearly for many who formed the Gaelic readership of the century, and who were neither academics nor tradition-bearers, this cannot have been the perspective in which they viewed their poetry. There is, indeed, one academic who articulates what must have been a common view. Donald MacKinnon, first incumbent of the Chair of Celtic at Edinburgh, time and time again in his literary criticism (written in Gaelic) expresses a reaction against the merely verbal virtues of traditional poetry, developed, in his opinion, at the expense of intellectual range and grasp. To MacKinnon, the eighteenth-century religious poet Dugald Buchanan has a unique intellectual quality but the yardstick of excellence is *Oisean* ('Ossian'). MacKinnon was not a great critic, his views on Ossian particularly seem muddled, and his opinions were opposed by other Gaelic scholars of his own time. But if we fail to see that his testimony is representative of the feelings of nineteenth-century Gaels trying to come to terms with the modern world, we shall also fail to understand a whole dimension of the history of Gaelic poetry.

NOTES

1   W J Watson *Bardachd Ghaidhlig* (Edinburgh, 1918) pp xxxiii and xix.
2   D Stewart *Sketches . . . of the Highlanders of Scotland* (Edinburgh, 1822) Vol 1, p 467.
3   Traditional; there are several variants.

4 M F Shaw *Folksongs and Folklore of South Uist* (London, 1955, Repr Aberdeen, 1986) pp 92–3.
5 Ibid. pp 94–5.
6 T Sinton *The Poetry of Badenoch* (Inverness, 1906) p 345.
7 *See* R MacLeod 'Ministearain an Arain' in *Trans Gaelic Society of Inverness*, Vol 52.
8 J Matheson *Oran na h-Eaglais* (Edinburgh, 1836).
9 This and following citations from J MacInnes 'Gaelic Spiritual Verse' in *Trans Gaelic Society of Inverness*, Vol 46.
10 Translation in D S Thomson *Introduction to Gaelic Poetry*, p 222.
11 Translation in M MacDonell *The Emigrant Experience*, pp 20–7.
12 Translation in D S Thomson op. cit., p 241.
13 J H Jackson *A Celtic Miscellany* (London, 1951), p 294.
14 V Blankenhorn 'Traditional and Bogus Elements in "MacCrimmon's Lament"' in *Scottish Studies*, Vol 22, pp 45–67.

FURTHER READING

MacDonell, Margaret, *The Emigrant Experience* (Toronto, 1982).
MacGill-eain, Somhairle, *Ris a' Bhruthaich* (Stornoway, 1985).
Thomson, D S, *An Introduction to Gaelic Poetry* (London, 1974).
——(ed) *A Companion to Gaelic Studies* (Oxford, 1983).

Chapter 21

The Study of Folk Tradition

MARY ELLEN BROWN

All times and all places exhibit a lively traditional culture and nineteenth-century Scotland is no exception. The published literature contains ample evidence of this facet of culture, illustrating as well the Scot's particular interest in the traditional aspects of culture—both at home and abroad: collections of ballads, songs and narratives, descriptions of customs and beliefs and sometimes their analyses attest to the impulse to look beyond oneself and one's own specific cultural environment. From Walter Scott to William Motherwell, from Andrew Lang to James George Frazer, a number of nineteenth-century Scots looked to the narratives and songs—and sometimes their meaning and significance—which circulated orally and informally and had been handed down from generation to generation, implicitly recognising that their recurrence and repetition signalled their importance, both as art and as cultural text.

The interest in folk tradition—particularly its artistic literary forms—is best seen as two parallel though quite distinct approaches. Representative Scots largely outwith Scotland found themselves looking at world-wide evidences, cross-cultural material—at narratives, often labelled myth, which were thought to contain references to belief and custom which illustrated the similarity of all cultures; thus the study of aspects of tradition enabled universalistic analyses. Often referred to as 'armchair' scholars because of their reliance on data gathered by others (and of varying degrees of accuracy and reliability), they used art to understand culture. Scots at home foregrounded evidences of native traditional art—ballads, songs, *märchen* and legend—often recognising that such material offered ample evidence of a Scottish culture; thus many of the collections of texts are presented and framed with nationalistic sentiments. Drawing their information from earlier publications and manuscripts as well as from the mouths of then contemporary Scots, their work collectively illustrates the existence and persistence of Scottish culture despite political union with England. Different as these two approaches are, they yet share an interest in and positive valuation of aspects of oral culture; while each approach reflects specific interests and concerns of the nineteenth century, the published works continue to have literary and cultural resonance.

James George Frazer is the ideal representative of the universalistic approach. Born in Glasgow in the 1850s, nurtured in Calvinism, he was educated at the University of Glasgow and then at Trinity College, Cambridge where he spent the remainder of his life. At Glasgow he acquired a thorough classical background from G G Ramsay and was stimulated to search for absolute laws of nature by the physicist, Sir William Thomson, later Lord Kelvin. These influences prepared him for his introduction to both W Robertson Smith and his interest in comparative religion and the anthropological theories of Edward Burnett Tylor. Any discussion of Frazer and particularly his monumental work *The Golden Bough* must begin with an exploration of the cultural views of the times and Tylor's work in particular.

Tylor articulated a theory of cultural evolution—consonant with the Victorian frame of mind—which assumed that all cultures go through the same stages in their development—progressing from savagery to barbarism, and finally to civilisation, represented by late nineteenth-century Western Europe. The thrust of development is ever upwards. Cultures in the same stage of development then are everywhere basically the same and a scholar might reconstruct the prehistory of a particular culture by assuming its similarity to any other culture. Furthermore, in the advance to later stages of a culture, holdovers or 'survivals' remain as evidence of the stages left behind. These materials—beliefs, customs, narratives—often seem dysfunctional and anomalous. When compared with similar materials from earlier, less developed cultures, however, their original meaning, significance, and function become clear. These cultural assumptions and the comparative method used to illustrate them provided the intellectual bases for the work and contributions of Frazer. Thus in *The Golden Bough* Frazer juxtaposes materials from primitive peoples, classical civilisations, and contemporary 'survivals' to understand a legend or myth about the priesthood at Nemi; in doing so he simultaneously dealt with the evolution of human thought.

First published in a two volume version in 1890, the third edition, published between 1907 and 1915 in twelve volumes, is considered the definitive version. While the basic questions and theoretical framework remain the same, the comparative data is greatly expanded in the third edition. The work seeks to explain certain curious, even tragic aspects about a presumed ritual periodically reenacted:

> The myth to be explained concerned the rule of priestly succession at the sacred grove of Diana at Nemi, in the Alban hills of Italy. The lake (Nemi) and the grove were sometimes known as the lake and grove of Aricia, after a town some three miles away. The Priest-King of this sacred grove spent his time with drawn sword around a certain tree in the grove, constantly on guard. He had succeeded to his title by murdering his predecessor with a sprig of the mistletoe bough which grew high up on the tree, and he, in turn, was destined to be murdered by a successful challenger in the same manner. He defended himself successfully only so long as his powers of awareness, skill, and strength suffered no deterioration; as soon as he started to slip, he was murdered and the murderer reigned in his place.[1]

Using comparative material from all over the world, Frazer sought to answer several questions: why did the priest have to kill his predecessor? why did he pick the branch first?

The myth/ritual Frazer sought to understand was not an isolated example, for he uncovered similar materials from diverse times and places, suggesting that the impetus for the myth/ritual at hand was worldwide. His ability to illustrate through his massive data a connective tissue tying all peoples together was and remains inspiring. Drawn from different stages in culture's development, his examples collectively reveal the 'tendency, with the growth of civilisation, (for materials) to dwindle from solemn ritual into mere pageant and pastime'.[2] Frazer's technique is analogical, a mental characteristic he also attributes to early humanity: early narratives of the slain god, of death and resurrection, involve human enactments or representations of the observed cycle of nature. In fact, human life and nature were thought to be closely linked by early humankind. The priest at Nemi in an earlier form would have been a god, devolved here to a priest, elsewhere to a king. The god/king/priest is often equated with corn, harvested and milled in the fall, planted and grown again in the spring. Frazer discusses in great detail early beliefs about the separation of soul from body, both in sleep and in death, that is temporary and permanent, and suggests that the mistletoe at Nemi contains the soul, the life force, the essence of the god; thus it was necessary for the new priest to acquire that soul before assuming the priesthood. The former priest—once god and sometimes king—must die, relinquish his position, or be killed at regular intervals to insure the well-being of the people. Again, the assumption/analogy was made in the minds of early humanity that there was a connection between their health and well-being and that of the priest/king/god. Even further, the health of the priest/king/god was integrally tied in with the status of nature: the old, enfeebled priest would negatively effect nature's fertility; thus he must be removed and replaced by a more effective/healthy priest for regeneration to occur. Not infrequently the old priest/king was also a scapegoat, made to represent all that was evil, negative, all that might impede rebirth. The priest killed his predecessor than because he was no longer protecting the people, and he had first to break off the golden bough of mistletoe because it contained the very essence of the god through whom the life-saving connection with nature was made.

Frazer saw narratives and their imbedded beliefs as reflections of the attempts of humanity to deal with certain recurring situations, as illustrations of the ways all peoples have sought to control and regulate their environments. Early attempts to understand and control were based on magic; and magical principles, articulated by Frazer, become the interpretative device for understanding the vast data assembled for *The Golden Bough* and other works. Magic, according to Frazer, is based on two simple principles of thought: the law of similarity which assumes that like produces like and that effect resembles cause, and the law of contact or contagion, based on the belief that things once associated continue to be so even after the physical connection is severed. By the law of similarity, a magical practitioner might assume that imitation will produce the desired effect; by the law of contagion, the practitioner assumes that action done to an object will effect the person with whom the object was once associated. Corporately, these two principles or laws are referred to as Sympathetic Magic, both misapplications of the association of ideas; for the law of similarity errs in thinking that things that seem alike are alike, and the law of contagion errs in thinking that things once associated remain so.

Defining magic as 'a spurious system of natural law as well as an abortive art'[3] Frazer divides magic into the theoretical and practical. Theoretical magic involves an abstract system of natural laws, a set of rules which determine events throughout the world. Practical magic, on the other hand, refers to that which people do to arrive at desired ends. The primitive magician knows only practical magic or false art, never analysing the principles which lie behind the actions. At first, magic is practised by individuals for their own benefit. The development of public magic, which benefits or injures the whole community, introduces a public figure—a magician—and represents an important development in the evolution of society. The magician becomes a man of rank, perhaps a chief or king; and some of the ablest and most ambitious are, of course, drawn to the role. Achieving status, the magician seeks to serve the public rather than self; by tending 'to place the control of affairs in the hands of the ablest man: it [public magic] shifted the balance of power from the many to the one: it substituted a monarch for a democracy, or rather for an oligarchy of old men.'[4] Thus public magic and the rise of the magician/king are important steps in the development of culture, for— according to Frazer—savage democracy is conservative, tied to the past, and mediocre; a monarch must appear for progress from savagery: 'The rise of one man to supreme power enables him to carry through changes in a single lifetime which previously many generations might not have sufficed to effect; and if, as will often happen, he is a man of intellect and energy above the common, he will readily avail himself of the opportunity.'[5] Further, Frazer suggests that public magic 'has contributed to emancipate mankind from the thralldom of tradition and to elevate them into a larger, freer life, with a broader outlook on the world,' adding that 'if it [magic] is the child of error, it has yet been the mother of freedom and truth.'[6]

Magic assumes implicitly that a practitioner can bring about the desired result. And everywhere that magic is found, the same simple ideas of association either by resemblance or contiguity form the basis of the practice, though erroneous. At some point those of superior intellect recognise that they have no real power to control, that the effects they seek to produce occur anyway. It seems natural then to attribute control and power to something stronger, perhaps like human beings, and to humble oneself to those powers. Thus religion arises, attributing the governance of nature to superior powers who need to be both conciliated and propitiated. With the evolution of religion comes the idea of sacred leaders or kings with divine power, often identified with the forces of nature. And precautions, mostly in the form of taboos—things not to do—surround the king; for his well being affects the welfare of the people. Not infrequently, there is a mingling of magic and religion with a priest-king wooing and propitiating the gods as well as performing rites which of their own accord are thought to bring about the desired results.

Frazer assumes that magic came first in the evolutionary chain, for it is everywhere the same. Religion, on the other hand, is diverse, though based on the belief in superior, personal agents above humankind, a concept which requires reflection, intelligence and the recognition of humanity's weakness and impotency in controlling nature. In time, however, religion evolves to science, which like magic earlier, assumes the uniformity and order of nature, that one who knows the causes can put much into motion and make things happen. Both magic and science represent humanity's attempts to discover how to govern natural phenomena. The age of science, however, brings right premises and techniques, acquired in civilisation, realising at last the dream of the age of magic. And this is for the good: 'It is probably not too much to say that the hope of progress—moral and intellectual as well as material—in the future is bound up with the fortunes of science, and that every obstacle placed in the way of scientific discovery is a wrong to humanity.'[7] Elsewhere Frazer goes further, postulating the eventual demise of science: 'In the last analysis magic, religion, and science are nothing but theories of thought; and as science has supplanted its predecessors, so it may hereafter be itself superseded by some more perfect hypothesis, perhaps by some totally different way of looking at the phenomena—of registering the shadows on the screen—of which we in this generation can form no idea. The advance of knowledge is an infinite progression towards a goal that for ever recedes.'[8]

The Golden Bough 'depicts, in its sinuous outline, in its play of alternate light and shadow, the long evolution by which the thoughts and efforts of man [*sic*] have passed through the successive stages.'[9] More particularly the work deals with the age of magic and the mingling of magic and religion, where Sympathetic Laws are resorted to frequently. The killing or death of the priest/king imitates nature's change of seasons; intercourse between the king and his consort, sometimes herself a goddess, insures fertility. The king's very touch may have the power to cure; the soul of the god may be transferred from former to present priest. Thus similarity and contagion are illustrated over and over again in Frazer's work by the use of analogies.

As a cultural explanation, the message of *The Golden Bough* is no longer viable: cultures are far more diverse than he, Tylor, Andrew Lang, and others assumed; cultures develop at different rates and in different ways calling into question the satisfying, but inaccurate concept of unilinear, progressive evolution, everywhere culminating in civilisation. On a more particular level, Frazer's work errs like the thought of his savages and barbarians, by over-reliance on analogy: he assumed, without knowledge of a cultural context, that similar effects (texts of myths and beliefs) resulted from similar causes. In Frazer's defense, he perceptiently anticipated in a general way subsequent criticism when he said, 'what we call truth is only the hypothesis which is found to work best'[10] and when he articulated his feeling that his 'contribution to the history of the human mind consists of little more than a rough and purely provisional classification of facts gathered almost entirely from printed sources.'[11] Failing as social science, his work has yet succeeded as art.

The ample quotes throughout this discussion have illustrated Frazer's penchant for encapsulating certain ideas compellingly. His vivid descriptions of places and events further heighten his communicative ability. Understandably, his rhetoric and descriptive talent, together with his mastery of analogy and metaphor for sometimes symbolic and imagistic effect have called attention to and appreciation of his style. The structure of *The Golden Bough* too has often been subject of comment for its nonchronological, thematic ordering, developing often in concentric fashion—sometimes equated with sonata form. But most of all, the work and Frazer have been singled out for making accessible in an ordered fashion mythic ideas, cyclical theories, and for providing an extended example of the archetypal pattern— the quest, here the quest for the meaning of a ritual rather than a more narrative, literary quest with worldwide analogues. A work intended to reveal the secrets of humanities's intellectual development has become a literary sourcebook for artists who have selectively utilised and been influenced by its parts.

Frazer's *The Golden Bough* is a monumental example of a Scot's look- ing to traditional culture—especially to the distant past and to far flown cul- tures—for understanding of humankind's development in general. And he was not alone. Andrew Lang—anthropologist, journalist, poet, classical scholar, historian, writer of children's stories, literary critic—espoused and worked with many of the evolutionary ideas of Tylor and Frazer. His collective works, however, have not had the cumulative literary impact of Frazer's productions. Perhaps the very diffuseness of his interests and pub- lications precluded their use as sourcebook; perhaps, too, the theoretical bent of his anthropological and folkloristic disquisitions and his distance from the primary data about which he was writing have also limited the usefulness of his work today; for he often foregrounded theories which today have been discarded or drastically revised. His definition and discussion of the ballad in the 11th edition of the *Encyclopaedia Britannica* is a case in point.[12] Lang urges the employment of the comparative method in looking at aspects and incidents of ballads which contain traces of old beliefs and customs and which have world wide distribution, ignoring more useful comparison of whole texts if kinship is sought. He further suggests that ballads grew out of the custom of singing and dancing and were a result of communal improvisation, their repetition among other characteristics suggesting their origin in dance. This proposition too has long been questioned as a universal explanation. However Lang's assertion that most study of the ballad has been for literary reasons is perhaps well taken and brings us to the second approach to traditional culture, mentioned at the outset: the examination of oral literary tradition at home for nationalistic reasons.

A particular interest in Scottish cultural attributes had begun rather late in the eighteenth century, perhaps a delayed response to the monarchical (1603) and parliamentary (1707) union with England. Not political in nature, but frankly cultural, an informal movement seems to have sprung up con- cerned with foregrounding evidences of a distinctly Scottish heritage: Mac- pherson's Ossian, the 'untutored' works of Robert Burns, and the profusion of ballads and songs found in early publications, in manuscript collections, and in the mouths of many 'unlettered' and some 'lettered' Scots gave ample encouragement to the cultural nationalists. Perhaps the most lasting result of this movement, often felt to be a salvage operation, was the fascination with the ballad which peaked in the first quarter of the nineteenth century in the editions of 'national' song published by Walter Scott, James Hogg, Peter Buchan, Charles Kirkpatrick Sharpe, Robert Chambers, George Ritchie Kinloch, William Motherwell and others. Many of these collections are prefaced by introductions which make clear the nationalistic stimulus: 'By such efforts, feeble as they are, I may contribute somewhat to the history of my native country; the peculiar features of whose manners and character are daily melting and dissolving into those of her sister and ally';[13] 'The origin of the historical ballads of Scotland requires no investigation; they have sprung up, like the greater part of the popular poetry of all uncivilised nations, among the people themselves, as the record of their most interesting events; and little can be collected regarding them, but a few incidental notices, from successive historians, of those which were popular in their time';[14] 'The ancient Ballads of Caledonia are venerated by those lovers of their country who delight in the native imagery of their homes, and in hearing the martial and warlike deeds of their forefathers said or sung in the enchanting voice of their fair countrywomen.'[15] And such works as Scott's *Minstrelsy of the Scottish Border* have been called 'great national works' and the *Minstrelsy* is said to have done for Scotland what Percy's *Reliques of Ancient English Poetry* (1765) did for England, providing a national collection and sourcebook for poets.

In reality, of course, neither Percy's *Reliques* nor Scott's *Minstrelsy* are national collections in the strict sense of the word, for much of the material included is international, certainly shared in part by other Northern and Western European nations. Early in the nineteenth century, Robert Jamieson had called attention to Scandinavian parallels to Scottish balladry and had developed a theory—the Anglo-Norse Theory—which postulated that Scandinavians had brought and left ballad materials in Scotland on their many forays; thus he suggested a Scandinavian origin for many presumed Scottish ballads. John Finlay, on the other hand, pointed to French sources. Later comparative studies were to reveal additional parallels in ballad stock. Nonetheless, the materials claimed for Scotland do reflect Scottish versions of widespread ballads and those versions have often been identified as especially artistic, as particularly worthy of note. Thus the multiform quality of the ballad—'it manifests itself in many texts'[16]—enables a given ballad to be both national and international; and the national versions of the international stock of ballads deserve a place in Scottish literary history, as one kind of artistic heritage: 'Folk literature . . . is the literature of traditional culture, that is, the literature perhaps created by but certainly transmitted by word of mouth rather than written or printed document; it is the literature of tradition as distinct from the literature of print.'[17]

The texts that made their way into published collections, then, had originally been sung and recited by people, transmitted orally and aurally. Some nineteenth-century gatherers of balladry collected material from those who knew them; others relied on earlier collections in manuscript or printed form. Since many ballad enthusiasts were poets or would-be-poets themselves, collected or available versions often had a 'helping hand' before they were presented to the public in published form. Since texts straight from the mouths of the 'country folk' lacked polish and did not fit existing standards of literary taste, they needed fixing. And the texts needed fixing to present the Scottish heritage in the best possible light. Clearly too the poet/ballad presenters were responding to their own aesthetic sensibilities and were doing on a reflective level what oral possessors and creators of ballad materials were doing on a less conscious, reflexive level. The fact of the matter is, then, that many collections of Scottish ballads have their problems, pointed out most succinctly by James Hogg's mother: 'An ye hae spoilt them a' thegither. They were made for singing, an' no for reading; an' they are nouther right spelled nor right setten doun.'[18] Nonetheless, numerous collections appeared, some as texts to be read, others with piano accompaniments to facilitate drawing room singing. Despite their questionable status as reflections of genuine oral tradition, the printed versions stimulated interest, imitations, and encouraged the singing of the songs and the recognition that Scotland's oral literary inheritance was indeed worthy of note.

Looking back, one figure stands out not only for his collection and his criticism of current editorial principles, but also for his perspicacious, forward looking discussion of the ballad as an oral literary genre: William Motherwell, West country journalist, antiquarian and poet, recognised balladry as an important cultural artifact. And he collected and encouraged others to collect materials to add to the national stock. Andrew Crawfurd, an invalid doctor from Lochwinnoch,[19] is but one of the contributors to Motherwell's 1827 work—*Minstrelsy: Ancient and Modern*. Motherwell was well aware of the international scope of much ballad material and many particular ballads, but stressed Scottish versions and materials presumed to be of Scottish origin. In fact half of his lengthy introduction provides a chronological survey of the publication of presumed 'Scottish' examples. Like Scott, Finlay, and Buchan quoted earlier, he saw ballads as a 'curious and interesting species of national literature transmitted even to the present day,' calling them a 'portion of national literature'; 'they convey to posterity, that description of song which is peculiarly national and characteristick; that body of poetry which has inwoven itself with the feelings and passions of the people.'[20]

Unlike many of his ballad compatriots, however, Motherwell saw no need for editing, valuing oral transmission as 'a safe and almost unerring guide.'[21] His criticism of the kind of editing described earlier is amazingly direct and in keeping with twentieth-century standards for collections of folk materials: 'The tear and wear of three centuries will do less mischief to the text of an old ballad among the vulgar, than one short hour will effect, if in the possession of some sprightly and accomplished editor of the present day, who may choose to impose on himself the thankless and uncalled for labour of piecing and patching up its imperfections, polishing its asperities, correcting its mistakes, embellishing its naked details, purging it of impurities, and of trimming it from top to toe with tailor-like fastidiousness and nicety, so as to be made fit for the press.'[22] In criticising many of the liberties taken with oral material, he goes further, saying, 'Some of these offenses against truth and correct taste, are of a very deep, others of a lighter shade of criminality, but be they what they may in magnitude, all are alike deserving of unmitigated condemnation' which is exactly what he reserves for Allan Cunningham's editing, described as a 'wholesale mode of hacking, and hewing, and breaking the joints of ancient and traditionary song.'[23]

In line with his very clear preference for unedited, unpolished, unvarnished 'truth', Motherwell recognised that 'the same story is told after a different fashion in one district of the country, from what it is remembered in another' and further that 'all versions . . . are entitled to be considered as of equal authenticity.'[24] Such sentiments clearly militated against the conflations and editing typical at the time and illustrate his intimate knowledge of oral tradition also reflected in his identification of recurring ballad qualities. He recognises commonplaces as key repeated elements which aide both memory and composition. He suggests several categories or levels: there are commonplaces at the phrase level, commonplaces which involve recurrent descriptions of 'certain actions in one uniform way'; and commonplaces which control the structure of the whole so that 'the outline of the building and the effect of the whole remain unchanged.'[25] Such commonplaces serve as the building blocks of composition 'as a kind of ground-work, on which the poem could be raised. With such common-places indelibly fixed in his memory, the minstrel could with ease to himself, and with rapidity of extemporaneous delivery, rapidly model any event which came under his cognizance into song.'[26] Thus Motherwell anticipated the concept of oral formulaic composition.

He suggests that the action of the ballad begins at once and proceeds in a straightforward fashion with no backward glances to fill in missing information. The telling is elliptical and the metre irregular—'licentious and incorrect'[26]—concealed in performance by the music/tunes to which texts are inextricably bound. The spare, often incomplete narrative hints at an audience familiar with the story and necessitates a degree of participation: 'much is always left for imagination to fancy, and for the feelings of the auditors, to supply, roused as they cannot fail to be, by the scenick picture rapidly and distinctly traced before the mind's eye.'[28] Furthermore, he suggests that in actual performances, singers often preface their materials with historical information and explanatory details—a recognised technique for filling out the narrative. Singers of song not infrequently localise and rationalise materials and express belief in the veracity of the accounts rendered in song. Motherwell describes his unwitting brush with such deep belief: 'from no discourteous motive, but from sheer ignorance of this important article of belief, I have unfortunately for myself, once or twice notably affronted certain aged virgins, by impertinent dubitations touching the veracity of their songs, an offence which bitter experience will teach me to avoid repeating, as it has long ere this, made me rue the day of its commission.'[29]

Touching on a topic of considerable concern in his day and time, Motherwell assumes the minstrel authorship of original materials then circulating as ballads among a particular portion of the population with a taste for simply told accounts of potentially real incidents. Thus the story materials have moved from castle and hall to lowly house and hut—a decline in status. Nonetheless they deserve a place in the history of Scottish literature albeit he thought their time was almost over: 'the changes which, within this half century, the manners and habits of our peasantry and labouring classes, with whom this song has been cherished, have undergone, are inimical to its further preservation.'[30]

Motherwell like many ballad enthusiasts in nineteenth-century Scotland was interested in ballad material as one aspect of Scottish literature, transmitted orally. Like others in his day and time he attributed their origins to minstrels and assumed a loss in class status for the ballads then circulating—an assumption which is accurate for only a limited number of texts. His prediction that the ballad would disappear overstates what actually happened: the ballad changed; new forms of oral literature developed. And the changes have been tied, as he incompletely suggested, to larger societal changes—in particular the technological revolution and such concomitant developments as the rise in literacy.'[31] Motherwell's insistence on scrupulous editorial principles, his recognition of the equality of all versions, his anticipation of oral formulaic composition in his discussion of 'commonplaces', his recognition that ballads are more than text and include a tune, and his comments on performance mark him as the premier ballad scholar of his time, often overshadowed by the more literarily prominent Walter Scott.

Scott, Motherwell and all the many ballad editors, collectors, enthusiasts who span the nineteenth century, collectively made available an incredible body of ballad material. Many Scottish versions of the international body of balladry have been justly singled out as particularly aesthetic renditions by such noted critics as Francis James Child—the late-nineteenth-century American compiler of 'classic' ballads. Cumulatively the editions and collections offer a lasting monument to Scottish oral artistry, which stimulated interest in this kind of literature—'folk literature'—simultaneously providing models for poets and imitators who found the form, themes, and 'commonplaces' of traditional balladry useful exemplars. The nationalistic impulse which stimulated the interest in ballads provided then—taking all the published material into account—a sourcebook for national pride and poetic inspiration.

Such works as *The Golden Bough* and Motherwell's *Minstrelsy: Ancient and Modern*, Scott's *Minstrelsy of the Scottish Border* show Scottish interest in folk literature, in aspects of traditional culture—albeit a selective interest. These works focus on few genres—narrative and song—and thus together touch on only a small portion of folk literature or traditional culture extant then and now: they might have looked to folk speech, drama, dance, riddles, proverbs[32] and genres of traditional material culture such as house types, costumes, agricultural procedures, foodways[33] in order to present a thorough picture of the values, concerns and aesthetic preferences of people in traditional culture. Nineteenth-century students of folk literature and traditional culture tended, however, to limit their focus to a few genres and, as has been suggested, to provide general schema into which the folk literature might be put—Frazer's universalistic approach, Motherwell *et al*'s nationalistic.

The work of the universalists was global in scope, and clearly too expansive; the nationalistic approach was Scotland-centred and perhaps too constricted. Both perspectives abstracted material from the cultural contexts where they had life and vitality—the people who told the myths and legends and honoured the beliefs, the singers of songs—and gave the assembled texts meaning in isolation. Both perspectives shared a view of the 'folk' as less developed segments of culture or society—perspectives which very much reflect the particular societal milieu of the scholars. Both approaches fit as well the nineteenth-century penchant for gathering data, facts, for all the works described here might be seen as compilations. However incomplete in data analyses, the publications of both perspectives have served and continue to serve as sources of information, as sourcebooks of inspiration, providing a lasting tribute to traditional culture and folk literature, being repositories of materials of a particular time and place.

NOTES

1   Abram Kardiner and Edward Preble, *The Studied Man* (New York, 1963), p 82.
2   James George Frazer, *The Illustrated Golden Bough*, Mary Douglas (ed), illustrated by Sabine MacCormack (Garden City, New York, 1978), p 118.
3   James George Frazer, *The Golden Bough: A Study in Magic and Religion*, 3rd edn, revised and enlarged, 12 vols (London, 1911–15), I, p 53.
4   Ibid., p 216.
5   Ibid., p 217.
6   Ibid., p 218.
7   Frazer, *Illustrated*, p 249.
8   Ibid.
9   Kardiner and Preble, p 74.
10   Frazer, *Illustrated*, p 98.
11   James George Frazer, *Man, God, and Immortality* (New York, 1927), p 47.
12   *Encyclopaedia Britannica* 11th edn, s. v. 'Ballads'.
13   Walter Scott, *Minstrelsy of the Scottish Border* (Kelso, 1802), I, pp cix–cx.
14   John Finlay, *Scottish Historical and Romantic Ballads, chiefly ancient* (Edinburgh, 1808), I, p xi.
15   Peter Buchan, *Gleanings of Scarce Old Ballads with Explanatory Notes* (Aberdeen, 1891), preface.
16   David Buchan, *Scottish Tradition: A Collection of Scottish Folk Literature* (London, 1984), p 6.
17   Ibid., p 1.
18   Sigurd Bernhard Hustvedt, *Ballad Books and Ballad Men* (Cambridge, Mass, 1930).
19   E B Lyle (ed), *Andrew Crawfurd's Collection of Ballads and Songs* (Edinburgh, 1975), I.
20   William Motherwell, *Minstrelsy: Ancient and Modern* (Glasgow, 1827), pp x, v.
21   Ibid., p iii.
22   Ibid., p iv.
23   Ibid., pp v, xcvii.

24   Ibid., pp v, vi.
25   Ibid., pp xix, xi.
26   Ibid., p xxiii.
27   Ibid., p xvii.
28   Ibid., p xiii.
29   Ibid., p xxvii, note.
30   Ibid., p cii.
31   For a discussion of this point *see* David Buchan, *The Ballad and the Folk* (London, 1972).
32   *See* as an example Robert Chambers, *Popular Rhymes of Scotland* (Edinburgh, 1870).
33   Alexander Fenton, *Scottish Country Life* (Edinburgh, 1976) includes an example of the kinds of material which might be examined.

FURTHER READING

Child, Francis James, *The English and Scottish Popular Ballads* (Boston, 1882–1898).

Frazer, James George, *The Golden Bough: A Study in Magic and Religion*, 12 vols (London, 1911–15).

Hustvedt, Sigurd Bernard, *Ballad Books and Ballad Men* (Cambridge, Mass, 1930).

Motherwell, William, *Minstrelsy: Ancient and Modern* (Glasgow, 1827).

Scott, Walter, *Minstrelsy of the Scottish Border* (Kelso, 1802).

Vickery, John B, *The Literary Impact of 'The Golden Bough'* (Princeton, 1973).

Chapter 22

Exile and Empire

ALAN MACGILLIVRAY

In his short and admittedly inferior novel, *The Surgeon's Daughter* (1827), Sir Walter Scott makes his anti-hero Richard Middlemas exclaim upon the allure of India for an ambitious young man.

> 'Oh, Delhi! oh, Golconda! have your names no power to conjure down idle recollections?—India, where gold is won by steel; where a brave man cannot pitch his desire of fame and wealth so high, but that he may realize it, if he have fortune to his friend?'[1]

These sentiments were felt by many Scotsmen from the middle of the eighteenth century onwards. Like Middlemas, they realised that their proving years 'had better be spent in India, where much may be done in a little while, than here, where nothing can be done save just enough to get salt to our broth, or broth to our salt.' Where was the attraction of spending 'years in this infernal wilderness, cruizing after crowns and half-crowns, when worse men are making lacs and crores of rupees'?[2]

It would no doubt be wrong to ascribe base motives of financial greed to all the young Scotsmen on the make in the later eighteenth century as they took ship for India or North America or the West Indies. Yet those were the days before the more complex nineteenth-century motivations of imperial government service or missionary zeal or scientific knowledge had emerged with their recognised channels of entry through the armed and civil services and the various sponsoring societies. It was the major trading companies like the East India Company or the Hudson's Bay Company and its rival the North-West Fur Company, along with a multitude of lesser trading houses, that drew the lairds' sons and the lads o' pairts and education in the greatest numbers overseas with the hope of the fortune, at least in Scottish terms, that would enable them to return in middle life to their own land and a secure comfortable position in society. Menie Gray, the surgeon's daughter herself in Scott's novel, returns to her native village and 'appeared to find her only pleasure in acts of benevolence which seemed to exceed the extent of her fortune, had not her very retired life been taken into consideration.'[3]

Undoubtedly Scotland as a whole, and local communities in particular, benefited from the infusion of fresh capital and the dissemination of knowledge about the wider world that attended the return of these voluntary exiles to their poor and isolated homeland. John Galt treats this in two of his novels.

Mr Cayenne in *Annals of the Parish* (1821), a loyalist planter from Virginia, brings great benefit to the district of Ayrshire in which he comes to rest in peppery middle age. Galt treats him kindly, and through the eyes of the Reverend Micah Balwhidder we can see that this eighteenth-century 'nabob' is an instrument of social change for the better within the context of an Ayrshire parish. However, when we meet Mr Rupees in Galt's later and more ironical novel, *Last of the Lairds* (1826), we find that the new wealth is being used for the baser purposes of ostentation and the accumulation of a great estate at the expense of poorer neighbours. The Laird of Auldbiggings exclaims bitterly against this practice:

> 'Ye see, when Mr Rupees the Nawbub came hame frae Indy, and bought the Arunthrough property frae the Glaikies, who, like sae mony ithers o' the right stock o' legitimate gentry, hae been smothered out o' sight by the weed and nettle overgrowths o' merchandise and cotton-weavry, he would fain hae bought Auldbiggings likewise, and sent that gett o' the de'il and the law, Caption, to make me an offer; but I was neither a prodigal son nor an Esau, to sell my patrimony for a mess o' pottage, so I gied him a flea in his lug, and bade him tell the Nawbub to chew the cud o' the sin o' covetousness, the whilk is disappointment.'[4]

The Biblical references here very clearly indicate the nature of the tensions that must have afflicted many a Scottish community at that time: the resentment of the traditional landowners, the legitimate stock, against the incomers of dubious origin, alien tares among the homegrown corn; the fear of natural parochial hairy Esau that a sophisticated far-travelled smooth Jacob will unfairly buy out his birthright; the annoyance of the stay-at-home son that the world-wandering ne'er-do-weel ultimately gains a higher reward and more favour in the eyes of the nation. Mr Rupees, on the other hand, for all his self-flattering stories and boring anecdotes of India, puts his side of the matter very pungently:

> '(The people of Scotland) are quite as well disposed to esteem those who, by their own merits, have made their own fortunes, and have brought home from other countries the means of improving their native land. I have myself spent more money here, Dr Lounlans, on Nawaubpore, than all that the Mailings, since the Ragman's Roll, have had to spend, whether got by thieving in days of yore, or by rack-rents and borrowing in our own time.'

He is savagely contemptuous of the stay-at-home Scots:

> '... the daft and the imbecile ... constitute the majority of the nation at large; for, you know, that every man of sense and talent seeks his fortune abroad, and leaves only the incapable and those who are conscious of their deficiencies at home—'[5]

This, of course, takes us back to the sentiments of Middlemas in *The Surgeon's Daughter*, but with the emphasis more on the poor-spiritedness of the Scottish people than on the poverty of the Scottish environment. Mr Rupees does not speak for his creator, but the alacrity with which Galt again and again set out from Scotland on one commercial or literary venture after another suggests that the main attraction, the zest and adventure of life, lay furth of Scotland.

It is the setting out that is the decisive act, not the returning, nor even the writing about the experience. Leaving aside those transported against their will in the convict ships, the (sadly) much larger number of the guiltless and the exploited who emptied the glens and filled the emigrant ships, and the high proportion of the male population of Scotland who enlisted and put on a red uniform to fight for the Queen, there still remains a significant element, men 'of sense and talent' certainly, educated and articulate equally certainly, moved by ambition or idealism, who voluntarily undertook Scotland's nineteenth-century quest. Many of them chose at some point during or after that quest to write about it. Whether or not what most of them wrote was literature in the accepted sense is arguable; what is certain is that they found a wide readership among the nation's loyal subjects, proud and avid to hear about the strange world being opened up by English enterprise. Scotland's quest, whatever it was, unfolded within that English imperial enterprise; and, although to twentieth-century Scottish sensibilities that seems deplorable, the wandering Scots who undertook it do not seem to have cared a jot. As they left their village schools or their academies or the English schools to which their prosperous parents had sent them, the important thing was to be off and away, into the East India Company service or the trading house in Canada or Jamaica, and out into the wider world that Scots had been attracted towards since the Middle Ages.

In the case of Alexander Mackenzie, however, the trip from Stornoway to the Hudson's Bay Company was interrupted by some formative years in New York and Montreal. For this survey he marks the starting-point, since, although his great journey was made in 1793, it was 1801 before Scotland could read his *Voyages from Montreal, on the River St Lawrence, through the Continent of North America, to the Frozen and Pacific Oceans*. This crossing of the continent, several years before the American expedition of Lewis and Clark, was described by him in a concise narrative which reveals his genuine interest in the Indians he encountered and at times tried to help. Another interest comes through in the lists of words in two Indian languages which he includes in the account. Yet, while he writes in the main tradition of nineteenth-century exploration with his clear descriptions of people and places and vivid recounting of the events of the journey, he has a rather appealing vagueness about his position at times. The moment of his actual entry into the Pacific Ocean is attended by no expressions of elation:

> At about eight we got out of the river, which discharges itself by various channels into an arm of the sea. The tide was out, and had left a large space covered with sea-weed. The surrounding hills were involved in fog. The wind was at West, which was ahead of us, and very strong; the bay appearing to be from one to three miles in breadth. As we advanced along the land we saw a

great number of sea-otters. We fired several shots at them, but without any success, from the rapidity with which they plunged under the water. We also saw many small porpoises or divers. The white-headed eagle, which is common in the interior parts; some small gulls, a dark bird which is inferior in size to the gull, and a few small ducks, were all the birds which presented themselves to our view.

This interest in wild life was not entirely scientific, as he reveals slightly later:

I had flattered myself with the hope of getting a distance of the moon and stars, but the cloud of weather continually disappointed me, and I began to fear that I should fail in this important object, particularly as our provisions were at a very low ebb, and we had as yet no reason to expect any assistance from the natives. Our stock was, at this time, reduced to twenty pounds weight of pemmican, fifteen pounds of rice, and six pounds of flour, among ten half-starved men in a leaky vessel, and on a barbarous coast. Our course from the river was about West-South-West, distance ten miles.[6]

How often, as the century proceeds, do we find the leaders of expeditions expressing similar gloomy sentiments about their situation, even at a moment of success, and juxtaposing them with the routine details of directions and distances?

Perhaps it is a Scottish characteristic to speak or write reductively about success, even one's own, and to be conscious of the supposedly crowning moment being undermined by drawbacks and tainted by contradictory elements, even by absurdity. When John Galt set out to found the new town of Guelph in the Huron Tract of Upper Canada in 1827, even before misfortune fell upon his Canada Company operation, he was aware of how close the solemnity bordered upon the ridiculous:

. . . after endeavouring to dry ourselves, and having recourse to the store-basket, I proposed to go to the spot chosen for the town. By this time the sun was set, and Dr Dunlop, with his characteristic drollery, having doffed his wet garb, and dressed himself, Indian fashion, in blankets, we proceeded with Mr Prior, attended by two woodmen with their axes.

It was consistent with my plan to invest our ceremony with a little mystery, the better to make it be remembered. So intimating that the main body of the men were not to come, we walked to the brow of the neighbouring rising ground, and Mr Prior having shown the site selected for the town, a large maple tree was chosen; on which, taking an axe from one of the woodmen, I struck the first stroke. To me at least the moment was impressive,—and the silence of the woods, that echoed to the sound, was as the sigh of the solemn genius of the wilderness departing for ever.

The doctor followed me, then, if I recollect correctly, Mr Prior, and the woodmen finished the work. The tree fell with a crash of accumulating thunder, as if ancient Nature were alarmed at the entrance of social man into her innocent solitudes with his sorrows, his follies, and his crimes.

. . . After the solemnity, for though the ceremony was simple, it may be so denominated, we returned to the shanty, and the rain, which had been suspended during the performance, began again to pour.[7]

Mackenzie the explorer and entrepreneur chose to write only incidentally to his main business, whereas Galt, for us today, is mainly a literary man whose business ventures smack almost of the irrelevant. Yet, objectively, both were important in the development of Canada as a nation and the writing that came of that major involvement has its own significance as documentation of real experience aimed at informing and motivating the reader. Galt's two Canadian novels, *Lawrie Todd, or The Settlers in the Woods* (1830) and *Bogle Corbet, or The Emigrants* (1831), may not be rated along with his *Tales of the West*, the 'theoretical histories' of Ayrshire, but they have a detailed realism that commended them to many readers. This realism and immediacy coming out of personal experience of exciting faraway places was a major factor also in the initial success of another venturer into the Canadian wilderness. R M (Robert Michael) Ballantyne spent a number of years as a clerk in the Red River Settlement for the Hudson's Bay Company and out of this came *The Young Fur Traders* (1856), *Ungava* (1858) and a major share for the author in the development of the comparatively new genre of boys' adventure story. His best-known book, *The Coral Island* (1858) signalled the expansion of his literary territory into a wider empire. In his stories the pervading message to the reader is of the romance and attraction of the wider world; they are advertisements to the young of the Old Country that there is a New World for them to enter and possess; and they will enter it not as exiles but as first citizens. To the writer of the 'Canadian Boat Song', it was indeed a sad separation:

> Fair these broad meads—these hoary woods are grand;
> But we are exiles from our fathers' land.
> ... Yet still the blood is strong, the heart is Highland,
> And we in dreams behold the Hebrides.[8]

In the Nova Scotia and Red River settlements many a Highland heart did 'beat heavily beyond the Atlantic roar', but for these others we are considering, the dreams of Scotland were not allowed to figure very large in a generally outgoing and unreflective involvement in new experience.

The most extreme exponent of this attitude wrote not about Canada but about the West Indies. Michael Scott, a Glasgow man, whirls the reader away in the breathless pell-mell narrative of *Tom Cringle's Log* (1836), a succession of sea-fights, violent deaths, drinking parties, farcical situations, vivid descriptions and sentimental asides very reminiscent of Smollett's picaresque novels. There is no time to stop and think, hardly a moment to register new characters before they are whisked off to their fates or dropped out of sight. Through all this roisters the young naval officer hero, cruising the Caribbean on the King's business, making jokes about the Irish and other foreigners, delivering himself of unthinking racist comments about negroes and Hebrews, admiring the ladies of all colours, declaring himself frequently to be true blue English.

Paradoxically, however, he is prone to larding his colloquial narrative with a multitude of Scots words, with the occasional qualification, 'as we say in Scotland'. He meets up with several Scots characters, reminding us that many a transported felon or rebel ended up in the West Indies as an indentured servant and worked himself into freedom and some prosperity. Tom Cringle even encounters a 'negro Scotchman . . . the spirit of Nicol Jarvie conjured into a blackamoor's skin!'—who turns out to have been born in the 'good town of Port Glasgow'.[9] Cringle's friend, Aaron Bang, becomes progressively more Scots in speech as he philosophises; and Tom himself, developing a mental allegory about how his Conscience is beset by personified temptations, creates the moral figure of Mistress Adversity,

> a wee outspoken—sour—crabbit—gizzened anatomy of an old woman—'you ne'erdoweel, Tam' quoth she, 'is it no enough that you consort with that scarlet limmer, who has just yescaped thorough the winday, but ye maun smoor my first-born, puir Conscience, atween ye? Whare hae ye stowed him, man—tell me that.'[10]

At first sight this contradictory Scots element sitting uneasily within an English frame of reference could be either Michael Scott pandering to the tastes of his Scots readers (*Tom Cringle's Log* was first published in instalments in *Blackwood's Magazine* between 1829 and 1833) or an authorial confusion between himself and his English hero. However, what may be more likely is that this reflects an attitude born of more than a hundred years of Union; the idea that, although you may have been born in Scotland and have Scots speech and feelings, when you have put on an English uniform or have undertaken English imperial business, you have in fact become an Englishman. It is not even necessary to insist, as twentieth-century Scots defiantly do, that you are British; the assimilation is complete, and you may commit the ultimate treason of making stereotyped gibes at your own countrymen—In *Tom Cringle's Log* a parasitical growth strangling the life out of a magnificent cedar tree is blithely described as 'the Scotchman hugging the Creole'.[11] A minor character, Don Ricardo, is revealed as being Scottish by birth and upbringing but Spanish in his identification with society in Cuba; yet, 'in his mountain retreat, sole master, his slaves in attendance on him, he was once more an Englishman, in externals, as he always was at heart, and Richie Cloche, from the Lang Toon of Kirkaldy, shone forth in all his glory as the kind-hearted landlord.'[12] This is Tom Cringle the Scoto-English naval officer speaking, but he articulates an attitude which is probably central to the understanding of Scotland's 'literature of Empire', the desire to identify with the imperial English drive—the Scotchman hugging the Englishman, not to draw out the life but to add to it and to be assimilated into it.

Nowhere did this happen more clearly and more triumphantly than in India. The smallness of the ruling group of Europeans and their need to show a united front to the multitudes that they governed; the code of loyalty, first to the East India Company, and later to the Government service; the military tradition within which so many of the expatriates worked: all these considerations must have had a strong bearing upon the tendency of the Scot in India to conform to English expectations, to seek assimilation. Especially so when a fair number of the Scots entering the Indian service appear to have been of elevated, even aristocratic, birth and breeding. At the highest level, the appointments were political: early in the century, Gilbert Elliot, the first Earl of Minto, was Governor-General; in the middle years, the tenth Earl of Dalhousie; and, just outside our period, in the first decade of the twentieth century, another Minto, the fourth Earl, ruled as Viceroy. The Border Elliots had come far. Under the first Earl of Minto, other Scots rose to prominence, becoming Governors of Madras and Bombay: Sir Thomas Munro, Sir John Malcolm and Mountstuart Elphinstone. All of these men wrote extensively, even copiously. What they wrote arose mainly out of their official responsibilities: letters, memos, reports in all cases, but much more than that in the cases of Malcolm and Elphinstone, who sought a wider readership with their histories and accounts of diplomatic missions. The achievements of Munro, Malcolm and Elphinstone in the establishment and government of British India were immense and would need whole books to describe and assess; their writings show that they were not solely men of action but were also thoughtful, observant and far-sighted.

Thomas Munro is the closest of the three to our image of the young Scot bent on self-advancement abroad, if only because it was the failure of his father's business in Glasgow after the confiscation of family properties in Virginia that led directly to his sailing to India as a cadet in the East India Company. After his Glasgow University studies in mathematics and chemistry, his reading of literature and his learning of Spanish, this was a picaresque turn in his fortunes reminiscent of Smollett's hero Roderick Random, whose adventures he so much enjoyed. It led him to active military service and administration of a district in South India; to an awareness that the real people of India, the peasants, deserved proper justice and would best receive it on a direct local level; to the Governorship of Madras and to death from cholera. As a writer he was a man of minutes and memos and letters, but in their clear observation of Indian life and society and their direct expression they have a literary merit. He also diagnosed the English imperial disease that is still with us:

> Our Government will always be respected from the influence of our military power; but it will never be popular while it offers no employment to the natives that can stimulate the ambition of the better class of them. Foreign conquerors have treated the natives with violence, and often with great cruelty, but none has treated them with so much scorn as we; none has stigmatized the whole people as unworthy of trust, as incapable of honesty, and as fit to be employed only where we cannot do without them. It seems to be not only ungenerous but impolitic, to debase the character of a people fallen under our dominion; and nothing can more certainly produce this effect than our avowing our want of confidence in them, and, on that account, excluding them as much as possible from every office of importance. [13]

The administrative world of India at the start of the century was a small one and Munro made friends with his fellow Scots, John Malcolm and Mountstuart Elphinstone. Sir John Malcolm seems to have been everybody's friend and was even well known to the Nabob, Mr Rupees, in John Galt's *Last of the Lairds*: 'Canning, I'm told, calls my friend Sir John, Bahaddar Jaw . . .'[14] He well deserved the title 'Bahadur Jah' bestowed on him for his military valour by his Indian admirers, and also the nickname 'Boy Malcolm' for his boyish enthusiasm in all that he undertook. 'What would you do', he was asked as a twelve-year-old candidate for the East India Company service, 'if you met Hyder Ali?' 'I would draw ma sword and cut aff his heid', was the reply that gained him acceptance. The drive and energy this Eskdale man brought both to soldiering and to politics and administration was matched by his application to writing. The pun in Canning's reference to 'Bahaddar Jaw' is to his loquacity of speech, but there is a similar bulk of writing; Malcolm himself makes fun of this, referring in his initially anonymous *Sketches of Persia* (1828) to 'Sir John Malcolm's ponderous quartos' already written on the subject. Malcolm had been sent on a first diplomatic mission to the Shah of Persia by the Marquis of Wellesley (Wellington's older brother); on the way he had made a treaty with the ruler of Oman, and he had been a great success at the Persian Court. From this, and from his second mission to Persia, entrusted to him in 1808 by Gibby Elliot of Minto, came the 'ponderous quartos', *A History of Persia* (1815), and the *Sketches*, a lively entertaining account of his travels and observations in a land little known by Europeans, interspersed with Persian traditional stories and other anecdotes to make a pleasing narrative for the general reader.

The conversations he reports having with the Shah of Persia illustrate this well. At times there is an echo of Swift's Gulliver explaining Europe to the King of Brobdingnag. Malcolm himself is the Elchee, or Envoy.

> The visit was at its commencement very formal, but the king, evidently desirous to give it another character, said to the Elchee, 'I have heard a report which I cannot believe, that your king has only one wife.' 'No Christian prince can have more,' said the Elchee. 'O, I know that, but he may have a little lady.' 'Our gracious king, George the Third,' replied the Envoy, 'is an example to his subjects of attention to morality and religion in this respect as in every other.' 'This may all be very proper,' concluded his majesty of Persia, laughing, 'but I certainly should not like to be king of such a country.'[15]

Malcolm was popular with the Peacock Throne and was granted a special Order of the Lion and the Sun. Some of this popularity no doubt came from the ability to pay a subtle compliment, such as this from a soldier to the follower of the Prophet:

> After a number of questions on the mines of South America and the arts and manufactures of Europe, the king said, 'All this is astonishing! Persia has nothing but steel.' 'Steel, well managed', said the Elchee, 'has, from the beginning of the world to the present day, commanded all other riches.'[16]

In his long and fruitful life, Malcolm also found time to write a fair amount of not very good poetry, a life of Lord Clive and *Sketch of the Political History of India*. Politics, however, brought him some bitterness. Because Malcolm had been associated in earlier years with the Marquis of Wellesley, distrusted in London for his lofty and extravagant manner and policies, he was denied a Governorship, first in Central India and then in Bombay, until his more junior colleague Elphinstone had retired. However, he at last received his reward and ended his long Indian career as Governor of Bombay.

There are interesting parallels and contrasts to be drawn between the lives and careers of John Malcolm and Mountstuart Elphinstone. Malcolm was much more the soldier, yet the civilian Elphinstone fought a victorious battle against the Marathas. Elphinstone was the more scholarly, yet it was Malcolm who wrote the more assiduously. Both could see clearly what the present situation demanded and could deal decisively with it, yet Elphinstone had the clearer vision of what it was all about in the long run. He believed in and promoted education for the Indians at a time when the English imperial purpose had scarcely been identified, and wrote while in Bombay:

> ... it may not be too visionary to suppose a period at which (the natives) might bear to the English nearly the relation which the Chinese do to the Tartars, the Europeans retaining the government and the military power, while the natives filled a large proportion of the civil stations and many of the subordinate employments in the army.[17]

A century later that had come to pass. Some years earlier, Elphinstone had been even more prophetic:

> The most desirable death for us (the British in India) to die of should be the improvement of the natives reaching such a pitch as would render it impossible for a foreign nation to retain the government ...[18]

The main literary productions of Elphinstone are a *History of India* and his description of Afghanistan as perceived by him on his mission there in 1808, the parallel undertaking to Malcolm's second mission to Persia. These two diplomatic initiatives, along with Charles Metcalfe's embassy to the Sikhs in the Punjab, were Lord Minto's response to the alliance between Napoleon and Czar Alexander of Russia. The intention of each envoy was to win friends and extend British influence in a sensitive area between British and Russian territory. Elphinstone's visit to Afghanistan did not produce significant political results but his book, *An Account of the Kingdom of Caubul and its Dependencies* (1815), remained the authoritative source for many years. The emphasis of the book is firmly on information: there is only a comparatively brief introduction dealing with Elphinstone's own mission before we are taken into a geographical description and sections on the inhabitants, the tribes and the royal government, and appendices on the history, language and other matters. It is clearly and interestingly written without any striving for literary effect, and, to a generation exposed to sensational journalism and television images of strife in Afghanistan, it comes as a relief to read quiet facts which go below the surface and, even after one hundred and seventy years, tell us more about the land and its people than the modern media.

There is a massive literature on India written by Scots of many ranks and professions, as a 1986 exhibition at the National Library of Scotland made clear.[19] Some of the most perceptive and entertaining accounts of the developing British Raj were naturally written by women. Maria Graham, in her *Journal of a Residence in India*, cast a shrewd and critical eye over the scene in the early years of the century; later came Emily Eden and Charlotte Canning.

One of the most praised books by a female observer was Emily Eden's *Up The Country: Letters written to her Sister from the Upper Provinces of India* (1866). In this journal of the Governor-General's progresses between 1837 and 1840, life's variety is looked at from the standpoint of the First Lady of British India. Emily Eden was half-Scottish; her mother was Eleanor Elliot, sister of the first Lord Minto, who married into the Eden family. George Eden, Emily's bachelor brother, became Governor-General in 1835 and his unmarried sister accompanied him to Calcutta as his hostess and wrote a series of letters home about her experiences.

Perhaps it is the epistolary style of *Up The Country* that makes it so successful. The letters are vivid, chatty and amusing, written in a colloquial sisterly tone, as much concerned with trivia as with great occasions. She describes dinners, dances, tiger-shoots, meetings with Indian princes, sketching and painting excursions (she was quite a talented artist), the luxuries and inconveniences of public life—all with a sharp eye for detail and a ready wit. Frequently her personal feelings come through strongly, as when she is moved by the sights of famine and poverty; she actually bought two orphan girls who were being badly treated and deposited them in a Calcutta orphanage for a kinder upbringing. The two clearest impressions that come across from her letters are of the massive ridiculous lumbering apparatus of the Governor-General's retinue—12,000 attendants, plus camels, elephants, horses, tents and baggage, to be uprooted and shifted a few miles further along the road every day—and the almost desperate concern of the English expatriates to maintain their links with home and create the illusion of an English social life—eagerly awaiting the latest volumes of Lamb or Dickens to come in the packets and flinging themselves into balls, dramatic evenings and receptions during the Simla season. It is an English world that Emily Eden describes, and, although she can quote from *Annals of the Parish*, hers is an English viewpoint. Nevertheless, like Munro and Elphinstone, she has a wider and longer perspective. One is tempted to wonder if perhaps a Scottish cast of thought enabled them to see the imperial institutions rather differently from the majority of the English around them. Emily Eden expresses both a sense of the merit of the Indians and a regret for the manners of the English towards them. She recognises the plight of the Anglo-Indian community, and she has a vision of the future reversal of English fortunes in India. Over all, she comes across as a sensible, warm and entertaining woman and writer. In later years, with India behind her, she enjoyed a little success as a novelist. Of her two novels, *The Semi-Attached Couple* (1860) and *The Semi-Detached*

House (1859), the first was in fact written but not published before she went to India. The characters are Border Eskdales and Douglases, but the spirit and style are totally English.

At first sight, Charlotte Canning's Journal[20] looks like a more superficial view of life at the top in India. Of Scottish origins on both sides of her family, Charlotte Stuart had married the up-and-coming Charles Canning, who was appointed Governor-General in 1856 in succession to Lord Dalhousie. Her Journal of their time in India begins with the trivial social round of the Governor-General's wife, occasions of the kind that Emily Eden could describe sardonically. If this were all that her Journal contained, it would not be worthy of note. However, within a few months of her arrival in Calcutta, Charlotte is describing the events of the Indian Mutiny as if from the Royal Box. Her record of that great assault upon English power and complacency, from the first stirrings of discontent among the sepoys, the early rumours and the initial false official optimism through the catalogue of disasters and the desperate search for reinforcements to the successful outcome in which her husband showed himself to be generous and statesmanlike, makes fascinating reading and vindicates the Journal as a significant document. Nothing later in her writing matched up to it, and indeed tragedy followed close upon the heels of the Cannings' success. Three years later, with Canning now a Viscount and the first Viceroy of India, Charlotte died suddenly of fever, and her grief-stricken husband survived her by only a few months.

It would require much research to prove the soundness of the idea that articulate homegrown Scots became less significant in the official life of the Empire as the century wore on. It was probably true of India with, first of all, the growing reliance of the East India Company upon the products of the East India College at Haileybury and, later, the way in which the examinations for the Indian Civil Service favoured the classically trained products of the English public schools and the Universities of Oxford and Cambridge, as has been suggested by George Davie in *The Democratic Intellect*. The lads o' pairts were perhaps most successful when the Empire was still to a large degree a freelance commercial undertaking; when it became a bureaucratic machine, the job specifications were devised to secure employment for the owners' offspring. Yet, in commerce and the army, in exploration, in the missionary fields, in a host of practical and executive areas, the Scots were still to the fore; fewer of them, however, come to our notice as able to write interestingly for the general reader.

The explorers are exceptions to this trend. They write the great continuing saga of discovery for the avid reading public. From Alexander Mackenzie in Canada, as we have seen, James Bruce, with his *Travels to Discover the Source of the Nile in the Years 1768–73*, and Mungo Park, with *Travels in the Interior of Africa* (1799), the habit is established of the journals that had been kept under circumstances of sometimes incredible hardship and suffering being edited for general publication. Mostly they are of great scientific and geographical interest; at their best they are also personal records of vital human experience, revealing some wit and style. Africa is the stage for much of the movement. Hugh Clapperton followed Mungo Park to West Africa in the

1820s. James Augustus Grant went with Speke to discover the source of the White Nile in Lake Victoria, but unselfishly let his leader reach it alone, similarly playing second fiddle in his book, *A Walk Across Africa* (1864)— 'You have had a long walk, Captain Grant', said the Prime Minister, Lord Palmerston, thus inspiring the title. Joseph Thomson pioneered a direct route across Kenya to Uganda, later publishing *To The Central African Lakes and Back* (1881).

Above all, it is David Livingstone who must be given precedence in Africa among the Wandering Scots. He was truly a wanderer. It has been written of him (by Alan Moorehead) that, unlike the other explorers, who proceeded in a straight line to fulfil a purpose or object and then return home, Livingstone travelled in circles, with his mission beginning and ending in Africa. This made him more part of Africa than any others of his generation, so that when he wrote his great accounts of his missionary travels and explorations, the readers sensed his passion and sympathy reaching out to stir their feelings and arouse them to involvement. The evil of the slave trade in Africa was one of his major concerns. It runs like a bloodstained black thread through his three journals, *Missionary Travels* (1857), *Expedition to the Zambesi and its Tributaries* (1865) and *Last Journals* (posthumously in 1874), with one violent episode or encounter after another, and harrowing scenes in abundance.

> When endeavouring to give some account of the slave trade of East Africa, it was necessary to keep far within the truth, in order not to be thought guilty of exaggeration; but in sober seriousness the subject does not admit of exaggeration. To overdraw its evils is a simple impossibility. The sights I have seen, though common incidents of the traffic, are so nauseous that I always strive to drive them from memory. In the case of most disagreeable recollections, I can succeed, in time, in consigning them to oblivion, but the slaving scenes come back unbidden, and make me start up at dead of night horrified by their vividness.[21]

The theme of *Heart of Darkness* is visible in Livingstone's narrative decades before the horrors of the Congo appalled the European conscience. Another foreshadowing of a later issue of guilt occurs in his first journal from Africa. Early in his labours, when he was still principally a missionary and teacher, Livingstone had had a prickly relationship with the Boers in Southern Africa and diagnosed their condition long before the rest of the white world:

> I attempted to benefit the tribes among the Boers of Magaliesberg by placing native teachers at different points. 'You must teach the blacks', said Mr Hendrick Potgeiter, the commandant in chief, 'that they are not equal to us.' Other Boers told me, 'I might as well teach the baboons on the rocks as the Africans', but declined the test which I proposed, namely, to examine whether they or my native attendants could read best.'[22]

The nineteenth-century involvement of Scots in Australia, as recorded in their writings, is as marked as their achievements in Canada, India or Africa, although there may be a contrast in scale. Lachlan MacQuarie, Governor of New South Wales, did keep his diaries of tours in his territory, including Van Diemen's Land, between 1810 and 1822, but they found their readers only in the columns of the *Sydney Gazette*. Like Galt in Canada, he was concerned to found new towns for settlers but he was as likely to be admonishing the settlers who were already there on the need to pay more attention to their own personal cleanliness and comfort and to build better houses to live in, to be lecturing convicts and to be organising the setting up of street signs. Compared with the Nabobs in India, his daily round was one of mundane normality, doing a dull necessary job with efficiency; similarly, his writing is concise and factual with the bare minimum of conventional literary touches. The best stories from Australia did not receive proper literary treatment. One wishes that Angus McMillan from Skye had continued his *Journal of a Cruise from Greenock to New Holland* (1837) to deal more fully with his exploration of new territories in New South Wales, to articulate clearly the dream of a 'Caledonia Australis', a new Scotland of the South, that would accommodate the flood of emigrants from the Scottish Highlands, and to reveal how this dream crumbled before the prosaic absurdity of the English bureauractic foundation of Gippsland (named after a Governor). What he did write was contained only in a letter.[23]

We have to turn to *The Journals of John McDouall Stuart* (1864) for something resembling a heroic story. Stuart tried over a period of five years to make a crossing of the Australian continent from south to north. After one or two failures, he made it, despite shortages of food and water, weakness of both men and horses, a severe fall from his horse, sufferings from scurvy which nearly blinded him, and the suspicion and hostility of aborigines. On the way he observed birds, collected plants, examined rocks for gold, fixed the centre of the continent, named many landmarks and kept his eloquent journal. His style is factual and detailed but his sufferings are exposed clearly and feelingly. Yet there is time for humour, as when he describes meeting an aborigine who greets him with a Masonic sign, which he is able to return.

The tidewash of Scottish emigration was worldwide during the nineteenth century. No continent, no ocean was without its flotsam and jetsam from the wreck of Scotland's failure to provide a harmonious and prosperous community for all her people. The blame was not totally to be laid at the door of the Scottish people themselves, but in a large measure it was their fault, for reasons that lie outside the scope of this essay. The human jetsam cast up on the empty continents of the world found a permanent lodgement there; when the settlers or their children found a writing voice, their work became part of the new literatures of Canada, the United States, Australia or New Zealand. The flotsam, whom we have basically been considering, tended to bob around the world for a few years and then return with the currents—old age, retirement, official posting, the sense of a mission completed—either to their starting point or, frequently, to a more congenial English locality. Their writings are part of their official memorials.

We have already touched on some of the characteristics of this writing. It was the direct expression of people looking outward on the world, not inward to their own mental processes. It was not 'literary' in an aesthetic sense but it was designed to communicate significant matters to a reader of middlebrow tastes and accordingly used some basic literary modes and conventions to facilitate the communication. We can see a reliance on journals, histories, sketches, accounts; there is interesting narrative, detailed and vivid description, commentary frequently of a moral or sympathetic kind, flashes of humour or self-deflating near-mockery, and a personal first-person voice to give authenticity to the tone. The emphasis is firmly on content rather than on technique, for it is a basic premise of the writer that the subject matters to the reader as it does to the writer. It is assumed that the reader wants to 'know', more so than to be merely diverted. Many of the writers are conscious that they were significant actors in the events they are describing, yet there are very few egos on display. It is as if there is an acceptance of a duty to be fulfilled: to enlarge the store of human knowledge and to educate the reader. It is felt that knowledge is power, and by 'knowledge' is meant the accumulation of facts about the real world. The reader's mental map of that world must have its blank spaces filled in with names and features and coloured with confident understanding just as the tantalising empty areas in the atlases were acquiring the lines of rivers, the shapes of great lakes and a proud wash of protective red coloration. Perhaps this duty is an aspect of Scottishness in the writers, a legacy of the education many of them had experienced in their own burgh or village school classroom from dominies trained in a harder discipline than the study of Latin and Greek classics. On the other hand, we can find that many of those we have been examining here had upbringings that were not typically Scottish in the educational sense. This is not really a contradiction, for the nineteenth century was a time when the official ethos of society, to which most of our subjects subscribed, was particularly close to the Scottish Calvinist ethic promoted in schools and churches.

Finally, as we have seen, the writing, though Scottish in attitude and purpose, contained no awareness of Scottishness as anything more than a continuing aberration within an English pattern of culture and nationality. Even David Livingstone could speak of 'my principles as an Englishman'. No doubt this is to be deplored, but it is a fact that cannot be argued around. There may be an argument that Scots today might wish to develop, that in some way this separation of self from national or cultural roots vitiated the expression, diminished the writing, produced the same visible malaise as can be perceived in the writings of the Kailyard. If there is evidence of this, it in no way diminishes the actual achievement of these writers, which was to have performed with honour in the world of action and to have transmitted this real experience effectively either as fact or as fiction to an interested circle of typical readers.

It has not been the purpose of this essay to consider that other group of articulate Scots who, for one reason or other—ill health, commercial necessity, a sense of alienation—chose to live and work for much of their adult lives beyond Scotland.[24] The writer or artist in exile is a romantic figure in most Western societies. His is a different and more diverse psychology from that of the servant of empire. The motivating impulses behind Thomas Carlyle or

James Thomson or George Douglas Brown or George MacDonald deserve
and have received fuller treatment elsewhere. However, it would be fitting to
end this essay with reference to that most far-flung of Scottish exiles, Robert
Louis Stevenson.

While Scotland's 'literature of Empire' moves beyond the optimism and
enthusiasm of the early century into a serious and businesslike mood that is
sutained throughout the heyday of Victorian and Edwardian imperial complacency, Stevenson strikes a more pessimistic *fin de siècle* note. His writings
from the Pacific, *In The South Seas* (1900) and *Vailima Letters* (1895), have
much to say about the effect of Western man upon weak and vulnerable
societies. The fatal impact was already producing its destructive results, and
not only upon the original inhabitants. The opening words of *The Ebb-Tide*,
which Stevenson wrote with Lloyd Osbourne, stress the Western intrusion:

> Throughout the island world of the Pacific, scattered men of many European
> races and from almost every grade of society carry activity and disseminate
> disease.[25]

But the emphasis in this short and powerful novel is upon the corruption that
takes hold of Western man, even in apparent Paradise. The images of disease,
drunkenness, degradation and homicidal greed that pervade the story of
Herrick and his companions sailing to and invading Attwater's Island take
on a universal and allegorical significance beyond their seeming localisation
in place and time. If we think back to Richard Middlemas and his lustful
visions of limitless wealth won by violence, we can see that they are not really
separated by a century of years and a hemisphere of distance from the South
Seas. They are the same, and, in Scott's novel, Middlemas undergoes the
same debasement.

Stevenson's gloomy vision seems to put Scotland's nineteenth-century
imperial writers into a bleaker context. However much good many of them
did in their own spheres, however free most of them remained from the
corruption of wealth and power, they were all ultimately shipped together on
a doomed vessel bound on a tainted and dubious quest. They performed
nobly all the tasks required of them and wrote up the log clearly and efficiently
before they took their severance and departed. Yet because of the destination
and fate of the great ship of Empire, these worthy crew members now carry
a degree of apparent blame and their reputation has suffered. Herrick in *The
Ebb-Tide* had an insight into his fate:

> He had complied with the ebb-tide in man's affairs, and the tide had carried
> him away; he heard already the roaring of the maelstrom that must hurry him
> under.[25]

The ebb-tide of history and political opinion has carried most of the writers
dealt with here away from the consciousness of modern Scotland. It may be
time that a new flow of thinking about their lives and writings should bring
them back.

NOTES

1 Sir Walter Scott, *The Surgeon's Daughter*, Melrose Edition (Edinburgh, 1898), Ch. IV, p 42.
2 Ibid., Ch. IV, p 43.
3 Ibid., Ch. XIV, p 131.
4 John Galt, *The Last of the Lairds* (Edinburgh, 1976), Ch. VI, pp 25–6.
5 Ibid., Ch. XVII, p 73.
6 Alexander Mackenzie, *Voyages from Montreal, etc.*, in Walter Sheppe, *First Man West* (California, 1962), pp 231–3.
7 John Galt, *Autobiography* (London, 1833), vol 2 (Epoch Sixth), Ch. IX, pp 58–60.
8 'Canadian Boat Song', Anonymous (but sometimes attributed to John Galt), in R L Mackie (ed), *A Book of Scottish Verse* (London, 1967).
9 Michael Scott, *Tom Cringle's Log* (London, 1969), Ch. V, p 108.
10 Ibid., Ch. XII, p 263.
11 Ibid., Ch. XIV, p 337.
12 Ibid., Ch. XIV, p 339.
13 Sir Thomas Munro, Letter to Lord Hastings, 12 November 1818, given in Rev G R Gleig, *Life of Sir Thomas Munro* (London, 1830), vol 1, pp 519–20.
14 John Galt, *The Last of the Lairds* (Edinburgh, 1976), Ch. XVII, p 74.
15 Sir John Malcolm, *Sketches of Persia*, vol 2, Ch. XVIII, p 132.
16 Ibid., Ch. XVIII, p 135.
17 Mountstuart Elphinstone, Letter to Governor-General, 1823, quoted in Philip Woodruff, *The Men Who Ruled India*, vol I (London, 1953), p 243.
18 Mountstuart Elphinstone, Letter to Sir James Mackintosh, op. cit., p 221.
19 Scotland and India: Exhibition 7 June–21 September, 1986, National Library of Scotland, Edinburgh.
20 Charlotte Canning, Journal Letters, given in Augustus Hare, *The Story of Two Noble Lives* (London, 1893).
21 David Livingstone, *The Last Journals of David Livingstone in Central Africa* (London, 1880), vol 2, Ch. VIII, p 212.
22 David Livingstone, *Missionary Travels and Researches in South Africa* (London, 1857), Ch. II, pp 37–8.
23 Angus McMillan, in T F Bride, *Letters from Victorian Pioneers* (Melbourne, 1898).
24 Equally it has not been considered appropriate to deal with the significant figure of the Scottish soldier in the nineteenth century. From the Napoleonic Wars at the beginning of the century through the colonial campaigns, the Indian Mutiny and the Crimea down to the second South African War at the end of the century, a host of Scots of all ranks from private to general experienced war at first hand, and some wrote about it. A collection of these writings has still to be made. The soldier stands at the edge of exile, separated from his home and family but probably less affected by his strange surroundings than the administrator, the explorer or the missionary, since he is an instrument of policy rather than an independent agent and it is in the interests of this policy that he should be unreflective about his area of action and its inhabitants.
25 Robert Louis Stevenson and Lloyd Osbourne, *The Ebb-Tide*, Works of Robert Louis Stevenson, Vailima Edition, vol XVIII (London, 1922), Ch. I, p 5.
26 Ibid., Ch. VIII, p 141.

FURTHER READING

Bumsted, J M, *The People's Clearance 1770–1815* (Edinburgh, 1982).

Calder, Jenni (ed), *The Enterprising Scot* (Edinburgh, 1986).

Donaldson, Gordon, *The Scots Overseas* (London, 1966).

Galbraith, J K, *The Non-Potable Scotch* (London, 1964).

Gibb, Andrew Dewar, *Scottish Empire* (London, 1937).

Hill, Douglas, *The Scots to Canada* (London, 1972).

Mackay, Donald, *Scotland Farewell—The People of the 'Hector'* (Edinburgh, 1980).

Macmillan, David S, *Scotland and Australia 1788–1850* (London, 1967).

Moorehead, Alan, *The White Nile* (London, 1960).

Royle, Trevor, *Death Before Dishonour—The True Story of Fighting Mac: Major-General Sir Hector Macdonald* (Edinburgh, 1982).

Smailes, Helen, *Scottish Empire* (Edinburgh, 1981).

Watson, Don, *Caledonia Australis—Scottish Highlanders on the frontier of Australia* (Sydney, 1984).

Woodruff, Philip, *The Men Who Ruled India*, vol I (London, 1953).

Chapter 23

Scottish Drama in the Nineteenth Century

ALASDAIR CAMERON

As we all know, from 1756, when John Home's *Douglas* was first produced in Edinburgh until, depending on your critical position, either 1897, when J M Barrie's *The Little Minister* was produced in London, or 1914, when J A Ferguson's *Campbell of Kilmohr* was staged by the Glasgow Repertory Theatre, Scotland had no drama. Indeed, until the recent pioneering work of Michael Booth and others convinced us otherwise, the established critical consensus on nineteenth century English drama was equally severe. It was summed up by Dame Una Ellis Fermor when she wrote 'the history of English drama . . . is one of steady decadence from the end of the great Jacobean period until the middle of the nineteenth century'.[1] However, after that, English drama, with a little help from Oscar Wilde, began a tentative ascent towards the glorious dawn of George Bernard Shaw. Scottish drama remained decadent slightly longer.

If drama is examined only with the tools of conventional literary criticism, then the study of the drama produced by Scots and in Scotland during the nineteenth century yields poor pickings. If, however, Scottish drama is seen as the raw material for the Scottish theatre, as dead until brought to life on the stage, as something to be measured, not just by the quality of its language and ideas, but by its popularity with audiences, its national significance, its appeal to actors, its interest for historians, its reflection of social attitudes and so on, then, though there are few masterpieces, Scottish drama between 1800 and 1900 offers a cornucopia of riches. The Scottish stage provided hundreds of plays by Scots, plays for and about Scotland and the Scottish people. These ranged from the solemn Gothic tragedy, *De Montfort*, by Joanna Baillie, to the equally solemn Celtic gloom of Fiona MacLeod's *The Immortal Hour*; from the unashamedly commercial plays of W H Murray to the closet tragedies of Professor Robert Buchanan; from W Barrymore's *Wallace* and Isaac Pocock's *Rob Roy* to R L Stevenson's *Deacon Brodie* and J M Barrie's *The Little Minister*.

The early part of the century is particularly rich in plays and this is hardly surprising, for, until about 1870, Scotland had a distinct 'national drama' and, between 1810 and 1851 at the Theatre Royal, Edinburgh, a 'national theatre'. Scottish writers, especially Sir Walter Scott, were responsible for some of the most frequently revived works on the English stage. The nineteenth century theatre's thirst for dramatic novelty, stimulated by the lengthy programmes offered each evening, meant that every corner of Scottish literature and history was ransacked to provide mainpieces, curtain-raisers, after-pieces, pantomimes and harlequinades. The subjects chosen ranged from the obvious, like Mary, Queen of Scots, to the seemingly unstageable, such as *Tam O'Shanter*.

Burns's poem inspired at least five plays as well as a pantomime and a harlequinade. Part of its attraction came from the fact that through the medium of chapbooks, engravings by Wilkie and Landseer and the widely exhibited sculpture of James Thom, the poem was known all over Britain. The fate of Tam at the hands of English adaptors was, however, sometimes bizarre. In 1834, H R Addison constructed a play in which Tam wanted to marry his daughter Jeannie off to Souter Johnnie and the plot revolved around her attempts to thwart the match. These included several accomplices dressing up in white sheets, pretending to be ghosts in Alloway Kirk and dancing around to the words 'Tyrant, tyrant know thy doom/Elfin sprites prepare his tomb'; a far cry from the, 'hornpipes, jigs, strathspeys and reels', of the original. Gone too is Tam's wife, 'gathering her brows like gathering storm'. Instead, Dame Shanter tells her daughter that 'Tam is a wee faulty, [but] he's a gude mon. I dinna like irritating him.'[2] Similarly a *Harlequin Tam O'Shanter and His Auld Mare Meg* at Astley's Equestrian Amphitheatre in 1843 adds to the poem a tableau of the 'Fairies of the Magic Thistle', with a marvellous mechanical thistle and additional verses, like the following:

My Tam, how is't, ye dirty loon,
That in your bed ye are sae late.
You weel deserve your back aboon,
A switch to teach you better state.[3]

Though such adaptations were not for the purist, they did capitalise on the enormous popularity of Burns and, for at least fifty years, brought his work, in however diluted a form, to new audiences north and south of the Border.

Early in the century, there was an almost insatiable appetite all over Britain for plays about Scotland, the land of mountains and mystery. This owed a great deal to the Romantic imagination and to writings like Macpherson's *Ossian* which had been dramatised in various forms towards the end of the eighteenth century. Ossianic eulogies on the landscape of the Highlands and Islands were plundered to provide the settings for plays as diverse as Joanna Baillie's *The Family Legend*, C E Walker's *The Warlock of the Glen* and J R Planché's *The Vampyre* set, not in Transylvania, but on Staffa. The *Vampyre* was written for the English Opera House in London. The Ossianic connections and romantic appeal of Fingal's Cave for English audiences are obvious:

The Curtain rises to slow Music, and discovers the Interior of the Basaltic Caverns of Staffa—at the extremity of which is a chasm opening to the air—the moonlight streams through it, and partially reveals a number of rude sepulchres.[4]

For much of the century, theatre in Scotland was dominated by the Theatre Royal, Edinburgh. It was here that the phrase 'national drama' was invented to appeal to the patriotism of the prosperous. It described any play with a historical Scottish setting, usually adapted from a novel by Sir Walter Scott, and containing liberal sprinklings of Scottish music, Scottish dancing, spectacular scenery and tartan soldiery. Scott himself was actively and weightily involved in the affairs of the theatre and numbered its manager from 1815 to 1851, W H Murray, and many of the best actors amongst his friends and championed performances of works by other Scottish dramatists, notably Joanna Baillie.

It is perhaps unfair to imply that Joanna Baillie was a protegée of Sir Walter Scott's, as she was a famous author before they became friendly, but, sadly, that is how she is now best remembered and her *Plays on The Passions* (1798 to 1836), written 'to deliniate the stronger passions of the mind', and which made her one of the most celebrated writers of her time, are now largely forgotten. These were avidly read and each new volume was awaited, with the eagerness which would attend the discovery of a 'Ms. play of Shakespeare or . . . a missing novel of Scott's'.[5] Unfortunately these plays were not destined to have the same success on the stage. Even when her play *De Montfort* (1798), which illustrated the passion of hatred, was performed by Sarah Siddons and John Philip Kemble, 'critics were by no means unanimous in their approval of the piece'.[6] In Edinburgh, Sir Walter Scott engineered a production of *The Family Legend*, one of her *Miscellaneous Plays*, as the first play in the season of 1810. The piece met with a gratifying response, partly as a result of the Scottish interest of its subject, a feud between the Campbells and the Macleans set in Mull and on the Mainland, partly because Scott had insisted that authentic tartans (green for the Campbells contrasting with red for the Macleans) be used. The play however was a short-lived sensation and was never revived.

Part of the problem the modern reader has with Joanna Baillie's plays is their awkward, overblown and anglicised poetic style, which is rarely fitted to the subject. In *The Phantom*, for example, a 'musical drama' of rivalry and illicit love set in the Highlands and in Glasgow, the characters address each other as 'thou' and 'thee' and none speaks Scots. The play begins with a brief attempt to incorporate individual Scots words into her pseudo-Shakespearean style:

Enter ALLEN

1st high.   Welcome, brave Allen! we began to fear
            The water-kelpy, with her swathing arms,
            Had drown'd thee at the ford.
2nd high.   Faith did we, man! thee and thy shelty too.
Allen.   Am I so late? There's time enough, I hope,
            to foot a measure with the bonnie bride,
            And maidens too.—'Tis well I'm come at all:
            I met the ill-eyed carline on my way.
1st high.   And suffer'd scath by her?

> *Allen.*   Ay, scath enough:
> My shelty, in the twinkling of an eye,
> Became so restive, neither switch not heal
> Could move him one step further.[7]

But, by the second scene, Baillie drops these picturesque additions and writes in plain English. In her few poetic plays with a Scottish setting, not even the servants speak in Scots and the incidental songs, unlike, for example, Planché's *The Vampyre*, are not 'favourite national airs' but Baillie's own songs in English. However, on the rare occasions when she forsakes the grand poetic style and writes in prose and in Scots, her efforts have much more life than the enervated Shakespearean blank verse she felt it her moral duty to produce. In *Witchcraft* (1834), a play about the 'witch-craze' set in Renfrewshire, she tried to capture the 'language made use of [by] the lower and higher characters [which] is pretty nearly that which prevailed in the West of Scotland about the period'.[8] The play's construction is weak but she certainly succeeded in creating, especially in the scenes of the witches' incantations, a far more vigorous dramatic language than she had before. The denouement of the drama occurs in Paisley Market Square with faggots piled high round the stake, when in the nick of time a messenger arrives to announce that witch-burning has been banned by Parliament. The Provost then offers the crowd a wedding and a funeral in compensation but they are bitterly disappointed and shout:

> Voices: My certes! the deil has been better represented in the House of Parliament, than a' the braid shires in the kingdom. Sic a decree as that in a Christian land—To mak Satan triumphant!—There'll be fine gambols on moors and in kirkyards for this, I trow—Parliament forsooth! we hae sent bonnie members there, indeed, gin these be the laws they mak[9]

Baillie chose to write mainly in the poetic tragic mode because she believed it 'fitted to produce stronger moral effect' but she was following in a long line of Scottish writers of blank verse from the famous, like John Home, to the forgotten, such as Samuel MacArthur, whose play, *The Duke of Rothsay, a Tragedy*, set in Falkland Palace, is practically indistinguishable from the work of any other dramatist of the genre. The most successful practitioner of the style, only by virtue of his superior craftsmanship, was Baillie's contemporary, Sheridan Knowles. An Ulsterman, long resident in Glasgow, he had a fruitful career as principal dramatist to the 'eminent tragedian' William Macready. The two first met in Glasgow where for a time Macready's father ran the Theatre Royal and where Macready had served part of his apprenticeship. Their partnership produced some of the most successful plays of the day including *Virginius* (1820) and *The Hunchback* (1832). Knowles' style, which like Baillie's has proved unrevivable, was best described by Bulwer Lytton, who wrote in a letter to Macready:

> I say when a door is to be shut, 'Shut the Door'. Knowles would say, as I think he has said somewhere, 'Let the room be airless'. Probably he is right.[10]

Sheridan Knowles did, however, prove that verbose poetic tragedy could, in the hands of a skilled performer, mean both financial and artistic success and many Scottish writers tried their hands at the genre. Indeed, taken together, the poetic dramas of Joanna Baillie, James Hogg, John Galt, Lord Byron and Scott himself, temper Edwin Muir's contention that Scotland had 'no great burst of poetic drama'.[11] The burst, with its peak around 1820, is there; it was just not very great.

One reason for this lies in the excruciatingly self-conscious and apologetic way in which most of these writers faced their task. Sir Walter Scott, for example, in the preface to his drama, *Halidon Hill* (1822), wrote, 'the drama (if it can be termed one) is in no particular either designed or calculated for the stage',[12] and he went on to warn anyone who attempted to produce it that they did so at their peril. John Galt's distancing of himself from his tragedies was even more complete:

> These Dramas are the sketches of pastime, and as such are offered to the public. MADDALEN was written in the Lazzaretto of Messina, to lighten the captivity of quarantine; CLYTEMNESTRA during a passage from Sardinia to Gibraltar; AGAMEMNON in the course of my voyage from that fortress to Ireland; ANTONIA, while obliged to perform a second quarantine in Cork harbour; and LADY MACBETH, at subsequent intervals, when I could contrive no better way of employing my attention. In compositions so hasty, polished correctness ought not to be expected. I think it would be easier to write others than to make these more worthy of perusal, by any application which I might exert; and I have printed them, because I do not think that they ought to be destroyed.[13]

Galt held the view that 'the solemn drama . . . might be rendered capable of exciting a degree of pathetic sympathy', and, like Baillie, seemed to find English a more appropriate language for moral uplift. Galt, Hogg and Scott were quite capable of writing vigorous and idiomatic Scots, but, when faced by the drama they all turned to insipid English. Hogg's *The Haunted Glen*, a dramatic fragment, though written about the abduction of Lu, a Scottish Prince, by the Fairies, is no earthy folk-tale but a colourless confection in English, with fairies called 'Snowflake' and 'Dew', which ends with a Scots song of 'more than usually revolting sentimentality'. Hogg's later play *All Hallow Eve* (1817) has been recently revived with some success, however.

Scott's disdain for the use of Scots in serious drama probably sprang, like Galt's, from his enslavement by the dead hand of Shakespeare. Galt wrote that

> With respect to the style, I consider the characteristics of the British dramatic verse as having been fixed by Shakespear; and his successors, in my opinion, would shew as bad a taste in attempting to introduce a new manner, as in imitating the obsolete quaintness peculiar to the writers of his age.[14]

Unfortunately, he did just that. However, Scott's emulation of the style of Shakespeare resulted in flattering comparisons being drawn by reviewers.

The *New Edinburgh Review* said of *Halidon Hall,* 'we do not believe that anything more essentially dramatic . . . has appeared in England since the days of her greatest genius.'[15] A modern critic might perhaps treat *The Doom of Devorgoil,* for example, somewhat less charitably:

> ELE.   Fy on it, Flora; this botch'd work of thine
>   Shows that thy mind is distant from thy task.
>   The finest tracery of our old cathedral
>   Had not a richer, freer, bolder pattern,
>   Than Flora once could trace. Thy thoughts are wandering.
> FLO.   They're with my father. Broad upon the lake
>   The evening sun sunk down; huge piles of clouds,
>   Crimson and sable, rose upon his disk,
>   And quench'd him ere his setting, like some champion
>   In his last conflict, losing all his glory.
>   Sure signals those of storm. And if my father
>   Be on his homeward road—
> ELE.   But that he will not.[16]

Compared with the Scots, or even the English, which Scott employed in his novels, this is sorry, convoluted stuff. It is difficult to believe that this author's novels contained some of the pithiest dialogue and most enduring characters to appear on the nineteenth century stage.

The vogue for stage adaptations of Scott's novels really began with Isaac Pocock's version of *Rob Roy MacGregor,* in 1818, but before that, there had been many attempts to get the formula right. The most successful of these had been William Terry's 'Terrifications', as Scott called them, of *Guy Mannering. The Lady of the Lake* had also proved popular, even though its first performance in Edinburgh in 1810 when it was produced as a lavish spectacle, with 'views taken from life', had been a failure, in spite of being widely advertised and eagerly looked forward to in the newspapers. By the time Scott died in 1832, most of his novels and poems including even *Anne of Geierstein* and *The Lord of the Isles,* had been adapted for the stage. Sometimes novels would reappear in unusual disguises. *The Heart of Midlothian,* for example, was adapted as *The Lily of St Leonards* and *The Bride of Lammermoor* as *The Spectre at the Fountain.* Some novels were constantly reworked, *Ivanhoe,* for example, gave birth to over thirty plays and operas. But perhaps the most famous and certainly the most enduring of all adaptations were those of *Rob Roy MacGregor.*

Rob Roy became the 'national drama' *par excellence,* mixing as it does Highlands and Lowlands, an emotional espousal of the Jacobite cause contrasted with Bailie Nicol Jarvie's arguments on behalf of the Union and overall sense of balance and clear view of Scottish history. All the adaptations kept much of the spoken Scots and preserved the memorable Scottish characters, including the 'Dougal Craitur', and Bailie Nicol Jarvie himself; and though the Pocock adaptation, for example, only dramatises the last third of the novel in any detail, by skilful dramatic workmanship it captures the essence of the work and rigorously adheres to Scott's vision.

Rob Roy is also remembered as the play which saved the Theatre Royal Edinburgh and turned it, under the management of Mrs Henry Siddons and her brother, W H Murray, into the foremost theatre in Scotland. Its final accolade came in 1822 when *Rob Roy*, with the famous actor William Mackay as the Bailie, was given a Royal Command performance before George IV and Scott himself. W H Murray was also a practised adaptor of Scott and a playwright, author of *Gilderoy* and *Crammond Brig*. Also called *The Guidman of Ballengeich*, the latter is based on a story from Scott's *Tales of a Grandfather* and tells the story of James V and a humble farmer, Jock Howison, whose daughter he rescues from imminent dishonour. In his autobiography, Peter Paterson, a strolling actor in Scotland, attributed the frequent revivals of this play to the fact that actors were usually allowed to eat the boiled sheep's head which the King was served by Jock, to great royal amusement.

Between 1800 and 1870, with the Theatre Royal Edinburgh at its heart and a network of theatres in every Scottish town from Dumfries to Elgin, it was possible for a Scottish actor to spend all of his or her professional life in Scotland and, with the existence of a national drama, to play a series of satisfying Scottish parts. Many actors chose to move to London but, there too, given the popularity of Sir Walter Scott, they could be sure of having the chance of playing some Scottish characters. Similarly writers who wished to put Scotland on the stage had the opportunity to do so and still see their plays widely performed. But by the 1870s, thanks to the spreading railway system it became possible to tour London plays almost as soon as they had been premiered in the capital. London became the manufacturing centre and sole exporter of most of the theatre seen in the country. Syndicates of theatre owners some based in the South bought up most of the major theatres in Scotland and, rather than being the home of independent companies, these became receiving houses for endless London tours. From the 1870s to 1909 Scotland had little or no independent theatre. In 1909, Alfred Wareing, inspired by the Abbey Theatre, and in reaction to the domination of Scottish Theatre by touring companies from the South, tried to found a Scottish theatre in Glasgow to develop 'a purely Scottish Drama . . . national in character, written by Scottish men and women of letters'.[17]

The new social status of theatre-going in London, where it had become an after-dinner diversion, coupled with the economics of touring, had led to a trend towards only a single play being performed each evening and one piece having as long a run as possible. This led to a drastic cut in the number of plays required and when the fashion in drama moved towards Mayfair melodrama, playwrights were further restricted to what would make money. Until J M Barrie had established his reputation, Scottish writers who wanted to write for the London stage and wanted their plays to be commercially successful usually had to forsake writing about Scotland. If they wanted to write plays about Scottish history, or write in verse, then their only option was to write 'closet-dramas', to be read, rather than performed. Of the many writers who chose to compose for the study rather than the stage, perhaps the best known are John Davidson and William Sharp, 'Fiona MacLeod'. But, apart from Rutland Boughton's operatic adaptation of MacLeod's *The*

Immortal Hour, neither writer owes his reputation to his plays. Davidson is remembered as a poet and MacLeod as a rather fanciful novelist, philosopher and poet.

John Davidson's plays were mainly written in the 1880s, early in his career, and among his first dramatic essays was, as seems almost inevitable, an unstageable historical panorama about a Scottish hero, in this case, *Robert the Bruce: A Chronicle Play*, which was described by Hugh MacDiarmid, with no supporting evidence, as 'our best historical play'. Davidson was drawn to the drama partly by his need to make money. Although his plays seem written to be read, Davidson would possibly have welcomed a commercially successful play and he experimented with many different dramatic forms, including adapting from the French and using Allan Ramsay's *The Gentle Shepherd* as a model.

Perhaps his most stageable play is *Scaramouche in Naxos* which contains some lovely lyrical writing. This play, an early version of *Ariadne auf Naxos*, was only given its first performance in 1986.[18] It consists of equal measures of ponderous dialogue and evocative descriptive verse, such as this spoken at the approach of Bacchus and Ariadne:

> Silenus.   He comes in all his state: the chariot-wheels
> Like silent billows roll; from side to side
> The tigers' heads between their velvet paws,
> Like lilies eyed with flame, sway noiselessly,
> Or, poised on high, breathe odours to the moon.
> Taller than Ariadne by a head
> He stands with her upon the chariot-floor:
> They have been lovers since he found her here:
> His arm is round her neck; one loyal hand
> Droops on her shoulder, and the other holds
> A careless rein: her face lifts up to his
> the deep, sweet melancholy of desire;
> And he looks down, high mystery in his eyes—
> The passionate love of these sweet centuries;
> Unstaunched, uncloyed.[19]

In spite of all his experiments, Davidson was unable to find a formula for writing successful plays. William Sharp or 'Fiona MacLeod', on the other hand, equally study-bound, had a definite theory of dramatic writing. Just before his death, he was engaged on a seven-play cycle, to be called *The Nature of the Soul, a Psychic Drama*. In the event he only completed two parts, *The House of Usna* and *The Immortal Hour*. In his Preface to *The House of Usna*, Sharp tells us that his reasons for writing a 'psychic drama', are partly concerned with the outworn conventions of the modern stage and the scenic illusions of the stage carpenter. Unfortunately he died too soon for the reforms of Edward Gordon Craig and Adolphe Appia whose ideas would have been much to his taste. Sharp also disliked the materialistic intellectual theatre of Ibsen, introduced to Britain by another Scot, William Archer. MacLeod claimed that the world was crying out for his Psychic Drama, wherein thoughts and ideas and intuitions shall play a more significant part than the acted similitudes of the lesser emotions, which are not so much the incalculable life of the soul as the conditioned energies of the body.[20]

'At this bitter and dry theatre of the intellect', he continued, 'the modern soul cannot quench its thirst for the infinite and absolute'. What Sharp offered the modern soul was plays set in a misty and mysterious Celtic past. Though he claimed his inspiration from the Greeks, and his dramatic form from the French neo-classical drama, his plays about the loves, feuds, fights, betrayals and deaths of such legendary figures as Maeve, Concubar and Usna owe much to the Symbolist dramas of Maeterlinck or the early plays of W B Yeats, like *The Land of Heart's Desire*. Sharp, however, was more than just an idle dreamer and as President of The London Stage Society, an organisation dedicated to produce 'plays of artistic merit which are not likely to be performed in the commercial theatre', he took practical steps to reform the stage. The Stage Society were allowed to present *The House of Usna* in 1900 but *The Immortal Hour*, for which he is better remembered, was not performed in Sharp's lifetime, only gaining popularity in the 1920s, when it was made into an opera by Rutland Boughton and Sharp's lyric, 'How beautiful they are/The lordly ones/Who dwell in the hills,/The hollow hills', became for a time a 'soprano standard'. However, as is perhaps inevitable with a drama of the psyche, dramatic situations which perhaps had lived in the mind of their creator seem rather lifeless by the time they reach the printed page.

Much less well known than MacLeod was another Scottish 'closet' dramatist, Professor Robert Buchanan. He, by coincidence, had a namesake who, though he lost all the money he made, was possibly the most successful Scottish dramatist before Barrie. Professor Buchanan was the author of two extensive 'Tragic dramas from history', one based on the life of James I and the other on the life and death of William Wallace. Like many contemporaries who believed the theatre to be too frivolous for serious consideration, Professor Buchanan did not write his plays with performance in mind. *Wallace* is written in the style of Joanna Baillie, with high-flown sentiments and leaden blank verse. Again no-one speaks Scots and everyone is addressed as 'thee' or 'thou'. In the final moments of the play, when Wallace has been led off to his execution, King Edward cries 'am I doomed/To be for ever stunned with Scotland! Scotland!' To which Gilbert Grimsby defiantly answers, 'Sir king, thou art', and vows that his sword shall never 'visit his scabbard' till Scotland is free.[21] This may seem a little pale in comparison with W Barrymore's melodramatic version of the events written in 1817. His play ends with Wallace being led away and almost instantly executed off-stage while his wife runs in frantically, shrieks in horror as she sees him being hung, drawn and quartered, finally sinking sobbing into the arms of a Scottish nobleman, as the curtain falls. One might argue that Professor Buchanan should have perhaps visited melodramas a little more often as you can't, as Shaw observed, 'be too stagey on the stage'. However, the melodramatic ending effectively turns the play from a national tragedy into a personal one, so rendering it safe.

The other Robert Buchanan, a journalist as well as a playwright, is now principally remembered for his attack on the 'Fleshly School of Poetry' of the pre-Raphaelites, an attack which he later retracted. In the 1880s he was the author of a string of stage successes, mainly mounted at the Vaudeville Theatre and mostly adapted from great works of English fiction. The best of these were *Sophia* (1886) from *Tom Jones, Joseph's Sweetheart* (1888) from *Joseph Andrews* and *Clarissa Harlowe* (1890). He later turned to European literature and produced a version of *Crime and Punishment* entitled *The Sixth Commandment* (1890). Buchanan was the quintessential nineteenth century dramatic 'hack', writing on commission, always for cash and producing plays to order for actors such as Cyril Maude and his wife Winifred Emery and for society celebrities like Lillie Langtry.

Money was also the main motivating factor for R L Stevenson's interest in the theatre. In collaboration with W E Henley he hoped to write a play for the London stage which would make both their fortunes. None of their three attempts made them any money, and only *Deacon Brodie*, eventually given a few performances in London in 1882, met with Stevenon's approval. He even called *Admiral Guinea* 'low, black, dirty, blackguard, ragged . . . vomitable, simply vomitable', but for his 'poor old' *Deacon Brodie*, he had greater affection.[22]

Deacon Brodie is interesting, both as a study of the eponymous hero, revered Deacon by day and common thief by night, and as a first draft for *Dr Jekyll and Mr Hyde*. The play contains some gripping scenes and is often very effective, though for some reason Stevenson did not make use of the historical irony that the Deacon was hanged on a gibbet of his own design, preferring to have him shot by a Bow Street Runner, Hart, an early example of the omniscient detective who was to play such an important role on the commercial stage in the twentieth century. Neil Munro's verdict on Stevenson's plays that 'although the soliloquies and asides and the creation of atmosphere charm in private reading . . . on stage the brilliance of the writing fails to make up for their inability to rouse emotion',[23] seems fair. The plays have had occasional revivals, but have never met with much success.

Outstanding amongst all the Scottish writers who chose the stage was James Barrie. Though his period of absolute pre-eminence did not come until the early twentieth century, by 1897, when *The Little Minister* was first produced, he was already showing signs of that mastery of stagecraft, which even his most vociferous critics acknowledged. R L Stevenson's description of Barrie as a 'genius' is often quoted to decry Stevenson's critical faculties, but this view was widely shared by his contemporaries. After a few respectable attempts at drama, with *Walker, London* (1892) and *The Professor's Love Story* (1894), *The Little Minister* made Barrie's reputation. George Blake described the original novel as a 'hopeless and utterly impossible tangle . . . in the coldest fact ridiculous . . . to say nothing of its technical blemishes',[24] but Barrie's reworking of it into a play at least tightened up the story's construction and dispensed with most of the clumsy narrative framework. However some of the characters, are made much less complex, in particular, Nanny Webster, who, in the novel is a tragic figure on the threshold of the poorhouse, but in the play becomes a rather bland, sweet old lady.

As always, Barrie springs surprises. The play begins in a countryside rife with Chartist unrest, with the weavers of Thrums up in arms against their oppression by the local landowner. But, out of this promising confrontational beginning comes Lady Barbara ('Babbie') a free spirit in gypsy attire, destined to bewitch the new minister of the village, Gavin Dishart. This 'faery woman' is almost a sexual fantasy figure and like all such fantasies when exposed to the light of day, seems faintly embarrassing. Her exoticism sits rather uneasily in the Auld Licht setting and what attracts her to the rather colourless minister is never adequately explained. Elders and townspeople are however well-drawn and there are moments of realism, such as the plea by Micah Dow not to upset his father lest he drink and beat him. These offer a welcome contrast to, for example, the Oedipal excesses of the Nanny Webster scenes. Yet again though, all criticism must be qualified by the play's immense popularity. *The Little Minister* was frequently revived, both in Britain and in the United States, where three film versions of it were produced.

By the end of the century, the only place where Scottish plays, performed in Scots and by Scottish actors, were regularly mounted was in the 'geggies', portable wood and canvas theatres which toured the small towns and poor areas of the couantry. Their repertoire was Shakespeare, melodrama and the 'national drama', all three often truncated, but always sincerely played, and most important for the national drama, kept alive. Many of the older geggie actors were those who had performed Scottish roles at the major theatres before they became touring houses. Younger performers, like Will Fyffe, sometimes moved into Music Halls, performing sketches of Scottish life and character which drew on their apprenticeship as Dandie Dinmont, the Dougal Craitur and Bailie Nicol Jarvie. Because of a complete change in theatrical fashions, the 'national drama' written mainly for the upper-classes in Edinburgh ended up as part of the staple theatrical fare, for the working classes in the city and country. However, the features of the 'national drama', its mixing of genre, its use of music, its direct audience involvement and above all its use of Scots, lived on in Pantomime, Variety and Music Hall and this tradition eventually fed back into the mainstream of Scottish Theatre in the twentieth century.

Despite all the evidence to the contrary, Kurt Wittig, in *The Scottish Tradition in Literature* (1958),[25] could still write that 'not until the twentieth century was there anything that can properly be called a Scottish theatre or a Scottish tradition of drama'. He, like so many others, could not find a theatrical tradition in Scotland because they were looking on library shelves. William Power writing on 'The Drama in Scotland' in 1924, had searched further, but was unimpressed by what he found:

> the average Scottish historical play was beneath contempt, as was also, indeed, the average Scottish play of any kind. The once-famed 'Cramond Brig' is a witless and doltish production. Poor imitations of insipid English comedies make up most of the work of writers like John Burness (a cousin of Robert Burns), Sergeant Archibald McLaren, and Archibald Murray; illiterate fustian, vulgar facetiousness, and blustering British jingoism. Worst of all were the

execrable hotch-potches of high-falutin, humorous dialogue, sentiment and song, fighting and dancing, that were concocted from the Waverley Novels. The only non-historical Scottish play I have come across that has a single gleam of real interest is a fantastic mind-picture, hopeless for the stage, called 'Marrying for Money,' by a young schoolmaster named Stuart Ross, who was afterwards known to the theological world as 'Saladin'.[26]

In that 'hopeless for the stage' we have all the contradiction between drama as theatre and drama as literature. Perhaps if Power had thought of most of the plays as opera libretti, as incomplete without the music, dancing and scenery of a performance, then they might have made more sense to him. Obviously such wholesale denunciation is open to endless debate. Power was writing at a time when the Kailyard had been harvested but nothing had yet grown to replace it. He was also writing from a nationalist position which maintained that Scotland was not being taken seriously in the theatre.

From a survey of Scottish drama in the nineteenth century what does seem strange is that there was no dramatic equivalent of the fictional tradition of *The House with the Green Shutters*. But without an independent theatre this would have been impossible. London audiences were not even allowed to be interested in the 'real life' of their own country and anything which showed a Scotland on stage which was other than 'quaint' would have seemed boring and provincial. Like England, Scotland had to wait until well into the next century before the mainstream theatre took her economic and political problems seriously. As any social comment or local references were restricted to the Music Hall stage or the Pantomime, it was little wonder that by the end of the century, Scots had stopped taking the theatre seriously.

The century began and ended with Scotland on the stage a paradigm for somewhere romantic, mysterious and unreal. But, though one must give due regard to Barrie's psychological subtlety, by 1900 the nobility and seriousness of an Ossianic vision of Scotland had been replaced by a patronising Kailyard notion of a picturesque backwater. 'Real' theatre had become synonymous with the touring companies who arrived by train one Sunday and left by train the next. Because of this distortion of Scottish drama, it is hardly surprising that in 1907, the National Burns Club could lament publicly the lack of any 'great' plays about Scotland, except *Macbeth*,[27] but in doing so, they ignored a rich vein of drama. Perhaps the plays did not live up to the Burns Club's notion of imperishable classics of World Theatre, perhaps they would have disapproved of *Harlequin Tam O'Shanter*, but the whole tradition in which such plays had thrived had been destroyed. The Burns Club forgot that 'great' plays only grow from great traditions.

NOTES

1   Una Ellis-Fermor, *The Irish Dramatic Movement* (London, 1939), p 3.
2   H R Addison, *Tam O'Shanter* (London, 1834).

3   *Harlequin Tam O'Shanter*, Lord Chamberlain's Collection, British Library.
4   Reprinted in *The Hour of One*, Wischhusen (ed) (London, 1975), p 88.
5   John Genest, *Account of the English Stage* (Bath, 1832), vol 8, p 335.
6   Ibid., vol 7, p 466.
7   Joanna Baillie, *Collected Works* (London, 1853), p 570.
8   Ibid., p 613.
9   Ibid., p 641.
10 *Bulwer and Macready* (Urbana, Ill., 1958) p 96.
11 In Edwin Muir, *Scott and Scotland*, Alan Massie (ed) (Edinburgh, 1982), p 10.
12 Sir Walter Scott, *Halidon Hill* (Edinburgh, 1822), p i.
13 John Galt, *Tragedies* (London, 1812), p iv.
14 Galt, p iii.
15 Sir Walter Scott, *Poetical Works* (Edinburgh, 1847), p 721.
16 Ibid., p 748.
17 Prospectus quoted in *The Glasgow Herald*, 19 March 1909.
18 In the University Drama Studio, Glasgow University, by the Department of Theatre, Film and Television Studies.
19 John Davidson, *Plays* (London, 1894), pp 279–280.
20 *The Collected Works of Fiona MacLeod*, vol 7 (Poems and Dramas) (London, 1919) p 304.
21 Robert Buchanan, *Tragic Dramas* (Edinburgh, 1868) p 117.
22 *Letters of R L Stevenson* Colvin (ed) (London, 1911), vol 2, pp 235–6.
23 Neil Munro in *The Bookman* extra R L Stevenson number, 1913.
24 George Blake, *J M Barrie and The Kailyard School* (London, 1951), pp 68–9.
25 Kurt Wittig, *The Scottish Tradition in Literature* (Edinburgh, 1958).
26 'The Drama in Scotland', *Scots Magazine*, vol 1, No. 1 (1924), p 4.
27 Reported in *The Glasgow Herald*, 28 January 1907.

FURTHER READING

Baynham, Walter, *The Glasgow Stage* (Glasgow, 1892).
Dibdin, James, *The Annals of the Edinburgh Stage* (Edinburgh, 1888).
White, Henry A, *Sir Walter Scott's Novels on the Stage* (Yale, 1927).

GENERAL BIBLIOGRAPHY

GENERAL AND POLITICAL HISTORY

Campbell, R H, *Scotland Since 1707* (Oxford, 1965).

Checkland, Sidney and Olive, *Industry and Ethos: Scotland 1832–1914* (London, 1984).

Cheyne, A C, *The Transforming of the Kirk: Victorian Scotland's Religious Revolution* (Edinburgh, 1983).

Devine, T M and Mitchison, R, *People and Society in Scotland: Vol. I, 1760–1830* (Edinburgh, 1988).

Drummond, A L and Bulloch, J, *The Scottish Church 1688–1843: The Age of the Moderates* (Edinburgh, 1973).

—— *The Church in Victorian Scotland: 1843–74* (Edinburgh, 1975).

—— *The Church in Late Victorian Scotland: 1874–1900* (Edinburgh, 1978).

Ferguson, William, *Scotland 1689 to the Present* (Edinburgh and London, 1968).

Fry, Michael, Patronage and Principle; *A Political History of Modern Scotland* (Aberdeen, 1987).

Harvie, Christopher, *Scotland and Nationalism: Scottish Society and Politics 1770–1977* (London, 1977).

Hutchison, Ian, *A Political History of Scotland 1832–1922* (Edinburgh, 1985).

Lenman, Bruce, *Integration, Enlightenment and Industrialisation 1746–1832* (Toronto and Buffalo, 1981).

Mathieson, William, *Church and Reform in Scotland* (Glasgow, 1916).

Meikle, Henry, *Scotland and the French Revolution* (Glasgow, 1912).

Smith, Donald, *Passive Obedience and Social Protest: Social Criticism in the Scottish Church 1830–1945* (New York, 1987).

Smout, T C, *A History of the Scottish People 1560–1830* (London, 1969).

—— *A Century of the Scottish People 1830–1950* (London, 1986).

CULTURAL HISTORY

Anderson, R D, *Education and Opportunity in Victorian Scotland* (London, 1983).

Brown, Callum, *The Social History of Religion in Scotland Since 1730* (London, 1987).

Carlyle, Thomas, *Reminiscences* (1881) (ed. Ian Campbell) (London, 1972).

Chapman, M, *The Gaelic Vision in Scottish Culture* (London and Montreal, 1979).

Cockburn, Henry, *The Life of Lord Jeffrey* (Edinburgh, 1856).

—— *Memorials of His Time* (Edinburgh, 1856).

—— *Journal, 1831–54* (Edinburgh, 1874).

—— *Circuit Journeys* (Edinburgh, 1888).

Craik, Sir Henry, *A Century of Scottish History* (2 vols) (Edinburgh and London, 1901).

Crosland, T W H, *The Unspeakable Scot* (London, 1903).

Daiches, David (ed), *A Comparison to Scottish Culture* (London, 1981).

Davie, George, *The Democratic Intellect: Scotland and her Universities in the Nineteenth Century* (Edinburgh, 1961).

Durkacz, V, *The Decline of the Celtic Languages* (Edinburgh, 1983).

Fyfe, J G (ed), *Scottish Diaries and Memoirs 1746–1843* (Stirling, 1942).

Hechter, Michael, *Internal Colonialism: The Celtic Fringe in British National Development, 1536–1966* (London, 1975).

Houston, R A, *Scottish Literacy and the Scottish Identity* (Cambridge, 1985).

Humes, W M and Paterson, H M (eds), *Scottish Culture and Scottish Education 1800–1980* (Edinburgh, 1983).

Jeffrey, Francis, *Contributions to the Edinburgh Review* (4 vols) 1844.

Knowles, Thomas, *Ideology, Art and Commerce: Aspects of Literary Sociology in the Late Victorian Scottish Kailyard* (Gothenburg, 1983).

Lockhart, John Gibson, *Peter's Letters to His Kinsfolk (1819)* (ed William Ruddick) (Edinburgh, 1977).

—— *Memoirs of the Life of Sir Walter Scott* (Edinburgh, 1837).

Marshal, Rosalind, *Virgins and Viragos: Women in Scotland 1080–1980* (London, 1983).

Masson, David, *Edinburgh Sketches and Memoirs* (London and Edinburgh, 1892).

—— *Memoirs of Two Cities: Edinburgh and Aberdeen* (Edinburgh and London, 1911).

Miller, Karl, *Cockburn's Millennium* (London, 1975).

—— *Doubles* (Oxford and New York, 1985).

Miller, Hugh, *Scenes and Legends of the North of Scotland* (Edinburgh, 1835).

—— *First Impressions of England and Its People* (Edinburgh, 1847).

—— *My Schools and Schoolmasters* (Edinburgh, 1854).

Muir, Willa, *Mrs. Grundy in Scotland* (London, 1936).

Nairn, Tom, *The Break-up of Britain* (London, 1981).

Oliphant, Margaret, *Annals of a Publishing House: William Blackwood and his Sons* (2 vols) (Edinburgh, 1897).

Saunders, Laurence, *Scottish Democracy 1815–1840: The Social and Intellectual Background* (Edinburgh, 1950).

Scott, Sir Walter, *The Journal* (ed William Anderson) (Oxford, 1972).

—— *The Letters of Malachi Malagrowther* (1826) (intro P H Scott) (Edinburgh, 1981).

Somerville, Alexander, *The Autobiography of a Working Man* (1848) (intro Brian Behan, London, 1967).

Thomson, Derick, *A Companion to Gaelic Studies* (London, 1983).

Wolfe, J N (ed.), *Government and Nationalism in Scotland* (Edinburgh, 1969).

Young, Douglas, *Edinburgh in the Age of Sir Walter Scott* (Oklahoma, 1965).

LITERARY HISTORY

Aitken, W R, *Scottish Literature in English and Scots: a Guide to Information Sources* (Detroit, 1982).

Campbell, Ian, *Kailyard: A New Assessment* (Edinburgh, 1981).

Craig, David, *Scottish Literature and the Scottish People 1680–1830* (London, 1961).

Daiches, David, *Literature and Gentility in Scotland* (Edinburgh, 1982).

Donaldson, William, *Popular Literature in Victorian Scotland: Language, Fiction and the Press* (Aberdeen, 1986).

Grieve, C M, *Contemporary Scottish Studies: First Series* (London, 1926).

Hart, Francis, *The Scottish Novel: A Critical Survey* (London, 1978).

Henderson, T F, *Scottish Vernacular Literature* (Edinburgh, 1910).

Kinsley, James (ed), *Scottish Poetry: A Critical Survey* (London, 1978).

Lindsay, Maurice, *History of Scottish Literature* (London, 1978).

Millar, J H, *A Literary History of Scotland* (London, 1903).

Muir, Edwin, *Scott and Scotland: The Predicament of the Scottish Writer* (London, 1936).

Open University (Donnelly, Hearn, Norquay and Calder), *Scottish Literature: A Study Guide* (Edinburgh, 1984).

Power, William, *Literature and Oatmeal* (London, 1935).

Royle, Trevor, *Precipitous City: The Story of Literary Edinburgh* (Edinburgh and New York, 1980).

—— *The Macmillan Companion to Scottish Literature* (London, 1983).

Smith, G Gregory, *Scottish Literature: Character and Influence* (London, 1919).

Thomson, Derick, *An Introduction to Gaelic Poetry* (London, 1974).

Watson, Roderick, *The Literature of Scotland* (London, 1984).

Wittig, Kurt, *The Scottish Tradition in Literature* (Edinburgh and London, 1958).

For help with the glossing of Scots and Gaelic terms the reader is referred to the following:

Macleod, Iseabail, Martin, Ruth and Cairns, Pauline (eds), *The Pocket Scots Dictionary* (Aberdeen, 1988).

Robinson, Mairi (editor-in-chief), *The Concise Scots Dictionary* (Aberdeen, 1985).

MacLennan, Malcolm, *Gaelic Dictionary* (Edinburgh, 1925) (repr. Aberdeen, 1985).

For further information the *Scottish National Dictionary* and *A Dictionary of the Older Scottish Tongue* will prove helpful.

INDEX

The index is arranged word-by-word. Titles of works appear twice, under title, and listed with the author.

Abbey Theatre 435
Aberdeen Free Press 212, 213
Aberdeen Herald 362
Academy 330
Account of the Kingdom of Caubul and its Dependencies, An 419–20
acculturation 392
Adam Bede 111
Adam Blair 109, 239–40
Adam, Dr Alexander 17
Adamson, Robert [photographer] 34
Addison, H R 430
Addison, Joseph 95, 225
Admiral Guinea 438
adventure stories 291, 294, 296, 298, 299, 301, 305
Adviser, The 205
Aestheticism 293
Afghanistan 419
Africa 421–3
Agamemnon 433
agricultural revolution 44–5, 135
Alec Forbes of Howglen 181, 218, 227–8, 248, 278–80, 281, 285
Alexander, Czar of Russia 419
Alexander, William 7, 10, 26, 211–14, 223, 224, 227, 236, 310, 326
 and vernacular revival 212
 Authentic History of Peter Grundie, The 212
 'Baubie Huie's Bastard Geet' 213
 'Couper Sandy' 213
 'Francie Herregerie's Sharger Laddie' 213
 Johnny Gibb of Gushetneuk 2, 26, 35, 36, 211–12, 213, 218, 225, 226–8, 232, 236, 249–50, 325–6

 Laird of Drammochdyle and his Contemporaries, The 212–13, 236, 249, 251
 Life Among My Ain Folk 211, 213–14, 249–50
 'Mary Malcolmson's Wee Maggie' 213
 My Uncle the Baillie 213–14
 Ravenshowe and the Residenters Therein 213
 Sketches of Rural Life in Aberdeenshire 212
Alison, Sir Archibald 33, 175, 176
 History of Europe 176
Alison, Prof William Pulteney 33
All Hallow Eve 433
Alton Locke 182
Amateur Emigrant, The 294
American revolution 116
An Claigeann 'The Skull' 383
An Cogadh Naomh 'The Holy War' 386
An Creideamh Mór 'The Great Faith' 384
An Gaisgeach 383
Anglo-American Copyright Treaty 29
Anglo-Norse Theory [ballads] 403
Annals of a Publishing House 173, 193
Annals of the Parish 110, 112, 114, 116, 117, 119, 120, 218, 224–6, 241, 269–70, 321, 324, 412, 420
Anne of Geierstein 434
Anster Fair 340
Antiquary, The 69, 74
Antonia 433
'Apologia' 141
Apostle of the North *see* MacDonald, Rev Dr John

Appia, Adolphe   436
Arabian Nights   281
Archer, William   14, 436
Ariadne auf Naxos   436
Ariosto, Lodovico   73, 78
Arnold, Matthew   346
Arnold, Thomas   155
Ascent of Man, The   51
Astley's Equestrian Amphitheatre   430
At the Back of the North Wind   229,
    276
Auden, Wystan Hugh   280
Auld Licht Idylls   316, 439
'Auld Man's Farewell to his Little
    House'   95
Austen, Jane   1, 72
    Emma   67, 241
Australia   422–3
Authentic History of Peter Grundie, The
    212
authors, high number   28
autobiography, as literary form   38
Autobiography (Galt)   108–9, 116
Awakening of George Darroch, The   30
Ayrshire Legatees, The   109–10, 112–
    13, 114
Aytoun, William Edmonstoune   8,
    173, 178, 184, 197–8, 199
    'Firmillian'   198
    'How I stood for the Dreepdailly
        Burghs'   197
    'How we got up the Glenmutchkin
        Railway and How we got out of
        it'   197, 239
    Norman Sinclair   175, 239

B V *see* Thomson, James
Bagehot, Walter   68
Bailey, Philip James   198
Baillie, Joanna   431–3, 437
    De Montfort   429, 431
    Family Legend, The   430, 431
    Miscellaneous Plays   431
    Phantom, The   431–2
    Plays on the Passions   431
    Witchcraft   432
Bain, Alexander   178
ballads   7, 397, 402, 403–6
Ballantyne, John   66
Ballantyne, Robert Michael   178, 415
    Coral Island, The   415

Ungava   415
Young Fur Traders, The   415
Balliol College, Oxford   55, 57
Balmorality   8, 27
Barclay, Sheriff of Perth   43
Bards of Angus and the Mearns, The
    355, 357
Bards of Galloway, The   355
Barrie, Sir James Matthew   226, 230
    a 'British' writer   26, 206, 435
    contributions to *The British
        Weekly*   180, 200
    kailyard work   251, 309, 311,
        312–17, 329, 353
    Auld Licht Idylls   316, 439
    Little Minister, The   233, 312, 429,
        438–9
    Margaret Ogilvy   329
    Peter Pan   10
    Professor's Love Story, The   438
    Sentimental Tommy   240–1, 329–
        30
    Tommy and Grizel   240–1
    Walker, London   438
    Window in Thrums, A   233–4
Barrymore, W   437
    Wallace   429
Barthes, Roland   163
Basil Lee   224, 241
Battle of Egypt, The   380–1
Battle of Holland, The   380
'Baubie Huie's Bastard Geet'   213
Baxter, Charles   174, 175
'Beach at Falesa, The'   271, 295, 302–3
'Bean Thorra Dhamh'   384
Beattie, James   321
'Beattock for Moffat'   170
Beethoven, Ludwig van [composer]   97
Begg, James   34–5, 50, 53
Beleaguered City   230
Bell, John Joy
    Wee MacGreegor   10, 242
Bentham, Jeremy   160
Beside the Bonnie Briar Bush   233, 309,
    312, 314, 316, 329–30
Bible   327
    Ecclesiastes   158–9, 160, 161
    Psalm 122   89, 93
Bildungsroman   38
Biographia Literaria   108
Black Arrow, The   296–7
Black Dwarf, The   79

Black, William 8, 36, 138, 170
  Macleod of Dare 234–5
  'Penance of John Logan, The'
    235
  Princess of Thule, A 330–1
Blackie, John Stuart 2, 173, 174
  178–9
Blackmore, Richard Doddridge, *Lorna
  Doone* 234, 242
Blackwood, John 173
Blackwood, William (publisher) 26,
  98, 321
  and *The Chaldee Manuscript*
    192–3
  and Galt 109–10, 112, 114
Blackwood's Edinburgh Magazine see
  Blackwood's Magazine
Blackwood's Magazine, formerly
  Edinburgh Monthly Magazine 3–4,
  94, 95–6, 114, 125, 133, 139–41, 143,
  171–3, 177, 178, 192–8, 217, 232, 233,
  236, 239, 321, 337, 416
Blaikie, W G 58
Blair, Alexander 147, 194
Blake, George 309, 312–13, 353, 359,
  368
Blake, William 92, 103, 345
  'Energy is eternal delight' 97
  'Little Girl Found, The' 92
  'Little Girl Lost, The' 92
  'To Mercy, Pity, Peace and Love'
    92, 99
Blind Harry, *Wallace* 218
Blue Lagoon, The 137
'Bodkin, Tammas' see Latto, William D
Bogle Corbet 114, 415
Bombay 417, 419
Bonaparte, Napoleon 134–5
Bonar, Horatius 179
Book of Martyrs 386
Borges, Jorge Luis 153
Bosanquet, Bernard 57
Boswell, James 339
Bothie of Tober-na-Vuolich 29
Boughton, Rutland 435, 437
'Boy's Poem, A' 342
'Boy's Song, A' 90, 338
'Braes o' Balqhidder' 360
Brecht, Bertolt, *Mother Courage* 100
Brewster, Sir David 171, 179
Bride of Lammermoor, The 72, 79, 81,
  243, 434

Bridie, James *see* Mavor, Osborne
  Henry
British Idealists school 55, 57–8
British Weekly, The 180, 200, 313
Brontë, Charlotte 219
  Jane Eyre 146
  Shirley 111
Brontë, Emily 219
Brougham, Lord Henry Peter 172, 177,
  190, 191, 196
Brown, George Douglas 10, 28, 180,
  240, 241, 305, 310, 425
  House with the Green Shutters, The
    170, 181–2, 185, 219, 228, 231,
    243, 246–55, 271, 330, 353, 440
Brown, George Mackay 217
Brown, Dr John
  Horae Subsecivae 178
  Rab and His Friends 29
Brown, Dr Thomas 2, 128
Brownie of Bodsbeck, The 8, 96–7,
  218, 223–4, 234, 325
Bruce, James, *Travels to Discover the
  Source of the Nile in the Years 1768–
  73* 421
Brunton, Mary
  Discipline 237
  Emmeline 237
  Self-Control 237
Buchan, John, Lord Tweedsmuir 4,
  8, 9, 38, 199, 231, 242
  John Burnet of Barns 234, 242
  Life of Sir Walter Scott 14
  Watcher by the Threshold, A 234
Buchan, Peter 204, 403, 404
Buchanan, Dugald 393
  An Claigeann 'The Skull' 383
  An Gaisgeach 383
Buchanan, George 197
Buchanan, Prof Robert 429, 437
  Wallace 437
Buchanan, Robert Williams 337, 345–
  6, 438
  Joseph's Sweetheart 438
  'Outcast, The' 346
  'Scaith o' Bartle, The' 346
  Sixth Commandment, The 438
  Sophia 438
  'Widow Mysie, The' 346
Buckle, Henry, *On Scotland and the
  Scotch Intellect* 3, 4, 6
Bunyan, John 276, 293

Pilgrim's Progress, The   30, 93,
    218, 221, 241–2
Buonaparte, Napoleon   419
Burger, Gottfried August   109
Burgher Church   156, 164, 171
Burke, Edmund   136, 144–5
Burness, John   439
Burns, Robert
    alluded to   2, 7, 24, 26, 74, 89, 92,
        97, 103, 120, 133, 139, 143–4,
        146, 148, 156, 161, 176, 180, 197,
        206, 218, 221, 242, 309, 328, 341,
        345, 358–9, 361, 367, 402
    Mackenzie's review of the
        Kilmarnock Edition   189–90
    'Cottar's Saturday Night, The'
        370
    'Does haughty Gaul invasion
        threat?'   18
    'Holy Willie's Prayer'   240, 245,
        247, 341
    'Jolly Beggars, The'   218
    'Man's a man for a' that, A'   360–
        1
    'Tam o' Shanter'   240, 430
    'Vision, The'   92
Burton, John Hill   173, 176
Byron, Lady   285
Byron, Lord George Gordon   109, 138,
    191, 281, 326, 337–40, 342, 360, 433
    Childe Harold's Pilgrimage   67,
        339
    Don Juan   339–40
    'English Bards and Scotch
        Reviewers'   191, 340

Cadell, Robert   66
Caird, Edward   8, 57, 58, 178
Caird, Dr John, 53–4, 57, 58
    Scotch Sermons   53
Calcutta   420
'Caledonia Australis'   423
'Caledonian antisyzygy'   102–3, 317
Calvinism   156, 158, 270–1, 280–1, 283,
    287–8, 302, 397, 424
Calvinist minister   384–5, 390
Campbell, John Francis   7
Campbell of Kilmohr   429
Campbell, Thomas   109
Canada   413, 414, 415, 421, 422–3
Canada Company   414
'Canadian Boat Song'   197, 415

Canning, Charles   421
Canning, Charlotte   420, 421
Carlyle, James (father of Thomas)
    156, 157
Carlyle, Jane Welsh (wife of Thomas)
    157–8, 175, 182
Carlyle, Thomas   1, 2, 9, 10, 24, 25,
    37–8, 66, 153–66, 182–3, 191, 219,
    326, 353
    on *Blackwood's Magazine*   95
    on Hogg   103
    on John Wilson   174
    move to London   4, 13, 14–15,
        171, 172, 175–6, 196
    on revolution   5, 135
    Chartism   154–5, 159
    French Revolution, The   153–8,
        164–6, 183
    Latter-Day Pamphlets   155
    On Heroes and Hero-Worship   154
    'On History'   158, 161
    Past and Present   154–5, 218
    Reminiscences   156, 164, 170–1,
        183–4
    Sartor Resartus   153–64, 171, 183,
        230
    'Signs of the Times'   158, 160
Carnegie, Andrew   177
Carswell, Catherine, *Open the Door!*
    11, 237–9
Cassell (publishers)   368
Castle Warlock   285
Catriona   218, 223, 230–1, 241, 242,
    297, 303, 323, 331, 332
'Celtic Gloom'   378
'Celtic Twilight'   8, 11, 235, 393
Cervantes Saavedra, Miguel de, *Don
    Quixote*   98
'Chaldee Manuscript, The'   95, 192–3
Chalmers, Thomas   5, 9, 32–4, 37, 47–9,
    54, 58, 135, 171, 174–5, 179, 184, 314–
    15
Chambers, Robert   175, 198–9, 204, 403
    Vestiges of Creation, The   55
Chambers, William   175, 198–9, 204
Chambers' Edinburgh Journal see
    Chambers's Journal
Chambers's Journal   198–9, 204, 337
'Chants for Churls'   344, 355, 367
chapbooks   203–4, 340, 430
'Chapter on Dreams, A'   293
Chartism   154–5, 159

Chartists 5, 50, 439
'Chaunts for Churls' *see* 'Chants for Churls'
Cheap Magazine, The 204
Cherrie and the Slae, The 240
'Chieftain Unknown to the Queen, A' 365–6
Child, Francis James 7, 406
Childe Harold's Pilgrimage 67, 339
Child's History of Scotland, A 8–9
Chisholm, Lord Provost of Glasgow 45–6
Christison, Sir Robert 171, 173, 175
Christ's Kirk on the Green 89
Chronicles of Carlingford 238, 263
Church of Scotland 5–6, 16, 18–20, 30–5, 49–50, 52–3
  disestablishment campaign 52
  see also Disruption
Church in Scotland, influence and role of 3, 6, 24, 34, 45–7, 50–4, 59, 315
City of Dreadful Night, The 14, 178, 180, 230, 342, 347–8
City of the Plague 137–8
Clapperton, Hugh 421–2
Clarissa Harlowe 438
Clark, Mary, 'Bean Thorra Dhamh' 384
Classical Gaelic 384
Claverhouse *see* Graham of Claverhouse
Clearances 7, 12, 18, 44, 377, 378, 379, 383, 387–92 *passim*
Cleg Kelly 242
Cleghorn, James 192
Clive, Lord Robert 419
Clough, Arthur Hugh 155
  Bothie of Tober-na-Vuolich 29
Clouston, W A 7, 27
Clytemnestra 433
'Coast of Fife, The' 291
Cockburn, Lord Henry Thomas 1, 2, 5, 9, 31, 32, 177, 191, 196
  on Disruption 6, 19
  on Edinburgh/Scotland 14–15, 171, 172, 174–5
  on industrial revolution 24
  on Scots language 16, 327
  Life of Lord Jeffrey 14–15
  Memorials of His Time 10, 337
Coleridge, Samuel Taylor 71, 72–3, 109, 133, 135, 137, 276, 277, 281, 338
  his conservatism 136, 140–2
  Biographia Literaria 108, 192
Colvin, Sidney 347
commonplaces [in ballads] 405, 406
'commonsense' philosophy 2–3, 6
'Commonwealth man' 31
Conan Doyle, Sir Arthur 199
Confessions of a Justified Sinner see *Private Memoirs and Confessions of a Justified Sinner, The*
Congested Districts Board 45
Conrad, Joseph 302, 305
  Heart of Darkness 422
Consider the Lilies 247, 255
Constable, Archibald (publisher) 65–6, 120, 190, 191, 192, 321
Copyright Treaty, Anglo-American 29
Coral Island, The 415
Cottagers of Glenburnie, The 237–8, 321
'Cottar's Saturday Night, The' 370
'Counterblast Ironical, The' 346
'Couper Sandy' 213
Covenanters 115
Crabb Robinson, Henry *see* Robinson, Henry Crabb
Crabbe, George 217
'Crabbed Youth and Age' 293
Craig, Edward Gordon 436
Crammond Brig 435, 439
Craobh-sgaoileadh an t-Soisgeil 'The spreading of the Gospel' 386
Crawfurd, Andrew 404
crime 49, 51
Crime and Punishment 438
Crimean war 343
Crockett, Samuel Rutherford 169, 180, 200, 206
  a kailyard writer 231, 309, 311, 313, 315–16, 329, 353
  Cleg Kelly 242
  Lilac Sunbonnet, The 233, 234, 310
  Men of the Moss Haggs, The 234
  Raiders, The 234
  Red Cap Tales 331
Crofters Act (1886) 315
Crofters' Party 44
Cromwell, Oliver 156
Cronin, Archibald Joseph 255
  Hatter's Castle 247

Cross, Mary Ann *see* Eliot, George
Crossriggs 238–9, 271–2
'Cruel Mother, The' 93
'Crystal Palace, The' 349
culture, Scottish, and epic
  philosophical poetry 25–6, 28
Cunningham, Allan 405
Cunningham, Andrew 233
Cunninghame Graham, Robert Bontine
  see Graham, Robert Bontine
  Cunninghame
Cursory Reflections 108

D C Thomson Group 26
Dalhousie, 10th Earl 417, 421
Dallas, E S 173
Dalyell, J G 193
Dante, Alighieri 276
D'Arcy Thompson Class Club 175
Darwin, Charles 55
  Descent of Man 56
  Origin of Species 56
Darwinism 51, 58, 293
David Elginbrod 227–8, 275, 279
Davidson, John 1, 9, 230, 337, 345,
  347–9, 353, 435–6
  'Crystal Palace, The' 349
  'In the Isle of Dogs' 349
  'Last Journey, The' 349
  'Matinee' 349
  Ninian Jamieson 241
  Pilgrimage of Strongsoul 241–2
  Robert the Bruce: A Chronicle Play
    436
  Scaramouche in Naxos 436
  'Snow' 349
  'Testament of John Davidson,
    The 349
  'Thames Embankment, The' 349
  'Thirty Bob a Week' 348
  'Wasp, The' 349
Davidson, Thomas, *Memorials* 38
De Montfort 429, 431
De Quincey, Thomas 131–4, 173,
  194, 328
Deacon Brodie 429, 438
'Dean of Guild, The' 112
'Death of Mairi, The' 392
'Death of the Widow's Child, The' 392
Defoe, Daniel 224, 296
Delacroix, Ferdinand Victor Eugène
  [painter] 97

Δ 'Delta' *see* Moir, David Macbeth
Denovan, John C 175
Depression (1842–43) 24, 33–5
Descent of Man 56
Destiny 237, 266
Dialectic Society 175
Dickens, Charles 1, 72, 125, 155, 157,
  184, 345
'Disagreeables' 338–9
Discipline 237
Disraeli, Benjamin, Earl of Beaconsfield
  Lothair 169, 180
  Sybil 218
Disruption of the Church of Scotland
  3, 6, 12, 19–20, 24, 30–5, 49, 59, 169,
  174, 179, 181, 198, 314, 325–6, 365,
  390
Diz ony o' You Chaps ken Aboot Jesus?
  205
Dobell, Sydney 198
Docherty 255
Doctor's Family, The 264–6
'Does haughty Gaul invasion threat?'
  18
'Dominie, The' 338–9
'Domsie' 314
Don Juan 339–40
Don Quixote 98
Donal Grant 285
'Donald MacDonald' 90
Donn, Rob 8
Doom of Devorgoil, The 434
Dostoevski, Fyodor Mikhailovich 153
  Crime and Punishment 438
  Notes from Underground 160
Douglas 429
Dr Jekyll and Mr Hyde 154, 230, 245,
  292, 295, 299–300, 438
drama, Scottish 429–40
'Drama in Scotland, The' 439–40
'Dreamings of the Bereaved' 362
Dreamthorp 7
Drummond, Henry 54, 179
  Ascent of Man, The 51
  Natural Law in the Spiritual World
    51
Drummond, Peter 205
Dryden, John 93
  Works, ed Scott 67
Duke of Rothesay, The, a Tragedy 432
Duke's Children, The 36
Dumfries and Galloway Courier 182

Dunbar, William 7, 92
Duncan, Rev Henry 182
Dundas family 3
Dundas, Robert 32
Dundee 23, 312
Dundee Advertiser 207, 209
Dunfermline Press 209
Dynamiter, The 230
Dürer, Albrecht 348

Earthquake, The 111
East India Company 411, 413, 416–18, 421
Ebb-Tide, The 295, 302–3, 305, 425
Ecclesiastical and Religious Statistics of Scotland, The 53
Eco, Umberto 153, 163
Economist, The 14
Eden, Emily 420, 421
  Semi-Attached Couple, The 420–1
  Semi-Detached House, The 420–1
  Up the Country 420
Eden, George 420
Edgeworth, Maria 217
Edinburgh 294
Edinburgh Bailie, An see *Some Remarkable Passages in the Life of an Edinburgh Baillie*
Edinburgh Monthly Magazine see *Blackwood's Magazine*
Edinburgh Review, The 19, 31, 65, 129, 139, 141, 143, 172, 177, 190–1, 193–4, 196, 321, 337, 340
Edinburgh Weekly Journal 16
education in Scotland 3, 6, 16, 24, 25, 37, 39, 47–9, 51–2, 59
'Edwin of Deira' 342
Effie Ogilvie 262
Eglinton, Earl of 196
Elect Lady, The 279, 285
'Election, The' 226
Eliot, George 111, 198, 266
  Adam Bede 111
  Felix Holt 36
  Middlemarch 241
  'Scenes of Clerical Life' 173
Eliot, Thomas Stearns 27, 326, 347–8
'Elizabeth, or The Exiles of Siberia' 203
Eliot, Eleanor 420
Eliot, Gilbert, 1st Earl of Minto 417, 418, 419, 420

Elliot, 4th Earl of Minto 417
Elliot, Walter, *Scotsman's Heritage, A* 173
Elphinstone, Mountstuart 417–20
  Account of the Kingdom of Caubul and its Dependencies, An 419–20
  History of India 419
Emerson, Ralph Waldo 154, 155, 171, 182
Emery, Winifred 438
emigration, from Highlands and Islands 44, 379, 388–9, 392, 423
Emma 67, 241
Emmeline 237
Empire, British 3, 7, 10, 18, 27, 411–40
Encyclopaedia Britannica
  Biblical commentaries 56
  Frazer on the ballad 402
  Scott's essays 67
'Energy is eternal delight' 97
enfranchisement, of Scots males 43
Engels, Friedrich 24
English Act (1870) 35
'English Bards and Scotch Reviewers' 191, 340
Enlightenment, Scottish 2, 5, 6, 17, 27, 58, 189
Entail, The 8, 9, 110, 113, 115–16, 118, 119, 219, 234, 243, 246, 247–8, 251, 253, 268–9, 322, 324
'Essay on Commercial Policy' 107
Essay on the History of Civil Society 33
Eugenics 45–6
Evangelical 'Men' 385
Evangelical Movement (Revival) 383–8
Evangelicalism, Protestant 3, 5, 6, 7, 9, 30–3, 379, 389–90
Evergreen, The 20
evolution, cultural 398–402
Evolutionary Utilitarianism 58
Evolutionism 51
Excursion, The 191
Expedition to the Zambesi and its Tributaries 422

Fables 240
Factory Girl, The 236
Faerie Queene, The 93
Family Legend, The 430, 431
famine, in Highlands and Islands 44

Faulkner, William 91
Felix Holt 36
Ferguson, Adam 58, 83
    Essay on the History of Civil Society 33
Ferguson, J A, *Campbell of Kilmohr* 429
Fergusson, Robert 2, 7, 89, 120, 206, 345, 367
    'Election, The' 226
Ferrier, James Frederick 2, 6, 8, 126, 129, 173, 179, 193
Ferrier, James Walter 175
Ferrier, Susan 266–8, 270, 322
    Destiny 237, 266
    Inheritance, The 9, 237–8, 266–8, 269
    Marriage 237–8, 266–8, 269
fiction *see* serial fiction
Fielding, Henry
    Joseph Andrews 438
    Tom Jones 72, 75, 438
Findlater, Jane 310
    Crossriggs 238–9, 271–2
Findlater, Mary 310
    Crossriggs 238–9, 271–2
Fingal's Cave 430
Finlay, John 403, 404
Fios thun a' Bhaird 'A Message to the Poet' 392
'Firmillian' 198
First Reform Act 116
Flaubert, Gustave, *Madame Bovary* 241
Flemington 242–3, 247
'Fleshy School of Poetry' [pre-Raphaelites] 438
Fletcher, Phineas, 'Purple Island, The' 281
folk tradition 7, 9, 27, 312, 397–407
Forbes, J D 8, 173–4, 175
Foresters, The 232
Fortunes of Nigel, The 66, 70, 71, 72
Foulis, Andrew 339
Foulis, Hugh *See* Munro, Neil
Foulis, Robert 339
Foxe, John, *Book of Martyrs* 386
'Francie Herregerie's Sharger Laddie' 213
Fraser's Magazine 154
Frazer, Sir James George 7, 27, 397–402

Golden Bough, The 398–402, 406
Free Church 6, 24, 32–5, 37, 49, 51, 53, 56, 59, 310, 313, 314, 326
French revolution 5, 116, 135–6
French Revolution, The 153–7, 164–6, 183
Freud, Sigmund, 'Seventeenth-century Demonological Neurosis' 101
friendship and RLS 292–3, 297–8, 300–1
Froude, James Anthony 155
Fyffe, Will 439

Gaberlunzie Man legends 29, 93, 218
Gaelic Bible 379, 384
Gaelic poetry 377–93
Galt, John 74, 107–20
    alluded to 1, 5, 7, 8, 10, 24, 29, 36, 177, 196, 207, 217, 223, 240, 245, 252, 266, 322, 353, 423, 433
    compared with William Alexander 226
    devil metaphor 246
    founding of Guelph, Huron Tract, Upper Canada 414–15
    and Scots language 74, 329, 330, 332
    Agamemnon 433
    Annals of the Parish 110, 112, 114, 116, 117, 119, 120, 218, 224–6, 241, 269–70, 321, 324, 412, 420
    Antonia 433
    Autobiography 108–9, 116
    Ayrshire Legatees, The 109–10, 112–13, 114
    Bogle Corbet 114, 415
    Clytemnestra 433
    Cursory Reflections 108
    'Dean of Guild, The' 112
    Earthquake, The 111
    Entail, The 8, 9, 110, 113, 115–16, 118, 119, 219, 234, 243, 246, 247–8, 251, 254, 268–9, 322, 324
    'Essay on Commercial Policy' 107
    Gathering of the West, The 326
    Lady Macbeth 433
    Last of the Lairds, The 110, 112, 117, 119, 224, 326, 412–13, 418
    Lawrie Todd 114, 415
    Life of Byron 109
    Literary Life 108–9, 111, 112, 114

'Maddelen' 113, 433
Majolo, The 111
Member, The 113, 116–17, 328
Omen, The 246
Provost, The 113, 117–18, 224,
240–1, 245, 252, 324, 328
Radical, The 224
Ringan Gilhaize 112–13, 115,
224–5, 234, 324
'Seamstress, The' 324
Sir Andrew Wylie 110–11, 113–14,
119, 224–6, 227–8, 232, 234, 246,
329
Steamboat, The 114, 234, 324
Tales of the West 114–15, 116,
415
Tragedies 113
Garibaldi, Guiseppe 343, 368
Gaskell, Elizabeth Cleghorn 184
Gathering of the West, The 326
Geddes, James Young 344–5
'Glendale and Co' 10, 344
'Man and the Engine, The' 344
'People's Theatre, The' 344
'Work of Art, A' 344
Geddes, Patrick 2, 38, 176
Evergreen, The 20
'geggies, the' 439
Geikie, Archibald 170, 171, 173
General Assembly 6, 18–20, 31–4
Gentle Shepherd, The 73, 219, 436
George, Henry 44
George IV 196, 326, 341, 435
German Romanticism 281
Gibbon, Lewis Grassic *see* Mitchell,
James Leslie
Gide, André 101
Gilderoy 435
Gilfillan, George 175
Gilfillan, James 199
Gilian the Dreamer 240–1
Gillespie 235, 243, 247–8, 249, 254–5
Gippsland 423
Gladstone, William Ewart 12, 29–30,
36
Glasgow 23–4, 43, 312, 417
and municipal socialism 58
'Glasgow' 236, 341, 342
'Glasgow boys' [painters] 11
Glasgow Herald 330
Glasgow Poets, The 355
Glasgow Repertory Theatre 429

Glasgow University chair of Scottish
History and Literature 11
Gleig, George Robert, *Subaltern, The*
234
'Glendale and Co' 10, 344
'Gleniffer' 360
'Gloomy Winter' 360
Godly Commonwealth 33, 34
Godwin, William 38, 107–8
Goethe, Johann Wolfgang von 183
Werther 109
Wilhelm Meisters Lehrjahre 157,
183
Wilhelm Meisters Wanderjahre
183
'Gold Digger of California, The' 204
Golden Bough, The 398–402, 406
'Golden Key, The' 229
Golden Leaves from American Poets
342
Goldsmith, Oliver 225
Good Words 54, 179, 233, 331
'Goodly Ironmaster, The' 357
Gordon, George 25
'Gossip on Romance, A' 298
Graham of Claverhouse, John, 1st
Viscount Dundee 97
Graham, Henry Grey 287
Graham, Maria, *Journal of a Residence
in India* 420
Graham, Robert Bontine Cunninghame
28, 178
'Beattock for Moffat' 170
Gramsci, Antonio 148
Grant, Elizabeth, of Rothiemurcus 178
Grant, James 8
Romance of War 234
Grant, James Augustus 422
Walk Across Africa, A 422
Grant, Peter 287
Oran nam Misionaraidh 'The Song
of the Missionaries' 386
Gray, Alasdair 245
Lanark 70
Gray, David 337
'Luggie, The' 340
Great Exhibition (1911) 11
'Great Muckle Village of
Balmaquhapple, The' 90, 338
Green, Thomas Hill 55, 58
Gregory, D F 173
Greig, Gavin 7

456 INDEX

'Grey Wolf, The' 229
Grieve, Christopher Murray 9, 11, 25–6, 160, 231, 332, 333, 337, 346–8, 363, 436
    on John Wilson 127–9
    'Of John Davidson' 349–50
Grimm Jacob Ludwig Carl 27
Grimm, Wilhelm Carl 27
Grundtvig, N F S, Bishop 32
Guidman of Ballengeich, The 435
Gunn, Neil Miller 11, 217, 249
    Lost Glen, The 235
    Silver Darlings, The 231
Guthrie, Dr Thomas 49–50, 53
Guy Mannering 71, 79, 270, 434

Haldane, Richard Burdon 38, 57
Haliburton, Hugh *see* Robertson, James Logie
Halidon Hill 433, 434
Hamilton, Elizabeth, *Cottagers of Glenburnie, The* 237–8, 321
Hamilton, Janet 10, 343, 358, 367–73
    'Local Changes' 368–9
    'Oor Location' 370–2
    'Our Local Scenery' 372
    'Plea for the Doric, A' 343, 373
    'Rhymes for the Times, I' 343
    'Rhymes for the Times, IV—1865' 372–3
    'Wheen Aul' Memories, A' 369–70
Hamilton, Thomas 217
    Youth and Manhood of Cyril Thornton, The 239
Hamilton, Sir William 2–3, 6, 171, 173, 174, 175, 179
Hamlet 275
Hanna, William 32
Happy for the Child 247
Hardenberg, Friedrich Leopold von 276, 279
Hardie, James Keir 50, 54, 176, 247
Hardy, Thomas 91, 114, 305, 309
    Mayor of Casterbridge, The 118, 251
Harlequin Tam O'Shanter and His Auld Mare Meg 430, 440
Harp of Perthshire 355
Harp of Renfrewshire, The 355, 357
Hatter's Castle 247
Haunted Glen, The 433

'Have You Signed God's Promise?' 205
Hawthorne, Nathaniel 240, 245
    'Minister's Veil, The' 245
    Scarlet Letter, The 245
    'Young Goodman Brown' 245
Hay, John MacDougall 10, 240, 241, 305
    Gillespie 235, 243, 247–8, 249, 254–5
Hazlitt, William 133, 142–4, 293
Heart of Darkness 422
Heart of Midlothian, The 1, 79, 80–1, 169, 218, 219–24, 225, 230, 232, 243, 244, 254, 270, 321, 323, 434
Hegel, Georg 192
Henderson, T F, *Scotch Vernacular Literature* 11
Henley, William Ernest 175, 292, 300–1, 303, 309, 438
Henryson, Robert 7, 92
    Fables 240
    Testament of Cresseid, The 218, 240
'Hermit of the Colorado Hills, The' 204
heroic poetry and Gaelic literature 378, 392, 393
Hester 238, 261–3, 266, 271–2
Highlands, landlord policy in 44–5
Hill, David Octavius [painter]
    'Signing of the Deeds of Demission, The' 34
    'Sun Pictures' 34
Hill, Frederic 50
History of Europe 176
History of India 419
History of Persia, A 418
History of the Sufferings of the Church of Scotland 96
Hodder & Stoughton 200, 313
Hoffman, Ernst Theodor Wilhelm 154, 276
Hogg, James 89–103
    alluded to 1, 2, 7, 8, 10, 133, 177, 180, 196, 217, 223, 236, 240, 245, 254, 281, 360, 361
    and *The Chaldee Manuscript* 192
    devil metaphor 246
    influence on John Wilson 127
    Noctes Ambrosianae 144, 194–5
    poetry 337, 339, 345
    Scots language 206, 324, 330

song collection 403–4
All Hallow Eve 433
'Auld Man's Farewell to his Little House' 95
Basil Lee 224, 241
'Boy's Song, A' 90, 338
Brownie of Bodsbeck, The 8, 96–7, 218, 223–4, 234, 325
'Cruel Mother, The' 93
'Disagreeables' 338–9
'Dominie, The' 338–9
'Donald MacDonald' 90
Edinburgh Bailie, An see *Some Remarkable Passages in the Life of an Edinburgh Baillie*
'Great Muckle Village of Balmaquhapple, The' 90, 338
Haunted Glen, The 433
'Kilmeny' 91, 93, 230, 328, 338
'Laird of Lariston, The' 91
'Lock the door, Lariston' 95
'Love Adventures of Mr George Cochrane, The' 95
Mador of the Moor 93
'May of the Moril Glen' 94–5, 97
Memoir of the Author's Life 328
'Mistakes of a Night, The' 89
Mountain Bard, The 90, 103
'New Christmas Carol' 90
Pilgrims of the Sun, The 93, 230
Poetic Mirror, The 338
Private Memoirs and Confessions of a Justified Sinner, The 96, 100–2, 103, 154, 224, 240, 241, 245, 252, 324–5
Queen Hynde 94, 97
Queen's Wake, The 91–2
Scottish Pastorals 90
Shepherd's Calendar, The 223
Some Remarkable Passages in the Life of an Edinburgh Baillie 103, 224, 241
Spy, The 95, 192
'Thirlestane, a Fragment' 91
Three Perils of Man, The 97, 98, 102, 223–4, 230
Three Perils of Woman, The 97, 98–100, 224, 232
'Tibby Hyslop's Dream' 325
'True Story of a Glasgow Tailor, A' 338–9
'When the kye comes hame' 90

Winter Evening Tales 223
'Witch of Fife, The' 91, 93, 94, 340
Witches of Eildon, The 230
Hogg, Margaret (mother of James) 89, 404
Hogg, William (brother of James) 89
'Holy Willie's Prayer' 240, 245, 247, 341
Home, John 431
    Douglas 429
Homer 378
'Horace in Homespun' 328
Horae Subsecivae 178
Horner, Francis 190, 191
Horner, Leonard [geologist] 174
House with the Green Shutters, The 170, 181–2, 185, 219, 228, 231, 243, 246–55, 271, 330, 353, 440
House of Usna, The 436, 437
Housman, Alfred Edward 120
'How I stood for the Dreepdailly Burghs' 197
'How we got up the Glenmutchkin Railway and How we got out of it' 197, 239
Hudson's Bay Company 411, 413, 415
Hughes, Thomas, *Tom Brown's School-days* 38
'Humble Remonstrance, A' 298
Hume, David 107, 139, 179
Humphry Clinker 239, 321
Hunchback, The 432
Hunt, James Henry Leigh 142, 192–3
Hutcheson, Francis 2, 221

Iain Gobha na Hearadh 388–9
Ibsen, Henrik 37, 309, 436
    Master Builder, The 251
    Peer Gynt 37
    Pillars of Society 251
Idealism 55, 57–8
Idealism, German 154, 160, 162
'Idiot Boy, The' 130
'Ille Terrarum' 346
Immortal Hour, The 429, 435–6, 437
In the Footsteps of the Creator 55
'In the Isle of Dogs' 349
In the South Seas 425
India 18, 411, 416–17, 420–1, 422–3
industrial revolution and urbanisation 5, 9, 16, 18, 23–4, 28–9, 33, 35–6, 44,

135–6, 157, 211, 213, 217, 236, 312–13, 315, 354, 358–9, 361–2, 368, 370–3
Inheritance, The 9, 237–8, 266–8, 269
Inland Voyage, An 294
Innes, Cosmo 176
Irish revival 235
'Iron Shroud, or, Italian Revenge, The' 203
Irving, David 178
Irving, Edward 35, 177, 182
Islands, landlord policy in 43–5
Isle of Palms 137–8
Italian, The 109
Ivanhoe 196, 218, 434

Jacob, Violet, *Flemington* 242–3, 247
Jamaica 413
James, Henry 72, 292, 294, 298, 303
James V 338
James VI 91
Jamieson, Robert 403
Jane Eyre 146
'Jeanie's Grave' 362
Jeffrey, Lord Francis 2, 15, 171, 172, 176, 182, 324
    editor, *The Edinburgh Review* 65, 129–30, 177, 190–2, 196, 340
    and John Wilson 138–41
    and Scots language 38
Jenkins, Robin 242, 245, 255
    Awakening of George Darroch, The 30
    Happy for the Child 247
Jessie Melville 209–10
John Burnet of Barns 234, 242
'John Cheap the Chapman' 203
John Nicholson 246–7
Johnny Gibb of Gushetneuk 2, 26, 35, 36, 211–12, 213, 218, 225, 226–8, 232, 236, 249–50, 325–6
Johnson, Dr Samuel 95, 164, 339
    Lives of the English Poets 67
Johnston, Ellen, 'Last Sark, The' 357
Johnstone, Mrs, 'Mrs Mark Luke; or West Country Exclusives' 332
'Jolly Beggars, The' 218
Joseph Andrews 438
Joseph's Sweetheart 438
Journal (Cockburn) 15–17, 24, 172, 174
Journal (Scott) 13, 16, 68

Journal of a Cruise from Greenock to New Holland 423
Journal of a Residence in India 420
journalism, a new occupation 209
Journals of John McDouall Stuart 423
Joyce, James 70
    Ulysses 93
'Justice—a Reverie' 364–5
Justice of the Peace, The 247

Kailyard school 5, 27, 29, 59, 137, 170, 180, 181, 184, 198, 200, 212, 232–3, 234, 236, 304–5, 309–17, 326, 329–30, 353–4, 424, 440
Keats, John 72–3, 142, 147
Keddie, Henrietta 310
Kellas, James 35
Kelso Chronicle 26
Kelvin, Lord *see* Thomson, Sir William
Kemble, John Philip 431
Kesson, Jessie 239
Kidnapped 20, 218, 223, 230–1, 234, 241, 297, 298–9, 300, 303–4, 305, 331–2
'Kilmeny' 91, 93, 230, 328, 338
Kingsley, Charles, *Alton Locke* 182
Kinloch, George Ritchie 403
Kirk *see* Church of Scotland
Kirsteen 218, 228, 238, 249–51
Knowles, Sheridan 432–3
    Hunchback, The 432
    Virginius 432
Knox, John 156

Labour movement 28, 315
Lady of the Lake, The 338, 434
Lady Macbeth 433
Laidlaw, William 102
Laing, David 178
Laird of Drammochdyle and his Contemporaries, The 212–13, 236, 249, 251
'Laird of Lariston, The' 91
Lake District 132–3
Lake school 136, 139, 191
Lanark 70
land agitation 5, 388, 389
Land of Heart's Desire, The 437
'Land of MacLeod' 382–3
Landseer, Sir Edwin Henry [painter] 430

'Monarch of the Glen, The'   235
Lang, Andrew   14, 27, 178, 397, 401, 402
Langtry, Lillie   438
Last Journals   422
'Last Journey, The'   349
Last of the Lairds, The   110, 112, 117, 119, 224, 324, 412–13, 418
'Last Sark, The'   357
Latter-Day Pamphlets   155
Latto, William D   35, 199, 206–8, 236, 249
Lauder, Sir Thomas Dick   285
    Wolf of Badenoch, The   234
Lawrence, David Herbert   309, 310
Lawrie Todd   114, 415
Lay of the Last Minstrel, The   68, 73, 79, 81, 337–8
Lays of Ancient Rome   136
League Journal   205
Lee, Jennie   38
Lee, John   53
Legend of Montrose, A   79
Leigh Hunt, James see Hunt, James Henry Leigh
Leng, John   207, 210
Leonard, Tom, ed, Renfrewshire Poetry from the French Revolution to the First World War   355
Leslie, John   171, 179, 193
Letter to a Friend of Burns   139–40
Letters of Malachi Malagrowther, The   4–5, 16–17, 67, 81–2, 84
Letters on Demonology and Witchcraft   67
Lewis, Clive Staples   278, 280
Lewis, Matthew   267
Lewis, Percy Wyndham   127
libraries
    Airdrie   28
    and fiction   203, 206
    Greenock   120 n1
Life Among My Ain Folk   211, 213–14, 249–50
Life of Byron   109
Life of Lord Clive   419
Life of Lord Jeffrey   14
Life of Mansie Wauch, Tailor of Dalkeith   178, 197, 199, 233
Life of Napoleon Buonaparte   67
Life of Sir Walter Scott   14
'Life-Drama, A'   342

Lights and Shadows of Scottish Life   98
Lilac Sunbonnet, The   233, 234, 310
Lilith   229–30, 275, 277
Lily of St Leonards, The   434
Lindsay, Sir David, Satire of the Thrie Estatis, Ane   218, 224
Linklater, Eric   11, 245
Lister, Joseph   6
literacy, universal   28, 203, 206, 214, 313
Literary History of Scotland, A   275, 353
Literary Life   108–9, 111, 112, 114
literature
    local   353, 355–7
    popular see serial fiction
Literature and Oatmeal   182
'Little Girl Found, The'   92
'Little Girl Lost, The'   92
'Little Match Girl, The'   345
Little Minister, The   233, 312, 429, 438–9
Lives of the English Poets   67
Lives of the Novelists   67
Livingstone, David   422, 424
    Expedition to the Zambesi and its Tributaries   422
    Last Journals   422
    Missionary Travels   422
Livingstone, William   8, 391–2, 393
    Fios thun a' Bhaird 'A Message to the Poet'   392
'Local Changes'   368–9
'Lock the door, Lariston'   95
Lockhart, John Gibson   102, 134, 140, 177
    and Carlyle   155
    and The Chaldee Manuscript   192–3
    'Cockneys' attacks   142–3, 173, 192
    editor, The Quarterly Review   13, 14, 125, 171, 172, 196
    Adam Blair   109, 239–40
    Matthew Wald; The Story of a Lunatic   239–40
    Memoirs of the Life of Scott   17, 66, 193
    Peter's Letters to His Kinsfolk   10, 171, 239
London Stage Society, The   437
Lord of the Isles, The   434

'Lords of Labour, The' 342
Lorna Doone 234, 242
Lost Glen, The 235
Lothair 169, 180
Lounger, The 189
'Love Adventures of Mr George
 Cochrane, The' 95
'Lowden Sabbath Morn, A' 346
'Lucy Spence's Last Advice' 240
Lucy the Factory Girl 209–10, 211
'Luggie, The' 340
Luther, Martin 155
Lyell, Sir Charles [geologist] 55, 174
Lyrical ballads 129–31
Lytton, Lord Edward Bulwer- 173, 432

['Mac'—M', Mc and Mac are all treated
 as 'Mac']
Mac an t-Saoir, Donnchadh Bàn 8,
 235
MacArthur, Samuel, *Duke of
 Rothesay, The, a Tragedy* 432
Macaulay, Thomas Babington 14, 172
 Lays of Ancient Rome 136
Macbeth 440
MacColl, Evan, 'Death of Mairi, The'
 392
M'Combie, William 212
'MacCrimmon's Lament' 392
McCulloch, Horatio [painter] 235
MacCunn, John 57
MacDiarmid, Hugh *see* Grieve,
 Christopher Murray
MacDonald, Mrs Charles Edward
 (George's grandmother) 286
MacDonald, George 1, 10, 26, 36,
 180–1, 183, 219, 223, 275–88, 310, 312,
 326–7, 328, 337, 425
 Alec Forbes of Howglen 181, 218,
  227–8, 248, 278–80, 281, 285
 At the Back of the North Wind
  229, 276
 Castle Warlock 285
 David Elginbrod 227–8, 275, 279
 Donal Grant 285
 Elect Lady, The 279, 285
 'Golden Key, The' 229
 'Grey Wolf, The' 229
 Lilith 229–30, 275, 277
 Malcolm 225, 227–30, 232, 278–9,
  329, 330

Marquis of Lossie, The 227–9,
 278–9, 286–7
Phantastes 227, 229–30, 275–7,
 281–3
Portent, The 229
Princess and Curdie, The 229, 276
Princess and the Goblin, The 276
Ranald Bannerman's Boyhood 233,
 280, 281, 331
Robert Falconer 181, 227, 278–80,
 285–7
Salted with Fire 275
Sir Gibbie 227–30, 241, 279, 285,
 327
'Story of the Sea-Shore, A' 283–5
'Wow o' Rivven, The' 229
MacDonald, Rev Dr John 387–8, 391
MacDonald, Ramsay 36
Macfarlan, James 341, 342–3, 345
 'Lords of Labour, The' 342
 'Midnight Train, The' 342
 'Ruined City, The' 342
 'Street, The' 342
 'Wanderer of the West, The' 342–3
McGonagall, William 345
 'Little Match Girl, The' 345
MacGregor, James 387
McIlvanney, William, *Docherty* 255
MacIntyre, Duncan Ban *see* Mac an
 t-Saoir, Donnchadh Bàn
Mackay, William 435
Mackenzie, Alexander 413, 415, 421
 Voyages from Montreal . . . 413
Mackenzie, Henry 95, 189–90, 193,
 196, 232, 253
 Man of Feeling, The 154, 219
Mackenzie, J S 57
MacKinnon, Alexander 380
 Battle of Egypt, The 380–1
 Battle of Holland, The 380
MacKinnon, Prof Donald 393
Mackintosh, Charles Rennie
 [architect] 11
'MacKrimmon's Lament' 393
MacLachlan, Dr John 391
McLaren, Sergeant Archibald 439
MacLaren, Ian *see* Watson, Rev
 John
MacLean, John
 An Cogadh Naomh 'The Holy
  War' 386
 Craobh-sgaoileadh an t-Soisgeil

'The spreading of the Gospel' 386

MacLennan, J F 27

Macleod of Dare 234–5

Macleod, Donald 54, 58

'MacLeod, Fiona' *see* Sharp, William

MacLeod, Neil 391
  'Death of the Widow's Child, The' 392

Macleod, Norman 4, 53–4, 179, 233
  Old Lieutenant and His Son, The 234
  Starling, The 233–4

McMillan, Angus, *Journal of a Cruise from Greenock to New Holland* 423

Macmillan's Magazine 327

M'Neil [poet] 367

Macpherson, James 392, 430

MacPherson, Mary *see* Mairi Mhór nan Oran

MacQuarie, Lachlan 423

Macready, William 432

Madame Bovary 241

'Maddelen' 113, 433

Mador of the Moor 93

Madras 417

Maeterlinck, Maurice 437

'Maggie Lauder' 340

magic, principles of [Frazer] 399–401

Maginn, William 133, 140, 173

Magnum Opus 67, 69, 70

Mahomet 155

Mairi Mhór nan Oran 'Big Mary of the songs' 8, 235, 390–1

Majolo, The 111

Malcolm, Sir John 417–19
  History of Persia, A 418
  Life of Lord Clive 419
  Sketch of the Political History of India 419
  Sketches of Persia 418

Malcolm 225, 227–30, 232, 278–9, 329, 330

'Man and the Engine, The' 344

Man of Feeling, The 154, 219

'Man's a man for a' that, A' 360–1

Mansie Waugh see *Life of Mansie Waugh*

Margaret Ogilvy 329

'Markheim' 230, 294–5

Marmion 18, 73, 190–1, 338

Marquis of Lossie, The 227–9, 278–9, 286–7

Marriage 237–8, 266–8, 269

Marrying for Money 440

Martin, Sir Theodore 29

Martineau, Harriet 125

'Mary Malcolmson's Wee Maggie' 213

Mary, Queen of Scots 91, 430

Masson, David 14, 179

Master Builder, The 251

Master of Ballantrae, The 8, 20, 231, 240, 241, 245, 248, 291, 295, 298, 300, 301, 302–3, 332–3

Matheson, Donald 389

Matheson, John, *Oran na h-Eaglais* 'The Song of the Church' 385

'Matinee' 349

Matthew Wald; The Story of a Lunatic 239–41

Maude, Cyril 438

Mavor, Osborne Henry 11

Maxwell, James Clerk 6, 173

'May of the Moril Glen' 94–5, 97

Mayor of Casterbridge, The 118, 251

Melville, Herman 219, 245

Member, The 113, 115–17, 224, 328

Memoir of the Author's Life (Hogg) 328

Memoirs of the Life of Scott 66, 193

Memorials of His Time (Cockburn) 337

Memorials (Davidson) 38

Memories and Portraits 293

Men of the Moss Haggs, The 234

Merchant's Daughter, The 210–11

Merry Men, The 230, 243, 247, 294–5

Metcalfe, Charles 419

Middlemarch 241

'Midnight Train, The' 342

'Mile an' a Bittock, A' 346

Mile marbhphaisg ort a shaoghail 'World, a thousand shrouds upon you!' 384

Mill, John Stuart 58, 155, 177, 182

Millar, John Hepburn 13, 103, 217, 309, 310
  Literary History of Scotland, A 275, 353

Miller, George 204

Miller, Hugh 1, 2, 5, 6, 9, 10, 37, 175–6, 177, 184, 199, 353
  In the Footsteps of the Creator 55
  My Schools and Schoolmasters 37–8

Milton, John 73, 93, 161, 281, 343
  Paradise Lost 367

'Minister's Veil, The' 245
'Minstrel, The' 360
Minstrelsy: Ancient and Modern 404, 406
Minstrelsy of the Scottish Border 67, 68–9, 90, 91, 403, 406
Minto, Earls of *see* Elliot
Mirror, The 189–90
Miscellaneous Plays 431
Miss Marjoribanks 238
Missionary Travels 422
'Mistakes of a Night, The' 89
Mitchell, James Leslie 9, 217, 249, 255
    Scots Quair, A 218, 219, 228, 231, 332
    Sunset Song 35, 226–7
Mitchell, John, 'St Rollox Lum's Address to his Brethren, The' 357
Mitchison, Naomi 11, 239
'Mitherless Bairn, The' 362
Moderates 3, 32–3
Modern Accomplishments 237
Modernism 161
Moir, David Macbeth 173, 178, 207, 217
    'Canadian Boat Song' 197, 415
    Life of Mansie Wauch, Tailor of Dalkeith 178, 197, 199, 233
Moir, George 173
'Monarch of the Glen, The' (Landseer) 235
'Monitor's Song' 364
Montaigne, Michel Eyquem de 293
Montgomerie, Alexander
    Cherry and the Slae, The 240
Moore, George 360
More, Hannah 109
Morris, William 177
Morrison, John *see* Iain Gobha na Hearadh
Morrison, Nancy Brysson 239
Mother Courage 100
Motherwell, William 7, 397, 403–6
    Minstrelsy: Ancient and Modern 404, 406
Mountain Bard, The 90, 103
Mountain Lovers, The 235
Mrs Grundy in Scotland 3, 4, 247, 250, 252, 317
'Mrs Mark Luke; or West Country Exclusives' 332

Muir, Edwin 11, 23, 25, 29, 38, 317, 433
    Scott and Scotland 4
    Scottish Journey 23
Muir, John, *Story of my Boyhood and Youth, The* 38
Muir, Thomas, of Huntershill 17
Muir, Willa 11, 217, 239, 248
    Mrs Grundy in Scotland 3, 4, 247, 250, 252, 317
Muirhead, J H 57
Munro, Neil 9, 233, 438
    Gilian the Dreamer 240–1
Munro, Sir Thomas 417–18, 420
Murchison, Sir Roderick Impey [geologist] 174
Murray, Archibald 439
Murray, W H 429, 431, 435
    Crammond Brig 435
    Gilderoy 435
    Guidman of Ballengeich, The 435
Music Halls 439, 440
My Schools and Schoolmasters 37–8
My Uncle the Baillie 213–14
'Mysterious Miner, The' 204
myth 217–35, 280, 397–402, 407

Napier Commissioners 45
Napier, McVey 171
Napoleon *see* Buonaparte, Napoleon
Napoleonic Wars 17–18, 91
National Burns Club 440
nationalism *see* Scottish nationalism
Natural Law in the Spiritual World 51
Nature of the Soul, a Psychic Drama 436–7
Neaves, Lord Charles 173
Neill, A S 38
Nettles, Jenny (folksong heroine) 100
New Arabian Nights, The 230, 294
'New Christmas Carol' 90
New Edinburgh Review 434
New Monkland 28
New Review 309
New South Wales 423
New Zealand 423
Newbolt Committee 25
newspaper press 26, 205–14, 235–6, 313, 326, 354–5
Nicoll, Sir William Robertson 4, 179–80, 200, 231, 313, 315

Nietzche, Friedrich Wilhelm 153
Ninian Jamieson 241
Niven, Frederick 255, 310
    Justice of the Peace, The 247
Noctes Ambrosianae 126, 135, 144
'Noctes Ambrosianae' 95, 98, 103
Non-Intrusionists 31, 33–4
Norman Sinclair 175, 239
North America 411
North Briton 210
North, Christopher *see* Wilson, John
North-West Fur Company 411
Notes from Underground 160
Nova Scotia 415
Novalis *see* Hardenberg, Friedrich
    Leopold von

O'Connell, Daniel 32
'Of John Davidson' 349–50
Oisean 'Ossian' 8, 235, 379, 387, 391,
    392, 393, 402, 430
'Olalla' 294–5
Old Lieutenant and His Son, The 234
Old Mortality (Scott) 1, 70, 79–81, 84,
    218, 220–1, 234, 243, 244, 332
'Old Mortality' (Stevenson) 301
Oliphant, Margaret 7, 8, 9, 10, 13–14,
    26, 178, 181, 184, 198, 219, 223, 237,
    261–66, 310, 329
    Annals of a Publishing House 173,
        192–3
    Beleaguered City 230
    Child's History of Scotland, A 8–9
    Chronicles of Carlingford 238, 263
    Doctor's Family, The 264–6
    Effie Ogilvie 263
    Hester 238, 261–4, 266, 271–2
    Kirsteen 218, 228, 238, 249–51
    Miss Marjoribanks 238
    *Passage in the Life of Margaret
        Maitland* 264
    Son of the Soil 265
Omen, The 246
On Heroes and Hero-Worship 154
'On History' 158, 161
On Scotland and the Scotch Intellect
    3, 4, 6
On the Eve 241
One Hundred Modern Scottish Poets
    355–6, 357
'Oor Location' 370–2

Open the Door! 11, 237–9
Oran an t-Saighdeir 'The Soldier's
    Song' 381–2
Oran na h-Eaglais 'The Song of the
    Church' 385
Oran nam Misionaraidh 'The Song of
    the Missionaries' 386
'Ordered South' 293
Origin of Species 56
orthography, Gaelic 377
Osbourne, Lloyd 425
Ossian 8, 235, 379, 387, 391, 392, 393,
    402, 430
'Our Local Scenery' 372
'Outcast, The' 346
'Overgate Orphan, The' 364
Owen, Robert 107–8

Pae, David 209–11, 236, 249–50
    Factory Girl, The 236
    Jessie Melville 209–10
    Lucy the Factory Girl 209–10, 211
    Merchant's Daughter, The 210–11
    St Mungo's City 236
Paine, Thomas 146, 341
    Rights of Man, The 232
Palmerston, Henry John Temple, 3rd
    Viscount 422
pantomime 439, 440
Paradise Lost 367
Park, Mungo, *Travels in the Interior of
    Africa* 421
parochial schools 47–8
*Passages in the Life of Margaret
    Maitland* 264
Past and Present 154–5, 218
Pater, Walter 293, 295
Paterson, Peter 435
patronage 5, 6, 31–3, 35
Paul's Letters to his Kinsfolk 67
Payne, James 204
Peel, Sir Robert 155
Peer Gynt 37
Peerie, Moses, 'Goodly Ironmaster,
    The' 357
'Penance of John Logan, The' 235
People's Friend see People's Journal
People's Journal 35, 199, 205–6, 207–
    9, 236, 337
'People's Theatre, The' 344
Percy, Thomas, *Reliques of Ancient*

English Poetry 403
Persia, Shah of 418
Perversion of Scotland, The 30
Peter Pan 10
Peter's Letters to His Kinsfolk 171, 239
Phantastes 227, 229–30, 275–7, 281–3
Phantom, The 431–2
Pharsis, A Romance of the Isles 235
Phineas Finn 9, 36
Picken, Andrew 233
Pilgrimage of Strongsoul 241–42
Pilgrims of the Sun, The 93, 230
Pilgrim's Progress, The 30, 93, 218, 221, 241–2
Pillars of Society 251
Pindar 378
Planché, James Robinson, *Vampyre, The* 430, 432
Playfair, Lyon 173
Playfair, Prof 193
Plays on the Passions 431
'Plea for the Doric, A' 343, 373
Pocock, Isaac, *Rob Roy MacGregor* 429, 434–5
Poe, Edgar Allan 125, 138, 204, 340, 342, 345
Poetic Mirror, The 338
poetry
    epic philosophical 25–6, 28
    Gaelic 377–93
    local, in newspaper press 355–8
    Scottish 10, 337–49
Pollock, Robert 233
popular party 32
Portent, The 229
Power, William 13, 311, 314, 353, 359
    'Drama in Scotland, The' 439–40
    Literature and Oatmeal 182
Praeterita 38
Prelude, The 78
Prince Otto 292, 297–8, 300, 301–2
Princess and Curdie, The 229, 276
Princess and the Goblin, The 276
Princess of Thule, A 330–1
Pringle, Thomas 192
Pringle-Patterson, Seth 57
Private Memoirs and Confessions of a Justified Sinner, The 96, 100–2, 103, 154, 224, 240, 241, 245, 252, 324–5
Professor's Love Story, The 438

'Prometheus Unbound' 97
Provost, The 113, 117–18, 224, 240–1, 245, 252, 324, 328
'Purple Island, The' 281

Quarterly Review, The 13, 125, 171, 191, 193, 321
Queen Hynde 94, 97
Queen's Wake, The 91–2

Rab and His Friends 29
Radcliffe, Ann, *Italian, The* 109
Radical, The 224
Ragged Trousered Philanthropists, The 250
Raiders, The 234
railway transport 15–16, 29, 217, 435
Rambler, The 95
Ramsay, Allan 7, 120, 206, 343, 345, 367
    Gentle Shepherd, The 73, 219, 436
    'Lucy Spence's Last Advice' 240
    'Vision, The' 92, 218, 240
    'Wealth or the Wuddy' 252
Ramsay, Edward Bannerman, Dean of Edinburgh, *Reminiscences of Scottish Life and Character* 29, 169, 180
Ramsay, G G 398
Ranald Bannerman's Boyhood 233, 280, 281, 331
Randall Press, Stirling 204
'Rauf Coilyear' 218
Ravenshowe and the Residenters Therein 213
reading, recreational 203, 206, 209, 211, 214, 313
Red Cap Tales 331
Red River Settlement 415
Redgauntlet 68, 69, 70, 71, 74–5, 77, 78–9, 234, 241, 243, 246, 250, 251, 322–3
Reform, Parliamentary 5, 171, 183
Reformation 115, 116
Reich, Wilhelm 101
Reid, Thomas 2, 107–8, 109
Religious Tract and Book Society of Scotland 205
religious tracts 204–5
Reliques of Ancient English Poetry 403
Reminiscences (Carlyle) 37, 156, 164, 170–1, 183–4

Reminiscences of Scottish Life and Character   29, 169, 180

Renfrewshire Poetry from the French Revolution to the First World War   355

Rhymers Club   349

Rhymes and Recollections of a Handloom Weaver   344, 359–64

'Rhymes for the Times, I'   343

'Rhymes for the Times, IV'—1865   372–3

Richardson, Samuel, *Clarissa Harlowe*   438

Riddell, Henry Scott   175

Rights of Man, The   232

Ringan Gilhaize   112–13, 115, 224–5, 234, 324

Ritchie, David G   57–8

Rizzio, David   91

Rob Roy   74–7, 79, 221, 243, 244, 246, 434

Rob Roy (*MacGregor, play*)   10, 429, 434–5

Robbers   109

Robert Falconer   181, 227, 278–80, 285–6

Robert the Bruce: A Chronicle Play   436

Robertson, J M   28
    Perversion of Scotland, The   30

Robertson, James Logie   178, 328
    'Horace in Homespun'   328
    'Sketches of Scottish Life among the Ochils'   328

Robertson, Dr William   116, 176

Robinson, Henry Crabb   131, 138, 147

Roderick Random   417

Rodger, Alexander   341

Roman de la Rose   290

'Romance of the Texan Pampas'   204

Romance of War   234

Romantic influences   7, 107, 109, 111, 118, 120, 164

Romantic poetry, English   136–7, 143, 148

Rosebery, Archibald Philip Primrose, 5th Earl   29–30

Rosencrantz and Guildenstern are Dead   100

Ross, Stuart, *Marrying for Money*   440

Rousseau, Jean-Jacques   107–8

Royal Commission (1843)   24, 34

Royal Society, The   175

Ruddiman, Thomas   2

'Ruined City, The'   342

Ruskin, John   14
    Praeterita   38

'Rusticus' *see* Alexander, William

Sabbatarianism   46, 49, 52–3, 59

St Ives   292, 304–5

St Mungo's City   236

'St Rollox Lum's Address to his Brethren, The'   357

Salted with Fire   275

Sartor Resartus   153–64, 171, 183, 230

Satire of the Thrie Estatis, Ane   218, 224

Saturday Review   14

Savigny, Karl von   27

'Scaith o' Bartle, The'   346

Scaramouche in Naxos   436

Scarlet Letter, The   245

'Scenes of Clerical Life'   173

Schiller, Johann von   157, 183
    Robbers   109

'Scholar's Funeral, The'   139

Scotch Sermons   53

Scots language   7, 15–16, 24, 26, 38, 198, 321–33, 372–3
    vernacular   9, 236, 311–12, 358, 361
        in popular literature   205, 206–9, 211–12, 214

Scots Magazine   89

Scots Quair, A   219, 231, 332

Scotsman   37

Scotsman's Heritage, A   173

'Scotsman's Return from Abroad, The'   346

Scott and Scotland   4

Scott, Michael   337
    Tom Cringle's Log   234, 415–16

Scott, Sir Walter   65–84
    alluded to   1–12, 14, 15, 18, 24, 25, 26, 28, 36, 120, 125, 133, 136, 156, 171, 176, 177, 183, 185, 192, 206, 207, 217, 226, 325, 328, 330, 353, 358, 360, 392, 397, 404, 406
    on *Childe Harold* (Byron)   67
    and *The Edinburgh Review*   190–1
    on *Emma* (Austen)   67
    and the English stage   429, 431, 433, 435

essays in *Encyclopaedia Britannica* 67
George IV, 1822 visit to Edinburgh 196, 326, 341, 435
and Hogg   90, 92–3, 95, 100, 102, 134
his nationalism   13, 16–17, 315
his poetry   337–40
his politics   33
romance-realism models   244–5, 246
values of society   227–8
Anne of Geierstein   434
Antiquary, The   69, 74
Black Dwarf, The   79
Bride of Lammermoor, The   72, 79, 81, 243, 434
Doom of Devorgoil, The   434
Fortunes of Nigel, The   66, 70, 71, 72
Guy Mannering   71, 79, 270, 434
Halidon Hill   433, 434
Heart of Midlothian, The   1, 79, 80–1, 97, 169, 218, 219–24, 225, 230, 232, 243, 244, 254, 270, 321, 324, 434
Ivanhoe   196, 218, 434
Journal   13, 16, 68
Lady of the Lake, The   338, 434
Lay of the Last Minstrel, The   68, 73, 79, 81, 337–8
Legend of Montrose, A   79
Letters of Malachi Malagrowther, The   4–5, 16–17, 67, 81–2, 84
Letters on Demonology and Witchcraft   67
Life of Napoleon Buonaparte   67
Lives of the Novelists   67
Lord of the Isles, The   434
'MacKrimmon's Lament'   393
Magnum Opus   67, 69, 70
Marmion   18, 73, 190–1, 338
Minstrelsy of the Scottish Border 67, 68–9, 90, 91, 403, 406
Old Mortality   1, 70, 79–81, 84, 218, 220–1, 234, 243, 244, 332
Paul's Letters to his Kinsfolk   67
Redgauntlet   68, 69, 70, 71, 74–5, 77, 78–9, 234, 241, 243, 246, 250, 251, 322–3
Rob Roy   74–7, 79, 221, 243, 244, 246, 434

Surgeon's Daughter, The   411, 412, 425
Tales of a Grandfather   83–4, 435
Tales of My Landlord   79
'Two Drovers, The'   233, 243
'Wandering Willie's Tale'   323
Waverley   1, 8, 65, 70–1, 73, 74–5, 76–7, 79, 80, 84, 219–21, 233, 237, 239, 240–1, 243, 244, 245, 255, 270, 321–2
Woodstock   84
~ ed
 Sir Tristrem   67
 Works of John Dryden, The   67
 Works of Jonathan Swift, The   67
Scott, William Bell   337
'Witch's Ballad, The'   340
Scottish colourists   11
Scottish Colportage Society   205
Scottish History Society   20
Scottish Home Rule [Association]   12, 20, 28
Scottish Journey   23
Scottish Liberal Party   20
Scottish National Portrait Gallery   20
Scottish 'national theatre'   10, 427
Scottish nationalism   1, 2, 4–5, 9, 10, 11, 17, 25, 28
and ballads   397, 402–3, 406–7
Scottish Pastorals   90
Scottish Poor Law   33–4
Amendment Act (1845)   49
Scottish Realism, school of   107–9, 111, 120
Scottish Rights Movement   35
Scottish Temperance League   205
Scottish Text Society   20
Scottish Vernacular Literature   11
'Seamstress, The'   324
Selector, The   204
Self-Control   237
Semi-Attached Couple, The   420–1
Semi-Detached House, The   420–1
Sentimental Tommy   240–1, 329–30
'Serf' *see* Thom, William
serial fiction   206, 209–14, 291, 354–5
serialisation *see* serial fiction
Seth, Andrew   57
'Seventeenth-century Demonological Neurosis'   101
Shairp, John Campbell   173, 179
Shakespeare, William   84, 281, 439

Hamlet   275
Histories   115
Macbeth   440
Tempest, The   286–7
Sharp, William   8, 9, 36, 230, 254, 310, 327, 436–7
  House of Usna, The   436, 437
  Immortal Hour, The   429, 435–6, 437
  Mountain Lovers, The   235
  Nature of the Soul, a Psychic Drama 436–7
  Pharsis, A Romance of the Isles   235
Sharpe, Charles Kirkpatrick   403
Sharpe, Prof   193
Shaw, George Bernard   429
Shelley, Percy Bysshe   71, 72, 107, 109, 138, 276, 281, 340
  'Prometheus Unbound'   97
Shepherd, Nan   239
Shepherd's Calendar, The   223
Shirley   111
Siddons, Mrs Henry   435
Siddons, Sarah   431
'Signing of the Deeds of Demission, The' 34
'Signs of the Times'   158, 160
Silver Darlings, The   231
Simpson, Sir Walter   175
Sinclair, Catherine, *Modern Accomplishments*   237
Sinclair, Sir John, *Statistical Accounts* 24
Sir Andrew Wylie   110–11, 113–14, 119, 224–6, 227–8, 232, 234, 246, 329
Sir Gibbie   227–30, 241, 279, 285, 327
Sir Tristrem   67
Sixth Commandment, The   438
Sketch of the Political History of India 419
Sketches of Persia   418
Sketches of Rural Life in Aberdeenshire 212
'Sketches of Scottish Life among the Ochils'   328
Sloan, Edward L, 'Weaver's Triumph, The'   357
Smiles, Samuel   177
Smith, Adam   3, 118, 130, 139, 160
Smith, Alexander   8, 26, 177, 198, 353
  'Boy's Poem, A'   342
  Dreamthorp   7

'Edwin of Deira'   342
'Glasgow'   236, 341, 342
'Life-Drama, A'   342
Smith, G Gregory   184, 317
Smith, Iain Crichton, *Consider the Lilies* 247, 255
Smith, John   8, 235, 391–2
  'Song for Sportsmen, A'   389
  'Spirit of Kindliness, The'   390
  'Spirit of Pride, The'   390
Smith, Sydney   19, 172, 190
Smith, William Robertson   6, 7, 27, 56, 398
Smollett, Tobias George   176, 415
  Humphry Clinker   239, 321
  Roderick Random   417
'Snow'   349
social problems and reform   9, 28, 47, 49, 52, 54, 59, 315
'Some Portraits by Raeburn'   270–1
Some Remarkable Passages in the Life of an Edinburgh Baillie   103, 224, 241
Son of the Soil   265
'Song for Sportsmen, A'   389
Sophia   438
Soutar, William   11, 363
Southey, Robert   109, 137
'Spaewife, The'   346
Spark, Muriel   245
'Spasmodic' school of poetry   198–9
Spectator, The   14, 95, 189
Spectre at the Fountain, The   434
Speculative Society   175
Speke, John Hanning   422
Spencer, Herbert   33, 56
Spenser, Edmund   73, 78, 276, 281, 338
  Faerie Queene, The   93
'Spirit of Kindliness, The'   390
'Spirit of Pride, The'   390
Spy, The   95, 192
Starling, The   233–4
Statistical Accounts   24
Steamboat, The   114, 236, 324
Steele, Sir Richard   95
Stephens, Henry   173
Sterling, John   158
Sterne, Laurence   70
  Tristram Shandy   154
Stevenson, Robert Louis   1, 5, 7, 8, 9, 10, 11, 36, 38, 169, 176–7, 180, 184, 219, 223, 225, 246, 254, 271, 291–305, 310, 353, 358

a 'British' writer   26
I Can Remember RLS (Masson)
   175
living out of Scotland   181, 345
his poetry   337
published in *Chambers's Journal*
   199
review of *Noctes Ambrosianae*
   126–7
Scots language   206, 328, 330, 346
Admiral Guinea   438
Amateur Emigrant, The   294
'Beach at Falesa, The'   271, 295,
   302–3
Black Arrow, The   296–7
Catriona   218, 223, 230–1, 241, 242,
   297, 303, 323, 331, 332
'Chapter on Dreams, A'   293
'Coast of Fife, The'   291
'Counterblast Ironical, The'   346
'Crabbed Youth and Age'   293
Deacon Brodie   429, 438
Dr Jekyll and Mr Hyde   154, 230,
   245, 292, 295, 299–301, 438
Dynamiter, The   230
Ebb-Tide, The   295, 302–3, 305,
   425
Edinburgh   294
'Gossip on Romance, A'   298
'Humble Remonstrance, A'   298
'Ille Terrarum'   346
In the South Seas   425
Inland Voyage, An   294
John Nicholson   246–7
Kidnapped   20, 218, 223, 230–1,
   234, 241, 297, 298–9, 300, 303–4,
   305, 331–2
'Lowden Sabbath Morn, A'   346
'Markheim'   230, 294–5
Master of Ballantrae, The   8, 20,
   231, 240, 241, 245, 248, 291, 295,
   298, 300, 301, 302–3, 332–3
Memories and Portraits   293
Merry Men, The   230, 243, 247,
   294–5
'Mile an' a Bittock, A'   346
New Arabian Nights, The   230, 294
'Olalla'   294–5
'Old Mortality'   301
'Ordered South'   293
Prince Otto   292, 297–8, 300, 301–
   2

St Ives   292, 304–5
'Scotsman's Return from Abroad,
   The'   346
'some Portraits by Raeburn'
   270–1
'Spaewife, The'   346
'Storm'   347
'Tale of Tod Lapraik'   323
'Thrawn Janet'   292, 294, 295, 333
'To S C'   347
'To S R Crockett'   346, 347
Travels with a Donkey   292–3, 294
Treasure Island   246–7, 291, 294,
   295–6, 297
Underwoods   327–8, 346
Vailima Letters   425
Virginibus Puerisque   293
Weir of Hermiston   231, 243,
   247–9, 251, 253, 254, 271, 295,
   298, 304
Stewart, Alexander   379
Stewart, Donald   379
Stewart, Dugald   108
Stirling Tract Enterprise   205
Stirling-Maxwell, William   176
'Stolen Beauty of Rio Grande, The'   204
Stoppard, Tom, *Rosencrantz and
   Guildenstern are Dead*   100
'Storm'   347
Story of my Boyhood and Youth, The
   38
'Story of the Sea-Shore, A'   283–5
Stowe, Harriet Beecher, *Uncle Tom's
   Cabin*   343
'Street, The'   342
'Stricken Branch, The'   365
Stuart, James, *Reminiscences*   38
Stuart, John McDouall, *Journals of
   John McDouall Stuart*   423
Subaltern, The   234
'Sun Pictures'   34
Sunday Post   26
Sunday schools   47
Sunset Song   35, 218, 226–7, 228, 332
Surgeon's Daughter, The   411, 412, 425
Swan, Annie S   200
Swift, Jonathan   70, 82, 155
   Works, ed Scott   67
Sybil   218
Sydney Gazette   423
Sym, Robert   194
syndication (of non-book material)   210

'Tale of Tod Lapraik' 323
Tales of a Grandfather 83–4, 435
Tales of My Landlord 79
Tales of the West 114–15, 116, 415
'Tam o' Shanter' 240, 430
Tannahill, Robert 340, 360, 361, 368
    'Braes o' Balqhidder' 360
    'Gleniffer' 360
    'Gloomy Winter' 360
    'Minstrel, The' 360
    'Yon Burnside' 360
Tartanry 27
Tempest, The 286–7
'Ten Years' Conflict' 3, 30, 33
Tennant, Charles 6–7
Tennant, William, *Anster Fair* 340
Tennyson, Lord Alfred 155
Terry, William, 'Terrifications' of *Guy Mannering* 434
Testament of Cresseid, The 218, 240
'Testament of John Davidson, The' 349
Thackeray, William Makepeace 1
'Thames Embankment, The' 349
Theatre Royal, Edinburgh 429, 431, 435
Theatre Royal, Glasgow 432
'theoretical history' 116
'Thirlestane, a Fragment' 91
'Thirty Bob a Week' 348
Thom, James [sculptor] 430
Thom, William 10, 341, 343–4, 358–67, 373
    'Chants for Churls' 344, 365, 367
    'Chieftain Unknown to the Queen, A' 365–6
    'Dreamings of the Bereaved' 362
    'Jeanie's Grave' 362
    'Justice—a Reverie' 364–5
    'Mitherless Bairn, The' 362
    'Monitor's Song' 364
    'Overgate Orphan, The' 364
    Rhymes and Recollections of a Handloom Weaver 344, 359–64
    'Stricken Branch, The' 365
    'Whisper Low' 363, 367
    'Whisperings for the Unwashed' 344, 366–7
Thomson, Alexander 50
Thomson, James 337, 340, 345, 347, 353, 425
    City of Dreadful Night, The 14, 178, 180, 230, 342, 347–8

Thomson, Joseph, *To the Central African Lakes and Back* 422
Thomson, Sir William, later Lord Kelvin 6, 398
'Thrawn Janet' 292, 294, 295, 333
Three Perils of Man, The 97, 98, 102, 223–4, 230
Three Perils of Woman, The 97, 98–100, 224, 232
'Tibby Hyslop's Dream' 325
Times, The 172
To the Central African Lakes and Back 422
'To Mercy, Pity, Peace and Love' 92, 99
'To S C' 347
'To S R Crockett' 346, 347
Tom Brown's Schooldays 38
Tom Cringle's Log 234, 415–16
Tom Jones 72, 75, 438
Tommy and Grizel 240–1
Tory Party 5, 33, 34, 35, 134–5, 140–1, 143, 191–2, 194, 196, 218
tradition 27, 397–407
Tragedies 113
Travels in the Interior of Africa 421
Travels to Discover the Source of the Nile in the Years 1768–73 421
Travels with a Donkey 292–3, 294
Treasure Island 246–7, 291, 294, 295–6, 297
Tressell, Robert, *Ragged Trousered Philanthropists, The* 250
Trials of Margaret Lyndsay, The 145–7
Tristram Shandy 154
Trollope, Anthony 114, 177, 297
    Duke's Children, The 36
    Phineas Finn 9, 36
'True Story of a Glasgow Tailor, A' 338–9
Tulloch, John 57, 173
Turner, Joseph Mallord William 153, 160
'Two Drovers, The' 233, 243
Tylor, Edward Burnett 398, 401, 402
Tytler, Patrick Fraser 176
Tytler, Sarah *see* Keddie, Henrietta

Ulysses 93
Uncle Tom's Cabin 343
Underwoods 327–8, 346

Ungava 415
Union of Scotland and England 5–6, 17, 83–4
United States 423
universities, Scottish 3, 6, 11, 17, 190, 197, 198
Up the Country 420
urban setting *see* industrial revolution
Useful Knowledge movement 204
Utilitarianism 51, 58, 160

Vailima Letters 425
Vampyre, The 430, 432
Van Diemen's Land 423
Variety 439
Vaudeville Theatre 438
vernacular *see* Scots language
Vestiges of Creation, The 55
Victoria, Queen 29, 326, 365
Virginia 417
Virginibus Puerisque 293
Virginius 432
'Vision, The' (Burns) 92
'Vision, The' (Ramsay) 92, 218, 240
'Voluntaries' 31, 34, 35, 49
Voyages from Montreal 413

Walk Across Africa, A 422
Walker, C E, *Warlock of the Glen, The* 430
Walker, London 438
Wallace 218, 429, 437
Wallace, Prof William 57
Wallace, Sir William 115
'Wanderer of the West, The' 342–3
'Wandering Willie's Tale' 323
Wareing, Alfred 10, 435
Warlock of the Glen, The 430
'Wasp, The' 349
Watcher by the Threshold, A 234
Watson, Rev John 4, 28, 180, 200
    kailyard work 251, 311, 313–16, 329, 353
    Beside the Bonnie Briar Bush 233, 309, 312, 314, 316, 329–30
    'Domsie' 314
    Young Barbarians, The 233–4
Watson, W J 378
Watson, William, Sheriff 50
Waverley 1, 8, 65, 70–1, 73, 74–5, 76–7, 79, 80, 84, 219–21, 233, 237, 239, 240–1, 243, 244, 245, 255, 270, 321–22

'Wealth or the Wuddy' 252
'Weaver's rebellion' 5
'Weaver's Triumph, The' 357
Weber, Max 28
Wee MacGreegor 10, 242
Weir of Hermiston 231, 243, 247–9, 251, 253, 254, 271, 295, 298, 304
Wellesley, Marquis of 418, 419
Werther 109
Wesley, John 30
West Indies 411, 415–16
Wheatley, John 23
'Wheen Aul' Memories, A' 369–70
'When the kye comes hame' 90
Whig Party 5, 34, 35, 37, 49, 54, 58, 140, 141, 142, 190, 191, 193, 212
'Whisper Low' 363, 367
'Whisperings for the Unwashed' 344, 366–7
Whistle-Binkie 340–1, 343, 355–7, 358, 361, 362, 367, 374
Whitman, Walt 10, 25, 153, 340, 344–5, 346
'Widow Mysie, The' 346
Wilde, Oscar 429
Wilhelm Meisters Lehrjahre 157, 183
Wilhelm Meisters Wanderjahre 183
Wilkie, Sir David [painter] 430
Wilson, Daniel 179
Wilson, John 3–4, 5, 9, 100, 103, 125–48, 177, 179, 182
    Carlyle on 170–1
    and *Blackwood's Magazine* 173, 192–7, 233
    university appointment 174
    'Apologia' 141
    City of the Plague 137–8, 194
    Foresters, The 232
    Isle of Palms 137–8, 194
    Lights and Shadows of Scottish Life 98, 232
    Noctes Ambrosianae 126–7, 135, 144, 171, 172, 194–5, 200, 236
    'Scholar's Funeral, The' 139
    Trials of Margaret Lyndsay, The 145–7, 232
Window in Thrums, A 233–4
Winter Evening Tales 223
'Witch of Fife, The' 91, 93, 94, 338
Witchcraft 432

Witches of Eildon, The   230
'Witch's Ballad, The'   340
Witness, The   37, 175–6
'Witty Sayings and Exploits of George Buchanan'   203
Wizard of the North *see* Scott, Sir Walter
Wodrow, Rev Robert, *History of the Sufferings of the Church of Scotland* 96
Wolf of Badenoch, The   234
Woodstock   84
women, condition of   9–10
Wordsworth, William   71, 72, 73, 109, 132–3, 137, 138–41, 147, 217, 281, 337, 338
    Excursion, The   191
    'Idiot Boy, The'   130
    Letter to a Friend of Burns   139–40

Lyrical ballads   129–31
    Prelude, The   78
'Work of Art, A'   344
Working Man's Friend   368
'Wow o' Rivven, The'   229
Wull't Last, 'Leez'beth? Wull't Last? 205

Yeats, William Butler   153, 349, 437
    Land of Heart's Desire, The   437
Yellow Book   349
'Yon Burnside'   360
Young Barbarians, The   233–4
Young Folks   331
Young Fur Traders, The   415
'Young Goodman Brown'   245
Youth and Manhood of Cyril Thornton, The   239